PEOPLE IN AUSCHWITZ

Hermann Langbein. Photograph © Alisa Douer; reprinted with permission.

HERMANN LANGBEIN

■ ■ ■

People in Auschwitz

TRANSLATED BY HARRY ZOHN

FOREWORD BY HENRY FRIEDLANDER

The University of North Carolina Press Chapel Hill & London

Published in association with the

United States Holocaust Memorial Museum

© 2004 The University of North Carolina Press
All rights reserved
Originally published in German as *Menschen in Auschwitz,*
© 1995 Europa Verlag GmbH Wien München

Published in association with the United States Holocaust Memorial Museum.
The assertions, arguments, and conclusions contained herein are those of the author
or other contributors. They do not necessarily reflect the opinions of the
United States Holocaust Memorial Museum.

The University of North Carolina Press gratefully acknowledges the
support of the Federal Ministry for Education, Science, and Culture, Vienna, Austria;
the Lucius N. Littauer Foundation; and the L. J. Skaggs and Mary C. Skaggs Foundation
in the publication of this book.

Manufactured in the United States of America
Set in Quadraat types by Tseng Information Systems, Inc.
The paper in this book meets the guidelines for permanence and durability
of the Committee on Production Guidelines for Book Longevity of the Council on
Library Resources.

Library of Congress Cataloging-in-Publication Data
Langbein, Hermann, 1912–
[Menschen in Auschwitz. English]
People in Auschwitz / Hermann Langbein ; translated by Harry Zohn ;
foreword by Henry Friedlander.
p. cm.
"Published in association with the United States Holocaust Memorial Museum."
Includes bibliographical references and index.
ISBN 0-8078-2816-5 (cloth : alk. paper)
1. Auschwitz (Concentration camp) 2. World War, 1939–1945—Prisoners and prisons,
German. 3. Holocaust, Jewish (1939–1945) I. Title.
D805.5.A96L3613 2004
940.53′1853858—dc22   2003020485

08 07 06 05 04   5 4 3 2 1

I have felt obligated to write this book

for the sake of the countless people who

carried on a struggle against inhumanity

even in Auschwitz and lost their lives—

especially in memory of

Ernstl Burger and Zbyszek Raynoch.

CONTENTS

■ ■ ■

FOREWORD
Henry Friedlander

■ ■ ■

The name Auschwitz has come to symbolize the criminality of Nazi Germany. It not only was Germany's largest concentration camp but also housed its largest killing center. In the end, combining assembly-line mass murder and the exploitation of slave labor, Auschwitz was the premier Nazi installation of the Holocaust.

But Auschwitz did not launch the wholesale extermination of people deemed undesirable by the regime. In September 1939, at the beginning of World War II, before Auschwitz even existed as a place of incarceration and murder, the German concentration camp system was already firmly established. The individual camps of that system—Dachau, Sachsenhausen, Buchenwald, Flossenbürg, Mauthausen, and Ravensbrück—had become infamous.

After the conquest of Poland, the Germans needed a new concentration camp to hold the large number of Poles who had been arrested as potential opponents to German rule. The search for the best site focused on Auschwitz, whose Polish name was Oswiecim. Its location at the juncture of the Vistula and Sola rivers made possible a large measure of isolation from the outside world. In addition, it provided essential railroad connections, being situated at the crossroads of Silesia, the General Government of Poland, the incorporated Wartheland, and the former states of Czechoslovakia and Austria. In early May 1940, Auschwitz was officially designated a German concentration camp, and SS Captain Rudolf Höß, who had served on the SS staff at Dachau and Sachsenhausen, was appointed commandant. About 1,200 Poles whose dwellings were on or near the proposed camp site were relocated, and soon thirty prisoners, all ordinary German criminals, arrived from Sachsenhausen, receiving Auschwitz prisoner numbers 1 through 30. In June, the first Polish political prisoners, including Polish Jews, were received at Auschwitz and were given prisoner numbers 31 through 758.

During 1940 and early 1941, the Auschwitz camp held mostly Polish prisoners; the remainder were German. This camp would eventually become the center of a system of camps, while its inmate population would be augmented with prisoners from all countries occupied by Germany. Known as the "main camp," it would house the administration of the Auschwitz complex.

In January 1941, officials of IG Farben, the large German chemical concern, visited the Kattowitz region as the possible site for the production of a type of synthetic rubber known as buna. They took an interest in Auschwitz because the camp could provide cheap inmate labor. Eventually, inmate labor constructed the Buna Works at Monowitz, a short distance from the main camp. Other German industries followed, employing Auschwitz inmate labor in various subcamps. In March 1941, Reich Leader ss Heinrich Himmler ordered the construction of a large camp for 100,000 Soviet POWs at Birkenau, in close proximity to the main camp. Most of the Soviet prisoners were dead by the time Birkenau was reclassified as a concentration camp in March 1942.

With the German invasion of the Soviet Union in 1941, the Nazi regime moved to implement the so-called final solution, the murder of the European Jews and Gypsies. At first, ss killing squads shot their victims in mass executions, but soon the killings were moved to newly built extermination camps, where the victims were gassed with carbon monoxide.

Assembly-line mass murder in gas chambers started with the systematic execution of persons with disabilities under a program euphemistically called euthanasia. Starting in the winter of 1939–40, six killing centers on German soil, each with a gas chamber and a crematorium, put to death about 80,000 disabled patients in less than two years. Thereafter the killing of the disabled ran parallel to the murder of Jews and Gypsies. Since the overcrowded concentration camps did not yet have the means for rapidly killing large numbers of people, the facilities of the euthanasia program were utilized. Commissions of euthanasia and ss physicians selected inmates for shipment to the euthanasia centers. In July 1941, victims began to be selected in Auschwitz.

Sometime in the summer of 1941, Himmler informed Höß, the Auschwitz commandant, that he had chosen his camp as one of the sites where the final solution would be implemented. Although the ss in Auschwitz would eventually copy the euthanasia method of mass killing—with gas chambers, crematoria, and the stripping of gold teeth from corpses—it used hydrogen cyanide, known by the trade name Zyklon B, rather than carbon monoxide. As an experiment, the ss tried out Zyklon B, otherwise used as a pesticide in concentration camps, to kill Soviet POWs in August 1941.

In February 1942, the first transports of Jews arrived in Auschwitz; the victims were gassed in the Old Crematorium at the main camp. In March 1942, the killing operation was moved to Birkenau, utilizing two farm buildings for this purpose. During the period March–June 1943, the construction there of four large structures, each housing a gas chamber and a crematorium, was completed. Soon, massive gassings commenced, claiming altogether about 1.1 million victims.

In November 1943, the expansion of the killing operation, of industrial activities, and of the inmate population at Auschwitz led to a reorganization of the camp structure, resulting in three camps, each with its own commandant: the main camp (Auschwitz I), Birkenau (Auschwitz II), and Monowitz (Auschwitz III). Auschwitz I did, however, retain some overall control. The commandant of the main camp served as post senior, and various central offices, especially the Political Department and the post physician's administration, were still located in the main camp.

The most intense period of killings at Auschwitz began in 1944 with the murder of Hungarian Jews, whose transports started to arrive in May. Jews continued to be brought from other European countries and were also destroyed en masse, as were the Jews from the so-called Theresienstadt family camp, established in Birkenau in September 1943, and the Gypsies held in the Birkenau Gypsy camp since February 1943.

In the fall of 1944, as the Red Army moved closer to Upper Silesia, the SS prepared for a possible withdrawal. Rumors soon spread that they would kill all inmates who knew too much, and first on the list were the Jewish inmates who had been forced to work in the Sonderkommando of the crematoria. On October 7, 1944, the Sonderkommando staged an unsuccessful uprising, damaging one of the crematoria. The gassings continued but at a reduced rate. Finally, as the front drew closer to Auschwitz, Himmler ordered a halt to the gassings, and in November 1944 the SS destroyed the crematoria. On January 17, 1945, the SS conducted the last roll call in Auschwitz. A day later, the camp was evacuated, and its inmates started on the death marches and death transports toward the interior of Germany. Only very sick inmates were left behind. On January 27, 1945, Soviet troops liberated the Auschwitz camp complex.

The final defeat of Germany revealed for the first time the extent of the Nazi regime's massive crimes. Pictures of the liberated camps and their surviving inmates appeared in the newspapers and cinema newsreels of the nations that had defeated Germany. But because the extermination camps had been located in the East and liberated by the Soviets, the pictures seen in the West were primarily of the camps whose inmates were liberated by the Western Allies. The best-known images came from Bergen-Belsen, liberated by British troops. The landscape of death there was shocking, but Bergen-Belsen had not been a killing center.

In the early postwar years, the public in the West did not distinguish between the extermination camps in the East and the concentration camps in the West. Usually, the term "death camp" was applied to both, a usage that has persisted. This began to change only in the 1970s, as greater public interest focused on the Holocaust and the extermination camps. But camps like Treblinka had disappeared, totally destroyed by the Germans. This was not true of Auschwitz, which had been far too large to eradicate. True, Monowitz and the subcamps had disappeared; only the factories constructed by the Germans survived. The main camp, however, remained almost intact and drew growing numbers of visitors. At Birkenau, which was difficult to maintain and preserve, the barracks were mostly gone; rapidly growing weeds covered virtually everything. Even so, today, the barbed wire is still there, as are the railroad tracks that led to the siding where the ss selected from the arriving transports those destined for the gas chambers. Despite the disappearance of the barracks, their chimneys stand here and there, creating an eerie landscape for the visitor viewing the camp from the lookout at the front gate.

Although we now have considerable information about Auschwitz and Birkenau, it comes mainly from archival sources and trial records. In the English-speaking world, the principal sources for Auschwitz are the memoirs of survivors. Most were written by lower-level inmates, whose perspective stemmed from their own experiences and the events in their immediate surroundings. The best of the Jewish memoirs undoubtedly is Primo Levi's *If This Is a Man*, and the best Polish memoir probably is Wieslaw Kielar's *Anus Mundi*.

Hermann Langbein's *People in Auschwitz* is a very different kind of memoir. Langbein occupied a crucial position as clerk to the ss post physician at Auschwitz; as an inmate functionary, he could see and know things not visible to the common inmate. And, as a member of the Auschwitz resistance, he had access to information not available to others. Langbein's account, which deals with the ss as well as the inmates, intertwines his own experiences with quotations from other inmates, derived from official sources as well as personal interviews, and from ss personnel, drawn from statements made in detention and at trial. Written in an objective, sober style, Langbein's book presents us with a narrative few others could have provided.

Hermann Langbein was born in Vienna in 1912 into an Austrian middle-class family; his father was a white-collar employee. His mother was Catholic; his father was Jewish but converted to Protestantism when he married. Langbein's mother died in 1924 and his father ten years later. Hermann attended a Vienna Gymnasium, an essential stepping stone for university attendance, receiving his diploma in 1931. He wanted to become an actor and therefore did not follow his older brother, Otto, into the university. Instead, he started his training at the Deutsche Volkstheater.

At this time, Langbein's general political outlook was leftist, but he did not yet have any party ties. He was definitely opposed to the German Nazis and the Austro-Fascists. He did a great deal of reading during this period, mostly works by progressive authors; in a later interview, he mentioned Upton Sinclair. His brother Otto, who influenced him greatly, joined the Communist Party in 1932, and Hermann followed him in January 1933. Langbein's term at the Volkstheater ended in 1933, and he subsequently appeared in a number of plays in various theaters. Arrested in 1935, he was jailed until 1937 by the Austrian fascist regime. After the Anschluss in 1938, Langbein fled to Switzerland with his girlfriend Gretl, also a member of the party. They made their way to Paris, where they met Otto and various communist friends. Langbein soon crossed into Spain to join the fight against Franco as a member of the International Brigade, while Otto, who was ill, and Gretl stayed in Paris.

By the time Langbein entered Spain, the war had already been lost by the republican side. Still, he was involved in bitter battles. Of course, everyone was looking toward the future, as Langbein's letters to Paris show. Gretl decided to emigrate to Australia; Langbein was less enthusiastic about going so far from Europe. Nevertheless, he studied English, thought about a future as an actor in Sydney, and even talked about marriage. Late in 1938, Gretl left for Australia while Langbein was still in Spain; world history separated them.

In April 1939, Langbein finally was permitted to cross the French border, only to find himself interned, as were most of the other members of the International Brigade. He was first in Saint-Cyprien, then in Gurs, and finally in Le Vernet. After the defeat of France, the Vichy regime handed the members of the International Brigade over to the Germans, and thus Langbein entered the world of the German concentration camps. The first one was Dachau. Following several weeks at hard labor, Langbein was assigned to the inmate infirmary, since he knew both shorthand and Latin. There he served as clerk for several SS physicians, including Dr. Eduard Wirths. In August 1942, Langbein was transferred to Auschwitz.

Being from Austria, which had been absorbed into the Reich, Langbein was classified in the concentration camp as a German, the most privileged type of prisoner. That privileged status was enhanced in Auschwitz because there the percentage of German inmates was even smaller than in camps such as Dachau and Buchenwald. Under the German racial laws, however, he should have been classified as a Jew. When he was registered in Dachau and asked about his lineage, he prevaricated, telling the clerk that his father was partly Jewish, a so-called *Mischling*, but that he did not know exactly to what degree, except that it would not usually classify him as a Jew. Surprisingly, no one ever followed up, and therefore he was also registered in Auschwitz as not being Jewish.

Langbein was transferred to Auschwitz because of the need there for extra personnel to assist in the battle against epidemics; he was assigned to the inmate infirmary in the main camp as a nurse. Within a short time, Dr. Wirths was transferred to Auschwitz as the post physician. He recognized Langbein and picked him as his clerk. As this book illustrates, in that position Langbein not only was privy to much confidential information, including the statistics of inmates killed and transports gassed, but also was able to influence Wirths to improve conditions for his fellow inmates. That privileged vantage point, plus his activities as a member of the resistance cell in the camp, gave him a feel for how Auschwitz functioned, a sense that few others could match.

In August 1944, Langbein was transferred to the Neuengamme concentration camp near Hamburg and then to various subcamps of Neuengamme. During the period of death marches and death transports, he fled from a transport. Shortly thereafter, provided with a pass by the U.S. Army, he returned to Vienna by bicycle.

Langbein proceeded to work for the Austrian Communist Party, organizing and directing party schools in various Austrian provinces. At this time, he met his future wife, Loisi, a journalist and party member; they were married in 1950 and had two children, Lisa and Kurt.

Slowly, Langbein became dissatisfied with life within the Communist Party and began to stray from the strict party line—reading, for example, Hemingway's novel about the Spanish civil war, For Whom the Bell Tolls, even though it lacked the party's stamp of approval. He always had been someone who spoke his mind; he did not easily compromise his convictions. Caught up in intraparty conflicts, he eventually became their victim. He was removed from his position in party education and was forced in 1953 to move to Budapest to take charge of the Austrian program on Hungarian radio. His disaffection increased as he saw the shocking reality of life in a Stalinist people's democracy. After about a year, he returned to Vienna to join the staff of one of the party papers. There he began to suffer under censorship that he found to be absurd. When the newspaper closed in 1955, Langbein earned his living as secretary of the International Auschwitz Committee and of the Austrian Concentration Camp Association, both dominated by communists.

Two events in 1956 led to Langbein's break with the Communist Party: the suppression of the Hungarian uprising and Nikita Khrushchev's speech to the Twentieth Party Congress in the Soviet Union. More and more, Langbein acted on his convictions even if they clashed with the party line. In 1957, his brother Otto left the party, but Hermann refused to drop out quietly. The most public of his activities was the organization of a telegram protesting the trial and conviction of Imre Nagy. As he likely knew it would, this led to his public expulsion from the party in 1958. Although the International Auschwitz Committee and the Austrian Concentration Camp Association were not communist bodies, he was soon pushed out of them and lost his entire income.

After 1958, Langbein turned to writing to make a living. Through connections, he received a contract from the publisher Europa Verlag and wrote a few books on politics. But his greatest interest lay in the Nazi past. After all, his opposition to Nazism and fascism had originally led him into the Communist

Party. In the Auschwitz resistance, he had worked with both communists and noncommunists. Following the war, he wanted to talk about the experiences of the camps and was angered when he found that none of the party leaders cared to find out what had happened in Auschwitz. In 1947–48, he wrote an account of his experiences but had difficulty publishing it. The book appeared under the title *Die Stärkeren: Ein Bericht* (The stronger: A report) in 1949.

While still secretary of the International Auschwitz Committee, Langbein had become involved in the effort to bring the Auschwitz criminals to justice. The first case in which he participated concerned the obstetrician and gynecologist Carl Clauberg, who had conducted sterilization experiments on Jewish female inmates at Auschwitz. Sentenced by the Soviets to hard labor, he was released to West Germany through a deal made by Konrad Adenauer. In the name of the International Auschwitz Committee, Langbein filed an accusation against Clauberg, who was arrested and died in jail awaiting trial. He later filed an accusation against Josef Mengele, providing the names of witnesses for the West German prosecutors, but Mengele disappeared from Argentina before he could be extradited. Even after he had lost his position with the camp committees, Langbein continued to provide help in the prosecution of war criminals, later as secretary of the noncommunist Comité International des Camps.

In 1958, Langbein filed an accusation against Wilhelm Boger, a former member of the Political Department at Auschwitz. This eventually led to the first big Auschwitz trial in Frankfurt, which opened on December 20, 1963, and ended on August 20, 1965. Langbein attended most of the court's sessions and, shortly after the verdict was announced, published a two-volume documentary account of the trial.

Langbein used the next four to five years to write a clear-eyed study of Auschwitz, drawing on his own experiences, as well as testimony at trials, and the accounts of fellow inmates. The book was published by Europa Verlag in 1972 as *Menschen in Auschwitz* (People in Auschwitz). As he told the Austrian political scientist Anton Pelinka, the use of the word *Menschen*, that is, "human beings," was meant to show that he tried his best to be objective, not to demonize even the SS. He did this in contrast to Benedict Kautsky, who in 1946 used the title *Teufel und Verdammte* (Devils and the damned) for his memoir of life in the concentration camps.

Until his death in Vienna in 1995, Langbein continued to write, participate in conferences, serve as secretary of the Comité, and speak to school classes as a witness. Wherever he appeared, he never indulged in self-dramatization. He would point out that his own condition as a political prisoner, who arrived in Auschwitz without kin, differed substantially from that of Jewish prisoners who arrived there with their families and soon realized that those dearest to them had been killed. He was always sure to discuss in his presentations about racial mass murder the fate not only of Jews but also of Gypsies.

I first met Hermann Langbein in 1987 at a conference in Hamburg. Later I also met him at a conference in Cologne and a few more times in Vienna. He always treated me like a comrade, insisting that we use first names and informal address. His attitude was probably due to the fact that he considered me a fellow Auschwitz survivor, although my three months in Birkenau could hardly match his experience. Still, I do remember enough to attest to the accuracy with which Langbein's book delineates the texture of life and of death there. As a fellow historian, I also can attest to the accuracy of his interpretation, which I share. I do not believe that one can explain Auschwitz as a horrible chapter in Jewish history alone; an explanation also must take into full account Gypsies and other victims. In the larger context, Auschwitz epitomized a total negation of the values of Western civilization. Langbein's skilled mixture of personal observations and historical knowledge makes his book unique among Holocaust memoirs. I am therefore very happy that an English-language translation of *Menschen in Auschwitz* finally is being published. All those, especially students, interested in the dark planet that was Auschwitz will profit from reading *People in Auschwitz*.

Introduction

Auschwitz prisoner Hermann Langbein, ca. 1940. Photograph from United States Holocaust Memorial Museum, courtesy of Panstwowe Muzeum w Oswiecim-Brzezinka.

AUTHOR'S RATIONALE

■ ■ ■

"What Auschwitz was is known only to its inmates and to no one else." This is what Martin Walser wrote under the impression of the Auschwitz trial in Frankfurt. "Because we cannot empathize with the situation of the prisoners, because their suffering exceeded any previous measure and we therefore cannot form a human impression of the immediate perpetrators, we call Auschwitz a hell and the evildoers devils. This might be an explanation for the fact that when we talk about Auschwitz, we use words that point the way beyond our world." Walser concludes his observation tersely: "However, Auschwitz was not hell but a German concentration camp."

Auschwitz was created in the middle of the twentieth century by the machinery of a state with old cultural traditions. It was real.

In that camp people were exposed to extreme conditions. This study will describe how both prisoners and guards reacted to them, for the people who lived in Auschwitz on the other side of the barbed wire had also been placed in an extreme situation, though it was quite different from the one forced upon the prisoners.

"No one can imagine exactly what happened. . . . All this can be conveyed only by one of us, . . . someone from our small group, our inner circle, provided that someone accidentally survives." These words were written by Zelman Lewental, a Polish Jew who was forced to work in the gas chambers of Auschwitz. He was tormented by the idea that posterity would never know what he had to experience. Since he had no hope of surviving Auschwitz, he buried his notes near one of the crematoriums. They were dug up in 1961, but only scraps could still be deciphered.

■ Many prisoners were plagued by the same worry as Lewental: that the world would never learn about the crimes committed in Auschwitz, or that if any of these became known, they would not be believed. This is how improbable a description of those events was bound to seem to outsiders. I still remember some conversations about this subject. The friends who voiced such fears perished in Auschwitz, but I survived and have borne the burden of a responsibility. We regard it as our task to keep insisting that lessons must be learned from Auschwitz.

For this reason many people have written down their experiences. Shortly after his liberation Viktor Frankl wrote: "We must not simplify things by declaring that some were angels and the others devils." Since then this obligation has gained even more weight. Nevertheless, I am aware of the limitations of one survivor's efforts to give an objective presentation of people in Auschwitz and their problems.

Each of us harbors his personally biased memories and has experienced "his" Auschwitz. The perspective of a person who was always hungry differed markedly from that of an inmate with a job; the Auschwitz of 1942 was quite different from the Auschwitz of 1944. Each camp of the large complex was a world of its own, and that is why many a survivor of Auschwitz will be able to react to individual descriptions by saying, "That's not how I perceived it" or "That's news to me." Since I did not skirt delicate subjects, there may be objections from some who believe that these should not be made public. I did not devise any theory about certain problems discussed in the literature and did not choose examples from the rich material to bolster one theory or another, and for that reason readers committed to some ideology might view my presentation with displeasure.

▧ Is it, then, necessary for me to justify my decision to present a comprehensive study despite such possible objections and my subjective orientation, which I could not and would not suppress? Perhaps the following circumstances will justify this decision.

Like all Austrian prisoners, I was regarded as a German in the concentration camp. Germans were even more privileged in Auschwitz than in other camps because there the percentage of Germans was smaller than in Dachau, Buchenwald, and other camps in Germany. Thus I was not crushed by the daily struggle for the most elementary things. As the clerk of the ss garrison physician (*Standortarzt*), I had no heavy physical labor to perform; I always had a roof over my head, never went hungry, and was able to wash myself and wear clean clothes. We Austrians differed from many equally privileged German political prisoners. These hated Nazism with all their heart, but in some instances they had hailed victories of Hitler's armies or at least regarded them with mixed feelings. By contrast, the politically persecuted Austrians also felt nationally suppressed. We saw our future only in the defeat of the German armies, and our vision was not narrowed by the inhibition of those who believed that what happened was done in the name of their people and that the crushing of Nazism would bring untold misery to that people and abandon it to the vengeance of those now being tortured. That is why the privileges deliberately granted by the camp administration to German inmates had less of a corrupting effect on politically aware Austrians.

My job afforded me a chance to look behind the scenes. However, the camp administration never saddled me with the kind of responsibility for fellow prisoners that every capo or block elder had. Hence I am able to analyze without any personal bias the problems connected with being an inmate functionary.

I was one of the top VIPs in the camp, but I lived in constant fear that the administration might find out that according to Nazi regulations I was not an "Aryan" but a "*Mischling*" (part-Jew). For as long as a Mischling was treated as a Jew, I had to be prepared to be thrust down the long scale from privileged German to Jew. This rendered me resistant to the condescending compassion a self-assured person might show for that lowest stratum, a feeling of pity that could so easily mingle with contempt.

I was interned as a fighter in the Spanish Civil War and as a communist, and thus I know from my own experience the additional problems faced by members of that party. Since I later broke with it, I gained the freedom and detachment that permit me to deal with problems concerning the conduct of communists in the concentration camps—questions that have elicited a variety of answers in the literature, depending on the political orientation of an author.

I was one of the leaders of the international resistance movement in Auschwitz. The tasks that we set ourselves required us to deal with many problems of camp life and transcend our selves and our current situation. By virtue of my position as the secretary of an SS leader, it was my special assignment to observe the SS men as closely as possible and to differentiate among them in an effort to exploit these differences and create chances to influence those men.

I spent only two years in Auschwitz, from August 1942 to August 1944, but this was the most eventful period. During my nine months in the bunker of Auschwitz I became acquainted with the most extreme situation of the prisoners, except for those assigned to the Sonderkommando (Special Commando) [charged with burning corpses].

However, all this did not initially give me the courage to tackle a presentation of the human problems. This study has had a long gestation period; the first outline is dated January 30, 1962, but I kept hesitating. It took the Auschwitz trial in Frankfurt to dispel my doubts about whether I already had the necessary detachment from my experiences to present them objectively. In Frankfurt I faced Josef Klehr, an SS medic who had just been arrested. I knew all about his heinous deeds. At that time, in the fall of 1960, all my painful memories returned, and for a long time I was haunted by the impressions made by that encounter. Five years later, at the conclusion of the big Auschwitz trial, at which Klehr was one of the defendants and which I attended as an observer, especially of Klehr's conduct, I no longer regarded that man as the omnipotent terror of the prison infirmary but as an aged, extremely crude criminal who defended himself ineptly. When I became aware of this transformation, I dared to set to work, and in February 1966 I began to study the sources.

■ There is an extensive literature on Auschwitz. Primo Levi begins his report about the camp with these words: "The need to tell the 'others,' to let the 'others' participate, had grown into such an immediate and urgent impulse in us that it challenged our other elementary needs. And it is this need that prompted this book, which means that it was written mainly for the sake of an inner liberation." He properly uses a plural pronoun, for many survivors of Auschwitz have put pen to paper out of the same urge.

As a rule, these reports were written quite subjectively, and this is what makes them valuable. Prior to their deportation, life had formed the authors in different ways, and they had different kinds of experiences in the camp. They varied in their abilities, their opportunities to observe, their honesty toward themselves, and their expressiveness. Their reports express all these differences, and each is a tessera in the total picture which no one can convey from his own vantage point.

Only a very small number of survivors of the concentration camps were qualified to record, immediately after their liberation, not only their own experiences but also the entire system of the Nazi concentration camps. Eugen Kogon, Benedikt Kautsky, and David Rousset did have the strength for such a presentation, and errors in detail that were unavoidable at the time do not diminish the importance of their pioneering work in the least.

A critical assessment of the various first-hand accounts can be undertaken only if we compare them with the facts now documented, for a comparison with one's own experiences would be too subjective.

When authors describe events that they have not personally witnessed, errors are understandable, because in the camps rumors tended to embellish anything that was out of the ordinary. There was hardly any author who was able to verify the truth content of a report based only on his own memory.

If an author errs in the description of something he has experienced, this should be a warning for the critical reader. For example, Henry Bulawko claims that upon his arrival at the train station he saw a sign with the inscription "Oswiecim." However, the town called Oswiecim had become part of Upper Silesia, and thus the station bore only the Germanized name Auschwitz, which has achieved such terrible fame. Miklos Nyiszli gives exact figures as well as the ranks of the ss men who were killed on October 7, 1944, during the rebellion of the Sonderkommando, to which he belonged: one first lieutenant (Obersturmführer), twenty-seven technical sergeants (Oberscharführer) and staff sergeants (*Scharführer*), and fifty-two privates first class (*Sturmmänner*). According to documents that have been preserved, only three ss men, all of them sergeants (*Unterscharführer*), were killed on that occasion, and twelve are said to have been wounded. Bernard Klieger's description of the sexual problem conflicts with all other reports. He speaks of an animalistic sexual voracity and describes its consequences thus: "Males and females did it almost like dogs. Wherever and whenever there was an opportunity, they rushed into each other's arms." This crass generalization is about as accurate as would be the observation that after a long internment everyone weighed eighty-five kilos, Klieger's weight, at the evacuation of Auschwitz.

It is altogether understandable that errors are most likely to be made in a chronological presentation of events. When former inmates are obliged to describe their experiences at trials, they are as a rule most uncertain in giving dates, for daily life in the camps offered too few clues. Elie Wiesel's statement that he lost his sense of time completely has general validity. Wiesel even got the date of his deportation wrong when he remembered that he arrived in Auschwitz in April. His prison number indicates an arrival on May 24.

A fanatical fixation on party politics can induce an author to produce a one-sided presentation. Oszkár Betlen betrays his partisan orientation when he writes: "Of the six clerks in the prison office, only Walser and I were communists, but the other four were decent people, too." However, despite this obvious one-sidedness Betlen is able to make many universally valid statements, and this is true of all first-hand reports that contain errors and distortions. A critical reader who has himself experienced Auschwitz is probably a better judge of what is valid and what cannot be accepted or generalized about than an outsider.

To be sure, methods such as those applied by Bruno Baum are bound to give anyone pause. His little book about resistance in Auschwitz was published in the German Democratic Republic in 1949 and reprinted in 1957 and 1961. Persons named in the first edition as heroes of the resistance were omitted from the later ones because they had broken with the Communist Party, while others were discovered as leaders of the resistance in the third printing because they were then enjoying the favor of the party's leadership.

In referring to my own experiences I usually draw on my book *Die Stärkeren: Ein Bericht* (The stronger: A report), which I wrote in the winter of 1947–48, when despite a certain detachment from those events my memory was still keen. Decades later it would not be possible for me to reconstruct conversations and events with more telling words than I did then. I wrote that report as a convinced communist and therefore kept silent about many things that communists would not like to read. In the present study I shall discuss problems of that kind by way of a supplement. To be sure, even in Auschwitz I did not share Betlen's view that people could be classified as communists and as others who can be "decent, too."

Understandably enough, surviving members of the ss have not had the same urge to write down their memories of Auschwitz as surviving prisoners did. Nevertheless, there are a few reports of enduring value, first and foremost the memoirs of Rudolf Höß, the commandant of Auschwitz, which he wrote in a Cracow prison. Even though he repeatedly attempts to whitewash his conduct, he does give an alarmingly accurate picture of the extermination camp and at the same time unintentionally paints a vivid self-portrait. We also have a report by Pery Broad, who wrote down in a British prisoner-of-war camp what he learned as a member of the Political Department [the camp Gestapo]. Even though he keeps silent about his own actions, he proves to be a keen observer. The concise diary entries of Johann Kremer, an ss physician and university professor, also have documentary value, as well as the merit of having been written on the spot rather than during Kremer's subsequent imprisonment.

Obtrusive attempts at whitewashing decrease the value of the reports that Wilhelm Claussen, an ss roll call leader (Rapportführer), and Maximilian Grabner, the chief of the Political Department, wrote during their imprisonment. Grabner's report is further devalued by his attempt to get even with ss men who testified against him before an ss tribunal in Auschwitz. In the paragraph in which Grabner deals with me, the falsity of his report is manifest.

As time elapsed and sources became known, authors who had no personal knowledge of Auschwitz frequently concerned themselves with related subjects. The first presentation of this kind is by Jan Sehn, the Polish examining magistrate who prepared the big Auschwitz trials in Poland. Despite the author's great conscientiousness, even this objective and sober study is not altogether free from errors. Thus Sehn writes that in early 1942 all non-German prisoners had a number tattooed on their left forearm. Actually, the order for this was not given until February 22, 1943. Implementing this order took considerable time; thus, for example, prisoners who were transferred from Auschwitz to Sachsenhausen had no tattooed numbers on March 13 of that year.

As the first comprehensive study of the Nazis' destruction of the Jews, Gerald Reitlinger's book Die Endlösung (The Final Solution), published in 1953, gained the reputation of a standard work. For this reason, some of its errors were uncritically adopted by other authors, frequently without a reference to the source. A few small misstatements shall be recorded here. Reitlinger mentions "two physicians from Poland, Entress and Zinkteller." The two physicians were indeed from Poland, but in Auschwitz Entress, as an ethnic German, wore the uniform of an ss physician, and Zenkteller (not Zinkteller) was there as a Polish inmate physician. By mentioning them together, Reitlinger is misleading. Elsewhere Reitlinger writes that Arthur Liebehenschel was the commandant of Auschwitz until February 1944, but he actually held this position until May 9 of that year. Reitlinger also states that fear of being called to account some day caused the SS physician Kremer and his kind to put bogus diagnoses on death certificates. When I was a prisoner, I had to submit to Kremer and his colleagues piles of such certificates for their signature. Neither Kremer nor any other SS physician added any diagnosis, for the prison clerks had to do this beforehand. In most cases the diagnosis was indeed a fantasy, but the SS physicians rarely read them before signing and only groaned about all the signatures that were required of them. Kremer was in Auschwitz in the fall of 1942. Neither I nor anyone else who dealt with SS physicians at that time, prior to the German defeat at Stalingrad, noticed any indication that a member of the SS was afraid of ever being called to account for his activities in Auschwitz.

An awareness of Reitlinger's insignificant errors will give readers a more critical attitude toward the data published by that author, information that was copied by many others and added to the general confusion about the numbers of those who were killed in Auschwitz.

In his characterization of Höß, the historian Joachim C. Fest evidently relies on the commandant's autobiography and ignores other sources. Thus he describes Höß's "pronounced moral sense" as an outstanding characteristic of the commandant of Auschwitz. Höß depicted himself as a loving family man, but he had an affair with an inmate of the camp and tried to starve that woman to death in a stand-up bunker when that relationship became known. Certainly this is not compatible with a pronounced moral sense or with unselfishness, a quality that Fest also discerns in Höß. He appropriated so much property from the deportees that two railroad cars were required when Höß left Auschwitz with his family.

In his book *Die unbesungenen Helden* (The unsung heroes), Kurt R. Grossmann cites Heinz Kraschutzki's greatly embellished portrait of the SS physician Moench, who reportedly joined the SS only to save his Jewish wife. When he was arraigned in a Cracow court, the entire audience is supposed to have cried, "Free him!" In point of fact, the wife of Dr. Münch (the correct name) was not Jewish, and the physician joined the SS because he hoped this would further his career as a hygienist. Some former inmates testified in his favor, and so Münch was the only person acquitted in the Cracow trial, but there is no other report about spontaneous dramatic shouts in the courtroom.

Christiane Klusacek is another author who has perpetuated a legend. In her little book *Österreichische Wissenschaftler und Künstler unter dem NS Regime* (Austrian scholars and artists under the Nazi regime), she writes that when Alma

Rosé, the well-known musician and conductor of the women's orchestra at Auschwitz, was asked to play while people selected for the gas chamber were being taken away, she spontaneously jumped on a truck transporting the condemned. Klusacek concludes her report with these words: "On the rolling truck she plays that great song of freedom, the Marseillaise." Rosé did die in Auschwitz, but not so melodramatically.

About publications like those of Paul Rassinier there is nothing to say. Anyone who doubts whether there were gas chambers in Auschwitz and tries to devalue the memoirs of Höß, which contain a precise description of the gassing procedure, by saying that they can be deciphered only like hieroglyphs is beyond any criticism. Höß's handwriting is quite legible, and none of the SS men charged with crimes have attempted to deny that there were gassing facilities in Auschwitz.

I am sorry to say that I did not have access to all the literature on Auschwitz. Since there is no reasonably complete collection anywhere, I had to do quite a bit of searching and traveling. In only a few cases was I able to have reports in languages unfamiliar to me translated, and thus I could not take cognizance of many Polish descriptions. On the other hand, my work was facilitated by having several unpublished manuscripts placed at my disposal and by having use of my enormous correspondence with survivors of Auschwitz as well as a large number of conversations. Finally, while I was working on this book, I had fragmentary reports checked by persons with first-hand knowledge of the episodes presented in them. I was aided by the fact that conversations with former inmates, including those I had not known in Auschwitz, soon produced an atmosphere of trust, whereas outsiders often complain about the difficulty of getting such former prisoners to speak frankly.

In my work I was guided by a principle enunciated by Andrzej Wirth in his postscript to the Auschwitz tales of Tadeusz Borowski: "To get at the truth about mass murder in the twentieth century, one must not demonize the murderers or apotheosize the victims. What needs to be indicted is the inhuman situation created by the fascist system." I would only replace "fascist" with the more precise term "Nazi," for there have been various fascist systems but only one Auschwitz. In this I agree with Günter Grass, who wrote: "What happened before Auschwitz is subject to different categories of judgment. The machinery of destruction has always existed, but only its perfection turned it into a category. What was new and unprecedented was not the particular cruelty of individuals but rather the anonymous smoothness of clerical work that has to be called diligent, and it was this newness in its human pallor that we, distancing ourselves from it, call inhuman."

THE CAMP AND ITS JARGON
■ ■ ■

A description of people in Auschwitz and their problems presupposes a knowledge of the system of the concentration camps and an explanation of the lingo that developed there, in particular of concepts that were typical of Auschwitz and became part of that camp's language.

The first concentration camps were built immediately after the Nazis' accession to power in 1933. In the course of time they developed a system of controlled self-government by the inmates that was based on the Nazi leadership principle (*Führerprinzip*). Each unit housing prisoners was called a block and headed by a block elder (*Blockältester*), and a dormitory elder (*Stubenältester*) was in charge of barracks. All reported to a camp elder (*Lagerältester*). Basically, all prisoners had to work. They formed labor details headed by capos (or, in the case of large details, by senior capos and junior capos). These functionaries were identified by armbands with the proper inscription. They enjoyed extensive privileges and frequently had unlimited power over their subordinates. The functionaries did not have to work, but they were called to task if the camp administration determined that there was something wrong in their camp, block, or detail.

An incident that was by no means isolated may illustrate how the SS expected this instrumentality to work. One day the SS camp leader (*Lagerführer*) decided that there had been a general decline in discipline, and so he ordered all capos to come forward after the evening roll call and had each given five lashes. "From now on, see to it that the entrance of the work details is improved." Quite a few of the capos passed those punitive lashes on to their subordinates.

Seeing to it that their men marched as *zackig* (snappily) as possible, an extreme form of the bullying practiced at Prussian military posts, was only part of the capos' duties. They were also responsible for their details' workload. If the output did not correspond to the norm, the capos had to "bend over the buck," as the German capo Willi Brachmann put it, explaining that this practice was ordered to make the capos see to it that the work went well.

Richard Böck is one of the very few SS men who have been willing to testify. When he was called to Frankfurt as a witness, he prepared a manuscript that contained this passage: "If an inmate was no longer up to the labor, the capos and junior capos had to beat him. If a commando leader or block leader happened upon the scene, things really got rough. 'Capo, come here!' Boom!

'Can't you hit any harder?' At that point the capo appeared to be beating his victim as if his life depended on it. Again. 'Capo, come here! Finish him off!' If the capo did not hit hard enough, he usually got his face slapped or his butt kicked by a boot."

On the other side of the ledger, the camp administration granted the inmate functionaries privileges that ordinary inmates did not even dare dream about. They were given preferential treatment when it came to lodging, clothing, and food, and they could claim rights that distinguished them from the bulk of the prisoners. An underling had no chance to lodge a complaint against a capo or block elder; these men could mete out punishment and even kill as they saw fit. If an inmate functionary announced a "departure through death," usually no one asked about the cause of death. The numbers had to be correct, and the roll call had to be in order; that was all the camp administration cared about.

In this way a hierarchy was systematically built up among the prisoners that was to act as an extended arm of the camp leadership, carry terror to the remotest parts of the camp, and keep it active even when no ss man was in the camp (for instance, at night). Once inmate functionaries had incurred guilt in the service of their masters, there was a simple way to make them their obedient tools: a capo or block elder could be stripped of his armband at any time and pushed down the hierarchic ladder. However, once he had lost his armband and with it the protection of the camp leadership, he was fair game for the revenge of those he had tormented. Often a threat that this protection would be removed was sufficient.

▓ In regard to jobs, Germans were given preferential treatment. In addition to his number, each inmate had to wear a triangle (called a *Winkel*) that indicated the type of imprisonment. In the case of non-Germans, the triangle bore an initial indicating their nationality: for example, "P" for Poles and "F" for the French. The color of the triangle indicated the reason for the imprisonment. Political prisoners wore a red triangle and thus generally were called Reds; inmates who had been committed to the camp because of their criminal records and were listed as "professional criminals" wore a green triangle and were known as Greens. Other colors, those designating antisocials (black), Jehovah's Witnesses, and homosexuals played no significant part in the hierarchy of the prisoners in Auschwitz—except for the women's camp, where prostitutes with black triangles had important functions. Underneath their triangle, which indicated the country from which they had been deported, Jews had to wear a yellow triangle whose tip pointed upward, and with their six points the two triangles formed a Star of David.

The differences among the prisoners were indicated not only in this graphic fashion; in fact, the contrasts and conflicts among the various groups were deliberately emphasized and even exaggerated. Commandant Höß summarized the rationale for this as follows: "No camp administration, no matter how powerful, would be able to lead and keep a tight rein on thousands of inmates without utilizing these contrasts and conflicts. The more numerous the opposing forces among the prisoners and the fiercer their power struggles are, the easier it is to run the camp."

Konrad Morgen, an SS judge acquainted with several concentration camps, testified in American captivity that the prisoners' self-government was balanced in such a way that there was a permanent rivalry between political and criminal inmates.

Maximilian Grabner certified that, as a practical person, SS roll call leader Oswald Kaduk managed to "create a following of criminal prisoners that he unleashed on the political prisoners whenever an opportunity arose."

Where German political prisoners set the tone, we speak of a Red camp, and camps in which German criminal prisoners did so are referred to as Green camps. Höß, who had had years of experience in camps when he was entrusted with the development of Auschwitz, once stated that from the viewpoint of those running a camp ten Green functionaries were better than a hundred SS men.

To be sure, groups with identical insignia were anything but homogeneous. The camp population included not only political prisoners who were active opponents of Nazism, but also persons who had told political jokes while drunk or who had been caught participating in the illegal slaughter of animals. Ella Lingens reports about German women sent to a camp with red triangles because they had relationships with Poles. On the other hand, there was an occasional Green whose transgressions were political in nature—for example, the forgery of documents in order to provide members of an underground organization with false papers.

It needs to be emphasized that not all Greens were willing tools of the SS and that not all Reds performed their functions in a spirit of comradeship. Nevertheless, camps governed by Greens were rightly feared. In a Red camp the political prisoners were able to exercise a kind of moral supervision over inmate functionaries, and this had a good effect. Because of the natural antithesis between the Reds and the Greens and also because of the camp administration's tactic of playing these factions off against each other a bitter underground struggle raged between them in all concentration camps.

As far as jobs in the camps were concerned, Germans were given first choice and Jews received certain functions only in the final phase, particularly in satellite camps that housed Jews almost exclusively. Among the other nationalities identified as "Aryans" (and we shall have to use this unscientific designation to avoid awkward circumlocutions), the Poles achieved a certain privileged status in Auschwitz—not because the SS granted it to them, but because in the early period Auschwitz had mostly Polish prisoners, which meant that they filled key positions in the prisoners' administration for which Germans were not suited because of their small number or their lack of intelligence. The Poles used every opportunity to help their compatriots obtain better positions. This privileged status was expressed linguistically as well, for Polish or Polonized terms frequently became part of the camp jargon. Thus many prisoners referred to a block elder as Blokowy (feminine form: Blokowa) and called a dormitory elder Stubowy.

German criminals were sent to the camps because of their prior convictions, German political prisoners because of their real or at least presumed opposition to the regime, and "Aryans" from other nationalities because of their usually even vaguer enmity toward the Third Reich; but the Jews from almost all countries under German domination were deported solely because of their Jewish descent. For that reason there were even greater differences among these Jews than among other groups of inmates. The Gypsies were the only other group that suffered the same "total" fate under the Nazis.

■ The inmates were differentiated not only by their insignia. Every prisoner also had to wear a number sewn to his clothing. Unlike the practice of many other camps, Auschwitz did not reassign the number of an inmate who died or was transferred, which means that each number indicates when its bearer came to Auschwitz. In all camps a sort of aristocracy of low numbers came into being. People in Auschwitz regarded the "millionaires," as those with a six-digit number were called, with a certain disdain. That camp, however, was different in one respect: When I was transferred to Auschwitz after fifteen months in Dachau, I was still regarded as a "novice" in the latter camp because of my number. In Auschwitz, on the other hand, I was counted as an "old-timer" after just a few months. This indicates that in an extermination camp the fluctuation was that much greater.

Women received numbers of a different series in Auschwitz, beginning with number 1, and when a Gypsy (Zigeuner) camp was established, its inmates also had special series of numbers, one for men and another for women, with a "Z" preceding the number. On May 13, 1944, the camp administration ordered that Jewish newcomers be given numbers of a new series, one preceded by an "A." At a later date an additional series with a "B" was started.

■ In the camps the inmates knew one another by their first names. Polish names were always used in their short form—for instance, Staszek for Stanislaw, Tadek for Tadeusz, Józek for Jósef, and Mietek for Mieczyslaw. I use such forms in the present study, and with some German names as well. Since Rudolf Friemel was generally known as Rudi, I call him that here.

As the camps grew—and Auschwitz became the biggest after it had been expanded into an extermination camp—their administrative machinery became more and more complex. Numerically and intellectually, the guards were incapable of running this machinery without friction. Among the prisoners there were many who had the ability to perform even complicated administrative tasks, and it was from their ranks that the offices and other administrative centers were staffed. The camp leadership regarded the daily roll call as most important. Despite all new arrivals and transfers, admissions to and releases from the infirmary, deaths, work orders outside the camp area, and the like, the roll call had to balance. The inmates who had to write reports or perform similar functions were interested in complicating the administrative machinery even further to demonstrate their indispensability. In this endeavor they were aided by the SS's marked tendency toward overbureaucratization.

Every individual in the machinery could be capriciously replaced at any time if he displeased his superior. However, the camp leadership was dependent on the entire machinery of the inmates' self-government, for its removal would have led to the breakdown of the entire camp. Despite all of the SS's efforts, the prisoners who were part of that organization managed to stick together, and thus they constituted a certain force.

Inmate functionaries and those who held key positions in the administration and important work details were regarded as part of the camp elite. The living conditions of these VIPs were quite different from those of the hoi polloi, and more so in Auschwitz than in the ordinary camps.

These masses were constantly harassed by a system of barbaric punishments and absurd orders that were practically impossible to carry out. The camp leadership liked to impose collective punishments that were designed to set one group of prisoners against another. Extension of roll call, punitive calisthenics, or withholding of food were intended to make the mass of the prisoners angry at the inmate who had incurred the displeasure of the leadership. At an early hour the inmates were forced to engage in an exhausting race to wash, make their beds, go to the latrine, and get coffee. Bruno Bettelheim, who became familiar with such races in other camps, has described them as follows: "By sunrise a struggle of all against all with all its tensions, humiliations, and depressions had already taken place. An inmate was forced to engage in it in the morning even before a guard had entered the camp. The SS, which was as yet invisible, had compacted the prisoners into a mass of human beings who were unable to abreact their anger and despaired because of their impotence."

This wearying struggle was continued in the evening after the SS had left the camp. "Our evening in the barracks after finishing a long workday should not be regarded as a rest. It must be thought of as another ordeal," writes Pelagia Lewinska, who became acquainted with the women's camp at Birkenau. That a VIP was largely able to avoid this stressful daily struggle was not the least of the benefits of his status.

The official abbreviation for *Konzentrationslager* was KL, and this form appears in documents and written statements by SS men, but in everyday speech the abbreviation KZ prevailed, both among the prisoners and their guards.

Every KZ had an inmate infirmary, and in Auschwitz it was called the Häftlingskrankenbau (HKB). The prisoners entrusted with its operation wore an armband with the inscription "Lagerältester HKB."

■ In every camp a commander was in charge of the guards. The camp itself was operated by one or more SS protective custody camp leaders (*Schutzhaftlagerführer*). Below them in authority were the SS roll call leaders, who in turn were superior to the SS block leaders (*Blockführer*). The latter were SS men, usually of a low rank, who were in charge of one or more blocks. They should not be confused with the block elders, who were prisoners. The labor details (*Arbeitskommandos*, called *Kommandos*) were headed by an SS commando leader (*Kommandoführer*).

The chief SS physician, who was in charge of everything connected with health services and some things unconnected with health, had the title SS garrison physician in Auschwitz. He was the superior of the other SS physicians, and they in turn were assisted by medics of various ranks (*Sanitätsdienstgrade*, or SDG). The infirmaries were not supervised by the SS camp leaders, the SS roll call leaders, or the SS block leaders, but by the SS physicians and the SDG. This was to be of special significance in Auschwitz.

Every camp had a Political Department, which in addition to performing administrative tasks functioned as a camp Gestapo. The head of this division in Auschwitz reported to the Gestapo in nearby Katowice, while all others reported to the SS Economic and Administrative Central Office (Wirtschaftverwaltungshauptamt, or WVHA) in Oranienburg near Berlin.

The SS called its officers "Führer" (leaders). The highest rank held by an SS officer in Auschwitz was that of SS lieutenant colonel (*Obersturmbannführer*). The commandants Höß and Liebehenschel as well as Joachim Caesar and Ernst Möckel, who headed the agricultural and administrative institutions, held that rank.

■ In all camps corruption assumed grotesque dimensions. SS men had inmates work for them in camp workshops. The higher their rank and the greater their influence, the more extensive were their orders. Raw materials that were in short supply and thus were to be reserved for the arms industry were freely used for such orders. An inmate who wanted to stay alive also had to "organize," to use the common expression for appropriating goods from stockrooms, larders, or kitchens, because the officially distributed rations were inadequate. A distinction was made between stealing and "organizing." If someone helped himself to the property of a fellow inmate, he was treated as a thief and severely punished by his comrades. "Organizing," however, was regarded as honorable and commendable. Anyone who was able to do this without attracting attention and being caught was generally respected.

In Auschwitz the opportunities for such "organizing" were far greater than in regular concentration camps, for the Jews transported to the extermination camp were told they were being resettled and ordered to take along anything that might be of use in building a new existence in the East. On their arrival in Auschwitz, everything was taken from them, and their belongings were sorted by a prisoner labor detail and checked for hidden valuables. Everything was there—not only food and medicine, alcohol and clothing, but also jewelry, diamonds, gold, and money in many currencies, especially dollars. The Polish inmates called the barracks in which this property was inspected, sorted, and stored "Canada"—to them presumably a symbol of legendary riches. This expression gained currency and was used even by the SS. The detail that had to work there and thus had the best chances to "organize" became known as the Canada Commando.

As happened in all concentration camps, prisoners were sent to Auschwitz by various offices of the Gestapo and the detective forces (Kriminalpolizei, or Kripo). After the camp had been designated an extermination camp for Jews, and later for Gypsies as well, the Reich Security Main Office (Reichssicherheitshauptamt, or RSHA) directed transports of people earmarked for killing there; these were commonly referred to as RSHA transports. Unlike other prisoners, those sent to Auschwitz under these auspices were not brought directly to the camp but made to leave the train at the *Rampe* (ramp), as the railroad siding was called, and usually subjected to a "selection." This meant that those who appeared to be unfit for work were immediately sent to a gas chamber, while those fit for work were added to the inmate population. In this way the camp had a steady influx of fresh laborers, and therefore the SS carried on periodic selections among the inmates in order to kill in the gas chambers those who were no longer able to work and to have their tasks performed by new arrivals. Along with "Canada," "ramp" and "selection" became standard terms in Auschwitz.

THE HISTORY OF THE
EXTERMINATION CAMP
■ ■ ■

"The ss state appeared in the metallic glow of its totality as a state in which an idea was realized," wrote Jean Améry, who had been thrust into that state, the world of the concentration camps run by the ss.

Hannah Arendt, who was able to analyze this state from a distance, wrote: "The concentration and extermination camps serve the machinery of total power as experimental laboratories that investigate whether the fundamental claim of totalitarian systems—that it is possible to exert total domination over human beings—is correct."

Elsewhere Arendt writes: "Terror is the nature of total dominance. In countries with a totalitarian government, terror has as little to do with the existence of opponents of the regime as the laws in constitutionally governed countries are dependent on those who break them." Hannah Arendt points to a problem that students of the system of the Nazi concentration camps have to confront:

> Just as the stability of a totalitarian regime depends on isolating from the outside world the fictive world of [totalitarian] "movement," so the experiment of total domination in the concentration camps hinges on its being safely insulated from the world of all others, the world of the living, even within a country with a totalitarian ruler. This insulation is connected with the singular unreality and implausibility that are inherent in all reports from the camps and constitute one of the main impediments to a real understanding of the forms of total domination that stand and fall with the existence of the concentration and extermination camps, for, however improbable this may sound, these camps are the actual central institution of the totalitarian power and organization machine.

If one wants to study the power that a totalitarian regime can achieve over people as well as the influence that this untrammeled violence had on various individuals, it seems most expedient to investigate those central institutions. Our study is limited to Auschwitz, which was a concentration camp before it was turned into an extermination camp. In this respect it differed from Treblinka, Belzec, Sobibor, and Chelmno, which served as extermination camps exclusively. In those camps only a small number of prisoners were kept alive for as long as they were needed to operate the machinery of extermination.

Their fate is comparable to that of the Sonderkommandos in Auschwitz. Only Majdanek was, like Auschwitz, both a concentration and an extermination camp. However, it existed for a shorter period of time and was considerably smaller than Auschwitz. Very few inmates of that camp survived; most of them wound up in Auschwitz, which became the biggest extermination camp and at the same time the concentration camp with the largest number of inmates. About 60,000 prisoners who had been in Auschwitz were liberated in 1945. Many of them have rendered testimony, and numerous documents have been preserved. The information derived from these sources can apply to all Nazi extermination camps.

Those who had to live in those places were subjected to hitherto unknown and even unimaginable conditions. Opposing any comparison of Auschwitz with Dachau, Jean Améry writes: "Dachau was one of the first Nazi concentration camps and thus had, if you will, a certain tradition. Auschwitz was not established until 1940 and was subject to daily improvisations to the very end. In Dachau the political element predominated among the prisoners, while in Auschwitz the overwhelming majority of the prisoners consisted of completely apolitical Jews and politically rather unstable Poles. In Dachau the internal administration was largely in the hands of political prisoners, while German career criminals set the tone in Auschwitz." In Monowitz, where Améry was interned, the camp elder wore a green triangle until the very end.

I was transferred to Auschwitz from Dachau. When, at the Auschwitz trial in Frankfurt, I was asked about the difference between the two camps, I called Dachau a kind of idyll by comparison with the other camp. In response to the same question with reference to Buchenwald, his first place of internment, the Czech Arnos Tauber used the same term. Ernst Toch, who was transferred to Auschwitz from Sachsenhausen, said that he had thought he had a chance in his previous camp but lost that belief in Auschwitz. Heinz Brandt who was in the same camps as Toch, wrote: "Sachsenhausen was hell, but a hell that could be comprehended. Auschwitz is a jungle of murder, looting and slavery."

In Dachau, the first Nazi concentration camp, the ss developed a system that was adopted by all other camps. After the outbreak of the war, the character of the camps was changed radically by the steadily increasing number of non-German prisoners and the substantial growth of the camps. This made the German inmates a privileged minority.

Auschwitz is situated between Cracow and Kattowitz, an area that became part of Upper Silesia after the German occupation of Poland. The early history of the camp hardly differed from that of the other concentration camps established during the war. An ss Central Office report dated January 25, 1940, indicates that a plan to build a camp near Auschwitz was conceived early that year. In early May Rudolf Höß, the SS camp leader in Sachsenhausen, was appointed commandant of Auschwitz. He brought along not only the SS roll call leader Gerhard Palitzsch but also thirty German inmates who were to fill the most important jobs within the prisoner hierarchy. Almost all of these were criminals who already had performed such functions to the satisfaction of the SS. On June 14, 1940, the first 728 Poles arrived in Auschwitz, and the history of the camp begins with that fact. Further transports of Polish prisoners followed in short order.

On only one occasion [during the early period], on August 29, 1940, did prisoners of another nationality arrive in Auschwitz—again Germans from Sachsenhausen who were intended to meet the need for capos and block elders in the expanded camp. June 6, 1941, marked the first arrival of a unified group that did not contain any Poles; it was from neighboring Czechoslovakia.

In every newly established camp, the early period of development was particularly difficult for the inmates. Those Poles who managed to survive it had gained camp experience and tended to develop a feeling of superiority toward those who arrived after the camp had been fully built. The three-digit and four-digit numbers on their prison garb were a kind of badge that proved they had survived the hardest period, a documentation frequently respected even by the SS. In this way the Poles achieved a privileged position.

In the summer of 1941, the commandant of Auschwitz was ordered by Heinrich Himmler in a private conversation to expand his camp and get it ready for the "final solution of the Jewish question." This expression was a Nazi euphemism for the murder of the Jewish people. Höß did not remember the exact date of that confidential conversation, nor does it appear in any document.

In October 1941 construction was started on a camp complex of hitherto unknown dimensions about three kilometers northwest of the camp, later known as the main camp (*Stammlager*). Approximately 250 barracks were to house 200,000 prisoners. This new camp was called Birkenau, the German version of Brzezinka, the name of the Polish town that was destroyed to make way for the new construction. Russian prisoners of war who had been sent to Auschwitz in the fall and winter worked on it, and almost all of them perished. Of more than 1,300 men only 200 survived; according to a Russian who testified at the Frankfurt trial, the survivors were regarded as something like "objects in a museum" and given better treatment. The Birkenau complex of camps began to house prisoners in March 1942, but not all plans for expansion could be carried out by the time of evacuation.

"When one speaks about a camp, it is not sufficient to give the name of the camp. Even if one looks at the same period, the inmates of the same camp lived on different planets depending on the kind of work they had to do." This statement by Benedikt Kautsky applies to Auschwitz even more than to other camps, and it is especially true of the difference between the main camp, with its relatively orderly conditions, and the camp jungle of Birkenau.

■ In the process of executing Himmler's order, the SS began to search for some method of killing many people simultaneously and without great expense, and in September 1941 it had recourse to poison gas for the first time. The first victims were Russian prisoners of war and men from the infirmary who were unfit for work. The poison gas Zyklon B, which was stocked in Auschwitz for the extermination of vermin, found favor in the eyes of the camp leadership, for it offered the SS a chance to kill numerous people rapidly and with only a small number of guards and executioners. Herbert Jäger has pointed out another benefit that this form of killing brought the SS: "The inhibiting effects of the mass shootings (practiced by the Einsatzgruppen [SS operational groups] in the East up to that time), which once caused even Himmler to blanch, probably were the reason for the later murders in gas vans and gas chambers."

In this context Otto Ohlendorf, the leader of such an Einsatzgruppe, told his judges about the "humanization" of the mass murder. To be sure, this humanization did not refer to the victims but to the perpetrators, who were to be spared the emotional burden of nonstop shootings.

Andrzej Wirth has pointed out another significant consequence of this type of killing: "The relationship between a murderer and his victims has become anonymous. The murder itself results from a large number of partial decisions made by a large number of people who have neither an emotional nor an intellectual connection to the object of the murder." With this statement and his question "What is the cause and where does the effect begin?" Wirth touches on a problem that is encountered by anyone studying the reactions of people who participated in the mass murders in Auschwitz.

In the early period Polish Jews were already sent to Auschwitz along with Polish "Aryans," and they were automatically assigned to the penal company. Willi Brachmann, who came to Auschwitz as a capo with the second Sachsenhausen transport, testified that in those days all Jews had to work in the gravel pit. According to Brachmann, the SS camp leader ordered Roman, the capo of the detail, to finish off the Jews assigned to him: "I don't want to see any Jews!"

Two farmhouses that had survived the razing of the village Brzezinka were turned into gas chambers, and in January 1942 the first wholly Jewish transports (from nearby Upper Silesia) were murdered there. As in all extermination camps, the SS in Auschwitz forced the inmates to relieve them of all the labor connected with the removal and incineration of the corpses. Those who were assigned such tasks formed the so-called Sonderkommandos.

From March 26, 1942, onward, the RSHA directed all Jewish transports to Auschwitz; the initial ones came from Slovakia and France. At first all the Jews became inmates of the camp, but since the first transport included Slovakian women, it was necessary to establish a women's camp. Some blocks in the main camp were detached for that purpose, but on August 16 the women's camp was shifted to Birkenau, which was totally unprepared for this. As Höß put it, "The women's camp always had the worst conditions in every respect."

In the beginning all the deportees who arrived on RSHA transports were added to the camp population, but later these transports were subject to a selection. Documents indicate that the first such selection took place on July 4, 1942.

The deportation trains rolled day and night. Soon the makeshift gas chambers were insufficient, and four big crematoriums, each with a built-in gas chamber, were erected in Birkenau. Electric elevators took the corpses to the ovens. The modern buildings of extraordinary dimensions — in the two larger crematoriums it was possible to squeeze 2,000 people into each gas chamber — were the pride of the main construction office of the Waffen-SS and police.

These dates mark the period in which Auschwitz was expanded into an extermination camp. I shall not devote much attention to the preceding period, which may be called a sort of prehistory. The following figures will illustrate the speed with which the camp grew after the beginning of the RSHA transports. Between June 1940 and late March 1942, approximately 27,000 inmate numbers were given out, and during the following year, by March 1943, around 135,000 people received such numbers in Auschwitz.

The daily mass killings soon became routine. The selection of new arrivals, who usually did not suspect anything, at the ramp was done as quickly as possible, and the deception was kept up to the very end. SS roll call leader Oswald Kaduk testified in Frankfurt that the SS had been ordered not to administer beatings at the ramp so as to avoid panic among the victims. Rudolf Vrba, an inmate who had to work at the ramp for an extended period of time, confirmed that these orders were usually obeyed.

The constant threat of being selected as unfit for work, the stench of burnt human flesh that enveloped the camp complex, and the knowledge of daily mass murders placed anyone who was permitted to stay alive in Auschwitz in an unprecedented situation and confronted him with unparalleled problems. These were most crassly perceptible in Birkenau, where the extermination facilities had been installed. Seweryna Szmaglewska writes: "Anyone who falls into a leaden sleep after the daily drudgery is bound to be shaken awake by the screams at the ramp. Their realism burrows into the depth of consciousness, irritates and arouses."

Those ordered to guard the victims and operate the machinery of murder were also confronted with problems entirely different from those faced by, say, guards in Buchenwald or Dachau. Life in an extermination camp put everyone in an extreme situation, though it was extreme for those living outside the barbed wire in an entirely different sense from the victims.

The presiding judge at the big Auschwitz trial in Frankfurt, a man pledged to sober objectivity and striving for detachment, at the time of sentencing summarized his impression of the trial in these words: "Behind the entrance gate of the Auschwitz camp was the beginning of a hell that cannot be imagined by normal human brains and expressed in words."

The physician Désiré Haffner, an inmate of Auschwitz to whom we owe an incisive and reasonably objective study of Birkenau, has given this concise summary of what happened in the extermination camp: "The mass murder in Auschwitz is characterized by its long duration and the considerable number of its victims. The number of the children and babies killed there is in the hundreds of thousands."

What differentiates the mass murder in Auschwitz from other mass murders in history is that it was carried out without an element of excitement or passion. This mass murder was logical, dispassionately planned, carefully studied, and coolly implemented. Its planning was the result of close cooperation among politicians, chemists, physicians, psychiatrists, engineers, soldiers, and others. Its implementation required the disciplined and methodical support of a large-scale organization with branches in all European countries. This organization also encompassed the utilization of the property of those murdered, including their corpses. Gold was removed from their teeth, women's hair was used for special textiles, and even their "ashes were used as fertilizer or scattered over the Vistula River," as stated by Johann Gorges, an SS sergeant who worked in the crematoriums. Zofia Knapczyk recalls that the fields of the Babitz farm were fertilized with them. The ashes were also used to level the bottom of the fish ponds in a village called Harmense and to build a dam between it and another village, Plawy. Human ashes also served as insulating material under floors. Inmates who had to do this work found mixed in with the ashes eyeglass frames, bits of jaws with teeth in them, and similar things.

■ Birkenau was different from the main camp, and there were great differences between the conditions in 1942 and those in 1944. For this reason, we need to provide, first, a rough outline of the history of the extermination camp before we present the human problems found there.

In the course of the two and a half years of the camp's existence, various influences produced a change in its climate, the primary impetus being the general developments during this period.

In the early years of Auschwitz, the system that had been developed in all concentration camps before the war prevailed. Labor was intended as punishment, and, in keeping with this philosophy, assigned work frequently was as senseless as it was torturous. The literature on the concentration camps contains numerous examples. Rocks had to be carried from one place to another quickly, carefully stacked there, and then rushed back to the old place. The SS never completely abandoned this method of torture, but even before Auschwitz was expanded into an extermination camp, change was in the air, for the war economy needed workers. The great effect that this had on the camps is documented in a letter from Himmler dated January 26, 1942; in it he informed the inspector of the concentration camps that he planned to send 150,000 Jews in the next four weeks because "the coming weeks will bring the camps great economic tasks and assignments."

In order to provide the steadily more demanding arms industry with workers, satellite camps were built in the vicinity of all camps near factories, mines, or quarries and fitted out as labor camps. This eliminated the prisoners' long trek to their workplaces, which had restricted the utilization of their energies. In the summer of 1942, the first labor camps were built near Auschwitz. In October of that year, a labor camp was built at the Buna Works of IG Farben, a few kilometers east of Auschwitz. It was later called Monowitz after the neighboring town, and as the biggest satellite camp it became the headquarters of all other labor camps. This development was accelerated after the defeat at Stalingrad. There were thirty satellite camps in all, though not all at the same time. New camps were built all the time, but occasionally one of them was discontinued.

A striking new expression may be found in internal memos of the camp administrations from this period: extermination through labor. This explains why not all deported Jews were immediately sent to the gas chambers: those capable of working were to be used in the arms industry before they died. Consequently, as the center for the "final solution of the Jewish question," Auschwitz rapidly developed into the most populous KZ. Even though the quoted phrase clearly demonstrates that the basic philosophy had remained the same, the prisoners were able to benefit from the new system to some extent.

From that time on, there was less brutality. Stanislaw Kaminski, a Pole who was in Auschwitz from the beginning, writes: "At first the SS and the capos ran wild and murdered everywhere. After 1942 this eased up somewhat, and after 1943 the inmates with jobs had an entirely different attitude." As Kaminski's compatriot Józef Mikusz puts it matter-of-factly, "In 1943 there was less killing in Auschwitz than there had been before."

This may have been due to the fact that in the early period Poles were the preferred victims of the SS and that they were later replaced by Russian prisoners of war and subsequently by Jews. The reason for this change in attitude is clear: flogging a skilled worker will diminish his output rather than increase it. A specialist was not easy to replace, and this inhibited the indiscriminate beating up of prisoners or the making of "selections" when they were ill. There were a number of relapses, to be sure, for many SS men and capos could not part with their favorite system of beatings and naked terror. Also, the inhibitions against brutality did not apply to work details that had to perform unskilled labor.

Nevertheless, one can draw the simple conclusion that, in the course of the extermination camp's history, manual killing increasingly gave way to industrialized killing. The four large and modern crematoriums had rendered laborious and exhausting killing by hand inefficient.

At that time, the administration of the concentration camps also realized that slave labor is unproductive. In the case of easily supervised work in the open air, the most brutal terror, extreme punishments, and a network of informers can enforce optimal performance, but these methods do not work where skilled labor is involved. In the arms industry, prisoners were increasingly used for tasks that could not be easily monitored by nonspecialists. For this reason the SS instituted a system that was to function like the piece rate of freelance workers. On March 5, 1943, Himmler ordered Oswald Pohl, the head of the WVHA, to devote himself intensively to all the questions of a system of piecework among the prisoners. This resulted in the distribution of bonus slips.

Like many other things in Auschwitz, this system underwent a grotesque distortion. Only on rare occasions was it possible to buy something useful with such a bonus slip. Toothpaste and toilet paper had always been desirable items, and a visit to the camp bordello, which had been established around that time, could also be paid for with bonus slips. The expected effect was reduced by the fact that the commander of the detail frequently did not give them to the most efficient workers but rather to those who did the best "organizing" job for him. In the beginning, bonus slips could be given only to "Aryan" prisoners; but when more and more Jews were used in the arms industry, an order dated November 19, 1943, stated that they, too, were to be rewarded for good work. Prisoners who had to do the heaviest labor, such as excavation workers, were not eligible for this bonus, for terror sufficed to force the desired performance out of them.

At that time an order was issued to shorten the roll call. At first the prisoners often had to stand for hours at the roll call place in military formation and in any kind of weather until the procedure was finished. Later the time for these roll calls was substantially reduced.

Around that time the receipt of packages was permitted. In a circular dated October 30, 1942, the commandants of the concentration camps were informed that Himmler had permitted all "Aryan" prisoners, with the exception of Russian citizens, to have packages sent to them. However, it was some time before this permission was put into practice. Jan Stehn states that while the prisoners were informed of this opportunity in late December 1942, there was no appreciable flow of packages until February 1943. A letter written by the Polish resistance in early April says that packages "with the normal weight of three kilos are permitted at present." In those days this appears to have been a novelty.

Wanda Koprowska, a Pole deported to Auschwitz around that time, writes in her memoirs: "For the past few weeks we have been receiving packages from home. Our joy knows no bounds." Though empty bags indicated that the censors of those packages did some pilfering, "the main thing was that they did not touch the bread. I received such packages twice a week until June 1944, and so I had enough for myself and others."

At their hearings after the end of the war Grabner, the head of the Political Department, and SS roll call leader Claussen accused each other of having been involved in thefts at the parcel office, and both admitted that there were large-scale thefts there. The capo of that office participated, and as usual the SS allowed him to do so.

The release of packages exacerbated the differences among the various groups of prisoners. This privilege was not extended to Jews, Russians, and Gypsies or to those whose relatives had no chance to procure additional food in wartime and others who had for their protection assumed a false name and thus could not get in touch with their family members. According to my observations, Poles received the largest number of packages and the most nourishing ones, and the Czechs were in second place. I do not remember members of other nationalities receiving a large number of packages. Presumably, a pronounced solidarity on the part of the Poles and Czechs who were still living in freedom was responsible for the large number of packages. It may be due to a lack of such a solidarity that, for example, Germans did not receive anything like that amount of additional foodstuffs. To be sure, many German prisoners never asked their relatives for packages because by virtue of their positions they did not need them.

Prisoners who could count on the regular receipt of packages gained in prestige. They were more likely to be assigned to a better detail and given pref-erential treatment in their block. Even when they were sick, they could count on "pull." The prisoner Otto Wolken, who worked as a physician in the quar-antine section of Birkenau, writes that the mortality of Poles was consider-ably lower than that of other nationals, and he attributes this to the fact that even the most indigent Pole received packages. Wolken remembers that the mortality rate of Poles increased in the last phase of the war, when the postal service in large parts of Poland was disrupted and no food packages arrived.

▓ During the period under discussion here, Himmler's order of December 16, 1942, to intern the Gypsies—who, like the Jews, were to be exterminated—took effect. A section of Birkenau was equipped as a Gypsy camp. On Feb-ruary 26, 1943, the first Gypsy transport organized by the RSHA arrived in Auschwitz, and it was followed by others in rapid succession. The Gypsies were not subjected to a selection on arrival, but all persons on a few of the transports, mostly those from the East and suspected of epidemics, were im-mediately murdered in the gas chambers. The Gypsy camp was set up as a family camp.

Benno Adolph, who briefly served as an SS physician at that camp soon after its establishment, recalls that in those days German Gypsies arrived there wearing Wehrmacht uniforms and military decorations. Adolph testified that "some of these Gypsies were directly taken to the KL Auschwitz." Kazimierz Czelny confirms that there was a sergeant who wore an Iron Cross First Class, and Dr. Hans Eisenschimmel saw a Gypsy who arrived at the camp with the same decoration on his uniform. Eisenschimmel, who worked in the property room, was able to make such observations because, unlike what happened with the Jews who came on RSHA transports, the possessions of the Gyp-sies were not immediately taken to Canada. SS Corporal (Rottenführer) Franz Wunsch, who was in charge of setting up the Gypsy camp, admits that four members of the Wehrmacht who were in uniform and even a captain with an Iron Cross First Class arrived at the camp with the greeting "Heil Hitler!" Dr. Franz Lucas, another SS physician at that camp, gave this characteriza-tion of the conditions (as part of his defense): "Conditions in the Gypsy camp were catastrophic. Practical help was impossible because any proposals for improvements foundered on the attitude of the camp administration. The only thing that was done was the occasional supply of some whitewash and dyes."

Adolf Eichmann, the organizer of all RSHA transports, told an Israeli mag-istrate that no one intervened on behalf of the Gypsies. Evidently there was even more prejudice against this ethnic group than there was against the Jews, and the prejudice was perceptible among the prisoners in Auschwitz as well.

■ Other changes in the camp's atmosphere were due to an internal development caused by the frequent transfers from one camp to another that were ordered by the central administration.

In the fall of 1942 Himmler ordered that all concentration camps in the Reich be made *judenfrei* (free of Jews) and that the Jews be transferred to Auschwitz. A substantial transport from Buchenwald was subjected to a selection, and those who were classified as fit for work were sent to the newly established satellite camp Monowitz on October 30, 1942. These included a unified, communist-led group that had gained a wealth of camp experience and practice in conspiratorial activities in Buchenwald. By virtue of its experience and its solidarity, this group managed to occupy influential positions in the newly emerging system of prisoner self-government, particularly in the prisoners' infirmary.

Erich Kohlhagen states that the constant increase in the number of inmates, almost exclusively Jews, forced the camp administration to employ Jews as well. The SS gave preference to German Jews for linguistic reasons; the large group of arrivals from Buchenwald included many Jews from Germany and Austria with years of experience in concentration camps. "Even if some Jews did not measure up," Kohlhagen writes, "and did not behave as one might have expected them to, I would like to state that in general their attitude was exemplary."

> This was also one of the main reasons why there was always friction and agitation between the bad elements from the Reich on the one hand and the Jewish leaders and decent Germans and Austrians on the other. In the course of time, so much harmony developed among the inmates' leadership, which consisted both of Jews and of "Aryans," that those who opposed the community were simply shunted off, usually to a coal mine. (Kohlhagen is evidently speaking about the period after November 1943, when the labor camps, including the dreaded coal mines, were already under the administrative supervision of Monowitz.) In this way they brought with them a record that made it impossible for them to repeat their antisocial behavior in the new camp.

Things also began to improve in the infirmary of the main camp when prisoners were transferred from another camp. A description of this favorable development must be preceded by a discussion of conditions in the HKB.

■ Prisoners dreaded being sent to the infirmary, for the admission procedure was as follows: Anyone who announced that he was sick was taken to the Outpatient Department after the morning roll call. There he had to undress and wait for the SS physician. The patients were compelled to stand in a corridor or in an adjoining room because the SS physician did not want to breathe air polluted by them. When the SS physician arrived, the *Arztvormelder* (medical presenters), as they were called in the camp lingo, had to line up in front of him, and he quickly decided the fate of each patient on the basis of a brief report by the inmate physician. A patient could be admitted to the infirmary, declared to be healthy and sent back to the camp, or selected to die if the SS physician gained the impression that his capacity for work could not be restored quickly enough. The proximity of the extermination facilities and the steady stream of fresh labor through RSHA transports prompted the camp administration to kill workers who were worn out, especially Jews who were, after all, to be "exterminated through labor." In the Frankfurt courtroom, Stanislaw Klodzinski, a nurse in Block 20, described the fate of those doomed to die by an SS physician:

> In the morning or at noon those selected were taken to a side entrance of Block 20 wearing only a shirt and wooden clogs and carrying a blanket. Those unable to walk were put on a stretcher. After they had been lined up in the corridor, the block clerk (*Blockschreiber*) received the list of those under his control, the SDG arrived, the doorkeeper cried, "*Achtung!*"—and from this moment on no patient could leave his room. It was deathly quiet in the block. Every patient there knew what was going to happen. Most of those selected didn't know what was in store for them. Then the SDG proceeded to Room 1, which had white windows and was usually kept locked. To the left of the door was a small table on which lay a set of syringes and long needles as well as a bottle containing a yellowish pink liquid: phenol. The room also contained two stools, and a rubber apron hung from a hook on the wall. In a corner were some rubber shoes. Two Jewish prisoners had to bring the first victims in.

For a time Imre Gönczi was one of the two men who had to escort the victims. He gave the following description of their last walk:

> A number was written on each victim's chest with indelible ink. Then I had to lead one after another through the dark curtain that hung in the corridor. Escorted by an inmate, the victim had to sit down, and Klehr, the SDG who did most of the killings, in his white coat injected the victim directly in his heart. The victims died immediately after emitting a soft sound, as though they were exhaling. Their bodies were dragged across the corridor and into the washroom. In the evening the van from the crematorium came, backed up in front of the gate, and the corpses were loaded on it.

Klehr himself gave the court an expert report: "The prisoner had to sit on a stool. I palpated his chest to see where to position the syringe and then aimed the needle directly at his heart." Referring to the victims' behavior, he said, "I assume they knew what was happening to them." Klehr claimed he did not remember anyone screaming and concluded his report by saying that "they were completely apathetic."

In the lingo of the camp this procedure was called *Spritzen* (injecting). A letter smuggled out to Cracow in November 1942 by the Polish resistance organization in the HKB states that "thirty to forty people, among them four to six Poles, are killed every day by means of injections into the heart with a ten-cubic-centimeter syringe containing 30 percent phenol." Most of the victims were Jewish, and according to the letter they were already earmarked for such a death when they were just slightly ill. Evidently, the SS physician who made selections devoted more attention to the type of imprisonment than to the medical picture.

Camp physician Friedrich Entress, who organized the injections and for a long time selected medical presenters in the manner detailed above, testified as follows on April 14, 1947, when he was under American detention: "Around May 1942 I first learned in Auschwitz about the order concerning euthanasia. This order was issued to the camp by Dr. Lolling, a high-ranking medical director of the camps. In accordance with it, incurable mental patients as well as those who had incurable tuberculosis or were permanently unfit for work were to be subjected to euthanasia by means of injections. In the fall of 1942 that order was extended to include sick inmates who could not be cured within four weeks." Entress was wrong about the time because documents prove that injections were introduced in Auschwitz as early as the fall of 1941.

The prisoner Wladyslaw Tondos, a pulmonary specialist who headed the TB section in the block for infectious diseases, testified in Nuremberg shortly after the end of the war that, on orders from Entress and Dr. Jung, those suffering from tuberculosis could not be treated in 1941 but were killed, initially by intravenously administered poison and later by injections directly into the heart. This witness remembered that in the first quarter of 1942 approximately 200 TB patients were murdered on orders from Entress.

■ On August 20, 1942, seventeen prisoners were transferred from Dachau to Auschwitz as nurses to combat the typhus epidemic raging there. In accordance with Dachau tradition, they were not chosen because they were the best qualified to fight this infectious disease but because they were regarded as troublemakers. There was not a single physician among those seventeen— in those days physicians in Dachau had little chance to be on the staff of the infirmary—but there were four clerks, including myself. All were German (as an Austrian, I was officially considered a German), and all but one wore the red triangles of the political prisoners.

A small number of Germans with a red triangle had come to Auschwitz earlier, but this transfer marked the first arrival of a unified group. It remained together in Auschwitz as well, for all were assigned to the infirmary, which held a key place in the inmate self-government. All of us had camp experience, and many had already fought together against the administration in Dachau.

As it happened, a few weeks later a new ss garrison physician was transferred to Auschwitz, someone who was clearly different from all other ss physicians. These changes produced "a kind of revolution in the infirmary," wrote Wladyslaw Fejkiel, who was well acquainted with conditions in the HKB.

The first result was that the key positions in the HKB were occupied by political prisoners as early as spring 1943. From there began the struggle against the predominance of the Greens in the camp, and this trend transcended the main camp. Ludwig Wörl was the first Red camp elder who came to the newly erected infirmary in Monowitz. Without his help, the former Buchenwald prisoners could not have achieved the influence that they were to exert. Through transfers from one camp to another, the ss unintentionally saw to it that there was a fruitful exchange of experiences among the prisoners. Wörl was a member of the group transferred from Dachau.

Another result was the moderation and eventual discontinuation of the injections. Because I became the clerk of the new ss garrison physician, Dr. Eduard Wirths, and am therefore acquainted with the circumstances that led to this development, I shall quote here from my Bericht.

Wirths is under orders from Berlin to combat the typhus at any cost. The main reason for this order was that the illness had spread to the troops, and it was feared that the epidemic would spread to the entire surrounding area. This is what I learned from the correspondence.

He is trying, first of all, to rid the camp of lice. The blocks are being disinfected, the laundry is monitored, and constant lice checks have been ordered. He even wants to have a poster made and is consulting me about the caption.

"Herr Doktor, may I say something?"

"Yes." He looks at me quizzically. He gave me quite a bit of dictation today, wove in a few personal remarks, and asked me my opinion. Once he stopped dictating and looked at me as though he wanted to add something, but then he went on with his dictation. Now he is leaning back in his chair. I am sitting on the other side of his desk with my shorthand pad on my knees.

"The most important thing in fighting this epidemic is that the inmates shouldn't be afraid to come to the infirmary when they feel sick. After all, typhus is spread by a louse that transfers the blood of a typhus patient to a healthy person. As long as sick people run around in the camp, you won't get rid of the typhus."

"Naturally. But why don't the sick people come to the infirmary? They have to be isolated, of course." His astonishment seems genuine. Is he really ignorant of what goes on in the infirmary? Shall I go on?

"Out with it, Langbein." The whole time I've been meaning to have a frank discussion with Wirths. I can't believe that he will turn me over to the Political Department; we already have too human a contact for that. Today there is a good opportunity.

"I'd have to speak about things that no inmate of the camp is allowed to know, Herr Doktor. At least he mustn't admit that he knows them. Shall I go on?"

"Yes." He looks at me in surprise. There is leaden silence in the room. "You have nothing to fear."

"Most of those who come to the infirmary aren't cured but injected. This is known in the camp. Above all, every person with a suspected case of typhus thinks about it. If someone has a fever accompanied by a headache, then he'll do everything he can to avoid having to go into the infirmary. With a high fever, they go out with the work details, and if it's at all possible, they are hidden somewhere by their comrades during the work period. As a result, typhus remains in the camp, and you, Herr Doktor, cannot change that by issuing orders."

"You said that the patients are being injected. What do you mean by that?" He looks as if his question is meant sincerely.

"Phenol is injected into their hearts. A few dozen a day. And from time to time the whole block for infectious diseases is sent to the gas chambers, nurses and all."

"No!"

"I saw it with my own eyes in late August."

"I wasn't here then."

"But there are daily injections even now." He rises and walks up and down with long steps and creaking boots. What's going to happen now?

"This method of fighting disease can't lead to anything. As long as the inmates have to be afraid of the infirmary, there will be typhus in Auschwitz."

He stops at the stove. "Does the camp physician, Entress, know about the . . ."—he hesitates a bit—"about the injections?"

"Dr. Entress selects and ss Technical Sergeant Klehr injects."

"No!" I nod only once. Then it's quiet in the room. A gust of wind rattles the window.

"If only there were someone to rely on!" It sounds as if he were talking to himself.

When Wirths questioned Entress about this, the latter tried to persuade him that he was selecting only incurable tuberculosis patients for injections. On the basis of Dr. Lolling's order, Wirths believes that killing these patients is unavoidable because they cannot be cured under the conditions that exist in Auschwitz and constitute a source of infection for as long as they live. In the face of such arguments, I am powerless, and so I have to provide Wirths with clear evidence that Entress is not selecting only TB patients. For as long as Bock, a Green from the first Sachsenhausen transport, is camp elder at the infirmary, I fail to get solid evidence. However, I do make some progress when Ludwig Wörl is transferred back to the main camp from Monowitz and assumes that position. In my book I give this description of my collaboration with him:

A few days later Wörl sends me the proof. The messenger Tadek, a discreet young Pole, brings me an envelope containing a temperature curve and a note from Wörl that says, "A German was injected today despite my protest and without an examination." The fever chart tells me that the patient is a sixty-two-year-old German criminal who was admitted to the infirmary yesterday and immediately examined. The X ray showed no sign of disease. Diagnosis: Feverish gastroenteritis. Therapy: bed rest, diet, bolus alba.

In the afternoon I am in Wirths's office. When he has finished his dictation, I do not get up. "Is there something on your mind again, Langbein?"

"Yes, Herr Doktor." I hand him the chart. My voice has sounded hoarse and so I clear my throat.

"What about it?"

"Dr. Entress selected this man for an injection today because he has incurable TB."

"TB? But there is no pulmonary diagnosis. It's gastroenteritis."

"Herr Doktor, you didn't believe me when I told you that Dr. Entress sends prisoners to be injected without first examining them. This chart proves that I am right. And that's the way it is with all the others, but since the others are not Germans, no fever charts are kept and there are no written records of examinations."

"But I've given Dr. Entress express orders . . ." He stops in a state of excitement, for he always gets angry when he senses that his orders are first . . . "Ontl, tell Dr. Entress to come here right away."

After the sergeant has left, Wirths asks me whether I have anything else on my mind. I tell him that Entress is sure to guess that the chart came from Wörl and that I have no right to put Wörl at risk. Wirths assures me that nothing will happen to Wörl or to me.

I concluded my account of this momentous conversation with these words: "When I am already at the door, Wirths says in a soft voice: 'I ought to be grateful to both of you.' ss men are out in the corridor, and I can't let them see that I am overjoyed. I pass them with a serious, diligent mien and go to my little office. On the next day there are no injections, nor are there any the following day. Otherwise nothing has changed. No indication, no word."

The results are described in letters from the Polish resistance organization. In November the number of injections was given as thirty to sixty, but a letter smuggled out to Cracow in late April 1943 says: "About ten injections a day." In the first half of May the following information was sent out of the camp: "General relaxation. The patients stay in the infirmary until they are completely cured and their strength has returned." At the same time calcium gluconicum is requested because patients with active tuberculosis could also be treated: "We already have 100 sufferers from this disease." At a later date Dr. Entress was transferred to Monowitz, and Klehr also left the main camp.

The clerk of Block 20, Stanislaw Glowa, who knew the number of those killed by injections of phenol, testified that, between the spring of 1942 and late 1943, 30,000 people in his block were killed in this way. Stanislaw Klodzinski estimates the number of these at 25,000 to 30,000 and adds that 90 to 95 percent of them were Jews. An unnamed Polish major whose memoir appeared in the United States in November 1944 writes that an "Aryan" had to be gravely ill to be injected, whereas 80 to 90 percent of the Jews who were sent to the infirmary were murdered in this fashion.

In exceptional cases Germans were among those injected, and it was this fact that made the discontinuance of this method of killing possible. However, even later some inmates were killed by having phenol injected into their hearts. Hans Sauer, the last block elder of Block 20, gave the following testimony under oath: "In a case known to me, Germans were among those injected; it happened around May or June 1944. They were eight or ten criminals who had been sent to Auschwitz from Breslau. I assume that this was done on special orders."

Désiré Haffner, the chronicler of the infirmary in the men's camp at Birkenau, confirms that the improvement of living conditions was not limited to the main camp. Haffner writes that beatings were forbidden in early April 1943. "Even if this prohibition is only a theoretical one, the scenes of cruelty and blood lust that we were accustomed to witnessing are now the exception." Haffner adds that in those days a primitive washing facility was installed, the food was improved, and a change of underwear every two weeks was ordered. Typhus also waned in the Birkenau men's camp.

The result of such improvements may be seen in the number of deaths. Despite the typhus epidemic that broke out in the newly populated Gypsy camp in May 1943 — a letter from the resistance movement speaks of up to thirty deaths a day — the percentage of dead in relation to all internees was reduced from 15.4 in March 1943 to 10.3 in April and 5.2 in May. This reduction cannot be attributed only to the more favorable season. We have no comparative figures for the women's camp and know only the number of deaths, but these show the same trend. In March 3,991 women died, in April 1,859, and in May 1,237. Stanislaw Klodzinski speaks of a "normalization of infirmary life in a positive sense" in 1943 and 1944.

▓ To be sure, one should not lose sight of the relative value of ideas such as "improvement" and "normalization." Selections continued to be made, especially in the infirmaries of the labor camps. The victims were taken to the gas chambers either directly or with an intermediate step in the HKB in the main camp or in Birkenau.

Robert Lévy reports that almost every Saturday patients were transferred to the HKB in Birkenau from satellite camps, particularly the murderous coal mines. According to Lévy, "Many young men were included." Some could be saved, but most of them were the victims of the next selection. The young prisoners asked whether death by poison gas was painful. Older ones wrote farewell letters that never reached their addresses, and many begged to inform the world at a later date of what had happened.

I have given the following description of such a transfer to the HKB of the main camp:

In front of a block of the HKB there is a Sanka (Sanitätskraftwagen, ambulance). "Medical transport from Golleschau," says the gatekeeper. They are coming out of the vehicle now; the sight of these walking skeletons is always frightening. One can tell that the last man out is at death's door by his complexion and his pointed waxen nose. He is piteously feeble and cannot negotiate the three steps leading to the block gate by himself. But when he reaches the double door, he clings with his two skeletal hands to the part that is closed. His eyes tell me that he is panic-stricken and does not want to enter. At first the doorman drags him, but this doesn't work. He yells at him in Polish, but the patient does not understand him or doesn't want to. I look for his number and insignia: He is a Jew; who knows what country he is from and what his mother tongue is? Was he an artisan or a scholar, a merchant or a profiteer, earlier, when he still had a life? Now he stands there and clings to the wooden door with all the strength of a creature who refuses to die. The doorman slaps his fingers with a wooden stick, but the man won't let go.

Far more drastically than former prisoners, the accused Stefan Baretzki, a former block leader, described for the Frankfurt court in the harsh, intense speech of an ethnic German the fate of the prisoners who were transferred to Birkenau from the satellite camps. "Let me explain about the *Muselmänner* [a term used to denote feeble, apathetic inmates of both genders] from the satellite camps. There's just a transfer and a handing-over. Usually the patients come on Saturday at noon. They always go to section B II d, and those coming from the satellite camps are sick anyway. On Monday they're presented to the physician. The prisoners who are handed over don't even come to the camp. As a block leader I'm not allowed to open the gate. Being handed over means to go to the gas chamber." When he was asked whether the patients had to disrobe, Baretzki answered:

> Yes, they took off their clothes, but not in the camp. If they're admitted to the camp, it has already happened. You've got to picture it this way: On Saturday a car or two comes, a man stands by the gate, another block leader is in the room, and a guard has a slip of paper in his hand. The car stops in front of the gate; the driver says, "This is a transfer"; I open the gate; the car drives in; and now there are two different kinds of people in it. The driver doesn't wait; he just dumps his load, and now the two types of prisoners are all jumbled up. How are you going to tell them apart and get all their numbers? The old man (the ss camp leader) is going to eat me alive if I sign transfers into the camp. So I call the camp elder and tell him: "Danisch, leave them all standing there!" They're not coming into the block, for they'd just louse it up. They'll get into the washroom, but only at night, and during the day they'll stand outside. On Monday morning they'll be registered for rations, but they won't get anything to eat until noon. The people who are being handed over won't get any food even then because they're practically dead.

That is how Baretzki remembered the routine that continued while conditions in the infirmaries were being normalized.

■ The fall of 1943 witnessed the most momentous changes in the personnel of the camp administration. I learned about events that contributed to these changes.

As a reaction to the requirement to report an ever increasing number of prisoners employed in the arms industry, a demand that grew ever more insistent after the defeat at Stalingrad, the head physician of all concentration camps sent a circular to all of the garrison physicians. In it, he ordered them to decrease the number of deaths in their camps. According to my observations, such circulars rarely produced changes. Wirths, however, took the order seriously, for it offered him a chance to take a stance against the mass killings of prisoners, and to do so without incurring the reproach that he was too soft on the inmates. I knew about the order, observed Wirth's reaction, and endeavored to provide him with documents that would enable him to intervene effectively.

The conduct of Entress clearly proved that Wirths could not rely solely on the reports of his camp physicians and medics. To prevent prisoners detailed to work in the infirmaries from becoming known as his informants and thus being put at risk, I proposed that every camp physician or SDG give a weekly report indicating how many deaths were reported in his camp every day. One benefit of this was that if, for example, an average of ten to fifteen deaths per day were to be reported for his camp, but that number soared to seventy-five on a weekday, it was evident that around sixty people had been killed that day. This would not have been the case with summary reports.

The Political Department maintained a prison in the basement of Isolation Block 11. From time to time it lined up prisoners against the Black Wall that had been erected at one end of the locked courtyard between Blocks 10 and 11 and shot them. The official report said, however, that the men murdered in this way had been transferred to the infirmary and died of some disease there. I called the SS garrison physician's attention to the discrepancies that these bunker selections caused in the daily mortality figures for the main camp and explained the reason for it. The following conversation is again drawn from my Bericht.

> "That won't do," said the garrison physician. "The Political Department must bear the responsibility for these deaths. Why doesn't Entress report this to me?"
>
> "Herr Doktor, I believe there are many things you aren't told about."
>
> "List for me the days with high figures. But is that really so?"
>
> "Yes sir."
>
> "How do you know?"
>
> "I know it from inmates who wouldn't repeat this to you or any other member of the SS."
>
> "But I need some proof."
>
> "In Auschwitz it is very hard to find proof that people are being murdered." At that point I thought of something. "Herr Doktor, you would find proof in the death records of the main camp. All deaths are entered there

together with a diagnosis and the time of death. In the case of those who die in Block 11, there are never temperature charts or medical histories. So all you need to do to get proof is to ask for these."

Wirths rings. He always acts so quickly. Ontl, his sergeant, comes in. "Ontl, I'd like to see the death records of the main camp right away."

The stone is rolling, but in what direction? Now there will be a clash with the Political Department. I overhear a conversation over the field telephone in which Entress and Klehr are ordered to report to the garrison physician. I have little appetite this noon.

Tadeusz Paczula, the roll call clerk of the HKB, was ordered to bring all the death records to the SS infirmary. As he later remembered, there were so many volumes that he had to use a handcart. I continue quoting from my book: "It seems that there really was a catastrophe. Yesterday it wasn't possible to talk with Wirths, he was very nervous and curt. Today he dictates only a letter to Lolling, his superior, in which he asks to be transferred from Auschwitz. As the reason for his request he states that SS Second Lieutenant (Untersturmführer) Grabner, the head of the Political Department, told the camp commandant that Wirths's conduct was unbecoming of an SS officer. This was surely in connection with the reports from Block 11."

■ At that time an accident triggered an investigation of corruption. After the end of the war Dr. Konrad Morgen, the SS judge in charge of the investigation, gave the following report: "The police of the Protectorate [of Bohemia and Moravia] determined that there was illegal trafficking in gold in the Protectorate, and these acts were traced to Berlin. The Customs Investigation Department in Berlin-Brandenburg identified persons on duty in Auschwitz and turned the investigation over to the SS and police court in Berlin. This is where I learned of it, and I assumed responsibility for the investigation of this trafficking."

When he appeared as a witness at the Auschwitz trial in Frankfurt, Morgen added:

The investigation of SS men in the Auschwitz concentration camp was triggered by a package found in the army post office. Because of its striking weight it was confiscated, and it turned out that it contained three gold nuggets, one the size of a fist and two smaller ones. It was high-carat dental gold that was sent by a medic on duty in Auschwitz to his wife. I estimated that this amount of gold corresponded to about 100,000 corpses if one considered that not every person has gold fillings. It was incomprehensible that the culprit had been able to stow away such a large amount of gold without being noticed.

That was not the first affair of this kind. Robert Mulka, who was a legal officer in Auschwitz for a time, remembered that an exceptionally valuable diamond ring was found in the possession of an ss sergeant at the dental office in the Hotel de Kattowitz. The sergeant, who was on leave at the time, was searched on orders from Mulka, and gold ingots were found in his luggage. Mulka, who was well acquainted with the general corruption of the guards because of Canada, drew no particular conclusions from this and simply told the Frankfurt court, "I don't know what his punishment was."

Dr. Morgen, however, took the case more seriously and went to Auschwitz. There he quickly learned of the mass extermination but saw no way to expand his investigation in that direction. Dr. Gerhard Wiebeck, his deputy, later endeavored to explain to the Frankfurt judges the limitations of that commission's authority: "We had to combat corruption and actions that crossed the line—for example, unauthorized killings." More closely questioned, the ss jurist responded: "An investigation of general killings was not permitted. I heard that the extermination of the Jews had been verbally ordered by Hitler." That ss judges considered such an order entirely possible and were deterred from investigating such extensive and evident crimes by no more than a reference to a verbal order by the Führer is more revealing of the conditions of that time than lengthy analyses.

The investigation by Morgen and his group showed that Grabner was responsible for murders that "crossed the line." The large-scale gassing of Jews was reported in Berlin with the notation sb, standing for *Sonderbehandlung* (special treatment), a euphemism for killing. This made Morgen conclude that the Central Office desired these killings. However, those who were lined up against the Black Wall and shot were not reported in this camouflaged fashion but were listed as having died of natural causes. From this Morgen concluded that it was not certain that the Central Office approved of these killings. Besides, most of the victims of the Political Department were Poles, but Hitler's verbal order of the extermination was supposed to refer to Jews. For this reason Morgen looked into the shootings, and in the course of this research he came into contact with Wirths. In 1946 he testified as follows:

With a gleam in his eyes, the garrison physician pointed to the precipitate decline of the high numbers since his arrival. (He meant the number of deaths. On a wall in his office was a large table with graphs depicting the number of prisoners and the number of deaths. I had provided him with the documentation for these statistics.) At the same time he mentioned Grabner, who had suggested that pregnant Polish women be killed. This the physician had rejected as incompatible with his professional duties. Grabner had not relented, and there was a showdown in the commandant's office, though neither Rudolf Höß nor Robert Ernst Grawitz, whose title was Reich physician SS (Reichsarzt-SS), said anything about it. When I happened to walk up to him, Wirths was facing a terrible conflict and asked me, "What shall I do?" I told him that what he had done—namely, a downright refusal—was absolutely right and that I was going to arrest Grabner the next day.

Dr. Gerhard Wiebeck also confirmed that Wirths supported the commission in its investigation of Grabner: "The garrison physician was an adversary of Grabner and kept a daily journal in which he gathered material against him. When the camp was evacuated, he told me, 'If you need documents, I can give you some.'"

Grabner was dismissed and arrested in October 1943, and this step led to others. On November 11, Camp Order 50/43 contained an announcement that SS Lieutenant Colonel Arthur Liebehenschel would replace Commandant Höß. Dr. Rudolf Mildner, the Gestapo chief of Kattowitz and Grabner's superior, was also transferred. That man had presided over the dreaded courts-martial in the bunker block, events that regularly ended with mass executions. Utilizing the situation, Wirths also managed to obtain the transfer of Dr. Entress, a confidant of Grabner.

This change in commandants was accompanied by a tripartition of the camp, which had become the largest complex of all concentration camps. The main camp was designated as Auschwitz I, the Birkenau camp complex was called Auschwitz II, and the labor camps that had proliferated at various arms factories and were centralized in Monowitz were collectively called Auschwitz III. Each of these camps was given its own commandant, but they were not completely independent. Liebehenschel was both the commandant of Auschwitz I and SS senior garrison commander (Standortältester) of Auschwitz and thus the superior of the commandants of Auschwitz II and III. The Political Department and the medical system remained the same for all three camps. Prisoners could still be transferred without the formalities normal for a transfer from one KZ to another, and their records remained centralized. At a later date Auschwitz I and II were recombined.

This radical change certainly cannot be explained by assuming that an unsuspecting administration first learned of the crimes in Auschwitz from reports of the investigating committees. That this was not the case is demonstrated by the fact that although Grabner was arrested as a scapegoat, Höß was promoted to department head in the central administration of all concentration camps. This was done even though the SS investigating committee had uncovered not only his complicity in the mass murders that "crossed the line" but personal offenses as well. Also, Mildner, Grabner's superior, received a leading position in Denmark. Entress was appointed to the position of SS garrison physician at Mauthausen and finally promoted to the rank of SS captain (*Hauptsturmführer*). Wirths had steadfastly refused to propose him for this overdue promotion.

These transfers are attributed to information that had leaked out of Auschwitz. Stanislaw Dubiel, an inmate who worked as a gardener at Höß's villa, testified on August 7, 1946, that he had been able to overhear snatches of a conversation between Himmler and Höß in the garden. According to him, Himmler said that Höß would have to leave Auschwitz because the British radio was reporting too much about the extermination of prisoners in Auschwitz. Höß is said to have declared that his activities in the camp constituted good service to the fatherland. This statement was overheard by Sophie Stipel, a Jehovah's Witness who was also employed in Höß's villa. Wilhelm Boger testified on July 5, 1945: "When news about the mass deaths in Auschwitz went beyond the unsuspecting German people and reached the world in the fall of 1943, changes were suddenly made in the leading positions in the camp and in the Gestapo at Kattowitz (Dr. Mildner)." In the Cracow prison Grabner stated that Höß could not remain in Auschwitz any longer "for reasons of foreign policy."

Liebehenschel started a new epoch in the history of Auschwitz. His first reforms related to Block 11; after all, the capricious shootings in that block had provided the impetus for all of the changes. Liebehenschel stopped the periodic selections with subsequent shootings in the bunker. It is true that this did not end executions, but these were carried out away from the camp, in the crematoriums of Birkenau. The new commandant ordered the destruction of stand-up cells, which offered no means for sitting or lying down and which were used to punish inmates. He proclaimed a general bunker amnesty and later had the Black Wall torn down. In addition, he rescinded the order to shoot any prisoner trying to escape; all sorts of things could be interpreted as preparations for such an escape, and under the guise of this order it had been easy to eliminate any prisoner who was out of favor. From now on, escapees who had been caught and were in the bunker awaiting their executions were transferred to another KZ. In the Auschwitz trial at Cracow, where Liebehenschel was among the defendants, the Pole Marian Bialowiejski testified that Liebehenschel had forbidden the Political Department to lock inmates in the bunker without orders from him. He is said even to have barred members of that department from entering the camp without his express permission.

A conversation that I was once able to have with Commandant Liebehenschel was consequential, and therefore I shall reproduce it here. Even the events that led to it were extraordinary. I was locked up in the bunker at the time Grabner was relieved of his position. Following an intervention by the ss garrison physician, Grabner's successor, Hans Schurz, ordered my release. On the day before that happened, Józef Cyrankiewicz was brought there, having been accused of preparing his escape. A search of his possessions turned up a wig, highly incriminating evidence. Via the clerk of the bunker block, Jan Pilecki, we were in contact with Józek, as Cyrankiewicz was known among us in the resistance movement. We sent him news of the change of commandants and the hopes connected with it.

One day Józek wrote us that Stanislaw Dorosiewicz had come to see him in the bunker and invited him to join him in an escape. That man, the block elder of Block 15, was as well known as he was feared. Since he was a trusty of the Political Department and was in charge of many informers, he was called *Spitzelcapo* (informer capo). As a consequence of his connections he evidently had grasped the reasons for Grabner's dismissal more quickly than anyone else, and he thought his preferential position would be jeopardized if the activities of the Political Department were subjected to closer scrutiny. He could easily gain access to the strictly isolated bunker. At that time Józek already knew that Dorosiewicz had betrayed him. Since he was bound to regard his offer as a provocation, he wrote us that we could use his information as we saw fit and need have no scruples regarding the informer. What happened next is in my *Bericht*:

> After a long nocturnal conversation (with Ernst Burger) we reached a decision. We must run the risk. After all, I have a new lease on life, and it is no longer mine alone. Józek must be saved!
>
> I say to Wirths at the next opportunity: "Herr Doktor, I recently told you about the informers in the Political Department. Today I have a case that clearly shows the methods with which they are working." After telling him about Józek and the block elder, I say: "As long as the informers use such methods in the camp, there will always be attempts to escape from it. The informers are the ones who cause unrest in the camp."
>
> Wirths listens with interest. It seems that he is gathering evidence against the Political Department. "Put that in writing. A simple note will do. I believe ss Lieutenant Colonel Liebehenschel will be interested." Then he goes on dictating letters.
>
> He drives off but returns shortly and rings. "I've seen the commandant, and he was satisfied with your report. He opposes working with informers in the camp and would like to know what you would advise us to do with the informer in question."
>
> This is better than I expected. "He can't do anything yet. If he has the in-

former interrogated, he will of course deny everything, and it goes without saying that the Political Department will back him up. There is no proof of the conversation. Now we have to wait and observe the informer. The only important thing is that nothing is done to the Pole in the meantime."

"No, the commandant took down his number."

Today I find it hard to sit quietly in front of my typewriter and bang out long, boring lists. I'd really like to tell everything to Zbyszek (a Pole in our detail) and the others, but I'm not saying anything. I write the lists and think of Józek.

The next day the whole camp talks of nothing else. This is what our messenger tells me: "The Blockowi (a Polish form of Blockältester that was in general use) of 15 has escaped. With the Jew from Canada—you know, the informer. The two took with them an SS sergeant from the Political Department whom they know well. They told him they knew a spot near the camp where gold is buried. He guided them through the chain of guards, then they killed him on the other bank of the Sola River and were gone."

The SS is on alert and searches the entire area. Wirths is also excited: "Have you heard?" I just nod. "Isn't that the informer you told me about yesterday in connection with the Pole? The one I told the commandant about?" "Yes sir." "So that's all correct." "Yes."

The Kalendarium issued by the Auschwitz-Birkenau State Museum says that Dorosiewicz escaped with Hersz Kurcwajg on December 21, 1943, and that the resistance movement issued an urgent warning because it feared that Dorosiewicz would continue his informing activities on the outside and reveal contacts with the camp. Dorosiewicz, who murdered Kurcwajg, was not apprehended. I shall continue quoting from my book:

In the afternoon SS Sergeant Richter comes to our office in a state of excitement. "Langbein, grab your notepad and come with me. The garrison physician is in the commandant's office and phoned to say that he wants you." This is it. The SS officer on duty in the office takes me right to the commandant's office. Padded double doors. "Inmate No. 60-3-55 at your service." Dark furniture, including a big desk. Behind it Commandant Liebehenschel and facing him, with his back to me, the garrison physician. My heart is pounding, and my nerves are no longer that strong. "So there you are. Yesterday's report from you was very valuable to me." A brief pause. Then Wirths says: "Langbein, tell the commandant what you told me about the informers in the camp." "Yes, go ahead." "Lieutenant Colonel, I have a request to make." "What is it?" "May I speak as if I weren't an inmate?" Another brief pause. "Yes, please talk quite frankly." "Then I beg you not to ask me where I got my information. We prisoners know many things, but we aren't allowed to know anything." "I don't care about that." "That informer not only advised the Pole to escape now, but he brought him to that point by threatening and blackmailing him on earlier occasions." "Nothing will be done to the Pole. I shall take a personal interest in this case." "I don't know whether you will be able to prevent it, Lieutenant Colonel. The Political Department has a great variety of methods. I spent more than two months in the bunker myself." "On what charge?" "On suspicion of political activities." He furrows his brow. "I'm sure this suspicion will surface again and that there will be enough testimonials once the Political Department finds out that I told you that today's escapee was its main informer." "You are forgetting that I am the camp commandant." He is angry, and thus I am on the right track. "As long as I'm here, you won't be sent to the bunker again. Captain, let me know immediately if anything happens to him." Wirths nods: "Yes sir."

I don't know whether I should leave now. "What else do you have to report about the camp? You are well informed, aren't you?" He doesn't sound ironic or dangerous. "May I answer freely again?" Liebehenschel nods. "There are two especially bad things. One is the informers. They keep the whole camp in a state of agitation and are the cause of most escapes." "And the second thing?" "The dominance of the Greens in the camp. Camp elders, block elders, and capos are usually Greens, and they are bent on making life in the camp even harder than it ordinarily is. They steal food, and harass and beat people. In this way they also diminish the prisoners' capacity for work. There are, of course, exceptions, but the rule is bad enough." "Are you of the opinion that political prisoners would do a better job running the camp?" "Yes sir." Wirths looks at me, nods lightly, and appears to be satisfied. "That will be all." "Beg permission to leave."

I immediately notified Ernst of this conversation, and he passed this information on to Józek in the bunker. That was a good thing, for Liebehenschel sent for Cyrankiewicz, who was now able to testify in the same spirit. There were quick results. I quote from my report again:

One day Wirths tells me that the commandant would like to have a list with the numbers of all informers known to me. I immediately go to the camp and speak with Ernst. "Sure, we'll give him such a list. Once you start the informer story, you've got to finish it. The list won't increase our risk, except, perhaps, if he asks you where you got the numbers." "Then I'll repeat what I said before—namely, that I can't say anything about it."

Józek agreed as well. Upon his release from the bunker he, Tadek (Holuj) and Ernst wrote down the numbers. A few days later a transport to the

Flossenbürg concentration camp is put together, and all the informers on our list are on it. Sighs of relief are heard throughout the camp. No one can explain this development, least of all the informers themselves. They try hard to get out of the transport, but all their tricks are in vain. Everywhere they are told, "Express orders from the camp Commandant."

Erwin Olszowska, a roll call clerk (Rapportschreiber), testified as follows at the Frankfurt trial: "When in the winter of 1943–44 the chief informer of the Political Department, Dorosiewicz, escaped and murdered an ss man, the new camp commandant ordered no reprisals. By way of punishment Gerhard Lachmann, a member of the Political Department, was transferred. In those days the bad influence of the abominable informer system seems to have been noticed. On February 8, 1944, a special informer transport to Flossenbürg was put together."

Soon after my intervention, Liebehenschel appointed Ludwig Wörl as the first "Red" camp elder. That man saw to it that an increasing number of Reds were made block elders, and this ended or at least greatly reduced beatings by inmate functionaries. The predominance of the Greens in the main camp was over.

Jenny Spritzer, who worked in the Political Department, writes: "Everyone felt an enormous relief when one day Höß, the camp commandant, was appointed to a higher position in Oranienburg and replaced by Liebehenschel. The new commandant was aghast at the conditions in Auschwitz and immediately abolished capital punishment. Even the hanging of unsuccessful escapees was prohibited, as was the beating of inmates during interrogations, at work, or anywhere else." To be sure, the author adds that these prohibitions were not observed by everyone.

Artur Rablin, a trusty assigned to the commandant and, as such, in a position to make good observations, has described inspections by Liebehenschel that were different from those of his predecessor. He visited the kitchen and asked (for example), "How does the soup taste?" and did not insist that everyone stand at attention in his presence.

Owing to the tripartition of Auschwitz this change did not have equal effects everywhere. It was least effective in Birkenau, where the dominance of the Greens remained untouched, but even there the new developments were somewhat perceptible.

Mathilde Hrabovecka, who knew the women's camp from the first day to the last, told me that in those days most of the German prostitutes, who had hitherto occupied key positions, were relieved of them. She remembers that in the end hardly any "Blacks" were in a position to give orders. As has already been mentioned, prostitutes had to wear the black triangles of antisocials.

According to statistics relating to the quarantine section in Birkenau, there was a marked decrease in random killings in that period, a result of the change in leadership in that section of the camp. At the time its head, Schillinger, was replaced by Johann Schwarzhuber.

That Liebehenschel let himself be influenced by prisoners is unusual but not unprecedented. Kogon reports that German capos occasionally complained to the commandant of Buchenwald, Hermann Pister, about SS men who had maltreated inmates, and that these complaints were successful.

In those days something blossomed that had previously been unknown in Auschwitz: hope. The selections of *Muselmänner* in the camp ceased. It is true that transports were subjected to selections at the ramp every day and that the crematoriums burned constantly, but there now was hope that Auschwitz could lose the character of an extermination camp at least for those who had already been admitted to it. Together with good news from the fronts this improved the atmosphere of the camp.

■ Appearances were deceiving. This is what I wrote about it in my *Bericht*:

Today the messenger Tadek comes to me with a note. "Read it right away!" Ernst wants me to come to the camp as soon as possible. "What's going on, Ernstl?" "They've put together a transport to the gas chambers again. All Jews. For the time being they locked them up in the bath barracks. There are more than a thousand of them. Try to reach the commandant via Wirths. Perhaps it'll be possible to stop this."

I stand at the window the entire time looking for Wirths, who is outside the camp, to enter the infirmary. But his wide car with its light brown military paint does not turn into our street until evening. Finally he rings. I come right away, but his sergeant is already in front of his desk and has presented a folder for the physician's signature. "Take this down," he says and dictates unimportant things. I have to keep quiet and take it down in shorthand while a thousand people are locked up in the bath who want to live but are going to be gassed within the next few hours.

Ernst is already waiting for me on the camp road. "Have you been able to do something?" "No, I didn't have a chance. Are they gone?" "Before the roll call the trucks were here. So it's starting all over again." I can see it in every face: Death has again come closer to everyone. Were the last few weeks only a dream?

The next day I speak with Wirths, and he speaks with the commandant. "The commandant knew about the transport. It wasn't done behind his back, as you may think, Langbein. The action was ordered directly from Berlin, by the Labor Assignment Office (Arbeitseinsatz). They have been informed that there are too many prisoners in the camp who are not completely fit for work."

This first camp selection after a considerable hiatus was discussed in the Auschwitz trial at Frankfurt. ss roll call leader Oswald Kaduk confirmed what Wirths had told me: "At that time Liebehenschel tried to get Berlin not to send that transport to the gas chambers, but Berlin was in favor of gassing. The selection was made by Max Sell, the head of the Labor Service (Arbeitsdienst)."

Franz Hofmann, then ss camp leader at the main camp, said in his defense at Frankfurt: "It is not true that a selection was made in Liebehenschel's absence. A selection was made in Block 2a, and 400 to 500 prisoners were chosen. Afterwards, however, there was a discussion with Liebehenschel, and on this basis he went to Berlin to prevent the gassing. He came back and told me, 'Hofmann, these people won't be gassed.'"

Hofmann went on to say: "The first selection in Liebehenschel's term was in January 1944, and this was ordered by Berlin." After his sentencing Hofmann told me in prison about another attempt by Liebehenschel to slow down the machinery of extermination. Defects in the ramp gave him an opportunity to report to Berlin that the railroad siding would have to be repaired before new transports could be directed to Auschwitz. However, the Central Office did not permit even a temporary stoppage of the exterminations.

Another campaign of mass murders was also ordered directly from Berlin. On September 8, 1943, 5,006 Jews were transferred from Theresienstadt to Auschwitz with the notation "sb (Sonderbehandlung, special treatment) six months." They were housed in a special section of Birkenau which, like the Gypsy camp, was run as a family camp. These Jews were not assigned to any work details, and were permitted to write letters (they were even required to notify their relatives) and to receive parcels. To illustrate conditions in Birkenau, it may be stated that despite this preferential treatment 1,140 inmates of that family camp died within six months. When that time had elapsed, those still alive were killed in the gas chambers on March 9, 1944. Only about seventy young inmates were exempted from this murderous action.

▧ Liebehenschel stayed in Auschwitz for only six months, and another change of commandants worsened the atmosphere in the camp. On May 8, 1944, Rudolf Höß appeared in Auschwitz again and assumed the function of an ss senior garrison commander, but three days later Richard Baer replaced Liebehenschel as the commandant of Auschwitz I. The measures that followed in rapid succession indicated the reason for this change. Höß reinstated his proven assistants in the key positions of the extermination machinery from which they had been removed. On May 16 the first three trains from

Hungary arrived, and the biggest campaign of extermination began, directed against the Jews from Hungary and Siebenbürgen, a territory that had been annexed by Hungary. Evidently, the central administration had not regarded Liebehenschel as the appropriate man for the smooth completion of this unparalleled mass killing. "On some days the arrivals were simply wild," wrote Oswald Kaduk. "Five transports had already arrived by half past ten one morning." As had been done in the early period of the camp, the corpses were burned on pyres that were set up in the open air next to the crematoriums, for the capacity of the ovens was insufficient.

In the final phase of the war, the arms industry urgently needed additional workers, who were to be distributed among the numerous labor camps that tightly ringed all concentration camps. For this reason those who had been found fit for work at the initial selection and allowed to live were "put on ice," as the SS called it—that is, they had to wait in Section B II c of Birkenau and in an unfinished section of that camp for their transport to one of the work camps. Since they were not slated to remain in Auschwitz, these prisoners did not receive Auschwitz numbers, and thus their numbers can only be estimated.

The new section of the camp reproduced the indescribable conditions that had had such devastating consequences in the Birkenau women's camp and later in the Gypsy camp. The absence of even the most primitive hygienic facilities and the lack of water caused a mortality rate that was especially high even by Auschwitz standards. In the camp lingo, the new section was called "Mexico." The inmates had received neither prison garb nor camp blankets, and so were now given all sorts of blankets that had been amassed in Canada from the belongings of deportees. When they walked around draped in blankets, the colorful scene evoked Mexico.

Baer followed Höß's policies, though not with the same energy. Paul Steinmetz, an SS master sergeant (*Hauptscharführer*) with administrative duties that enabled him to observe the work of the various commandants, came to this conclusion: "While a certain improvement had been effected under Liebehenschel, conditions under Baer soon became as bad as they had been under Höß. This involved not only the prisoners but the SS as well."

Not all of Liebehenschel's reforms were rescinded, however. After its most important informers had been transferred, the Political Department was unable to achieve the unlimited dominance that it had had under Höß. Under Baer, Greens were given important functions again, but the Reds retained their key positions, at least in the main camp. In Birkenau, the dominance of the Greens had never been broken, but, as a result of developments at the fronts, brutal acts of the SS and capos were less frequent than they had been in Höß's time.

Höß left Auschwitz on July 29, when the Hungarian campaign was essentially completed. Baer received the title SS senior garrison commander.

On orders from the central administration the inmates of the Gypsy camp were gassed on August 1. The prisoner Regina Steinberg, who as the clerk of the Political Department of that section was best situated to observe events, has made this statement about some exceptions: "Those Gypsies were summoned who had fought in the front lines and had been transported from the front to the camp at the time of Easter 1944. Pery Broad, who headed the Political Department for this section of the camp, told them that if they agreed to be sterilized, they would be released. Those who agreed were transferred to the main camp, sterilized, and sent back to us. On the day of the liquidation, or the day before, they were transferred to the quarantine section of Auschwitz."

A man involved in this action testified before the court as follows: "Before the liquidation of the Gypsy camp, those who had served in the Wehrmacht were sent to Ravensbrück to be sterilized. Afterwards we were supposed to volunteer for army duty and be readmitted to the Wehrmacht in 1945. The others were gassed. I was wounded in 1945."

Even before that, exceptional instances occurred in which it was possible to be released from the camp in return for sterilization. A Gypsy woman who was married to a German front-line soldier was sent to Auschwitz with her child. The child became ill, and the mother tried all sorts of things, for she was afraid to go to the infirmary, which did not have a good reputation. When she was at her wits' end, she implored Dr. Mengele in the HKB to help her child, for her husband was wearing the same uniform as the physician. This gave Mengele pause; he asked her some questions, examined the child, and prescribed medicine that helped. Some time later he sent for the Gypsy woman, told her he had checked her statements, and would recommend that she and her child be released if she agreed to be sterilized. The woman had no choice, and the two actually went free. Although they are still alive, their lives are destroyed.

■ The Russian front came closer. In July 1944 Russian troops liberated Majdanek near Lublin, the second KZ that had been expanded into an extermination camp. Acting hastily, the panic-stricken administration ordered the evacuation of the prisoners—especially the Germans—who had not already been killed and also attempted to obliterate all traces of the mass extermination. This attempt was unsuccessful, and in light of this failure, which afforded the Allies some insight into the methods of exterminating human beings, the Auschwitz administration began to prepare for the liquidation of the camp. First, the admission authority's documents revealing the scope of the extermination campaign were burned. Even before then, the central administration had ordered the transfer of Russian and (particularly) Polish prisoners to other camps, where there was no nearby Polish population with whom they could establish contact. The transfer of Poles increased in the second half of 1944.

The machinery of extermination, which had been greatly enlarged for the slaughter of Hungarian Jews and, subsequently, of the inhabitants of the Lodz ghetto, was dismantled, and the Sonderkommandos were reduced—that is, the superfluous prisoners were killed. Knowing the fate that threatened them, members of this detail organized a desperate attempt at breaking out. On October 7 they were able to blow up a crematorium, but they could not escape their fate.

RSHA transports were still rolling into Auschwitz. On November 3 SS officers for the last time decided the life or death of new arrivals with a movement of their hands. Then the machinery of extermination, which had been in operation for more than two and a half years, was stopped, and in late November 1944 Himmler ordered the destruction of the extermination facilities. Only Crematorium IV remained intact so that the corpses from the Auschwitz camps could be burned. A member of the Sonderkommando had recorded in a chronicle that later was dug up near a crematorium in November 1953: "Today, on November 25, they began to demolish Crematorium I. Crematorium II is next." This entry ends with the words: "Now we, the 170 male survivors, are on our way to our women. We are convinced that we are being led to our deaths. Thirty people were picked to stay in Crematorium IV. Today, November 26, 1944."

On January 17, 1945, the advancing Russian armies forced the SS to order the evacuation of Auschwitz, and it was accomplished by the nineteenth of the month. Patients and members of the nursing staff stayed behind, and so did some inmates who thought they might have a better chance of survival if they hid in the camp than if they participated in the evacuation march in the wintry cold. After days of uncertainty, those who had stayed behind were liberated by Russian troops on January 27.

On the evacuation marches, all those who could not go on were shot, and the others were taken to Mauthausen, Buchenwald, and other camps. This last chapter in the history of the camps was characterized by overcrowding, a breakdown of provisions and services, and constant evacuations and death marches. Neither those marches nor the final phase of the camps, as illustrated by the piles of bodies of people who had starved to death and were found by the Allies in Bergen-Belsen, are the subject or background of this study. It will conclude with the day on which Auschwitz ceased to be a concentration camp.

NUMBERS

■ ■ ■

Because the Auschwitz system never assigned the same number twice, it is possible to make a rather accurate survey of the prisoners registered in that camp—that is, those who were admitted in the regular way or, having arrived on an RSHA transport, were classified at the ramp as fit for work. Those who were immediately taken from the ramp to the gas chambers received no inmate number and were not registered anywhere, and thus their numbers can only be estimated.

According to the documents collected and processed in the Auschwitz-Birkenau State Museum, 405,000 people had to live in Auschwitz for varying lengths of time. In addition, some tens of thousands were "put on ice" in Birkenau at the time of the Hungarian campaign or at a later date to await their transfer to labor camps in Germany. These prisoners remained unnumbered, and so their numbers cannot be reconstructed exactly. Also, approximately 300,000 people, predominantly Poles from the vicinity, were locked up in Block 11 of the main camp awaiting a court-martial as prisoners of the police. Only those admitted to the camp on a court order were given a number, and they have therefore been included in the figure of 405,000. The great majority were immediately shot and remained unregistered. The 405,000 consisted of almost exactly two-thirds men and one-third women.

The documents permit us to learn about the fate of these inmates. Some 261,000 died in Auschwitz—that is, they were murdered. The number of those released can be ignored; with some exceptions only Poles who revealed themselves as ethnic Germans and Germans who volunteered for the special Dirlewanger Unit of the SS were released. An even smaller number of prisoners successfully escaped from the camp. The great majority of those who survived the extermination camp were transferred to another camp, either with one of the numerous transports that kept shuttling from one camp to another or on one of the evacuation marches. Only a rough estimate of the number of those who perished on those death marches or in other camps can be given. If one estimates that in the spring of 1945 60,000 "Auschwitzers" regained their freedom, this figure is probably not too low.

Some extant documents indicate the nationalities of the prisoners. Two letters from the resistance movement that have been preserved in Cracow reveal the ethnic composition of the camp on May 11, 1943, and on August 22, 1944. On the first of these dates, 2.7 percent of the prisoners were registered as Germans, but by August 1944 this percentage had declined to 1.9. The main camp had the highest percentage, 5.6. Germans were employed for the most part in the camp's administration office. Promises and pressure induced Upper Silesians, who spoke both Polish and German, to sign the ethnic list; as soon as they had done so, they were registered as Germans. Next to the thin upper crust of Germans, the Poles were the most influential ethnic group. Originally, they were in the overwhelming majority, but after Auschwitz's expansion into an extermination camp their percentage declined. In May 1943 it was 30.1, but in August 1944 only 22.3. At that time it was highest (29.5 percent) in the Birkenau men's camp and lowest (18.6 percent) in the women's camp.

Because of the steady RSHA transports, the number of those who had to wear the Star of David grew constantly despite the high mortality rate of this group, which was subjected to the worst treatment. On May 11, 1943, 57.4 percent of all prisoners were registered as Jews, and by August 22, 1944, this percentage had risen to 64.6 (and to 68.2 in the women's camp). This figure includes neither the Jews who were "put on ice" in Mexico nor those who were doing forced labor in the satellite camps. The percentage of Jews in the work camps was much higher; thus it has been reported that in Jaworzno 80 percent of all inmates were Jews and in Günthergrube 95 percent.

Another list, smuggled out of the camp by the resistance movement, contains the Jews' countries of origin as of September 2, 1941. Most of the men were from Poland, and next came those deported from Hungary, France, Holland, and Greece. In the women's camp the deportees from Slovakia were in fourth place after the Jewish women from Poland, France, and Greece.

Of other ethnic groups only the numerically strongest are mentioned. On May 11, 1943, it was the Czechs with 5.9 percent; on August 22, 1944, the Russians with 9.4 percent. Most of the latter were in Birkenau; in the main camp on that day, the count of Russians amounted to just over 5 percent. The marked decrease in the number of Czechs — only 81 on September 2, 1944 — was the result of an order from the central administration to transfer the Czech prisoners to camps with better living conditions. The regime was trying to dampen the unrest that the high death rate in Auschwitz had caused in Czechoslovakia. For the same reason the transfer of French prisoners was ordered as well, but this was not handled so rigorously, for on September 22, 1944, there still were 325 Frenchmen on the roll call in Auschwitz. The statistics of the last roll calls in the main camp and the Birkenau men's camp, held on January 17, 1945, have also been preserved. On that day 2 percent of the inmates were French, and the number of Czechs had decreased to 24 individuals. The percentage of Poles (8) and Russians (3) had also declined greatly by that time; this was the result of numerous transfers of these nationalities in the months before the evacuation. Few of the Germans who had not been conscripted for the

Dirlewanger Unit had been transferred to other camps, for the camp administration did not regard them as dangerous and most of them were in what seemed to be indispensable positions. Thus the percentage of Germans at the last roll call had risen to 11, and as late as early December 1944 Germans were transferred to Auschwitz from Mauthausen.

The countries of origin of the surviving prisoners are also indicated by a compilation made after the liberation of Auschwitz. Eduard de Wind, a Dutch physician who had stayed behind with the sick prisoners, published the nationalities of 2,690 persons who had been interrogated by the Russian medical legal commission. Since the Jews were no longer compelled to identify themselves as such, they stated their nationality on the basis of the countries from which they had been deported. Though this makes it impossible to determine how many of these 2,690 were Jews, it is probably safe to describe most of them as persons persecuted for "racial" reasons. Almost 28 percent of the patients were Poles, and more than 22 percent stated that they were Hungarian or Romanian citizens (Jews from Siebenbürgen identified themselves as citizens of Romania again). A little less than 13 percent were citizens of France and barely 1 percent of Czechoslovakia. Almost 7 percent came from the Soviet Union, less than 6 percent from Holland, and more than 5 percent from Yugoslavia. The other patients gave Greece, Belgium, and other states as their homelands.

Some information about the number of prisoners in the various Auschwitz camps has been preserved. The main camp had the steadiest population— 18,437 on January 20, 1944, and 14,386 on July 1 of that year. By August 22, 1944, it had risen to 17,070 again. As I remember it, the population probably fluctuated between these figures in the second half of 1942 and in 1943 as well, and it was to decline drastically because of transports of Poles just before the evacuation.

The population of the Birkenau men's camps (for a long time there were several, in addition to the quarantine section and a section that housed the infirmary) fluctuated between 22,061 (on January 20, 1944) and 15,000 (an approximate figure given by the camp administration on April 5, 1944). In July and August of that year, figures in excess of 19,000 were mentioned. At the last roll call on January 17, 1945, there were only 15,317 prisoners in the main camp and the Birkenau men's camp.

There were greater fluctuations in the women's camp. While the resistance movement gave a population of 27,053 women on January 20, 1944, this number declined to 21,000 by April 5, 1944, and rose to 31,406 by July 12 and to 39,234 by August 22 of that year.

The Gypsy camp housed a total of 10,849 women and 10,094 men. The Auschwitz-Birkenau State Museum estimates that fewer than 3,000 of them were transferred to other camps. It cannot be ascertained exactly how many had died before the liquidation of that section of Birkenau.

In another section of the camp, which was run as the Theresienstadt family camp, 15,711 Jews from Czechoslovakia had to spend six months waiting for their deaths. Before the second gassing campaign on July 11 and 12, 1944, around 3,000 people were sent to labor camps.

Kazimierz Smolen, the director of the Auschwitz-Birkenau State Museum, has estimated that approximately 120,000 persons were housed in the various sections of Birkenau. This estimate includes those prisoners in Mexico who waited without a number to be sent to a labor camp.

The population of the labor camps grew steadily. On January 20, 1944, 13,288 prisoners were registered in Auschwitz III, and by April there were 15,000. By July 1, 1944, the figure had risen to 26,705 and was probably 10,000 higher at the time of the evacuation. Monowitz, the largest labor camp, housed 6,571 inmates on January 20, 1944; that figure rose to 10,000 in June and to approximately 10,500 in December.

▦ In March 1944 I managed to smuggle out of the camp statistics that showed for each month the percentage of deceased inmates in proportion to the population. For 1942 I took these figures from the quarterly reports that I was able to examine in the files, and the figures for 1943 and for the first three months of 1944 were based on the monthly reports that Wirths had dictated to me. I took the death figures from the weekly reports that listed those who died each day.

These figures clearly indicate the conditions under which the inmates lived. While in the third quarter of 1942 an average of 20.5 percent of the prisoners were registered each month as dead, an average of 3.6 percent per month died in July, August, and September 1943. The document that covers the period up to March 1944 gives the lowest mortality rate for October: 2.3 percent. In the first quarter of 1943 an average of 4.8 percent of all prisoners died each month; the figure had been 20.4 percent in the same quarter of the preceding year.

It is possible to compare the figures for the first quarter of 1944 month by month. In January 1943, 19.1 percent died; in January 1944, 13.2 percent. In February the corresponding percentage of the dead amounted to 25.5 in 1943 and 6.1 in 1944. The February 1943 number is the largest known. For March the figures are 15.4 percent in 1943 and 10 percent in 1944. The latter figure is given as an estimate in the document, for I completed it before I had all of the March statistics.

As compared to the maximum reached in the worst period of Auschwitz, the second half of 1942 and the first two months of 1943, the number of deaths had already declined considerably under Höß as commandant. The reforms of Liebehenschel were clearly evident, and they would have become even more so had a typhus epidemic in the women's camp not caused a drastic rise in the number of deaths. In July 1943 there were 1,133 deaths in the women's camp, 1,433 in August, 1,861 in September, and 2,269 in October. In November, when there was a change of commandants, the number declined to 1,603, but in December it climbed to 8,931, a number reminiscent of the worst times. The number of deaths has been preserved only for the first half of January 1944; it was 2,661.

The high figure for March 1944 is due to the killing of the members of the first transport, who had been housed in the Theresienstadt family camp and were murdered six months after the transfer on orders from the central administration. The resistance movement sent a chart to Cracow that contains the monthly death figures for the women's camp for February 1943 to mid-January 1944 and also indicates the number of those who died in the camp and those who were killed in the gas chambers. These figures are broken down; under four different rubrics are listed "Poles," "Other Aryans," "Jews," and (in German) "Gas." In the following account of this document, two obvious mathematical errors have been corrected, though these add up to no more than forty.

In those eleven and a half months 19,761 inmates of the women's camp died and 11,940 were gassed. The influence of the season and of the typhus epidemic in late 1943 had a striking effect on the number of deaths. September and October brought the lowest numbers, 690 and 724, but in March 1943 there were 2,189, in December 4,684, and in the first half of January 1944 1,961. The largest number under the rubric "Gas" is given for December as well: 4,247. This rubric has a line for the months of June, July, and November; evidently there were no selections in the camp then.

Polish women made up 21.7 percent of all the deceased registered in the camp. This rubric, too, indicates great fluctuation. Between February and April more than 39 percent of those who died were Poles, but the percentage declined to 4.3 for September to November. Of all who died in the camp, 37.8 percent were "other Aryans." Their percentage was highest in the relatively favorable months September and October: 72. During that period, transports of "Aryan" women, which included no Poles but a large number of Russians, were directed to Auschwitz.

The percentage of Jewish women who died in the camp was 40.5. Their mortality rate was highest at the end of the period covered by the report; between November 1943 and mid-January 1944 it amounted to 54.2 percent. To this number must be added those listed under the rubric "Gas," for Jewish women were the first victims of the selections in the camp. This means that

60 percent of those who died or were murdered were Jews. While there are no documents to show how many Jewish women, Polish women, and "other Aryans" were interned in the women's camp at that time, these figures speak for themselves.

Some statistics that happen to have been preserved give us a chance to learn about the differences in the treatment of Jews and "Aryans" as well as the different conditions in 1942 and 1943.

Between April 17 and 29, 1942, when RSHA transports were not yet subject to selections at the ramp and all prisoners were admitted to the camp, 2,845 Jews arrived in Auschwitz on four transports from Slovakia. By August 15 of that year only 182 of them were still alive. Even though there are no exact figures, there can be no doubt that the fate of the other people on the RSHA transports, all of whom were admitted to the camp in its early phase, was similar. In those days many transports from Slovakia were directed to Auschwitz, and those who survived had to go through periods in the camp that left an indelible mark on many of them. These data should be borne in mind when reading later in this book the account of the behavior of Slovakian women on the first transports.

On January 17, 1943, 230 "Aryan women" arrived in Auschwitz; on April 10 of that year 73 of them were still alive and on August 3, 57. Charlotte Delbo, the chronicler of that transport, emphasizes that such a low death rate in the women's camp was "unique in its history." She attributes this exceptional situation to the fact that these women were political prisoners who knew one another and practiced solidarity.

The difference is clear: 93.6 percent of the Jews deported in April 1942 died within the first four months, while 24.8 percent of the "Aryan" Frenchwomen deported in January 1943 were still alive after more than six months.

That the fate of privileged Germans in Auschwitz differed from what awaited this group of prisoners in other camps is proved by our transport. Our group of seventeen men was transferred from Dachau in August 1942. Within the first few months six of us died of epidemics that spared no group of prisoners.

■ These figures also prove that for all those deported the first weeks and months were the worst. After that, no member of our transport died. Of the group of Frenchwomen, 68.3 percent lost their lives in the first two and a half months in Auschwitz. During the next four months, almost 22 percent of the survivors from the early period died. We may assume that the mortality figures of the Slovaks who survived the terrible early period dropped markedly as well.

Statistics prepared by the Auschwitz-Birkenau State Museum shed light on the relationship between mortality and the length of time spent in the camp. They give the weekly death rate of Jews who were deported in fifteen transports between April 15 and July 17, 1942. Of these, 3.06 percent died in their first week in Auschwitz, and the percentage increased quickly in the following weeks, amounting to 5.32 in the second week, 6.2 in the third, and 11.32 in the fourth. After that, the mortality rate stabilized; it was 11.04 in the fifth week, 10.75 percent in the sixth, and 10.45 in the seventh. These statistics prove that those who survived the most horrendous early period had better chances. In the eighth week the mortality rate was 7 percent and in the ninth 8.7 percent, but then it declined rapidly. It was 6.1 percent in the tenth week, 4.78 percent in the eleventh, 3.3 percent in the twelfth, and less than 2 percent thereafter.

Wojciech Barcz, a Pole who was interned in Auschwitz from the first day to the last and to whom we owe valuable observations, wrote: "It is a fact that most of the prisoners in the camp perished within the first three months after their arrival. The reason was that the devitalizing nature of the system hit an unprepared human being with enormous force and, as it were, crushed him intellectually, so that he was ready for impending death. After three months something like a resistance after an inoculation developed, at least in mental terms."

■ Finally, there are statistics about those who were left behind at the evacuation of Auschwitz because they were sick, unable to walk, or hidden. In the women's camp, 4,428 women and girls and 169 boys remained. The Russian troops found approximately 4,000 persons there on January 7; the others had been shot or had died or had escaped from the camp in the ten days between the evacuation and the liberation. On the day of the liberation, around 1,880 people were in the infirmary of the Birkenau men's camp and 1,200 in the main camp. Eight hundred and fifty prisoners who were unable to walk remained in Monowitz, and 200 of these died in the aforementioned ten days, a period vividly described by Primo Levi. In Fürstengrube 250 patients stayed behind, and all but approximately two dozen of these were massacred by an SS squad after January 27. Six hundred stayed behind in Jaworzno; some inmates were killed when the camp was fired at, but most of them were liberated by Russian troops as early as January 19. The number of those left behind and liberated in Blechhammer cannot be determined.

This means that the arrival of Russian troops restored the freedom of at least 7,650 people in Auschwitz, but many of those could no longer enjoy it. On February 6, 1945, functionaries of the Polish Red Cross counted only 4,880 survivors in the various Auschwitz hospitals, which amounts to a difference of 2,770 people. It cannot be determined how many died in the first ten days of freedom (in many cases the change of diet had a devastating effect), and how many people, most logically Poles, had the strength to head for their homes. A committee of Russian medical examiners found 536 corpses and determined that in the case of 474 of them death had resulted from total exhaustion. Such mass deaths continued for a time. On February 28 two former inmates were buried in a mass grave. According to a report by Leo Vos, eighty-two of those liberated in Blechhammer died.

This is what the available figures tell us about the fate of the 405,000 persons who were imprisoned in Auschwitz.

■ The number of those who were selected immediately after their arrival in Auschwitz and were murdered in one of the big gas chambers is far greater. Because those deportees were not registered, their numbers can only be estimated, though we do have partial figures. Georges Wellers has calculated that of the 61,098 Jews who were sent to Auschwitz from France between July 29, 1942, and August 11, 1944, 47,976 or 78.5 percent were victims of the selections at the ramp. Danuta Czech came to a similar conclusion—that 76.6 percent of the Jews deported from Greece were killed in the gas chambers immediately upon arrival; of a total of 54,533 deportees, only 8,025 men and 4,732 women were admitted to the camp. Between July 17, 1942, and September 5, 1944, fifty-seven trains from Holland brought 51,130 persons to Auschwitz; 18,408 received an inmate number, but 64 percent were immediately killed with poison gas.

Since these statistics cover only a small part of the RSHA transports, anyone who wants to get an idea of the magnitude of the extermination campaign must resort to estimates.

The admission division of the Political Department was the only office that preserved carbon copies of the reports that were sent to Berlin and revealed the number of those destined for death during the selection at the ramp. Those copies were destroyed by the SS when an evacuation of the camp became likely, but Kasimierz Smolen and Erwin Bartel, prisoners who had been employed in that office, made calculations before the destruction of the documents. At that time they arrived at figures between three and four million. Before his escape in April 1944, Rudolf Vrba attempted to gain an idea of the scope of the extermination campaign because he wanted to tell the world about it. His estimate is noteworthy for several reasons. He first worked at the ramp and then became a clerk in Birkenau, where he had an exceptional insight into the situation, and he has an unusually good memory for figures. Vrba arrived at a figure of 3.25 million. To be sure, the most extensive campaigns of extermination, in which the Hungarian Jews and the inhabitants of the Lodz ghetto were among the victims, did not begin until after Vrba's escape.

Members of the SS have dealt with this subject as well. At his hearing in Nuremberg, Höß gave the figure of 2.5 million, but later he reduced it. It is not clear whether his estimate refers to his tenure as the camp's commandant or to the entire period. On July 30, 1945, the SS physician Friedrich Entress testified at Gmunden that two to 2.5 million people were killed in Auschwitz. When he was challenged, he conceded that it might have been five million. Entress had no contact with the camp after his transfer, and so his vague estimate probably refers only to his period of employment in Auschwitz.

Maximilian Grabner, who headed both the Political Department and its admissions division, the only office permitted to record the number of those gassed immediately after their arrival, testified in Vienna on September 16, 1945. "There were so many deaths that I completely lost count and today cannot state how many prisoners were murdered. But during my term as head of the Political Department it was at least three million." Grabner was transferred from Auschwitz in October 1943, around the same time as Entress. When SS Technical Sergeant Wilhelm Boger, who was also attached to the Political Department, was questioned in 1945 about the number of deaths, he responded that there were more than four million, but two decades later he reduced that estimate substantially. Unlike Entress and Grabner, Pery Broad, also a member of the Political Department, testified in March 1946 not as a defendant but as a witness, and he stated that a total of 2.5 or three million prisoners were gassed. All these statements were made shortly after the end of the war, when each informant's memory was still fresh and none of those interrogated had been influenced by other estimates or calculations. Because these testimonies were given independently of one another, they permit us to draw some conclusions regarding the actual number of victims in Auschwitz.

An objection that is occasionally raised, namely that killings of such a scope would have been impossible from a purely technical point of view, has already been refuted by Höß. "It would not have been difficult to destroy even more people," he told the American psychologist G. M. Gilbert in a Nuremberg prison. "Killing was easy. We didn't even need guards to push them into the gas chambers; they simply went in because they assumed they would take a shower there, and instead of the water we turned on the poison gas. The whole procedure went very quickly." The burning of corpses was harder and took more time. When the gas chambers were in maximal use, corpses were burned on wood piles in the open air next to the crematoriums. The SS did not want to have this action limited by the capacity of the ovens.

The incredible scope of the killings and the uncertain and largely unknown estimates of persons able to give first-hand information later led to calculations and speculations that deviated much more from one another than the estimates of those who had been in Auschwitz. This only increased the uncertainty about the total number of those murdered in the extermination camp Auschwitz, and often this uncertainty was fomented intentionally.

Finally, I would like to point to a grotesque consequence of the bureaucracy. It afforded Jews whom the Nazis persecuted not only because of their origin but also because of political activities against them better chances of survival than it gave to Jews who were persecuted only for "racial" reasons. A Jew who was sent to Auschwitz because of a political offense did not arrive on an RSHA transport but on one of the many transports that were directed to Auschwitz from German prisons. Hence he did not have to undergo a selection, for he was accompanied by a Gestapo file, whereas those deported to Auschwitz on an RSHA transport had no such file. If at a later date he fell victim to a selection because of physical weakness, the Political Department pulled him out of the ranks of those earmarked for death. Before those selected were taken to the gas chamber, their numbers were sent to that department, and anyone who had a file there was removed from the list.

An acquaintance of mine owes his life to this practice. The Viennese Pepi Meisel, a member of the Communist Party, was sent by that party from Belgium, where he had immigrated, to Austria in order to engage in political activity there with false papers that identified him as a foreign worker. He was soon captured by informers. The file that accompanied him when he was sent to Auschwitz contained references to his political activity. Meisel was safe from camp selection, but there was no doubt that sooner or later the Vienna Gestapo would notify the camp administration that he had been sentenced to death. We helped Meisel to escape successfully.

Eduard de Wind tells about a Dutch jazz trumpeter, Lex van Weren, who also owed his life to the fact that he had been sent to Auschwitz as a Jew with a file. De Wind's report does not say whether that man was able to survive the entire concentration-camp period. Anton van Velsen reports about Wilhelm Schwed from Vienna, whom the same practice saved from gassing, though he was later shot at the Black Wall.

The respect for files could for a while keep German Nazism from exterminating human beings like vermin.

The Prisoners

UNDER THE POWER
OF THE CAMP
■ ■ ■

In a sociological study of the concentration camps, H. G. Adler, who had first-hand experience of them, writes: "The problems of Nazism represent nothing but an extreme—admittedly insanely extreme—special case of conditions or possibilities that are encountered in modern society all over the world, at least latently and often manifestly. . . . Cruelty and deindividualization are what make a concentration camp possible; both have to be systematically fostered for it to exist and become what it is: a place of absolute and ultimate subjugation beyond the bounds of a life worth living."

Adler also refers to the Nazi leadership principle (Führerprinzip), which "extended to the concentration camps and, because of their closed society, assumed its purest form there. The 'positive' hierarchy of the free ss was continued among the enslaved prisoners as a 'negative' hierarchy." Olga Lengyel, who recorded her experience in Birkenau, picks up on this idea: "The greatest crime committed by the Nazis against the prisoners may not have been their extermination in the gas chambers but the frequently successful endeavor to form the prisoners after their own image, to turn them into bad persons."

Because the ss had every conceivable resource at its disposal, it was even able to blur the boundary line with which it separated people in Auschwitz from one another: the electrically charged barbed wire. Willi Brachmann, a Green capo and certainly not one of the worst, may serve as proof of the blurred line between inmates and guards. A quarter century later, when he told the court about his fellow prisoners under his command, he casually used the expression "my inmates."

The fact that fluid borders between the two sharply divided groups of people in Auschwitz were created by the other side as well is an indication of the limits that human nature imposes on a totalitarian system even where it has established its most unrestricted dominance. For the time being, Viktor Pestek, an ss man who escaped from Auschwitz together with an inmate and returned to the camp in order to help others escape, may suffice as evidence for the crossing of the boundary set by the ss leadership.

One result of contact between two such antithetical groups of people was that prisoners were even integrated into a special ss unit; according to ss theory, Germans had "Führer qualities" even as prisoners. In practical terms, the ss thought that these qualities were developed particularly in career criminals, and that is why they recruited German Greens for the Dirlewanger Unit. Another result was that some members of the ss were punished for favoring prisoners, and a few were even imprisoned for that reason.

This means that any description of people in Auschwitz must heed Benedikt Kautsky's warning that "nothing is falser than a simple black-and-white picture." Since the present study deals with extremes in human behavior under the conditions of an extermination camp, more space is given to a description of people whose reactions differed from what was expected of them than to an account of standard reactions. This applies to those prisoners who allowed themselves to be misused as an extension of their oppressors. Olga Lengyel's reference to the camp leaders' responsibility for crimes committed by their lackeys as well retains its validity. The same is true of the guards, and there too exceptions (that is, human emotions) are more interesting than the rule.

■ Everyone who was placed in the milieu of a Nazi concentration camp experienced a shock that the camp administration deliberately exacerbated by its especially brutal treatment of new arrivals. The shock caused by confrontation with an extermination camp was even more enduring.

Even though I had already become acquainted with the ss system in Dachau, came to Auschwitz in the company of good friends, and there met like-minded persons who familiarized me with the special qualities of an extermination camp, my first encounter with the machinery of destruction was still a great shock. In Dachau I had hoped to survive the camp, but in Auschwitz I quickly lost this hope. As a clerk in the infirmaries of the two camps, I received impressive visual instruction. In Dachau we spoke of a bad day if ten or more deaths were to be reported, but in Auschwitz we used seven typewriters on day and night shifts to prepare just such reports.

An incomparably greater shock was suffered by those who had not come from another concentration camp but had enjoyed freedom before being sent to Auschwitz, who had no friends and thus had to cope with everything alone, who were not privileged like us Germans or Austrians, and who at the ramp were brutally separated from their relatives, whose fate they would soon learn. In addition, experienced inmates could hardly help someone who suffered the consequences of a shock. The fact that people in Auschwitz had few chances to think of matters that did not directly concern them was not the only reason. A host of informers made it risky to converse openly with someone whom one did not know well and who had as yet no camp experience. A thoughtless remark or reaction could mean mortal danger not only for the novice but also for his informant. Officially, an inmate was not supposed to know anything about the machinery of mass extermination, and talking about it was taboo. Precisely at the time when a helpless new arrival had the greatest need for support, he remained woefully isolated.

The arrival shock, which was most painful for those persecuted for "racial" reasons, has been described many times—for instance, by Dr. Erwin Toffler, who was eighteen when he entered the camp in the spring of 1944: "I thought I was dreaming. Even today the whole thing seems like an ugly dream to me. The selection, the noise, and the smell of smoke awakened me, and it was clear to me that I had arrived at the last stop of my life."

Zdenka Fantlova, who was transferred from Theresienstadt to Auschwitz in October 1944 as a young girl and sent to a labor camp after a few weeks, writes: "Auschwitz was such a terrible shock for me that my memories of it and everything I experienced there appear to be shrouded in a veil of mist. During my entire stay there, it felt as though someone had hit me on the head. For a long time I was unable to comprehend that what I had experienced was reality. I stopped thinking and feeling. That was the only help given us by nature to preserve our health."

Eduard de Wind sums up his experiences as a physician who treated many fellow sufferers by saying that in most cases the very first impressions were forgotten. "It was a shock phase in which a profound regression of the entire personality took place. For a brief period of time, the inmates lived in a kind of dreamlike state."

Like Fantlova, Grete Salus was deported to Auschwitz from Theresienstadt in October 1944. Shortly after her liberation she wrote down her first impressions of the extermination camp. "As soon as we jumped out of the railroad car, we were engulfed and, half unconscious, floated along toward something horrible that we could only sense deep in our subconscious. Now everything unfolded with breathtaking speed. Only some of it remained fixed, like flash photography, but everything else did not penetrate into our consciousness." Salus has this to say about the greatest shock, which was caused by the tearing asunder of families at the ramp: "At first my husband and I were still together. People did and said senseless things—a last clinging to something real and familiar. A female friend of mine passed some chocolates around; my husband took a piece and said: 'I'll be right back, I'm going back to the train to take this chocolate to my sick friend.' This was the last time I saw my husband, and these were the last words I heard from him."

There are numerous descriptions of first impressions of the camp. Salus has summarized hers as follows: "*Schneller, schneller, schneller* (faster, faster, faster)—it still rings in my ears, this word that from now on hounded us day and night, whipped us on, and never gave us any rest. On the double—that was the watchword; eat, sleep, work, die on the double. . . . I often asked people with the same experiences what their impressions were on their arrival in Auschwitz. Most of them weren't able to tell me much about it, and almost all of them said they were utterly addled and half dazed, as though they had been hit on the head. They all perceived the floodlights as torturous and the noise as unbearable."

Albert Menasche has described how the word *schnell* cast a shadow over everything from the very beginning. Max Mannheimer's impression: "Move— *dalli*—seems part of the camp lingo." Norbert Fryd speaks of a "new incarnation of the *ruck zuck* (chop-chop) type."

Hanna Hoffmann has retained this memory of her arrival in Auschwitz in December 1943: "The door of the railway car was torn open. Outside striped figures were running around. They dragged us off the train pushing, beating, and shouting, 'Leave your luggage! *Schneller, schneller, schneller*, line up by fives.' Outside, one of the striped men whispered to me, 'Don't get on the truck, it's going to the gas!' and loudly, 'Get on the truck quick!' One after another is grabbed and thrown in a truck. We are not given any time to think it over."

Edith Bruck, who was twelve when she arrived in Auschwitz on a transport from Hungary in the spring of 1944, has reported that Jewish women from Poland and Slovakia gave her advice while their hair was being cut. Between barked orders, they whispered to her that an inmate should never admit to being under sixteen or over forty-five years of age. Bruck has this to say about her condition: "I was as though drunk, and I could not manage to focus my mind on anything."

Elie Wiesel remembers a similar episode. After he and his father had left the carriage at the ramp, an inmate asked him how old he was.

> "Going on fifteen."
> "No, eighteen."
> "No," I replied. "Fifteen."
> "Listen to me, *dummkopf*."
> Then he asked my father his age, and the answer was, "Fifty years."
> The man was even more enraged now. "No, not fifty. Forty. Understand? Eighteen and forty." Then he disappeared into the night.

Nina Weilova, who was deported to Auschwitz from Theresienstadt, remembers what Czech inmates whispered to them when they helped them get out of the railway carriage. "Don't tell them that you're sick; otherwise, you go to the gas chambers."

Jacques Furmanski has given this description of his first night in the camp: "It is significant that during that night I did not think of myself and that my mind was not troubled by any memory of the past. I was the object of a diabolical experiment that was being made on me, or in me. I thought that this was just an individual reaction on my part, but my comrades confirmed that they had been in the same state as well." Furmanski tried to explain this emptiness: "I believe that the multiplicity of the terrible impressions that were concentrated on one day crushed us completely. A horrendously heavy weight lay on us and in us. It took us a long time to free ourselves from this pressure."

This is how Julien Unger captured his first impressions of life in the Birkenau camp in 1943. "Even things that could make life a little easier—some soap, a bath, etc.—are here occasions for suffering and drama." As the reason for this, he identifies "the prevailing contempt for human beings that spells the end of any community."

Eugen Kogon put it succinctly. "Terror renders an average person helpless and frequently overwhelms even strong personalities for a period of time."

To veteran inmates, helpless, distraught, and disoriented newcomers presented a picture of misery that rarely inspired compassion; far more frequently it provoked contempt from people who were stronger and incomprehension on the part of those who had become inured. It even spawned some sadistic jokes.

I remember the lecture given to us new arrivals by Karl Kapp, the camp elder of Dachau. No SS man was present in the washroom, but Kapp acted as though he were a member of the SS as he talked about our future . . . imperiously, threateningly, and fully aware of his power and our powerlessness. Yet Kapp had himself been imprisoned as a political opponent of the Nazis and knew that we, Austrian volunteers in the Spanish Civil War, had fought against Nazism.

Oszkár Betlen has described the welcoming speech given by Tadek, a young Polish dormitory elder, to a group of prisoners transferred from Buchenwald to Auschwitz in the fall of 1942, when all Jews were concentrated in Auschwitz. With his hands on his hips and his legs spread apart, he said: "This is Auschwitz!" Betlen adds: "He seemed to enjoy saying this, as though he were proud of the camp in which tens of thousands of his compatriots had been murdered." Tadek said in his speech: "They've sent you here to croak. Anyone who opens his mouth or doesn't keep things in order will leave through the chimney all the sooner."

I have described an episode from the spring of 1944 when the first transports of Hungarian Jews arrived in Auschwitz. At that time a group of new arrivals were assigned to Block 4 in the main camp, where my friend Ernst Burger was block clerk.

I go with Ernst to the cellar, where the majority of new arrivals are housed. A capo is talking to them, and we listen. He asks them about Hungary, how things look on the outside. Then a Hungarian asks: "Can you tell me where my parents and my wife are? I said farewell to them on our arrival, and they were put on a truck. A gentleman from the ss said older men and women should get on the trucks so they wouldn't have to walk so far. But I haven't been able to see them here yet."

"You jackass, you'll never see them again. Your wife has been singing hallelujahs for quite a while now, and your parents are coughing; you see, they swallowed a bit too much gas."

The capo looks around triumphantly. He must think he made a delightful joke. The Jew smiles crookedly, incredulously.

If someone met acquaintances who had been in the camp for some time, this is what happened in some instances, according to Marc Klein: "On our first evening in the camp, French colleagues who had been in the main camp for some time sought me out in the quarantine section in order to get news of France, and they cautiously revealed the terrible secret of Birkenau. There were a few comrades, to be sure, who implored us not to give credence to those sinister rumors. At a much later date I understood that these encouraging remarks had been nothing but pious lies."

As Klein says, it was weeks or months before the new arrivals slowly comprehended the purpose of the arrival selection.

■ When a prisoner had weathered the arrival shock, he was subject to the camp life of the nameless persons that were crammed into the blocks. Jean Améry has described the consequences of the "compression of human masses in the narrowest spaces." Since the victims "constantly saw, smelled, and touched one another, they were deindividualized and turned into an opaque mass of flesh." As a result they were "nothing but a surfeit to one another." Jenny Spritzer observed the same thing: "The camp made a person mean and egotistical, and anyone who did not help himself with his elbows invariably perished—except for very lucky souls who had pull and were helped in that way."

Observing himself and others, Elie A. Cohen concluded that the will to survive crowds out any other thoughts. He was not interested in the fate of his fellow prisoners. "The instinct of self-preservation is very strong," he writes. All too quickly one could become a person who lived in extreme fashion in the "here and now," as Eduard de Wind put it, or who lived "only in the present, without past or future" (Grete Salus). Viktor Frankl reports a constantly recurring sigh that all of us probably still remember: "Another day gone by!"

The average prisoner was not able to be alone anywhere for even a minute. Everywhere he was constantly surrounded by a hectic crowd that was forever foraging for something edible. Louise Alcan describes her furtive nocturnal visits to the latrine where she could enjoy being alone: "I stay there in order to enjoy some quiet and solitude. The ambiance may not be ideal, but we are in the camp and I have no choice." The unceasing noise made by an excessive number of people crammed into one block strained the nerves to the limit of the bearable. "Eight hundred nervous women crammed into a small space," writes Alcan, "produce permanent disquiet. The only thing I appreciate about the roll call is the quiet."

Désiré Haffner had the strength to describe the consequences of the loss of individuality in Birkenau, where it was at its worst, with the detachment of a physician: "The feelings of the unfortunate prisoners soon become blunted, and a state of inurement and indifference to suffering develops. These prisoners confirm the observation that an organism readily reduces its receptivity to outside stimuli of exceptional intensity if these stimuli are repeated regularly and with the same strength. The deaths of others, and even the probability of one's own impending death, no longer make an impression. People do not even turn their heads when they hear the screams of prisoners being strangled, and I have seen some who ate while having to witness hangings." Viktor Frankl confirms this total devaluation: "Suffering, sick, dying, dead people—all these are such familiar sights after a few weeks in the camp that they can no longer stir the emotions."

A report by Teddy Pietrzykowski, a Pole from the first transport, confirms this observation. Teddy, who worked in the SS infirmary, was able to observe from a trapdoor the gassings in the crematorium opposite that building. "The first time I saw it," Teddy told me, "I felt physically ill. The second and third time also hurt, but after that not as much. Then I didn't watch any more."

On account of the everyday nature of death, people hardly thought about the fact that they would have to die, but only wondered how their death would come. "People had conversations," writes Jean Améry, "about the length of time it would take for the gas to be effective in a gas chamber. They speculated about the painfulness of death by phenol injections. Should they wish for a blow on the head or a slow death from exhaustion in the infirmary? . . . For an inmate death had no sting—none that hurt, none that stimulated thought. This may explain why a camp inmate was tormented by fear of certain types of death but rarely had a fear of death as such." Judith Sternberg-Newman confirmed that concisely when she wrote: "I feared death less than I feared beatings."

I became aware of the blunting of my feelings with a shudder when my friend Hiasl Neumeier died of typhus. We had been transferred from Dachau to Auschwitz together; he became block elder of the infection block and was infected there. During his illness I visited him every morning before our detail set out for work. When I came to his room one morning, the nurse told me that Hiasl's corpse was in the washroom. Because he was a block elder, his body had not been taken to the mortuary immediately. In the washroom I saw Hiasl's body, which was wrapped in a sheet. At a later date I described my emotions: "I am quite empty—not sad but empty." I was gripped by fear at that time: "I tell myself not to become blunted."

Without a kind of thick skin that covered one's emotions, it was impossible to exist in Auschwitz. It was easy to forget that a newcomer had not yet grown such a protective skin, and for that reason such a person's bewilderment, emotional outbursts, and dismay frequently inspired mockery and contempt.

■ When a person had survived the first and hardest period, become familiar with the camp laws, and established connections, he or she gradually became an "old inmate." This type is characterized, according to Eugen Kogon, by demonstrative hardness and emotional primitivism. It developed more clearly in camps with a long tradition and a greater percentage of Germans who had been interned for years than it did in Auschwitz, where there was constant change.

In accordance with an unwritten law in all camps, new arrivals were assigned hard physical labor, whereas "old numbers" were more likely to get a good detail. The SS did not have to enforce this law rigorously, for it was respected by the inmate hierarchy. A good detail was accompanied by better accommodations in blocks that were not so crowded, received more food, and had fewer beatings. What was at least as important for those who were members of a good detail and bore an old number was that they were able to procure better prisoners' garb. That the old adage "clothes make the man" had greater significance in a concentration camp than elsewhere may be illustrated by an episode described by Georges Wellers. Serving as a nurse in the Monowitz infirmary, he wanted to help a friend who was still on the lowest rung of the camp hierarchy. Wellers dressed carefully and visited him in his block. He behaved like a big shot, smoked ostentatiously, though this was strictly prohibited to an ordinary inmate, and stood in the middle of the corridor so that everyone who wished to pass had to beg his leave—in short, he made sure that those in charge of the barracks noticed what acquaintances his friend had, for he knew that a bit of the glamour he exuded as a VIP would be reflected on his poor friend. As a matter of fact, the latter's standing rose markedly after that visit.

Prisoners who owned clean clothes without patches, wore shined shoes, and were always clean-shaven were respected even by the SS, at least up to a point. As the secretary of the SS garrison physician I was able to procure all these things, for members of the SS were interested in the cleanliness of inmates whose work brought them in contact with them. I had sewn a breast pocket on my prisoner's coat, the tacitly accepted privilege of a clerk. When I walked through the camp with full awareness of the impression made by this attire, I was fairly safe from the capricious harassment of even the most aggressive functionaries, prisoners that any inmate who did not stand out from the crowd had to guard against. A made-to-measure suit was capable of preserving a life in Auschwitz.

"Old numbers" were bound together by a certain solidarity. Alfred Wetzler reports (under the pseudonym Jozef Lanik) how a block elder in Birkenau hesitated to proceed against an inmate with a low number who had behaved disrespectfully and finally dropped the matter "because otherwise he would have made an enemy of every older inmate."

All too often, "old hands" looked down contemptuously on those who were least equipped for the merciless struggle for existence. Primo Levi has commented on this as follows: "The social structure of the camp is based on the suppression of the nonprivileged by the privileged." And Bruno Bettelheim writes that "the fear of sinking to the subhuman strata was a strong spur to engage in a class struggle against them."

Erich Altmann remembers a frequently heard argument that was used by old hands to justify their harsh treatment of newcomers and that others must have heard as well: "This is a paradise now. In 1940 and 1941 we had to suffer much more. Why should you be better off?" Others heard that same sort of reasoning which stuck in Altmann's mind.

Friedel de Wind was given a hard time in the experimental block by Jewish women from Slovakia who had been appointed dormitory elders. "They had a miserable time of it, and now they feel they have to make life miserable for us as well. 'If you'd been in Birkenau in those days, you'd be long dead.' That's what they tell us, and this is why we have to endure all their brutality. Always the system of taking out one's feelings on others."

Kogon's interpretation of this frequent boasting about earlier suffering is that the old hands attempted to "preserve their superiority in the concentration camp" by debasing the new arrivals. Benedikt Kautsky believes that once an inmate who has had to undergo a personality change acclimates, he becomes "aggressive, cantankerous, mistrustful, and in extreme cases even treacherous. . . . Since the great majority of the inmates adopt these characteristics, even a placid person must assume an aggressive stance, for otherwise he would not be able to stand his ground."

■ Added to this personality change is a tendency that has been observed by psychologists with first-hand experience of a camp. If a person is interned in a rigorously run camp for an indefinite period of time, his psyche regresses to that of a child. Just as a child is completely defenseless against the orders of a strict father, an inmate must constantly be terrified of the whims of an all-powerful SS man.

There is some merit to assertions that because of their total dependence in the KZ inmates tended to demonize their guards. "They viewed the SS men as powerful adversaries and claimed they were not even human," writes Bruno Bettelheim on the basis of experience gathered in Dachau and Buchenwald before the war, and he points to a benefit of this schematic oversimplification: "This enabled an inmate to submit without debasing himself." Bettelheim even goes further by stating that the stereotype permitted a prisoner to "identify subserviently with the great power of the SS. Then he was able to enjoy the limited security produced by complete submission and participate in the power of the SS in a circuitous fashion."

On the basis of his experiences in Auschwitz, Elie A. Cohen asserts that prisoners identified with their oppressors with mingled feelings of hate and love, contempt and admiration. Other psychologists who had to experience the KZ reached similar conclusions. Eugen Kogon speaks of an adaptation of friend to foe: "The antithetical types develop similarities in their primitive way of thinking, in their feelings, their military demeanor, tone, and corruption."

It is possible that some survivors of concentration camps will reject such conclusions indignantly, and I am sure that all such persons can adduce examples to refute the general validity of these theses. But has our memory not preserved many contrasting examples as well? It was not just capos, block elders, or corrupt criminals who aped SS men in their brutality, their capriciousness, and even their outward appearance. How many prisoners liked to wear breeches and boots, provided they were able to "organize" such apparel, how many copied the bellowed commands of the SS and tried very hard to appear as little Führers in their domains? I remember a young Jew who had been assigned to a good labor detail and used this opportunity to procure tight-fitting breeches and boots. Even though he hated the Nazis with a passion, he was visibly proud of his smart and dashing military appearance. Persons of this type who unconsciously strove for assimilation adopted from their masters their contempt for any weakness as well, and their aggressive impulses were directed against the weakest.

A typical scene described by Tadeusz Borowski may serve to demonstrate the extent to which the Nazi master morality held sway: After the food has been served, the coveted second helping is distributed. "The capo points his cooking spoon at those who are to be given a second helping. Only the better workers, the stronger and healthier prisoners receive it. A sick, weak person has no right to a second bowl of nettle soup. Not a drop of it can be wasted on people who will go through the chimney anyway."

Seweryna Szmaglewska speaks of an "odd reversal of concepts. Everyone who is weak, helpless, and sick is persecuted, punished, trampled"—and not only by the SS but by many prisoners as well.

With unsparing frankness Tadeusz Borowski reports how the anger of the inmates who had to clear the dirt, feces, and corpses of the deportees from the trains at the ramp was directed at these new arrivals. "The ramp gets on your nerves, you get angry, and it is easiest to vent your rage on the weaker persons."

Elie Wiesel did forced labor in the Buna Works together with his father. One day the prisoners acted clumsily as they loaded diesel motors, and this so enraged their capo Idek that he started beating them with a pole, hitting Wiesel's father. The son, a young boy at the time, tried to get out of Idek's range; later he described his feelings in these words: "If I felt hatred at that moment, it was not directed against the capo but against my father." After all, it was his clumsiness that had caused Idek's fit of rage. "What has life in the concentration camp made out of me?" asks Wiesel.

The prisoners' assimilation to the life standardized by the SS led to excesses that remain all but incomprehensible to outsiders. Gerda Schneider, a camp elder, had been imprisoned as a communist for many years before she was sent to Auschwitz. Many people have testified that she used her position courageously to help her fellow sufferers. Anna Palarczyk, a block elder directly subordinate to Schneider, confirms this but adds: "She had been imprisoned since 1933 and was no longer normal, for she beat people."

Another example may illustrate how this could come about. Margit Teitelbaum was dormitory elder in Block 23. One day someone from her barracks was missing at the roll call, and the SS was furious. It turned out that a Jewish woman from Holland had hidden in a pallet. Since Teitelbaum was responsible for all inhabitants in her barracks, she was given twenty-five lashes on her behind with a whip in front of all those assembled. The Dutch woman was shot.

Such methods frequently served their purpose. Those in charge used any means to enforce the discipline for which they were responsible. Whipping proved to be the most effective method, and so it was preferred by the camp leadership. Katarina Princz told me that a block elder once beat her cousin because she, being completely exhausted and sick, had concealed herself at roll call time. Princz concluded her story with a question: "Didn't she do the right thing?" This remark will be understood only by someone who is familiar with the methods of the SS.

An episode from the trial of Karl Kapp, the camp elder of Dachau, indicates the extent to which the system of holding an inmate functionary responsible for those under his control influenced the thinking of old prisoners. One of the charges against him was that he had told the ss that he suspected an in-mate who had concealed himself in the camp of having attempted to escape. As could have been foreseen, the prisoner was shot. In the fall of 1960 about a dozen former inmates of Dachau with extensive camp experience testified before a Munich court that, "in view of the ruthless reprisals that the entire camp had to endure because of a missing inmate and considering the great un-collegiality of an attempted escape," the action of the camp elder was justified. In the declaratory part of its judgment, the court summarized this testimony as quoted above, but the indictment had still reflected the well-founded view that the concealed inmate's life would probably have been saved and he would have got away with a lesser punishment if Kapp had, for example, reported that he had fallen asleep.

The ss granted German prisoners the aforementioned privileged position because its experience with long-time German inmates had frequently been similar to the Kapp episode and also because this was in line with their master-race theory. Werner Krumme, who was deported to Auschwitz from Breslau as a political prisoner and was given a leading position in the Labor Assignment Office in his first month, concisely summed up the privileged position of the Germans by saying that "the few Germans in the camp were needed."

Ella Lingens reports that any female German prisoner who was not too old and in reasonably good physical condition was able to become a forewoman in the camp after the first week. The Germans were to be corrupted by extra food, better lodging, and care in case of illness. Lingens emphasizes that "we were supposed to feel ourselves to be members of the master race (Herrenvolk) even in the concentration camp."

According to Höß's report, prisoners from the German Reich "almost al-ways received the better positions, and thus all their physical needs were met. Anything they could not obtain in the regular way they 'organized.'" Höß also describes the source that made such procurement possible. "After the cam-paigns against the Jews got going, there was practically nothing that could not be procured. And the upper-level functionaries had the requisite freedom of movement, too."

When the inmates of Auschwitz had their numbers tattooed on their left forearms, the Germans were exempted from this practice. No tattoos were ordered for them in any other camp either. Evidently, the ss thought that Ger-mans, and only they, might be released some day.

Poles were definitely not favored by the camp administration. The privi-leged position they occupied in Auschwitz was due to their ethnic solidarity, which transcended even serious political conflicts, and their camp experience. This was not always so; the early period was the worst for them. However, ac-cording to Tadeusz Paczula, as early as 1941 "the ss gave all its attention to the Russian prisoners of war; several wagon loads of corpses left the camp every day." This eased and frequently even saved the life of others, and these others were mainly Poles. Wladyslaw Fejkiel writes that "1941 and 1942 were the worst years for the Poles. Later the Jews came, and this gave the Poles more peace."

The camp leadership deliberately played Germans off against Poles, and this was another reason why it was so hard for good relations to develop between the ethnic groups that set the tone for the camp. Even those Germans who had been sent to the camp as political opponents often found it hard to relate to Poles. Fejkiel has addressed this problem: "They made the same mistake that the Poles frequently made: they generalized. They believed that every Pole had to be a fascist, willy-nilly, or infected by fascism. Similarly, the Poles often regarded even friendly German communists as enemies and simply took it for granted that they must not become friends or collaborate with them."

Many Poles learned German in Auschwitz to avoid being ruined. In the early period only prisoners who understood that language reasonably well were assigned to a good work detail. At a later date Polish was accepted as the second language of the camp. Thomas Geve, who was transported from Berlin to Auschwitz as a mere child, reports that in his block all announcements were made in Polish and then translated into Russian. Anyone who was not familiar with these announcements and committed a violation had to expect severe punishment. Not understanding the language was no excuse, and so Geve was forced to learn Polish.

■ Among the Poles anti-Semitism, which ss men fostered with every means at their disposal, continued a tradition. Their anti-Semitic tendencies were promoted by their fear that their hard-won privileged position would be jeopardized if the general discrimination against the Jews, which had initially prevented the latter from being assigned to desirable labor details, abated. This explains the frequent wholesale condemnation of the Poles in the camp as anti-Semites. Thus Benedikt Kautsky speaks of a "robust anti-Semitism among criminals and social misfits" and characterizes Polish criminals and fascists as "mercilessly anti-Semitic." Henry Bulawko portrays the majority of the Polish inmates as "born anti-Semites" whose patriotism and hatred of the Germans could not diminish their aversion to Jews. Dr. Aron Bejlin cannot forget the Polish physicians in Birkenau who assured him that they would stay in Auschwitz for another ten years if Hitler eventually succeeded in making Europe Jew-free (judenrein). Krystyna Zywulska remembers being told by an inmate that while the methods were horrible, they did solve the Jewish problem in Poland. "This may sound paradoxical," concluded the Polish woman, "but we owe this to Hitler." Fejkiel correctly observed that generalizations are wrong. Anyone who had a chance to become better acquainted with Poles, which was not easy, found that many of them fought against anti-Semitism vigorously and courageously, though without letting it jeopardize their tight-knit solidarity.

In the HKB, which offered the greatest opportunities to help one's fellow inmates, the effects of anti-Semitism among the prisoners were most clearly apparent. Vilo Jurkovic recalls that at first the Polish prisoner hierarchy in the HKB was "against everyone" and only pro-Polish. "Anti-Semitism was a good lightning rod," he writes, and therefore it often was "the primary practical expression of this negative attitude." Like Jurkovic, Igor Bistric was deported to Auschwitz from Slovakia in the spring of 1942, and he met Jurkovic while serving as a clerk in the HKB. Years later Bistric described his situation as one of the first Jews on the staff of the HKB. "In the infirmary, members of the Polish intelligentsia were serving as nurses and clerks. They gave us to understand that we were not welcome because they thought we were after their jobs." Bistric has not forgotten his superior, a Pole named Szary who gave him more than one beating, but he emphasized that several Poles in the HKB always behaved in comradely fashion. He specifically named Dr. Adam Zacharski, Tadeusz Paczula, and Jurek Czubak, men whom I also learned to respect.

Ella Lingens reports about a Polish nurse who said that she was against the Jews and the only reason she did not discriminate against them was that she did not want to support the SS men in their extermination of the Jews.

Tadeusz Holuj has described the following scene in the HKB of the main camp that took place after the SS had once again selected sick inmates to be put to death.

"Don't worry, they're all just Jews," said the small, stocky dormitory elder as he cut some margarine in tiny pieces. "They don't need anything anyway," he proclaimed frankly. "Why feed the patients who are bound for the gas chambers? It's better if we eat this ourselves." "Oh, Herr Stubenältester, let these people have a few bites to eat," reasoned the block barber Kamioner, a Polish-French Jew, a bit later as he was shaving the dormitory elder and rubbing his face with cologne that he had obtained somewhere. "Kamioner, you jackass," laughed the dormitory elder. "In a little while you're going to see Abraham again, too."

Kamioner became pensive and fell silent. It was a bad day for him, for he had lost two relatives and eleven acquaintances whom he was supposed to shave before they were carted off. He had not been up to that. "I still have too soft a heart," he said as he bribed a few patients with minor illnesses to perform this duty for him.

Holuj has described a conversation between Felek, the block clerk, and Kamioner:

"You Jews nailed Christ to the cross and that's why you're under a curse, my boy, until the end of time. This is your atonement," said Felek calmly and seriously. Kamioner was indignant. "I'm a simple Jew and you're a lawyer. You graduated from a university and say such ugly things. They're not true . . ." He wanted to speak more sharply, but he got scared and did not want to incur any danger, and so he only sighed and started to tell a French anecdote with a smile. Kamioner, who was born in Poland and raised in France, was a philosopher. With his clear, penetrating mind he grasped the full repulsiveness of a situation in which some of the inmates justified the mass destruction of the Jews and even rejoiced that "Hitler was taking care of this unpleasant matter"—on their behalf, of course. He tried to explain to his "Aryan" customer in his own fashion: "Well, all right, they'll exterminate us little Jews, but they won't get their hands on the big ones. They are in England and America, and one day they will demand information about us."

In March 1943 the Political Department claimed to have uncovered a Polish conspiracy among the personnel of the infirmary in the main camp and attempted to impress the SS garrison physician with that information. The following conversation between Dr. Wirths and me ensued:

"There are a great many Poles on the infirmary staff, Langbein."
"Yes sir."
"It's a clique—one person sticks up for another. Do you agree that the Poles have a secret organization in the infirmary?"
"Certainly not, Herr Doktor. It's only natural for one man to help another. I help every decent Viennese whenever I can."
Wirths looks at me and smiles. By now I know how I have to speak with him. He appreciates comradeship.
"In any case, there are too many Poles on the infirmary staff. This will have to be changed."
"May I make a suggestion, Herr Doktor?" He nods. "It goes without saying that any nurse helps his compatriots more than others. But not all nationalities are represented on the nursing staff. Couldn't, for example, Frenchmen and Czechs be used as nurses?"
"Fine. Bring me their numbers, and I shall request them."
I can see that he likes my proposal, and so I dare to go further:
"Can't Jews be added to the staff as well? After all, the sick Jewish inmates are supposed to get well, too, because they are also needed in the full

mobilization of workers. There are a considerable number of Jewish physicians in the camp. Would it be possible to employ them on a trial basis and then add the capable ones to the staff?"

I said this very fast, because his face had indicated that he did not like this idea so much.

At this point he interrupted me. "But then the sickroom would have to be organized in such a way that the Jewish inmate physicians do not treat any Aryans—because that is impossible." He emphasized the last words.

"Yes sir, Herr Doktor, that would be easy to arrange."

He reflects and then springs into action. "Take this down: To the head of the Labor Assignment Office, with a copy to the commandant's office. I request the identification of all Jewish inmates who are physicians by profession and their transfer to the HKB." After a pause: "Here is an addendum: This is by way of implementing the order of the WVHA—look up the number of this order, you know which one I mean—that the inmates' capacity for work be exploited to the greatest possible degree."

Soon thereafter the Polish monopoly in the infirmary was broken as Czechs, Frenchmen, and members of other nationalities were employed as nurses. Due to the machinations of SS medics and anti-Semitic superiors in the HKB, on more than one occasion Jewish physicians who had been placed on the infirmary staff on the basis of that order were not allowed to practice medicine but had to do dirty work, yet this change basically opened up an avenue that eventually led even Jewish physicians to influential positions.

Dr. Golse, who was deported from France to Auschwitz on an RSHA transport on July 20, 1943, reports an "extraordinary stroke of luck" that caused him to be assigned to the HKB as a physician after two days in quarantine, while the other men on this transport who had passed the selection were assigned to work in a mine without consideration of their profession. It soon became the rule, however, that physicians and pharmacists were pulled out of the mass of people at the ramp.

■ It stands to reason that the Jews did not constitute a homogeneous group, for they came from a great variety of environments; had different professions, philosophies, and languages; and did not have the same religious ties. Benedikt Kautsky writes: "Conditions were complicated by the fact that in wartime Jews of many nationalities met in the camps and instead of displaying solidarity felt enmity toward one another. In line with the camp's tendency toward generalization, the 'Poles' now stood opposed to the 'Germans,' the 'Dutch' to the 'French,' and the 'Greeks' to the 'Hungarians.' It was by no means unusual for one Jew to use arguments against another Jew that were not very different from those of the anti-Semites."

Elie A. Cohen states that anti-Semitism, which can be observed among Jews in normal life, really became perceptible in Auschwitz. Cohen, who was from Holland, was struck by the antagonism of Dutch Jews toward Jews from Poland.

The camp administration favored German Jews primarily because of their linguistic ability. Jews who knew neither German nor a Slavic language, for example most of those from Greece and Italy, had the hardest time. In Block 7 of the Birkenau HKB, to which prisoners marked for death were transferred, André Lettich observed the effect that this differentiation had even there. Jews from Germany, who had to wait for the gas chambers in the block together with their fellow sufferers from other countries, demanded privileged treatment from the nursing staff and threatened to complain to the ss if they did not receive it.

Max Mannheimer, who came from Czechoslovakia, writes: "The Dutch Jews are dying like flies. The Jews from Poland, many of them craftsmen or workmen, are the hardiest. They are in better physical shape, too, not as pampered as those from Holland or Czechoslovakia." Like the Jews from Poland, the Slovakian Jews were used to the climate and by virtue of their previous life were in better shape than, for example, the Jews from Greece, who had a hard time coping with winter in the camp.

Like French "Aryans," Jews from France had to deal with additional difficulties, for the Nazi propaganda about the degenerate French was effective with many prisoners as well. Georges Wellers points to another reason for the general dislike of them: Poles were not able to forget France's passivity during Hitler's attack on their country. The rapid defeat of France in the spring of 1940 dealt the coup de grâce to the reputation of the French. Thus Julien Unger was greeted by a Slovak with the following words: "I owe it to you Frenchmen that I now have a number with 30,000 on my arm. You talked a lot, but when it was time for action, you were screwing girls. The war against you was won before it started."

Grete Salus from Slovakia, whose mother tongue is German, remembers the uncomradely behavior of many Czech Jewish women toward their fellow sufferers from Hungary. The camp administration favored German-speaking Czech women.

With full awareness that generalizations should not be made lightly, I would like to say a few words about the reputation of various "Aryan" national groups. Czechs, who for linguistic reasons had an easier time of it than, say, Frenchmen, enjoyed a good reputation. Russians were regarded as mistrustful and wild. The reputation of Yugoslavs was extraordinary; this applied particularly to women, for there were not many men of this nationality in the camp. This may have been due to the great sympathy for a people that was fighting so courageously and also to the fact that many Yugoslavs were sent to the camp because they were suspected of having collaborated with partisans. The bonding of a combat community could be perceived among them, though the political conflicts between groups engaged in defensive action were also noticeable in the camp. Frenchwomen set the tone in the underground organization of the women's camp.

■ "To him who has, more will be given; and from him who has not, all will be taken. The heaviest and dirtiest labor was assigned to the weakest prisoners, and by way of compensation they were also given the least peace and the least gratification. The lightest and socially most prestigious work was done by the stronger inmates, and on top of that they usually received bonuses and opportunities for obtaining additional rations."

This camp law, as formulated by Benedikt Kautsky, favored the younger over the older. Young prisoners found it easier to adapt physically to camp conditions, and they were also more likely to adopt the master morality that requires an underling to snap to attention before his superior and to react to every order with a loud and clear "Jawohl!" This morality also presupposes that an inmate is ready to trample mercilessly on underlings in the execution of orders. As a result of their general demoralization, older prisoners frequently let themselves go completely, while younger ones were more likely to adopt the ss morality of contempt for all weakness. A young sporting type who adapted in this fashion was in the administration's good graces. David Rousset observed that it became the right of the young to insult the old, to beat them and displace them. All respect for old age was gone. When Oszkár Betlen admonished a young fellow in Monowitz not to be so rough on elderly inmates, he received this reply: "We're supposed to respect these people? They don't have enough class not to wipe their runny noses on their neighbors' jackets!"

Suzanne Birnbaum reports about Polish and Slovak girls who were proud of being, by virtue of their jobs, the superiors of much older French, Dutch, or Hungarian "ladies," whom they could push around. Elie Wiesel has given us a thumbnail sketch of a young tyrant: "Edek, the capo, was our master and our king. This red-cheeked young Pole with the movements of an animal loved surprising his slaves and making them howl with fear. A mere youth, he enjoyed having such power over grown-ups." Vilo Jurkovic, who was interned in Auschwitz for two-and-a-half years, believed that the power given to a young man at age twenty or less almost always went to his head: "They subsisted on the glory of being a superior," he concludes.

The younger a person was when he was thrust into an extermination camp, the more defenseless he was against such influences. Elie Wiesel reports about a child named Jankel, who was known as the little prince: "Well nourished and wearing warm clothes, the little prince walked around the barracks and evoked envy, fear, or pity." He enjoyed the favor of the all-powerful block elder; "he had ruled a nation of old men, he had forced his law upon them, his whims, his will. His power was an illustration of the grotesqueness of the situation. Thousands of men trembled before a child who was only amusing himself."

Feinstein observed a father and his son at the distribution of bread in Birkenau. The father, who was completely run-down, shook all over; his son, who was around eighteen, had a bit more strength. The young man greedily devoured his ration, but his father pressed his against his chest. No sooner had the son wolfed his bread down than he looked around quickly, snatched away his father's portion, and stuffed it in his mouth. "He was all chewing jaws. The old man emitted a scream with his last strength. The block elder came and took both men away. They never came back." Feinstein assumes that the SS man who observed this scene was bound to regard it as confirmation of the Nazi theory about subhumans and probably could not even conceive of the idea that a concentration camp could transform human beings as it had transformed that son.

▓ Georges Wellers became familiar with the block in Monowitz that housed young men between fifteen and eighteen. He reports that this block had the greatest number of thefts and was devoid of any feeling of solidarity. In Auschwitz, where "old" was an altogether negative concept, people were considered old much earlier than in normal life. Wladyslaw Fejkiel has attempted to define the concepts of "young" and "old" under the conditions that existed in Auschwitz. "It is known that the vitality of young people is always greater than that of older ones. I regard as young those who have not passed the age of thirty-five. In our situation people between eighteen and thirty had the greatest endurance. I observed that inmates below or above that age always displayed symptoms of starvation earlier. It appears that in our part of the world persons under age eighteen have not reached their full physical development yet." Eduard de Wind, a professional colleague of Fejkiel, has described a forty-five-year-old prisoner as "very old by camp standards."

There are a small number of documents that indicate the age structure of the prisoners. For example, we have a book that lists the names and ages of inmates who were sent to the bunker. Of 2,137 inmates in this book, 48.8 percent were under thirty years of age, 3.3 percent over fifty, and seven of the latter were over sixty. A German Jew who was already seventy-five was sent to the bunker and shot there. He had not arrived in Auschwitz on an RSHA transport; otherwise, he would undoubtedly have become an instant victim of the selection at the ramp.

Nine hundred and thirty-two personnel sheets of the Blechhammer sub-camp have been preserved. This camp was not integrated into the Auschwitz complex until April 1, 1944, when the chances of survival had risen even for elderly prisoners, and for this reason one must be cautious about drawing conclusions for other camps and other time periods. The youngest prisoner was fourteen, the oldest fifty-eight. Those between twenty and twenty-five constituted the most strongly represented age group; people of that age had the greatest chance of survival. Over 64 percent were younger than thirty-five and only 10 percent older than forty-five.

Another age statistic permits more valid conclusions than the two mentioned above, which cover randomly assembled groups of persons. Within the framework of the big Auschwitz trial in Frankfurt, 244 survivors of the camp testified. As a rule, the witnesses called were people with ample camp experience whose positions had enabled them to see more than average inmates did. At the time of their internment, more than 68 percent were under thirty-five (young by Fejkiel's standards) and 45.5 percent even younger than thirty. Among the Germans and Austrians, the age structure differed markedly. Of the seventy-eight witnesses who were over thirty-five when they were deported to Auschwitz, twenty-five were members of these nationalities, while only sixteen German and Austrian witnesses were under thirty-five when they first experienced Auschwitz. Their age reduced their chances of survival far less than it did those of the average inmate. Many Poles with years of camp experience were among the youngest witnesses in Frankfurt; thanks to their intelligence and knowledge of languages, numerous Polish university and secondary-school students from the first transports had been able to cope with the camp better than the others.

In its preferential treatment of young inmates, the camp administration sometimes went so far as to exempt them from the program of extermination that called for the killing of all persons unfit for work. Attempts were made to establish courses in masonry for prisoners who were too young to work in order to alleviate the shortage of trained masons. Prisoners have claimed to have taken the initiative in the establishment of such schools. However, that such young fellows were admitted to the camp rather than being immediately taken to the gas chamber was surely something that even the most privileged prisoners could not achieve. Adolf Weiß remembers that the first masonry school was established in Birkenau in June 1942 and that he was twenty when he attended it together with 1,000 Jews, mostly from Slovakia and France, who ranged in age from fifteen to twenty-five. A Polish Jew called Mudek was the capo, and the foremen were "Aryans." Thorough instruction was given in two barracks.

Weiß also remembers the end of the school. One day a capo needed a hundred men to unload potatoes, and he was assigned that number of trainees, including Weiß . When they came marching back from their work, they found the two barracks half empty. A group of high ss officers on an inspection tour had been shown the masonry school. They were evidently not convinced of the value of that institution, for immediately after the inspection half the pupils were taken to a gas chamber and killed there. The others were assigned to various work details the next day. Weiß landed in a construction squad.

The Pole Czeslaw Kempisty was fifteen when he attended a masonry school in the main camp in the winter of 1942–43. The school was administered by a German Green capo, and regular instruction was given by a Polish professor. The makeup of the pupils was mixed, and after the completion of their training they were assigned to construction squads working on the expansion of the camp. Many of these young men could not cope with this heavy labor. Kempisty had already dropped out of the school on account of illness.

Thomas Geve was fourteen when he was assigned to a masonry school in the main camp in the winter of 1942–43. He states that his fellow trainees were thirteen to eighteen years of age. In "this sole asylum for youths," as Geve calls it, there were 400 lads from Russia, the Ukraine, Czechoslovakia, Germany, Austria, and Poland. Geve specifically mentions young Gypsies from Czechoslovakia and Jews from Greece and Poland. With one exception the teachers were Jews who had been chosen for their knowledge of languages.

A masonry school was also set up in Monowitz, where 100 to 200 youths ranging in age from nine to sixteen were trained for three months. After that, they were assigned to the appropriate labor details, making room for other young inmates. This school was under the supervision of chief engineers of the IG Farben Works and was administered by Eduard Besch, a German political prisoner. According to Wassermann, Besch beat prisoners, but others remember him favorably.

Some children were employed as camp messengers and were treated as a kind of curiosity, while every day an enormous number of children of all ages were killed in the gas chambers.

The "weakness" that some members of the ss had for children manifested itself most distinctly during the liquidation of the Theresienstadt family camp. At that time the block leader Stefan Baretzki, a man feared for his brutality, was among those who begged the ss camp leader to spare the lives of the young inmates. At a later date, when he was questioned in court about his motivation, that primitive ethnic German replied: "Well, we had nothing to do in the camp, but we always went to the children's theater, and so we were already used to the children."

Maurice Cling, who was fifteen when he arrived at the camp in 1944, collapsed at work during the first snowfall because of utter exhaustion and was determined not to get up. However, a capo who had treated him brutally up to that time astonished him by suddenly displaying compassion and saving his life. Protected by a directive from the German capo, Cling remained in the infirmary until the evacuation. "Don't kill this little fellow, don't send him to the crematorium!" Cling ascribes his rescue to the sympathy of the capo; he could not have known that the gassings had already stopped at that time. Nevertheless, the attitude of the capo remains remarkable; even brutal types were much more likely to display compassion for young prisoners than for old ones.

▦ Added to all that has so far been described was the fact that in Auschwitz everything was incalculable and nothing impossible. From a logical point of view, and even if viewed from the perspective of the exterminators, much remained inexplicable. No one was safe from surprises, and in exceptional cases these could have a positive effect.

Inmates who had come into direct contact with the machinery of destruction were eventually killed as bearers of secrets—this was a rule. However, the female clerks of the Political Department, the bunker trusty, and the male nurses who had to carry the corpses out of the bunker cells after the first trial gassing—all remained alive. Wojciech Barcz, one of those nurses who had expected to be killed, said: "On many later occasions, too, I learned that among the ss there were again and again surprises and inconsistencies."

Even to a person with a lot of camp experience, nothing appeared impossible, and this may explain the naïveté with which even "old hands" gave credence to promises of ss men.

Staszek Slezak may serve as an example. This Czech, born in 1920, was charged, as a professional, with the maintenance of the X-ray equipment used by Dr. Horst Schumann for his experiments in sterilization in Birkenau. Schumann had such a good relationship with this inmate that he sometimes shared his breakfast with him. Artur Rablin, who also worked for Schumann for a short time, wondered about "the great cordiality between these two men." Rablin remembers Slezak, who trusted Schumann "implicitly," telling him that if he ever got out of the camp, he would owe this to Schumann, for he was advocating his release. Rablin, who was afraid of what would happen to him as a bearer of secrets, sought and found a way of getting out of the dangerous work in the immediate vicinity of the experiments on human beings, and he advised his friend Slezak to change his detail, too. But the latter trusted

Schumann's promises more than he did his friend's counsel. When it finally dawned on Slezak that he would not be released, it was already too late to get another assignment, and the Political Department frustrated such an attempt. In early January 1945 Slezak was transferred to Mauthausen together with other bearers of secrets—Polish capos of the Sonderkommando—and shot there. The choice of such a roundabout way evidently represented an attempt by the ss to shroud the fate of bearers of secrets in mystery.

Leo Vos, who was interned in the Blechhammer labor camp in Upper Silesia together with other Dutch Jews, reports that the integration of this camp into the Auschwitz complex in April 1944 initially brought improvements. The roll call was shortened, enabling the inmates to get a little more sleep; the distribution of food was better organized; and the laundry was changed more frequently. The inmates of Blechhammer did not notice until later that this integration had brought them into the sphere of an extermination camp.

It was characteristic of an "old" prisoner that he feared any change. Grete Salus was able to closely observe this type of person marked by camp life: "Thanks to their knowledge of all of the camp tricks, their living conditions were bearable, but they feared any change, for this would force them to start all over again on an unfamiliar footing. Of course, there were gas chambers and deaths, but that hardly bothered them. They knew about death here, but thanks to their experiences and connections they could often obtain an extension and even hope to escape death altogether. But they did not know the death that awaited them if there was a change; to that kind of death they were vulnerable, without knowledge, like all the others."

Adelaide Hautval reports about the victims of the experimental Block 10. Since they were never told what purpose those experiments were to serve, they had to fear everything imaginable, including the possibility that they were the subjects of artificial insemination and might give birth to deformed children. Added to this fear was the pain of the surgical procedures. And yet, Hautval writes, "the instinct of self-preservation is so strongly anchored in human beings that most women were so afraid of being transferred to Birkenau that they preferred this hell, which at least left them one hope: 'Perhaps they will let us live afterward!' Only one group of Jewish women who had already had one operation refused another and preferred a transfer to Birkenau, where they faced extermination. We remember their courage with a great deal of sympathy."

Friedel de Wind, one of the "guinea pigs" in that block, secretly wrote her husband, an inmate of the camp, a letter in which she described the fate of those women. "Yesterday was a special day. We marched almost as far as Birkenau. That is where I had seen Lotte Spittel and the other girls, including the French communists, who had refused to undergo the experiments. They and seventy others were transferred three weeks ago. It is horrible to see the women in Birkenau. How they have changed! They are completely bald and barefoot; on their bodies they have nothing but a piece of jute tied together with string. These are not women anymore; they are sexless creatures."

Johanna Nachemstein gave this simple testimony: "I tried not to protest (as she was brought in for experiments) because I knew from my colleagues that every four or six weeks there was a transport to the gas chamber. I did it to prolong or save my life."

■ On March 3, 1943, the central administration ordered the transfer of 1,000 Polish prisoners who were healthy and fully fit for work to each of the following camps: Buchenwald, Flossenbürg, Gross-Rosen, Neuengamme, and Sachsenhausen. These men had ample camp experience, and the idea was to reduce the percentage of such experienced Poles in Auschwitz for security reasons. When all good work details were checked for Poles with low numbers, there were numerous interventions by commando leaders who had been bribed. At that time and later, when there were more transfers of Poles from Auschwitz, all kinds of ruses were employed because everyone wanted to get out of these transports. Höß commented on this as follows: "Although the general conditions in Auschwitz were anything but good, no Polish inmate wanted to be transferred to another camp. As soon as they found out they were to be transferred, they pulled all strings to be exempted or deferred. In 1943, when a blanket order came to transfer all Poles to camps in the Reich, I was swamped with petitions from all factories that claimed that these workers were indispensable. None of them could do without the Poles. The exchange simply had to be effected by force and by percentages."

To the motives cited above by Salus it should be added, in the case of the Poles, that in Auschwitz they could hope to strengthen their connections with their homeland. They also knew that in Auschwitz the Poles occupied a hardwon top position in the camp hierarchy that they had in no other camp. However, quite a few Czechs and Frenchmen managed to get out of the transfer transports, after the central administration had ordered that these nationalities be transferred to less endangered camps. When the Austrian Ella Lingens was transferred to Dachau in November 1944, she at first felt—as she writes—nothing but fear and depression. These feelings were caused by separation from dear friends and by the necessity to start all over again.

The German Werner Krumme was declared unworthy to bear arms and was sent to Auschwitz because he had refused to divorce his Jewish wife. The death of his wife in the camp removed the reason for this unworthiness, and Krumme was conscripted into the Wehrmacht. Since he had a privileged position in the Labor Assignment Office, he strove with some success to delay his release from the camp. Simon Laks and René Coudy report that Kopka, an ethnic German and head of the Birkenau camp orchestra, was anything but overjoyed when he was sent to the quarantine section in preparation for his release. Both cases, however, represent rare exceptions. In the camp Krumme and Kopka had everything that was at the disposal of a VIP and for entirely understandable reasons the thought of serving in the German army after their incarceration was not an unalloyed joy.

Zalman Kleinmann reports how he, together with other adolescents from the Theresienstadt family camp, swindled his way onto a transport that was leaving Auschwitz. Ana Novac describes her transport from Auschwitz after three weeks in the camp as the most beautiful departure of her life. This is supplemented by H. G. Adler in his account of the terror spread in Theresienstadt by every transport to parts unknown. "Only for those who landed in Auschwitz did a transport lose its paralyzing horror, its almost transcendental nature, for now they knew the possibility or certainty of ruin." Like Novac, Adler had to wait for a few weeks in 1944 in the shadow of the crematoriums of Auschwitz to be transported to a labor camp.

■ In an extermination camp every criterion of normal life is bound to fail. This was Auschwitz: gas chambers, selections, the processions of human beings who marched to their death like puppets—designated by David Rousset as the most horrible thing of all—as well as Canada with its inexhaustible abundance even in the last year of the war; the Black Wall and the bloody tracks on the camp road that marked the path of the vehicles in which prisoners who had been shot were taken to the crematorium; the anonymity of death that inhibited any martyrdom, and boozing bouts of prisoners and their guards. Auschwitz taught a sensitive person like Grete Salus to make this confession: "Much as I would like to, I cannot write a heroic epic about people. All I can say is that a human being should never have to endure as much as he can endure, and never should a human being have to see that there is no longer anything human in the highest degree of suffering."

Starvation was as much a daily phenomenon in Auschwitz as the sight of capos who had stuffed themselves. There were all kinds of epidemics, from noma, a disease that produces holes in the cheeks of children, to typhus, the camp disease of Auschwitz. Any reasoning person had to conclude that there was no chance of leaving Auschwitz other than through a chimney, and yet this insane hope could never be completely stifled: perhaps a string of lucky accidents will permit me to slip through and survive. For anyone who wore an SS uniform or even the armband of an inmate with a function, killing someone whenever they felt like it was a trivial matter, one hardly worth mentioning. And yet, in this same Auschwitz a never-ending struggle for the lives of friends was carried on by nameless companions in misfortune, a fight that never let up despite depressing failures and obvious hopelessness. A resistance movement that fought terror with some success was also part of Auschwitz. "Each one of us did something that at least touched his or her human dignity," wrote Grete Salus. Is there a survivor of Auschwitz who can question this statement? Being inured to death and suffering; greedily grabbing any chance of enjoyment; going dead while still alive; choosing to expose oneself to additional dangers; smuggling medications into the camp—all this added up to Auschwitz. Some were able to drink champagne in Auschwitz, and no one knew in the morning what the day would bring. There were inhumane punishments for trifling transgressions—for example, if an inmate did not keep the respectful distance of three paces from an ill-humored ss man. On the other hand, there were ss men who had affairs with female prisoners. It was possible to bribe ss officers, but an inmate had to be wary of good friends, for anyone could turn traitor if he was tortured by the Political Department. All too often Auschwitz was covered by a cloud that exuded a sweetishly insipid smell, the smell of burnt human flesh.

In Auschwitz nothing was inconceivable, no extreme too harsh. Anything was possible, literally anything. People lived there until they were killed. How did they live? How did they cope with life in Auschwitz?

THE MUSELMANN

■ ■ ■

In accordance with the Auschwitz law of giving the weakest the hardest time, the worst conditions were to be found in the Birkenau women's camp. Pelagia Lewinska has described these as follows:

> No lights. The blocks are never lit. Movement and noise as in a beehive. Women's voices in various languages (Polish, French, Czech, Russian) that are devoid of energy and feeling. Here and there the gleam of small burning candles. This illumination does not permit a wide view, but it is possible to make out the broad outlines of the barracks, which is divided by beams in such a way that boards are placed on three tiers, each one meter high. Living beings emerge from them as from sheds. The barracks resembles a huge barn that is twenty-four meters long and ten meters wide. It has no ceiling but is covered directly by a roof. In lieu of boards the well-trodden ground is covered with bricks of different sizes. The barracks was built in accordance with the principle that there should be maximal room for sleeping. The beams on three levels along the walls and in the middle of the barracks support the bunk beds. Wooden beams separate the barracks lengthwise into bunks; each of these is around two meters wide and deep and no more than a meter high. There is only room for three if a woman wants to move a bit more freely and turn around without bumping her neighbor. In an area of four square meters it is not easy to provide room for more. In spite of this the blocks that had to house 800 to 1,000 persons are so jam-packed that seven or eight women have to share a bunk. Since the floor of the lowest level is formed by bricks, a woman has to crawl in as into a doghouse; there she lies on the moist bricks and is completely without air. The uppermost level touches the roof; in the winter water comes in, and in the summer the women's heads roast. The only things to lie on are paper pallets with a bit of wood wool; in each bunk there are at most three such pallets and one blanket. If a woman wants to reach the topmost bed, she has to step on the lower bunks. The inmates are terribly hemmed in as they climb to their beds. In that narrow bunk they have to organize their entire life, which is really reduced to eating and sleeping.

When Lewinska was admitted to that camp, it had been in operation for five months, and the very worst defects were already a thing of the past. In August 1942, 15,000 women were the first to be transferred to the camp. The appearance of these inmates has been described by Désiré Haffner: "Their skeletal appearance, their shaved skulls, their blood-streaked bodies, their scaly skin—all this made it hard for an observer to recognize them as women. The lack of any hygiene was even more perceptible among them than in the men's camp because of the pungent odor that came from their blocks, the smell of thousands of women who had not been able to wash for months. Their work is as hard as the men's, and as a rule they are even worse dressed. They are usually seen bareheaded and barefoot, and sometimes they are naked."

Seweryna Szmaglewska observed the columns of prisoners marching off to work from the nearby Birkenau men's camp:

> Prisoners marching five abreast keep streaming out of the gate. Now the capo pulls his cap off, screams in the direction of the marching columns, "Caps off!" and runs toward the ss men. There is something almost shameful about the sight of the shaved heads of the defenseless prisoners, who obediently march past some armed Germans, and there is something utterly repulsive about the figure of the capo, who stands at attention and presses his cap against his striped pants as he makes his report. The second gate is opened, and one column after another march out. And again there is a capo, and there are rows of five, the same thing over and over again. All are equally skinny and equally black. Those shaved heads are alike, and everywhere those fingers stretched out against the trouser seams. Thus they march, like a big, lifeless army, to the last parade. New columns keep streaming out of the camp, and they are easily counted. The first thousand have marched past, two thousand, ten thousand. They march and march. If your father, your brother, or your son were among them, you would not recognize him, for these emaciated figures are all alike. A young lad has the same furrowed face as an old man.

■ While still under the shock of arrival, nameless new inmates faced a merciless struggle for their bare existence in a world that was so very different from the one they had known.

"Just survive, survive, that is what it is all about," writes Franciszek Jazwiecki retrospectively, "and the forms of survival are extreme and disgusting, they are not worth the price of living." Nevertheless, prisoners were forced by their instincts to seek a way of surviving.

In the quarantine section, which Julien Unger likened to a menagerie with defenseless animals that were subjected to drills by tamers without compassion, there began the struggle for a second helping of camp soup, water, a better bed, a bit of blanket—in short, the most elementary things. The result of this drill has been described by Max Mannheimer, who was sent to the Birkenau quarantine section from Theresienstadt in early February 1943:

Dr. Beck from Ungarisch-Brod is lying in the lowest bed with a high fever. We drag him out and prop him up for the roll call. The next day he is at death's door, and two inmates try to take the dying man's shoes off. He has good ones, and shoes mean a lot in this cold and mud. The inmates scuffle and the stronger wins. A few minutes later Dr. Beck is no longer alive. We say Kaddish. His body is put outside the block, and he is counted at the roll call. He is not the only one, for several corpses are delivered from other blocks, and a work detail that deals with the dead arrives. That is what happens every day. Now I know what quarantine means: a sieve with big holes.

The footwear of dying people was not the only desirable item. Ella Lingens writes: "I have seen how blankets were snatched away from dying women with the words 'You don't need this any more.' "

In the spring of 1944, when the Jews from Hungary, a veritable flood, were awaiting their further fate crammed together in the unfinished Mexico section, a relentless fight broke out, as reported by Carl Laszlo, over "who would spend the night sitting up and who would lie down. The more or less bad physical position, the constant need to watch for thieves of shoes or bread, and the stale air" deprived sleep of its function to regenerate energy. In a barracks with enough sleeping room for at most 300 people, 1,000 prisoners had to lie on a bare concrete floor without bunk beds or straw.

A person with camp experience could very quickly tell whether a newcomer could survive or would perish. Robert Waitz, a physician who was able to observe new arrivals in Monowitz, estimates that it was possible to tell in eight or ten days. Anyone whose willpower was crushed by the burden of the camp soon bore the marks of impending death on his face.

Those destroyed human beings were called *Muselmänner* in Auschwitz, and later this designation was used in other camps as well. I heard it the first time when I came to Auschwitz; in Dachau inmates who were in poor shape were called, in the Bavarian dialect, *Kretiner* (cretins).

Physicians have given a precise description of the *Muselmänner*'s condition. Wladyslaw Fejkiel, probably the most experienced among the inmate physicians, has provided this clinical picture:

The symptoms of starvation may be divided into two stages. The first is characterized by a great weight loss, muscular weakness, and progressive decline in kinetic energy. During this stage there was as yet no serious damage to the organism. The patient's only symptoms were slowness of movement and debility. Apart from a certain excitability and typical irritability, there were no emotional changes. It was hard to discern a boundary line between the first and the second stages. In some patients the transition was gradual; with others it came very rapidly. It may be estimated that the second stage began when the starveling had lost one-third of his normal weight. In addition to further weight loss his facial expression began to change. His gaze became clouded, and his face assumed an apathetic, absent, mournful expression. His eyes were veiled and his eyeballs hollow. His skin began to turn a pale gray, had a paper-thin, hard appearance, and started to peel. It was very susceptible to all kinds of infection, particularly scabies. The patient's hair became shaggy, lusterless, and brittle. His head became elongated, and his cheekbones and eye sockets stood out. The patient breathed slowly and spoke softly with a great effort.

At this stage edemas appeared, and their size depended on the length of the starvation. They appeared first on the eyelids and feet, the location being governed by the time of day. In the morning, after a night's rest, they were most visible on the face, and in the evening on the feet and legs. As the starvation proceeded, these edemas developed and, in the case of people who had to do a lot of standing, spread to the thighs, buttocks, scrotum, and even to the stomach. In addition to the swellings, there was diarrhea, and often diarrhea developed before the swellings.

At this stage, the patients became indifferent to everything that went on around them and detached themselves from all ties to their environment. If they could still move, they did so slowly and without bending their knees. As a consequence of their low body temperature, which was usually thirty-six degrees Centigrade, they shivered from the cold.

Anyone who observed a group of patients from a distance had the impression of seeing praying Arabs. This accounts for the designation *Muselmänner* that was current in the camp for starving prisoners.

Janina Kowalczykowa observed in the infirmary female *Muselmänner* (in the camp lingo women inmates who were in bad physical and emotional shape were called such):

Starving, weakened, and constantly freezing patients liked to gather around the stove in the infirmary barracks, or rather, by the brick chimney canal that ran lengthwise through the barracks. Often the patients sat on this canal as on a bench, and this caused serious burns, up to the third degree, on the back of the thighs and the buttocks. Sometimes the patients did not even feel the burns.

One case I witnessed was that of a female patient at an advanced stage of starvation whose soles were chewed off at night by rats in such a way that on the surface only the carefully preserved tendons were left. The woman did not react at all. After a bandage was applied, she lived for two more days.

The Polish professor Jan Obrychi has published his observations in the infirmary of the main camp. "Apathy and drowsiness (became apparent), a slowing down and weakening of the entire life process, particularly the psychic kind. Such patients had bad vision and hearing. Their apperception, association, train of thought, and any kind of reaction had slowed down. As a result they carried out orders more slowly; this was misinterpreted as a sign of passive resistance and occasioned bestial torture on the part of SS men and (inmate) functionaries."

Désiré Haffner has given this description of the *Muselmänner* in the Birkenau men's camp:

What impressed one most about the appearance of the prisoners was their extreme emaciation. In a few days they lost ten, twenty, thirty, and even forty kilograms. This striking weight loss is accompanied by a total atrophy of the muscles. The zygomatic arches become more prominent, the cheeks are hollow, the jawbone protrudes. The patient's limbs have become mere bones covered with withered, wrinkled, scaly, gray and yellow skin; the thorax is like a wasp waist; the ribs project; the intercostal spaces are sunken; and the abdomen is hollow. The gluteal muscles are the only ones that are still intact and have preserved a certain tone. Intestinal protrusion is frequently observed. The weight of these cachectic adults fluctuates between twenty-five and thirty-five kilograms.

Coupled with this rapid muscular atrophy, the rapid weight loss is striking. Soon we shall not be able to recognize our comrades whom we have not seen for only a few days.

The inmate Otto Wolken, who served as a physician in the quarantine section of Birkenau, was able to save records that indicate the height and weight of seven prisoners. One inmate, who was 156 centimeters tall, weighed 28 kilograms; another, who was 167 centimeters tall, had a weight of 34.5 kilograms; and a third was 171 centimeters in height and weighed 35.5 kilograms. Here are the remaining statistics: 173 centimeters and 39 kilos; 175 centimeters and 39.5 kilos; 180 centimeters and 36.5 kilos; 180 centimeters and 43 kilos. A Polish commission that examined patients left behind in Auschwitz in May 1945 recorded the weight of a woman, who was born in 1914 and was 160 centimeters tall, as 25 kilos; another had a height of 155 centimeters and a weight of 23 kilos. It may be assumed that Wolken and the Polish commission recorded extreme cases, but these were not rare.

The Dutch physician Eduard de Wind has also provided a description of a *Muselmann*: "I watched young people sink into a state of total apathy in a few days. A Dutch physician was accidentally kicked in the heel. He developed a mild inflammation, went to bed, and died four days later without displaying any clear symptoms. This can be called a form of suicide."

Aron Bejlin summed up his observations as follows:

The *Muselmann* stage is the final phase of malnutrition. It is very interesting to observe how a person who reaches this stage begins to talk constantly about food. There are two subjects that the inmates of Auschwitz regard as taboo: the crematoriums and food.

By way of conditioned reflexes, talking about food stimulates the production of stomach acid and thus increases hunger, which is why one should not talk about eating. If someone lost control and kept talking about meals he had eaten at home, this was the first sign that he was turning into a *Muselmann*. We knew that such a man would soon not react any more, that he would lose interest in his surroundings and stop obeying commands. His movements were going to become slow and his face masklike; his reflexes would stop functioning, and he would become incontinent without noticing it. He was not going to rise from his pallet but would remain lying on it motionlessly—in short, he would turn into a *Muselmann*, a corpse standing on swollen legs. When we had to come out for roll call, we would place such men against the wall with their arms raised. It was only a skeleton with a gray face that now leaned against the wall without moving, for it had lost its sense of balance.

■ Fejkiel also mentions the uncontrollable mania for fantasizing about food. "The *Muselmänner* showed some signs of life only when they saw food, or when their eyes or ears received some impression that evoked thoughts of food." Every day strong inmates had to carry the soup kettles from the kitchen to the infirmary. On one occasion dozens of *Muselmänner* flung themselves at the soup carriers "like locusts," overturning the kettles. "The starving attackers laid into the mixture of soup and earth and slurped it up while lying on their bellies. After a short time the camp road had been licked clean; both the soup and the dirt were gone."

Kitty Hart remembers a similar scene in the women's camp: "Some soup had been spilled during the transport. The inmates stretched out on the ground and licked the spilled soup from the dirty ground. Others rummaged around in the garbage for potato peels."

Tadeusz Paczula remembers "a very likable prisoner, a professor at the Warsaw Graduate School of Business. One time some cheese was served that teemed with worms and was so runny in the literal sense of the word that even the most desperate starvelings decided to forgo this delicacy. The professor, however, requested this side dish and consumed it with the greatest appetite without paying any attention to the live creatures in it."

Fejkiel has not forgotten the jurist "in whose pallet we found after his death two thick bundles with all kinds of original recipes that he had hidden there."

At one time Max Mannheimer was quite close to becoming a *Muselmann*, but some strokes of luck restored him to life. He describes his condition quite unreservedly: "I eat the potatoes unpeeled, and I keep my eye on those who are still strong enough to peel their potatoes. I beg them for their peels. I eat them. No, I wolf them down. Like an animal. As if I were afraid. Perhaps of the envy of the other peel eaters. I am ashamed—and keep a sharp eye on the peelers."

"I know about the futility of those hunger fantasies," writes Primo Levi, "but I cannot escape the general rule, and thus I see dancing in my mind's eye the macaroni that my friends and I had just prepared in an Italian refugee camp when we were suddenly informed that we would be transported here the next day. We were just about to eat the macaroni (it was so good and yellow and firm), but, like blockheads and idiots, we left it uneaten. If we had only known! Could this happen to us again? . . . What an absurdity. If there was any certainty in the world, it was this: it won't happen to us again."

Elsewhere Levi writes: "Fourteen days after my arrival I already experience real hunger, the chronic hunger that free men do not know, that produces dreams at night and dwells in every limb of our bodies. My own body is no longer mine; my belly is bloated, my limbs are withered, my face is swollen in the morning and hollowed in the evening." In his memoir Levi includes what may be described as a refrain: "Who could imagine a time with no hunger? The camp is hunger. We ourselves are hunger, living hunger."

"My only interest," writes Elie Wiesel, "was my daily soup and my piece of bread. Bread and soup—that was my whole life. I was all body, and perhaps even less: an emaciated body."

Albert Menasche writes: "We were practically like wild animals. Our only activity was to escape being beaten with clubs and above all to get some food. Our greatest desire was to end the hunger pangs."

Henry Bulawko describes how three Greek Jews in the satellite camp Jaworzno chased a dog and stole some bones from him.

This is what Lucie Adelsberger, a physician, had to say on the same subject: "Anyone acquainted with hunger knows that it is not just a vegetative, animal sensation in the stomach, but a nerve-shattering agony, an attack on the entire personality. Hunger makes a person vicious and corrupts his character. Many things about the inmates that rightly appear monstrous to an outsider

become comprehensible and partly excusable from the perspective of hunger."
Adelsberger confesses that hunger made her cry like a little child.

■ Maria Elzbieta Jezierska has described the depths to which a person can
sink if the voraciousness of a convalescent is added to the chronic hunger of
a *Muselmann*. "Having survived typhus, Paula lies in the infirmary and with a
terrible, corrosive, murderous envy stares at those who were able to 'organize'
a bowl of soup. 'To kill and then possess a bowl of soup'—that is what she
is thinking." Jezierska continues with her description, which could not have
been fabricated:

> Paula feels a horrendous hatred well up within her, the monstrous envy
> of a beggar. She can feel the sweaty, hot, disgusting bodies of the typhus
> patients that had been thrown together with hers on this bunk bed that was
> designed for only one person. Now she raises her head. If you only croaked
> at long last!
>
> It's true; a few weeks earlier she was one of these and like them moaned
> softly and piteously all night long. Sweat and urine ran down her body,
> too, and she was as defenseless against bedbugs as they were. But then she
> passed out. And these vile people stay awake! What use do they have for
> food? And yet they guard it like the healthiest prisoners.
>
> Seething with rage, Paula stares at the pointed nose of the Novak woman
> that juts upward, like a dead person's. Near the top of her pallet Novak has
> a box in which she collects bread. She gobbles the soup, even though Paula
> has warned her that it would harm her. But she eats ravenously despite her
> diarrhea, and then she soils her bed.
>
> Paula looks daggers at the barely living profile of the woman whose dirty
> heels are under her shoulders. Every night she wonders whether her time
> has come. Novak is getting weaker and weaker, and there is no chance that
> she can get up to use the pail. Novak cannot even lift her body, and the only
> thing she can still do is to put her bread ration in the box. As she does so,
> her eyes gleam feverishly.
>
> Novak's hollow eyes flash when bread is distributed, and her hand is
> stretched out like a red root to receive it. She holds the bread and tenderly
> presses it against her bosom, as a mother does with her child, but her hand
> is as firm as the claw of a hawk. As if bewitched, Paula stares at the other
> woman's bread and she cannot avert her eyes all day. For the first time,
> Novak has been too feeble to put the bread in the box.
>
> Evening has come and Novak is not dead yet. Paula looks around quickly.
> No, no one will see it. Cautiously she moves closer to Novak and listens.
> No, she is definitely no longer conscious. Cautiously, carefully she touches

the bread and tries to remove it from the hand of the moribund woman, but in her death struggle her fingers have closed so tightly around the slice of bread that Paula is unable to remove it. Paula trembles, in her thoughts mutters curses and obscenities, and tugs at Novak's hand harder and harder, obeying the commands of life in the face of death.

She can feel the body beside her slowly getting colder. At last! Paula calls the night guard, who drags the dead body down. Paula gets hold of the box, but the bread in it is mildewed. Nevertheless, Paula eats everything that is not completely green. Two days later she dies amid excruciating pain. From under her pallet her neighbors pull out a box with a few uneaten pieces of bread. These are not mildewed.

Judith Sternberg-Newman saw how inmates stole bread from their dying comrades and ate it even if it was soiled by excrement. She confesses that she pulled a concealed bread ration from under the body of a woman who had just died.

Gisella Perl's experiences as an inmate physician in Mexico were as follows: "I was always busiest after the food rations had been distributed. There were bloodied heads to bandage, broken ribs to treat, and wounds to clean. I worked and worked even though I knew full well that it was hopeless, for the next day everything would start up all over again and even the patients would probably be the same."

Tadeusz Borowski has described how people could be driven beyond all limits:

Twenty Russians were to be shot in Birkenau, and all prisoners had to line up and watch the execution. In addition, they would have to go without supper by way of punishment. "Ready, set, fire!" said the commandant without raising his voice. The carbines barked and the soldiers jumped back a pace to avoid being spattered by the smashed skulls. The Russians tottered and plopped down like heavy sacks, smearing the stones with blood and splattered brains. Putting their carbines over their shoulders, the soldiers quickly walked off in the direction of the watchtower. The corpses were temporarily dragged under the barbed wire. The commandant and his retinue got into a Skoda that, emitting gas clouds, backed out of the gate.

No sooner had the graying, tanned commandant driven off than the silent crowd, which had kept pressing forward toward the road, emitted an ominous growl and rushed up to the bloody stones, where there was a thunderous outburst. The cudgels of the block and dormitory elders, who had been summoned from all over the camp, quickly drove the rioters back into their barracks. I was standing on the side of the place of execution and was not able to come up close. But the next morning, when we were herded out to work again, a run-down Estonian Jew who was carting pipes with me kept assuring me zealously that a human brain was really so delicate that it could be eaten raw, without cooking it.

And here is Borowski's definition: "One isn't really hungry until one regards another human being as something edible."

Until the end, the pain caused by chronic hunger remained the predominant feeling. Jacques Furmanski reports about a comrade who was destined for death at a selection and had nothing to say but to request a piece of bread: "The only thing I have left is the ability to eat! Eat! Die with a full stomach!"

When the number of those taken to the crematorium was so small that it would not have been cost-effective to fill a big gas chamber with Zyklon B, the victims were shot. A member of the Sonderkommando has described such a shooting, and his notes were unearthed at a later date: "A group of emaciated, starving Jews was brought in from some camp. They undressed in the courtyard and one by one went to be shot. They were terribly hungry and begged for a piece of bread to sustain them for the short time they still had to live. Inmates brought a large amount of bread. The eyes of the new arrivals, which had been dimmed by the horrendous hunger, blazed in a wild outburst of joy. With both hands they seized a piece of bread and devoured it greedily while they were climbing the stairs to be shot."

■ What was harder to bear, hunger or thirst? This question was posed to the nameless people interned in Birkenau. In the main camp the water supply was sufficient for inmates to quench their thirst, though they had to fight for a place in the washroom. Kazimierz Smolen has put it concisely: "The sanitary and hygienic conditions in the main camp were miserable, but those in Birkenau were truly hopeless." Simon Laks describes conditions in the Birkenau men's camp in the summer of 1942, when it had housed prisoners for only a few months. "There was no water in the camp. There was only one operational pump, and it was reserved for the kitchen. Anyone who wanted a few drops had to pay for them with bread."

On August 16, 1942, the women's camp was moved to section B I of Birkenau. Hilda Horakova has provided a description of the early period of that camp: "There was only one well, and some corpses had fallen into it. We had to push those bodies down so we could draw some water." Anna Palarczyk also comments on that well, which was part of the kitchen, though she does not remember any corpses in it. At night women tormented by thirst crept there, though it was forbidden to do so. Occasionally, a secret attempt to draw water from the well caused a feeble woman to fall in and drown. Anna Palarczyk, who had been deported in mid-August 1942, was not able to wash until Christmastime, and even this was possible only because a friend had been able to "orga-nize" a kettle with water.

Dounia Ourisson-Wasserstrom, who arrived in Auschwitz a month before Palarczyk, writes: "At first I washed with tea, which was an undetermined brown liquid, but in winter I washed with snow."

On January 27, 1943, some Frenchwomen arrived at the women's camp, which by then had been in operation for almost half a year. Among them was Maria-Claude Vaillant-Couturier, who later testified in Nuremberg about the water supply:

When we arrived, there was only one faucet for 12,000 inmates. The water was not potable and flowed only intermittently. This faucet was located in the washrooms for Germans, and the only access was past guards, Ger-man criminals who beat us unmercifully. Hence it was almost impossible to wash or to clean one's underwear. In more than three months we were not able to put on clean underwear. When there was snow, we let it melt so we could wash with it, and in spring we used, on our way to work, the same puddle of water at the edge of the road for drinking and washing our shirts and pants. Then we washed our hands in the dirty water.

Marie-Elisa Nordmann-Cohen confirms this account when she writes: "Most of us did not wash for a few months, unless we were able to do so with snow or rainwater." Charlotte Delbo, who arrived in Auschwitz on the same transport, remembers vividly that "those who remained in Block 26 lived there for seventy-six days without being able to wash." In those days an inmate re-ceived only an eighth of a liter of herbal tea daily.

Shortly after the end of the war Zofia Litwinska testified as follows: "I was assigned to clean the latrines. We had to wash them with our hands. Inmates were very eager to get this job, because it allowed them to wash a bit."

Kitty Hart observed the following conditions as late as April 1943: "At the exit some liquid was distributed. It had been a long time since I had had any-thing to drink, and so I was terribly thirsty. Finally it was my turn and they poured something in my rations cup. It was a foul-smelling, dark, blue-gray herbal brew. I smelled it, tasted it, and was nauseated. Two girls next to me conferred: 'Shall we drink it today or wash with it?' They decided to share one portion and use the other one for washing. They also warned me not to drink too much, for otherwise I would get diarrhea."

After she had familiarized herself with the camp, Kitty Hart saw only one way to get water: "In the sauna there was water, but only VIPs had access to it. If an ordinary inmate tried to get in, she was given a beating and thrown out. I realized that it was especially important to be better dressed if one wanted to make an impression and not to be regarded as an ordinary prisoner." But how was a dirty, stinking inmate to obtain good clothes or be assigned to a detail where she could "organize" such things? Only on rare occasions was it possible to break through the vicious circle.

Hermine Horvath has given this description of the Gypsy camp: "Since there was no water, feverish inmates often drank urine. The pails in which they relieved themselves were used to serve us food after they had been washed."

Things were not much different in the quarantine section of Birkenau as late as spring 1944. André Blécourt reports how he sneaked out of his barracks at night in order to enjoy drinking water from a nearby ditch into which inmates had urinated and in which there were dead rats.

When the Mexico section of the Birkenau camp began to receive prisoners in the spring of 1944, conditions there were if anything worse than those in the early period of the women's camp. Katalin Vidor has described the following scene: "Zoska blurts out, 'Hope to God it doesn't rain!' 'No, it shouldn't stop raining,' interjects a woman, cups her hands to get some water from a puddle, and slurps it down. A group of women washes in the puddles, for there is only one kind of water: the kind that is bestowed by heaven."

In his primitive mode of expression, the block leader Stefan Baretzki described to the Frankfurt court the conditions in that section of the camp.

> There were a few thousand women in the Mexico section. They slept on the bare ground, they didn't even have a blanket. Only one barrel of water was brought there every day. I was ordered by the Labor Assignment Office to take such a barrel there. The people from the orchestra carried the water in. Jewish women from Slovakia (evidently inmate functionaries) were in there, and they begged us: "Bring more water!" But that was hard for me. I can't bring water again until noon, when no one notices it, when the other guards are away. The female wardens in Mexico agreed that I should bring water. And now and then I brought water at noon. The inmates gave the guards cigarettes for it, but I didn't take any.

Later Baretzki told me that Cylka, the camp elder, had bribed the guards. He also stated why these practices were not stopped: "When I talked with SS camp leader Schwarzhuber about it, he kept telling me, 'That's none of your business, it's high time for you to understand that these are Jews!'"

Henryk Porebski, who was in charge of maintaining the electric installations in Birkenau, has called attention to one cause of the chronic lack of water in that camp complex. The four big crematoriums needed a lot of water, and so the construction people installed pumps that were to be used primarily for the crematoriums.

In March 1941 Professor Zunker was asked to test the water in Auschwitz. He came to the conclusion that it was not potable and should not even be used as a mouthwash. As a result the guards received sufficient supplies of mineral water. On August 31, 1942, the SS physician Johann Paul Kremer entered in his diary: "The water is polluted and so we are drinking seltzer, which is distributed free of charge (Mattoni)."

■ Chronic hunger and thirst; the separation from relatives that, as soon became apparent, was permanent; the utter hopelessness of ever getting out of the Auschwitz mill—all this turned human beings into *Muselmänner*. Here is how Jean Améry describes this type: "The so-called *Muselmann*, as an inmate who was giving up on himself and had been given up by his comrades was called in the camp lingo, no longer had a space of consciousness in which good and evil, nobility and meanness, intelligence and stupidity could confront one another. He was a walking corpse, a bundle of physical functions in its death throes."

Vilo Jurkovic has also provided a portrait of the *Muselmann*: "That was a bag of skin and bones, an emaciated human being barely able to drag himself along and devoid of will and strength, a person with a nasal discharge that ran down his mouth and chin, a dirty person clad in rags and often completely lice-ridden, suffering from severe diarrhea, with a resultant soiling of underwear, a person with sunken or bulging eyeballs—a true picture of misery, weakness, hopelessness, and horror!"

The SS physician Hans Münch diagnosed in *Muselmänner* not only a complete indifference to their surroundings but also a shattering credulity. That credulity is probably the reason why many of them allowed themselves to be deceived by the transparent maneuvers of the camp administration when a selection doomed them to death. The American psychologist Martin Wangh regards the obsequiousness that was sometimes displayed by *Muselmänner* as a consequence of their general devitalization.

Benedikt Kautsky has concerned himself with indications that an inmate was deteriorating and about to become a *Muselmann*:

A decline in personal hygiene was the surest indication of impending danger. Particularly in the winter, washing was regarded as a superfluous loss of calories; inmates resisted getting fresh air into their block and went to bed in their clothes. This change usually coincided with an inmate's tendency to shun any avoidable physical exertion; his gait became slow and shuffling, and his energy at work was reduced to a minimum. Naturally, this filthy, brutish, slothful creature became the target of all sorts of brutal acts and jokes. In point of fact, it was really difficult for a dormitory elder or foreman to cope with a person who reacted only to the strongest forms of pressure.

Kautsky goes on to say: "There were many inmates who did not get up at night to relieve themselves. As a consequence of the high water content of the food, the number of pathological bed wetters was extremely high, but there were quite a few inmates who became bed wetters because they lacked self-control."

There were other factors that frequently inhibited prisoners from going to the latrine at night. Leo Diamant has mentioned one: "On several occasions I saw in the morning the corpses of inmates who had been shot during the night by guards in the watchtowers when they were leaving the block to visit the toilets. This is why we stayed in the block and relieved ourselves into the mess tin."

Like many others, Kautsky observed that numerous intellectuals let themselves go, but "it would, of course, be wrong to see in this slackening of physical self-discipline only a characteristic of the intellectuals." Their decline to the level of a *Muselmann* was more noticeable than that of others, and this led to generalizations that Kautsky rightly rejects.

And what about the death of the *Muselmänner*? Jakob Laks writes laconically that "an acquaintance of mine died one morning while putting on his pants," and Maria-Claude Vaillant-Couturier observes that "the organism was so weakened that a person died the way a clock stops." She has this to say about the reaction of the survivors: "She has stopped suffering. But we have to carry her to the camp now."

Jurkovic explains why a *Muselmann* became an object of contempt and disgust rather than compassion on the part of his fellow inmates: "The *Muselmann* condition was dreaded by the inmates because no one knew when he might suffer such a fate himself and be a certain candidate for the gas chamber or another kind of death." Added to this was the fact that *Muselmänner* frequently provoked the anger of the others: "These were creatures in the final stage of humanness who acted only like unreasoning animals." Viktor Frankl observed that they reacted only if they were yelled at, "but even this often failed, and then it really took great self-control not to strike out at them, for in the face of the apathy of others one's own irritability assumed immeasurable dimensions."

These inmates posed ever new problems for those who had anything to do with them. For example, they crawled out of sight at roll call time even though they must have known that all those lined up had to remain standing until the last missing inmate had been found.

■ Julia Skodova had already come perilously close to the *Muselmann* stage when she was assigned to a detail that was housed in the ss staff building under incomparably more favorable conditions. For the first time she was able to take a morning shower in the basement of that building because the administration wanted inmates whose work brought them in contact with the ss to be clean. "It's breathtaking," she writes. "Warm water flows from the showers, and it can even be regulated. No, this luxury can't be described. It's what a blind man must feel like when a miracle has restored his eyesight." She has given this description of her first day in this new workplace: "One day passed during which I was hungry but not beaten or hounded, one day during which I wasn't soaked by the rain or scorched by a merciless sun. This one day sufficed to make me a human being again and let me grasp the suffering of others, not just my own." Skodova has described this transformation as follows:

> We are beginning to feel that we are human beings. Physically we are incomparably better off, but we are all the more severely and more frequently beset by mental depressions. Because as long as a person cannot think of anything but hunger and filth, as long as one is tormented by thirst and pain, as long as one cannot satisfy the most elementary human needs, concepts like "parents," "home," "forest and flowers" are hidden somewhere in the depths of consciousness and very rarely penetrate to the surface. But if you have already eaten your bread and are lying in a bed without fleas and lice, then all this comes to the surface of consciousness and begins to torment you. I have never cried here. Despite all the misery and terror that I have experienced here, my eyes have remained dry, but when I lie in bed now, I am shaken by sobs.

Pelagia Lewinska mustered the energy to keep herself from sliding into a *Muselmann*'s death:

> After their daily work and a roll call that lasted for hours, the inmates finally had time to rest. And precisely at that moment they had to think of cleaning themselves. It is dark and rainy, the dirty camp road is slippery, and every step makes one sink into the mud. The latrines with the water taps (which later were installed in the women's camp) are on the other side of the camp. We are utterly exhausted.
>
> We have to get up. Only a few inmates are capable of such an exertion. If we didn't feel the urge to go to the latrine, none of us would muster the necessary strength. But for us this meant more—an act of will with the aim of mastering difficulties, proving capable of making this little effort, giving clear evidence of unmistakable resistance. In our case this was a protest that was meant to say: We won't let ourselves go.
>
> As for me, the fact that I forced myself to clean my shoes was proof that I still was my own master. Most of the time the efforts I made were utterly futile. The next morning my shoes were, after a few steps, as dirty as they

had been the night before, and yet every evening my clean shoes proved my unbroken will. After we had marched into the camp half-dead from fatigue, I began to clean my shoes.

In Monowitz there were facilities for washing, albeit inadequate ones, but the inmates were given neither towels nor soap. As a consequence, Georges Wellers and Robert Waitz write, "the majority of inmates washed only infrequently and even then very superficially."

Primo Levi reports:

After a week's imprisonment, I've lost any urge to be clean. I walk through the washroom and see my friend Steinlauf, who is almost fifty, rubbing his bare neck and shoulders with little success (he has no soap) but with great energy. He sees me, grabs me, and asks me directly and sternly why I am not washing. Why should I? Would that help me? Would someone like me better if I did? Would that lengthen my life by as much as a day or an hour? On the contrary, it would shorten my life because washing is work and thus a waste of energy and calories. Doesn't Steinlauf know that after a half hour under the coal sacks there will no longer be any difference between him and me?

Levi, who had become convinced that all of them had already begun to die, rejected Steinlauf's notion, but the latter taught the young Italian a real lesson. Levi continues:

I am sorry that I have forgotten Steinlauf's clear and sensible words, the words of a former royal imperial noncommissioned officer, holder of the Iron Cross 1914–1918. And I regret having to translate his shaky Italian and the simple speech of a good soldier into my own language, the language of an unbeliever. But this is the gist of what he told me, and I did not forget it then or later:

Precisely because the camp is a big mechanism that is intended to degrade us to the level of animals, we must not become animals. Even in this place it is possible to stay alive, and we must have the will to do so, if only to report about it later and bear witness. For our existence, it is important to do anything to preserve at least the structure, the shell, the form of civilization. Even though we are slaves stripped of all rights, exposed to all insults, and destined for certain death, we have one chance left, and, because it is the last one, we must defend it with all our strength. It is the chance to withhold our consent. From this it follows that we must wash our faces without soap and dry them with our jackets. We must shine our shoes— not because it is required but out of self-esteem and cleanliness. We must walk erect and not shuffle in our wooden shoes—not as a concession to Prussian discipline but in order to remain alive and not waste away.

Not every inmate who was in danger of being felled by the first shock met a Steinlauf in time. The sensitive observer Primo Levi has explained more clearly than anyone else could have why the *Muselmann*, that icon of Auschwitz, must be near the beginning of a study on the subject of people in an extermination camp:

They, the *Muselmänner*, the lost ones, are the nerve of the camp, the nameless, ever renewed, and ever identical mass of mutely marching, toiling nonhumans in whom the divine spark has been extinguished and who are already too enfeebled to really suffer. One hesitates to describe them as living or to call the death that does not frighten them a death, because they are too exhausted to grasp it. They populate my memory with their faceless presence, and if I could concentrate all the suffering of our time in one image, I would select one that is familiar to me: a careworn man with a bowed head and bent shoulders whose face and eyes do not betray even a trace of a thought.

THE INMATE AND DEATH

■ ■ ■

A *Muselmann*'s fate in an extermination camp was preordained. From time to time inmates who could no longer march briskly, those who were bandaged, and emaciated persons whose fitness for work seemed doubtful—in short, the *Muselmänner*—were "selected."

The camp administration never made an official announcement about the purpose of these selections and the fate of the selectees. If it gave out any information at all, it pretended that the prisoners had been transferred to another camp, or something of that sort. Since there were frequent transfers and every ss camp leader attempted to use such occasions to get rid of inmates who were a burden on the camp, including *Muselmänner*, doubts about the purpose of a selection could arise—not so much among old hands, who were able to observe all measures soberly and with detachment, as among those directly affected, whose situation Katalin Vidor has described in these terms: "If a person has reached a stage of utter helplessness, he begins to hope: perhaps not ... perhaps ... perhaps ..."

In late 1942, when I was recuperating in the HKB of the main camp, I could see through the window how selectees were treated. In my *Bericht* I wrote:

Sudden noise. The familiar roar of the capos, the dreaded intonation of ss commands. I go to the window.

In front of my window there is the tangled barbed wire. There is little space between the block and the wire. People are now being herded. ss men bark commands. Ahead of them, capos busily run around and randomly beat with their clubs the crowd of inmates jammed together.

I'm sure they've rounded up the *Muselmänner* again. This has happened a number of times. On such days the ss roll call leader picks out from the details marching off to work in the morning all those who attract his attention and do not appear to be fully fit for work. A black day for the camp.

"Strip completely!"

Now they have to undress in the cold, helped along by screams and beatings.

Most of them surely know what is going to happen to them. I can read it in their faces. Thinking that he is not being observed, one man stealthily and quickly puts on his clothes again, but a capo catches him. I can hear the blows and his screams through my window. Everyone wants to be the last to take off his clothes. Perhaps the terrified inmates hope that this will enable them to cheat their way out of their fate.

"Faster, faster! On with it!" In the background stands an ss man with his legs apart.

Now everyone has undressed. Pitiful skeletons. Their numbers are taken down, and they are chased into the block. The sun is shining, and the snow is glistening and merrily dripping from the roof. No one is in front of my window; all I can see are big piles of dirty prison clothes along the wall. Then I hear footsteps and muted voices from the corridor. I look outside. Now there are long lines of naked inmates. The clerk of our block walks up to each one with file cards in his hand, compares names and numbers, and writes each inmate's number on his chest with indelible ink. The corpses in Auschwitz bear that number on their chests; these inmates are already counted among the dead, and there has to be order. (In late 1942 not all inmates had had their numbers tattooed.)

How they look at me, these freezing skeletons, as if I could help them, as if I were to blame for what is to come. I quickly close the door again.

How must such a human being feel, standing naked in a corridor and waiting to be loaded on a truck that will take him to the gas chamber?

But I don't hear any motor vehicle drive up. Those men are still there each time I have to cross the corridor on my way to the toilet. Some are apathetic and in a squatting position, others have flickering eyes. Do they still have hope—are they still seeking a way out? Those who sit are repeatedly roused; the corridor has to be clear. It was in the morning, after the early roll call, that I saw them being herded together in front of my window. Now it is evening, and they haven't had anything to eat all day. And why should they still be fed? If they want to drink, their only resource is water from the toilets.

Now many are lying down. They are too weak to fear the blows that are intended to shake them awake. Three of them are lying in front of my door, and I have to step over them if I want to leave the room. One is dead, but the two next to him are still alive. There is little difference among these three.

The ss had forced a feeling of utter impotence on the inmates. Among the numerous accounts of the methods they used for this is a scene described by Hanoch Hadas to the Frankfurt court: "I had been assigned to a street-cleaning detail and was loading garbage on a truck near the kitchen. Baretzky, the block leader, walked through the camp, called an inmate, and slapped his face. In an effort to protect his face, the inmate raised his hand. 'What, you want to hit an ss man?' roared Baretzky and rained blows on the man, trampling him after he had fallen down. Then he took the wooden handle of a shovel, placed it across the inmate's neck, stepped on it, and seesawed until the inmate was dead."

So a prisoner was not even allowed to raise a protective hand if an SS man wanted to beat him. *Muselmänner* were in no condition even to think of self-defense. As Kogon has observed, "To expect them to resist would mean to misinterpret their mental state. They simply could not go on." Added to this is the fact that fellow prisoners who came into contact with selectees as clerks, nurses, or in other functions and were bombarded with questions usually supported the administration's attempts at deception. Wellers reports that, like many of his colleagues on the staff of the Monowitz infirmary, he answered questions like "They aren't taking us to the crematorium, are they?" by saying they were going to be sent to another camp for rest and relaxation. Wellers added to this white lie by saying, "This is an absolutely sure thing," but afterward he wondered whether it would have been better to tell the victims the truth and thus rob them of all hope in their last hours.

Even a person who faces certain death is not indifferent to the way he must die. Every inmate knew from ample experience that if SS men felt provoked by an act of disobedience, they were capable of engaging in indescribable tortures before the end was to come.

Jacques Furmanski has reported about his leave-taking from a friend who had become the victim of a selection. On many earlier occasions this friend had told him, "They aren't going to get me. They'll have to pay dearly for my hide. I'll know how to die." Now the friend pressed his hand and said, "Be good, old boy, and keep your courage up." "I remained mute and numb in the most awkward situation of my life," writes Furmanski about that moment. "I didn't know how to reply. Inside me I felt an imperative need to tell him, 'Defend yourself, at least show something, we'll support you!' But as he was standing before me, I felt that he was already far from us, that he had gone away and was no longer thinking of anything."

Most of the victims of selections were Jews; in fact, only they had to line up for some selections. That is why the phenomenon of innumerable people allowing themselves to be led to their death knowingly and without attempting to resist has sometimes been described as typically Jewish. I agree with Georges Wellers when he terms the fact that the overwhelming majority of prisoners let themselves be herded to their destruction "like sheep" (as has often been written) as typical of Nazi concentration camps. "Aryans" behaved the same way in the same situation, and the only difference is that for them this situation arose less often.

A Polish officer, an inmate who frequently had to help with the loading of selectees onto trucks, has characterized their bearing as follows: "As a rule the victims remained relatively calm, and they always remembered to say, 'Do not forget the retribution!'" He remembers two brothers, one of whom was selected. His brother killed him in order to spare him the ride on a truck to the gas chamber.

Do not forget the retribution and do not forget the victims—these may have been the last thoughts of many who were still capable of thinking. Thus there once was a Hungarian inscription in a Birkenau barracks from which victims of a selection had just been driven out. These words had been written on the wall with blood: "Andreas Rappaport—lived sixteen years."

■ Isolated instances of resistance, escapes from death in a gas chamber, and demonstrations in the presence of the murderers have been documented. Thus Erich Altmann has recorded the end of Meilech Herschkowitz, a former theater director. When that man was selected, he spoke to an ss man who knew him from occasional Sunday performances: "I have been selected and am to be burned. Can't you help me?" The ss man replied, "There's nothing I can do." "Don't you think, Herr Unterscharführer," continued Herschkowitz, "that if I have to die, I deserve a bullet?" "You're right," replied the ss officer, pulled out his revolver, and shot the inmate. This happened in Birkenau in January 1944.

Eduard de Wind recalls an Italian Jew who escaped from the block in which selectees were waiting for transportation to the gas chambers and cheated his way onto the Bauhof detail. There he carried bags of cement all day in order to prove his fitness for work and was praised by the foreman for his diligence. Despite this, the ss camp physician had him removed and the block elder punished because he had not prevented the inmate's escape from the isolation block.

Other attempted escapes were more successful. Ella Lingens reports about a Jewish woman who sneaked out of the infirmary after a selection had been announced and tried to get into another block that had not been threatened with a selection. However, the block elder did not dare to admit a stranger while the block was locked. Thus the escapee hid under a pile of corpses in front of the barracks and had to stay there for four or five hours in the wintry cold until the selection was over.

A sixteen-year-old Frenchwoman has described her flight, together with a friend, from Block 25, in which selectees had to wait for transportation to the gas chamber. Because she was very thin, she was able to slip through the bars of a window. "It may seem strange that we waited all night before we tried this relatively easy route of escape," she writes, "but we could not have done it at any other time without being immediately noticed and betrayed. You see, it was to be expected that a block elder or dormitory elder would see us, or other prisoners who would have tried to do the same thing, and then everything would have been ruined."

The following incident occurred in the Birkenau men's camp in late 1942. A father and a son named Bentschkowski were housed in Block 8. The father, who was around forty-five years old, was the owner of a small textile factory in Paris, and the twenty-year-old son was a comfort and support to his father, who became more feeble every day. One evening the young man returned from work with a bloody face and a head full of bumps. He had been so badly beaten that he was not even able to eat his piece of bread. The next day, when the morning roll call was as usual followed by the command "Labor details, line up!," the young Bentschkowski dragged himself back to the barracks and collapsed. He was not able to rise and join the lineup. His father did not want to leave him and lay down on the ground next to him. An inmate who was working as a roofer and thus had a good chance of observing events has described what happened next.

> Suddenly I heard bloodcurdling screams that were followed immediately by the admonition "Sh'mah Yisrael!" (Hear, O Israel!). I watched how the people who had been lying around were loaded onto trucks like inanimate objects. Among them were the father and the son, my neighbors in the barracks. The father cradled the mauled head of his son in his hands and called out so loudly that it echoed in the empty camp: "Sh'mah Yisrael! Sh'mah Yisrael!" And now something happened that I had never experienced before. When those doomed to die were lying on the truck and the transport began to move, other voices joined in the prayer, which invigorated the almost lifeless human beings once more. We could see arms strengthen and frail bodies totter upward for a moment. When they saw us on the roof, they called out to us, "Avenge us if you ever get a chance!" One of the men on the truck started to sing, and in the middle of the human tangle were the father and the son, kneeling and embracing.

Many women will always remember another scene. Frenchwomen who were being taken to the gas chamber in a truck intoned the "Marseillaise." This demonstration of an unbroken will immediately before death was unusual.

Tadeusz Paczula remembers the end of an engineer named Popper, "a very cultivated man" who had come on an RSHA transport from Slovakia. In the early period, when all Jews were assigned to the penal company, Popper was sent from there to the infirmary, suffering from cellulitis. One day it was ordered that all Jews were to be discharged from the infirmary no matter what their state of health was. Paczula bid Popper goodbye with these words: "Tadek, tomorrow morning I won't be alive any more. . . ." Paczula did not know what to say to console him. "Both of us knew that this was the truth," he wrote later. "The next day, when the SS men started to manhandle the members of the penal company, Popper hurled himself at one of the SS men, who drew his gun and shot him."

These were exceptions to the rule. The rule was that the inmates, being exhausted unto death, an apathetic mass, let themselves be directed wherever the all-powerful SS pleased. The following incident was reported to David Rousset. Selectees who knew their fate were being escorted to the gas chamber. An old man whose legs could no longer carry him sat down on the way. An escort yelled at him, "If you don't go on, I'll mow you down!" The old man quickly blurted out, "No, don't kill me, I'll go on," whereupon he got in line again on the way to the gas chamber. Every minute of even the paltriest life retains its value.

When the Birkenau family camps were to be liquidated, the situation was different. Thousands who knew one another because they had been interned together for a long time and were in better physical condition than the *Muselmänner* found out that they were to be killed. Even though SS men used any means to camouflage their actions, their true purpose could not remain hidden from those who had been forced to live in the immediate vicinity of the gas chambers. In the Theresienstadt family camp, a Jewish block elder named Bondy, speaking in Czech, urged the inmates not to board the trucks as ordered by the SS. Bondy was knocked down by capos whom the camp administration had summoned to the family camp for this liquidation from other parts of the Birkenau complex. Bondy was regarded as a "hard" block elder who was capable of slapping faces. Ota Popel is said to have attempted a warning also and to have suffered the same fate as Bondy. The SS had to exert its full brutality in the liquidation of the Gypsy camp as well, because all tricks intended to persuade the Gypsies to board the trucks willingly failed.

The inmates destined to be killed by phenol injections in the infirmary behaved much like those selected to die in the gas chambers. Klehr, a medic who killed more people by means of such shots than any other SS man, later gave this expert explanation in a courtroom: "They knew what was in store for them, but they did not offer any resistance. They were completely worn out, all skin and bones."

Here, too, there were well-remembered exceptions. Stanislaw Glowa, a block clerk, reports about a Russian who arrived at the camp in a prison van in the summer of 1942 and was taken directly to Block 20 and into the room in which Klehr had assembled some inmates who had to assist him with his injections. Glowa heard Klehr yell and ran to him. "I saw Klehr sitting on the man with a syringe in his hand," he writes. At a later date Glowa learned that the Russian had grabbed a stool and attacked Klehr with it, but he was wrestled to the floor. Josef Farber remembers that a nurse whom Klehr had selected for injection yelled that he was healthy. "Later we took his corpse away," writes Farber laconically.

■ Pery Broad, who was present at the bunker selections as a member of the Political Department, has described the behavior of those doomed to die. "From the overcrowded narrow cell comes a nauseating stench. A prisoner calls out, '*Achtung!*' and with an apathetic expression the emaciated figures in their filthy blue and white rags line up in a row. With the indifference of people whose will to live is already broken they submit to the procedure that follows, a decision between life and death that they may already have survived more than once."

I witnessed this procedure six times myself and have described my first confrontation with the commission as follows: "I have already seen the vehicles leave Block 11 as well as the trail of blood that they left in the camp. Well, it may not be so bad. Am I trying to comfort myself with lies? Don't I know perfectly well that Auschwitz is bad, terribly bad? How many death notices have I written myself, giving the cause of death of murdered men as pneumonia or cardiac arrest. Will my relatives at home also receive such a notice?"

After the first bunker selection, I was familiar with how this procedure played out and described it as follows:

Jakob (the bunker *Kalfaktor* [handyman]) told me at breakfast that we should sweep well today. I know what that means. I divide the bread and the onions that I received from Robert into thirteen portions. "Better save it. Then those who are left will enjoy it more." Nevertheless, we eat together. Then the waiting. The last hours for most men. If thirteen people with strained nerves are crowded together in such a small space, you begin to loathe everyone. Oh to be alone! A key turns in the lock. The ss camp leader's voice is too loud for the little cell.

"Cell 8, housing thirteen inmates. Inmate 60-3-55." He looks at his list and motions with his hand: "Step aside, stay." Behind me is a very young inmate who has been planning to escape, as desperate as he is childish and worn out. He would never have made it. "Out!" Then there is a fifteen-year-old Jew from Warsaw who drank coffee from a canteen while at work without knowing that it belonged to an ss man. Now he, too, is ordered out of the line, but he does not blanch. He spoke about dying like an old man. Another one, another one.

Pery Broad has given this account of the shootings in the block yard:

An exceptionally strong inmate from the cleaning staff (undoubtedly Jakob) quickly brings in the first two victims. He holds them by their forearms and presses their faces against the wall. When they turn their heads to the side, someone commands, "*Prosto!*" (straight ahead, an indirect confirmation by Broad that most of those were Poles). Although these walking skeletons, some of whom had for months been leading a miserable life in the stinking cellar cells, an existence that one would not inflict on an animal, could barely stand on their legs, many of them called out in this last second, "Long live Poland!" or "Long live liberty!"

Ota Fabian, a corpse carrier who had to be present at numerous shootings, reports that some Poles prayed, sang their national anthem or called out slogans. Fabian remembers "Long live liberty!" and "Your turn will come!"

For a time I was incarcerated in a cell whose ventilation shaft led to the yard near the Black Wall. Thus I was able to count the shots, but I heard only one shout; it was in Russian, and all I could make out was "Stalin." I was prepared to shout, "Long live free Austria! Down with fascism!"—because I did not want to be shot without speaking. I realized that such a last demonstration could not have much of a response, and might have none at all. The possibility of active resistance did not occur to me. The victims were led to the courtyard where several armed SS men were waiting for them, singly or in pairs, and thus any resistance would have been quickly squelched. Another inhibiting factor was that naked victims were confronting uniformed murderers.

There was one attempt at active resistance, and the Pole Alfred Woycicki has described it as follows: "On October 8, 1942, two hundred persons transported to the camp from Lublin were shot. Eighty inmates were added to this group and taken to Block 11, where they were ordered to strip. They refused, and there was an uprising in the hallway. The block was locked and so was the entire camp. Around 3:00 P.M. a large group of SS men came to the bunker, and the executions were carried out. The vehicles that carried the corpses to the crematorium left trails of blood on the camp road."

Wladyslaw Fejkiel has also reported about this attempt. Dr. Henryk Suchnicki, a Polish army physician, and Genio Obojski, a vigorous young lad from Warsaw, were summoned together with other inmates and taken to Block 11. Like all experienced inmates, Suchnicki knew what this call meant, very calmly bid his friends farewell, and said, "I won't be such an easy mark; those sons of bitches will be surprised!" He and Obojski are said to have attacked the SS men. Machine-gun fire could be heard in the camp, and that is how the SS ended this action. The *Kalendarium* prepared by the Auschwitz-Birkenau State Museum lists this episode under October 28, 1942.

While the majority of the victims of camp selections were Jews, those shot at the Black Wall were primarily Polish officers and intellectuals.

It will probably never be possible to establish whether the so-called Budy revolt in October 1942 was a desperate attempt at an uprising or a capricious massacre. Because not a single inmate survived, we are dependent on accounts of ss men, and the most detailed report was given by ss Corporal Pery Broad. At that time, the satellite camp Budy housed the women's penal company. German prostitutes were the inmate functionaries, and Jewish women had been assigned to that company. According to Broad, the majority of them were from Poland and the Ukraine, but commandant Höß remembered that they were primarily Frenchwomen. They must have received exceptionally bad treatment even by Auschwitz standards. Broad, who had been ordered to Budy together with other members of the Political Department on the morning after the massacre in order to investigate its causes, has described what he saw there:

> On the ground behind and beside the school building (which housed the penal company), dozens of maimed and blood-encrusted female corpses are lying around helter-skelter, all of them wearing only shabby prisoners' shirts. Among the dead some half-dead women are writhing. Their moans mingle with the buzzing of huge swarms of flies that circle over sticky pools of blood and smashed skulls, and this produces a peculiar kind of singing that initially baffled those who came on the scene. Several corpses are entangled in rigid positions in the barbed wire; others appear to have been pushed out of the open dormer window.

Broad claims to have learned the cause of the massacre from survivors. ss guards goaded the German inmate functionaries into beating the Jewish women. As a result the favored German women had a bad conscience and lived in constant fear that at some future date the women they were torturing would have an opportunity to take revenge and turn them into victims. According to Broad, the massacre was triggered by a German prostitute, Elfriede Schmidt, and an ss guard who was having an affair with her. Maximilian Grabner, the head of the Political Department, also testified that in those days some interned female criminals had forbidden relationships with ss guards. "They were afraid that a Jewish inmate might betray them, and so they staged a revolt and used the opportunity to exterminate the majority of the inmates (Jewish women)." Höß also remembered this massacre: "What the Greens did to those Jewish Frenchwomen! They tore them to pieces, killed them with axes, choked them — simply horrible." The ss closed this case in line with its tradition. The Jewish women who were still alive were murdered on the spot, and six German inmate functionaries were killed by phenol injections on October 24. This saved the camp administration the embarrassing task of reporting guards for breach of duty.

■ All these incidents constitute exceptions to the rule, which was that the overwhelming majority of those who were taken to the gas chambers, the lethal injections, and the Black Wall obeyed their murderers without resisting. In their behavior, no difference based on their nationality or type of imprisonment could be discerned. Eugen Kogon has made some additions to the previously mentioned decisive factors that produced this phenomenon. In his last hours a religious person would feel defiled by the blood of others. A person governed by a sense of political responsibility was probably restrained by the familiar ss system of reprisals that always hit uninvolved people as well. Finally, Kogon believes that "masses never have a will—unless they receive it from the outside or from individuals within their ranks" and that any panic inhibits the mind and the will.

Liebehenschel, the new commandant of Auschwitz, temporarily stopped camp selections, but in January 1944 all Jews were forced to line up again. At that time Dr. Alfred Klahr, a leading Austrian communist who had to wear the Star of David, urged the leaders of the resistance movement to stage a general rebellion in an effort to offer some resistance to the renewed destruction of the Jewish inmates. Though Klahr's opinion carried weight with us, we rejected his proposal. A general uprising would have had no chance of success, for the Russian front was still very far away and the groups of Polish partisans in the neighboring mountains were weak. It would have been possible to make some ss men join us in death, but it was certain that all inmates would be cruelly exterminated, including those who knew nothing of the uprising and would not have participated. We could not assume the responsibility for such consequences. That we had made the right decision was subsequently confirmed by the fact that 60,000 people, including Jews, survived the imprisonment in Auschwitz. However, my conscience was not clear then or later, and it is significant that I did not include in my *Bericht* this episode, which had made a deep impression on me.

■ Even though it was extremely difficult even to think of rebelling against the masters who operated the machinery of destruction in a commanding manner, inmates frequently strove to save acquaintances from destruction. This was often done by bribing ss men. Robert Waitz reports how an inmate suffering from chronic nephritis was spirited out of a transport bound for the gas chambers after Gerhard Neubert, the SDG of Monowitz, had received a bribe of a hundred dollars. Jan Trajster remembers a similar incident: for a bribe of fifty dollars and a liter of schnapps, Neubert removed the name of Zawadzki, a Jew who had been deported from France, from the list of those to be gassed. Leon Stasiak was able to save a North African named Siradien by giving an ss man ten dollars. Evidently bribes were common in Monowitz, but they were possible in Birkenau as well. Barbara Pozimska owes her life to a bribed ss man who took her out of the death block. However, only an inmate who had access to the treasures of Canada was able to help acquaintances in this way.

Carl Laszlo has described how he helped a friend save his son who was stuck in an isolation block together with other selectees. Laszlo's friend had managed to smuggle a diamond into the camp, and with this precious stone Laszlo gained access to that block. "The block elder was a Pole, the block clerk an Austrian Jew. I asked both of them to take me to their room, where I proposed that they release the boy in exchange for the diamond. They didn't seem at all surprised, but examined the stone carefully, nodded to each other, and about ten minutes later I escorted the boy to his father." Laszlo found out how the block functionaries were able to arrange this. They grabbed another inmate on the camp road, and the count was correct again. This indicates the frightful problems that were inevitably connected with many individual rescue actions.

With the aid of a block elder, Jacques Furmanski was able to change an endangered friend temporarily into an "Aryan" and thus keep him out of the selection lineup. "I was trembling with fear that the deception would be revealed. All of us know the punishment: the indiscriminate detention of everyone. A terrible responsibility. At the time I had no clear conception of the risk."

■ The overwhelming majority of those who were murdered in Auschwitz never even entered the camp, for they were escorted to the gas chambers immediately after leaving the trains.

The measures taken by the ss to camouflage their real intentions worked well. From the camps where the victims were put on trains for "resettlement in the East" to the gas chambers, which were made to look like showers, everything was a perfect deception. Rudolf Vrba, who had to work at the ramp for a long time, has addressed this point. "The treatment of new arrivals by the ss was variable; it depended on the condition of the transport that arrived in Auschwitz, but also on the mood of the ss men who were involved. If 10 or 15 percent of the people on the transport had died on the way to Auschwitz, there was not much to conceal, and the newcomers could not be impressed by politeness. Thus the ss treated such people brutally. However, if they gained the impression that the prisoners had no idea of what awaited them in Auschwitz, they treated them with relative courtesy."

Dr. Sigismund Bendel, a survivor of the Sonderkommando, remembers that as late as June 1944 the ss managed to deceive people who had been deported from the ghetto at Lodz. While they were being led to the crematorium, ss

Master Sergeant Moll told them that they were to bathe and that hot coffee would be ready for them afterward. This announcement was greeted with applause. When some children did not want to be put off until later and cried that they were thirsty, the ss had some water brought to them. Bendel emphasizes that "the deception was kept up to the last moment."

Deportees who were not sent to Auschwitz from Poland but from more distant countries, and not as late as mid-1944 but in 1942 and 1943, were much easier marks for such deceptive maneuvers. True, rumors circulated about the gassing facilities and the radio broadcasts of the Allies reported about them, but these reports sounded so improbable that people refused to believe them. Many years later Berlin Jews testified that while British broadcasts had informed them about the extermination of the Jews and they had in this connection heard the word "gassing" for the first time before they were deported to Auschwitz in March 1943, "we did not believe it. There were all kinds of rumors, but the full scope was simply unimaginable."

Despite the harsh visual lesson that they had already received, Jews doing forced labor in the Blechhammer camp, which was not far from Auschwitz, could not believe the rumors about the gas chambers and mass extermination that reached them in 1943. Added to this was the fact that Jewish functionaries who knew about the machinery of destruction did not pass on their information. This is true of the leadership of the Jewish "self-government" in Theresienstadt and the responsible heads of the Jewish organization in Hungary. Both received detailed information about what was going on in Auschwitz by escapees from the camp, but they kept silent even when the deportations from Theresienstadt and Hungary began. Rumkowski, the elder of the Lodz ghetto, went even further as he zealously fostered doubts about the credibility of rumors that spoke of a mass extermination.

This is why Jews from the Lodz ghetto were, as late as mid-1944, as clueless as in Bendel's description. This is why the name Auschwitz did not "stir any memories or evoke any fear" (Elie Wiesel) when they read it at the railroad station. This is why, as Krystyna Zywulska attests, they had no idea what fate awaited them. This is why, as Dov Paisikovic reports, they innocently entered the buildings with the strikingly high smokestacks. The ss camp physician Entress, who was frequently at the ramp before being transferred in October 1943, testified that he had the impression that "many prisoners on transports from the East already knew when they arrived in Auschwitz what was in store for them, and thus there were terrible scenes." Apparently the deceptive maneuvers of the ss worked with others. Thus Thomas Geve reports that in the spring of 1944 Hungarian Jews in Birkenau desperately inquired about the children's camp. When these new arrivals were separated from their children in the selection, the ss calmed them by saying that the children would be housed in a separate children's camp. Every day the women saw flames coming out of the chimneys of the nearby crematoriums and were pursued by the odor of burned human flesh, and yet they refused to believe the truth. Occasionally children were allowed to live, and so the mothers regarded this as an indication that the lies of the SS might be the truth after all.

Only in exceptional instances were inmates who came into contact with new arrivals at the camp able to inform the latter. Since it was impossible to put a guard beside each prisoner, it would have been possible to circumvent the rule that talking was strictly forbidden. However, an inmate could not predict the reaction of a new arrival. Sometimes people were so perturbed by hastily blurted-out information about gas chambers and mass murder that they asked SS guards whether people were really being gassed. Such questions were possible because the SS men, being interested in conducting the selections as smoothly as possible, often did not behave harshly, while the inmates who had to clear the railroad cars were urged to hurry. Any inmate who issued a warning faced a cruel death if the camp administration found out about it. An additional consideration has been pointed out by Tadeusz Borowski: "It is an unwritten law of the camp that human beings who are about to die are lied to until the last moment. That is the only admissible form of compassion."

■ Only someone who did not merely sense or fear the fate that awaited him but knew it precisely could have made a desperate attempt to offer resistance outside the gas chambers. The SS had seen to it that any such attempt was bound to be futile. The area was fenced about with electrified barbed wire and guards stood behind machine guns in the watchtowers. All stages, from detraining to entering the gas chambers, were completed quickly, and the victims were constantly urged forward, which left no time or opportunity for any communication. That left only the possibility of taking one or another henchman with him when an inmate was sure that he was going to be murdered.

Such acts of desperation were committed. The best known of these is the rebellion of the Jews who were transferred from Bergen-Belsen to Auschwitz on October 23, 1943. Those 1,700 Jews, who, according to Höß's testimony in Nuremberg, were predominantly from the East, recognized their situation when they were escorted from the ramp to a crematorium. Höß has described what followed:

A transport from Belsen had arrived. When approximately two-thirds of the prisoners, mostly men, were already in the gas chambers, a mutiny broke out among the other third, who were undressing in an anteroom. Since the inmates on the cremation detail could not cope with this, three or four SS noncommissioned officers entered the room with their weapons in order to speed up the undressing. In the process the electric wires were torn, the SS men were attacked, one was killed, and the others were disarmed. Since that room was completely dark, a wild shooting match developed between the SS guards at the exit and the inmates inside. When I got there, I had the doors locked and the gassing process of the first two-thirds stopped. Then I entered the room with flashlights and the guards, and we herded the inmates into a corner. From there they were taken, one by one, to a room adjoining the crematorium and shot with a small-caliber rifle on my orders.

On that occasion the notorious SS roll call leader Schillinger was so seriously injured that he died on the way to an infirmary in Kattowitz. Wilhelm Emmerich, an SS sergeant, was also wounded and had a limp after his release from the infirmary. Rumor has it that a female dancer wrested an SS man's revolver away from him when he was trying to tear her clothes off. Zelman Lewental believes that this uprising was triggered by a young Jew.

Other acts of desperation at the gas chambers have not been so exhaustively documented. On May 25, 1944, several hundred Hungarian Jews broke out and attempted to hide in the underbrush near the crematoriums and in ditches. Three days later there was another attempt to break out. In both instances the guards used searchlights to ferret out the escapees and shot them. The resistance movement sent a report about this to Cracow.

Efraim Stiebelmann once observed the following event: "A transport from Lodz arrived, and Mengele chose those who would work and those who were to be gassed. A woman with a daughter aged thirteen to fourteen did not want to be separated from her. Mengele ordered a guard to take the girl away from her by force, whereupon the woman attacked the guard, hit him, and scratched his face. Mengele drew his pistol and shot mother and child. I saw this clearly." Stiebelmann also learned about the consequences of this deed. "After that, Mengele also sent the people from the transport who had already been chosen for labor to the gas chambers with these words: 'Away with this shit!'"

Krystyna Zywulska remembers approximately 300 young Jewish women who had been transferred from Majdanek. They were admitted to the camp but taken to a gas chamber at night, probably because they had offered resistance. Zywulska bases her conclusion on statements by the girls, with whom she was able to talk beforehand, and also on the fact that after this action an SS man was seen with a bandaged eye.

How many similarly desperate acts were there to which no one can bear witness? A chronicle that was buried near one of the crematoriums by a member of the Sonderkommando lists acts of resistance and commemorates inmates who went to their death proudly. To be sure, it also records instances in which a person's will to resist was broken in the last moment. Toward the end of 1942 young Jews from Przemysl planned to attack their murderers, and they had already concealed knives in their sleeves. A physician from the same transport betrayed this plan to the SS. After a guard had assured him that he had thereby saved his life and that of his wife, the physician reassured the young men, whereupon they stripped without making use of their weapons. When they were all in the "showers," the SS also pushed in the physician and his wife. Then the door to the gas chamber was locked.

SS camp leader Franz Hofmann, who supervised numerous acts of extermination, put it concisely when he said on October 24, 1961: "Naturally there were disturbances among the inmates who had been selected to die. Then I had to intervene in order to restore law and order."

■ The idea of ending one's life and thus all tortures and degradations suggested itself in Auschwitz. Bruno Bettelheim, who did not have first-hand experience of extermination camps, extended the idea of suicide greatly when he called the docility of the inmates who let themselves be taken to the gas chambers without resisting "a form of suicide that does not require the energy normally needed to decide on it and plan it." Bettelheim argues that, "from a psychological point of view, most inmates in the extermination camps committed suicide by going to their death without resisting."

I have reservations about this theory, for I observed too often how despite the obvious hopelessness *Muselmänner* tried everything imaginable to get out of selections or attempted to improve their appearance by slapping one another's faces to get red cheeks. Only when all their efforts had failed did they allow themselves to be led impassively to their death.

If one does not define suicide as loosely as does Bettelheim, there were fewer suicides in Auschwitz than one might assume. Carl Laszlo writes that suicides were extremely rare in the camp, "possibly because that would have been too cowardly." The psychiatrist Paul Matussek reports that 10 percent of the survivors interviewed by him said they had thought of committing suicide in the camp. Hannah Arendt calls the rarity of suicides in the concentration camps astonishing and attributes this to "the destruction of individuality after the murder of the moral person and the extermination of the juristic person." Those who made their observations in a camp express this more concretely. Wladyslaw Fejkiel gives the following reason for the small number of suicides: "This fact may be explained by the systematic starvation. A starving person is indifferent to the problem of death and incapable of attempting suicide. The few suicides in Auschwitz that are known to me were committed by inmates who were hardly emaciated."

Benedikt Kautsky has a different explanation for the same phenomenon: "A striking observation that I made of myself and that was confirmed by a number of comrades was that at a point where I thought I would have to collapse for physical or moral reasons my instinct for self-preservation appeared in the guise of defiance. 'Surely you aren't going to do those pigs the favor of killing yourself!' This was an argument that one applied not only to others but much more effectively to oneself."

Georges Wellers supplements Kautsky's reflections by pointing out that, according to his observations, many inmates, apart from personal motives, clung to life so they might bear witness at a later date. Simon Laks confirms this for himself: "I had firmly resolved not to go to my death willingly, come what might. I wanted to see everything, go through everything, experience everything, absorb everything. To what purpose, when I would never have an opportunity to scream the result of my discoveries out to the world? Simply because I did not want to exclude myself, exclude the witness that I could be."

In investigating the reasons for the small number of suicides, Kautsky evidently has politically aware inmates in mind and Fejkiel the average kind. Their arguments supplement each other and overlap. Where an encounter with death was a daily occurrence, the quest for death lost its special and possibly seductive nature.

Nevertheless, prisoners did end their lives—more frequently in the early years of utter hopelessness than toward the end of the war. To them, a form of suicide suggested itself that was the surest and required the least energy: "going into the wire." In front of the electrically charged barbed wire that fenced the camps in there was a death zone. Anyone who entered it was shot at from the watchtowers, and those who were not hit were sure to be killed by contact with the wire. Tadeusz Paczula reports that in the early period of Auschwitz, when the inmates had to stand during the long roll calls after hard work, shots frequently rang out. They were aimed at those who had gone into the wire. In those days suicides aroused "no attention, no one was surprised, no one felt sorry for anyone else, and the general indifference allowed no emotions to develop."

At a later date, when the machinery of destruction was in place in Auschwitz, Josef Neumann had to make a daily inspection of the fences surrounding the sections of the Birkenau camp. As a corpse carrier, he had to collect the dead bodies. This is what he wrote about it: "As a rule, those who ran into the fence at night were suicides. Their numbers varied. It was very high in transports from Holland, and I remember that at one time it rose to thirty. There were fewer from the Slovak transports, perhaps five to ten. Eight to twelve probably was the daily average. Most of those who ran into the wire were newcomers, but there were also some who had been in the camp for some time."

Josef Neumann had to rely on his memory when he gave these figures twenty years later, but the physician Otto Wolken kept statistics in the camp that he was able to conceal. They cover the quarantine section, where the new arrivals characterized by Neumann and others as especially prone to commit suicide were sent, and the period between September 20, 1943, and November 1, 1944. Of a total of 1,902 inmates recorded as dead, only two are listed as having been electrocuted and one as having been strangled. The other modes of death registered by Wolken do not indicate suicide. It is, of course, possible that Neumann's figures refer to a period before the fall of 1943 because Simon Laks and René Coudy also report that in the summer of 1942 shots could frequently be heard in Birkenau at night. They describe the reactions of Poles with low numbers when Jews in the camp orchestra took their lives: "When the number of musicians who had committed suicide the night before was higher than usual, one of these gentlemen called us together and said: 'You sons of bitches, I warn you. If you continue to run into the wire, I'll kill all of you like dogs!'"

There is conflicting information about suicides in the Theresienstadt family camp. While Jehuda Bacon, who was a child at the time, remembers that the number of suicides there was high immediately after their arrival in Auschwitz but declined afterward, Hanna Hoffmann, who made her observations as an adult, states that only a small number of inmates went into the wire. Only when this hitherto privileged special camp was about to be liquidated did many inmates break down and carry out their threat (to commit suicide).

In some cases the proximate cause of suicide is known. Aron Bejlin, a physician interned in Birkenau, was asked by a Dutch physician who had just arrived in the camp where he could meet his wife and children, from whom he had been separated. Bejlin told his colleague the truth, which the Dutchman at first did not believe; but when he was able to confirm it, he touched the electrified fence. Vera Alexander remembers a Hungarian Jew who was able to smuggle her small child into the camp. When the SS took it away from her, she went into the wire at night.

Other forms of suicide have been reported as well. Maurice Schelleken remembers that a Dutch physician took poison which he had been able to smuggle into the camp and conceal. Pery Broad writes the following about Russian prisoners of war who were forced to build Birkenau in the winter of 1941–42: "Hunger drove people insane. Every evening wagon loads of corpses were taken to the Auschwitz crematorium. Half-dead inmates who were no longer able to endure the indescribable torment voluntarily crept onto these wagons and were killed like cattle."

Even after the end of the early and most terrible period of the new camp, some cases of that type of suicide were recorded. Charlotte Delbo observed women who voluntarily went to Block 25, where the victims of camp selections had to wait for transportation to a gas chamber. When an SS man came to inspect this death block, which was normally locked tight, they slipped in behind him. A Czech inmate who wanted to die wangled his way twice into the selectees. Friends saved him both times. He survived his time in the camp.

Dounia Ourisson-Wasserstrom has reported the following incident: "One day I walked through a barracks and saw naked corpses on the floor. Something was stirring among the dead; it was a young girl who was not naked. I pulled her out to the camp road and asked her, 'Who are you?' She answered that she was a Greek Jew from Saloniki. 'How long have you been here?' 'I don't know.' 'Why are you here?' 'I can't live with the living any more, and so I want to be with the dead.' I gave her a piece of bread. In the evening she was dead." Two Yugoslav women are said to have committed suicide in Brody by jumping into a cesspool and drowning.

Can the following incident reported by Feinstein also be described as a suicide? One day the penal company did not march off to work but was ordered to stand in front of the block. SS block leader Eckardt ordered the block elder to supply fifty corpses by evening because space was needed for new arrivals. Emil, the capo, a notorious murderer who wore a green triangle, asked the waiting inmates whether anyone was tired of living. "Volunteers, come forward! I'll do it quickly, cleanly, and painlessly!" According to Feinstein, a few dozen inmates came forward. "The first one was a sixteen-year-old lad from Prague. He bent over a stool and said gently, 'Capo, do it fast!' The capo's club came down on the boy's neck. 'Next!'" This happened in February 1943.

Sometimes special circumstances caused the suicide of inmates who were safe because of their good positions in the camp. The German capos Reinhold Wienhold and Walter Walterscheid took their lives in the bunker, evidently because they feared that they would be tortured by the Political Department. On October 27, 1944, when the attempted escape of the Austrian Ernst Burger, a leader of the resistance movement, and of three Poles had been betrayed, all of them took the poison that they had prudently procured, for they knew that anyone subjected to the inhuman torture of the Political Department might break down. Being anxious to interrogate prisoners who had tried to escape, the SS immediately ordered that the stomachs of these men be pumped out, but in the case of the Poles Zbigniew Raynoch and Czeslaw Duzel it was too late. In the summer of 1943 Orli Reichert, the camp elder in the infirmary of the women's camp, attempted to kill herself. After friends had brought her back to life, she explained that she could no longer endure the constant sight of death.

Perhaps Anna Sussmann has given the clearest answer to the question why the number of suicides was surprisingly low, and thereby the clearest refutation of Bettelheim's thesis. In 1944 she was lying in the infirmary and had reason to fear selection, which primarily involved Jewish women. This is how she described her feelings: "My heart said honestly and deliberately that it would be better if they took *me* rather than anyone else, but at the same time I found myself wishing that I might be lucky once more and not be gassed yet. 'Just don't let them catch you!' cried a passionate voice inside me. How did it happen that I had two wishes at the same time? Yet in those days my condition was such that I would have greeted death as a welcome friend." A short time before this she had given birth to a child that had been taken away from her and murdered.

The following sentences from a document that Zelman Lewental buried near a crematorium could be deciphered: ". . . What does not distinguish them is the fact that every person is governed in his subconscious by a psychic will to live and an endeavor to live and survive. A person makes himself believe that he is not concerned with his own self but only with the general welfare. He would like to survive for one reason or another, out of one consideration or another, and for this purpose he invents hundreds of excuses. And the truth is that one wants to stay alive at any price."

One fact has been confirmed by all prisoners who experienced bombardments by Allied planes. The inmates did not fear them even though they were not allowed to go into shelters. Elie Wiesel is among those who described how the inmates rejoiced when the Buna Works were bombed, though their barracks shook and a direct hit would have caused hundreds of casualties. "Every bomb that exploded filled us with joy and made us trust life again," he writes. Erich Kohlhagen remembers that the bombing of the Buna Works on August 20, 1944, killed thirty-eight inmates and wounded numerous others. Krystyna Zywulska describes the first air-raid alarm that sounded in the women's camp as "the most beautiful music." When the immediate vicinity of the camp was bombed for the first time and the barracks shook, the prisoners prayed for the longest possible duration of the bombardment.

MUSIC AND GAMES
■ ■ ■

Death was as much of an everyday phenomenon as chronic hunger, and bloody tracks on the camp road did not attract much attention; but in the same camp concerts were given. When Auschwitz was built, it was already a tradition of the Nazi concentration camps to form an orchestra of inmates. It had to play marches when the labor columns marched out and in—not only because the ss cared about adding a pseudomilitary touch to camp life, but also because this kind of music helped the prisoners to march through the gate briskly and in precisely aligned rows of five, which enabled the ss to make an easy count.

As early as January 6, 1941, inmates started rehearsing in Block 24 with instruments that they had been permitted to receive from their homes. Because the camp at that time housed Poles, among whom there were enough qualified musicians, the orchestra was composed of Poles.

In keeping with the camp administration's need for prestige, the orchestra not only played in the camp after the morning roll call and before the evening roll call but also gave concerts, which usually took place on Sundays in front of the commandant's villa. To enable the musicians to practice, they were given a rehearsal room in Block 24. Soon these rehearsals led to concerts for the prisoners as well. Tadeusz Borowski has described such a rehearsal: "The concert hall is directly under the brothel in Block 24. It was rather crowded and noisy. The audience stood along the walls; the musicians were scattered throughout the room, sat wherever they could find a space, and tuned their instruments. Opposite the window there was a small raised podium. Doubling as a conductor, the kitchen capo climbed up on it, and the potato peelers and that guy from the truck (oh, I forgot: the musicians usually peel potatoes and drive trucks) started playing."

Jerzy Brandhuber has described the effect of a concert:

Sunday evening; in the background the kitchen, a building with a mansard roof and a flower garden next to it. At the stand the musicians, inmates in white suits with red braids. A big symphony orchestra, as hard-working as may be found anywhere, with breaks only for page-turning. And all around a crowd as in a spa, only it is white and blue, a crowd standing right across the road.

And then there were informal concerts. On rainy Sundays the orchestra did not play outside. Quiet in the concert hall; only a few persons sit or stand around forlornly.

At the piano a Hungarian virtuoso. As a Jew he is not permitted to play in the orchestra, and so he plays when the music room is vacant. He actually plays for himself. He wears a shabby suit, the white and blue kind, and he plays and plays. When I look out the window, I forget; I don't see the red walls or the comrades walking outside. He plays Mozart, Beethoven, Schubert, Bach. And then he suddenly intones Chopin's Funeral March. When he stops, he sits motionless with his hands on the keys. All of us understand one another.

I have frequently heard others express the words with which Brandhuber concludes his report: "That was the only moment at which I forgot the camp around me." Thomas Geve writes that there can be no other place where one could feel the effect of music more deeply. He was thirteen when he listened to concerts in Auschwitz. On more than one occasion I stood in that rehearsal hall and felt more clearly than ever before or afterward the power of music, which proclaimed that there was a human world beyond Auschwitz, which was able to put individual features on the faces of the listeners, which managed to dissolve the inert, gray mass that constantly surrounded us, which helped to keep inmates from drowning in the everyday life of the extermination camp.

The Polish percussionist Czeslaw Sowul remains unforgotten. Every movement of his always lively face spread good humor. The jokes that he always had at the ready gained him a certain fool's privilege from the ss, and he skillfully exploited it.

■ The fame of the Auschwitz orchestra goaded the leaders of the other camps into action. Soon orchestras were playing in the men's and women's camps of Birkenau, in Monowitz, in Golleschau (which had more than twenty instruments and put on concerts for the ss garrison), and in Blechhammer. An orchestra formed in the Gypsy camp achieved renown.

The most graphic description was given by Simon Laks and René Coudy, members of the Birkenau camp orchestra that was founded in the summer of 1942. Because that camp did not have so many Polish musicians, the ban on Jewish members, mentioned above, was not enforced, though the capo had to be an "Aryan." "He was given his position on the basis of his presumed German nationality," write Laks and Coudy. "Of course he constantly browbeat us Jewish musicians, gave us the most improbable orders, and made our hard life even harder. The nucleus of our orchestra consisted of about fifteen inmates that had been sent from Auschwitz I, where there had been a big orchestra for a long time. These had numbers between 2,000 and 16,000 and thus were absolute masters over us novices. Most of them made unrestrained use of their power." In the early period the members of the orchestra were subject to the periodic camp selections. Laks and Coudy give a clear account of the changes made in the course of time: "Our splendid music room has become a mecca for the SS and the VIPs of the camp. Almost every evening jolly tunes may be heard in our block. There is singing and dancing. The SS puts on ostentatious birthday celebrations, and the men have the inmates serve them schnapps." The authors do not say that the inmates also had to "organize" this booze, for this is self-evident to any "Auschwitzer."

An orchestra was established in the Birkenau women's camp as well. Since the head of the camp, Maria Mandel, was a music lover, this orchestra could be conducted by Alma Rosé, a Jew. Her father had been the concertmaster of the Vienna Philharmonic and founder of the world-famous Rosé Quartet. Alma, who continued the family tradition, married a Dutchman and was deported from Holland in 1943. In Auschwitz she was housed in the experimental Block 10. When the birthday celebration of a VIP was being planned, a request for a violinist was made. Rosé came forward. Her virtuoso playing so impressed the female wardens in attendance that they told the head of the camp about her. She arranged for Rosé to be transferred to the women's camp and appointed her the conductor of the orchestra.

Even in Auschwitz Alma Rosé remained an artist with all her soul. She turned those female instrumentalists into an orchestra that programmed works by Verdi and Chopin, Strauß and Tchaikovsky. Uncompromising in orchestrating and rehearsing this music, she was always on the lookout for new scores and instruments. According to Seweryna Szmaglewska, Rosé "conducts calmly, as though she were seeing nothing around her. She is controlled, and her graceful movements seem to be devoted only to the music." Alica Jakubovic, a camp messenger who was able to listen to rehearsals, asserts that she never loved music as much as she did when Alma Rosé was playing. Manca Svalbova has described her friend in these words: "She lived in another world. Music to her meant her love and her disappointments, her sorrow and her joys, her eternal longing and her faith, and this music floated high above the camp atmosphere." "She was not only a famous artist but also a wonderful comrade," write Laks and Coudy.

We owe the following description of the women's orchestra to Lucie Adelsberger:

Music was something like a lapdog of the camp administration, and the participants were clearly in its good graces. Their block was even better tended than the clerk's office or the kitchen. Food was plentiful, and the girls from the orchestra were neatly attired in blue cloth dresses and caps.

The musicians were quite busy; they played at the roll call, and the women who were returning from work exhausted had to march to the rhythm of the music. Music was ordered for all official occasions: the speeches of the SS camp leaders, transports, and hangings. In between, the musicians served to entertain the SS and the inmates in the infirmary. In the women's camp the orchestra played in the infirmary every Tuesday and Friday afternoon undisturbed by all the goings-on and selections around it.

Even though Alma Rosé was in a far less favorable position than her colleague in the main camp, the Polish kitchen capo Nierychlo, she did not curry favor with the camp administration as obsequiously as her male counterpart. On the contrary: sometimes she stopped the music because female SS guards were loudly conversing and laughing. When friends warned her that she might be punished for this, her response was brief: "I can't make music that way." The guards quietly took note of this rebuke by inmate Rosé.

Manca Svalbova has likened Rosé to a bird that cannot get used to being confined in a cage and repeatedly bloodies its wings. The camp also took into its grasp this sensitive artist, who lived in a world of music as if on an island in the sea of the Birkenau barracks. Alma Rosé died on April 4, 1944. The day before she had still been healthy. Legends have formed around her death. Some people believe that she poisoned herself. Rosé had frequently visited the Theresienstadt family camp; when its inmates were gassed a few weeks before her death, she was a broken woman. Others claim that she was poisoned by jealous inmate functionaries.

■ Music exerted its effects even in camps in which no orchestra played. Lex van Weren, who had been transferred together with other Dutch Jews to the Jawischowitz coal mine, where there were particularly harsh working conditions, was pulled out of the labor detail by the camp elder when he discovered that van Weren, a professional jazz trumpeter, could play the French horn that the elder had "organized" for himself. At Christmastime Lex had to play "Silent Night, Holy Night" for the SS roll call leader all evening long. As a reward he was assigned to barracks duty and did not need to go down into the mine. After some time only fifteen of the 300 Jews who had come to Jawischowitz with van Weren were still alive—among them Lex van Weren, whose artistry and French horn had saved his life.

Seweryna Szmaglewska tells about a fifteen-year-old Greek girl named Alegri who had a wonderful voice and whom her superiors frequently asked to sing while she worked. "Alegri starts singing, and the first word of her song, which now resounds over the ponds and meadows of Upper Silesia, is 'Mama.' It sounds exactly the way it sounds on all Polish lips and has the accent to which Polish ears are accustomed. And this word, in which lie longing and love and an outcry, keeps recurring in the refrain."

Szmaglewska has committed to memory another Greek tune as well: "Alegri sings another song. It begins with the words 'O thalme chasis,' which are said to mean 'Oh, come back!' A song of longing. The word 'nostalgia' recurs several times. The song is exceptionally melodious, and its semitones of mourning and longing speak to all of us." Alegri perished in Auschwitz; music was not able to save her life.

Zofia Posmysz has described a woman in the satellite camp Budy who because of her beautiful voice was called the "Singer." She had to sing for the SS guards their favorite songs. "One day a Latvian sentry gave her the rest of his noonday soup and advised her to wash her face with urine to keep her fair complexion and protect her face from the strong sun. Another time an SS corporal asked her how old she was and for what reason she had been sent to Auschwitz." Posmysz points out how unusual such a personal interest in an inmate was. Although the "Singer" was in the penal company, she was exempted from the hardest labor. In return the Polish woman had to learn the German text of the songs and sing them during work breaks.

Emilio Jani, an Italian singer, was also given privileged treatment because of his voice, and thus he titled his memoir "I Was Saved by My Voice."

The concerts of classical music in Block 24 made a profound impression on me, but when I think of music in Auschwitz, banal songs also come to mind. The unusual situation in which I heard them probably contributed to the deep impression they made. I had to await my fate in a bunker cell. For a while another cell housed a German who would sing when the sound of doors and keys indicated that no SS man was in the cellar. He evidently sang while standing close to the door of his cell, for his voice was quite audible. Soulfully and sobbingly he kept singing "Have you up there forgotten about me?" Since then this melody [from a Lehár operetta] has never failed to evoke for me the atmosphere of the bunker in Auschwitz. When I was sent to the bunker, a simple hit song grabbed me the way a piece of serious music rarely has. This is what I wrote about it:

> Now they've got me, and I am utterly defenseless. The sounds from a radio come blaring in through the window. The guard room must be above me.
>
> Shall I get out of here alive? What shall I have to go through until that day comes?
>
> I walk up and down. After all, I have always prepared myself for this eventuality, and I have always known that I was taking risks. When four million have died in Auschwitz, I shall know how to die as well. The shadow of the barred window slowly creeps along the wall.

I sit down. Oh, it'll be hard. The radio plays a new song; the first measures are soft and enticing, and then a female voice can be heard. It sounds quite close: "Franzl, all of Vienna sends you greetings . . ." All of Vienna sends you greetings! I am hot and lie down on the blankets.

It's probably an ordinary tearjerker, but I feel as though I said farewell while listening to this song.

■ In Auschwitz there was not only music-making but sports as well. As early as spring 1941 soccer games were played in the main camp. Tadeusz Borowski has described a soccer field in a section of Birkenau that was adjacent to the crematoriums. Jehuda Bacon, a child at the time, played there, and on one occasion so did the dreaded block leader Stefan Baretzki. Siegfried Halbreich tells about soccer matches in the Monowitz indoctrination camp. It goes without saying that only better-nourished inmates were able to participate in sports. Marc Klein remembers soccer battles between well-nourished VIPs that were often watched by SS men.

Games were even played in the courtyard of the crematorium. Miklos Nyiszli describes a game of SS against SK—that is, guards versus inmates on the Sonderkommando. Nyiszli reports that the spectators got excited, laughed, and screamed as at any playing field in the world.

The SS most consistently supported boxing. Teddy Pietrzykowski, a Polish amateur, was probably the best-known boxer in the main camp. On a work-free Sunday in the spring of 1941, German capos boxed and SS men watched. After the capo Walter, a professional boxer, had beaten his partners, new ones were sought, and this was the incentive: "Anyone who boxes with Walter will get bread." Teddy came forward and forced Walter to give up. Walter gave him not only bread but also margarine and sausage, and he saw to it that Teddy was assigned to a "nourishing" detail: the cow shed. The SS men became fired up and "organized" real boxing gloves; the head of the kitchen detail, an enthusiastic spectator, rewarded Teddy after each fight with a kettle of soup. Teddy estimates that he boxed against thirty or forty persons in Auschwitz. SS men watched regularly and made bets. When Teddy was put on a transport to Neuengamme in the spring of 1943, the head of the kitchen detail gave him boxing gloves, and Teddy actually did some boxing in Neuengamme as well.

Tadeusz Borowski has provided a description of what may have been a bout between the capo Walter and Teddy. He recalls a conversation among spectators while a German capo named Walter was fighting a Pole in the old laundry: "Look. At work he (Walter) floors a *Muselmann* with one blow if he wants to, and here—three rounds and nothing. And he even got punched in the mouth. Too many spectators, it seems, huh?"

Boxing bouts were put on in the satellite camp Janina as well, and Max Kasner remembers that these were the hobby of Kleemann, the ss camp leader. In the summer of 1944 the gentlemen from the mine administration watched a bout. ss roll call leader Wilhelm Claussen, who was responsible for the sports activities of the garrison, boasted when he was an American prisoner of war that he had promoted boxing among the inmates; he tried to present himself in a good light by saying, "Didn't I sit among them at almost every bout, and didn't they breathe a sigh of relief when I entered the ring myself?" To the inmates who participated, such bouts brought very concrete advantages — namely, additional food rations.

At a later date the camp administration also organized the showing of films. I saw Zarah Leander for the first time in Auschwitz, though I remember the overcrowded room and the stifling bad air more distinctly than the actress or the movie. Thomas Geve, who was almost a child at the time, has described the effect of a film on him. The very different world of elegance and the family life depicted in it made the greatest impression on him. As a Jew he would have been barred from such showings, but through the good offices of a German criminal he was able to watch. Geve remembers that only Germans and Poles received tickets at the time. Marc Klein concludes his description of a screening with these words: "How little a person needs to free himself from the anxieties of the world that surrounds him, no matter how cruel these may be!"

Only Louise Alcan has supplied a different reaction to showings of films. She writes that half of the female inmates of Rajsko declined to attend such a showing. Hössler, the head of the camp, who was in attendance, is said to have asked the women afterward whether they were satisfied now. Alcan believes that Hössler was trying to mock the inmates or divert them from dangerous thoughts, but I don't agree. Sometimes devilish intentions are read into every measure of the ss. On the basis of my experience I feel that the shrewdness of the ss should not be overestimated and that the indifference and thoughtlessness born of total desensitization as well as the effects of bureaucratic schematism should not be underestimated. I believe that screenings, sport events, and concerts were organized because every camp administration responded to a need for prestige and none wanted to be outdone by another. Films and projectors were available to the garrison, and so it took no additional effort to use them in the camp as well.

I have precise knowledge of one incident. One day posters were affixed in the inmates' quarters on which a big louse was depicted with these words in German and Polish: "A louse — your death." This poster is frequently described as the height of mockery, for the death that the poster warned against was repeatedly dealt the inmates by the ss. I know the background. The superior of the SS garrison physician was pressing for a vigorous fight against the typhus epidemic in Auschwitz that had spread to the garrison and the civilian population. Since this illness is carried by lice, the infestation of lice had to be eliminated. The SS garrison physician wanted to gain the cooperation of the prisoners and asked me one day whether we should not prepare a poster calling for war on lice. I reacted positively because I wanted this project to add another inmate to our good commando. In this way we actually managed to get the Polish artist Zbigniew Raynoch, generally called Zbyszek, as a draftsman. Designing the poster was his first task, and later he was given other graphic assignments. Zbyszek stayed with us, which means that the poster helped a prisoner.

■ Soccer, boxing bouts, Zarah Leander behind electrified barbed wire, Beethoven concerts by inmates for inmates in the extermination camp — it may be that some who learn about this cannot comprehend that the victims were prepared to listen to music and watch movies in Auschwitz. Anyone who does not approve of this would logically have to blame the prisoners for not committing suicide, for the instinct of survival makes a person seek diversion wherever this is possible.

To be sure, for the gray mass of pariahs there were neither movies nor sports nor concerts.

CANADA

■ ■ ■

"Organizing," the name given to the appropriation of institutional property that had not yet been distributed, was part of the tradition of the Nazi concentration camps. It offered the guards a welcome opportunity to enrich themselves, and the prisoners had to "organize" if they did not want to perish.

Jean Améry has described the dilemma faced by everyone: "Inmates always had to be clean-shaven, but it was strictly forbidden to own a shaving kit, and visits to the barber were possible only every other week. A missing button on a garment with zebra stripes was punishable, but if one was lost at work, which was unavoidable, it was virtually impossible to replace it."

Georges Wellers enumerates an inmate's options if he lost his cap. He either had to steal a comrade's or have a friend whose position gave him an opportunity to "organize" one. Without a cap an inmate was subject to beatings and punishments that might spell his end.

Emil Bednarek has described the same problem from the perspective of a block elder. "During the night the inmates stole one another's shoes or cut the buttons off the coats. In the barracks they bloodied one another, and in such cases I gave beatings to both factions. When the inmates marched off and an ss man standing next to the block leader's room ascertained that someone's coat had no buttons, the block elder was called and given a beating."

Primo Levi, who gathered his experiences in Monowitz, as did Améry and Wellers, has given this graphic description of the practice that developed from this necessity to "organize":

In accordance with camp regulations shoes have to be blacked and polished every morning, and the ss holds every block elder responsible for the observance of this regulation by every inmate of his block. This would lead one to assume that every block is periodically given a supply of shoe polish. This is not the case, however; there is an entirely different mechanism. I must point out that in the evening every block receives a quantity of soup that is significantly larger than the sum of the regular rations. The surplus is distributed at the discretion of the block elder, who first takes care of his friends and protégés and gives appropriate portions to the sweeper, the night watchmen, the lice inspectors, and all other VIP functionaries of the block. The remainder (and every conscientious block elder sees to it that something is always left) is used to make purchases. Everything else follows logically.

Those inmates who have an opportunity in Buna to fill their mess bowl with grease or lubricating oil (or something else, for any blackish or fatty substance is deemed suitable) go from block to block after they return in the evening until they find a block elder who is out of this article or who wants to stock up on it. For the rest, almost every block has its own supplier, who is paid a daily rate for delivering the grease whenever stocks are low.

Another example from the main camp will illustrate how even the most conscientious block elders were forced to "organize." Inmates there were quartered in brick houses, and the block leaders always checked to see if everything was clean and the walls in the rooms and corridors were not scratched. If scratches were found, punitive drills, withholding of food, and the like were ordered.

In the camp everything had to be done quickly. In the morning a prisoner had to try to be the first in the washroom in order to find a space. Inmates had to line up quickly for the roll call because stragglers were threatened with a beating. When food was distributed, it was advantageous to find a place at the head of the line, since this offered a better chance of getting a second helping. Up to a thousand inmates lived in a block. The hallways were narrow, and because of the constant pushing and crowding, a consequence of the never-ending hurrying and scurrying, the walls became scratched and dirty in short order. A good block elder had to see to it that his block was repainted before any punishments were meted out. However, he never received paint officially; it was easy for him to "organize" it, for there were plenty of labor details that were given it. But a block elder needed some form of payment, and only one was available to him: the rations that were delivered to the block.

De Wind described how a block that had been newly assigned to the infirmary was painted: "The paint for the beds and doors was paid for with bread and margarine, and the patients received that much less." This sort of thing was certainly not done stealthily. SS roll call leader Oswald Kaduk gave the following example to the Frankfurt court. "If a block elder stopped by the block leader's room to request permission to leave the camp and said, 'I'd like to go to the painters to 'organize' paint for my block,' I let him go."

A block elder who wanted to spare his charges bullying and punishment also had to bribe the block leader. If the latter was taken care of by the former, he was willing to listen. Under these circumstances a block elder was sorely tempted to put some of the food rations aside not only for purposes that served everyone but also for himself and his protégés.

The former German block elder Emil de Martini reports with unsparing frankness that starting from the block elder down to the block barber so much of the food rations was diverted that these men had enough. "There also were block elders who cut their block leaders in on the looting, and at each distribution of portions they slipped them four or five packages of margarine at the expense of the inmates." Emil Bednarek, the block elder of the penal company, was reproached with dividing a loaf of bread into five or even six portions rather than four. De Martini explained how this could be managed: "Anyone who dared to lodge a complaint against a capo or a block elder inevitably went up the chimney."

■ The same block elder who heedlessly curtailed the rations was honestly outraged and acted harshly if a bread thief was caught in his block. The morality of the camp decreed that already distributed bread could no longer be "organized," and any infringer was persecuted as a transgressor against camaraderie.

Rudolf Vrba has described the conditions in Block 18, where thefts of bread were common: "We lived among wolves, in a pack of famished, merciless wolves." He tells what happened when inmates took the law into their own hands:

It was night. Suddenly a cry of despair and a scream rang out: "My bread . . . my bread!" We heard the shuffling of half a dozen feet, a dull thud, a jumble of soft imprecations, and an outcry that was stifled and became a moan. Then, silence. In the narrow passage between the bunks I saw a blurry figure lying face down. An elderly inmate in the bunk below mine bent forward and observed everything with silent curiosity. "What's going on?" I asked him.

"Some dirty pig stole a *Muselmann*'s bread. The poor devil was too weak to get up and take it back."

"And what happened then? Did the others beat him up?"

"They beat him to death, of course. There is no point in just beating such a bastard." This was the law in Block 18: if a man stole your food, he was killed. If you were not strong enough to execute the judgment yourself, there were executioners. It was a brutal justice, but it was just, for robbing a man of his food was murder.

Yet even the harshest justice could not completely contain theft. Olga Lengyel indicates that some inmates achieved perfection in stealing: "Mothers from respectable families who would never have been capable of appropriating anything at all steal here without the slightest scruple." Once a spoon was stolen from her by the wife of one of the wealthiest Hungarian industrialists. Lengyel concludes that "only a person possessed of extraordinary moral strength was able to keep his instincts in check in Birkenau." Macha Ravine observed women who once occupied a worthy place in society grimly fighting for tatters of dresses. The Pole Józef Stemler reports about a public prosecutor who stole bread from a peasant, and I remember clergymen who also became bread thieves.

The following observation by Eugen Kogon applies not only to Buchenwald: "There were plenty of directors and high government officials who as inmates of a KL, even when they didn't really need to do so, pounced on buckets filled with potato peels in order to obtain scraps of food, or who became bread thieves."

It was not just the general demoralization and the naked struggle for existence that brought human beings to that point. "Can a person understand what it means to have a cold without a handkerchief or diarrhea without a piece of paper?" This question by Erich Altmann may indicate the compulsion that gripped those who misappropriated the possessions of their comrades.

■ In Auschwitz the corruption, the system of "organizing" that dominated all camps, assumed unimaginable dimensions, for in the extermination camp there was Canada. Among the possessions of the deported Jews that were taken from them at the ramp there were (frequently concealed) valuables of all kinds. Before the luggage was sorted and registered, anyone was free to appropriate whatever he liked; this applied to both inmates and the SS. All he had to do was to gain access to Canada and find a way of taking the appropriated objects away. In this endeavor members of the SS and inmates had to cooperate because an inmate who was "organizing" had to bribe an SS man not to check him and an SS man who wanted to appropriate something in Canada needed the aid of prisoners, since he could not rummage through the mountains of goods and choose something without being noticed. Otto Graf, who worked for a time in the financial section of the garrison administration, gave a Viennese court an impressive description of conditions. His job was to sort and count the money that had been taken from new arrivals at the camp. "Trunkfuls of money came in, and someone had to step on the bills, forcing them down, before the trunk could be closed." One can imagine how easy it was for people to help themselves before the trunks were full.

To be sure, opportunities were quite variable. A guard in a watchtower had to settle for scraps, while an SS man whose function gave him access to the camp found ways of getting to Canada. A member of the labor detail that had contact with Canada was able to help himself if he was smart enough to take care of all those who were privy to the practice. Inmates who worked on details like SS Kitchen or Slaughterhouse were able to get hold of barter objects that helped them obtain goods from Canada. Those who worked in the gravel pit or on road construction were excluded from "organizing." Inmates whose work gave them freedom of movement were able to reach Canada on secret paths, but every avenue there was blocked for the anonymous inmates who were never able to escape the control of their superiors. While such inmates desperately rummaged through the garbage in search of something edible, VIPs in privileged positions spurned the camp cuisine.

The social gradation that I encountered in Dachau and Neuengamme and that lifted a functionary far above the gray mass of nameless inmates shrinks into insignificance if one compares it with the difference between a VIP in Auschwitz and a *Muselmann*.

Höß has given the following description of conditions in Auschwitz:

> The Jews' valuables created enormous and insurmountable difficulties for the camp. They were demoralizing for the SS men, who were not always strong enough to resist the temptation of the readily accessible valuables. Even the death penalty and severe prison sentences were not sufficient deterrents. For the inmates the Jewish valuables opened up undreamt-of opportunities, and most attempts to escape are probably connected with this. With the easily obtained money as well as watches, rings, and the like, anything could be procured from SS men and civilian workers. Alcohol, smokes, food, false papers, weapons, and ammunition were everyday matters. In Birkenau male inmates gained access to the women's camp at night, and they even bought off some guards. Naturally, this had a bad effect on the general discipline in the camp. Those in possession of valuables were able to buy better workplaces, the sympathy of capos and block elders, and even long stays in the infirmary with the best of care. Despite the strictest supervision it was impossible to rectify this situation. The Jewish gold was a disaster for the camp.

The only thing missing in this graphic description is the fact that the general corruption could not be kept in check because even the commandant helped himself with both hands.

Ota Kraus and Erich Kulka have described from an inmate's perspective Canada's impact in Birkenau, where it was strongest because the barracks that housed Canada directly adjoined that complex of camps.

> Many precious things were hidden in the clothes and shoes left behind by the destroyed Jewish transports. The Canada inmates who sorted those objects brought secretly and daringly very valuable things into the camp. In

return for these they received food, clothes, shoes, alcohol, and cigarettes that were smuggled into the camp by civilian employees and ss men. An inmate who was doing some "organizing" was instantly recognizable, for he was better dressed and better nourished. This, to be sure, was exploited by the ss men and the inmate leadership. They persecuted such "organizers," checked up on them, and blackmailed them. Thus a veritable system of bribery developed that was based on the law of the jungle. In their work details capos had whole groups of inmates who had to "organize" for them. If one of them was caught "organizing," however, his capo never stood up for him, but, on the contrary, denied having had any connection with him.

With a serious demeanor ss men went from block to block and pretended to conduct searches, but the only purpose of these visits was the blackmailing of the block elders, who had to provide them with anything they wished. If a block elder wanted to fulfill these wishes, he had to pressure those inmates who were able to procure the things for the ss men. In return he gave them a favorable position in the block, increased their food rations, and treated them better. If an inmate was in danger of being reported, he was able to save himself by means of his connections. The ss had informants among the inmates, who for a bribe arranged that no report was made. This corruption extended to the office of the camp commandant, where a report could be stopped if enough gold and cash were involved.

Albert Menasche, a member of the detail that had to collect and load the luggage of the deportees at the ramp, reports about veritable pacts made between guards and inmates. Gold, jewelry, and similar valuables found by the inmates at the ramp were to be turned over to the guards; in return the guards permitted the prisoners to keep food and clothing.

Stefan Baretzki testified in court as follows: "As a block leader, I had to go to the ramp periodically when a transport arrived. All I had to do was to take the inmates of the Canada detail there, and then I could have left. But I did not leave because there was something to 'organize' there. After all, I was hungry, as were the inmates."

Rudolf Gibian, a member of the Canada detail, told the same court that the guards did not care only about food. One day he learned that his mother had arrived on a transport. After he had found her and briefly spoken with her, he selected from the possessions that his detail had to load those of this mother in order to take them to the camp, which was separated from the ramp by an electrified fence. "This is how I did it," said Gibian. "I put a clock on the ground, showed it to the guard, and asked him to help me. The ss guard took the clock and left, whereupon I threw the package over the fence."

■ The higher the rank of an ss man and the more influential the function of an inmate, the greater the bribe. Once Jerzy Pozimski, of the Labor Service in the main camp, gave his superior, ss Sergeant Wilhelm Emmerich, a whole shoe box full of watches. He was able to procure so many because everyone wanted to be in the good graces of the Labor Service. It goes without saying that after receiving such gifts Emmerich was obliged to accommodate Pozimski when he had special wishes. Pozimski, whose job was to provide the ss men in his office with food, told me the following story. His highest ranking boss, ss Captain Heinrich Schwarz, had been invited to the wedding of an ss man on his staff. He sent for Pozimski and ordered him to prepare a gift basket with bottles containing various alcoholic drinks. The basket was there on time, and Schwarz did not ask Pozimski how he had been able to procure it. Pozimski summed up his activities by saying, "I 'organized' for everybody."

A story told me by Alexander Princz illustrates how closely the general corruption bound inmates and guards together. As a coachman Princz visited all camps and had excellent opportunities to transport "organized" goods on his horse-drawn carriage. One day ss Technical Sergeant Moll, who was in charge of the crematoriums, summoned him to the women's camp. Moll, who knew Princz, ordered him to take a sack to be given him by Anna Franz, the chief of the ss kitchen, to his house, Number 184. Moll met Princz in the block leader's room and told the guard who had escorted him to take care of the horses. After giving him the order Moll pointed at the guard and added: "That bastard needn't know about it." Without Princz's help Moll could not have got the sack out of the camp, and henceforth Princz did not have to fear Moll, who made the whole camp tremble.

Krystyna Zywulska knew a German Jew—she remembers only his first name, Rolf—who was able to bribe ss men to let him wear the insignia of a German instead of the discriminatory Star of David.

To be sure, inmates had to be wary even of those for whom they "organized," for on more than one occasion an ss man did an inmate in because he was an accomplice to the thefts.

Canada was the source of all riches. Kitty Hart, who was assigned to the Canada detail as a young girl after she had had hard times on other labor squads, has provided a graphic description. Once she had become acclimated to her new detail, she was able to "put on fresh underwear and new clothes and shoes every day. We slept in nightshirts of pure silk and even smuggled bedsheets, the most striking luxury in Auschwitz, into our block. When our underwear and dresses got dirty, we simply threw them on the big pile from which we had picked them out. After a few weeks I was myself again. My skin turned white and my abscesses healed, soon leaving only scars. My bones no longer poked out at my knees and everywhere."

Simon Laks and René Coudy, who were able to visit Canada as members of the Birkenau orchestra, have given this report: "The girls who work there have everything—perfume, cologne—and they look as if their hairdos were the work of the top hairdresser of Paris. Apart from freedom, they have everything a woman can dream of. They also know love; the proximity of men, both inmates and ss men, makes this inevitable. . . . Ten meters from their barracks, on the other side of the barbed wire, rise the rectangular chimneys of the crematoriums that burn constantly, burn the owners of all the goods that these admirable creatures sort in these barracks."

Kitty Hart has described life on this detail:

It was a splendid summer. The sun was hot, and we, who had been assigned the night shift, found it hard to sleep during the day. We usually got up in the early afternoon, and if the weather was fair we lay on the grass in front of our barracks, sunbathing and splashing water over ourselves to cool down. Often we danced and sang, and we even formed a little band. We began to laugh and joke again. I spent many hours reading books that those destined for gassing had taken along on their transport to Poland. Our situation was surely one of the most insane in the whole world. All around us were the screams of the dying, destruction, the smoking chimneys that darkened and polluted the air with the soot and the stench of charred corpses. I suppose what we primarily cared about in those days was not to lose our minds, and that is why we laughed and sang even so close to the flaming inferno.

Kitty Hart sums up her experiences in these words: "It is astonishing what body and soul can endure if they have to. One can get accustomed to almost anything." Anyone who could not get accustomed did not survive Auschwitz. Because young persons could adapt more easily than older ones, details like Canada were staffed primarily with girls.

■ Bernard Klieger has unsparingly formulated the conclusions that he, a VIP, drew from this special situation: "In Auschwitz I lived better than many of my comrades, and I did not feel that this was immoral. In a KZ no one has the right to observe otherwise valid moral rules." Many of those who were interned in Auschwitz for an extended period had to pay the same price.

Seweryna Szmaglewska has reported where this could lead: "Once again a big transport arrived. Pillars of smoke indicated that the crematoriums were in operation. In the evening the Clothing Depot Commando came marching back to the women's camp." Szmaglewska overheard the following conversation: "Well, Licy, who arrived today?" "A wealthy transport. Oh, this underwear, these shoes . . . and those eats! All I can say is: Canada!"

Szmaglewska knew Licy, a Jew from one of the first Slovak transports: "You poor child, you've already spent three years of your youth in the camp. You can sing soft, longing songs from the Tatra Mountains. You can be so good, so comradely and obliging. Sometimes you are very sad. Your hot-bloodedness, your too long suppressed vitality, and your youthful élan have manifested themselves at the most inappropriate time. Your unbridled lust for life is making you blind." Szmaglewska observed that Licy did not constitute an exception: "The motto 'Enjoy the moment!' carries away many. A Jew covered with dirt mindlessly beats on an empty barrel with a hammer and rhythmically sings a melody from [Schubert's] *Rosamunde*: 'Organize' while there's still time, 'organize,' for tomorrow you'll be sent away from here."

On the basis of her experiences, Szmaglewska writes: "The whitewash of principles and the veil of good manners that under normal circumstances permit a little person, a nobody, to cope with many situations without realizing, or without others realizing, what a cipher he is drop off like flaking scales." This attentive observer gives an incisive description of the demoralization that emanated from Canada: "Once someone has reached for things that are still warm and felt joy in doing so, the bliss of ownership begins to affect him like hashish. In the everyday tumult of events, no change may be noticed in him at first. The developing greed is not even as annoying as a grain of sand in one's eyes, but it still grows and grows and grows, filling one's thoughts and drawing people under its spell. Perhaps this is also a form of oblivion, like the alcoholism of the ss men."

ss Corporal Pery Broad writes: "The proverb 'One man's doom is another man's boon' was probably never applied as aptly as in this extermination camp."

Canada skewed all values to the point of grotesqueness. For example, Manca Svalbova reports that in the women's camp it was possible to trade a diamond ring for water, which was scarce there, or buy quinine tablets with a bottle of champagne or elegant stockings. Krystyna Zywulska remembers a prisoner who swapped a diamond that he had discovered sewn into an article of clothing from Canada for an apple, which he gave to a sick friend. Seweryna Szmaglewska's statement that "it is easier to obtain a Swiss watch with a golden strap than to have a moment's peace and quiet" illustrates the inversion of all values. In Auschwitz watches were more than timepieces. Laks and Coudy report that a wristwatch was the badge of someone who knew how to "organize" in the camp, a kind of passport with a visa for survival.

■ Canada not only helped vips lead a life that many ss men envied, but, as Höß correctly observed, the resistance movement also used this source for its purposes.

Medicines from Canada had a special significance for the camp. Tadeusz Szymanski has indicated the methods used to bring these in. His compatriot Tadeusz Myszkowski was the orderly of SS Master Sergeant Bernhard Walter, the head of the Identification Service, and enjoyed his full confidence. Walter provided him with a pass that gave him access to his apartment, which was outside the big cordon, where Myszkowski made breakfast for him, shined his shoes, and performed other personal services. When Walter was finally ready to go to his office in the camp, Myszkowski followed him and carried his briefcase. At the camp gate Myszkowski properly reported his return while his boss took the briefcase. Myszkowski now put medicines in it. The briefcase was never inspected because at the critical moment, while passing through the gate, it was in the hands of the SS man. When they arrived at the camp, Myszkowski had to empty the briefcase, which means that he could safely take out the smuggled medicines.

Robert Lévy has confirmed that medicines smuggled by the Sonderkommando into the Birkenau infirmaries were "of immeasurable benefit" there.

In October 1942, when a satellite camp was built right next to the Buna Works of IG Farben, the new construction included an infirmary. Within a short time it had an operating room, a laboratory, X-ray machines, and even apparatuses for electroshock treatments. Everything was "organized" by prisoners from the IG plant in which they were doing forced labor. It goes without saying that all SS men knew where the equipment came from. In fact, when the infirmary was inspected, they bragged about the good facilities, and no one asked about the provenance of the valuable instruments. Even an old steam engine was (illegally) rolled from the IG plant into the camp and was used to heat and disinfect the infirmary. With its help the camp became "recognized as epidemic-free," as Felix Rausch proudly put it. If, however, an anonymous inmate was caught in the IG plant stealing a piece of wire to tie his shoes or a bag of cement, which he planned to put under his shirt as protection from the cold, he was punished as a saboteur. Such "crimes" sometimes drew death sentences.

Canada was as much a part of Auschwitz as that army of the living dead, the *Muselmänner*. Both extremes existed in a grotesque juxtaposition in the shadow of the crematoriums.

THE VIPS

■ ■ ■

When one speaks of VIPs in Auschwitz, one thinks of German career criminals, especially those brought to Auschwitz to help build the camp who proudly bore the inmate numbers 1 to 30, just as one thinks of inmates who had to wear the Star of David when one speaks of *Muselmänner*. There were, of course, VIPs who were neither criminals nor Germans, just as there were "Aryan" *Muselmänner*, but the VIP type was formed by Greens. From the beginning the camp administration granted them privileges in order to turn them into their tools. Bernhard Bonitz reported frankly that "the conditions in 1940 were rosy compared to Sachsenhausen." Bonitz was one of the first thirty who had been brought in from Sachsenhausen.

Two Poles who experienced the camp in its early period have provided characterizations of it. Józef Mikusz said that in those days every inmate functionary gave beatings, and Jerzy Pozimski wrote: "People beat and kill one another even under normal conditions, let alone under those created by the SS in Auschwitz."

This is what Wetzler and Vrba wrote in their report shortly after their escape from Auschwitz: "To them, beating an inmate to death is no crime. Someone simply records that inmate number such and such has died. The mode of death is quite immaterial."

Based on his ample experience as an inmate of German penal institutions from 1923 to 1928, as a guard in concentration camps between 1934 and 1945, and after the end of the war as a prisoner in Nuremberg and Poland, Höß answered his own question as to why capos and senior inmates so often mistreated their subordinates:

Because they wanted to curry favor with like-minded guards and to show how efficient they were. Because this could bring them benefits and make their lives as inmates more pleasant—but always at the expense of their fellow prisoners. However, the opportunity to behave and act in this way was given them by the guards, who either watched the goings-on with indifference and were too lazy to stop them or who approved and even encouraged this conduct because of a low-down, mean disposition, who derived satanic pleasure from inciting one inmate against another. . . . Even types who had always been helpful and good-natured in ordinary life on the outside were capable of mercilessly tyrannizing their fellow prisoners in the harsh confinement if this could make their lives just a little more bearable. But inmates with egotistical, cold, even criminal dispositions disregarded the distress of their fellow inmates all the more heartlessly and unmercifully if this brought them the slightest advantage.

Höß is silent about something that his deputy Hans Aumeier freely admitted in captivity—namely, that in Auschwitz block elders were selected for their positions because of their sadistic temperament. He testified that most of them were career criminals. Zenon Rozanski has described their indoctrination. One day, at a time when there were as yet no gassings and selections, Jews were, as usual, assigned to the penal company. The ss commando leader ordered all inmates with green triangles to line up. Rozanski quotes from the speech he made: " 'You have been chosen to be foremen because of your good leadership. I don't need to explain what your duties are. In the camp you have had the time and the opportunity to become acquainted with them. The inmates whose superiors you are becoming are Jews. I only want Aryans on my detail, understand?' The Greens responded in unison, 'Yes sir.' After that we went into the camp. The new VIPs were already carrying the badge of their power: cudgels." Rozanski concludes his account with this pithy observation: "That evening, thirty-seven corpses were carried into the washroom."

A sadistic strain may have been a greater determinant among inmates in leadership positions than among guards because they had been locked up for years, and it was more evident in career criminals who had spent a major part of their lives behind bars and were more morally unstable than others.

Julien Unger has posed this question to himself: "Who forced the inmate functionaries to do the work of the executioners even in their absence?" Here is his answer: "Sadism, derived from their lords and masters, brought them to a point where they forgot that they were themselves inmates."

However, this alone cannot explain the conduct of many VIPs. Life in an extermination camp lacked perspective—it being a place where neither epidemics nor the camp leadership spared an inmate functionary and VIPs were often killed because the ss began to feel threatened by these bearers of secrets—and this caused many prisoners to live from one day to the next and think only of the advantages that might be obtained at a particular moment. A future after the camp remained beyond all imagining. If, however, the KZ was accepted as the basis of a life, a VIP was tempted to adapt to the tone and methods of his masters. Once such a person had gained their favor he was able to procure pleasures that could make him forget his sad situation. The KZ and with it the ss became the measure of all things.

"Power and prestige," writes Benedikt Kautsky, "were extraordinarily effective precisely in this environment, which was designed to oppress people. It was, of course, impossible to feel free, but this lack of freedom was much less of a heavy burden if one could give orders to others. The power that a person wielded was enormous, and the social distinction between this upper crust of VIPs and the dregs of inmates was more glaring than the distinction between the middle class and the proletarians in a democratic state."

The German Green became the symbol of a zealous and self-satisfied henchman of the SS. "A violent person could beat others to his heart's content," wrote Kautsky, "a thief and cheat could rob his comrades and deprive them of their food, and even a sex offender could indulge himself."

If an inmate functionary wanted to, he could lead the kind of life that has been described by Robert Waitz: "(The Greens) are very proud of their custom-made striped suits; they have the barber give them a facial massage, rub their faces with cologne and treat them with hot napkins. They obtain meat, sausage, and fruit in return for the blankets, sheets, pullovers, shirts, jewelry, and money that they steal from Canada. Then alcohol and foodstuffs are brought into the camp from the factory in which the barter is made. On their return to the camp, certain labor details are completely safe from the frisking of the guards because their capo knows how to grease the palms of the SS." Waitz, who describes his experiences in Monowitz, points out that the Greens always emphasized that they were "Aryans"—and from the German Reich to boot.

If an inmate functionary was disobedient, the camp administration cut him down to size. SS camp leader Aumeier testified that "if an inmate who had been ordered to administer corporal punishment did not accept the order, he received the same punishment."

Oswald Pohl, the former head of the WVHA, which was in charge of all concentration camps, and Hermann Hachmann, the former adjutant of the commandant of Buchenwald, gave expert testimony about the dilemma in which inmates with positions found themselves. In 1949 both men were in the Landsberg prison, which also housed a former inmate functionary who had been sentenced for atrocities committed in Flossenbürg. Here is an excerpt from their testimony on behalf of this prisoner: "An inmate was subject to the law of unconditional obedience. Beyond that, he had no claim to any rights. Any privileges granted him were determined by the offices in charge of the concentration camps. . . . It was not possible for an inmate to volunteer for any job or to refuse to accept a position that he was ordered to fill. He was ordered what to do. An inmate's refusal to obey an order was cause for the harshest punishment."

If an inmate functionary who had incurred guilt in the service of his masters lost his privileges, he was defenseless against the vengeance of his fellow inmates. Once someone became a henchman, he reached the point of no return. This gave rise to situations like the one in the Kobier satellite camp in which around 150 inmates had to fell trees and process wood between October 1942 and September 1943. Friedrich Skrein reports that the ss decided each morning, when the labor squads marched off, who would be killed that day. Those selected were then tortured by two Green capos until they attempted to flee from this torture and were shot by a guard "while trying to escape."

Otto Wolken observed the extent to which positions could be pushed. The block elder of Block 8 in the Birkenau quarantine section, a certain Rudolf Oftringer from Lörrach, is said to have made a bet with Kurpanik, the block leader, to see whether Kurpanik could kill an inmate by shooting him in the neck from a distance of fifty paces. The bet was for a bottle of schnapps.

Max Mannheimer has described a block elder in the Birkenau quarantine section who was called "Tiger": "When he raises his arm to strike, he wears leather gloves for the sake of the sound effect. I observed only one person who was not felled by one blow from this beanpole of a block elder. This one failure enraged the man, for his prestige had declined. He never worked without spectators."

I heard about a Green capo in the main camp who, in order to demonstrate a new grip to a colleague, called a Jew who happened to be passing by and used him to show how he could kill someone with one blow. The demonstration was successful. No one took notice of it.

After the end of the war, many an inmate functionary was taken to court to answer for crimes committed in the camp. A Bremen trial at which Helmrich Heilmann was a defendant brought to light circumstances that incriminated that man, who had initially been in the Flossenbürg concentration camp as the wearer of a green triangle. In that camp he was a functionary who treated those in his charge in comradely fashion. Evidently this disappointed his superiors, and Heilmann landed in the penal company. The court was able to ascertain that the tortures and torments to which he was subjected there had done permanent physical damage. He knew that the ss wanted to "finish him off." Finally he got lucky and was assigned to a transport to Auschwitz—the last test, as the ss camp leader threateningly told him. In Golleschau, a satellite camp of Auschwitz, he "stood the test" as a capo, but witnesses confirmed that he gave beatings only when superiors were near. The Bremen court, which sentenced him for attempted murder, stated that "through arbitrary actions of a violent authoritarian regime he was put in a position where he committed criminal acts that were alien to his nature."

Heinous deeds of a fellow inmate made a greater impression on the prisoners than those of the ss. Höß confirmed this when he wrote: "No arbitrary act, no matter how mean, nor bad treatment from the guards hits them (the prisoners) as hard and has such a grave emotional effect on them as the behavior of their fellow prisoners. Having to watch helplessly and impotently how such senior inmates torture their fellow inmates is precisely what has such a crushing effect on the whole psyche of the prisoners."

I have had to witness so many things since then, but to this day I remember vividly how shocked I was when as a new arrival in Dachau I observed the infirmary capo Sepp Heiden beating a sick inmate with all his strength and uncontrollably trampling on him after he had fallen. Heiden was an Austrian with a red triangle, and his brutality upset me far more that the sight of SS men giving beatings.

■ I have already said and shall repeat here that not all those who wore a green triangle in the KZ and were given positions abused their power over their fellow inmates, and many political prisoners were in no way different from the typical Green functionaries. In the early period of Auschwitz, a Red could as a rule obtain an armband and thereby gain power only if he was able to adapt to the Greens. "Rather than the SS man, it is the inmate with a red triangle robbing and killing his comrades who serves as the most shattering symbol of the concentration camps," writes Benedikt Kautsky. "He was living proof that the mentality of violence corrupts and ruins those who display it even when they have themselves become victims of violence." Eduard de Wind indicates how things could come to such a point when he characterizes his block elder in these terms: "Paul was not a bad person and did not administer beatings, but he had been in the camp too long to have much compassion."

The development of the fronts in the course of the war made many inmate functionaries think about the impending end of the camps and thus also of their having to answer for their actions—not to the present camp administration but to a subsequent human society. Thanks to the work of Dr. Wirths, the SS garrison physician, in the infirmaries of which he was in charge, and later the work of Commandant Liebehenschel for the entire camp, the mindlessly brutal VIP did not remain predominant as a type everywhere until the end. Not every prisoner had an opportunity to observe this, and negative examples are always better remembered. Hence it is not surprising that many generalizing judgments have been made. Thus Viktor E. Frankl writes succinctly that the capo types "assimilated to the SS psychologically and sociologically and collaborated with it." He speaks of a negative selection and diagnoses "megalomania *en miniature*" in them. Based on his observation, the capo types did not feel *déclassé* but practically *arrivé* in the camp. Primo Levi does not differentiate either when he writes that the political VIPs (he names Germans, Poles, and Russians) vied with the criminals in brutality.

Frankl probably was not in Auschwitz long enough to register differences. In 1944 Levi evidently did not encounter those inmate functionaries with red triangles in Monowitz who quietly used their positions for the general good. The commentators who gained an insight into the dynamics of the inmate hierarchy in that camp have confirmed that there were a considerable number of them.

■ The picture of the Greens who set the tone as camp elders may explain why others have been overlooked. Bruno Brodniewicz bore the inmate number 1. He was the first camp elder and decisively influenced the camp atmosphere, which has been described by Tadeusz Paczula: "From the beginning the SS and the Greens instituted a reign of terror. They complemented and even vied with one another in murdering."

Emil Bednarek, who became block elder under Brodniewicz and later had to face the Frankfurt court, described for that court a speech that Brodniewicz once gave to an assembly of block elders. "You know what you have to do. Make sure that everything is clean and proper, and if someone doesn't toe the line, strike him or you'll get a whipping yourself!" Willi Brachmann, a Green capo whom the SS had also brought in from Sachsenhausen, has characterized the all-powerful camp elder as follows: "Brodniewicz was a beast. He was king of the camp. What he ordered had to be done."

If Brodniewicz appeared on the camp road in the evening, there soon was an empty space in the dense throng of the inmates around him, for nobody wanted to get close to him. Our very first encounter with this camp elder was typical. When I had been transferred from Dachau to Auschwitz together with sixteen Germans, Brodniewicz looked at us ominously and lit into us because we had not taken off our caps to him. True, in all camps every SS man had to be saluted in military fashion, with inmates snapping to attention and taking off their caps, but in Auschwitz the camp elder also asked to be saluted in this manner, at least while Brodniewicz was in power.

The best-known and most dreaded camp elder of the Birkenau men's camp was Franz Danisch. His favorite saying was "I recognize only workers and dead people." Fritz Hirsch, a German capo with a red triangle, told me how Danisch put this maxim into practice. After the labor details had left the camp, those no longer able to march stayed behind. One day Danisch ordered those Muselmänner to sit cross-legged, Turkish style. Then he went down the line and killed each man with his cudgel. According to Hirsch, the victims waited without any visible reaction until it was their turn. This is how Danisch cleansed his camp. In September 1945 Isaak Egon Ochshorn testified in Nuremberg that Danisch once told a column of Jews: "I, master over life and death of the Jews, shall now decide which of you will be gassed." Then he picked sixty-eight out of the one hundred, and when those begged for their lives, Danisch responded: "Anyone who can endure three blows from my club on his neck will be taken off the list, for he is viable." Many Jews bowed their heads to receive these blows, but then they collapsed under them and died. The camp administration appreciated this camp elder for relieving it of so many small chores.

However, Danisch could do more than murder and rage. "He was a virtuoso in playing the noble-minded and concerned protector of the hungry inmates," write Ota Kraus and Erich Kulka, who have reported the following episode:

A newcomer who had learned that the block elder would give him bread and margarine in return for gold entered the room in which Danisch, then only a block elder, and his clerk were having an opulent meal. Hesitantly the inmate pulled out his golden objects, which he had been able to smuggle into the camp, and showed them to the clerk with a request to give him food for them. "I don't want this! I won't hear of it! I don't need this! I don't do such things!" shouted Danisch. The inmate got flustered, realized he had come to the wrong place, and wanted to leave. Danisch turned to his clerk and said to him with a worried look: "Don't you see that the poor boy is hungry? Give him something to eat! Give him bread! Give him margarine! Just give him, give him, give him more!" The clerk handed some bread and margarine to the astonished inmate, who thanked him humbly, fairly oozing gratitude, bowed to the good block elder, and slowly put his gold in his pocket again. Danisch, however, jumped up and screamed at the clerk: "Have you gone mad? You're not planning to let him keep these things, are you? Take them from him and don't bring him bad luck. If someone finds this on him, he will go to the penal block, and that could cost him his life."

Simon Laks and René Coudy have reported how Danisch advanced to the position of camp elder:

The rapid rise of Danisch was a permanent subject of the inmates' conversation. In recognition of the services he rendered them by reporting even minor offenses, the Germans appointed him as a block elder to enhance the effectiveness of his vigilance vis-à-vis the inmates. One day, when there was a breach of discipline and the perpetrator could not be identified, the Germans ordered that all block elders be given twenty-five blows on their buttocks by way of punishment. When it was Danisch's turn, he refused to be flogged and made the following proposition to the SS men administering the beating: "Why do you want to beat me? What happened wasn't the block elder's fault. Only your camp elder is responsible for it. He is not up to his tasks. If you replace him with me, there won't be the slightest trouble. Then you will have a model camp, one that I shall create in a very short time." The Germans were astonished at such bold language from an inmate, but they accepted the challenge and named him camp elder on the spot. And Franz Danisch kept his promise. All inmates, from the lowliest to the most privileged, were terrified when they as much as saw him from a distance. He managed to do what his predecessor had attempted in vain: to militarize the terror.

His rapid rise may have been promoted by the fact that Danisch came from the same Upper Silesian town as SS roll call leader Oswald Kaduk. Alfred Wetzler overheard these two conversing in the Silesian dialect. Besides, Danisch had "bought" Kaduk's colleagues; he "organized" for them on a large scale and they gave him *carte blanche*. Eventually Danisch had consolidated his position to such an extent that he could venture a test of strength with the SS camp leader. Johann Schwarzhuber, a music lover, sponsored the camp orchestra, and Danisch was jealous of the musicians' privileges. One day the musicians prevailed on Schwarzhuber to excuse them from their work assignment so that they might make copies of some music. They had appealed to his pride in having an extensive repertoire for his orchestra. This exemption from work would have removed the musicians from the control of the camp elder, who assigned and supervised the work. Thus Danisch protested against the decision of the SS camp leader, pointing out that he was responsible for the output of the inmates in his charge and needed workers rather than copyists of music. Since the commandant had ordered that all inmates do useful work, Danisch knew how strong his arguments were. In point of fact, Schwarzhuber withdrew his permission.

Like Danisch, Brodniewicz was from a region in which both German and Polish were spoken. Both men understood these languages, the most important in the camp, and both were imbued with the hatred of Poles that in multilingual areas was more frequently encountered among Germans. In the eyes of the camp administration this constituted an additional qualification for a camp elder because it wanted harsh treatment of the Poles—the ethnic group that the SS men always watched with suspicion in Auschwitz. They regarded an understanding between German and Polish prisoners as something dangerous.

The first camp elder in Monowitz was Jupp Windeck, a German who first broke a law at the age of sixteen and eventually had twenty-three convictions on his record. Minor thefts were his specialty. He had been transferred from Sachsenhausen with the black triangle of an "antisocial." Before his appointment as camp elder he was a capo in the main camp. In a courtroom years later he described the life of a Green VIP: "A capo from the German Reich led a life of luxury as compared with that of the other inmates. We had enough to eat and also received clothes, watches, and jewelry, which we didn't need to take away from anyone." When he was asked whether he visited the camp brothel, Windeck replied: "I didn't need that. I had a girlfriend in the weaving mill." By that he evidently meant a female member of the Weaving Mill detail.

No one was able to observe Windeck better in Monowitz than Freddy Diamant, who was his assistant as a sixteen-year-old. In a courtroom Diamant described him as follows:

> A little man who always was a nobody and suddenly had power. This went to Windeck's head, and he did want to wield it. He was short and weak, and he wanted to compensate for this with brutality. He particularly liked to beat up feeble, half-starved, and sick inmates so brutally that they perished. When these miserable fellows lay on the ground before him, he trampled on them, on their faces, their stomachs, all over, with the heel of his boots. . . . The capos always strutted around the camp with brightly polished boots, just like the ss men. Nothing was more important to them than these boots. God help the man who dirtied Windeck's boots, for he could be murdered for that.

Both Windeck and Brodniewicz were punished several times while in the camp. The latter was in the bunker three times, and it should be noted that only shady deals on a large scale could cause the ss to take action against camp elders. After each punishment both men were given armbands again. Brodniewicz wound up as camp elder in the Jaworzno satellite camp, and Windeck was transferred to Birkenau. The camp administration could not do without such useful servants.

Paul Kozwara, who had received several sentences for fraud, became Windeck's successor in Monowitz. The reign of P.K. as this camp elder was generally called, brought some relief. Franz Unikower called this man, who was born in Upper Silesia in 1899, a "relatively good" camp elder and emphasizes that he whipped block elders if they did not distribute food fairly in their block. Robert Waitz has described P.K. as follows:

> He is a well-nourished giant who likes to hear himself talk and plays the part of a patron and supporter of the fine arts and sports. He greatly appreciates physical strength and can be impressed by it and sometimes also by intelligence. He gets a massage every day and surely lives better in the camp than he ever did in freedom. Sometimes he comes into the infirmary (in which Waitz served as a physician) and screams at the hapless *Muselmänner* because of their diarrhea. "You'll croak soon, all of you, and that's good. Why do you eat potato peels and such inconceivable *dreck*? You're real

shit-eaters!" His birthday is an occasion for events that seem worthy of a Rabelais. He is awakened by a serenade, and later in the day there are other concerts. All VIPs appear for a congratulatory visit, bringing gifts and flowers. The celebration is even more remarkable gastronomically, what with an abundance of kegs of beer, wine, liquor, meat, and cold cuts.

In the Theresienstadt family camp, Arno Böhm was appointed as camp elder. Hanna Hoffmann has described him:

> Our camp elder was a German, inmate number 8, a primitive sadist who had been sent to the KZ after committing several murders. He had an enormous craving for recognition. From our transport he picked out 600 young girls who were housed in the block in which he had a room. In that barracks there was an orchestra that had to play day and night, always the same hit songs. This is where the camp elder received "dignitaries" from the satellite camps. SS men frequently dropped in, and thus the girls in the block had "chances," which the camp elder encouraged. A few days after our arrival (in December 1943), he put on a Christmas show; the audience consisted of 100 young women from the entire camp who had been ordered to attend. We had to stand when he entered the room and applaud him when he whistled. He was accompanied by his runner; everyone in authority in the camp had one (a boy aged eleven to thirteen), but this one was of a special kind. In Theresienstadt we had been obliged to put him in a home for problem children, but now he marched along behind the camp elder in well-polished boots and dressed just like his master, faithfully copying all his movements.

■ Camp elders set the tone that block elders adopted in order to please their superiors.

The extent to which inmates were at the mercy of their block elders' whims is set forth in a report about Albert Hämmerle by Laks and Coudy. That man, who also wore a green triangle, was said to have sat down for breakfast only after he had slain a few inmates. One day Hämmerle underwent a striking change. He had acquired a new lover, a handsome young Pole with whom he had fallen in love and who exerted a moderating influence on him. The block breathed a sigh of relief. One day the Polish lad switched to another VIP, and Hämmerle raged in his block like a wounded beast. Only Laks, Coudy, and the other members of the camp orchestra did not have to fear him, for Hämmerle had them play sentimental pieces for him every evening.

Among the Green VIPs there were more harmless men as well. Robert Waitz has given this description of the capo of the Monowitz clothing depot:

(He is) around forty and a noted pimp who enjoys talking about his earlier life. As the lessee of a whorehouse in Berlin he had good opportunities for crooked activities, and he is proud of these to this day. Very elegantly dressed, he gads about all the camps (of Auschwitz III, whose headquarters was in Monowitz), and in some of them he has a little girlfriend whom he showers with presents. The ss men who accompany him also benefit from these tours, of course. This depot capo is also the initiator of theatrical performances to which the vips and other privileged persons in the camp are invited. The great mass of inmates—filthy, emaciated, poorly shaved and even more poorly dressed—are not admitted.

Simon Laks and René Coudy have sketched a portrait of senior capo Reinhold, who was in charge of all construction work in Birkenau and thus of all building material, 800 prisoners, and half a dozen capos. Reinhold, who had already been imprisoned for more than ten years for embezzlement, was the only "honorary inmate" in Birkenau. The reason for this unusual preferment becomes instantly clear if one knows that members of the ss, from top to bottom, ordered furniture and furnishings for their apartments from him. Reinhold took what was needed for this from the wood intended for the building of barracks. He did not "organize" only for the ss, of course. According to Laks and Coudy, it was rumored that he dined more opulently than the commandant. The best French and German wines, liqueurs, and whole liters of pure alcohol were at his disposal. When I questioned the former block leader Baretzki about this, his only reply was, "He had everything."

A vip's prestige required that he celebrate his birthday in a manner befitting his status. The camp orchestra in which Laks and Coudy played serenaded Reinhold on the morning of his birthday. The senior capo appeared in silken pajamas, generously distributed hundreds of cigarettes to the musicians, and offered them a few bottles of liquor while the vips flocked around him to offer their congratulations. All the while the orchestra was playing. Later, when the labor details marched off and he walked past the band at the head of his column, handsome as a prince, the musicians interrupted their playing to intone his favorite march. It is obvious that the celebrations of pashas followed the same scheme. None of the top vips wanted to be outdone by another.

▦ These descriptions should not lead one to make generalizations. Not every capo had the same opportunities as did senior capo Reinhold, and not every Green behaved like Danisch. Josef Farber had to work in the disinfection section and thus came in contact with new arrivals. He met a German Green who refused to accept a position in the camp; that man had murdered his wife and later died of typhus. Even among the notorious first thirty there were functionaries whom those who had to work under them remember as "very decent." Alwin Voigt had a good reputation, and so did another man, whom the Poles remember only as "Mateczka," which means "little mother."

The best-known and most shining exception was Otto Küsel, an inmate with the number 2, who from the beginning occupied the key position of head of the Labor Service. I have spoken about him with many survivors of Auschwitz and never heard as much as a hint of a negative memory of this exceptional human being. He was swamped with requests, for it was known in the camp that Küsel never turned anyone down imperiously, as did other functionaries. What inmate did not want to get a place on a good detail for himself or a friend? Of course, with the best will in the world Küsel was not able to fulfill all wishes. Decades later I was frequently asked for Küsel's address because survivors of Auschwitz wanted to thank him.

When I asked this Berliner, who had a good sense of humor and the talent to spread good cheer, in the fall of 1969 how he had managed to make no enemies, he said: "Of course, I wasn't able to help everyone who asked to be put on a good detail. When I had to turn someone down, I told him, 'Keep checking with me!' Eventually I was able to accommodate him. I assigned newcomers to the undesirable details, and transferred those who had been forced to work on these for some time to better ones."

Küsel escaped from Auschwitz after Christmas 1942. "I wouldn't have wanted to escape, for I had a good life in Auschwitz," he told me. As a universally liked VIP he had access to all sources, but the reason he decided to escape is characteristic of him. "The Poles on my detail wanted to flee. Mietek was an officer and had to expect that he would sooner or later be shot. The Political Department pursued all those whom it suspected of having been officers in the Polish army. My only options were to inform on them or escape with them, for if they had escaped without me, no one would have believed that I had not noticed their preparations. And then it would have been my turn. But I did not want to report them."

Küsel used this escape to rid the camp of the bloody tyranny of the camp elder Brodniewicz. The men escaped on a horse-drawn wagon that the Labor Service, which had many "connections," had managed to obtain. In the wagon, which was abandoned outside the camp area, the SS found a letter from Küsel that said that Brodniewicz had concealed treasures in the stove of the room he occupied as camp elder. Gold was indeed found there. Brodniewicz was taken to the bunker, and the camp breathed a sigh of relief.

After living in Warsaw for nine months and helping a secret Polish organization there, Küsel fell into the hands of the Gestapo and was taken back to Auschwitz. He had good fortune in misfortune because at that time there was a change of commandants. Liebehenschel's bunker amnesty benefited Küsel as well, and at a later date he was transferred to Flossenbürg together with other inmates who had been caught while trying to escape.

This man who could be as proud of his past as hardly another survivor of Auschwitz, who was offered honorary Polish citizenship in 1945, and who kept receiving tokens of gratitude is living in retirement in a Bavarian village and does not answer letters from his former charges—he is still ashamed of his past. As a young fellow he had received three sentences in a period of widespread unemployment and poverty, the last one at age twenty-four. This is what he told me by way of explaining his exemplary conduct: "Because of this past I had guilt feelings, and this is why I helped others."

▨ Many German political prisoners did not model themselves on someone like Küsel but adapted to the predominant type of Green VIP. Georg Berger was one of these. He specialized in murdering prisoners with gold teeth and collecting the gold. When it became known that he had killed a fellow inmate who had once been an SS man and was scheduled to be released from the camp, Berger went to the bunker and was shot there. Berger was twenty-one years old when he was given an armband and with it unlimited power.

Because he was a defendant in the Auschwitz trial at Frankfurt together with members of the SS, Emil Bednarek became better known than other wearers of a red triangle who had abused their power in Auschwitz. Bednarek was born in 1907 in Königshütte, where his father had assumed Polish citizenship when that Upper Silesian region became part of Poland. His national orientation was, like that of many Upper Silesians, conflicted. At the outbreak of the war he was mobilized as a Polish noncommissioned officer, but, according to his own statements, he went over to the Germans after twelve days, and in July 1940 he was sent to Auschwitz on suspicion of belonging to a Polish resistance organization. Since he was an ethnic German, he was soon made block elder. Jiri Beranovsky has given this concise description of conditions at that time: "Beatings were normal and they were administered by Bednarek, the dormitory elder, and the block leader. A bad salute was enough for a flogging." Pavel Danel testified as follows: "In my opinion Bednarek as a block elder was forced to beat the inmates. After all, beating was an everyday occurrence in Auschwitz." Karol Doering explained Bednarek's conduct to the court in these words: "He was a primitive person, and therefore the indoctrination in the camp could mold him." SS roll call leader Oswald Kaduk, once Bednarek's superior and later his fellow defendant, confirmed the statements of the former Polish prisoners: "The block elder had to slap a face now and then, because everything had to go chop-chop when the inmates were to line up for roll call."

Bednarek attempted to make the court understand the pressure he was always under as a block elder. He said that if anything went wrong, he was himself beaten by the camp elder, the block leader, and the ss roll call leader. "It was very hard," he said, "to maintain quiet, cleanliness, and order in the camp in accordance with instructions. I often had to intervene when there were thefts or brawls, and on a few occasions I had to do some whipping. If I had not given them those few whacks, the inmates would have received even more severe punishment because then I would have had to report them for stealing bread, for instance."

However, Bednarek did not merely slap a few faces; there is proof that he committed some murders when no ss man was present, which means that there was not even indirect pressure. Several survivors of Auschwitz were asked on the witness stand about Bednarek's motivation, and their responses are revealing. Stanislaw Klodzinski testified as follows: "I believe there was some cause each time. The inmate was clumsy, he had made his bed poorly, or something like that." Leon Uchwat, a friend of Bednarek, pointed to a typical motive: "When a person had been in Auschwitz for two or three months, he had reached rock bottom physically and morally. Bednarek did not like to see such inmates, and he thought that they would not survive anyway." Uchwat explained how hard it was to recognize a murder in Auschwitz: "Every day some prisoners died of natural causes. It is possible that one of those had been slapped in the face by Bednarek." According to him, flogging gave Bednarek no pleasure: "One could see that beating was disagreeable to him. On several occasions he gave extra food to an inmate after he had beaten him."

Like colleagues credited with a similarly large number of sins, Bednarek did not just rage but also helped. Józef Mikusz concluded his gravely incriminating testimony with these words: "When children between nine and fourteen came to the camp in late August or early September 1944, after the uprising in the Warsaw ghetto, Bednarek took them under his wing. In those days we barely recognized him; he had become a different person. He permitted us to bring the children everything—bread, soup, medicines. I don't think that anyone else in his position would have done so much for the children. His conduct in this period was 100 percent positive. On a later occasion I saw that he took good care of those children in Melk and Mauthausen (where they had been transferred after the evacuation in Auschwitz)." Other witnesses have confirmed this change in Bednarek, the causes of which were not clarified in the course of the trial.

Bednarek's tragedy became apparent when the former head of the Gestapo in Kattowitz was called to the witness stand. Bednarek, who had been arrested by that office, described excitedly how he was locked up in a coal cellar without a hearing and received twenty-five lashes with a whip. "If I hadn't been sent to the camp at that time, I wouldn't be sitting here today," he blurted out tearfully before breaking down. The tragedy was followed by a grotesquerie. Robert Kulka, who was sitting next to him in the dock, stroked the weeping man's hair paternally and soothingly. Fellow defendant Kulka was the former adjutant of the commandant of Auschwitz.

■ Numerous survivors who favorably remember inmate functionaries with red triangles have testified that men like Berger or Bednarek were exceptions to the rule. Mordechai Winekamien, who had been deported from Lodz in late August 1944, has not forgotten his block elder in Birkenau because he treated new arrivals "very decently." He remembers only that his first name was Hubert and that he was a German with a red triangle who had formerly been in Dachau.

Lucie Adelsberger, a physician in the Gypsy camp, has reported about Felix Amann, the capo of the disinfection section: "Three times a week, from five to six o'clock, there was 'staff bathing' with hot showers thanks to a benevolent capo, a politically outlawed German. This was a shining hour for us in the camp, for the capo responded to a few words of appreciation with even kinder ones, and let the warm water run on our bare bodies in abundant streams and not sparsely and amid blows, as in other camps."

Erich Kohlhagen writes about an Austrian named Aigner who headed the Electricity Commando in Monowitz:

> This Aigner was not only a fine person but also an outstanding capo, who showed all other capos how to lead a detail as a human being and an inmate. He did this without coming into conflict with the ss, which wanted high job performance and, most important of all, expected the capo to see to it that the inmates in his care had enough to eat, were well dressed, and had peace and quiet in the camp. He was the true father of the Jews in Monowitz. How many came running to him with their problems and worries! How many he saved from being sent to the coal mine, which would have spelled their doom, by bravely going to the ss camp leader or the Political Department and selflessly pleading their case.

In fairness to others who did not receive such a positive evaluation, it should be added that a capo who headed a detail consisting of skilled workers had much more favorable opportunities than one who was in charge of earth-works.

The Poles Erwin Olszowska and Alfred Woycicki treasure the memory of Franz Malz, a German political prisoner from Stettin who was the capo of the Identification Service. In the summer of 1943 Malz told ss Sergeant Jakob

Raith that the Germans were going to lose the war. The following day he was arrested by the Political Department and shot. The inmates on his detail were told to let this be a warning to them.

Alex Rosenstock has not forgotten the block elder Hans Röhrig, also a German with a red triangle: "When the Czech family camp was liquidated and capos and block elders were ordered to help the SS in getting the job done, Röhrig refused to participate. Schwarzhuber, the head of the camp, asked him the reason for his refusal, and Röhrig replied, 'I am not an executioner.' Whereupon he was ordered to cut his hair, which he had been allowed to grow as a privileged prisoner." According to Otto Kulka, who was in the family camp at the time and was spared the general carnage together with a group of adolescents, Röhrig was sent to the penal company but released again after a few days. Kulka emphasized that "this greatly increased his stature in our eyes."

When I think of German inmate functionaries with a red triangle whose conduct was exemplary, I particularly remember Hans Neumeier, a Bavarian communist who was not hardened or made insensitive by his long imprisonment in Dachau. In that camp he had become known for his refusal to punish his fellow inmates by flogging them. He was more inclined to accept such punishment himself than to beat another man. He and I were transferred from Dachau to Auschwitz together, and he was assigned to the infection block as a block elder. I often visited him in his miserable place where there were not even enough straw pallets to replace those soiled with the excrement of dying patients, where two patients per bunk had to be on three-tiered bedsteads and the nurse could not ascertain when someone on the third tier had died for the timely removal of his corpse, and where the SS kept selecting feeble inmates for death to the dismay of the nurses. I saw how none of this made Hiasl Neumeier lose his courage and how he did not flag in his efforts to help those entrusted to his care. He once told me with a laugh: "If the SS couldn't get us down in Dachau, we won't let the lice do it here, will we?" The lice did get him, however. He caught typhus in his infection block and died a slow and painful death. Only a small number of people will remember his self-sacrificing activities, for they lasted only a few short weeks. For me he will remain the model of a good comrade, a man to whom an armband meant an obligation and nothing else.

■ It has frequently been observed that despite their opposition to Nazism German political prisoners were not capable of distancing themselves from the Third Reich in a way that any other inmate of a concentration camp took for granted. Simon Laks and René Coudy mention the fifty-six-year-old block elder Josef Hofmann, a policeman from Breslau who had been sent to the camp for black-marketeering and enjoyed a good reputation in Birkenau. According to them, Hofmann was firmly convinced of a German victory as late as the evacuation in January 1945, believed in the promised miracle weapons, and regretted that he could not participate in the fight and victory in the ranks of the German army.

With reference to the first bombardments of the Buna Works in the summer of 1944, Primo Levi remarked sarcastically, and surely generalizing unfairly, that "even the inmates from the German Reich in the camp, including the political prisoners, feel in the hour of danger an attachment to blood and soil."

Karl Bracht, a German communist who had been imprisoned since 1936 and as a capo in Birkenau stood out from the Greens in a positive sense, told me two decades after the liberation with unmistakable pride that ss camp leader Schwarzhuber once called him his best capo in the presence of all others. The tendency of the camp administration to appeal to a solidarity of all Germans beyond the barbed wire led to a macabre incident that has been described by Otto Fabian, who as a corpse carrier was able to observe shootings at the Black Wall. "One time a man broke away from Jakob (who had to escort those destined for death at the Black Wall), pounded his chest, and cried out: 'This is how a German from the Reich has to croak.' This outcry did not keep the ss from shooting him, of course."

Primo Levi reports that at the time of the evacuation in Monowitz the ss appointed a German political prisoner named Thylle as block elder in the infirmary before leaving the camp with those able to march. Those unable to do so remained in the infirmary. "As a German he took this temporary appointment very seriously," writes Levi. "In the ten days before the disappearance of the ss and the arrival of the Russians, while everyone was waging a final battle against hunger, sickness, and the cold, Thylle made a thorough inspection of his new domain and registered the condition of the floors and the number of blankets (one for each person, living or dead)." Primo Levi characterizes this old communist as "petrified by ten years of wild and dubious camp life."

The last stage of my internment was Lerbeck, a satellite camp of Neuengamme, where I served as a roll call clerk. In early April 1945 we were evacuated to Fallersleben, which was also being prepared for clearance since the ss did not want any inmates to fall into the hands of the approaching Americans. When I was trying to turn the Lerbeck file over to the roll call clerk of Fallersleben in accordance with regulations, he had to point out that it was quite unimportant whether the record was correct or not because the ss had already lost track of such matters. At the time I was ashamed that I needed to be told that assignments made by the camp administration did not remain in force once the administration was gone.

In exceptional cases the ss released German inmate functionaries in order to use them as civilian workers in the camp area. Thus Erich Grönke, a criminal, was installed as head of the leather factory in late 1941, and in July 1942 Dr. Diethelm Scheer, a political prisoner, was employed as an expert fish breeder. Even two Polish surgeons, Dr. Wladyslaw Dering and Dr. Jan Grabszynski, who had proved themselves as assistants in human experiments were released in this fashion in 1944. Grabszynski did not take his civilian duties as seriously as Dering; rather, he used his freedom to join the partisans. Most of the releases from the camp with simultaneous assignments to civilian work were made by the central construction office. A dozen Polish or ethnic German architects gained relative freedom in 1943 and 1944.

■ The camp administration even considered the integration of inmate functionaries into the ss. Anton van Velsen, block elder and camp capo in Birkenau, received such an offer. He testified before the Frankfurt court: "In Auschwitz I was asked to volunteer for the ss as a Dutch officer, but I would have preferred Zyklon B in my lungs to an ss uniform on my body."

In my Bericht I have the following to say in this regard:

Today the ss infirmary is on red alert. Orderlies rush back and forth. The reason for the excitement is that Dr. Lolling, the chief physician in the WVHA, has announced his visit for today, and no one should attract his attention. It seems that the visit went well. Wirths is beaming and comes to our room, which he rarely does. We rise; I stand behind my little typewriter table and he leans on the other side of the table:

"You know, Langbein, the infirmary capo from Dachau, Zimmermann, has been released." After a pause, this sudden question: "Do you want to join the ss?"

The ss sergeant for accounting is also in the room; he is fiddling with something off to the side. When the question was posed, he turned around. So I just smile at Wirths. He smiles back; then he leaves.

The next time I come to his room alone, he broaches the same subject. "I told Lolling about you, and he told me that it is possible to take inmates who do especially good work into the ss and continue to work in the camp as ss men."

"Herr Doktor, if I have to be in a KZ, then only in the uniform I'm wearing now."

I don't know if Wirths would have tolerated this answer just a few months ago. Now he just looks at me, and his facial expression is no longer friendly. "But it would be better for you."

"Can I do something like that, Herr Doktor? You know the orders an ss man in Auschwitz must carry out. The inmates here are my comrades, even if I no longer wear their uniform tomorrow."

He looks through the window into the camp with its motley swarm of striped garments. It is the noonday break. "Your views do you honor." His voice sounds a bit disappointed. He senses that my answer is a judgment.

When the situation at the front worsened for the Germans, the ss made more frequent offers to German prisoners to put on its uniform. It is revealing that the ss first turned to the criminals.

On February 19, 1944, Himmler issued the following decree: "I want ss Lieutenant Colonel Dirlewanger personally to select from the antisocials and the career criminals in the concentration camps men who are between seventeen and thirty-five years of age, in exceptional cases up to forty, men who will volunteer for military service at the front for the purpose of rehabilitating themselves. Political criminals and key workers in the arms factories of the concentration camps are not eligible." Himmler initially limited the number of such volunteers from all camps to 800, but later these recruitments were stepped up considerably, and in the fall of 1944 German political prisoners were included as well. It need not be emphasized that Himmler's stipulation of a quota for each camp made the concept of "volunteering" problematical.

Tadeusz Borowski, an excellent observer, reports that one day Green inmate functionaries who were well known in the camp could be seen at a military drill in ss uniforms.

First they are taught to march, and then the leaders wait to see whether they will fit into the community. They are evidently quite taken with the community, for they try very hard. They have been together for just a few days and have already broken into the storeroom and swiped a lot of packages, made kindling wood of the canteen, and demolished the brothel. Why, so they say quite reasonably, should we let ourselves be beaten and stick our necks out? Who is going to shine our boots at the front, and who knows whether there are young lads there?

There they go, a whole horde of them singing "Tomorrow in our homeland." Notorious killers, all of them, one more notorious than the next: Sepp, the terror of all roofers, who mercilessly makes his charges work in the snow and the rain and will throw a person from the roof because of a badly hammered-on nail. Arno Böhm, number 8, a longtime block elder, capo, and camp capo who killed a dormitory elder if he caught him selling tea and punished every word spoken after the evening gong with twenty-five blows, the same man who wrote his aged parents in Frankfurt touching, albeit short letters about farewells and reunions. We know them all, every one of them.

Kaduk remembers three transports of released German inmates to the Special Dirlewanger Unit. Höß writes that Himmler kept ordering additional "volunteers." He appreciatively emphasizes that many inmates became valiant soldiers but also says that among the political prisoners there were numerous deserters. Dirlewanger Units also participated in massacres of the civilian population.

Political prisoners faced a momentous decision when they were asked to volunteer for Dirlewanger. We had agreed in Auschwitz that we would accept an invitation to join the Wehrmacht but would, if at all possible, resist being integrated into an ss unit. I was never put to the test. Neither in Auschwitz nor in Neuengamme, where I experienced the final phase of the war, were veterans. of the Spanish Civil War invited to come forward.

■ Originally, non-Germans received armbands only in exceptional cases. When more and more functionaries were needed later and the percentage of Germans decreased, a Polish capo was no longer a rarity, and even Jews received such an armband. The Pole Franz Nierychlo, who had been in Auschwitz since June 1940, became the head of the camp orchestra. Its members were assigned to work in the camp so they could be reached quickly at any time. Nierychlo became the capo of the inmate kitchen. Since he occupied a privileged position as conductor of the orchestra, he did not need to be especially submissive to the ss as a capo. Nevertheless, he gave beatings to members of his detail, and he is reputed to have killed, together with his ss chief Egersdörfer, seven inmates who had broken into the storeroom of the kitchen at Christmastime in 1941. Rablin remembers that the corpses were placed under the Christmas tree as a deterrent. That Pole has given this concise characterization of his compatriot: "His specialty was the drowning of Jews in water tanks." This imperious conductor was servile to the camp administration, and to please it he called a march that he composed "*Arbeit macht frei*" (Work makes you free). Following the example of Dachau, the ss had affixed this slogan to the entrance gate. As an ethnic German, Nierychlo was later conscripted into the Wehrmacht.

A statement by Elie Wiesel may suffice to demonstrate that my repeated warning against generalizations applies to Polish functionaries as well. Wiesel remembers that the block elder of Block 17, a young Pole, tried to make the first hours easier for him and other Jewish newcomers with comradely words and valuable advice. "These were the first humane words," writes Wiesel.

Block elders and capos appointed as their assistants dormitory orderlies and foremen who were like them. H. G. Adler has given the following description of the vIPs that he encountered in Birkenau in the fall of 1944: "The assistants emerge from their special rooms—block elders and block clerks

as well as dormitory orderlies, all strong young lads, some of them fantasti-
cally dressed up. Most of these are Poles and Germans who have been in the
camp for many years and almost feel at home here. They are hardly among the
lost ones, but their world has become natural to them because they no longer
know another. This is the only order; in this world it is possible to dominate
and spread terror, and one must know how to live a life at the edge of all life."

Samson Boeken testified on September 1, 1947, that a dormitory orderly
in Birkenau thought nothing of killing ten inmates, Jews from Holland, if he
could buy himself some vodka with their bread ration. This is said to have
happened in the summer of 1942.

Neither Adler nor Boeken mentions the color of the triangles worn by these
assistants of the block elders. It may be assumed, however, that most of them
were not career criminals, for the small number of Greens usually occupied
the top rung of the inmate hierarchy in Birkenau.

Thanks to the experienced Polish pedagogue Józef Kret, who was forty-
seven when he was assigned to the penal company in summer 1942, we have
a revealing study of a man who had reached the midpoint of that hierarchy.
Kret's dormitory elder, Józef Mitas, was a Pole from Upper Silesia, a locksmith
just under forty years of age. He was in charge of distributing food in the penal
block.

> He never stopped snapping at us as he poured a half liter of so-called tea
> (for two people) into our mess kit. He only interrupted himself to beat
> someone over the head with his ladle. Nothing escaped his attention.
> Whether someone sneaked to the head of the line, dared to talk, or put
> his bowl down clumsily—Mitas saw everything and immediately adminis-
> tered a beating. When there was nothing to criticize, he struck randomly
> anyway—as a warning, to keep his hand in, because it gave him pleasure,
> because that's what the block elder wanted, because Moll (the ss officer in
> charge of the penal company) demanded it, because the capos liked it, be-
> cause it consolidated his position as dormitory elder . . . and in any case,
> this was the penal company and not an ordinary detail.

This kind of grim pride in a particularly difficult detail was repeatedly encountered. Kret made a study of Mitas. "He had a view of people that he had acquired in a school of hard knocks," he wrote, "and he classified people's good
and bad points in an original way. Clumsiness, faintheartedness, and softness
could make him fly into a rage. The sight of slow awkward movements and
figures marked by apathy and resignation made him foam with rage. 'People,
where are your brains?' he would scream. 'You accursed intellectuals! Where
did you dumb people grow up and not learn how to help yourselves?'"

Kret asks how Mitas got that way. "Perhaps some long-repressed instincts were vented now that conditions in the camp were favorable to them. Perhaps a bad childhood had borne such bitter fruit. Or was this his way of trying to ease the worry about his own fate that was consuming him?" Even though Mitas had the function and privileges of a dormitory elder, he was also a member of the penal company, from which inmates could be called to the Political Department at any time, never to return. "Mitas did not want to kill people, but when his rage overcame him and he beat harder on a weak spot, he simply regarded this as the tough luck of the man he had beaten to death."

It was not just Poles who acted like Mitas, though they had the best chance of moving up in the hierarchy. Igor Bistric reports about a Russian dormitory orderly named Ivan who treated new arrivals in Birkenau so brutally that two and a half decades later Bistric could only call him a murderer. This Ivan was one of the handful of survivors out of the thousands of Russian prisoners of war who had been deported to Auschwitz in the winter of 1941–42.

■ Conditions in the women's camp were not much different. However, among the women the Blacks rather than the Greens dominated—that is, the "antisocials," mostly prostitutes. Only "German women with black triangles" were dominant among the inmate functionaries encountered by Wanda Koprowska in the satellite camp Budy in the spring of 1943. She described Sonja, the block elder, as "a horrible beast with a rather pretty body. She had been a streetwalker when she was free. She was never without her riding crop with which she would whip us for no reason at all." Her successor was named Eva and also wore a black triangle. She did not rage like her predecessor but preferred to lift a glass. "We don't know where she got her schnapps." When she was drunk, she maltreated the inmates of her block. The capo was Trude Richter, an "utterly illiterate" Upper Silesian. "Her cudgel helped us drag heavy rocks and beams," writes Koprowska.

Krystyna Zywulska mentions a Polish prostitute from Kielce who held the position of a camp capo in the women's camp. The Pole Stanislawa Starostka, generally called Stenia, who had been deported at the age of twenty-five and had initially impressed the camp administration as a block elder, was promoted to camp elder in the women's camp. At the Bergen-Belsen trial she was a defendant together with members of the ss. "If I wanted to help the inmates as camp elder," she said in her defense, "I had to gain the trust of the German authorities. I had to fight for every compromise." She claimed that this was harder for her than for German top functionaries.

Manca Svalbova, who experienced the women's camp from the beginning, writes that the majority of the vips lived well at the expense of their starving comrades. And more than that: the camp capos and block elders had more than once encouraged selections on the part of the ss with questions like

"What shall I do with all those *Muselmänner*?" If a selectee implored a block elder to help her, the answer she was likely to get was "Am I perhaps supposed to be gassed in your place?"

It goes without saying that there were also other kinds of functionaries among the women, as there were among the men.

In a story that was recorded by Meyer Levin, an inmate named Eva described her block elder, Lotta, evidently a Slovak Jew, though she is referred to as a Slovenian. "No matter how forbearing a block elder may have been, there were times when she had to strike, for many prisoners were in such a state that they no longer understood anything else. There were crafty women and evil women, thieves who stole bread, a spoon, or a comb, the half-crazed as well as those who had lost all human qualities and were filthy like babies in diapers. If there was a brawl, Lotta came out of her corner, dealt a few blows, and took things away. But she was not a sadist. When she did strike, it was hard and quick."

The type of "petrified" old inmate was represented in the women's camp as well. Kitty Hart describes a representative of this type, evidently a successor of Stenia. "At the head of the inmates of the entire women's camp was a camp elder, a German woman who had been interned in various camps for eight years as a political prisoner. She was known as a decent person, but the inmates still were afraid of her and tried to conceal themselves when she appeared. She had some helpers, and it was better not to cross their paths. They carried whips and used them abundantly and often unrestrainedly even when no German uniform was in sight." Kitty Hart knew that many an inmate functionary roared and occasionally flogged in the presence of ss men in order to forestall punitive measures on the part of the ss.

■ That an inmate functionary sometimes had to be strict even when no ss member was observing him may be illustrated by the following words of Herbert Buchhold, a former elder of Block 13. "During my time in Monowitz no epidemics broke out there, and this was largely to the credit of the camp elders and the block elders, who sometimes had to use violence to enforce cleanliness on the part of the inmates."

Lena Zoltanova reports an incident that clearly indicates how prisoners could form an erroneous opinion of their inmate overseers. In 1944 an acquaintance of hers was installed as block elder in the section of Birkenau that housed the recently arrived Jewish women from Hungary who had been found fit for work at the selection and had to await transportation to a labor camp. The roll calls there often lasted for hours, and many women were utterly exhausted from all that standing. Members of the ss made the friendly suggestion that those who felt tired or sick sit down on the side of the roll call area.

The block elder knew that with this invitation the SS wanted to save itself the bother of a selection, and the women who accepted it were later taken to the gas chamber. For this reason she warned the women who often were alarmingly naive, against sitting down, but of course she could not even hint at the reason for this warning if she did not want to risk her life. A few Hungarian women said, "But the SS has permitted us to sit down." No wonder that this made the block elder lose her composure and that she screamed at the women: "You stupid cows, remain standing! I forbid you to sit down!" Thus the unsuspecting Hungarian women got the impression that the SS was not so bad but the block elders were cruel. If they were transferred to a labor camp after a short time without having figured out what was up, they may never have suspected that the scolding block elder—who perhaps also beat people—had saved their lives.

Since Iris Langer had been deported with one of the first transports from Slovakia and thus was one of the "old hands" by 1944, she was appointed block elder in the same section of the camp. One day the SS physician Klein invited sick women to come forward so they could be sent to a sanatorium. Langer whispered in Hungarian to all inmates she could reach that no one should come forward, for of course she knew what Klein meant by sanatorium. Later she overheard Hungarian women say that the SS physician was better than the block elder, who had to wear a Star of David herself.

Once I mentioned to my friend Ernst Burger that I could not understand how inmates were capable of flogging their fellow sufferers and boasted that, even though I might be numbered among the VIPs, I never so much as touched anyone. Ernst responded, "It's easy for you to talk. As a clerk you bear no responsibility for others." He also told me how he had recently been forced to give a beating. Ernst, the clerk of Block 4, was well known and popular in the camp and always strove to use his popularity to provide relief for the inmates of his block. One day he once again managed to get an additional kettle of soup from the kitchen. When the inmates noticed that unexpected second helpings were in the offing, they wildly rushed at the men who were carrying the kettle to the block with their bowls, which inmates always kept handy by attaching them to their belts. If the pushing and shoving inmates had reached the kettle, it would certainly have been upset and the soup would have been spilled. Ernst screamed at the onrushing men to stop—then everybody would get something. There was no reaction. "What choice did I have?" Ernst asked. "I took one of the poles used for carrying the kettle and beat the inmates in the vanguard with it. Only then did they stop running. I shouted at the top of my voice that everyone should form a line, and now the soup could be distributed." An observer of this scene who did not know Ernst and the camp might have regarded him as a flogger.

■ Inmate functionaries had other problems to solve as well. For example, how was a block elder supposed to deal with an inmate caught stealing bread? If he reported him to the SS, the thief's life was as good as forfeited and collective punishment could also be expected. If he let the thief get away unscathed, he would be encouraging others to help themselves to their neighbors' bread. He was forced to set himself up as a judge and was easily tempted to wield judicial power even when it was not absolutely necessary.

Ella Lingens has described a case of arbitrary justice that she regarded as typical of the conduct of many communist functionaries. Two patients were lying on the same bunk bed in the infirmary. One of them had just received a parcel, but she was dying. The other woman, who, like many patients recovering from typhus, was ravenous, had appropriated the package while her neighbor was still alive. Others reported this incident, probably out of envy. Camp elder Schneider, a German communist whom long imprisonment had hardened, did not scream or hit, but instead said: "We shall take care of this matter ourselves. By stealing this parcel you have transgressed against the community, and now you shall work for this community." The convalescent woman was ordered to clean the room from now on. As a physician Lingens knew that the heart of the punished woman, which was still weak from her illness, would not stand the strain, and so she intervened. However, the camp elder, who like many other laypersons had gained her experience in inmate infirmaries, did not trust the judgment of physicians, and so she rejected this intervention. The patient died of heart failure a few days later.

Another case of arbitrary justice was reported by Franciszek Znamirowski during the proceedings against Emil Bednarek:

> I was assigned to the penal company in which Bednarek served as block elder. One time Bednarek beat a block elder named Franek, a Polish beast. When Franek was committed to the penal company, Bednarek first slapped his face, then forced him to put his head in the flue and gave him twenty-five whacks on his buttocks with a thick stick. This beating was administered because Franek pilfered things from inmate parcels. All inmates in Franek's block considered this fair punishment. I have heard it said that later, when Franek was transported to another camp, he was strangled by his fellow inmates.

Franek was well nourished and vigorous when this punishment befell him. Bednarek administered similar punishments to others who did not have a block elder's reserves of strength, and such cases could have a lethal result.

■ Should a prisoner whose sense of responsibility had not been destroyed by life in the camp have evaded the dangers connected with a function, or should he have incurred such risks to act in the interest of his fellow inmates? Eugen Kogon writes that in critical situations an inmate functionary's "only choice was between active help and a supposed retreat from responsibility, and experience showed that the latter caused far worse things."

With full knowledge of the dilemma frequently faced by a capo or block elder, I nevertheless repeatedly sought to convince responsible comrades to accept an armband. It would certainly have been easier for an individual to avoid accepting a position and to keep his conscience free from any burden, but in that case, how could the improvements that were effected in many camps have been achieved? How could the floggers and tricksters have been removed from their key positions? What would the camps have been like if all those whose morality had not been broken had refused to accept a responsibility? It was very difficult for someone who had agreed to wear an armband to find the right balance between what had to be done to keep a job and the influence connected with it and what already constituted an abuse of power. However, if a person considered the responsibility he incurred by refusing to assume a function, he did not shrink from this difficulty. Within the framework established by the SS, the VIPs in the camp could do a great deal, for good as well as for evil.

JEWISH VIPS

■ ■ ■

In the course of time the camp administration found itself obliged to entrust functions to Jewish inmates as well, for the percentage of "Aryans" kept declining. In a report compiled by Wetzler and Vrba after their successful escape in early April 1944, we read that in February of that year about half of the block elders in the Birkenau men's camp were Jews but that the central administration later ordered all Jews, with the exception of three from Slovakia, to relinquish their armbands. Because Wetzler and Vrba were block clerks and had used the greater freedom of movement afforded by their status to prepare their escape, all Jewish block clerks were also relieved of their duties. Czeslaw Mordowicz, who lost his position at that time, remembers that there were eight or ten Jewish block clerks, most of them from Germany.

In the main camp Jews had hardly any chance of getting an armband; there, the percentage of "Aryans" remained the highest.

In the labor camps that constituted Auschwitz III, Jewish prisoners were in the overwhelming majority. In these camps the inmates working in army factories had contact with civilians, and to prevent the spreading of contagious diseases the SS preferred to send new arrivals to these camps directly from the ramp. However, RSHA transports rolled to the ramp every day, and for that reason Jewish prisoners were for once able to reach even the highest rungs of the inmate hierarchy. Max Schmidt, the camp leader of Fürstengrube, testified: "At first a Jew was the camp elder, but after a certain point he was not permitted to perform that function any more."

Primo Levi reports what Monowitz, the central camp of Auschwitz III, was like in his time:

In 1944 only a few hundred of the old Jewish inmates of Auschwitz with the low numbers under 130,000 were still alive. (The number 150,000 was given out on September 1943, and men were considered "old" inmates after a few months). None of those survivors was an ordinary inmate on an ordinary detail and with ordinary rations. Those left were physicians, tailors, cobblers, musicians, cooks, attractive young homosexuals, and friends or compatriots of some camp authorities; also, especially ruthless, vigorous, and inhumane individuals who maintained themselves as capos, block elders, and in other positions (having been chosen by the SS, which in this regard displayed a satanic knowledge of human nature); and finally those who did not hold specific positions but by virtue of their craftiness and drive were always able to "organize" successfully and consequently could reap not only material benefits and prestige but also the forbearance and esteem of the camp administration.

Levi's description of the Jewish VIPs is just as unsparing as his characterization of the inmate functionaries who did not have to wear a Star of David:

The Jewish VIPs constitute a remarkable and sad human phenomenon. They are the typical result of the structure of the German camps. If you offer some individuals who live like slaves a privileged position, certain comforts, and the prospect of survival in return for a betrayal of the natural solidarity with their comrades, one of them will surely accept this offer. If he gets dominion over a handful of wretches and the power to decide their life or death, he will become cruel and tyrannical, for he knows that otherwise someone else who is considered more suitable will take his place. Furthermore, the entire force of his hatred, which could not be vented on his oppressors, will now come down senselessly on the oppressed. And he will not be satisfied until he has heaped the abuse that he suffered from those above him on those below him.

Many of those acquainted with conditions in Monowitz will reject sweeping statements of this kind as unfair. Levi himself realizes that he is generalizing when he writes: "During the entire endless year in the camp, I had neither the curiosity nor the opportunity to investigate the complex structure of the camp hierarchy. The gloomy structure of evil powers weighed on us as a totality, and our eyes were fixed on the ground." Levi is referring to a source of error that some commentators who have also made snap judgments may not have noticed. He is aware that a Jewish capo was under a stronger compulsion than an "Aryan" one and has this to say about his "Aryan" superior: "This capo is not giving us any trouble because he is not a Jew and hence is not worried about his position."

Some Jewish functionaries are remembered by survivors. Thus Henry Bolawko has described a foreman in Jaworzno, a young Lithuanian named Mosche. He always carried in his right hand the symbol of his rank, a stick, and he administered beatings with it. One day he opened his heart to Bulawko. His wife and three children were murdered in front of his eyes, and his house was destroyed. Mosche was religious and said his prayers every day. And every day he gave beatings.

Carl Laszlo reports about a Hungarian parliamentarian by the name of Fabian, who claimed to be a former government minister; he "gained an important position in the camp through dubious machinations and became one of the most disagreeable and meanest functionaries."

Karl Dubsky, who was sent to Birkenau in July 1942 because of his Jewish descent, has called his first block elder, a Polish Jew, a "beast." Tadeusz Joachimowski may have had the same man in mind when he wrote that the elder of Block 22 gave whippings and beat some inmates to death. His name was Pinkus, and he was originally from France.

Elie Wiesel remembers the elder of Block 57 in Monowitz who "beat an old man for lifting his cap too slowly" and flogged another man because he did not like his face. This wearer of the Star of David took another man's shirt because it was warm and also stole another man's shoes. Wiesel sums up his account by writing: "Yes, I knew the sadistic capos, and I have seen Jews who beat their brethren with a wild gleam in their eyes. . . . When these images come to life again, I am surprised that there were so few lost souls and poisoned hearts in this kingdom of the night where one breathed only hatred, contempt, and loathing of one's own self. What would have become of me if I had stayed in the camps longer—say, five, seven, or twelve years?"

■ In the women's camp, inmates from Slovakia with low numbers rose to the status of a kind of aristocracy. The first RSHA transports from that country in March 1942 contained primarily young girls; married Jewish women from Slovakia were not deported until a bit later. According to Aranka Krausz, who was deported at that time, those able to survive the hard early period usually left Auschwitz alive because after a year the Slovaks with low numbers already had better positions. Katarina Princz confirms that from the summer of 1943 onward every girl from the first Slovak transports who had survived had a good position. Princz came to Auschwitz with the same transport as Krausz. When Krystyna Zywulska was deported to Auschwitz in late August 1944, most of the block elders were Slovakian Jews.

The survivors of the first Slovakian transports are generally described as young girls. Anna Palarczyk remembers that the Slovakian Jews who were appointed block elders were nineteen, eighteen, or as young as seventeen years of age. Kitty Hart, who was sent to the camp in April 1943, has this to say about the Jewish block and dormitory elders from Slovakia: "They literally built the women's camp with their own hands. In the beginning there were many thousands of them; but only a few are alive today, and they occupy the best positions." Krystyna Zywulska believes that the early years in Auschwitz made the girls forget how things were then, and she asks herself: "What did we know about their suffering? Nothing." Lucie Begow, who arrived in Auschwitz in the spring of 1944 describes the Slovak women with low inmate numbers who had positions as the "camp generation," and she estimates that many of them were only sixteen to eighteen at the time. "With one exception their behavior was more German than that of the Germans."

Sura Zofia Herson-Nowak once overheard her block elder Sara Meisels, a young, tall, blonde Jew from Slovakia, say, "I have lost so many relatives here that I know no pity." Meisels gave beatings even when no guard was around.

Miriam Blits, a Dutchwoman who came to Auschwitz in 1944, has described her block elder Laura, a Polish Jew around twenty-two, as follows: "She gave beatings, got attacks of hysteria, and made us kneel for hours with our hands raised." Blits has also given this concise characterization of the Polish capo of the "shit detail": "I haven't seen a more evil creature in my life."

In January 1944 Hertha Ligeti was greeted by a block elder whom she describes as a very young and strikingly dressed Slovak woman: "She was wearing a flowered silk dressing gown and fur-lined slippers; her long blue-black hair was held together on her neck by an enormous sky-blue silk bow; her cheeks and lips were a vivid pink, her small hands were well-padded, and under her dressing gown her breasts were round and full. Next to her stood, like body guards, five girls who were not as splendidly dressed as she but who also seemed to be brimming with health. They were the dormitory orderlies (Stubendienste), called Stubowas, also Slovaks."

Wanda Koprowska says of her dormitory elder in the satellite camp Budy, a Jew named Henryka, that she demanded complete subordination; "otherwise, she would send us to a place we would not leave alive."

Hanna Hoffmann has given the following description of her first encounter with inmate functionaries in the sauna of Birkenau, where all new arrivals were taken: "From time to time one of the robust girls who work in the sauna—as we later learn, Slovak Jews who have been in the KZ for quite some time—comes and straightens out the rows of five (which new arrivals had to form) with the aid of a rubber hose. One of the Slovaks wants my jacket. Because I don't take it off quickly enough, she gives me a hefty slap in the face." Later Hoffmann struck up a conversation with that woman, who told her this: "My parents were immediately sent to the gas. I soon understood what matters. We've all become whores. You, too, will notice that this brings the greatest advantages." Hoffmann describes her in these words: "The girl looks quite indifferent. Empty eyes in a broad, bloated face. A sturdy, muscular figure. She is nineteen, but I would have guessed thirty."

Young Szuszi Gross quickly learned how one could get ahead in Auschwitz. Since the SS attached the greatest importance to military precision when the labor details marched out and in, the capos shouted rhythmically, "Left, two, three, four, left two, three, four," in order to keep everyone in step. When the newcomers had to march out on the first day, Szuszi Gross immediately seized the initiative and commanded loudly, "Left, two, three, four!" After four weeks she had already been made a dormitory orderly.

Eva Gabanyi, one of the women who heard bad things about Gross's conduct, remembers that in the hard early period Szuszi helped to keep up the inmates' morale. Katarina Princz, a childhood friend of Szuszi's, has told a story that illuminates this young girl's development as a block elder more vividly than descriptions of cruelties. One time Katarina became the victim of a selection, and inmates who knew her desperately appealed to block elder Gross to help her friend. "What am I supposed to do for her? Can she shine my shoes?" In her eyes, saving the life of her childhood friend would have made sense only then.

Ana Novac, who was deported with a transport of Hungarians in 1944, has given this portrait of her Slovak block elder: "Come to think of it, she is alive only when she is giving a beating. Then she comes to life like a tennis player who fell asleep during his training and finally starts a match. Her chin juts out and her beautiful, languid lips are pinched. For an instant she motionlessly eyes her victim. Then there flashes around her mouth that peculiar, somewhat evil, and a bit intoxicated smile that brightens her in the truest sense of the word. She swings her whip backward, only to make it whiz down with all her strength the next moment." Novac believes that the Slovak women could not forgive the newcomers for peacefully eating bread and butter in their homes when the Slovaks had to endure their worst years in Auschwitz.

Suzanne Birnbaum calls her dormitory elder, a young Slovak Jew named Elsa, a real panther. "She can't watch us laugh," she writes. The ss also found female sadists. Meyer Levin reports about a seventeen-year-old Jew, the assistant of her capo. "When she was administering a beating, she got excited and flogged until blood flowed."

Particularly well known in the camp was a woman named Cylka, who, according to Anna Palarczyk, was perhaps sixteen when she was deported from Slovakia. She received the armband of a block elder for Block 25, where the Muselmänner had to wait for their transport to the gas chambers. Cylka, who was pretty and very quick-witted, enjoyed the favor of the notorious ss roll call leader Anton Tauber, and this went to her head to such an extent that she raged unrestrainedly against her companions in misfortune. It was probably for this reason that she was later made camp elder in Mexico, where her conduct did not improve. To be sure, a few Slovak women have not forgotten that Cylka helped them. Anna Palarczyk explains the deep demoralization of this young creature by saying, "She had to put her mother on a truck that drove to the gas chamber." Other reports indicate that she tried very hard to get some water to the Mexico section that she headed.

Young Slovak women from the early transports were not the only ones who underwent such a development under the pressure of their experiences. Hanna Hoffmann has described her reception in the Theresienstadt family camp in these words:

The SS is gone. A woman's voice that resembles the roar of an animal calls out, "To the bunks! Get moving, you sows!" The voice is that of a woman I met in Theresienstadt. She runs around and deals out blows until she has finally intimidated the thousand women. She tells them in an imperious tone of voice: "From now on you are prisoners and have to do whatever I tell you because I am your block elder. Shut your trap or I'll belt you in the mouth. If you want to live here, you've got to obey. If there's no discipline, you'll all go into the gas." After a while she added: "All jewelry has to be turned in to me immediately because they'll take everything away from you anyway."

That woman was transferred to Auschwitz from Theresienstadt three months before Hoffmann was. Hoffmann has explained how she and other functionaries underwent such a change in this short period of time: "In the beginning they had Polish block elders who could maintain themselves in the KZ for years only by shedding all moral inhibitions. From them our people learned that the life of your neighbor has no value but, on the contrary, impairs your own existence. Anyone who wanted to live had to be ruthless and know how to beat and kill. Women who were quick to grasp this and were capable of acting in accordance with these laws gradually replaced the Poles in the leadership of the individual blocks." Hoffmann gives this additional picture of that section of the camp: "The real terror of the camp was Fischer, the new camp capo. He had already made a name for himself as an executioner in Theresienstadt, and here he added new luster to it. People knew that he was a psychopath and therefore unpredictable. He frequently ran amok through the camp, bent over and carrying a stick with which he beat everyone in his path." Fischer, who was broad-shouldered and slightly deformed, volunteered in Theresienstadt when the SS wanted one of the prisoners to function as an executioner. When he came forward, he said that he had worked in the anatomical and pathological institute and had acted as an assistant to the Prague executioner. Jehuda Bacon, who was almost a child when he arrived in Auschwitz, also remembers Fischer: "He had absolutely crazy whims, but he loved children and helped them."

Bacon also recalls an incident that seems typical of the atmosphere in this family camp. A friend of Bacon's who had come to Auschwitz with him was looking forward to a reunion with an acquaintance who had been transferred to the family camp from Theresienstadt before him. This acquaintance was now wearing the armband of a block elder, and Bacon's friend greeted him with these words: "Zdenek, I'm glad to see you again." The block elder's only response was two resounding slaps in his face.

◼ Grete Salus, a sensitive observer, has given a vivid description of her block elder, a woman she met in the fall of 1944:

> She ran and yelled all the time. In addition, she constantly listened for German inspectors who might be coming and worried about correct numbers at roll calls. The pressure of this position turned almost all these women into utterly merciless monsters and veritable hyenas. And all this for the sake of getting better accommodations, stuffing themselves to the point of bursting, and having a faint hope of rescue. These human beings saw nothing but death any more. Tomorrow we may no longer be alive and that is why we must eat today, get a piece of bread in exchange for a fine but useless silk scarf or vice versa, trade our only pair of stockings for a piece of bread.
>
> Such a block elder was pathetic. How her face and voice changed when she was talking to a German guard, how nimbly she moved, how submissive and charming she was! And yet one could sense fear behind all of it. Sometimes the ss guard treated her like her best friend, gave her a lot of freedom, often permitted her to visit other sections of the camp after the block was locked, and gave her other privileges of that kind. But none of this was certain or definitive. If such a guard had not slept well, had perhaps not made love to a man in two nights, or was simply in a bad mood, the sun of her favor was quickly eclipsed. In many such cases some trivial matter became the occasion for plunging the privileged person into the darkness of the dirty, anonymous mass. The next day one could already watch another block elder at work with the same fear and the same hope. These women strove to maintain their positions at any cost, and we had to pay the price.
>
> The more beatings such a woman could administer, the better she managed to oppress people, and the more she did for the smooth functioning of the machinery of murder, the more secure her position was. Some of them, but not all, definitely were amoral persons by nature. The majority of them had been made that by the terrible, enervating life that gnawed away at a human being like a running sore. These were people who had already gone through everything. Their relatives had been gunned down before their eyes, and they had been forced to watch their children being murdered in the cruelest way. They had become inured to human suffering because they had suffered too much themselves.

Grete Salus concludes her analysis with this remark: "These were people who had already forgotten that they ever led a life different from that of a KZ inmate. They lived only in the present, without a past or a future, and had become nothing but products of the camp." Continuing her attempts to fathom the reason for such a woman's behavior, Salus writes: "Our block elder had a small boy with her. He lined up for the roll call; the Germans saw him but left him alone. The woman had rescued the child, who was not hers, and by virtue of her position he was silently tolerated. We saw such children in a few other groups as well. She treated this boy in a touching fashion; he was well dressed, kept warm by being wrapped in the best woolen blankets, and looked the very picture of good health. Perhaps she did bad things only in order to save this little human life.

A Jewish woman from Slovakia who had been deported at age nineteen, soon obtained a position in Auschwitz, and later was bitterly attacked for abusing her power. She wrote this in her own defense: "Perhaps our shortcomings can be excused because we were young, inexperienced, and wanted to live. One false step might have meant that everything was lost, and there were certainly many missteps."

It was much harder for Jews to act in the interest of their fellow sufferers than it was for "Aryans," but several Jews did have the strength to do so. Jolan Groß-Deutsch has emphasized that Margit Bachmann was "very decent." Bachmann, who was on the first RSHA transport from Slovakia, wore the armband of a capo of the *Truppenwirtschaftslager* (garrison service center). Seweryn Praport praises the block elder of Block 6 in the Birkenau men's camp for behaving "very well" when Praport and many others arrived there in the fall of 1943. The block elder, whom Praport remembers only as Heinrich, was a Jew from Slovakia who might already have been fifty at the time. Numerous women and even three children owe their lives to Bozena Teichnerova, a young Slovakian nurse, who risked a great deal as block elder in the inmate infirmary to help others. Many of those she saved never found out how much they owed her.

Mala Zimetbaum, a young runner and interpreter in the women's camp, has been emphatically praised. A native of Poland who emigrated to Belgium as a child and was deported from there to Auschwitz in September 1942 at the age of twenty-two, she was soon given a very influential position in the camp on the basis of her knowledge of languages, her self-assurance, and her above-average intelligence. "Despite her position and her power she remained one of the few whose power did not go to their heads," writes Raya Kagan. "Unlike so many other VIPs, she did not become hardhearted." Mala warned patients when she heard about impending selections in the infirmary. Suzanne

Birnbaum has commented that it was one of Mala's duties to assign those discharged from the infirmary to details and that she was helpful to many inmates. Mala primarily concerned herself with Jewish women from Belgium and France, who rarely had influential acquaintances in the camp.

Kari Demerer, the Jewish camp elder of Blechhammer who had been deported from Germany, has been generally praised. Maria Rajs-Skowron affirms that when she was transferred to Blechhammer from another camp, in which a very bad Jewish elder had been in power, she thought she had come to a paradise. Gita Brandszedter-Szulberg emphasizes that inmates who had mistreated their charges were removed at Demerer's behest. The German Jew Lutz Hess, a night watchman in the Monowitz infirmary, may stand for many others whose comradely behavior has not been recorded. Samuel Graumann has reported about the man. As the ss physician Friedrich Entress later testified, wooden shoes could mean a death sentence for their wearers because they caused cellulitis. Good shoes, on the other hand, could save lives. One day Hess observed how a new arrival who had to strip for disinfection threw his good shoes out the window. He searched for him all over the camp in order to return these shoes, and his conduct can be properly appreciated only if one knows that all kinds of treasures could be obtained in the camp for a pair of good shoes. But this touching deed, which under Auschwitz condition seems unworldly, was not the only way in which Lutz Hess helped others. Rudolf Robert testifies that on two occasions Hess pulled him out of a group of selectees, thereby saving his life. Bergmann, a mine inspector, unwittingly gave Jewish inmate functionaries high marks when he demanded that the Jewish capos in the Jaworzno coal mine be replaced with "Aryan" ones because, in his experience, an increased output was to be expected under the direction of the latter.

CREATING ACCOMPLICES
■ ■ ■

In every prison and camp the guards seek and find persons who do their bidding in return for privileges. The more hopeless the situation of the prisoners, the easier it is for their masters. In an extermination camp the temptation to obtain better living conditions by acting as an informer was especially great. Besides, in Auschwitz the camp Gestapo had established a veritable informer factory in the bunker under its control. This is what I wrote about the subject in my *Bericht*:

> The swing is the Political Department's favorite form of torture. An inmate has to sit on the floor and draw up his knees. His hands are bound in front and pulled over his knees. A pole is placed under the hollows of his knees and over his lower arms, and the inmate is hung from this pole with his head down. Then he is rocked back and forth, and with each swing he gets a slap on his buttocks. All this would be bearable, but, worst of all, the tormentors hit his genitals. Boger, the notorious ss technical sergeant of the Political Department, takes direct aim at these. The inmates who are sent to the bunker have to strip and get only thin dungarees but no underwear. I never imagined that testicles could swell so horrendously and turn blue and green. Those coming from the swing cannot sit or lie for days. If someone has not talked despite this torture, he is picked up again after two days. By that time even the slightest touch is hellishly painful. If an inmate is put on the swing again, he has to be made of steel to keep his mouth shut.

> A Pole from my cell was given this treatment on the swing and sent for again after a short time. Since he evidently could not say what Boger wanted to hear from him but was not able to bear the pain, he stated that a compatriot of his, a man who was also incarcerated in the cell, was secretly corresponding with comrades in the camp. If I had not seen with my own eyes how badly that man had been mauled, I would have scornfully condemned him as an informer. Since then I have been cautious in my judgment and condemnations.

> I was spared such torture. All I can say is that I was firmly resolved not to betray anyone and anything, but I don't know whether I could have kept my resolution.

> By this method the Political Department was able to turn inmates into its confidential agents. In Auschwitz there also were informers who did not have to be forced to provide the ss with information. Most of those known through-

out the camp were Poles, for it was a primary interest of the Political Department to uncover contacts between Polish prisoners and the surrounding population as well as the Polish underground in the camp. Only a Pole could help it in this endeavor, and that is why it gave special privileges and options to Polish informers whose activities they considered promising.

Stefan Olpinski was a man who became unfavorably known. This Pole, who was born in 1898, had connections with Nazis and spoke on German radio stations before the war. The Political Department installed him in the infirmary as an informer. Experienced inmates were forewarned against him by the fact that he was the only survivor of a group of inmates who had been incarcerated in the bunker because of sabotage after a railway car had been set afire on a siding. Wladyslaw Fejkiel describes Olpinski as a fine figure of a man with agreeable manners who mastered several languages. He had his own room in Block 25, and no one really knew what detail he had been assigned to. He was reputed to have received several visits from his daughter and to be the only inmate who owned a revolver. Czeslaw Ostankowicz heard that Olpinski had two sons who served in the Waffen-ss.

Józef Lewandowski was another Pole placed in the bunker by the Political Department to sound out his cell mates. This was later confirmed by Klaus Dylewski, the ss sergeant of that department. This is what Jan Pilecki, the Polish block clerk of the bunker, told the Frankfurt court about Lewandowski: "I remember that one time a group of inmates was locked in the bunker under suspicion of having prepared an escape through a canal. Inmate Lewandowski was part of the group, and I had noticed that he had already come in with a group on several previous occasions and had always been the sole survivor." Klaus Dylewski testified that one time Lewandowski had himself been caught trying to escape and had saved his life by offering to become an informer.

Another important agent of the Political Department was the Pole Ernst Malorny, who was also over forty years of age. He lived together with Olpinski in Block 25.

■ The most dangerous informer in the main camp was Stanislaw Dorosiewicz. Born in 1908, he was deported to Auschwitz as early as July 1940 and was in charge of other informers in the camp. "We ran away from him as from the plague," writes Dr. Adam Zacharski, an experienced Pole. An incident I happened to hear about may characterize his modus operandi. In a conversation with a Polish block clerk, Dorosiewicz made this remark: "Strange that you haven't been in the bunker yet." Since the block clerk knew that Dorosiewicz had already informed on many Poles who had then been shot at the Black Wall, he told his block elder and friend, an influential German, about this remark. That man spoke to Dorosiewicz, who trivialized this incident and casually asked the block elder whether he had a good wristwatch for him. The block elder understood and promised to get him one, but it slipped his mind. In a subsequent conversation, Dorosiewicz gave some broad hints that he had heard something concerning the block clerk. The block elder remembered instantly, procured a wristwatch for Dorosiewicz, and the matter was over and done with. Not always did Dorosiewicz's actions end so harmlessly.

Not just little and little-known informers were dropped by the SS as soon as they had outlived their usefulness. Lewandowski, too, was shot by the Political Department during his fourth stay in the bunker. Klaus Dylewski had heard that Lewandowski's role as an agent provocateur in the camp had become known, and this rendered him worthless to Dylewski.

Olpinski became a victim of his compatriots' revenge. They sent him a beautiful pullover that contained typhus-carrying lice, and Olpinski was promptly infected. Since he suspected the connection, he resisted for a long time being sent to the infirmary. When this became unavoidable, the Political Department demanded that its protégé receive special care. The SS garrison physician, however, knew the role this informer had played and protected the Polish physicians and nurses whose treatment caused Olpinski to die of typhus. Malorny also paid for his treason with his life.

Dorosiewicz was cannier. When his all-powerful patron Grabner disappeared in the fall of 1943 and it became known that an SS legal commission was investigating the practices of the department he had headed, Dorosiewicz used his resources to reach a safe haven. Later Dylewski testified as follows:

> The former inmate Dorosiewicz was probably identical with an Armenian informer who occasionally came to the Political Department and gave it information about preparations for escapes and other goings-on in the camp. When he supplied information about attempted escapes, he was referred to me. I questioned him on several occasions and remember that he repeatedly made completely untenable and groundless statements. I know that one day he said something about hidden weapons and concealed jewelry; that case was then taken over by Lachmann. In making such reports Dorosiewicz was supported by a Jewish inmate whose name I no longer remember. When an SS man accompanied these two inmates to the presumed hiding place, they killed him and then escaped.

SS roll call leader Kaduk, who also remembered this dramatic episode, testified that the two "V-Leute" (*Vertrauensleute*, informers), as he expertly called the informers, had stated that gold was hidden near the fishponds. I have already mentioned Dorosiewicz's attempted provocation shortly before his escape as well as its consequences.

When the escape became known, the resistance movement wrote as follows to the Polish underground organization outside the camp. "It is absolutely necessary to set a trap for the camp informer Dorosiewicz. He is about thirty-five years old, has long hair, and is known to civilians in the area. His purpose is to expose camp contacts with the outside. He has to be either poisoned (he drinks schnapps) or shot, without hesitation and as quickly as possible." As I have already mentioned, this episode became an occasion for influencing Commandant Liebehenschel.

However, Dorosiewicz was able to elude the Poles' revenge. Even after the end of the war he continued to live unchallenged in his country. In fact, incriminating material gathered by survivors of Auschwitz was set aside by the leadership of the organization that was legally responsible for representing the interests of victims of Nazis in Poland. When an official charge was brought against Dorosiewicz, the Polish authorities did not react. My Polish friends explain this strange behavior by saying that Dorosiewicz was still practicing his profession, the only difference being that he now worked for the Russians rather than the SS.

In Birkenau the brothers Wacek and Franek Katarszynski had a reputation that was comparable to that of Olpinski and Dorosiewicz in the main camp. The Pole Józef Mikusz, a well-informed observer, has described these block elders as "real Polish devils who mistreated newcomers wherever they could." They, too, were under the protection of the Political Department and thus unassailable.

Members of other nations also played a shady role in Auschwitz. At his hearing in Frankfurt, the German Rudolf Kauer sketched such a graphic picture of his activities that no commentary is necessary: "I was transferred from Neuengamme to Auschwitz on a collective transport because I had had some trouble with the SS. At first I was in Block 13 of the main camp for a short time, and then I had a single room in Block 1. I had a pass and could move about freely in the camp. Between the main camp and Birkenau there was a road that was not guarded, and I was able to pass that stretch too. In the Political Department I had my own room in the barracks opposite the administration building. I had the run of the place and a permanent pass signed by SS camp leader Aumeier, but I never had to show it because everybody knew me."

At the preliminary hearing in Frankfurt, Kauer had provided highly incriminating and concrete evidence against the accused members of the Political Department, but at the trial he retracted his testimony. When he was questioned about Boger, all he said was this: "Boger had a bad reputation in the camp, but so did I." It is likely that he eventually became a nuisance to his SS patrons in Auschwitz, as had happened in Neuengamme, for in September 1944 he was surprisingly transferred to a camp near Litomerice. Kauer had been sentenced for high treason in 1933 and wore a red triangle.

The SS exploited the implacable enmity between an ultrarightist Ukrainian organization that was headed by the Bandera brothers and the Poles in Auschwitz. Kazimierz Smolen, the clerk of the admissions division, remembers that "the admitting office (for the members of the Bandera group) was the headquarters of the security police (Sicherheitspolizei, or Sipo) in Cracow, which also exercised special surveillance over the group. At its behest Stark (an SS man in the Political Department) took an interest in it. The group was housed together."

Dr. Nikolaus Klymyschyn, a surviving member of this group, has given the following frank characterization of its political position: "We asked the German government (after the invasion of the Ukraine by German troops) whether it wanted to be our friend or foe. By arresting us it showed that it was the latter."

For obvious reasons the SS recruited informers from this group. Bogdan Komarnicki has been described as one of the most dangerous. When he contracted typhus, a member of the Political Department threatened that ten Polish nurses would be done in if anything happened to Komarnicki. In a confession made in captivity, SS roll call leader Claussen mentioned another Bandera man who worked as a physician in the bunker block and notified the SS when inmates on the staff there tried to help those incarcerated in the bunker. Whether Boris Grawtschenko was also a Ukrainian is not known. Joseph Hermann has testified that Grawtschenko organized attempts at escape in Fürstengrube and then betrayed them to the SS. In the end he shared the fate of most informers. He became burdensome to his patrons and was put on a transfer transport. SS camp leader Schmidt made the Poles who had been assigned to the same transport aware of Grawtschenko's activities as an informer, and this presumably led to his being lynched.

Another informer became known through his assignment to find out who had smuggled out of the Union Works the explosives with which the Sonderkommando had blown up a crematorium on October 7, 1944. Israel Gutmann, a member of the Union Commando, writes: "I knew that informer; he was Eugen Koch, a half-Jew from Czechoslovakia and a foreman in my department." His conduct made him suspect. "While an inmate usually had an expressionless face when an SS man approached, Koch became submissive and groveling. He often spoke to SS men without having been asked." The suspicion intensified. "Without a particular reason he received permission to walk around freely in the plant. Sometimes he disappeared for several hours, and no one knew where he had gone. Finally he managed to get himself a young girl from Belgium. He declared his love, showered her with presents, and sounded her out without the girl catching on." In that way the SS discovered the division's external connections in obtaining explosives, and four girls were eventually hanged. As Bruno Baum reports, "Fate caught up with the bastard Koch in Mauthausen."

Anyone acquainted with the tragic effects of the informers' activities will understand why the camp breathed a sigh of relief when the new commandant Liebehenschel had the best-known informers transferred to another camp. However, this did not completely eliminate the deleterious informer system, as demonstrated by the fact that Kauer remained in the camp. Koch probably was not recruited as an informer until later.

■ The SS also enlisted the services of inmates for other duties. For an SS medic it was too much of a strain to inject poison into the hearts of dozens and sometimes even more than a hundred *Muselmänner* every day, and so inmates frequently had to perform this dirty chore for them. Both Josef Klehr, an SS medic, and Adam Zacharski, a Polish inmate who served as a clerk, have stated that Peter Welsch was the first prisoner who agreed to administer injections. Welsch, who came from Westphalia and wore the red triangle of a political prisoner, had been transferred to Auschwitz from Sachsenhausen and assigned to the infirmary as a block elder. Later he was transferred to the Birkenau infirmary as a camp elder and played an evil role there as well.

Welsch's work in the main camp was taken over by Poles: the officer Alfred Stössel, block elder in the infirmary, Mieczyslaw Panszczyk, and Felix Walentynowicz, all three of whom had arrived on the first transport of Poles, and Jerzy Szymkowiak, a former member of the Foreign Legion. Stanislaw Klodzinski, who was well acquainted with conditions in the infirmary, mentions an additional man who was said to have given injections, Dr. Landau. The most zealous of these was Panszczyk, who boasted of having killed 12,000 human beings with his own hands and enjoyed the fear that he spread. As a deputy block elder with no medical training, he loved to perform minor surgery, and it did not matter to him if in lancing a boil he occasionally also cut tendons and blood vessels.

In return for their help with killings, the men mentioned above enjoyed numerous privileges. Janusz Mlynarski remembers that for every murderous campaign they received a bonus of alcohol. I do not believe, however, that this alone induced those people to kill fellow inmates by giving them shots of poison. It is likely that an awareness of being on the side of those who so demonstratively flaunted their strength (these killings were accomplished when Hitler's victories had not yet been followed by defeats) and to be among the supermen who could kill without being accountable to anyone—in short, the intoxication with power of otherwise totally powerless men—removed the inhibitions that would under normal conditions surely have kept even these accomplices from killing someone every day.

The SS medics needed willing, skillful, and tireless accomplices. Such an activity could not be forced. That a man could refuse to give injections was demonstrated by Dr. Mikulas Korn. After Panszyczyk left Auschwitz, Korn was invited by the SDG Erich Hentl to take over his work. Even though he was a Jew and thus had to fear the consequences of a refusal more than any "Aryan," Korn did not accept the invitation. Nothing was done to him, and he survived Auschwitz.

It has been reported that Szymkowiak once had scruples. "He was generally known as a sadist," wrote Czeslaw Sowul, "and was used for killing campaigns. When children were taken to the infirmary early in 1943 to receive injections, he refused to administer them. SDG Herbert Scherpe called him a pig and slapped his face." Nevertheless, Szymkowiak did not kill these children. Wladyslaw Fejkiel remembers that Szymkowiak helped to preserve patients from those injections before Klehr, for reasons unknown to Fejkiel, prevailed upon him to administer them. Stössel's conduct, too, was not as unambiguous as Panszczyk's. As Czeslaw Ostankowicz has testified, Stössel saved many lives, and not just those of Poles. He warned comrades against informers and even used his power to get rid of dangerous specimens.

It was probably because of an abnormal disposition that Panszczyk became a murderous henchman. This is indicated by observations made by Adam Zacharski, who reports that Panszczyk was noticeably restless on mornings before injections but was calm and behaved normally after the killings in Block 20. Panszczyk, who had been a student at an art academy, once showed Zacharski a picture he had painted. It showed a Christ figure with a crown of thorns and a bloody face rising from a lake filled with blood instead of water.

Willingly performing services in the SS machinery of killing did not save those men's lives any more than it had saved the informers' lives. During an action against Polish officers, Stössel was shot at the Black Wall in March 1943. A short time before that, Stefan Boratyski had been imprisoned in the same cell as Stössel. He remembers that Grabner, the head of the Political Department, twice asked Stössel whether he was prepared to work for him. Stössel just shook his head; he did not want to buy his life in that way.

Szymkowiak was transferred to the Gypsy camp, where he succumbed to injuries in the summer of 1943. An operation could not save him. Evidently the revenge of his fellow inmates had reached him.

Panszczyk was transferred to Neuengamme after fellow Polish inmates had ousted him from the infirmary by threatening to reveal his homosexual activities. There, Poles who knew him from Auschwitz kept asking him whether he remembered this or that man, giving names of people to whom he had administered lethal injections in Auschwitz. He is said to have finally lost control, banged his head against the wall, and sought the protection of the commandant of the camp. He was assigned to a detail that had to look for bombs in nearby Hamburg, and that is where he died.

Only Peter Welsch survived the camp. He has been moving from place to place in Germany restlessly. Living on a pension, he has changed his place of residence half a dozen times in a few years.

■ The SS not only looked for accomplices in administering their injections but also used inmates as executioners. Leo Vos reports about a Jewish inmate who had a privileged position as a bath attendant in the Blechhammer labor camp, where the population was almost exclusively Jewish. In return for that he had to function as a hangman when the camp administration ordered an execution. When this bath attendant once again had to practice his second profession, the man sentenced to death with a noose around his neck called out to him: "A fine job you picked out for yourself!" This caused the bath attendant's nerves to snap; when he returned to his room, he moaned: "Who suffers more, the hanged man or the inmate who is forced to be a hangman?" This question may be called demagogic, primitively egotistical, or even provocative, but it does touch on a problem whose solution is not as simple as it may seem to an outsider. The case of "Bunker Jakob" demonstrates this vividly.

Jakob Kozelczuk, a Jew, came to Auschwitz from eastern Poland in late January 1943. On the ramp he attracted the attention of the SS because of his height and his unusual athletic build. Jakob was a boxer and rumored to have been the trainer of the German world champion Max Schmeling, though Schmeling denied this. Because of his physical attributes, the SS assigned him to the bunker as a *Kalfaktor* (handyman) for tasks formerly performed by a German and then by a Pole. The bunker assistant was supposed to be a man of exceptional strength, for he not only had to keep the place clean and distribute food under the supervision of an SS man on duty but also had to assist when the bunker was *ausgestaubt* (dusted off), as Grabner liked to put it. On such occasions the inmates of the cellar cells were taken up to the washroom and forced to undress, whereupon the *Kalfaktor* took them by twos to the Black Wall.

The bunker *Kalfaktor* enjoyed many privileges. Jakob lived by himself in a small room in the bunker block and was able to "organize" whatever he wanted in the camp, for who would not have wanted to be in Bunker Jakob's good graces? He could even establish intimate contact with women because they were also locked up in the bunker. Since the block leader on duty was often too lazy to go down to the cellar, Jakob opened the cells himself. I met Jakob shortly after I had been taken to the bunker, and this is what I wrote about it in my *Bericht*:

Collect my thoughts. First: Don't I have something on me? I search my pockets, but inconspicuously, so that others (in my cell) should not notice it. In my breast pocket there is a slip with numbers of Jewish inmates that Lokmanis gave me yesterday. I was supposed to see whether I could get them placed on a good detail. I've got to get rid of this slip, but how? I don't want to tear it up or throw it away in the presence of the others.

The door is open again. Now Lachmann (the SS man from the Political Department who took me to the bunker) is standing in the doorway. "Come." He beckons to me and asks Jakob, "Have you already frisked him?" "Yes, sir, Herr Unterscharführer, very carefully. All he has is a handkerchief." Jakob stands at attention.

"Take your shoes off!" He examines my shoes carefully to make sure I haven't hidden anything in them. I can hear my heart pound. "He'll be put on the other side. Solitary." Again we pass through two doors with iron bars and reach a dark hallway. This time Jakob unlocks the last door. An empty cell. I am alone. The slip of paper! I quickly pull it out, rip it into tiny pieces, and throw these into a pail that contains some liquid. Jakob lied to Lachmann. He has helped me.

If Lachmann had checked my pockets, not only my life but the lives of the bearers of those numbers would have been forfeited. During my detention in the bunker I confirmed the role that Jakob had been assigned at the bunker selections. I have described the first selection that I experienced in these words:

By now many people have been placed in my cell. One day the usual monotony is interrupted: "Clean up everything; the commission is coming." This is what Jakob tells every cell when coffee is given out in the morning. . . .

Keys. The clattering of the barred door. Footsteps, a lot of them. Then indistinct voices. No sound can be heard from us. All of us live with our ears. Now they are in our corridor.

"Be quiet, we can't hear anything." A few men push toward the door. "Line up, they're coming!"

We form a line, and I am at the head, facing the door. The creaking of a key. I feel my heart pound. The door is open. Grabner stands there, and next to him are Hofmann, an SS first lieutenant and deputy camp leader, and the SS roll call leader, as well as a few caps and faces that I don't know. Jakob is among them.

I can see all this all too clearly, as if it were a sharp photograph. I try not to let my voice betray my excitement when I speak. "Everyone give his number!" bellows the SS roll call leader. He grabs my sleeve and gives it a twist. "Inmate 60-3-55," I say and can't help thinking that it sounds like a telephone number. "Him I need right away. Out with him." The voice comes from behind, and I recognize it immediately as Lachmann's. Before I can start to go, I am dragged out. "But put him on the side; he's going to be interrogated." That was Grabner's voice, and he spoke to Jakob, who is now gripping my arm and dragging me to the end of the corridor.

"Nothing will happen to you," he whispers and then slaps my face. Perhaps he is afraid that someone has seen him speaking with me. I am led on. In the anteroom many men are lined up in quintuple file. Their faces are pale. Or is it the artificial light down here? Jakob pushes me into a dark corner. "Stay put here." I can't see or hear any more.

I stand there for a long time. Footsteps, voices, all the time footsteps and voices. Then commands: "Right face!" Then shuffling, clattering, marching.

How long have I been standing here? I've lost all sense of time. It is a long, dark moment between life and death. Jakob comes for me. I am alone with him. He leads me up through the bars and puts me in the corridor. Three men are standing there as well. The others—the many besides us—I haven't seen anywhere.

When I was brought back from the hearing, my cell was empty. This is all my *Bericht* says: "'Where have the others gone?' Jakob slams the door shut without responding."

After the next selections I knew both the ritual and Jakob's duties. "When the noonday meal is distributed, I look Jakob in the face," I wrote in my *Bericht*. "When our eyes meet, he nods to me, gently and sadly. Poor Jakob."

Jakob, whom the block clerk Jan Pilecki called illiterate, spoke a strange mixture of Yiddish and German, Polish and Russian. I observed him intently, the way an inmate observes everything that takes place outside his cell. One day he mentioned that he had been to South America, and from then on I communicated with him via scraps of Spanish; that way we could be fairly certain that we had no unwelcome eavesdroppers on our brief conversations when Jakob had to open the cells by himself. He gave me information and transmitted messages from me to prisoners in other cells.

Many people had similar experiences with Jakob. "Jakob made a lot of fuss," wrote Curt Posener, "but he also helped a lot. Sometimes he brought blankets and cigarettes." He gave Tadeusz Joachimowski news of accomplices and drew Stefan Boratynski's attention to an informer who had been locked up in his cell. Under the pretext that he needed him for cleaning, Jakob let Josef Neumann speak with an accomplice in another cell. Simon Slezak, who was tortured on the swing, gave this testimony: "I believe I owe it to Jakob that I got off relatively unhurt. He looked after me and cared for me very circumspectly, just as he cared for the other men who had been tortured." On orders from the Political Department Henryk Bartosiewicz was locked up in a stand-up cell of the bunker, where he was to be given neither food nor drink, but together with Pilecki Jakob found ways of feeding him secretly.

As a bunker *Kalfaktor*, Jakob also had to administer corporal punishment. Thomas Geve reports that experienced inmates rejoiced when they received this punishment from Jakob rather than from an ss man. He was a fearful sight when he counted out twenty-five whacks, but his blows hurt less than those of ss men. Joseph Hermann states that after he had been sentenced to receive twenty-five blows Jakob administered this punishment in such gentle fashion that he suffered no serious injuries but only bruises. How many others did Jakob help who can no longer testify to this?

In American captivity, ss roll call leader Claussen wrote that Jakob aided primarily his coreligionists. After my release from the bunker, I learned that my Jewish friends in the resistance movement had asked Jakob to help me because I was helping Jews in the camp. However, Jakob helped me right after my arrival in the bunker when that message could not have reached him yet. The testimonies of Bartosiewicz, Joachimowski, and Boratynski also indicate that Jakob helped not just Jews or persons on whose behalf Jewish friends had intervened with him.

On several occasions Jakob had to act as a hangman at executions in the roll call area. One day, when a Jew was to be hanged, the rope broke. Jakob was temporarily put in a bunker cell, and the condemned man was hanged again.

There are also negative judgments about Jakob. As far as I can tell, these are from persons who observed him performing his functions but did not witness his quiet relief actions. What should Jakob have done? If he had refused to do what was demanded of him, this would have been tantamount to suicide, for he wore the Star of David. If he had asked me at the time what he should do, I would surely have advised him to stick it out and continue to help as best he could.

On the other hand, many sheer opportunists defend themselves by saying that if they had refused to participate in atrocities, these would still have been committed, and possibly in even crueler fashion. Generally speaking, this argument is inadmissible even in the case of people caught in a predicament as inmates. Who can decide when it is correct to incur guilt in order to be able to help and when it is false?

After the war Jakob worked as a showman and strongman in Israel, where he died. Legal proceedings that had been instituted against him were dropped after the receipt of numerous exonerating testimonies.

If a prisoner became a collaborator of the SS, he had to reckon with the merciless revenge of his fellow inmates as soon as he lost the protection of the camp administration. This revenge was easiest when an informer was recognized after his transfer to another camp and before performing the same services there. Henry Bulawko reports about a Jew from Marseille who had been recruited as an informer by the Gestapo in France and was hunted down and beaten to death on his arrival in Auschwitz. I still remember how a newcomer was mercilessly chased through the camp by fellow prisoners until he finally ran into the high-tension wire and died. He, too, had betrayed others while still living in freedom and had been recognized. I was disconcerted by the savagery of this unmerciful hounding, but—like the overwhelming majority of my fellow inmates—I approved of lynch law in such a situation.

Abraham Matuszak testified how one day a traitor was stoned in Monowitz with the approval of the camp elder. Oszkár Betlen reports how in the same camp the capo of Commando 21, "one of the meanest fellows, a man who has the blood of many prisoners on his hands," was thrown into a filthy latrine, where he choked to death. Afterward, other capos who were also notorious floggers looked "timidly and worriedly at the human beings whom they had whipped and hounded only yesterday. What was in store for them? Wouldn't some of them be found suffocated in the latrine one day? For no one in the camp doubted that the capo of Commando 21 did not wind up at the bottom of the latrine by accident."

The SS was understanding in such cases of instant justice as long as one of its important agents was not involved.

Prisoners who took justice into their own hands did not always reach their goals. Judith Sternberg-Newman reports about a Croatian Jew named Schulz who mistreated the female inmates in his charge as the capo in the Union Commando. One evening Schulz was given such a beating that he was found the next morning lying in the snow in front of the barracks unconscious and with broken ribs. The camp administration saw to it that Schulz's injuries were healed; he returned to his post and is reputed to have given more severe beatings than before. However, according to a report by Ludovic Breiner, he did not escape revenge. Schulz was evacuated to Buchenwald, where he was appointed as a capo again. After the liberation, Polish Jews who had been forced to work under him drowned him in a tub used for purposes of disinfection.

An attempt to apply lynch law to the infamous SS garrison physician of the Birkenau men's infirmary, the Polish army physician Zenon Zenkteller, was unsuccessful. As long as he worked under the protection of the SS physicians, he was unassailable. When Poles with old numbers were transferred to other camps, Zenkteller was also scheduled to leave Auschwitz in the fall of 1944. The railway cars were still at the ramp in Birkenau when inmates began to beat the hated physician, and thus Zenkteller had a chance to beg an SS physician known to him for help. He was pulled out of the transport, taken back to the camp, and remained in his office.

I have already described how the vengeance of his fellow inmates caught up with Panszczyk in Neuengamme. Dov Paisikovic, who was assigned to the Sonderkommando, has reported a case of instant justice with a special background. In the summer of 1944 the Nazis liquidated the Lodz ghetto and deported the last inhabitants to Auschwitz. At that time Rumkowski, the Jewish elder of this ghetto, and his family were transported to Auschwitz and taken directly to one of the big crematoriums. Jews from Lodz were members of the Sonderkommando that had to work in this crematorium. They recognized the hated Rumkowski in the anteroom of the gas chamber and beat him to death. When I asked Paisikovic how the SS men reacted to this scene, his answer was, "They enjoyed it." Others claim that Rumkowski died after being shot in the neck by an SS man. However, since Paisikovic assured me that he was an eyewitness of the scene described by him, he is probably more credible.

With a few exceptions, those who sold themselves to the executioner in the extermination camp were not able to buy their lives, and yet even intelligent persons attempted this way of saving themselves. Under the conditions of Auschwitz, there was all too often a failure not just of character but also of intellect.

THE SONDERKOMMANDO
■ ■ ■

Only one of the many SS men who saw a gas chamber after it had been re-opened described his impression without sugarcoating it. Richard Böck tes-tified as follows on November 2, 1960: "The corpses were so entangled that it was impossible to recognize whom the various limbs and other body parts belonged to. I, for example, saw that one of the people who were gassed put his index finger a few centimeters deep into another man's eye sockets."

It was the daily duty of the inmates on the Sonderkommando to take those corpses to the ovens in the crematoriums or to the pyres.

Sigismund Bendel was assigned to this detail as a physician because mem-bers of this strictly isolated squad who took sick could not be admitted to the infirmary. Bendel, one of the very few survivors of the Sonderkommando, has presented the observations he was able to make with a certain detachment: "For two endless minutes one could hear people beating against the walls. Screams that no longer sounded human. After that nothing." After the gas chamber had been opened, the sight gave the impression that those locked in it had still engaged in a hopeless struggle against death. Entangled corpses full of blood oozed out of the chamber. The still warm bodies were handled by a barber who cut their hair and a dentist who extracted their gold teeth. "And now incredible hell broke loose. Men whom I knew, such as a learned lawyer from Saloniki or an engineer from Budapest, no longer had anything human about them. They were veritable devils. Amid blows from the cudgels and lashes from the whips of the SS, they ran like men possessed in order to complete their tasks as soon as possible. Thick black smoke rose from the pits. All this happened so quickly and was so unimaginable that I thought I was dreaming." Bendel concludes his account with these words: "An hour later everything was in order again. The men piled up the ashes that they took from the pit. Another transport arrived at Crematorium IV." That was everyday life in the Sonderkommando. Bendel testified about his own activity before a British military court in 1945: "I had to help if, for example, a man burned his feet in human fat." The inmates on the Sonderkommando had to douse the corpses with the fat that flowed from the pyres so they would burn better.

Not everyone of the few survivors of the Sonderkommando is prepared to speak about his experiences, and one must respect their silence.

Henryk Porebski, an electrician who had to take care of the installations of the crematoriums and thus came in contact with the Sonderkommando, knew that members of this detail had buried notes next to Crematorium II. It is due to his constant urging that seventeen years after the liberation of Auschwitz these documents were finally dug up. Despite the fact that these papers were carefully wrapped, they were not in good condition after all that time, and often only scraps of sentences could be deciphered. This is what can be read at the beginning: "Written by . . . exactly at . . . Sonderkommando of Crematorium II, Aug. 5, 1944 by Zelman Lewental, Ciechanow, Poland." Later it says: "No one can imagine exactly how things happened, for it is unimaginable that a precise account of our experiences can be given. . . . We, however—a small group of gray people who will give historians a rather hard time . . . but also the psychologists who want to know and investigate the mental condition of the people who tackled this dismal and dirty work; oh, that is interesting! But who knows whether these investigators will fathom the truth, whether anyone will be able to thoroughly . . ."

Dov Paisikovic remembers Lewental, who was probably twenty-five to twenty-seven at the time, walked with a stoop, and was exempted from the worst work because he did barracks duty. Paisikovic describes him as "exceptionally capable and decent." A year later a notebook of Lewental's was dug up near the ruins of Crematorium II; written in Yiddish, it also describes events involving the Sonderkommando, though only fragments could be deciphered. Other, less voluminous manuscripts by members of the Sonderkommando have been found and afford certain insights.

Anyone who wants to consider the conduct of members of a Sonderkommando must remember Lewental's warning. All comparisons are bound to fail. The boundary lines that were crossed by forced labor of this kind cannot be crossed even in thought after the fact. We have to take note of what may be learned about the existence and behavior of these human beings.

■ Only in the beginning did ss camp leader Schwarzhuber select from the Jews lined up in the Birkenau men's camp those who were assigned to the Sonderkommando. "He had a great eye for it," writes Szmulewski, who observed that Schwarzhuber made his choices not only on the basis of a strong build but also with regard to a man's physiognomy. Later it became the rule that young, vigorous people were assigned to the Sonderkommando straight from the ramp, before they had become acquainted with the camp. In exceptional cases persons were assigned to it by way of punishment—for example, Szyja Rosenblum in May 1944 because he had escaped from a labor camp and was wearing a German uniform when he was captured. Only a small number of "Aryans" were put on this detail: several Poles and Germans served as capos, and in April 1944 nineteen Russians, who had previously been members of a Sonderkommando in Majdanek, were assigned to it. According to Paisikovic, they were officers. When the scope of the extermination reached its zenith in the spring of that year, the Sonderkommando was expanded to a thousand inmates.

The SS tolerated the appropriation of food and alcohol by members of this detail. There was more than enough in the possession of the victims when they went to the gas chambers. Besides, valuables of all kinds were hidden in the clothes and belongings that they left behind in the undressing rooms next to the chambers; the members of the Sonderkommando had to remove those belongings, and the SS could not prevent the inmates from appropriating some of the valuables as well. The last items that the naked victims relinquished outside the door to the gas chamber were their shoes, which members of the Sonderkommando had to collect. Paisikovic told me that valuables were frequently hidden in these shoes: "It is understandable that people concealed in the last object that they were allowed to keep things that they wanted to retain if possible."

Many who were interned in Birkenau have observed members of the Sonderkommando. All that Lucie Adelsberger can say is that "these were no longer human countenances but distorted, demented faces." This is what Vrba and Wetzler wrote in their report after their escape: "The people on the Sonderkommando have separate housing. The other inmates have little contact with them, if only because of the terrible smell that emanates from them. They are always filthy, totally unkempt and seedy, and exceedingly brutal and ruthless. It is not unusual for one man simply to beat another to death." SS camp leader Aumeier later characterized the members of the Sonderkommando as "hulking, well-nourished Jewish inmates."

Tadeusz Joachimowski was roll call clerk in the section of Birkenau that housed the Sonderkommando in an isolated block. He has provided the following description:

When I went to Block 3 and entered the room occupied by the camp elder and camp capo, I saw a big table with a cloth of white linen at which about twenty Jews from the Sonderkommando were sitting. Karl Seefeld put platters with choice ham, sausage, fish, and other foods on the table, and those around it enjoyed the feast. After-dinner treats included chocolate and an assortment of fruit. With the exception of the Jews, those present selected whatever foods they fancied and filled their bellies. Only when pure alcohol and cognac were served did the Jews cheer up and drink in order to drown their sorrows.

Erich Altmann remembers the following statement by a member of the Sonderkommando: "A decent transport is finally coming again. I don't have anything sensible to eat anymore!"

Here are notes made by Seweryna Szmaglewska: "Sonderkommando—drunken Jews who treat their Jewish brethren who are destined to die just as the SS men do. A sad example of human aberration in the blazing jungle that is Birkenau. Even so, members of the same Sonderkommando venture to get close to the electric wire and bring the Jewish men and women in the camp last greetings from their relatives before they entered the crematorium. Sometimes they bring along some mementos, photos, or letters as a last sign of life." In fact, according to a report by Czeslaw Ostankowicz, inmates on the Sonderkommando, who, as Ostankowicz emphasizes, included good comrades, procured complete surgical equipment for the infirmary of the women's camp.

Krystyna Zywulska once asked an inmate on the Sonderkommando, whose intelligent appearance had attracted her attention, how he was able to do such work day after day. He sounded nervous and irritated as he replied:

Do you people think that I volunteered for this work? What was I to do? Sure, I could have gone into the wire, like so many comrades. But I want to survive. Maybe a miracle will happen! We could be liberated today or tomorrow. And then I want to take revenge as a direct witness of their crimes. If this work doesn't make you crazy on the first day, you get used to it. Do you think that those who work in a munitions factory have a much nobler occupation? Or the girls who sort the things in Canada so they can be taken to Germany? We're all working for them on their orders. Believe me, I don't want to survive for the sake of living. I don't have anyone anymore because they have gassed my whole family. But I want to live so I can report about it and take revenge. Do you think the members of the Sonderkommando are monsters? I tell you, they are like the others, only much more unhappy.

Elie Wiesel came to Auschwitz in the spring of 1944 together with Bela Katz, and the latter was immediately separated from the others because of his physical strength. Later Katz sent word to his friend that he had been assigned to the Sonderkommando, where he was forced to push his own father into the gas chamber.

Tadeusz Joachimowski became acquainted with a foreman on the Sonderkommando named Lewkowicz and commented on him as follows: "All his relatives had been killed in Auschwitz, and thus he did not have much to live for, except that he wanted to take revenge on the murderers." Survivors of Auschwitz have repeatedly reported that members of the Sonderkommando called out to them: "When you leave the camp, talk, write, and scream so the world may learn what is happening here!"

▧ Filip Müller is the only survivor who was a member of this detail for years. As a heating specialist, he was able to escape several liquidation actions. He has reported that many inmates were completely brutalized and desperate. A widely disseminated saying was "If we live just one hour longer, that is the only important thing." "Others were quite apathetic," he writes. "They didn't care about anything because they had no one anymore. These were not human beings but robots." Lewental wrote with awe-inspiring honesty: "I must tell the truth here. In the course of time some members of this group let themselves go to such an extent that we were simply ashamed."

All of them knew that they would themselves be killed in a gas chamber, just as earlier Sonderkommando members had been. Elie Cohen remembers that when members of the Sonderkommando were being taken to the gas chamber after a general lockup had been ordered in the camp, they spoke without visible fear about where they were going.

The camp physician Horst Fischer described for the court the liquidation of a Sonderkommando in these words: "First of all, the detail and ss Technical Sergeant Moll—well, how shall I put it? They drank alcohol, the inmates were also given alcohol, and when they were drunk, their quarters were locked, Zyklon B was poured through some window, and that's how they were killed."

For ss men it was so self-evident that all members of a Sonderkommando were to be killed that ss roll call leader Kaduk bristled when he was confronted in a Frankfurt jail with the testimony of a survivor of that detail: "It seems impossible to me that the witness should have survived Auschwitz as a member of the Sonderkommando. I know for certain that all the members of that detail were eliminated from time to time. Then none of them were left; even the inmate functionaries were included. One time I observed how a Birkenau Sonderkommando was taken to the main camp and killed in the small crematorium."

However, Kaduk overestimated the thoroughness of the camp administration in the final phase of the camp. When Auschwitz was being evacuated, the ss panicked and overlooked killing the surviving members of the Sonderkommando and other bearers of secrets who had mingled with the other prisoners in the general confusion. In Mauthausen, where most inmates had been transferred, the camp administration wanted to rectify the oversight and pick out the members of the Auschwitz Sonderkommando from the thousands of transfers. But because all prisoners already bore Mauthausen inmate numbers, some of them managed to evade this belated extermination campaign. Several prisoners escaped from the evacuation transport to Mauthausen and survived.

No fear of death, at the same time a mania for living just one hour longer, an apathy that made human beings descend to the level of brutish robots, and sophisticated escapes from extermination—these antitheses, too, point to the boundary lines beyond which questions must remain unanswered.

■ Such lines were crossed when an unfortunate individual was thrust into the Sonderkommando directly from the ramp. Dov Paisikovic, who was twenty when this fate befell him, remembers his first day on the Sonderkommando only too well. At that time the detail was being enlarged for the "Hungarian campaign." Together with 250 others, who like him had been selected from one of the first transports of Hungarians, Paisikovic had to carry and drag corpses from morning to evening out of the farmhouse that had been converted into a bunker for gassings and was being used again because the capacity of the gas chambers was insufficient. The ss kept driving them on. "We didn't even have a bite at noon or in the evening," writes Paisikovic. "We had to drag the corpses from the house to the pits, and then other inmates threw them in. Many of us jumped into the fire out of despair."

When 435 Jews deported from Corfu were assigned to the Sonderkommando on July 22, 1944, they refused to work there and were gassed. The *Kalendarium* compiled by the Auschwitz-Birkenau State Museum lists this action, which hardly anyone knew about. In Auschwitz heroism all too often remained unnoticed.

Henryk Porebski has called my attention to differences within the detail. The majority of inmates who had been assigned to transport corpses were jealous of the furnace men, who were not only spared this worst of jobs but as specialists also had better chances to survive the periodic exterminations. Porebski has this to say about those who had to clear the gas chambers: "I could not find any common language with them. They were completely imbued with the will to live, the will to survive this terrible fate that had been forced on them. They developed an inordinate zeal in their work, as though this was the price of their future life." On the command "Sticks out!" this unskilled majority of the Sonderkommando had to get clubs from a room in the crematorium and with the aid of them see to it that the orders of the ss were instantly obeyed. This command was given when the victims refused to undress in the anteroom of the gas chamber.

At the age of fourteen Jehuda Bacon belonged to a motorized detail that worked in the crematoriums in winter, collecting ashes that were scattered on the roads and paths. He also encountered people who were anything but bestial. One of them was Kalmin Furman, who was from Luna near Grodno, bore number 80,810, and was probably around twenty-five at the time. He was always friendly and helpful to the very young inmates and told Bacon his story. One time, when Furman was supposed to take his parents to be burned, he tried to hang himself but was cut down in time. Afterward, he was excused from working on corpses, but he received a special assignment: When SS men were shooting prisoners in a special room in the crematorium, Furman had to hold the victims' arms. If someone made a noise, he was held by his ear, which enabled the SS to take accurate shots at his neck. When I asked Bacon whether Furman ever indicated how he was able to endure this, he replied that Furman wanted to observe how men behaved before their death. When there were no shootings, Furman had to repair machines — on one occasion a sewing machine, as Bacon remembers.

The Pole Zdislaw Mikolajski was able to escape assignment to the Sonder-kommando. To be sure, conditions were exceptionally favorable at the time. Mikolajski had been a skilled worker in the SS dental clinic for a consider-able period of time when his boss, the SS dentist Dr. Schulte, ordered him to clean gold teeth that had been extracted from corpses. Mikolajski refused to obey this order, and Schulte did not insist on it and gave this order to another inmate. Mikolajski was able to do this because his boss appreciated him as a specialist and because, by working together, the two men had developed a certain personal relationship.

■ Mietek Morawa, who as a Pole had not sewn a Star of David on his inmate's uniform either, was twenty when he was taken from Cracow to Auschwitz in October 1940. He soon came to the attention of the head of the Political De-partment, for Morawa had to take care of the bicycles that SS men rode into the camp. Since Grabner noticed that Mietek was performing his duties con-scientiously and speedily, he assigned him work in the first crematorium when inmates were not yet killed with poison gas in Auschwitz. Morawa remained on this detail after the installation of the machinery of extermination. Grabner spared him at several liquidations of the Sonderkommando, and Morawa re-ceived the armband of a capo. As a VIP who had been on the same detail from the beginning, he became better known than all the others. When Paisikovic was assigned to him, Morawa was the senior capo of the Sonderkommando that had to work in Crematoriums I and II. No one knew more about the ma-chinery of extermination than he did. Acquaintances urged him to utilize his good relationship with Grabner and prevail on him to transfer him to another, less perilous detail. Grabner, however, calmed Morawa by assuring him that he was not in any danger. Even when the biggest campaigns of extermination were concluded in the summer of 1944 and Morawa's friends advised him to venture an escape, now that the members of the Sonderkommando were ex-pected to be murdered, Morawa did nothing, even though as senior capo he could have taken advantage of his freedom of movement and the long hair that he had been permitted to grow. Blind trust in the Political Department was probably not the only factor that kept him from acting, for on one occasion

Mietek tearfully told Kazimierz Smolen, whom he had met in the Gypsy camp, that he knew he would never get out of the camp. With the help of friends he finally tried to smuggle his way onto a transport that was leaving for another camp, but the camp elder Danisch recognized Morawa and pulled him out at the last moment. In the end Morawa had to take the path that Staszek Slezak and other capos of the Sonderkommando also had to take. In early 1945 he was transferred to Mauthausen together with these men and was shot there a short time before the liberation of that camp.

Judgments about Morawa differ. Poles who knew him well gave assurances that they never heard complaints about him and that he was "all right," but the verdicts of Jews were different. Filip Müller claims that Mietek was a rabid anti-Semite. "When Jews were being shot, he performed his duty—holding a victim's head—with pleasure, but when Poles were involved, he was desperate." Morawa's former block elder, a Polish "Aryan," recalls that other capos of the detail feared him. Tadeusz Joachimowski believes that young Mietek became so brutalized on the Sonderkommando because he saw nothing that could have aroused compassion in him.

Only those who accept this argument can fully appreciate the conduct of another senior capo who also became well known. Stanislaw Kaminski was, to be sure, much older than Morawa when he arrived in the summer of 1942 with a Jewish transport from Bialystok and was assigned to the Auschwitz Sonderkommando. Paisikovic has estimated his age at thirty to forty, and he describes him as short and of above average intelligence. Kaminski must have become a capo quickly, for André Lettich, who was assigned to the Sonderkommando as a nurse in January 1943 but was soon able to leave it, remembers that Kaminski already wore a capo's armband at the time.

There are many positive judgments of Kaminski. Henryk Porebski affirms that Kaminski frequently gave him gold and medicines to transmit to the resistance movement. In his attitude toward his fellow prisoners, he resembled another capo, the "Aryan" Polish teacher Józef Ilczuk, born in 1910, about whom Bacon has made this statement: "When there was nobody in the gas chambers, the capo permitted us to warm up there when we had finished our work." Like Morawa and Slezak, Ilczuk was killed in Mauthausen.

Kaminski's importance does not derive merely from the fact that he helped others. Several people have independently described him as a prime mover in the preparations for the uprising of the Sonderkommando, at least at a time when the groundwork had reached a stage where a revolt seemed possible to its organizers.

■ Earlier plans for a rebellion have become known. Adolf Weiß (from Slovakia) reports that he was assigned to a detail that worked on the construction of the crematoriums, and there he came in contact with members of the Sonderkommando, including compatriots from Holič. The capo of the Sonderkommando's night shift, also a Slovak named Weiß, wanted to bribe an SS man, had established contact with civilians outside the camp, planned a breakout, and hoped to find support out there. The capo of the day shift, a French Jew, learned of the plan and wanted to flee with the others, but they rejected him. (Adolf Weiß never learned the reasons for this refusal.) This caused the day-shift capo to betray the scheme to the SS—evidently because he feared that he would be killed if the escape was successful. The block in which those working the night shift were housed was surrounded and all the men were taken to the main camp, where they were gassed. Capos, junior capos, and foremen, as well as those assigned to the day shift, were shot in Birkenau. Alfred Wetzler remembers this shooting, and the Auschwitz *Kalendarium* reports about it under the date December 3, 1942. The traitor had already been killed with a spade by members of the night shift. Before the shooting Wetzler had received a letter from a man who wanted to participate in this attempted breakout in which he said farewell to his sister, who was also interned in Auschwitz. Adolf Weiß concludes his account with these words: "The next day the SS staffed a new Sonderkommando with Jews who had been deported from Sosnowitz."

This did not deter Kaminski and his friends. They were under pressure because, at the time of the large operation against Hungarian Jews and inmates of the Lodz ghetto, the Sonderkommando had been enlarged to nearly a thousand inmates (the figure 932 has been documented) and on the basis of past practice the liquidation of the Sonderkommando was to be expected. According to Paisikovic, at that time the Sonderkommando was composed of Jews from Poland, France, Czechoslovakia, Greece, and Hungary. Paisikovic also remembers a Dutch Jew. Shortly after the liberation, Slama Dragon stated that the Sonderkommando was largely comprised of 500 Hungarian and 200 Greek Jews.

When 200 members of the Sonderkommando were taken to the main camp in September and gassed there—something that despite all the efforts to keep it secret could not be concealed from the surviving members of the Sonderkommando—Kaminski suggested to the leadership of the resistance movement that a general uprising be organized. Since I had been transferred from Auschwitz in late August 1944, I did not find out more about it. However, Dawid Szmulewski reports that on two occasions Ernst Burger had discussions with members of the Sonderkommando in Birkenau, where he had managed to go. Burger could not be questioned about the substance of these discussions because he had been hanged in Auschwitz. However, at that time the leadership evidently could not decide on organizing a general uprising because it thought it could not assume responsibility for staking everything on one chance. As Henryk Porebski remembers it, he transmitted to the organizers in the Sonderkommando a message from Józef Cyrankiewicz, who urged them to avoid staging an uprising at any cost. Despite all this, Kaminski and two Greeks who had participated in an earlier discussion of these plans with Porebski decided to organize a rebellion of the Sonderkommando, which had nothing to lose. The name of one of the two Greeks has been passed along; Eduard de Wind writes about Errera from Larissa and Albert Menasche mentions Alexander Hereirra. While Paisikovic does not remember the name, he does recall that a very intelligent Greek who was known on the detail for his beautiful singing took part in the preparatory work. Even though at that time the leaders of the resistance movement in the camp could not make up their minds about organizing a general uprising together with the Sonderkommando, they did support the Sonderkommando's own resistance group to the best of their ability. Women who were working in the Union munitions factory smuggled explosives out, and those were used by the Sonderkommando to make hand grenades. Porebski has described them as "little tin containers filled with gunpowder, small stones, crumbled bricks, and a fuse." The resistance organization's vacillation engendered bitterness among those who had been planning an uprising of the directly threatened Sonderkommando. In a letter that was dug up later, Zelman Gradowski wrote: "We wanted to accomplish a great thing, but the people from the camp, some of the Jews, Russians, and Poles, held us back with all their strength and forced us to postpone the date of the uprising." In this connection Lewental goes so far as to say that they were left isolated and that "the Poles that were in contact with us doublecrossed us."

Tadeusz Joachimowski, who was employed as a clerk, heard about the plans for an uprising from Lewkowicz, a foreman. Lewkowicz was originally from Poland, but he had been deported from France, to which he had immigrated.

Russians were probably involved in the preparation as well, though Paisikovic says that they were not briefed about the plans because they drank a great deal and it was feared that they might make incautious remarks while intoxicated. Lewental has called the Russians "the best element of our action."

Alter Fajnzylberg, who was interned in Auschwitz under the name Jankowski and is among the few survivors of the Sonderkommando, testified at the Höß trial that the organizers of the uprising were in touch with prisoners who worked in the sauna and in Canada as well as with the small number of survivors of the Russian prisoners of war who had worked on the construction of Birkenau and with the women's camp. The group that planned the uprising saw to it that documents about the mass murder they had personally witnessed were buried. It is to Henryk Porebski's credit that the documents have been exhumed.

Kaminski did not live to see the uprising. He was shot by the ss, which informed the members of the detail that their capo had been executed because he had tried to kill an ss man. Survivors of the Sonderkommando surmise that Mietek Morawa might have betrayed Kaminski because the latter had just briefed him on plans for the uprising. According to Milton Buki, Kaminski told Mietek about his intentions when they were having drinks together, and Morawa then informed the ss. Lewental also writes that Mietek informed on Kaminski. The Greek man did not live to see the day on which the uprising began, for he had already been killed while trying to escape.

■ On Saturday, October 7, 1944, the headquarters of the resistance movement notified its contacts in the Sonderkommando that the camp administration was about to destroy this detail, which had 663 members on that day. Now quick action was of the essence. A German criminal who was serving as senior capo in Crematorium III evidently learned of the preparations and wanted to report them to the ss. In order to forestall this betrayal, the inmates killed their senior capo. According to another version, Max Fleischer, a member of the Sonderkommando, betrayed the planned uprising to an ss man, and this provoked the premature beginning of the revolt in Crematorium III. No matter which version is correct, the plan of a joint revolt in all four crematoriums failed in any case. The Sonderkommando in Crematoriums II and IV had no opportunity to join in the rebellion, and only the inmates who worked in Crematorium I managed to do so.

The rebels blew up Crematorium II, cut the barbed wire facing the women's camp, and broke out. The ss, which was instantly alerted, was able to quell the rebellion bloodily. The prisoners who were still found in the crematorium were shot there and the fugitives were hunted down. The next day, the Labor Assignment Office in Birkenau reported that the Sonderkommando consisted of 212 inmates. This jibes roughly with the numbers given by Fajnzylberg, who stated at the Höß trial that 455 were killed. As far as is known, no one managed to escape. Fajnzylberg mentioned that four ss sergeants were killed, but ss documents list only three — namely Rudolf Erler, Willi Freese, and Josef Purke. Fajnzylberg also said that twelve ss men were wounded. Crematorium III was rendered unusable.

Since none of the rebels survived, information about the organizers of the uprising can be derived only from secondary sources. Emanuel Mink and David Szmulewski, who were active in the resistance movement in Birkenau, give pride of place as organizers to Józef Warszawski and Jankiel Handelsman,

Poles who had emigrated to Paris and joined the resistance there. Warszawski was born in 1906, Handelsman in 1908, and both were experienced communists. Szmulewski also names Daniel Finkelstein, a Polish tailor who had also emigrated to France, Lajb Langfus, and a man he knew only by his first name, Ajzyk. Relying on preserved documents of the international resistance movement and testimony at the Höß trial, Danuta Czech identifies as organizers of the rebellion Warszawski, Langfus, Ajzyk Kalniak (presumably the man also named by Szmulewski), Zelman Gradowski, Józef Dresinski, and Lajb Panusz. It is known that three days after the rebellion Handelsman was locked up in the bunker with Wrobel and twelve other inmates and tortured to death there.

Eduard de Wind recalls a conversation that he had shortly after the evacuation of Auschwitz with Kabeli, a professor of literature at the University of Athens, who, like de Wind, had remained in the camp. Kabeli, who had served on the Sonderkommando for a year, named some Greek Jews whom he knew to have participated in the organization of the uprising: Baruch, Burdo, Carasso, Ardite, and Jachon.

Despite its bloody end, the importance of the rebellion cannot be overestimated. "This uprising showed the non-Jewish inmates of Auschwitz who shared the Jews' fate what Jews were able to do." That is a proud statement by Israel Gutmann, who was involved in smuggling explosives into the hands of the Sonderkommando. Ana Novac, who in October 1944 had already been transferred to a labor camp outside the Auschwitz complex, remembers a female physician's report that a crematorium was blown up in Auschwitz. "It was as though fear had been pushed aside and we were a head taller," she writes. That one can point to the uprising of the Auschwitz Sonderkommando in addition to the revolts in the extermination camps Sobibor and Treblinka means a great deal to Jews who are writing the history of their people during the period of Nazi rule.

Isolated acts of heroism and unimaginable brutalization—these existed in juxtaposition. If someone should seek an answer to the question why the members of the Sonderkommando who were destined to die did not at least clarify the situation for their fellow Jews, thereby prompting them to make some gesture of resistance, no matter how impotent, the following incident may serve as a reply. On one occasion a member of the Sonderkommando told those who had stripped in an anteroom of the gas chamber and were waiting to be taken to the bath what was in store for them in the adjoining chamber. Evidently the reaction of the victims betrayed this to the supervising ss men. As a deterrent, they shoved the warner into one of the ovens of the crematorium, and his comrades had to watch.

This is what we read on one of the sheets of paper buried by Zelman Lewental: "The whole truth is much more tragic, much more horrible."

THE INMATE INFIRMARY

■ ■ ■

Psychic shock and brutal physical terror, excessively hard and overlong labor, chronic malnutrition, and chaotic hygienic conditions—these were the causes of numerous illnesses in Auschwitz.

A number of inmate physicians have put on record their medical experiences. Wladyslaw Fejkiel, Désiré Haffner, and others published them soon after their liberation. Fejkiel's experiences came from the main camp, where this Polish physician worked for four years, first as a nurse, then as a physician, and finally as camp elder of the HKB. Désiré Haffner worked for more than two years in the HKB of the Birkenau men's camp. Otto Wolken, an inmate physician placed in the Birkenau quarantine section, kept records about illnesses and causes of death there from September 20, 1943, to November, 1, 1944. These have been preserved. Wolken has given the following commentary on his statistics: "The average population of the camp was 4,000 to 6,000 souls, who were housed in fourteen blocks. Since this was a quarantine section, the inmates remained there for only six to eight weeks, in rare cases twelve, and were used only for work inside the camp." According to these statistics, during this period of more than thirteen months, 4,023 persons were transferred from the quarantine section to the part of the Birkenau camp where the infirmary in which Haffner worked was located at that time. The number of people who died in the quarantine section was 1,902. Wolken's records contain information about the illnesses of these nearly 6,000 inmates. During the same period, 2,534 inmates of the quarantine section were selected to die in the gas chambers. No medical diagnosis of their maladies was made, and hence none shows up in the statistics.

Illnesses resulting from malnutrition supply the greatest percentage by far. Diarrhea, edemas, and the like were diagnosed in 42.7 percent of those transferred to the infirmary and 52.7 percent of the patients who died in the quarantine section. According to Haffner's observations, new patients frequently displayed edemas as early as the third or fourth day, and in elderly people these appeared on the first day. They were probably caused by chronic malnutrition and overtaxing of the heart. Haffner observed that the widespread diarrhea produced up to twenty and even fifty bowel movements per day. Latrines were usually located quite a distance from the barracks, and therefore every trip to the latrine was a strain on an inmate who had not been admitted to the infirmary. It was also risky because dangers lurked everywhere in the camp for a person who appeared debilitated.

Stanislawa Leszczynska identifies dysentery as the illness that caused the greatest casualties in the women's camp. "Since the bunk beds were on top of one another, the liquid bowel movement ran down on those lying below the sick women."

A letter from the Polish resistance movement to Cracow, dated November 24, 1942, says that in the main camp diarrhea produced the highest mortality rate, followed by typhus.

Patients with tuberculosis may be counted among those who suffered from the consequences of malnutrition; 33.8 percent of the patients who died in the quarantine section and 16.8 percent of those transferred from there to the infirmary had tuberculosis. Wolken's investigations showed that in 63 percent of these cases the tuberculosis had been contracted in the camp. Alfred Fiderkiewicz has described the consequences of this illness in the HKB of the Birkenau camp as follows: "Hunger, lack of space, unhygienic conditions, and the wet weather caused tuberculosis to spread rapidly. The mortality rate was very high. Every day between four and ten corpses were removed from each tuberculosis block that housed 130 to 140 patients. This continued until the evacuation of the camp." That most victims of a selection had been chosen because of their obvious symptoms of malnutrition cannot be proved statistically but is in line with the practice of the camp administration.

Typhus was a particularly dreaded disease—one feared by the SS as well, because, strangely enough, well-nourished people found it harder to get over this illness than undernourished ones. This observation was made by Fejkiel. Inmates who were transferred to Auschwitz from the Lublin prison brought in this epidemic in April 1941. Fejkiel estimates that in the main camp alone 10,000 to 15,000 inmates came down with typhus over the years. By the latter half of 1943 the epidemic had already abated in the main camp, and it could be contained in Birkenau as well. Haffner reports that in 1944 cases of typhus were rare in the men's camp. This is confirmed by Fiderkiewicz, who mentions that the typhus epidemic was brought under control in January 1944. In the first four months covered by Wolken's statistics (that is, in the fall of 1943 and the following winter), 401 typhus patients were recorded in the Birkenau quarantine section, and only one in the last six weeks. "Only after the completion of the sauna and the installation of disinfectant tanks in all camps was it possible to keep this epidemic under control," writes Wolken.

In the women's camp typhus was particularly virulent in the winter of 1943–44. At first the measures taken by the SS to disinfect the camp were totally inadequate. Anna Palarczyk reports that the clothes that came back from the disinfection station after the first delousing of the women's camp on December 6, 1942, were full of lice. The inmates developed initiatives of their own. Olga Lengyel remembers the struggle that "little Orli," her name for the camp elder in the HKB of the women's camp, carried on against the infestation of lice. Eventually typhus was brought under control in this section of the camp as well. A few satellite camps where cleanliness was a top priority of the SS remained typhus-free the whole time.

Typhoid fever could not be brought under control until 1943. Haffner remembers that in that year all inmates of Birkenau were vaccinated against this illness; this was the only general program of inoculations that became known. Paratyphoid, diphtheria, and malaria appeared in waves.

In all statements about infectious diseases contained in official documents, an unreliability factor should be kept in mind. Since the SS all too often fought epidemics in its own way—namely, by taking all sick patients, even those suspected of being sick and convalescents, to the gas chamber—nurses suppressed such a dangerous diagnosis wherever possible.

Wolken's statistics also indicate the incidence of another cause of death. In the period between September 20, 1943, and January 21, 1944, the cause of death of 18 percent of those who died in the quarantine section is given as "shot" or "frozen to death," which means "murdered." Later there was a marked decline in obvious murders.

▨ Despite the close contact with patients suffering from so many contagious diseases, the HKB was a desirable detail. Those who were assigned to work there had a roof over their heads, were excused from roll calls, and could get more to eat—because there were always patients with no appetite and dead people whose rations could still be obtained, since they were prudently not reported as having died until the number of required meals had been submitted. Finally, members of this detail belonged to the upper stratum of camp society, for experienced inmates fostered friendships with the HKB personnel.

To be sure, the work of a nurse differed basically from work on almost all other details. While most inmates worked only in order not to attract attention and to avoid being punished, the conscientious activity of nurses was in the interest of their sick comrades. The responsibility with which every nurse and physician was burdened often assumed superhuman dimensions. It was most difficult to bear in the worst camps, which means Birkenau, and there especially in its early period. André Lettich has provided the following description of Block 7, which was for a long time connected with the infirmary in the Birkenau men's camp:

> Even from a distance one became aware of a terrible stench from decaying and putrefying excrement. If one passed through the gate and reached the

yard (this block was surrounded by a wall two meters high), there was a truly horrible sight. To the left of the gate there were poor wretches with broken limbs, cellulitis, edemas, and every conceivable deficiency disease. A bit farther, other patients who seemed somewhat less frail and dragged themselves along. Lastly, at the far end of this hideous yard, corpses and living skeletons were intermingled. When we entered this courtyard in our first months in Birkenau, people who knew us stretched their imploring hands toward us from all sides and we heard heartrending screams: "Doctor, help us!" However, we were completely powerless, and so our help had to be limited to a few words of encouragement, hope, and comfort, a solace we ourselves lacked. This profusion of unimaginable human misery, this host of diarrheic patients and enfeebled prisoners, was a frightful sight. All were indescribably emaciated, most of them were almost completely naked, and their underwear and clothes, which had not been changed, were filthy all over. Three wooden boxes in the middle of the yard served as toilets. Those boxes, which were rarely emptied, overflowed, and thus an area within a radius of about two meters was flooded with urine. What a horrible sight it was when all those down-and-outers, the walking skeletons and ailing people, pitifully dragged themselves to those boxes, and, no longer able to stay on their feet, fell into the muck and struggled with death until it finally put an end to their pitiable situation.

Block 7 was a wooden barracks like the others. Over the door there was this cynical inscription: "Infection Department." If one opened the door, one's first spontaneous reaction was to step back and hold one's nose, the air was that repulsive, biting, stifling, and unfit for breathing. Everything was full of screams and moans. Eight or ten patients were lying on bunks that barely had enough room for five, and thus most of them had to sit up. In this jail for patients, all illnesses and every conceivable injury were represented. Typhoid fever, pneumonia, cachexia, edemas, broken arms and legs, fractured skulls, all helter-skelter. How could the physicians have treated these poor wretches even if they had been given a chance to do so — without medications and with paper bandages? It was impossible. Sometimes there were ten or fifteen aspirin tablets for 800 or 900 patients. And why tend to them and put on bandages when twice a week the nurses had to load all patients on trucks that took them to the gas chambers? The German method was the wholesale liquidation of the human material that only took up space.

How to describe the frightful sight of this departure for a scientifically conducted killing? All patients were driven out to the courtyard; and if there was not enough space there, they were lined up in rows of ten in front of the block. Since most of them were not able to stay on their feet, they were allowed to sit down in rows of ten, one between the legs of another. Often the number of the selectees was rounded off to the count demanded by the SS physicians by including the dead. If there were not enough corpses, the quota was reached by having the block elders add a few of those who had been excused from leaving with a labor detail because they were exhausted. This dismal sight presented itself to us regularly twice a week, on Mondays and Thursdays, in 1942.

In the Frankfurt courtroom, the Pole Adam Gawalewicz described this "waiting room for death," as Block 7 was called. He had been transferred there from the main camp—before the time described by Lettich—because he was no longer fit for work.

When we arrived, thirty or more *Muselmänner* were already there and told us they were the remnant of 1,200. Now we experienced the method of killing that had been used before the gas chambers were in operation. In two weeks we received twice or three times a liter of soup for three persons and twice bread weighing 1,400 grams for eight to ten persons. Every day we had to stand in front of the block, and sometimes the whole night. Drunken SS men came around and drowned inmates in vats. This besotted bunch included not only block leaders but also inmate functionaries, possibly from the penal company. One of them boasted that he could split a brain by striking it with his stick. There was a command: "Heads out!" Terrifying minutes ensued. Everyone asked himself: "Will he take a fancy to my head?" There was no medical help for us.

Gawalewicz told the court how he had managed to escape from this inferno. "At that time I became friends with a Polish comrade who had permission to visit our block. I recited Polish poems for him, and in return he gave me bread at the latrine." With the help of other friends, Gawalewicz was later transferred back to the main camp. If a confirmation was needed that Block 7 was furnished as a "waiting room for death," it was given by SS medic Josef Klehr. He disputed Gawalewicz's testimony in these words: "That was certainly not so. Inmates were never returned to the main camp. Every transfer meant that these people were liquidated."

In the women's camp, Block 25 was furnished as a counterpart of Block 7. Even though these two blocks constituted something extreme, which existed in this form only in Birkenau and not until the last period of this camp, they did shape the atmosphere. Even in the "normal" blocks of the infirmaries, an inmate was never safe from selections, and all too often the selections frustrated all of the medical personnel's efforts.

A passage from a letter smuggled out of the camp by a Pole forcefully describes the danger of despondency that threatened everyone in the infirmary who took his duties seriously: "On August 29, 1942, I had to watch as my acquaintances and comrades went to their death. I saw how the physicians' hands drooped helplessly. I spoke with one of them. He had tears in his eyes and could not control himself. So much toil, so many sleepless nights, so many patients snatched away from a cruel illness, and all this in vain." As part of the battle against typhus, the SS took the inmates of the infection block in the main camp to the gas chambers on that day. It may be estimated that of those 746 people 500 had already gotten over the critical stage.

At that time I was a clerk on the night shift of the HKB. I shall never forget the voice of the young Pole who came to our room on that day and told us that he had just been forced to help his father get on a truck. Falk reports about a young Belgian nurse who was able to retain her sister, a convalescent, in the infirmary for a time. She wanted to keep her from resuming the hard labor on her detail in a weakened state. After a surprise selection the nurse had to help her eighteen-year-old sister board a truck bound for the gas chamber. The nurse became completely apathetic and died soon thereafter.

The methods by which the SS forced the infirmary personnel to help with the extermination of those unfit for work are illustrated by what was done in the death block 25 of the women's camp. The daily reports indicated the numbers of the patients and the medical staff that were housed there. When the trucks arrived, the members of the SS, who avoided coming to this block, used the reports to determine the number of patients that had to be loaded on them. If there was a discrepancy, the SS ordered that it be supplemented with those on barracks duty. In this way the block personnel was forced to see to it that no one hid out in the dark block when a gassing campaign was in progress. The nurses could save their own lives only if a full complement of patients was on the trucks.

The SS was aware that the medical personnel sought and found ways of shielding acquaintances from selections, and thus it camouflaged these actions in the infirmaries in various ways. "One day the camp physician demanded a list of all malaria patients," writes Ella Lingens.

They were supposed to be transferred to a mosquito-free camp. I believed this and made such a list. Then a Czech physician said to me: "I beg you, put down only the seriously ill patients." I replied that a transfer would be the best thing for those suffering from malaria. "For God's sake," said the Czech woman, "what are you doing? They're all going to be killed." In response I removed three-fourths of the names from the list. But then the inmates were not taken to the gas chambers but transferred, and full of guilt feelings I told myself, "You should have put them all on the list." We didn't learn until later that those patients were taken to Lublin and gassed there. We simply never knew whether we were sending people to the gas or to freedom.

A satanic method was devised by the camp physician Heinz Thilo to deprive medical personnel of the chance to hide someone from his selections. From time to time he conducted reverse selections—that is, he selected those who were to be exempted from being transported to the gas chambers. This automatically doomed anyone who had been hidden before the selection, for his inmate number was kept in the roster of the block. When the trucks came, his number was called.

■ Other SS methods were also designed to break the spirit of the medical personnel completely. Robert Waitz reports that one time a patient was diagnosed with a perforated ulcer, and there was a state-of-the-art operation as well as expert postoperative treatment, but then the patient was sent to the gas chamber. Another inmate, a man who had been wounded in a bombing, was given a blood transfusion on special orders of an SS physician, but he, too, was gassed. Evidently the SS physician had lost interest in these cases.

Otto Wolken has summarized his pertinent experiences as follows: "What was possible one day was impossible the next. Patients were nursed back to health and given a special diet but gassed after their recovery. One inmate was badly beaten by an SS physician because as a nurse he had kept an incomplete medical record of a fellow sufferer, and then the patient was sent to the gas chamber. It was impossible to foresee anything." Even Oswald Kaduk, the former SS roll call leader, asked this question of the Frankfurt court: "In the infirmary there were inmates who were put on a diet for two or three weeks after an operation and sent to the gas six weeks later. Now I ask myself as a layman, Does this make any sense?"

That even the best intentions could have negative consequences in Auschwitz is demonstrated by Ana Novac's account of Birkenau in 1944. "Halina, the Polish block elder in the scabies block, was the most popular creature in the whole camp. Her kindness was legendary. Nowhere else was the distribution of bread so peaceful, were clothes so clean, was there so much singing. The majority of the inmates did not have scabies, and it was only because of Halina that they had come to the infirmary with all sorts of scratches and moles. The female physician could hardly cope with all those phony scabietics." Here is Novac's pithy description of the end of this idyll: "And now they've been taken away, the many malingerers and the few inmates suffering from scabies. Halina is standing in front of the barracks, leaning against the door and crying. The empty bunk beds will be disinfected." Novac does not deem it necessary to report who took them and where they were taken. For "Auschwitzers," that information is self-evident.

Those who had to accumulate such experiences reacted in the way that Georges Wellers describes. In late 1944 the inmates working in the Monowitz infirmary were ordered to record the inmate numbers of infirm patients. Supposedly, three blocks had been cleared for them where they could recuperate with better food and no work. Because the nurses distrusted the stated aim, Wellers and a Polish physician listed only sixty-eight especially enfeebled patients out of the 800 under their care in two blocks. In this case, however, those listed were in fact transferred to newly furnished special-care blocks where, until the evacuation, they were able to stay under incomparably more favorable conditions than obtained in the other blocks.

Any help given could spell ruin, and any help denied could mean trouble. The fatalistic mood that was created by the constant uncertainty and the permanent threat of the end has been described by Katalin Vidor, who writes that the "tired imagination" of those left behind after a selection left room for only one thought: "Tonight we'll have more room in the block, and that is the important thing at the moment. We're not interested in what tomorrow will bring."

Only when a selection involved or threatened acquaintances did this "tired imagination" receive a jolt. On numerous occasions I saw groups of selectees waiting to be carted off and did nothing. Only when I received timely notification that someone I knew had become the victim of a selection did I set everything in motion to save him, and a few times I succeeded thanks to my connections. Ella Lingens writes that the infirmary staff had been forced to realize that while the mass murder of the Jews was terrible, it was also inevitable. Only when we read a familiar name on a list of selectees were we forced to act. On such occasions we told ourselves that there must be a way of saving that inmate. "In most cases," writes Lingens, "we were forced to look on helplessly."

Tadeusz Borowski, a keen observer, writes: "The crematorium is part of our daily bread; there are a thousand cases of cellulitis and tuberculosis; we know what the wind and the rain are; we know about the sun and bread and turnip soup and work; we know how to keep from getting caught; we know serfdom and authority—because we have, so to speak, made friends with the beast."

▧ Tadeusz Paczula has recorded the consequences of the widespread demoralization in the inmate infirmaries. "There were smarty-pants who hung around the rooms in the infirmary in search of dying patients. When such a person saw someone 'at death's door,' he approached him, put his hands on his forehead and then under his head, said a brief prayer, and finally blessed the moribund person with his right hand while retrieving from under that person's head with his left hand a slice of bread, the existence of which he had verified during his initial inspection."

Every infirmary was a battlefield in the struggle for survival. Anna Sussmann recognized that in such a situation "one cannot and must not expect an average person who is leading a hopeless, brutish existence not to turn into an animal himself." She observed that female nurses stole packages from patients under their care.

Maria Zarebinska-Broniewska has described a compatriot of hers, the nineteen-year-old Pole named Pelagia, who was a cleaner and a sort of nurse's assistant:

> Regrettably, camp life brought out in her all the bad qualities that human nature can have. She was not only heartless and egotistical but also insanely greedy and concerned only with her own advantage. As soon as a patient received a package, Pelagia's attitude toward her changed instantly. She immediately evinced great interest in the patient's well-being, readily fluffed up her straw pallet, washed her, and promised to get her a fresh shirt or raw potatoes to make soup that evening. She was finally given something edible from the parcel, crawled back to her bed, stated with profound contentment that the most important things in the camp were food and impassivity, and then consumed her gifts. A few patients who received food packages regularly turned her into their obedient, faithful servant who did anything for them, was at their beck and call, and was ready to fulfill even their most capricious wishes. When seriously ill inmates received packages, Pelagia quietly took charge of them. Instead of swapping the contents of such a package for medicine, an injection, milk, or a clean shirt (unfortunately barter flourished), Pelagia consumed the food herself. She often said, "I'm eating the sausage of the woman who's lying there in a coma and is sure to die soon. And even if she comes out of it, the food will be spoiled by then anyway . . ." When the lights were turned off at night, one could hear the rustling of paper from her bed (she was unwrapping packages) and regular lip-smacking. Every day Pelagia grew plumper and fatter.

Zarebinska-Broniewska has made the following addition to the story of this nineteen-year-old. Pelagia had been in Auschwitz for a year and a half and had survived several illnesses as well as two months in the penal company. Almost all those who had arrived on her transport (from the Stanislau area) had died, but Pelagia was "healthy, cheerful, and doing splendidly. 'It's because I've learned how to live,' she said by way of an explanation."

Young people were most susceptible to such temptations, though Olga Lengyel says quite frankly that mature people succumbed to them as well. One day she and a friend who was also on the staff of the infirmary gave two aspirin tablets to a patient on barracks duty who was not seriously ill and had promised them platzkis, potatoes baked in margarine, in return. She describes how their scruples melted away when they savored the odor of those platzkis. "Under normal circumstances," she assures us, "neither I nor my friend would have made such a deal, but we were in Birkenau and hungry."

■ Even those who were not starving and hence were more likely to withstand all temptations faced a dilemma. Robert Waitz, a physician in the inmate infirmary at Monowitz, has given a vivid account of this.

> The physicians played a very important role. They tried to obtain medications, particularly sulfa drugs. These were stolen even from the SS infirmaries. The physicians endeavored to get sick or enfeebled comrades to the infirmary secretly and with the cooperation of clerks, thus sparing them an official admission, which was fraught with danger. Before selections they concealed emaciated and ill inmates; they also forged medical records and hid unfortunate inmates who were destined for the gas chamber. This very necessary activity of the physicians repeatedly confronted them with a dilemma. Either do nothing, which would have been a solution dictated by cowardice, or act, which would have meant that they could help only a limited number of people and turned a physician into a judge. Only those could be helped who had chances of recovering physically and morally after receiving such help. Making a choice is one of the knottiest problems that a physician who is worthy of that title can face.

The physicians in Monowitz decided to give the few medications to the youngest patients because they had the greatest chances of surviving. "There was no point in giving an old man sulfa drugs," said Siegfried Halbreich. Heartless though this may sound, it was impossible to evade such decisions in Auschwitz.

Ella Lingens has given this description of the same dilemma: "Shall I give the small number of cardiotonic injections at my disposal to a gravely ill woman who may die anyway? Or shall I divide them between two less seriously ill patients who might get well without the aid of these drugs? Shall I help a mother with many children or a young girl who still has most of her life ahead of her?"

Vilo Jurkovic, who worked at the TB station for a time, has described the courses of action that were taken to help the patients. The physicians "organized" raw calcium chloride, recrystallized and dissolved it, and then injected the patients with it intravenously. "Even though it did not act directly," writes

Jurkovic, "these injections were effective because the patient believed that something good was being done for him." In point of fact, this treatment reduced hopelessness, and the general condition of the patients improved.

All nurses had to "organize" medications. They were frequently able to do this only if they promised to give preferential treatment to a friend of the person who was able to procure medicines. Anyone who declined to do this had to do without additional medications.

Every selection in the infirmary confronted inmate nurses and physicians with decisions that could be evaded only at the cost of relinquishing their functions and thereby losing any chance to help. The inmate responsible for a barracks had to accompany the ss man who made selections. Sometimes the escort could use this opportunity to intervene helpfully—for example, by emphasizing that the inmate whom the ss physician wanted to select was a sought-after specialist or by pointing out that another patient had recently had such a speedy recovery that he would probably be fully fit for work in the near future. However, he was able to save only a fraction at best, and he had to decide on the spot in which cases he should intervene.

Sometimes the ss let the inmate personnel make preselections. Claudette Block remembers a young physician named Tamara who, like her colleagues, was ordered to make selections in her barracks. The order called for seventy patients, and Tamara would have had to select about twelve victims from the two barracks under her care. The first time that this was demanded of her, she did not select anyone. After she had to watch, as a result of her refusal, the capricious selection of the twelve victims, she resolved that the next time she would name those whose condition was hopeless.

Ella Lingens has described the conduct of the physician Ella Klein. "When there was a selection in her block, she would guide the camp physician to the patients for whom there was no hope. She regarded it as pointless to hide the seriously ill, for then he would have selected for gassing the more vigorous patients who might still have recovered. The others died anyway, and she would have had twice as many dead. What she said could not be refuted." Nevertheless, Dr. Klein was called to account in Czechoslovakia after the liberation.

Olga Lengyel cannot forget how the victims of a selection screamed like wounded animals at her and the other nurses as they were led out of the blocks after the arrival of the trucks: "Ihr auch!" (You too!).

Primo Levi tells about Henek König, who was deported from Transylvania at the age of fourteen and was the sole survivor of his family. He was appointed capo of the children's block because he was the strongest and had good connections with influential adults. When selections were ordered in that block, Henek made the choices. When Levi asked him soon after the liberation whether he regretted this, the adolescent replied, "Well, why should I? Was there another way of surviving?"

It may have been examples of this kind that led Hannah Arendt to this harsh conclusion: because the SS entangled its victims in its crimes, the inmates were forced to make ethical decisions that became absolutely questionable and ambiguous. By way of a rebuttal I shall quote what Margit Teitelbaum wrote about Maria Nowaczek, her block elder in the HKB: "With her help we were able to save the lives of many comrades at selections by substituting for the number of a selectee that of a moribund or already deceased woman. Nowaczek saved my own life by hiding me during a selection." She added that Nowaczek shared her food parcels with the inmates, including Jews. Some people who only observed Nowaczek escorting through her block an SS physician making selections might believe that she allowed herself to be degraded into a tool of the murderers. And how many continued to help despite all the discouragement!

Polish physicians diagnosed TB in the right lung of Bartosz Oziemkowski, a young Pole. "They managed to add me to the personnel of the infirmary as a gatekeeper," wrote Oziemkowski two decades later. "Every week they secretly gave me a pneumothorax. One physician guarded the door and another stood in front of the block, for if Klehr had found out that I was tubercular, he would surely have given me a lethal injection."

Even if there were only these examples, blanket judgments like Hannah Arendt's would have to be rejected. However, many more have become known and even more have remained unknown, be it because the saved were killed on another occasion or because they never learned whom they owed their lives to. Again and again, I hear from former prisoners words of thanks for nurses without whose help they would not have been able to leave Auschwitz alive. Many of the nurses have remained anonymous, and the inmates they saved remember at most their first names.

■ The prisoners who became generally known, however, were those who had been entrusted with the function of a camp elder in the HKB and always had to maintain a dangerous balance between the duties expected of such functionaries by the camp administration and the human obligations of someone who was better off and had some influence. They could not put the trust of their superiors, the SS men, on the line because if they lost it they forfeited all chances to help. If, however, they lost the trust of their fellow prisoners, they were soon isolated, able to rely only on their power and the masters from whom this power was derived. The camp administration expected them to participate in its program of extermination, and their fellow prisoners expected their help in surviving those killings.

The leadership of the HKB was observed closely and extremely critically. In Auschwitz and afterward, I learned a great deal about the camp elders. I have never heard or read anything negative about two of them: Orli Reichert-Wald, the German camp elder in the HKB of the women's camp, and Wladyslaw Fejkiel, the last camp elder in the HKB of the main camp.

Orli was a young girl when she was arrested in the spring of 1936 for her activities in an illegal youth organization, and after serving a prison sentence she was taken to the Ravensbrück concentration camp and then transferred to Auschwitz with the first women's transport. Many survivors have emphasized that despite her high position in the camp she never forgot that Nazism was the common enemy of all prisoners, and that she helped wherever she could. The most impressive testimonial is an incident described by Jeanne Juda. After the evacuation of Auschwitz, Juda was transferred together with other women to Malchow, a labor camp that was part of Ravensbrück. Some time later Orli also came to that camp. "The girls were delighted and cheered: 'Our Orli is with us again!'" If an inmate functionary who had abused his authority encountered a former subordinate again in another camp and did not have an armband as a symbol of power and protection, he received a different reception. Juda has made this concise judgment: "I know of no other functionary who remained as humane as Orli did."

Fejkiel has explained why he, like Orli, is judged differently from the other camp elders: "Compared to my predecessors, I was in a better situation because I was able to count on the support of a broad community irrespective of nationality. The international resistance organization and other groups of prisoners supported me." It is the great merit of these two camp elders that they solicited that support and integrated themselves into the organization in comradely fashion. They were able to withstand all temptations associated with the "Führer role" that the SS intended them to play.

It was not easy for Fejkiel to decide to accept the armband and the burden of a camp elder. In January 1944 an influential Pole and I tried to persuade him to hold that office. I promised him my support and told him that the SS garrison physician approved of his candidacy for the position that had been vacant since Dering's release from the camp. "I admit that these conversations surprised and disturbed me," writes Fejkiel. "I knew that I would be able to count on the support of a broad community of prisoners, regardless of their nationality. On the other hand, I was well aware of the tension in the camp and the infirmary, and because of this the position of camp elder hardly seemed attractive to me. I knew that someone in that position could do a great deal of good, especially if the support of numerous inmates could be counted on. But I also knew that clashes with the camp authorities were unavoidable and that they might send me to the bunker again. I had every reason to assume that there would then be no road back for me. After weighing all these factors, I was resolved to resist this appointment." Then, however, the informer Olpinski, whom he knew all too well, asked to speak with him. "Olpinski informed me that the commandant's office had just invited him to take over the position of camp elder in the infirmary, and he wanted to hear my opinion." Fejkiel congratulated him. "At the same time I decided not to resist any more but to accept the appointment. I realized that the Gestapo wanted to tighten its control over the infirmary with the aid of its best agent, and that could not be permitted."

Fejkiel was the first Pole in a high position who endeavored to moderate both an extreme Polish nationalism and the anti-Semitism among the staff of the HKB.

▪ The first camp elder in the HKB appointed by the camp administration was a Green who had been transferred from Sachsenhausen together with the first thirty German inmates in order to fill positions in the newly established camp. Hans Bock was presumably from Westphalia and is said to have been convicted of embezzlement. Emil de Martini, who served as a block elder under Bock, has said this about him: "He was not a bad man. He never beat an inmate or screamed at one. He helped patients to the best of his ability."

Tadeusz Kosmider has not forgotten that Bock once saved him from a punishment by the SS that could easily have cost him his life. When Igor Bistric, the clerk in the HKB, came down with diarrhea in the summer of 1942, Bock procured opiates and a special diet for him. This deed can be properly evaluated only if one considers that Bistric was a Jew and that it was unusual and even dangerous to help a Jew at that time. Fejkiel believes it is greatly to Block's credit that despite the prohibition then in force he put inmate physicians to work in the HKB, and he characterizes him as follows: "He was not a bad person, although a primitive man, rather loyal to the SS. He had certain 'weaknesses' that strained the situation in the infirmary to a great extent. He was a morphine addict and an admirer of young fellows whom he gathered round him and, even worse, entrusted with responsible positions in the infirmary."

I can confirm that I never saw Bock give a beating or heard him scream. Quiet and bent on preserving his authority, he did his job in a rather obscure fashion. He reminded me of a sly fox who shunted persons whom he sensed to be dangerous off to Birkenau or a satellite camp and who had good relations with others who could be useful to him. When he noticed that as the clerk of the SS garrison physician I had a certain influence on Wirths, Bock was friendly and helpful to me when this was not difficult for him. I associated with him whenever this seemed useful to me. Bock's weaknesses bothered me insofar as they inhibited him from taking a risk. For example, he did not support me when he noticed that I was gathering material against ss medic Klehr. Evidently that man, who terrorized the infirmary, knew too much about him, and Bock shied away from coming in conflict with him.

Eventually Bock was *geplatzt* (busted), as they said in the camp. The Political Department started a big investigation after his addiction and his affairs with young fellows had been revealed. The young Poles were locked up in the bunker, and Bock was transferred to Monowitz as a block elder and later to the satellite camp Lagischa as camp elder in the HKB. In this case, too, the camp administration did not completely drop a tried and tested German inmate functionary. Bock later died of drug poisoning. He may be regarded as an example of the type of functionary who, while not accepting the inhumane camp regulations, used his position of power primarily to obtain treats and palliatives for himself. For a VIP in the HKB, it was not difficult to "organize" narcotics, and Bock was not the only one who did so. The general demoralization encouraged many to use drugs. In the end Bock became a prisoner of his weaknesses, and as a consequence his good will could assert itself only in a limited way. It is to the credit of Dr. Wirths, the ss garrison physician, that Bock remained the only top functionary in an HKB who wore a green triangle.

Peter Welsch, who was from the same region as Bock, wore the red triangle of a political prisoner. He was a riveter and fitter who had been arrested as early as 1933 for planning an act of high treason and had been transferred to Auschwitz from Sachsenhausen with the second transport of inmate functionaries. He took Bock's place, and in contrast to him acquired the reputation of a strict superior. I have mentioned earlier that he was the first inmate who killed patients at the behest of the ss by injecting them with phenol. Bock, who did not get along with Welsch, saw to it that the latter was transferred to Birkenau in March 1942 as camp elder in the newly opened HKB. The French physician André Lettich met him there and has testified that Welsch personally "selected hundreds and thousands of our comrades for the gas chamber" and that he had a twenty-two-year-old Pole as his assistant.

Alex Rosenstock, who worked in the Birkenau dental clinic, and thus had a good opportunity to observe events, confirms that Welsch made selections independently. He believes he remembers the name of his young protégé, Jakowski, who is said to have raged even more ferociously than his master and friend. Désiré Haffner, a French physician, writes that metal worker Welsch boasted of having performed a few dozen amputations. This sort of thing, to be sure, was almost the norm in the concentration camps. For a long time the ss had barred inmate physicians from working in the infirmaries. (That Auschwitz was different in this respect is to the credit of the ss garrison physician, Dr. Wirths.) The inexperienced attendants were forced to improvise. Quite a few of them gained so much self-confidence and adopted the depreciation of all intellectuals displayed by the SS to such an extent that they opposed the employment of physicians even after the camp administration had relaxed its prohibition.

Welsch was locked up in the bunker in February 1943. He probably did not resume his position in the HKB after his release, though he remained in Auschwitz until November 1944. Welsch embodied the type of political prisoner who wore an armband and became a tool of the SS. If his activities are compared with Bock's, one is clearly reminded of how inaccurate it is to make generalizations like "the Green functionaries were bad and the Red ones good."

Former inmates have even more negative memories of another functionary in the Birkenau infirmary who also did not have a criminal past. Dr. Zenon Zenkteller came from Poznan and was a Polish army physician with the rank of colonel. As an informant of the SS and the leading inmate physician, he became the most powerful man in the HKB of Birkenau. "We accepted being beaten by locksmiths," writes Dr. Lettich with reference to Welsch, "by barbers or criminals. But that a physician in his fifties gave the most brutal beatings to his younger colleagues and even sent them to the gas chamber seemed a particularly repugnant crime to us." Lettich's compatriot and colleague Haffner shows restraint in calling Zenkteller's brutality toward patients and physicians one of his bitterest disappointments. On one occasion Zenkteller gave Vilo Jurkovic a "real slap in the face," even though he was a nurse with an old number. The reason? "He didn't like the way I spoke to him."

Judgments about this man are virtually unanimous. "The Polish inmate physician Dr. Zenkteller had a remarkable way of making a diagnosis," write Kraus and Kulka. "He faced the line of inmates who had reported that they were sick. Each one had to drop his pants, and if this was not done fast enough, Dr. Zenkteller helped by slapping faces. If he saw soiled underpants, he diagnosed the patient as suffering from dysentery, took down his number, and sent him to Block 7 in the camp B I b, where the inmate got nothing to eat." That block was the "waiting room for death" described by Lettich and Gawalewicz.

Alex Rosenstock calls Zenkteller a sadist who hit people indiscriminately, and not just when an SS man was around. Adolf Weiß told me that Zenkteller's beatings were worse than any capo's. Czeslaw Mordowicz observed how Zenkteller gave patients who were being admitted a beating and then asked them, "Are you healthy now?" Otto Wolken, a physician, was once beaten so badly by an SS man that he thought he might have some broken ribs. When he came to the infirmary, Zenkteller asked him: "What's wrong with you?" Wolken replied that he thought he had two broken ribs, whereupon Zenkteller barked at him: "Get out of here or I'll break two more for you!" According to Wolken, there was no SS man around whom Zenkteller might have wanted to impress with his energy.

In 1944 Zenkteller temporarily took the position of camp elder in section B II f, which served as an infirmary at the time, because the camp elder was ill. The block physician Alfred Fiderkiewicz reports that Zenkteller beat both dormitory orderlies and patients: "In an effort to please the SS physician, he bellowed and sent convalescents to the labor camp. When I protested, he threatened me with the SS physician."

Many—including Czeslaw Mordowicz, Mendel Eisenbach, Adolf Weiß, and Alfred Wetzler—have testified that Zenkteller also selected patients for gassing. To be sure, the selections observed by them were started by SS men and then completed by Zenkteller. Alex Rosenstock recalls that Zenkteller participated in deciding who was to die. Dawid Szmulewski confirms that during a diarrhea epidemic Zenkteller himself selected Dutch Jews with soiled underpants for death in the gas chamber. Only Franz Kejmar, a former capo, assured me that at his request Zenkteller removed some names from a list of selectees. When I questioned him about this, Kejmar said that "he did this without any bribe."

Even though Adolf Weiß emphasized that Zenkteller's every other word was *Saujud* (Jewish swine), anti-Semitism cannot have been the only force that drove this aging army physician to such excesses. Many survivors have testified that he treated everyone with equal brutality. Rosenstock knows that Zenkteller treated capos badly as well and made an exception only with those at the top of the inmate hierarchy. A statement by Rosenstock points to another factor that may have occasioned Zenkteller's conduct: "Mengele and the other SS physicians had respect for Zenkteller." Perhaps Zenkteller sought this respect in order to feel validated even in the garb of a prisoner without rights.

When Bock had been "busted" as a camp elder in March 1943, the SS garrison physician chose for the first time an inmate with the red triangle of a "political" for the influential top position in the HKB of the main camp. The Bavarian Ludwig Wörl had attracted his attention because as a camp elder he had displayed great energy in establishing the HKB in the newly built labor camp Monowitz. Wörl, born in 1906, was arrested as a communist on May 6, 1934, and taken to Dachau, where he had a hard time until he received a leadership position in the inmate infirmary. I remember the vigor with which he always fought for patients and against abuses, as well as his sensitivity and Bavarian pigheadedness.

His meritorious efforts in the development of the HKB in Monowitz have elicited general praise. He not only placed his great energy in the service of the patients entrusted to his care but prevailed on the authorities to employ

Jews from the Buchenwald transport as nurses in the Monowitz infirmary. As the head of the HKB in the main camp, Wörl had to deal with difficulties of another kind, and he was not equipped for them in equal measure. It was not a matter of building a new infirmary but of collaborating in an established HKB with experienced, self-confident Polish nurses and physicians, "Aryans" whom the SS regarded as suitable even for top positions, especially since SS physicians evaluated some of them as qualified medical men. Wörl, who had been trained as a medic but derived his experience from his years of work in the Dachau inmate infirmary, felt superior to medical men, and he reacted angrily when he was contradicted or met with silent refusal. Fejkiel writes:

> There is no doubt that the communist inmates from Dachau did a great deal to improve conditions in the infirmary. On the other hand, it must be noted that some of them, especially Wörl, a very honest man, took a number of careless and sometimes harmful measures. This was caused by the habits of old nurses with camp experience who thought that on the basis of their long service they were the equal of the physicians, something that often gave rise to deplorable incidents. After one of those incidents, the Pole Dr. Rudolf Diem, a trusty of the camp, had to leave the infirmary. These admittedly rare clashes with the physicians were grist for the SS camp administration's mill, for they undermined the inmates' unity and power of resistance.

I have to agree with Fejkiel to the extent that Wörl did not have enough knowledge of human nature to differentiate among the Poles on the infirmary staff. He did see through the bad elements, those who had been able to get ahead under Bock, and loathed the anti-Semites who occupied influential positions, but he disregarded those Polish nurses and physicians who were well-intentioned. With his support they would have been better able to combat all grievances than he was. After all, as Poles they would have had a better chance to succeed with their compatriots than any German inmate functionary, who was distrusted simply because of his nationality. Unfortunately, Wörl did not take the advice of the resistance movement in the camp. He did have contact with it but was not ready to involve himself in it, as Fejkiel did at a later date.

As regards the differences between Wörl and Diem, I cannot agree with Fejkiel. No matter how courageously Diem may have helped many compatriots, the influence that he exerted as an anti-Semite led to harmful results, given his key position as a physician in the Outpatient Department. In my view, Wörl cannot be blamed for removing Diem from his important position; I think the opposite. To be sure, I cannot approve of the method employed by

Wörl; he cast suspicions on Diem, and the Political Department locked him up in the bunker.

At a later date Dr. Wirths called Commandant Liebehenschel's attention to Wörl, and he was appointed the first Red camp elder for the entire main camp. He did many positive things in this position as well, and no one has denied that he was a man of goodwill. His courageous interventions on behalf of the Jews, the pariahs of the camp, are altogether praiseworthy. The reason for his failure in this position after a short time is that he was not able to cope with the dilemma faced by every top functionary. He did not want to become a tool of the camp administration, and he never became one, but he did not seek and find a way of gaining the confidence of responsible fellow prisoners who had the experience and influence to help him. Thus he was soon isolated and no match for the intrigues of malevolent people. The camp administration shunted him off to a satellite camp, and as camp elder in Günthergrube he made an important contribution to the normalization of conditions in that labor camp.

Wörl embodied the type of German prisoner that could be found in all camps. Before being arrested he had lived in modest circumstances, and after the liberation he resumed that lifestyle. In the camp he was given far greater power than he had ever had. The ss had made him a "Führer," and he did not have the strength to resist all the temptations offered by the Führer principle to those who were lifted out of the mass. Because he resolutely refused to descend to the level of a tool of the ss, he was not able to retain its favor. In his dealings with fellow prisoners, however, he asserted his authority as soon as he felt inadequately appreciated by them, not because they were ill intentioned but because they did not share his opinion on some question.

■ Wladyslaw Dering, a Polish surgeon, received the armband of a camp elder in the HKB as Wörl's successor. When Wörl was locked in the bunker by the Political Department in late 1943, the ss garrison physician was not able to solicit my advice on candidates for this key function, as he had done before Wörl and Fejkiel were appointed, for I had been taken to the bunker together with Wörl. He had heard good things about Dering from the ss camp physicians whom he had trained in general surgery and who appreciated his medical ability and his self-confidence. When Wirths appointed Dering camp elder, he broke with a taboo that barred physicians from being heads of infirmaries and according to Kogon was in force in all other concentration camps until the very end.

Dering, who was born in 1903 and arrived in Auschwitz in mid-August 1940 on the first transport from Warsaw, originally had a good reputation. He used his position as the physician in charge of the surgical section and his contacts with ss physicians to help many of his compatriots. However, he forfeited his good reputation when he participated in the sterilization experiments of Professor Clauberg and Horst Schumann. In order to determine the success of these experiments, the ovaries or testicles of the victims were removed after the surgery. Since neither Clauberg nor Schumann wanted to go to the operating room every day and Schumann was not even qualified to perform such operations, they looked for an inmate surgeon whom they could rely on, for after a procedure a surgeon's work can be checked only to a very limited extent. They came upon Dering, who had been recommended to them as a proven specialist.

At that time Dering's position was such that he could have refused to participate without putting his life or his job at risk. This is confirmed by Dr. Samuel Steinberg, who testified on February 5, 1945, that Dering told him he had once given an inmate an injection on orders from Dr. Entress without knowing what was in it. The inmate died after a few seconds. "When he saw that the inmate was dead," writes Steinberg, "he was frightened and said that he would never give injections again." This refusal, which had no consequences for Dering, must have been voiced in 1941 because subsequently everyone in the HKB knew what poison the ss used for injections. Two years later Dering's position was far more secure than it had been in the early period, and therefore a refusal entailed less risk than before. Dering, however, did not refuse, for he was an anti-Semite and the experiments were being made on Jewish women and men. Before this time Dering's attitude had had little practical effect because seriously ill Jews reached the operating table only in exceptional cases; they were injected or gassed. Clauberg skillfully promoted Dering's compliance by promising that he would fight for his release.

Eventually Dering participated in the human experiments with all his strength; in fact, he set (and boasted about) speed records in his operations and went so far as to use unsterilized instruments. His arrogantly anti-Semitic attitude toward the victims has been attested to by survivors. When an inmate whose testicles were to be removed protested against this procedure, Dering lit into him: "Stop yapping like a dog; you've got to die anyway."

At first I had a tolerable relationship with Dering, but it was abruptly destroyed. One day he laughingly showed me a tobacco pouch in the corridor of the block that housed the surgical section and asked me whether I noticed anything special about it. I didn't. "Take a close look. It has no seam. Have you ever seen such a pouch without a seam?" Dering proudly told me how he had obtained this rare object. He had had the scrotum of a victim of the sterilization experiments stuffed and tanned. That day marked the rupture of any friendship between us, though I had to guard against telling him my opinion frankly; Dering was too powerful, and the suspicion of being a friend of the

Jews was too dangerous. I was not the only person to whom Dering showed his pouch at that time.

Dering's further career developed in logical fashion. Since he knew that the Political Department had the last word when it came to releases from the camp, he gave it information. On May 16, 1945, when his memories were still fresh, Dr. Erwin Valentin testified that Dering as camp elder abruptly presented a Jewish physician named Zelnner and a nurse to the camp physician; whereupon the two had to get into a Sanka (*Sanitätskraftwagen*, or ambulance), and the clerks were ordered to write their death certificate. Valentin added that Dering did not like those two men. "Aryans" were also victims of Dering's whims; Kazimierz Czelny remembers that on one occasion Dering kicked his father, a compatriot and colleague of Dering's. Dr. Tadeusz Paczula has given this cautious and apt characterization of his compatriot: "Dering had an aversion to Jews, was full of himself, and loved boasting about his successes."

In January 1944 Dering reached his goal: he was released and signed a contract to work in Clauberg's clinic at Königshütte. "I saw him leave the camp with two big suitcases," writes Dr. Alina Brewda.

Dering's further fate is not without a certain tragic quality. In Warsaw friends from Auschwitz warned him against a Jewish committee that was investigating war criminals and also looking for him. His friends helped him leave the country in the summer of 1945. At first he hid out in British colonies in Africa, where he was so successful as a physician that he received a high decoration. When his wife learned about his actions in Auschwitz, she divorced him. Years later Dering, emboldened by the recognition of his work in Africa, dared to move to London, and he remarried there. All went well and no one inquired about his past, but then Leon Uris's book *Exodus* appeared; in it there was a brief statement about Dering's participation in the sterilization experiments. His second wife read this, but Dering denied that he had been involved in the human experiments in Auschwitz. She made her husband sue Uris for libel. Uris was prepared to provide documentary proof of his statement, and in spring 1964 a London court investigated Dering's activities in a lengthy and widely noticed trial. Among the witnesses were fourteen persons who had been operated on by Dering as part of the sterilization experiments. Dering was morally condemned. Because the number of operations cited by Uris was considerably larger than could be documented, the physician received compensation for the insult to his honor, but the jury found a halfpenny sufficient. Dering died shortly afterward, a broken man.

■ Dering was not the only person with whom the courts had to concern themselves after the liberation because of anti-Semitic acts in the camp.

The Pole Stefan Budziaszek was much younger than Dering; he was still a medical student when he was sent to the camp. He was soon put on the staff of the infirmaries and became camp elder in the HKB at Jawischowitz and later in the one at Monowitz. After the war Budziaszek became a resident of Hanover and Germanized his name to Buthner. Because serious charges were brought against him by former fellow prisoners, the German courts had to initiate legal proceedings. This is why there are numerous statements given as evidence about Budziaszek's activity in Monowitz.

Thus Norbert Wollheim declared that Budziaszek "personally made selections in the camp without the participation of ss men." Arthur Posnansky testified under oath that at smaller selections Budziaszek acted on his own and his superior, the ss medic Gerhard Neubert, only nodded. In the courtroom Ephraim Diament characterized him as "a zealous helper of the ss physicians" and Rudi Wachsmann portrayed him as "a fanatical, dangerous, and dreaded anti-Semite." Rudolph Robert confirmed Budziaszek's anti-Semitic attitude and its effects with these words: "He frequently turned away Jewish inmates who came to him for treatment, and so they had to continue to run around with gaping wounds. The Jewish inmates were afraid of this Polish inmate physician."

Jan Trajster told me about his impression that at selections Budziaszek was more unapproachable than Neubert. He also charges Budziaszek with having learned how to perform operations at the expense of the patients. He remembers that he once performed stomach surgery without having made a diagnosis simply to practice this procedure. Robert Waitz, a French professor, testified that Neubert and Budziaszek made preselections. "I clearly remember this," he wrote. "Sometimes these two presented such a large number of inmates to the ss physician that the latter could not accept all of them. I know that Dr. Fischer once told Budziaszek that 600 inmates had been presented to him for the gas chamber, but that he needed only 300. Budziaszek urged the ss physician to take all 600, but he did not prevail."

Oszkár Betlen claims that, generally speaking, the inmate physicians did all they could to inhibit the process of extermination and that Budziaszek was an exception. He remembers that at a selection a craftsman was presented. "The ss physician Fischer said that he was a tailor who could work in the camp. Camp elder Dr. Budziaszek said to Dr. Fischer that the man could not be used in the camp because there was no room for an additional tailor. Dr. Fischer yielded, and the man was sent to Birkenau for gassing. To avoid a repetition of this sort of thing, Dr. Fischer said about an inmate who was a chemist by profession: 'This man can definitely work for IG [Farben].'"

Betlen has given this characterization of the camp elder: "He was a Polish nationalist. It may be that he did something for Polish inmates, but he treated Jewish inmates and members of other nations badly."

Georges Wellers did not go to Monowitz until July 1944, whereas the observations cited above refer to an earlier period. Wellers states that Budziaszek helped him even though he had to wear a Star of David. Complaints about Budziaszek's anti-Semitic activities reached us in the main camp, and at that time I talked with Polish leaders of the resistance movement. Stanislaw Klodzinski recalls that he and Cyrankiewicz issued a warning to Budziaszek, and he believes that in general one could say both bad and good things about him. He is said to have helped many patients before he became a camp elder; but as soon as he become a "big man," he participated in selections and performed unnecessary operations. Dr. Vladimir Orlicky charges Budziaszek with having raged in the infirmary at Jawischowitz. He is reputed to have capriciously injected a patient named Mandelbaum, a Polish Jew born in 1902, with pus from the wound of a patient he had just operated on.

It must be mentioned that Budziaszek was very good at "organizing" equipment for his infirmary. Thus even electroshock treatments could eventually be given there, which also brought benefits of another kind. According to Georges Wellers, in October 1944 about a dozen mentally ill women were regularly taken from Birkenau to Monowitz, where they were given electroconvulsive therapy. This opened up an avenue for Monowitz prisoners to establish contact with their relatives in the Birkenau women's camp. Budziaszek did help Poles; Tadeusz Kosmider confirms that he was "the best comrade" for Poles. He, too, emphasizes that Budziaszek obtained everything imaginable for the infirmary.

Zenon Drohocki, who is personally indebted to Budziaszek, confirms that the latter managed to "turn the Monowitz HKB into a model for the other infirmaries" and describes him as "very capable as a physician and 'organizer,' a very good, helpful, and tireless comrade." To be sure, Drohocki cannot overlook the fact that his compatriot was not free of the anti-Semitism prevalent in Poland and believes that he was "not sufficiently prepared" to resist the current. Drohocki, an experienced inmate physician, also points to another factor that probably caused inmates to have a bad opinion of this camp elder: "Without the collaboration of the SS nothing whatever could be done, and certainly nothing good."

Years later Budziaszek told me, by way of defending himself, about the dilemma in which he found himself. Many inmates avoided going to the infirmary for as long as they could, even if they were sick, because they had heard about the selections. The SS camp leader noticed one time that numerous inmates on the labor details could hardly stay on their feet and dragged along the paper bandages that had opened as they marched out of the camp—in short, their sight offended his military eye, and thus he ordered that those unfit for work be identified in all blocks. No one had any doubt about the fate that awaited these men. Budziaszek received this order as camp elder, and he passed it on to the physicians who served under him. These physicians named only three of the several thousand inmates. Budziaszek asserted that "the physicians could come to me with this low figure, but I could not take it to the SS medic." A subsequent selection claimed 150 to 200 physically weak victims.

In retrospect Budziaszek criticizes those physicians for taking the easy way out and putting the burden of responsibility on him. If instead of three they had listed perhaps thirty or sixty, he could have desisted from the later selection, and the final result would not have been so unfavorable. Others have shown that in such a difficult situation only a trusting cooperation of the entire infirmary personnel could prevent one or another inmate functionary from becoming the tool of the SS. The power deriving from his armband probably went to young Budziaszek's head to such a great extent that he was incapable of developing a relationship based on trust with those serving under him.

■ Rudolf Diem, by contrast, was mature and experienced; he was forty-four years old when he was deported to Auschwitz. Many Poles praise him as the man who saved their lives. With the old Polish inmates in mind, Fejkiel calls him the "camp trusty." Servility was alien to Diem, and his imprisonment could not break his pride. However, his anti-Semitism led this army physician to save his compatriots by sometimes steering SS men making selections to Jews. His compatriot Holuj confirms that Diem harbored "an elementary hatred of Jews" and "actively contributed to their destruction."

I once saw Diem stand in the outpatient clinic before a row of naked inmates whom he had to examine so that he might present them to the SS physician the next day. No SS man was in the room. With his face contorted with rage, the otherwise very dignified-looking physician beat an utterly emaciated Jew who was standing in front of him with his stethoscope, evidently because he had not grasped an order. Vilo Jurkovic, who was able to observe Diem's conduct because he worked in the office of the HKB for an extended period, reports that Diem took it upon himself to send Jews for lethal injections without first presenting them to the SS physician, and he calls him a "helper of mass extermination." When Diem was transferred to the HKB in Birkenau, he evidently revised his attitude. Tadeusz Joachimowski has testified that Diem refused to execute Dr. Mengele's order to select Jews with these words: "I am an inmate, a physician, and a Pole, and that is why I can't do this." He knew that this meant dismissal from his top position.

The case of the physician Enna Weiß may illustrate that condemnations of leading functionaries in the infirmary must be considered with caution. "Many Jews hated her," writes Cilia Goldglas, "because they did not know that she did her very best for all." While everyone could see that the physician in charge accompanied the ss physician when he was making selections, an attempt by an inmate physician to help had to be done as secretly as possible. Weiß, who had been deported from Slovakia before she had completed her medical studies, was young as well as strikingly pretty and self-assured. That may have been why the ss physicians placed her in this influential position, perhaps prompting many older nurses and physicians to be envious of her.

I have asked many survivors their opinion of Weiß. Romualda Ciesielska, a Pole who was in charge of the children's block in the women's camp, characterizes her as "neither good nor bad" and adds that Weiß did anything to keep her position. Regina Steinberg-Lebensfeld said spontaneously: "She was very good; without her I wouldn't have survived." Jolan Groß-Deutsch also testified that Weiß saved her life when she was laid up in the infirmary with severe cellulitis. Iris Langer, too, was helped by Enna Weiß: "She was very kind to all Slovak women." Unlike these women, Claire Beja was not a compatriot of the physician, but was from Greece. She gratefully remembers that Weiß made it possible for her and her sister to stay on in the infirmary for a while after their recovery by having them knit baby clothes for an ss physician named König. Vera Foltynova also confirms that Weiß helped many patients. Why, then, do many survivors have negative memories of her? Foltynova explains this with a statement that has general validity: "Everyone was a bit power-crazed."

Anna Palarczyk's judgment seems to carry the greatest weight. As a block elder she was not dependent on the help of the inmate camp physician, and as a Pole she was able to observe the conduct of a Jewish inmate functionary objectively. Palarczyk confirms that Enna Weiß helped selflessly. She is reputed to have secretly switched selectees with dead inmates, saving some lives that way, and to have performed abortions at a time when every woman who was giving birth was taken to the gas chamber. "In everything she did her heart remained pure," writes Jeanne Juda, who got to know Enna Weiß quite well and esteems her.

■ The story of Dr. Maximilian Samuel, a respected professor of gynecology from Cologne, is bound up with the sterilization experiments that destroyed Dering's reputation. As a Jew Samuel had to emigrate to Belgium and later to France, from where he was deported to Auschwitz with his wife and daughter in late August 1942.

Dounia Ourisson-Wasserstrom, who worked in the Political Department, remembers that his arrival was announced with a note requesting the best possible living conditions for him. In point of fact, Dr. Samuel survived the initial selection, though on that occasion only thirty-nine out of 957 deportees were spared the gas chamber and Dr. Samuel was sixty-two years old at the time. His preferential treatment probably derived from the Iron Cross that he had received in World War I and his reported participation in the movement against the French occupation in Cologne. After imprisonment in Golleschau and Monowitz, Dr. Samuel was transferred to the experimental Block 10 of the main camp, probably in May 1943.

Judgments about his activity there are harsh. Dr. Dora Lorska, who was on the staff of that block, has criticized his overzealousness. Sara Spanjaard van Esso, who was locked up there as a test subject, characterized him as "a thoroughly loathsome person" who was "very zealous." In the Dering-Uris trial in London, many witnesses also mentioned Dr. Samuel, and on the basis of these testimonies Mavis M. Hill and I. Norman Williams have described him in their documentation as a sinister pest.

Everything connected with the strictly isolated experimental block was observed particularly closely by the resistance movement. We were quite aware that a Jewish physician could hardly evade an order to participate in experiments without endangering his life. Samuel's position was fundamentally different from Dering's, but the zeal he displayed was not forced on him. One time I cautiously indicated to him that an inmate participating in human experiments of the ss should not do more than what was absolutely necessary. Samuel brusquely rejected this by telling me that he knew what he had to do, and I immediately changed the subject. His reaction made it appear risky to speak of it again, and more plainly. The "Aryan" physician Dr. Adelaide Hautval refused to assist Samuel in experiments that he conducted on Schumann's orders. Samuel reported this to the ss, and eventually we learned that he also had contact with the Political Department.

One day the ss garrison physician asked me my opinion of Samuel. Dr. Wirths had occasionally asked me what I thought of functionaries in the infirmaries without giving a reason for his questions. Each time it turned out that he had asked my opinion because he had been considering a person for a leading position. After all I had learned about Samuel, I had reservations about helping him to an influential position, and so my answer was guarded. Wirths responded by saying that he did not think too highly of Samuel, and then he dictated something else to me. Soon thereafter Friedrich Ontl, the ss garrison physician's top sergeant, took Dr. Samuel to Birkenau, and the office was instructed to prepare his death certificate.

Should I have given Wirths a different answer? Upon sober reflection I conclude that I could not have reacted differently. Yet my thoughts keep returning to this question, and I wonder whether I unintentionally share the responsibility for that man's death.

Why did the ss kill Samuel before the conclusion of the experiments? Tadeusz Paczula believes that the ss "were evidently dissatisfied with him because of his talkativeness and unsavory appearance," for "Samuel's face was covered with a suppurating eczema and was repulsive to look at." Dering also stated that Samuel was eliminated because he was "old, useless, and full of eczemas," though he formulated the reasons differently in a London courtroom, saying that Samuel was arrogant, knew too much, and started quarreling with other physicians. De Wind learned from his wife, a "guinea pig" in Block 10, that prior to his disappearance Samuel had clashed with Clauberg. According to Dr. Alina Brewda, Samuel was convinced that her transfer to the experimental block as physician in charge meant his death. At that time he told her that he was an old man who was now superfluous, and he already regarded himself as a dead man because he was the bearer of secrets.

This, however, would not explain the zeal with which Samuel continued to carry out the ss's orders. Brewda supposes that the ss blackmailed him with regard to his daughter in Birkenau and describes him as a "confused old man." Tadeusz Holuj, a clerk in the block that housed Samuel, has probably come up with the best reason for Samuel's killing: "Dr. Samuel once wrote a letter to Himmler. I read it because all inmates who wanted to send letters had to submit them unsealed to the office. Dr. Samuel begged Himmler to spare his daughter Liselotte, who had been deported to Birkenau along with him at the age of nineteen, and referred to his meritorious service in World War I. As a frontline soldier he had been wounded, and later he was decorated for his opposition to the occupying forces in Cologne. He asked that his daughter be released because of these services. A few days later Dr. Samuel disappeared from the camp, and then his death was reported." Paczula also remembers that Samuel wrote similar letters to Himmler.

The type represented by Dr. Samuel in such extreme form was often encountered in Auschwitz, especially among older inmates—prisoners who despite their great intelligence and life experience, despite knowledge of the Auschwitz machinery of destruction, refused to face reality and harbored the insane hope that they could secure an exception for themselves. Years later I spoke with Dr. Hautval, who had been informed on by Samuel. She felt sorry for the old man and said: "I can still see him before me, sweating with fear."

▪ That extraordinary woman represents an entirely different type in great purity. Hautval was born in 1906 in Lorraine as the daughter of a Protestant pastor and given a strict religious upbringing. She received a medical degree from the University of Strassburg. After the Nazi occupation of France, she was arrested and while in prison protested against the bad treatment of her Jewish fellow prisoners. This was the answer she received: "If you defend the Jews, you will share their fate." Thus she was sent to Auschwitz on January 27, 1943, and assigned to the infirmary there. Soon she was asked by the ss garrison physician whether she could work as a gynecologist. At that time Hautval had already heard about the sterilization experiments and suspected that this question could be connected with them. Nevertheless, she gave a positive answer. When a London court questioned her about her motivation, she stated: "I wanted to know what kind of experiments they were, because it was possible that we could leave the camp some day."

In this way Dr. Hautval became acquainted with Block 10 and the experiments made there. When the ss garrison physician instructed her to assist Professor Clauberg in these operations, she told him that she was absolutely opposed to sterilizations. When the London court asked her how Wirths reacted to this refusal, she answered: "Dr. Wirths was surprised that a physician working as a psychiatrist regarded a method as bad when it constituted a selection aimed at preserving the purity of the race." She persevered in her point of view and justified it by saying that no one had the right to make decisions about the life and fate of others.

Dr. Samuel, who at the behest of the Luftwaffe physician Schumann removed ovaries of "guinea pigs" that had been destroyed by X-ray treatment, once brusquely ordered her to anesthetize a victim, a seventeen-year-old Greek girl, before the surgery. After Hautval had done this, she informed Samuel that she would henceforth not assist at operations of this kind, whereupon Samuel reported her to the ss.

Since Dr. Hautval occupied a key position in the London trial and Dering's defense was that any refusal would have posed an absolute risk to one's life, she was questioned at length. This was her response to the question why she had not refused to participate in the very first operation: "The reason was that I did not react quickly enough, and at that moment I was afraid of the consequences." This response explains why there were so few similar reactions. In Auschwitz people were repeatedly confronted with surprising situations. More than a quarter century after this incident, Dr. Hautval told me, by way of deflecting undue attention to her refusal, "Believe me, I am still bothered by the fact that I assisted Samuel at this first operation."

In the course of her testimony Hautval told the London court that after Samuel had informed him of her refusal, the ss garrison physician asked her whether she had not noticed that the Jewish women on whom these experiments were made were different from her. "I replied that there are different people who are different from me, beginning with the physician himself. Wirths made no response."

Dr. Hautval was transferred back to the Birkenau women's camp, where she again refused to participate in experiments, this time the ones conducted by Dr. Mengele. On August 16, 1943, a day Dr. Hautval has not forgotten, she was ordered to come to the Political Department the next morning. She needed no explanation of what that meant, and friends in the infirmary gave her sleeping pills. To this day she does not know how she escaped that danger. She never found out under what pretext her appearance before the camp Gestapo was canceled, but she surmises that Dr. Wirths and Dr. Weber from the Institute of Hygiene helped squash this affair.

Hautval, who resists any emphasis on herself, rejects all comparisons and judgments. She explains her conduct by saying, "I was fortunate enough to have higher values than life itself. I have other sides as well." Hautval's warning against rash judgments and self-righteous condemnations ought to be taken seriously.

Dr. Alina Brewda also stood up for the victims in the experimental block. The women on whom experiments were made and who as witnesses in a London courtroom accused Dering of misanthropic brutality testified that in those days Brewda was a kind of mother to them.

■ Before one dares to judge this person or that who had a function in an infirmary, one should always keep in mind the pressure under which every staff member worked. This pressure had the strongest effect on those who were at the very bottom of the inmate hierarchy. Jan Weiß testified about this at the Frankfurt trial. In Block 20 of the main camp, Jews were forced to help SS medic Klehr and his colleagues when he was killing the sick and the weak with injections of poison. "I had to remove the murdered men," said Weiß. "I had to take the dead from the injection room in Block 20 past the hallway to the washroom. Often I was only a half meter or a meter from Klehr when he was injecting. On September 29, 1942, Klehr murdered my father right in front of my eyes." When the presiding judge asked Weiß to describe this incident in detail, no matter how hard it might be for the witness, he continued: "At that time Klehr gave injections every day. My father was laid up in Block 21 with cellulitis in his left hand, and I frequently visited him. On that day my father was suddenly taken to Block 20. Two men were always taken to Klehr's room together, and one of these was my father. Klehr spoke to both of them. 'Have a seat. You'll now be inoculated against typhus.' I began to cry. He injected my father, and I carried him to the washroom." Weiß also explained why he remained mute: "I didn't tell Klehr at the time that this was my father because I was afraid he would tell me to take a seat next to him."

Despite the pressure that was on all of them, though to varying degrees, nurses and physicians did many positive things in the infirmaries of Auschwitz.

It is no accident that the resistance movement in Auschwitz gained a firm foothold among the personnel of the infirmaries, as it did in every other Nazi concentration camp. The infirmaries that the camp administrations had installed as "waiting rooms for death" were frequently transformed into cells of rescue and aid, though never completely and certainly not easily. Because this was possible, one may say with a detachment born of experience that it was proper to take positions in the infirmary. The moral burden that a person thereby shouldered for the rest of his life and the criticism from people who make judgments without knowledge of all connections and backgrounds were the price that had to be paid. What weighs more heavily on the scale is the awareness of a physician that he remained a healer even in Auschwitz and that of a nurse that he did not lose his human face even in death's waiting room.

THOSE BORN IN AUSCHWITZ
■ ■ ■

After the establishment of a women's camp in Auschwitz, the camp administration had to find an answer to the question of what would happen with children who were born in Auschwitz. The answer was in keeping with the general methods of the SS.

"When an expectant woman came to the camp in 1942," writes Anna Palarczyk, "neither she nor the child remained alive. I frequently saw newborn babies in the outpatient clinic. They continued to lie there until they died."

Here is a report by Julian Kiwala, who was assigned to the HKB of the women's camp as block elder from November 1942 to January 1943:

> One day a women's transport arrived from Zamosc, and it included five or six pregnant women. They gave birth in the infirmary. At first the mothers and the children received milk and white bread as additional rations. The children were added to the inmate population, and as a block elder I had to give a daily accounting of the numbers. One evening, when the children were about two weeks old, the SS medic Klehr remained in the block when we marched off (the male nurses slept in the men's camp). When I came to the block the next morning, those five or six children were no longer there. I found their corpses in the morgue and was able to determine that they had been given injections in the cardiac area.

"In 1943 an imprisoned woman was permitted to give birth, but her child did not have a right to live." That is how the Polish physician Janina Kosciuszkowa describes a change in orders by the SS. "The female nurse put the new baby in a water bucket and then burned it in the oven." The physician found out that it was much worse if the mother tried to save her child. One woman managed to hide her baby for five months, but then it was discovered and she was ordered to turn it over for destruction. Kosciuszkowa reports that this mother "pressed her son to her heart and went to the crematorium together with him."

Stanislawa Leszczynska adds that a prisoner who had been incarcerated for murdering her child was ordered to drown the newborn babies, and a German prostitute had to help her. "In May 1943 the situation of many children changed," she writes. "Blond and blue-eyed children were taken away from the mothers and sent to Naklo for Germanization." As far as she remembers, this involved a few hundred children, while 1,500 were drowned.

Dr. Kosciuszkowa recalls a group of pregnant women who were taken to the camp. Regardless of the state of their pregnancy, abortions were ordered for all of them. "Many of these women lost their lives," she writes at the end of her report.

On September 18, 1943, a girl born in the women's camp was the first baby who was given an inmate number and added to the camp population. The mother was a Pole from Kattowitz. Even after this, however, Jewish women were not allowed to give birth. If such a woman managed to conceal her pregnancy until delivery, which had to take place in the utmost secrecy and under unimaginably primitive conditions, the child had to die so that at least the life of the mother could be preserved.

"We stockpiled all the poison in the camp for this purpose, and it was not sufficient," writes Lucie Adelsberger, an inmate physician who had to deal with this problem in 1944. "Once no poison was available, and so the mother choked her newborn baby to death. She was a Pole, a good mother who loved her children more than anything. Three small children were hidden at home, and she wanted to live for them."

"My husband perished in Buna. Our first child was born in October 1943 in Birkenau and was given a lethal injection. Orli Reichert concealed me in the German infirmary, where Jewish women were not permitted to be treated." This is what a Jewish woman who had been deported from Germany wrote on the margin of a letter, written at my request, in which she recorded her experiences in Auschwitz. I suppose that such an occurrence can be reported only with extreme sobriety. Later this woman assured me that "I could have killed someone at that time." It took her a long time to feel normal again.

Adelsberger realizes that some mothers "did not forgive themselves and us." Because a Jewish mother could be saved only if her baby was poisoned and a miscarriage was pretended, "the Germans turned us into murderers" (Olga Lengyel). A female nurse had no other choice. Who will relieve her and her colleagues of the torment of memory?

A twenty-one-year-old Czech woman who was pregnant when she came to Auschwitz gave birth in the women's camp. Mengele refused to let the woman nurse her child and ordered her to ligate her breasts. Eight days later Mengele notified the young mother that she would be picked up the next day, and she knew that this meant death. When it was dark in the barracks, an unknown woman walked up to the desperate mother with a hypodermic syringe in her hand. "Give this to your child; it is a strong dose of morphine, and the child will die." "But I can't murder my own child!" "You've got to do it! I'm a physician and have to save human lives. Your baby is not viable—it's half-starved and has hunger edemas. I must save you, you're young." "After resisting for two hours I was so exhausted that I committed the deed." The young mother, who survived the camp, concludes her report with these words: "My child died slowly, very slowly, next to me." On the following day Mengele was notified of the child's death, and he acknowledged it by saying, "Well, you were lucky again. You'll go to work with the next transport."

Janina Kosciuszkowa noted the next development. "In 1944 Jewish babies were not murdered immediately after being born." However, the mothers had no milk, and no one had food for the babies. Krystyna Zywulska has reported that they cried, whimpered, grew weaker and weaker, became bloated, and died. Kosciuszkowa, who experienced the end of this episode, writes: "One day the news spread that mothers with infants were being gassed. The children who were still alive were 'liquidated,' and the mothers were hurriedly released from the infirmary and added to the camp population. The next day, a fellow prisoner discovered two live children wrapped in blankets, and we managed to save them." Zywulska states that those who had to witness this greeted the death of the children with a sigh of relief, for this seemed to avert the general killing campaign.

The camp administration did all it could to prevent secret births and abortions. Thus it announced one day that pregnant women would receive additional rations, be exempted from roll calls, and transferred to their own block. It even promised that both "Aryans" and Jews would be taken to a hospital to deliver. Such unexpected orders kept fostering the insecurity that the SS spread intentionally. "In late 1943 or early 1944," writes Kosciuszkowa, "a block was established for mothers with children from area of Witebsk and Dnjepropetrowsk. One day it was announced that the children were going to be taken to a different camp, and of course without their mothers. Screaming, crying, and outbursts of despair were in vain. The children left for parts unknown."

Anna Palarczyk remembers that in 1944 women were released who had given birth in the camp to babies fathered by SS men.

At the time of the Hungarian transports in 1944, women who had been found fit for work at the initial selection were gathered in Section B II c of Birkenau. Gisella Perl, who worked as a physician there, soon noticed that all pregnant women were taken away and gassed. In an effort to save at least the mother, it was her bitter duty to perform abortions. At a later date the SS gave the order to kill only the newborn babies and let the young mothers live. From then on, the abortions could be stopped and deliveries did not have to be secret anymore. "I was jubilant," writes Perl. There were 292 women waiting to give birth when Mengele surprisingly revoked this order and had all pregnant women taken to the gas chamber. In September 1944 abortions were permitted again and the killing of newborn babies was stopped. Even so, many of them died because their mothers were not able to feed them.

Immediately after the liberation, Dr. Otto Wolken testified that in the fall of 1944 a room was equipped for abortions in Block 2 of the Birkenau men's infirmary and that three inmate physicians had to perform this surgery.

■ For a time family camps were established in two sections of Birkenau; the Gypsy camp was in operation for a year and a half, and the Theresienstadt family camp for ten months. Families stayed together, and women were able to give birth. The first child was born in the Gypsy camp on March 11, 1943, when the family camp had been in operation for less than two weeks. From that day on, births were regularly registered. The physician Lucie Adelsberger has given the following description of the children, both newborns and those who were brought into the camp:

> The children's block in the Gypsy camp did not really differ much from the blocks of the grown-ups, but the plight of these poor little things was even more heartrending. Like the adults, the children were all skin and bones, without muscles and body fat; their thin, parchmentlike skin was chafed everywhere from being stretched over the hard bones of the skeleton and produced inflammation and ulcerous wounds. Scabies covered the malnourished bodies from top to bottom and drained them of the last bit of energy. Their mouths were corroded by noma ulcers that gnawed at the skin, hollowed the jaws, and riddled the cheeks like a cancer. In many children hunger filled the disintegrating organism with water, and they became swollen, shapeless lumps that could not move. Weeks of diarrhea dissolved their unresisting bodies until the constant drainage of substance left nothing.

> Many of those who had been unaccustomed to eating for such a long time no longer asked for food, but they all wanted something to drink; even those whose bodies had already accumulated an excessive amount of liquid kept begging for water. Thirst, unquenchable thirst, was one of the great torments of Birkenau. Water was forbidden because it was polluted; the three buckets with coffee or tea, a light-colored beverage, were like a mockery on the thousand parched throats in the block. Hunger destroys; thirst that is never quenched stupefies. No threat and no plea could keep the children from drinking. They traded their last bread ration for a cup of the dangerous water; and when they could hardly walk any more, they crept from their bunks at night and stealthily crawled on all fours under the beds to the buckets of dish water and swilled the dirty liquid down.

Hunger and thirst, along with the cold and the pain, kept the children from getting some rest even at night. Their moans swelled hurricane-like and resounded in the entire block until exhaustion caused them to abate, only to start a new crescendo after a brief pause.

The Gypsy Elisabeth Guttenberger has made this concise statement: "The first to die were the children. They cried for bread day and night, and soon all of them starved to death. . . . The children who were born in Auschwitz did not live long, either."

The main concern of the camp administration was to have each newborn get a tattoo with its inmate numbers so that its death could be properly recorded and the camp count was always correct. Since a baby's forearm, the place where grown-ups had their numbers tattooed, was too small for such an identification, the upper thigh was used. Entries were made in the register of births of the Auschwitz registry office that looked just like regular births. A physician was listed as the obstetrician. Julia Skodova, who worked in the registry, remembers clearly how careful those in charge were to avoid any irregularity in the register of births. The camp administration also provided some visual effects by building a playground in the Gypsy camp. "Like any proper playground, it had a merry-go-round with rocking horses and the like as well as all kinds of gym equipment, such as rings and parallel bars, and a wooden fence without barbed wire" (Lucie Adelsberger).

From the information received by the ss garrison physician, I had learned that at that time the mortality rate was greatest in the newly established Gypsy camp. I wanted to find out the reason for this and thought of a pretext to go there with a guard. Nurses took me through the HKB and also to the block that housed the women who were waiting to give birth. This is what I wrote about it in my *Bericht*:

Six babies are lying on a pallet of straw; they can't be more than a few days old. What a sight! Scrawny limbs and bloated bellies. On the bunk beds next to them lie the mothers—emaciated and with burning eyes. One of them softly sings to herself. She is best off, she has lost her mind. They lie there, wasted away, all skin and bones, many of them naked. They are evidently no longer aware of their nudity. "Come along, you shall see everything." A Polish male nurse whom I know from the main camp escorts me out of the barracks. A wooden shed has been built as an extension of the back wall: it is the morgue, which he opens for me. I have already seen many corpses in the kz, but this makes me recoil. A mountain of dead bodies at least two meters high. Almost all of them children, babies, adolescents. Rats scurry back and forth.

At that time I did not see the playground, the camp administration's show-piece that was always displayed to visitors.

Through tactically prudent actions, which will be described in the next chapter, the prisoners in the Theresienstadt family camp were able to secure preferential treatment for the children. They even managed to obtain butter and white bread as additional rations for mothers and children. Hanna Hoffmann, who was put in charge of distributing this additional food, found out how egotistical excessive deprivation can make a person: "One woman envies another; they are brutish in their greed. I can understand them and obtain more food for them. One has too little milk, and I must give her more *café au lait*—secretly, so the others won't notice. One inmate is sick and cannot nurse her child, and the other six mothers refuse to give her some of their milk. 'Let it croak; we can't raise it here. Our children mustn't get less.' Only after I bring them more food are they prepared to keep that child alive."

■ After the Warsaw uprising had been quelled in August 1944, another chapter in Janina Kosciuszkowa's chronicle of children's fates in Auschwitz was written. She describes "huge transports that suddenly came from Warsaw, elderly women, newborn babies, children, and adults. Again the children were taken from the mothers. Two blocks were set up, and they were the worst. Three hundred children in a block, ten per bunk—so crammed that it was almost dark. Unwashed, hungry, badly dressed, worn out from their experiences during the uprising and the days on the transport, the children fell prey to illnesses."

Romualda Ciesielska was appointed block elder in a children's block in the women's camp. She remembers that 800 children arrived from Warsaw at that time; 300 were taken to the men's camp and the others to her block. The youngest was two years old, and the upper limit was fifteen, but a few older youths were also admitted to the children's block. There was a lot of cheating, and thus a three-year-old Gypsy girl who had been saved by prisoners when all Gypsies were murdered was illicitly brought to the block. At first mothers with babies were also transferred there; but later they were taken to another block, and mothers were barred from entering the children's block. The children were secretly taught by female teachers. Beginning in September mothers with one child were taken to Germany to work—and later mothers with several children as well. According to Seweryna Szmaglewska, the last children's transport left Auschwitz in January 1945. In addition to Polish and Russian children, there were Jewish and a few Italian children in the camp. "All these children had eczema, lymphatic edemas, and scurvy. They were starved, poorly dressed, often barefoot, and had no facility for washing." Ciesielska recalls that when Auschwitz was evacuated, there were perhaps fifty or sixty children in her block.

Some statistics about children in Auschwitz have been preserved. According to a compilation by the Labor Assignment Office, 619 boys ranging in age from one month to fourteen years were living in Birkenau on August 30, 1944. On January 14, 1945, shortly before the evacuation, 773 male children and youths were registered. Mira Honel, who stayed in the camp to nurse the sick children, stated that 270 were liberated in Birkenau. A Russian commission examined these children and announced the results for 180 of them. Tuberculosis was diagnosed in seventy-two and frostbite in thirty-one children; forty-nine were suffering from utter exhaustion and twenty-eight from other illnesses. The oldest children were fifteen, and fifty-two were less than eight years of age.

The children brought something into the camp that could otherwise not get past the electrified barbed wire: feelings. This is what Maria Zarebinska-Broniewska has written on the subject:

On the camp road a little girl with long blonde pigtails kept running around; she was always very nicely dressed and wore an armband with "Runner" on it. That child was a Slovak Jew whose entire family had been murdered. Some ss woman had taken pity on the charming girl, who did not look Jewish at all, and saved her from death by burning. Lightheartedly threading her way between biers, she completed all errands very speedily. On warm summer days she often changed clothes twice or three times a day, and people regularly saw her in new dresses. She surely had no idea where these had come from, that they had been taken off girls her age who had just been incinerated or removed from their luggage.

Zarebinska-Broniewska says nothing about the further fate of this girl, but she does know what happened to another child who also enjoyed preferential treatment. "For a time a lovely three-year-old Gypsy boy who seemed to be made of chocolate could be seen near the guard by the gate, saluting whenever a German walked through it. He was the darling of the ss women, who were often seen holding the boy and his constant companion, a teddy bear. However, the career of this cute little Gypsy boy came to an end after a few weeks. He died."

A female nurse who took care of a six-year-old Yugoslav boy named Olek in the children's block has described her feelings when the boy put his arms around her neck and gave her a kiss. "For a year I had forgotten what tenderness is."

RESISTANCE

■ ■ ■

The system developed by the SS was intended to make not only resistance but also the very idea of it impossible. Again and again an inmate was shown in drastic fashion how impotent he was and how omnipotent even the lowest-ranking SS man was. Any thought of rebelling against such demonstrative omnipotence was supposed to seem absurd. Finally, the SS saw to it that no inmate who thought of resistance could hope that his deed would become known to posterity if he had to pay for it with his life. It would sink without a trace in the general chaos of destruction, and no one would ever bear witness to it. Heroes, however, are most likely to arise if they can hope that their actions will outlive them.

Nevertheless, acts of resistance against the authorities of the camp have been reported.

Charlotte Delbo has written about a Frenchwoman named Maria Alonso who struck back when she was beaten by a capo. She was beaten half to death and soon thereafter died of double pneumonia.

Ana Novac reports that Frenchwomen gave their Slovak block elder, who had threatened to send them to the gas, such a thrashing that she had to be laid up in her room.

Albert Menasche has told the story of Albert Benaviste, a Jew from Saloniki who had to work at the ramp. He called out in Greek to new arrivals who had been deported from his homeland: "You young mothers, give your children to an older woman near you. Elderly women and children are under the protection of the Red Cross." He had found out that a quasi-official announcement in a language the SS did not understand was less risky and much more effective than whispered warnings that might be misunderstood. If mothers took his advice, they could save their lives, for old women and children as well as women with children were destined to die in the gas chambers.

The Pole Teddy Pietrzykowski carried on a struggle against the enemy in his own way. He was a cleaner in the staff building where SS men with minor illnesses were treated. When one of these men was about to be released, Teddy had to get his clothes ready. From his friend Staszek Baranski he obtained lice infected with typhus that were kept in a bottle. This is what Teddy told me many years later: "I used this opportunity to put lice from the bottle under the coat collar of some SS men. I remember that four of them came down with typhus and died."

The best-known act of resistance was that of Maximilian Rajmund Kolbe, who deprived the camp administration of the power to make arbitrary decisions about life and death.

Kolbe, a Catholic clergyman, arrived in Auschwitz on May 29, 1941. When an inmate made a successful escape in July of that year, the administration ordered the reprisal that was usual at the time. The inmates of the escapee's block had to remain standing after the evening roll call. Karl Fritzsch, the SS camp leader, picked out fifteen men, and everyone knew that they would be locked up in a dark cell in the bunker where they would have to remain without food and water until the escapee was caught or they died. When Fritzsch directed a young Pole named Franz Gajowniczek to the bunker, he moaned: "My poor wife and children! What's going to happen to my family?" Another Pole, Dr. Franz Wiodarski, who had also lined up, has described what followed:

After the fifteen prisoners had been selected, Maximilian Kolbe broke ranks, took his cap off, and stood at attention before the SS camp leader, who turned to him in surprise: "What does this Polish swine want?" Kolbe pointed at Gajowniczek, who was destined for death, and replied: "I am a Catholic priest from Poland. He has a wife and children, and therefore I want to take his place." The SS camp leader was so astonished that he could not speak. After a moment he gave a hand signal and spoke only one word: "Weg!" (Away!). This is how Kolbe took the place of the doomed man, and Gajowniczek was ordered to rejoin the lineup.

Kolbe and his companions in misfortune had to spend almost three weeks in an unlit cell. On August 14 a lethal injection ended the suffering of the man whose bearing elicited the respect of the supervising SS men to the very end. Gajowniczek was able to survive the camp.

Teddy Pietrzykowski remembers Kolbe taking a walk with him and other Poles on Birkenallee, a road in the back part of the camp, after work and telling them about his missionary work in Japan. One time Teddy beat an inmate who had stolen bread from Kolbe. When Kolbe saw this, he told Teddy that he would not be allowed to come to him if he beat a fellow inmate.

Kolbe's deed was not the first of its kind. When the camp commandant ordered the first reprisal after an escape on April 23, 1941, and had ten comrades from the escapee's block locked in the bunker so they would starve there, Marian Batko, a forty-year-old secondary school teacher of physics from Chorzow, volunteered for this group. He died after four days in the dark cell. There is almost nothing about Batko's sacrifice in the literature.

■ Resistance in an extermination camp meant the protection of life. I have already shown how hard and often hopeless that was and how easily an inmate could become discouraged. Lucie Adelsberger has drawn attention to a factor that nevertheless induced many to keep trying: "Having to watch helplessly how another person is tortured and suffers without being able to do anything about it is one of the very worst things in the world." I agree with her. Never did I have such strong feelings of revenge as at such moments.

Added to this is the fact that anyone who was in a better situation as a functionary was drawn into the machinery of extermination in some way. Dormitory orderlies and block elders, capos and foremen, clerks and nurses—all of these had to serve the camp administration directly or indirectly in its campaigns of murder. Carl Laszlo has pointed out that the realization of either being among the moribund (if an inmate lost his position and was thrust back into the gray host of the nameless) or among the involuntary murderers was barely endurable. Only if a prisoner sought to use any opportunity to work against the machinery of killing, at least in a small way, could he have a bearable awareness of being lifted out of the mass of those who were constantly and directly threatened by death.

For an individual this was not as easy as it may seem in retrospect. One example may illustrate this. The most primitive form of help was to give some food to hungry inmates. Those of us who were clerks, cleaners, or assistants in the pharmacy or the dental clinic, comprising the SS Infirmary Commando, were among the more fortunate. Members of our detail had to get the food from the SS kitchen for SS men who were laid up in the SS infirmary with minor illnesses. By means of friendship with the inmates who worked in the kitchen, by bartering with generally desired medications that were "organized" in the SS pharmacy, and by bribing SS guards, we received more food than the patients needed. Whatever was left over was taken to the basement, where every member of our detail could eat it. The SS tolerated this sort of thing, for it was interested in good work by inmates on details that served them directly and knew that in the long run such work could not be exacted from undernourished inmates. Besides, the SS also profited from such activities. If the top sergeant in the SS infirmary needed anything, he asked our capo. Since we were interested in keeping him in a good mood, we did our best to fulfill his wishes.

Thus we did not go hungry. However, even with the best of intentions, we could share this nourishing SS food with others in only a very limited way. This was simplest in the case of inmates who were able to come to the SS infirmary under some pretext, but as a rule only the better-fed prisoners had freedom of movement. Anyone who suffered from chronic starvation had no chance to leave his workplace.

It was very dangerous to smuggle food into the camp. When the labor details marched back to the camp, spot checks were made; and if someone was caught smuggling, he was subject to harsh punishment and the loss of his detail. Of course, smuggling went on anyway, primarily the smuggling of the coveted medications from the SS pharmacy that were easier to conceal on one's body than food. Without any risk we could only share the camp food that we received on our block in the evening. Karl Lill and I gave our rations to two young Frenchmen. It seemed most practical always to help the same inmates, for only regular additional food could keep someone from descending to the level of a *Muselmann*. We chose French inmates because this national group had hardly any acquaintances who had some source somewhere. Our choice of young people was based on our camp experience that a young inmate had a better chance of weathering the dangers of camp life than an older one. In point of fact, those two Frenchmen did survive Auschwitz.

The same example also illustrates the role happenstance sometimes played. When I was sent to the bunker in August 1943, the Frenchmen were in the quarantine section that had been established on the floors of the isolated bunker block, for at that time all French inmates were scheduled to be transferred to other camps. The inmates in the quarantine section were allowed to take a brief daily walk in the walled-off courtyard of the block to which the windows of our cells opened as cellar shafts. The young Frenchman whom I had helped with my camp food found out that I was in the bunker and located my window. Through the bars he slipped me food and newspapers and also transmitted letters to my friends in the camp. If he had been caught doing this, he would have been a candidate for death.

■ Anyone who had the desire and the chance to offer resistance looked for like-minded people because there were too few opportunities for someone left to his own resources.

One group gained respect for its moral unity and purity: Jehovah's Witnesses. In Auschwitz there were hardly more than two dozen males, and they did not particularly stand out. There were a somewhat greater number of female Jehovah's Witnesses (a report dated August 1944 mentions 122), and they played an important role. Exploiting the principle of this religious community not to flee or appropriate the property of others even in exceptional situations, the SS employed female Jehovah's Witnesses as domestic help in the homes of leaders. Each woman was given a photo ID that entitled her to move about freely outside the camp area by day. All the female Jehovah's Witnesses that I met were proper, helpful, and friendly; they clearly rejected Nazism and did not let themselves be corrupted by their privileged position.

Maximilian Grabner, the head of the Political Department, testified that these Jehovah's Witnesses used the personal contact with SS leaders that their employment in their homes had given them to identify particular cases of

SS misconduct. For example, one of those women drew his attention to the cruelty of the guard Irma Grese.

Höß writes the following about these women, whom the SS liked to call Bibelwürme (Bible worms) or Bibelbienen (Bible bees):

> They worked as maids in the homes of SS families with many children, in the house of the Waffen-SS, and even in the home of leadership trainees, but primarily in farming establishments. They did not need to be supervised or guarded and did their work industriously and willingly, for that was Jehovah's commandment. Most of them were elderly German women, but there also were a number of young Dutchwomen. I remember a young Polish woman as well. For two or three years I had two older women in my home. My wife often said she could not take care of everything better than these two women. There also were some strange creatures among them. One worked for an SS leader and anticipated his every wish, but as a matter of principle she refused to clean uniforms, caps, and boots—anything connected with military matters.

A Jehovah's Witness was block elder in the staff building. When Julia Skodova spent her first night on the block, this elder, who was named Mizzi, came to her room and said in her Viennese German, "Gute Nacht, Kinder!" (Good night, children!). In that environment those friendly words seemed like a caress. Benedikt Kautsky observed that in some Jehovah's Witnesses loyalty to their beliefs intensified to the point of a deliberately fostered martyrdom.

■ There was another group that was able to play a special part by virtue of its ideological solidarity. It came to Auschwitz as a unified group with previous camp experience and was housed in Birkenau under less unfavorable conditions than most companions in misfortune. They were Zionists who had been transferred from Theresienstadt to the family camp in Birkenau.

A young man from Germany who had stood out in Theresienstadt was characterized by the chronicler of that camp, H. G. Adler, as a "physical education instructor and somewhat dictatorial male hero of young inmates, who was with his Zionist idealism, at least in the early period, the inspirational model, particularly of the smaller children." Nina Weilova, who had been deported to Theresienstadt at the age of ten, met this young man, who was named Fredy Hirsch, and describes him as follows: "There was no one who was so self-sacrificing and devoted himself to the children as much as he did." In the family camp Hirsch was given the function of a camp capo because, according to his co-worker Hanna Hoffmann, his "personality and appearance suited and even impressed the Germans from the beginning." Hoffmann mentions his elegant, always dapper appearance, his shrill whistle, and his Prussian discipline. Jehuda Bacon confirms that "he looked good and always wore clean clothes."

Fredy Hirsch used the impression he made on the camp administration to the advantage of the young people in the family camp and managed to secure a block for children between ages eight and fourteen. Hanna Hoffmann writes:

> Until then, the children were housed in various blocks together with elderly and sick inmates, and no one paid any attention to them. Their only activity was the roll call, and they disturbed the "discipline" of the block. Fredy picked out a few young people who had already participated in educational activities in Theresienstadt. . . . With their help he classified the 700 children who had up to then been mere numbers according to age and language. He procured for the children better food, which was brought to us from the Gypsy camp. Thanks to his good connections, he managed to obtain for the children's block some of the packages that arrived in the camp and did not reach their addressees—for example, those who had already died.

After Hirsch had managed to convince the camp administration that it was important for the children to learn German, a school of sorts could be established. "Of course, anything but German was taught, and only a few German sentences were drilled into the children just in case German visitors came to the block," writes Hanna Hoffmann. "We always had to be on guard. The SS frequently came to see how the children were doing and what they were learning. We taught sociology, Judaica, and so on in Czech. Then the children had to stand at attention and read off German poems for the 'guests.' It was due to the exemplary order in the block under Fredy's direction that the SS was pleased with it and frequently showed it off to the heads of other camps as a curiosity."

Otto Kulka, who was ten and a half when he lived in the children's block, said at a later date: "At that time I learned about Thermopylae and the story of the Maccabees." A chorus practiced, and a children's opera was performed. "I didn't know whether that was a kind of heroism or an absurd action," writes Kulka.

The teacher Hanna Hoffmann has mentioned the difficulties that impeded instruction under the conditions of Birkenau. Added to the space shortage and the lack of books, paper, and pencils was the fact that many children had never had any regular schooling: "In experience they were as old as we were and beyond that much more skeptical and even cynical, because in their short life they had had few opportunities to see anything good and beautiful. They could not believe in anything—or rather, they still believed in one thing: the omnipotence of the chimney that was smoking right in front of their eyes."

An exhibit of playthings made by the children was organized, and Hoffmann remembers that it was "greatly admired" by the ss. A girl decorated the children's block with pictures from Disney's *Snow White*, and "subsequently she became the sweetheart of our future camp elder." This decoration had other consequences as well:

> At the request of the Germans, who were impressed with the pictures, Fredy and the children rehearsed *Snow White* in German and performed it for the Auschwitz notables. We had to contend with great obstacles, for we had to make the stage, the scenery, and the costumes out of straw pallets, tables, stools, and clay. Staging this play took months. We overcame the linguistic difficulties, too, and the performance was a great success. Thanks to this performance, at least in part, the ss camp leader made a second block available as a day home for children aged three to eight and permitted mothers with children under ten and nannies to be housed in a separate block. This materially eased our work. We could now supervise the children in the evening and at night as well and were better able to prevent the children and their parents from bartering with the children's soup.

This ghostly idyll in the tempestuous sea of Birkenau was cruelly destroyed when the six-month grace period for the Theresienstadt transport expired. Even though it was bruited about in the camp administration that the members of this transport were being transferred to a labor camp, wild rumors, including optimistic ones, circulated. This happened in March 1944, and Hanna Hoffmann recalls that many prisoners hoped for a speedy end of the war. To be sure, she writes: "The only thing that gave us pause was that Fredy, who was among the best-informed inmates, walked around with a somber face, but it was impossible to get anything out of him."

Information about the impending extermination trickled through and aroused a desire to resist. Even though there could be no realistic hope of successfully averting the extermination, prisoners wanted to set Birkenau on fire, thereby giving a signal that could not remain unnoticed and at least postponing the general extermination for a certain period of time. Those who concerned themselves with such plans entrusted Fredy Hirsch with the leadership of this action because he had the necessary authority with the various rival groups in the family camp. When the resistance movement informed him on March 6 that the crematoriums were being made ready for the inmates of the family camp, he responded that he knew what his duty was. However, he did not give the signal for an uprising, and that evening he poisoned himself with Luminal. The next day the unconscious Hirsch and 3,791 others were taken to the gas chambers on trucks. He kept the reason for his final decision to himself.

The family camp also housed a later transport from Theresienstadt, and its members were not murdered at that time because their six-month grace period had not expired. Hanna Hoffmann reports that Fredy turned the leadership of the home over to the comrades from this block and sent greetings to friends in Israel. "He wrote that he had been 'friends' with the Germans, and even their confidant in the most intimate matters, but had never trusted them. They suggested that he stay in the camp with us (that is, with the members of the second transport). Fredy rejected this because he wanted to go with his children (from the first transport)."

It is to Fredy Hirsch's credit that eventually a group of young inmates escaped the general extermination. Inmates and SS men agree that they were pulled out of the group of those destined for death at the last minute because SS men who regularly visited the children's block and had formed a certain bond with the youngsters had requested this of SS camp leader Schwarzhuber, who was receptive to their arguments for the same reason.

■ As in the other Nazi concentration camps, groups were formed in Auschwitz that had been joined together in freedom by identical or similar political views. In a collective where everyone was controlled by like-minded inmates, an individual had the greatest chance of resisting all temptations to sink into the swamp of general demoralization.

Eugen Kogon observed that the leftist parties were the only aspect of the "social structure of the world outside the KL that was taken over unchanged, which means that their adherents found a piece of familiar psychic territory to which they could escape. The consequence was a better material start and a speedier retrieval of self-confidence, but also the danger of unrestrained primitivism and such a complete adaptation that it was no longer protective but ruinous."

In contrast to Buchenwald (where Kogon gathered his experiences), Dachau, or other camps that were in existence before the outbreak of the war, when Germans opposed to the Nazi regime were the primary prisoners, Auschwitz housed only a small number of Germans or Austrians with the red triangles of political prisoners. I have already pointed out that this triangle was worn not only by political opponents of the regime.

Resistance groups were formed in all of the Nazi concentration camps. This process was promoted by the imprisonment of many people who were trained in illegal organizational work, by the self-government of the prisoners on orders from a camp administration that with the growth of the camps was ever more dependent on the work of the clerks and functionaries, and by the fact that the prisoners were intellectually superior to their guards. In addition, the SS's system of constant transfers from one camp to another enabled prisoners to exchange experiences and establish contacts. After I had been earmarked for transfer from Dachau to Auschwitz, an Austrian active in the resistance movement in Dachau suggested that I get in touch with Ernst Burger. In point of fact, a resistance group had formed around that man in Auschwitz.

Bitter struggles between communist and social democratic groups have been reported from camps in which numerous political prisoners were interned. We have descriptions of an underground terror of communist groups in some camps where they were able to capture top positions in the inmate hierarchy—for example, in Ravensbrück, where Margarete Buber-Neumann experienced this terror. In Dachau I found out that even a socialist group that had gained power was capable of proceeding against communists. Together with other communists I was shunted off from Dachau to Auschwitz because we had begun to annoy the socialist group that dominated the Dachau infirmary. The ss only prescribed the numbers, and the socialist infirmary capo and his friends determined who had to go to Auschwitz, where typhus was raging.

Such internal struggles did not develop in Auschwitz—possibly because there were too few political prisoners or because the leadership of the international resistance movement was composed of communists and socialists from the beginning. Conflicts that were political in nature did exist within Polish groups, but these hardly affected the international organization.

The activities of a resistance organization in Auschwitz were hampered by different difficulties. The incomparably greater demoralization in an extermination camp and the considerably smaller number of those who were already accustomed to political activity, not to mention the unrestrained terror with which the Political Department dominated the camp, impeded an organized activity. All too often a prisoner deported to Auschwitz had been worn out, broken, and selected before a resistance group even had a chance to get to know him, especially if he had to wear the Star of David. Although I had opportunities to examine the card catalog of the new arrivals in the inmate infirmary, on more than one occasion I did not learn about the arrival of a Jewish acquaintance from my communist organization in Austria or the international brigades in Spain until after his death.

Kraus and Kulka write as follows from a Birkenau perspective:

Until 1943 two basic prerequisites for the formation of an organized resistance movement were lacking. For one thing, there was a great dearth of politically aware and progressive-minded inmates, and, for another, the unfavorable environs of the camp were an impediment. The latter factor was demonstrated by the experience of some inmates who tried to escape but could not make much progress in that terrain. . . . For a long time in the camp, there was a predominant feeling of absolute helplessness, which had the most debilitating effect, physically and mentally. Any thought of escape was immediately quelled by the fear of betrayal and, above all, by the condition of stolid submissiveness and apathy of the mass of prisoners, among whom there were only a small number of politically mature persons.

Anyone who could even think of resistance, or had a chance to think of anything, had to have risen from the lowest and widest stratum of inmates, whose thoughts revolved only around food and fear of beatings. Every resistance group had to begin by procuring bearable living conditions for those it had come to trust. That was the prerequisite of its activity, not its goal. Beyond this, such groups endeavored to secure influential positions for their members. Here is what Benedikt Kautsky says on the basis of his experiences in Monowitz:

> It was understandable that political prisoners who felt they had the ability to fill these positions claimed this power not for themselves but in the interest of the community. If they had not done so, life would have been even more unbearable in many camps than it actually was. Thus it was certainly in the interest of the inmates that the political prisoners held these jobs. From a personal point of view, however, if a person allowed himself to be enmeshed in that nest of intrigues, it meant a serious endangerment of his character, and it took considerable strength of character to avoid being corrupted by power or material benefits. This honorable credit must be given to a number of Jewish political prisoners of various persuasions in Auschwitz-Buna. But such shining examples of the genuine triumph that the human spirit and character were able to achieve even over the worst conditions must be contrasted with highly dubious figures, who show how far persons of complete integrity could go astray if they thought they were serving their cause.

Two examples from the main camp are suitable illustrations of Kautsky's observations. Ernst Burger and Dr. Heinrich Dürmeyer, both from Vienna and former functionaries of the Austrian Communist Party, were active in the leadership of the international resistance movement in the main camp—Burger from its beginning and Dürmeyer from January 1944 onward, shortly after his transfer from Flossenbürg to Auschwitz. Since I knew Burger from the international brigades, the requisite relationship of trust immediately developed.

When I met Ernst Burger in Auschwitz, he was already regarded as an "old hand." He could have claimed many privileges as the clerk of Block 4, but he chose not to. His natural comradeship with all prisoners, including members of other nationalities at whom he never flaunted his privileged status as a

"German," as well as his modesty, protected him from all the temptations to which a VIP was exposed: to command, to dominate, and to gain access to all attainable pleasures. Only a very few people suspected that Ernst occupied a key position in the resistance movement, but all who knew him respected him. That respect benefited the organization, for it had to work in a strictly conspiratorial way; thus the personal authority of every member was particularly important.

Heinrich Dürmeyer became capo of the detail SS Clothing Depot because the resistance movement considered this position especially important with regard to its plans for escapes and rebellions. In September 1944 he became a camp elder in the main camp. Both of these positions brought Dürmeyer into close contact with the camp VIPs as well as the SS, and he utilized this contact for the benefit of the organization. Despite our warnings, however, he participated in secret drinking bouts with Greens and SS men, his rationale being that this enabled him to get a lot of information and to influence members of the SS. This has been indirectly confirmed by SS roll call leader Claussen, who later wrote in prison: "How often did I send for the camp elder and talk with him over a glass of schnapps—not only in the line of duty but privately as well. . . . I have reason to state that he trusted me at least as a person."

In this way Dürmeyer alienated himself from the nameless prisoners with whom Burger always maintained good contact. At the evacuation of Auschwitz, which was a very difficult test for a camp elder, the consequences of this alienation became apparent. Those acquainted with the situation reproached Dürmeyer for failing to use as much as possible his undeniably great influence on the camp administration, gained by virtue of his intelligence and behavior, for the benefit of the community. They expected him to join a column of evacuees and try to prevent, or at least alleviate, the worst outrages. Instead, Dürmeyer left the camp in an automobile with other inmate VIPs.

Irmgard Jantsch, an Austrian woman who had delivered a baby in Auschwitz in May 1944 and as an "Aryan" was allowed to keep her child, seventeen years later recorded her memories of Dürmeyer during the evacuation: "After my arrival in the main camp with my daughter on January 17, 1945, I asked him to get warm clothes for my child from Canada, or at least permit me to take some. There was a stockroom, and many inmates took what they could. Dürmeyer declined my request with these words: 'That's completely out of the question. Others are freezing, too.' Then he left in the car of SS camp leader Hössler, whereas the evacuees had to march off on foot." Jantsch was possibly unaware of the circumstances that prompted Dürmeyer's reaction, which remain an open question. At the critical moment of the evacuation, he took the path that was most comfortable for him rather than the one that could have made him most useful to his fellow prisoners.

■ Anyone who attempts, after the fact, to describe resistance will understandably encounter great difficulties. Why should survivors of Auschwitz behave differently from someone who has weathered a critical situation and is afterward questioned about his resistance? Many people claim to have been there and to be giving authentic reports. Others who never encountered the organization that operated in the camp with strict secrecy are skeptical about all later reports. The only documentation is what may be read in the letters preserved in Cracow, and, understandably, these contain no information about internal matters of the organization. Hence only the later reports of members of this organization or notes of the guards can be used.

Anyone who wants to write about the resistance movement in Auschwitz must first provide a definition of resistance. If a prisoner shared his bread with a friend, that was an act of resistance against the SS's program of extermination. If someone concealed an acquaintance from those making selections, this was an even clearer act of resistance. On the following pages, however, the idea of organized resistance will be more narrowly defined. Only when an activity was not limited to helping a friend, compatriots, or like-minded people (in short, acquaintances), but rather when efforts were made to stave off a general worsening of the situation, to effect improvements, and to impede the work of the SS—when, therefore, the anonymous inmate was to be helped and the regime's machinery of destruction and war was to be harmed—then the concept of resistance will be used here.

This is certainly not intended to devalue the deed of a man who shared his bread with a friend or saved him from an action of destruction. The narrower definition is only used in an effort to concentrate on fundamentals.

A prisoner who was strong enough to behave consistently was encouraged to act in this spirit as soon as he had set himself the task of helping others. Roger Abada has described it accurately: "Surely there were limits to solidarity, and the death camps would not have continued as they actually were if the solidarity of the internees could have become fully effective." If someone felt solidarity with his companions and wished to take advantage of the possibilities afforded by his higher position to help them but kept bumping against these limits, the reactions could be as follows: to resign and be demoralized as a consequence or to seek organizational work.

I have already described the dilemma of a physician and a nurse who wanted to help those under their care. Those who worked in labor allocation, which was the second central location [besides the clothing depot] where help could be organized, had to make similar decisions. Usually the clerks received only general commands from the camp administration: so and so many inmates are to be assigned to this or that labor detail or to a certain subcamp. These commands had to be obeyed, and one was not allowed to bother the responsible ss labor allocation personnel with appeals. Within this framework the inmates assigned to labor allocation essentially had a free hand.

Oszkár Betlen, who worked in the clerk's office at Monowitz, where labor allocation for all subcamps belonging to Auschwitz III was coordinated, describes the dilemma he faced as a consequence of his job and his participation in the work of the illegal inmate organization. Who, for example, should he place on the list if the Gleiwitz I camp requested inmates? Betlen knew that the ss camp leader there was Moll, one of the most notorious members of the ss. "Under some pretext I could take one, two, or even three names off the list. But what if others were sent in place of those who were saved? Then I had the fate of those on my conscience." His comrades used one argument that finally helped Betlen dispel his doubts: "Since you cannot save all of them, you must first of all take care of those who will in turn save others."

Those who only heard of this dilemma, but not of the strength and courage of those who had not been broken by it, could draw such conclusions as were formulated by Hannah Arendt:

> By creating living conditions in which conscience no longer suffices and the good no longer can be accomplished under any circumstances, the deliberately organized plan to make everyone, including the victims, accomplices in the crimes committed by a totalitarian regime thus becomes "total." We know from several accounts to what degree inmates got entangled in the real crimes of the ss. The ss did this by assigning broad segments of the administration to inmates—criminals, political opponents, and Jews in the ghettos and extermination camps. In this way the victims were confronted with the insoluble conflict of whether to send their friends to their death or to help murder others whom they did not know. The important point is not that hatred is diverted from those who are really guilty (of course, the capos were more hated than the ss) but instead that the distinction between executioner and victim, between the guilty and the innocent, is destroyed.

Hannah Arendt has been harshly criticized for theses of this kind by many who have experienced the world of the Nazi concentration camps. Thus Jean Améry has characterized her comments as remarkably uncomprehending. She overlooked the fact that it was precisely the compunctions described by her that prompted many people to do more than merely help individuals at the expense of others. What was required for such acts was the moral strength to think beyond Auschwitz without any realistic hope of surviving Auschwitz. Another prerequisite was the good fortune of encountering like-minded people. To muster this moral strength, an inmate had to be in possession of his physical strength. Members of political parties were most likely to meet the first two requirements, and the third one, which was absolutely necessary, was found to varying degrees among the various groups of inmates.

In line with this thinking, Germans would have had to be most active and Jews least active in the resistance movement. Lucie Adelsberger has commented on the latter. "No Jewish inmate counted on ever leaving Auschwitz alive. We lived in the shadow of the chimneys both spatially and intellectually. The chimney was the alpha and omega of all conversations." Nevertheless, Jews worked in the resistance movement from the beginning, and the first resistance groups were formed by Poles rather than Germans, presumably because the very small number of Germans interned for political reasons were dispersed among the criminals. Whenever a German actively worked against the camp administration in the early period, like Otto Küsel in the Labor Assignment Office, he did so in contact with Poles.

■ In addition to the various Polish groups, one was formed around Ernst Burger. The Frenchman Roger Abada has described it as follows: "There already was an organization. It consisted of Austrian inmates and also included some Germans and Poles." In December 1942 Abada established contact with this group via the Viennese Rudi Friemel. At that time it also included Jews, but Abada evidently did not know this. Since any contact between "Aryans" and Jews was particularly dangerous, all connections with Jewish associates were limited to the absolute minimum. Tadeusz Holuj must have had this group in mind when he wrote that it was Austrian communists who took the initiative in organizing politically oriented illegal activities.

I have already reported about individual actions of the resistance groups and their results, which benefited everyone—for example, the struggle against the daily killings with injections of phenol in the inmate infirmary; the containment of beatings by inmate functionaries; the removal of criminals from key positions; and the successful fight against the deleterious informer system. The importance of the infirmary in all endeavors to counteract the extermination program has also been pointed out. That the people in this key location managed to put a stop to the camp administration's method of playing one national group off against another has been confirmed by Höß, who wrote that it was "all but impossible to retain our trustees in an infirmary."

Resistance groups also managed to listen to foreign broadcasts, most frequently those of the BBC, on radios that could be used by inmates who had to clean SS facilities before the men arrived for work. The dissemination of these news broadcasts counteracted the general demoralization, and more so as they became more positive in the course of the war.

After the leading Polish organization and the group that had formed around Ernst Burger had worked alongside each other for some time, the two groups were united in May 1943 and given a stable executive committee composed of two Poles and two Austrians. In addition to all other tasks, it undertook to deemphasize national differences in relation to the elementary difference that was graphically indicated by the striped uniforms of the inmates and the SS uniforms of the murderers. Progress in this area is one of the positive achievements of the Kampfgruppe Auschwitz (Combat Group Auschwitz), as this organization called itself.

■ Besides the saving of human lives, another task in the extermination camp forced itself on those who could think beyond themselves and the barbed wire: not to let the truth about the extermination methods of Nazism perish together with the victims. Ella Lingens writes that the following thought sustained many inmates: "We must survive so we can tell the world what we have seen and suffered." It stands to reason that it was primarily the Poles who were able to establish contact with the surrounding population and through it with the underground movement active in Poland. After some time Polish inmates who worked outside the camp area and Polish civilians employed in the area established a permanent contact by which a resistance movement in Cracow was regularly informed about what was happening in the camp. After the founding of the international organization in the camp, Józef Cyrankiewicz and Stanislaw Klodzinski carried on a continuous correspondence with Cracow. The letters sent to the camp from there were destroyed after they had been read. In Cracow, however, 350 letters from the camp have been preserved — just part of the extensive correspondence.

Other contacts were with neighboring Czechoslovakia. Three women who worked in the Waffen-SS's central construction office — Krystyna Horczak, Waleria Walova, and Vera Foltynova, one Pole and two Czechs — secretly made copies of plans of the camp and architects' drawings of the crematoriums with the built-in gas chambers, and these and other documents were sent to Czechoslovakia. Foltynova has described the motivation for this dangerous undertaking: "We were convinced we would never get out of that hell, and we wanted the world to know everything some day." Eventually they sent out three original plans that were stored in duplicate in the archive of the central construction office in the same way and also enclosed some other information about the camp — for example, about experiments with twins that Mengele made. Other documents they cemented in the washroom of their block. Their dormitory elder, the Pole Antonia Platkowska, helped them with this. The Czechs Foltynova and Walova were Jews but had been arrested because of their activity in the Communist Party.

Maria Stromberger, a nurse in the SS infirmary, helped me send reports about Auschwitz to my brother in Vienna, among other things an additional carbon copy of a secret monthly report that the SS garrison physician had dictated to me. From this my brother compiled facts and dates in a flyer that was disseminated by an underground communist group.

Because the leadership of the resistance organization had to acknowledge that the information about exterminations sounded so incredible that it was often bound to meet with skepticism, it decided to dispel doubts with the aid of photographs. In 1944 the leadership in the main camp instructed Dawid Szmulewski, who was active in the resistance movement in Birkenau, to procure photographs of the destruction. Stanislaw Klodzinski affirms that the Polish civilian Mordarski, who worked in the camp area, smuggled a camera into the camp. It was brought to the Sonderkommando in a food pail with a false bottom, and pictures were taken from the roof of a crematorium. The exposed film was brought back to the main camp where it was concealed in a tube of toothpaste and smuggled out of the camp by Helena Daton, who worked in the SS canteen. The photos were sent to Cracow with this covering letter: "We are of the opinion that the photos should be enlarged and passed on. . . . Urgent: Send as soon as possible two rolls of metal film for a camera size 6 × 9. Send the rolls as fast as you can!" These photos have become world-famous.

The Polish resistance movement in Cracow was in touch with London. When all connections were functioning, it sometimes happened that the BBC reported about occurrences in Auschwitz within two days. As I have already demonstrated, the radical change in the personnel of the camp administration in the fall of 1943 was due in part to the information disseminated about Auschwitz. Once we noticed how sensitive the Central Office was about news of this kind, a sensitivity that grew as the war situation became more unfavorable for the Germans, we systematically sent out detailed information about the SS's extermination program. This information did not fail to be effective and today constitutes important documentation.

At the beginning of 1944 names and personal data of those members of the SS who had played particularly prominent parts in the machinery of extermination were sent to London via this route, and the effect appeared promptly. Years later Hans Hoffmann testified as follows about his colleague Gerhard Lachmann, the notorious SS sergeant in the Political Department, who was on that list: "When I came to see him (in the Gypsy camp), he gave me his service pistol, which was now registered in my name. He also gave me his personal bicycle, which I was supposed to send to his sister. At that time he told me that his name had been mentioned on the British radio together with five other names in connection with crimes committed in Auschwitz. He recited those names, but I only remember Boger. He also mentioned that he was leaving Auschwitz for that reason and would receive a new military paybook with a false name." These demoralizing precautionary measures of the SS happened to become known in the case of Lachmann, but it may be assumed that they were taken in other cases as well. The SS sergeant Johann Piringer, who also heard that broadcast, remembers that Höß and Palitzsch were also sentenced to death on that occasion as well.

Long before that, the BBC in London had broadcast unequivocal threats against the SS—for example, in December 1942, when the commentator had this to say about the extermination of the Jews in connection with a report about a debate in the House of Commons: "For those in Germany who let themselves be misused as tools of the systematic extermination of another race with full awareness of what they are doing, there will be no room in the new postwar world. For such people there can be nothing but extermination. The members of the SS and all others who are participating in the planning and implementation of the Nazi policy of exterminating the Jews should take note of this." In Auschwitz this threat had no perceptible effect, perhaps because at that time belief in Hitler's victory was still too strong to let any fear arise, but surely a broadcast of more than a year later, in which specific SS functionaries were condemned to death, was very effective because it gave names and biographical details.

Eventually the resistance movement sent out plans of the camp that included the extermination facilities and called on the Allies to bomb these. It was expressly stated that a decision not to bomb should definitely not be based on the fear that inmates might also be killed. That this demand did reach the Allies is documented by a telegram from the British Embassy in Bern to the Foreign Office in London that was intercepted by the German monitoring service on July 5, 1944. This telegram describes the campaign to exterminate Hungarian Jews and makes this proposal among others: "Bomb the railway lines from Hungary to Birkenau. Zero in on the facilities of the death camp." The responsible authorities have never clarified why there was no such bombardment, even though at that time other targets in the immediate vicinity were reached by Allied air fleets.

In my opinion Bruno Baum went too far when he wrote shortly after the liberation that because of the documents sent out of the camp and Allied propaganda, conditions in Auschwitz improved to such an extent "that in the end the main camp became a model camp." However, such a trend may be documented.

■ The Polish underground organization in the vicinity utilized its connections to provide medicines for the prisoners. This kind of help was started early and constantly expanded. Poles who were living near the camp regularly gave medications to the Polish inmates on the Rajsko Garden Center detail. A touching letter that was smuggled out of the camp by Edward Biernacki indicates the scope of this action: "In June, July, and August (evidently in 1942) I brought around 7,500 cc vaccines as well as seventy sets of antityphus vaccine to the inmate infirmary. Other people also do this kind of work, and their results are certainly impressive. Rest assured that we shall not disappoint you in your wishes and hopes. For your readiness to make sacrifices and your remembrance, once more my heartfelt thanks."

In November 1942 the Polish resistance movement informed its friends in Cracow that the officially apportioned medications met about 20 percent of the demand and that another 10 percent were "organized" in the camp. The remaining 70 percent needed in the infirmary of the main camp were covered by medications that were smuggled into the camp. This report indicates that these medicines did not benefit all of the patients: "Poles constitute the greatest percentage (of patients in the infirmary of the main camp), about 50 percent, and we help only them." It is not certain whether this remark expresses the nationalistic egotism of the Polish resistance group in the infirmary or whether these words were written merely in line with the known attitude of the Cracow organizations. In any case, they underscore the importance of the international organization that was formed six months later. Several inmates and a Polish woman from the vicinity lost their lives in this relief action. They were caught smuggling and brutally put to death.

When "Aryan" inmates were allowed to receive packages, the resistance organization devised a less dangerous method of smuggling medicines into the camp. It arranged for packages containing medications to be addressed to deceased inmates. Polish prisoners who worked in the parcel office knew these addresses and smuggled the packages into the camp uncensored by the ss.

■ Connections with the outside world were also used for the organization of escapes. Since Himmler did not readily forgive the commandants of the concentration camps for high numbers of escapes, the most severe reprisals were occasioned by flights: making the entire camp population stand in the roll call area for up to twenty hours (after the first successful escape on July 6, 1940); condemning comrades of the escapee to starvation in unlit bunker cells; executing comrades in the roll call area en masse; at a later date, interning the escapees' parents in the camp and announcing this measure with placards. In keeping with a proven method, the camp administration assured itself of the capos' collaboration in preventing escapes by punishing them if a member of their detail had managed to escape during working hours. This caused many a capo to protect himself by having those in his charge line up and count off several times a day, a practice that enabled a quicker detection of any attempted escape. If an escapee was captured alive, he was publicly hanged in the camp, at least during the Höß regime. If he was shot in the pursuit, his corpse was displayed next to the camp entrance for all to see. In addition, an army of stool pigeons was mobilized to ferret out prisoners who had voiced thoughts of escaping.

Despite all this there was an unbroken chain of escapes and attempted escapes. Höß mentions that his superior Glücks wanted to replace him twice — "and only because of the unprecedented high number of escapes that caused the Reich Leader SS (Reichsführer-SS, or RFSS, that is, Himmler) to give him such a hard time."

This is confirmed by the following passage from the notes made by Grabner in prison: "Now, however, Berlin also applied so much pressure because of the escapes that Höß reported a greatly inflated number of inmates shot while trying to escape in order to appease those high-level gentlemen." Although Grabner's notes should generally be used with caution, this remark appears credible. It comports with Höß's report of a statement made by Himmler when he inspected Auschwitz in mid-July 1942. This is what Himmler allegedly told him on that occasion: "The escape rate in Auschwitz is unusually high and unprecedented in any KL. Any means, any means that you employ to anticipate and prevent escapes is all right with me! The escape epidemic at Auschwitz must disappear!" As a matter of fact, documents indicate that between July and October of that year 142 inmates were reported as shot while trying to escape.

It was easy to inflate the statistics by commending and giving special leave to every SS man who reported that he had prevented an escape. Since the circumstances under which he claimed to have done so were not investigated, it became the practice to feign flights and collect the reward. This was done most frequently with the aid of "cap tossing." An inmate with little camp experience had his cap torn from his head while he worked outside the camp and thrown beyond the cordon. Then an SS man screamed at the inmate and ordered him to retrieve his cap. If he obeyed, he was "shot while trying to escape." If the inmate disobeyed, he risked being killed even more cruelly for not following orders.

Many Green capos had been playing this game, but here, too, a generalization would be unfair. Alex Rosenstock mentions the following episode from Birkenau: "It was in 1942, when a great many inmates were being murdered in a sewage gas facility. Cap tossing was a great sport there. Then a capo from the German Reich named Hermann joined this detail. When an SS man once again tossed an inmate's cap over the cordon, the capo said to the inmate: 'Don't go, I'll get your cap.' He was not shot at." Rosenstock also writes that when food was distributed this capo made sure that everyone received equal rations. Hermann wore the black triangle of an "antisocial."

Sometimes reports of escapes were feigned for other reasons as well. Heinz Brandt has given an example. In the fall of 1944 two Gypsies managed to escape from a forest detail in the satellite camp Budy because the guards, who were ethnic Germans, had fallen asleep. When they awoke and noticed the escape, they shot the other nineteen members of the detail, reported a general rebellion, and claimed that they had managed to foil the outbreak of all but two inmates. In this way they garnered praise rather than censure.

■ However, there also were many genuine and not merely feigned attempts to escape. In the early period most of them were acts of desperation, and two of these mass outbreaks have become known. On July 10, 1942, about fifty inmates escaped from the penal company for men who had to dig the *Königsgraben* (ditch) in Birkenau. Thirteen were shot while trying to escape, nine did so successfully, and the rest were captured. As far as one can tell from the names of those shot and the successful escapees, they were all Poles. Grabner has stated that in those days the would-be escapees were primarily Polish intellectuals. According to him, with the exception of the German capos, all of the other members of the penal company were gassed. This act of desperation was probably prompted by the fact that in those days there was absolutely no chance for a non-German to survive in the penal company.

Soon thereafter a substantial number of Russians broke out of Birkenau. According to some reports, this happened on October 5, 1942, but Andrej Pogoschew, a survivor, thinks it was on November 6. At the evening roll call the absence of two inmates was reported. As was customary, inmate functionaries were ordered to conduct a search in the adjoining area inside the great cordon. In this instance the survivors of the transports of Russian prisoners of war who, as a form of public display, enjoyed certain privileges were ordered to participate in the search, and they used the opportunity to break out in the foggy dusk. Broad writes that nineteen Russians fled, and Pogoschew states that he fled with seventy comrades. He was not asked how many were later captured by the ss. Broad says only that the pursuit was not very successful. Kazimierz Smolen, the director of the Auschwitz-Birkenau State Museum, believes that over fifty people fled; he mentions that the Russians destroyed a watchtower and that more than ten managed to escape and join a partisan group that was active in the vicinity. Alois Staller, a German inmate functionary who participated in the search, remembers that sixty-eight Russians fled and fourteen corpses were returned to the camp.

Many survivors remember another escape. In May 1943 three Poles managed to escape from the Surveying Service Commando. The Political Department searched for accomplices and helpers. On July 19 twelve Polish members of the detail were hanged in the roll call area of the main camp in front of all of the lined-up inmates, and as a deterrent the corpses were left hanging for a long time.

In the early period many inmates fled spontaneously, quickly exploiting a favorable opportunity or out of despair, incurring any risk, but later on escapes were with increasing frequency carefully organized. The Combat Group Auschwitz prepared in the camp maps, provisions, medicines, and addresses of safe houses, and it established contact with Polish partisan groups in the vicinity that were to receive the escapees. The most important thing was to find inside the big cordon a secure hiding place that could not even be detected by police dogs, for as soon as a missing inmate was reported at the evening roll call, the ss sounded an alarm. Then the big cordon inside which most details worked during the day remained in place while a search was conducted in the area surrounded by it. If this search proved fruitless, the camp administration left the big guard chain that was normally there only during the day in place for three nights. Thus a fugitive had to stay in a hiding place inside the great cordon for three days and three nights and was not able to leave the camp area until the fourth night.

The resistance movement organized numerous escapes in this fashion, but the last and most important one failed. On many occasions two prisoners were sent out, frequently a Pole who was supposed to communicate with the helpers and a member of another nationality whose escape the organization considered important. In several instances the latter were Jews, and three of those are known to me by name. Two of them survived, but the third, who had escaped to Warsaw, was captured by the Gestapo there.

Legends have formed around some of these escapes. A case in point is Otto Küsel, a German inmate with the number 2 who fled from the camp together with three Poles on December 29, 1942, in a boldly planned escape. Nine months later Küsel was picked up in Warsaw and returned to Auschwitz, where, fortunately for him, the newly appointed commandant Liebehenschel had rescinded the order to execute all captured fugitives.

June 24, 1944, brought another particularly sensational escape. The Pole Edek Galinski fled in an ss uniform together with Mala Zimetbaum, a universally respected Jewish runner and interpreter. With the help of Poles both reached the Slovak border, but there they were captured, taken back to the camp, and publicly executed. (Liebehenschel had already been replaced by Baer.) In full view of the lined-up inmates of the women's camp, Mala was able to slash her wrists with a concealed razor blade, and with bleeding hands she slapped the face of an ss man—a dramatic act of rebellion at the end of a life that has remained in the memory of many.

Detlef Nebbe, the top sergeant in the commandant's office, testified many years later: "As is well known, safeguarding the camp was not easy. All sorts of incidents had to be expected; for example, there were massive attacks by the partisan movement. Also, some partisans tried to sneak into the camp area in ss uniforms." That this testimony does not merely express the self-importance of a man who loved to emphasize to German judges his "military duties" in Auschwitz is indicated by the fact that in the fall of 1944 twenty-nine of the 126 members of the Polish partisan group Sosienka, which operated in the vicinity of the camp, were fugitives from Auschwitz.

■ A number of attempts to break out of satellite camps that were not as closely guarded as the main camp or Birkenau have become known. When a drainage ditch was dug in Janinagrube in the summer of 1944, the camp administration discovered a subterranean passage that began near the latrine and went under the fence. It found out that a German, a Russian, and a third man of unknown nationality were planning to escape in this fashion. At a later hearing ss camp leader Hermann Kleemann testified as follows: "One time a criminal inmate from the German Reich was hanged because he had attempted to escape by digging a tunnel underneath the wire fence. This was reported by the inmates themselves because they feared the consequences." The execution of a German was unusual, and evidently this is why Kleemann remembered it more clearly than he did the executions of other inmates.

Another attempted escape in Janinagrube, also with the aid of an underground tunnel, was successful. At that time a German Green capo fled together with a young Polish Jew. This flight also happened in 1944, probably before the failed attempt mentioned by Kleemann. Both men got as far as Essen, most likely the German's hometown. There they were captured, brought back to the camp, and hanged in the roll call area of Janinagrube after the ss had informed the lined-up inmates that this would be the fate of all who dared to flee.

Josef Kierspel, the camp elder of Golleschau, recalls the flight in the summer of 1944 of the German capo Alois Reier, who was also from the Essen area and wore a red triangle. The escape was evidently attempted through a tunnel that had been dug from the washroom. The capo was ferreted out and shot. Kierspel also remembers the execution of an inmate in Golleschau. From the judgment that was read before the execution, Kierspel gathered that after attempting to escape the inmate attacked a police officer with a knife. This prisoner was executed in Golleschau but had not fled from this satellite camp.

The ss camp leader of Günthergrube, Alois Frey, testified as follows: "During my presence in Günthergrube, five inmates whose nationalities I no longer remember (they weren't Germans in any case) were publicly hanged. Those five had been planning to escape and had offered an ss man some money to help them. The man contacted by them was an ethnic German from the Balkans; I don't remember his name. He notified me of the inmates' plans, and I made a report to Schwarz, the camp commandant. Then the five inmates were removed from Günthergrube and publicly hanged a few weeks later." Ludwig Wörl, who was camp elder in Günthergrube at that time, remembers that four Jews were executed, and he believes that this escape was attempted in September 1944. Since others have also stated that four inmates were executed, Frey probably erred. It is possible that the fifth inmate died—that is, was murdered—in the course of the hearings. The victims were from the Auschwitz area. One of them is reported to have called out with a noose around his neck, "Fellows, keep going, don't be afraid!" This man, whose name was Fischel, used to be a cantor's assistant in Bedzin.

There was a similar incident in the satellite camp Fürstengrube. Henryk Kowadlo reports that a Jewish block elder named Grimm was executed together with two prisoners because someone had revealed that they had dug a channel for their escape. Dr. Miklos Udvardi is presumably referring to the same incident when he states that in late July or August 1944 five or six inmates were publicly hanged in Fürstengrube. As he remembers it, those hanged were Poles and Jews from Greece and Italy. Udvardi affirms that this was a conspiracy and that a radio transmitter was found in the block where Grimm was block elder.

Karl Dubsky, Theodor Weil, and others remember a failed attempt to break out of the satellite camp Jaworzno, also with the aid of a tunnel. Many of those involved—the reports range from nineteen to twenty-nine—were publicly hanged on December 6, 1943, after a Polish block elder had revealed their preparations. The camp elder of the satellite camp Sosnowitz, probably a Norwegian officer, was caught trying to escape and was hanged in the camp.

One escape has made the history books. Alfred Wetzler and Rudolf Vrba, who escaped from Birkenau on April 7, 1944, and reached Slovakia, their homeland, passed along their notes on Auschwitz to Jewish organizations as well as to a representative of the Catholic church; the notes were forwarded to the pope and Roosevelt, among others.

■ After a careful investigation of all preserved records, Tadeusz Iwaszko, a researcher at the Auschwitz-Birkenau State Museum, was able to document 667 escapes. He showed that at least 270 escapees were captured after escaping or were caught trying to escape. In the bunker book, the notation "back from escape" marks the listing of three inmates in 1941, fifty-nine inmates in 1942, and 119 the following year. In January 1944 five inmates were brought "back from escape" to the bunker. No entries have been preserved beyond that date. At a later date it was possible to obtain the addresses of around 100 escapees from Auschwitz. This means that at the very least 100 and at most 397 prisoners survived the flight and the subsequent life in the underground or among partisans.

Of the 667 prisoners who have been documented to have escaped, or tried to escape, only sixteen were women. Female inmates were most likely to attempt an escape from the penal company. For one thing, living conditions there were such that the women were ready to run any risk, and, for another, the penal company was for a long time housed in a satellite camp where the supervision could not be as tightly organized as it was in the main camp or the Birkenau complex.

It has been possible to determine the nationality of 481 of the 667 escapees. Over 48 percent were Poles, and Russians were the second largest group, with 19 percent. This may be due to the related language that permitted a Russian to communicate with Poles, to the especially brutal methods employed to annihilate Russians, and finally to the fact that almost all the Russians deported to Auschwitz were soldiers. In 1944 the approach of the Red Army must have induced many a Russian to flee, and there were an increasing number of escapes. Between April 19 and June 8, twenty-five Russian prisoners of war fled from Auschwitz, almost all of them in groups. On May 22 five Russians managed to escape together, and on May 27 another seven did.

Almost 16 percent of the fugitives were Jews. The documents do not indicate from what countries they had been deported to Auschwitz, but on the basis of known cases it may be stated that most of them were from Poland and neighboring Slovakia. The percentage is surprisingly high when one considers that for linguistic reasons many Jews had no opportunity to continue on their own after a successful escape. Besides, they had to cope with the anti-Semitism of the surrounding population on whose help they depended. When Edek Galinski was preparing to escape with Mala Zimetbaum, his friend and compatriot Wieslaw Kielar asked him whether in an emergency they could count on help from people in the vicinity if those people noticed Jewish features in Mala. Well, this was not the reason for the failure of this escape; but if Poles considered such matters, Jews certainly had to expect some trouble. After all, imprisonment in the camp had taken the heaviest physical toll on Jews. They were more strongly affected by a certain inhibition than those who could escape from the lowest rung of the inmate hierarchy, an inhibition that Elie A. Cohen has formulated as follows: "For years it was drummed into us that we must obey orders rather than think of taking an initiative, and eventually I was afraid of making any personal decision." This kept Cohen from thinking of escaping in the evacuation, even though it offered the most favorable opportunity to do so.

Six percent of those who attempted an escape were Gypsies, and there were almost as many Czechs who, like the Russians, could easily communicate with Poles and whose homeland was not far away. Although Germans undoubtedly were best qualified to break out of the camp, only 4 percent of all escapees were members of that nation. The obstacles they faced in freedom after their escape from the camp were greater than those of other groups. Since a lone German could not count on the support of the population, most of the Germans who decided to flee took along a comrade of another nationality.

The overwhelming majority of the fugitives were young. However, one of the escapees was a fifty-three-year-old man who had come on a Jewish transport from France. The youngest fugitives whose age became known were fourteen- and fifteen-year-old Gypsies. The elderly Jew and the Gypsy boys were caught and killed.

A little over 25 percent of the escapes were from the main camp, which was guarded most closely. From Birkenau, which housed many more inmates than the main camp, there were almost as many escapes as from all of the satellite camps together, even though the satellite camps offered the relatively best opportunities for flight. They were not as stringently guarded as the big camps, and it was easier for inmates working in the arms factories to establish contact with the outside world because there were non-German workers as well. In Birkenau the proximity of Canada, with its greater opportunities for bribes, enhanced the opportunities for a flight.

■ When inmates had to do forced labor in the arms industry, the resistance movement undertook a new assignment, sabotage. The cruelty with which the SS persecuted anyone who attempted sabotage may be illustrated by one example out of many. In the labor camp Blechhammer in January 1945, an inmate named Tuschenschneider was tortured and publicly executed. He had committed the crime of taking a piece of wire in the chemical factory where he worked in order to tie his shoes. A German master noticed and reported this. According to a report by Luzer Markowicz, Tuschenschneider and a Greek Jew whose number had also been taken down by the master, as well as a young French capo who was responsible for the labor unit to which both belonged, were sentenced to death for "sabotage."

Despite this terror the resistance movement did not shrink from the task of organizing systematic sabotage in armament plants. There is no comprehensive accounting of the occurrences. Thus only isolated results can be given, and this list cannot claim to approach completeness.

Roger Abada has testified that in the DAW (Deutsche Ausrüstungswerke) production declined by 50 percent within a few months after systematic sabotage had been organized. According to a report by Thérèse Chassaing, the successful activities of the women's detail that was assigned to work in the munitions factory of Union Werke were indicated by the daily complaints that grenades manufactured there had failed to explode. Often it was possible to render machines inoperative because of defects. In the Rheinmetall AG Düsseldorf, which operated a factory in Laurahütte, the inmates who worked in the engineering office found a way of damaging the mechanisms of the artillery manufactured there after it had already passed inspection. Thus they avoided being suspected of having caused these defects.

Sabotage was also carried on in the biggest factory in which inmates of Auschwitz worked, the Buna Works of IG Farben. On one occasion, defects in the power plant aroused suspicion. In the course of an investigation, the barracks that housed the senior capo of the cable-building detail was checked, and, according to Elie Wiesel, the ss found weapons there. The popular senior capo, a strikingly tall Dutchman named Jupp Snellen van Vollenhoven, was locked in the bunker and tortured but then released.

At that time a young Pole named Viktor Lies, who was also popular with everyone, was hanged. Franz Unikower, who was best informed as an inmate working in the Political Department in Monowitz, believes that Lies was executed because an informer had reported that he was preparing his escape.

When sabotage in arms factories became relevant, the resistance movement endeavored to smuggle cadres onto those details that offered opportunities for sabotage. There is no doubt that prisoners who had no contact with the Combat Group Auschwitz also committed sabotage. Finally, it must be mentioned that production in some factories was also sabotaged in a less risky way in cooperation with ss men and civilians employed in those plants. Inmates were glad to fulfill the private wishes of these masters and did work on the side instead of working on production. Such illicit work deprived the arms industry of much important raw material.

◾ In the final phase of the camp, Combat Group Auschwitz shifted the emphasis of its work again. What happened in the liquidation of Majdanek, the second extermination camp, in July 1944, when Russian troops approached the camp area, alarmed us. From reports by "Aryans" who were brought to Auschwitz, we learned that the mass of inmates were murdered at the liquidation, while the "Aryans" who were allowed to live let themselves be led away without any thought of fleeing, even though such an escape would have been possible in the initial confusion and prisoners had formed a secret organization. This taught us that it was our task to prevent a repetition of this sort of thing when Russian troops reached Auschwitz. In those days a special military leadership was added to the general leadership of the group, and other Polish resistance groups subordinated themselves to this military leadership. Its tasks were defined as follows in a letter directed to Cracow:

The military camp council is the joint leadership of all military combat groups. It organizes the military work in the camp, trains the cadres, forms combat groups, and assigns them tasks. The military camp council unites leading cadres that rely on military men of various nationalities as well as those who by virtue of their positions in the camp and through personal respect are gathering the illegal groups on the details and in some sections around themselves and in the decisive moment will be ready to sweep the fellow inmates in their sections along and subordinate them to the military command.

The cadres were assigned to details from which such important centers as the power station, the arms depot, the motor pool, and the telephone switchboard could be reached. Since the correspondence indicated that the partisan groups operating in the vicinity of Auschwitz, especially in the nearby Beskids, had several times been greatly weakened by the ss and did not seem properly prepared for vigorous cooperation in the event of a liquidation of Auschwitz, we decided to transfer part of the leadership to the outside to ensure a well-coordinated action at the decisive moment.

This escape was planned for August 1944. Ernst Burger, Zbyszek Raynoch, and I were to participate. On the eve of the projected flight we were informed that the partisans whom we were scheduled to meet at a prearranged place and who were going to arm us had been attacked. Our escape had to be postponed. I could not participate in it, for I was transferred to Neuengamme shortly after the failed attempt. Originally I was supposed to wear an ss uniform and escort out Ernst and Zbyszek, who would have retained their inmate's garb, as though I were taking them to work, but this was now canceled. In its new plan the organization again refrained from using the usual escape route, via the hiding place inside the camp area. The reason for this was that it had to be assumed that the ss would depart from its routine practice of keeping the great cordon in place for three nights when the fugitives included Germans known in the camp. In addition to Burger and Raynoch, three Poles were supposed to flee, for the escape was to be aided by two ss men who were to drive a truck with wooden crates to a place seven kilometers away. The crates were big enough to hide five men, and partisans were waiting at the meeting place. However, one of the ss men who had been recruited for this plan was a traitor. Instead of being driven to freedom, the five men were taken to the bunker on October 27, 1944. As soon as they became aware of the betrayal, they took the poison that they carried on them as a precaution. Since the ss wanted to learn what was at the bottom of this extraordinary attempt to escape, it had the stomachs of the prisoners pumped out. In the case of Zbyszek Raynoch and Czeslaw Duzel, this endeavor was too late, and they died before they could be tortured. At the meeting place the partisans were attacked, and Kostek Jagiello, who had escaped from Auschwitz four months earlier, was killed. Finally, the aforementioned ss man also betrayed Rudi Friemel and Vickerl Veseley, the two Austrian members of the resistance movement who had recruited the two members of the ss for the escape on the Motor Pool Detail.

A letter from the combat group to Cracow reports about their further fate:

Very urgent! According to our very accurate information regarding the five men incarcerated in the bunker for attempting to escape, a telegram from the commandant (Baer) has arrived in Berlin proposing that all five be condemned to death as a deterrent for trying to escape, persuading ss men to flee, and maintaining contact with the partisans. This information is strictly confidential. We, on the other hand, regard it as absolutely necessary to disseminate the following news to save the lives of our five comrades. "In Auschwitz a few political prisoners, Poles and Germans whose only crime was an attempted escape, face execution. They are the victims of the provocation of an ss man, the Romanian-German Viktor Roth, who persuaded them to flee in order to provide the camp authorities with fresh bloody victims." Add a call for retribution in whatever form you deem best.

These efforts were in vain. The execution was postponed once for a short time, but on December 30, 1944, a cross beam was put up on posts in the roll call area to serve for the last time as a gallows. Ernst Burger, who was still under thirty, was executed together with four comrades, two Poles and two Austrians. Thus members of the two nations that were prominently represented in the leadership of the Combat Group Auschwitz stood united under the gallows shouting battle cries that caused them to be beaten when the nooses were already around their necks.

Shortly before the evacuation of Auschwitz, there was an execution in the women's camp. On January 5, 1945, four young Jewish women were hanged in front of all the lined-up inmates because the ss had learned from informers and tortures that they had smuggled the explosives out of the Union arms factory that had been used in the uprising of the Sonderkommando. The four were Roza Robota from Ciechanow, age twenty-three, Ella Gartner, Toszka, and Regina. The family names of the last two can no longer be determined.

■ In the last chapter of the history of Auschwitz, the resistance movement was not able to play a decisive role.

In the fall of 1944 many members of the organization were assigned, in increasing numbers, to transports that were bound for other camps—even though the camp administration did not suspect that those involved belonged to the resistance movement, whose leadership was not identified until the very end. The isolated rebellion of part of the Sonderkommando meant an additional weakening. Finally the organization was, as Eugène Garnier put it, decapitated by the arrests on October 27. Then, too, the officer whom the Polish underground organization had sent to the Auschwitz area in order to keep up the contact with the organization in the camp fell into the hands of the Gestapo. He was carrying documents that gave the SS an outline of the illegal organization. A report from the commander of the security police in Kattowitz, dated December 18, 1944, describes the organization of the Polish underground movement; it indicates just how seriously the SS took this illegal activity. Here is an excerpt from the section headed "Inspector's Office, Bielitz":

> The district commander's office in Auschwitz plays a special role in this command. As some captured material indicates, the concentration camp in Auschwitz is also part of the AK (Armia Krajowa). The camp is serviced on behalf of the inspector's office by the "military council of the camp," the WRO (Wojskowa Rada Obozu). Contact with the camp is maintained by a number of persons, particularly the district commanders Danuta and the PPS man Kostka (PPS stands for Sozialistischen Partei Polens [Polish Socialist Party]). A certain "Rot" (cover name of Cyrankiewicz) was appointed as the AK commandant of the camp. He concerns himself particularly with making reports about the KL and transmits these to the area via a certain "Urban" (cover name of the Polish liaison officer who was captured by the SS). The reports about the Auschwitz camp contain information about the comings and goings of inmates, the structure of the camp, personnel, evaluation of SS leaders, the organization of the inmates, and plans for the future. Among the tasks of the WRO are preparations for the escape of inmates. Sending these on is the responsibility of the Bojowka organization, which was founded especially for this purpose and has connections with Cracow via various places of refuge.

Although the resistance organization no longer was at full strength in the final period, its spirit did not disappear, and it manifested itself in a declaration composed in the summer of 1944. Here is an excerpt: "Only an international collaboration based on solidarity and the fight for freedom give us the right to regard ourselves as comrades in arms struggling against the disaster that Hitler's fascism has brought upon the world." In keeping with this idea, the members of the Combat Group Auschwitz were active after the evacuation and transfer to other camps in the final phase, shortly before the liberation of those camps.

The results of the activities of the resistance movement in Auschwitz, which have here been briefly outlined, prove that prisoners found a way out of the dilemma that the ss wanted to force on them, the dilemma that offered them the choice of becoming casualties or involuntary murderers. They succeeded in throwing sand into the machinery of death.

The Jailers

THE GUARDS
■ ■ ■

"I pledge to you, Adolf Hitler, Führer and Chancellor of the Reich, my loyalty and bravery. I vow to you and the superiors appointed by you obedience unto death, so help me God." This is the formulaic oath taken by every member of the SS.

The obedience demanded of every SS man is defined in detail in the *Lehrplan für die weltanschauliche Erziehung in der SS und Polizei, erarbeitet und herausgegeben vom SS-Hauptamt* (Syllabus for the ideological education of the SS and the Police, composed and edited by the SS Central Office): "It is an obedience that is difficult because it stems from pure voluntarism and demands all the sacrifices that a man is able to make relative to personal pride, external honors, and many other things dear to him. It requires an unconditional commitment without the slightest hesitation as well as the execution of every order of the Führer even when an individual believes that he cannot personally accept it."

Added to this unconditional obedience is blind loyalty—"a matter of the heart, never of the mind," as Himmler preached. The words *"Meine Ehre ist Treue"* [My honor is loyalty] were engraved on the belt buckles of the SS men.

Hans Buchheim is one of the scholars who have investigated the factors that induced so many people wearing SS uniforms to commit deeds that appear unfathomable under normal circumstances. He makes the following comment on the obedience demanded of the SS. "It was not the obedience of a military man's fulfillment of duty that can be demanded of every citizen, but rather the obedience of an ideological fighter that was based on a loyalty that, as Himmler often emphasized, is demonstrated by a man doing more than his duty."

The psychoanalysts Alexander and Margarete Mitscherlich have pointed to other consequences of an unconditional submission to the "will of the Führer": "The fascination that emanated from Hitler and his demands of the nation partook not only of sadism but also to a great extent of masochism, a desire to subjugate oneself that was based on a tendency toward a desecration of authority much further removed from consciousness. Since the ideal of obedience was very binding, kicking against the pricks evoked in thought unbearable guilt anxieties that were compensated for with excessive subservience. What other people would be prepared to pursue the aims of their leadership, which were slowly revealed as delusional, with such patience and endurance even in self-destruction?" The previously cited definition of obedience by the SS Central Office contains a masochistic component.

The Mitscherlichs' analysis has led them to this conclusion: "If I identify with it (the idol) and magnify it to the best of my ability, I no longer feel the oppression emanating from it as a *Last* [burden] but as a *Lust* [pleasure]. In this way the idol, in our case the Führer, acquires the quality of uniqueness. To obey him becomes a pleasure, a distinction that will enter the history books."

Theodor W. Adorno has pointed to another side of this problem. "(It involves) a supposed ideal, one that plays a considerable role in traditional education generally, the ideal of hardness. The vaunted hardness that is to be inculcated means indifference to pain, and no clear distinction is made between one's own pain and the pain of others. Someone who is hard on himself earns the right to be hard on others and avenges himself for the pain whose manifestations he was not permitted to show and had to repress."

In addition to having drummed into them obedience to their Führer and other leaders as well as doglike loyalty and hardness, SS men had instilled in them the conviction that they belonged to an elite of whom more could be expected and demanded than of ordinary mortals. Herbert Jäger has made this point: "Typical of the mentality fostered by the SS is the avant-gardist notion that they were ahead of their time and had to take over the 'difficult tasks for which the nation in its totality was not yet ripe.' Thus the justification of a man's own actions was not really seen in an already existing world order but in an order still to be realized, which would sanction the terror retroactively once its 'necessity' had been generally recognized."

Eugen Kogon has summarized his experiences in this realm:

The aims of the SS did not require knowledge but consciousness: an awareness that they were masters, members of an elite—even within the NSDAP (Nationalsozialistische Deutsche Arbeiterpartei, or National Socialist German Workers Party)—and Praetorians; and an awareness that the world was divided between friends and enemies. All this involved a prestige that was easily augmented by a toughness and ruthlessness of manner, by behaving arrogantly and pitilessly, and by spreading fear. Critical thinking that presupposes an ability to make comparisons and differentiations and hence requires increasing knowledge would have diminished their striking power and "sicklied o'er the native hue of resolution." It would have appeared corrosive to them, dangerous, disloyal, "Jewish." It was not demanded by their consciousness, for which political doctrines were sufficient. They did not doubt the correctness of what their leaders told them (and what was so pleasant and frequently comfortable for them).

In the places that were equipped exclusively for the extermination of people, a handful of ss men sufficed to run the machinery of killing. Since Auschwitz was not only an extermination camp but also a concentration camp, and due to this dual function had become the biggest camp, a steadily increasing number of guards had to be stationed there.

At first Auschwitz was a small camp. Höß stated that in May 1940 he had at his disposal about fifty members of the Waffen-ss as guards and twelve or fifteen such men as staff for the expansion of the camp. A report dated March 1941 indicates that there were 700 ss men.

None of the extant documents indicates the size of the guard unit in the spring and summer of 1942, when the extermination of human beings was being organized, but it probably was not much lower than on June 20, 1943. A document bearing that date states "about 2,000." For December 1943 Höß gives the number of ss men as 3,000 guards, 300 on the staff, and 200 in the administration. In a document dated April 5, 1944, the number of guards is given as 2,950, but this figure evidently does not include the staff and administration. On September 8, 1944, the resistance movement sent out information intended to prepare the partisan units outside the camp for tasks that would arise when the camp was liquidated, and this document also contains the following information about the size of the guard unit:

Auschwitz I	1,119 ss men
Auschwitz II	908 ss men
Auschwitz III	1,315 ss men
Total	3,342 ss men

Altogether, the number of ss men who were on duty in Auschwitz was much higher, for they were frequently transferred—in the beginning predominantly from one kz to another and later to army units serving at the front. Höß estimates that during his term of office—that is, until November 1943—6,000 men of the Waffen-ss were in Auschwitz for some time, and he adds: "I assume that an additional 1,000 members of the Waffen-ss were replaced before the evacuation. Accordingly, 7,000 men of the Waffen-ss were in Auschwitz."

When the women's camp was established in March 1942, female wardens were sent to Auschwitz as well. Josef Kramer, the commandant of Birkenau, has stated that in the summer of 1944 around forty or fifty female wardens were on duty there.

The composition of the guard unit varied greatly and in the course of time became increasingly diverse. ss men who had been trained for years in the school of the concentration camps always constituted the core. They occupied the key positions and invariably set the tone, even toward the end, when they constituted only a very small minority.

Theodor Eicke, who was for a considerable period of time the commandant of Dachau, the first Nazi concentration camp, turned it into a model camp in the spirit of the ss and drilled the guard unit accordingly. When he was promoted to the position of inspector of all the camps at a later date, he saw to it that his methods were adopted by the other camps. "Dachau's leaders and men," wrote Höß, "are regularly transferred to the other camps in order to introduce the 'Dachau spirit' and make them somewhat more military and Prussian." Höß has described Eicke's principles of education in these words: "He said that there is no room for weaklings in his ranks, and such people would do well to get themselves to a monastery as soon as possible. He can use only hard, resolute men who obey every order in devil-may-care fashion. It is not for nothing that they wear the death's head insignia and a weapon that is always loaded with powerful ammunition."

Most of the top leaders of the Auschwitz troop were formed in accordance with this principle. Commandant Baer; ss camp leaders Aumeier, Hofmann, Hössler, and Schwarzhuber; chief administrators Möckel and Burger; and ss roll call leader Palitzsch had been fully integrated into the ss since 1933. The commandants Höß and Kramer began their careers in Dachau with low ranks a year later. All of them were successful because they had willingly adopted Eicke's indoctrination.

Others came to the ss in curious ways. Erich Dinges, born in 1911, claimed to have joined the motorized ss in March 1933 only because he, a passionate motorcycle racer, wanted to continue to participate in races. Richard Böck, born in 1906, played the trumpet in a band at Günzburg and like its other members joined the ss cavalry division in that town in 1934. Böck later explained this momentous step as follows: "If we wanted to continue to play music, we had no other choice because the SA already had a marching band." Despite their long membership in the ss, however, these two men did not go nearly as far as those mentioned earlier.

Hermann Rauschning, who was one of Hitler's confidants before he broke with Nazism, writes: "The selection of antisocial persons encumbered with hereditary defects for guard duty in the concentration camp was deliberate. I had the opportunity to learn something about this. Notorious drunkards and criminals were expressly selected from the military units of the party and assembled in special formations. Here we have the highly characteristic case of a true selection of subhumans for definite political tasks." According to Rauschning, who could only have found this out in the period immediately following Hitler's seizure of power, a complaint about the ss's abusive treatment of prisoners caused Hitler to explicitly designate terror as the most effective political method.

Konrad Morgen gathered his experiences as an ss judge in the course of his investigations of concentration camp guards in the war years. His judgment was that "the ss guards constituted a negative selection." In a Polish prison Höß complained that "Auschwitz had gradually become the personnel dumping ground of the IKL (Inspektion der Konzentrationslager [Office of the Inspector of Concentration Camps])."

■ All of this may be true. Even so, none of the attempts at an explanation that have frequently been made in recent decades can stand the test: it is not the case that a handful of deviants committed the crimes that a shuddering posterity has had to take cognizance of.

The physician Ella Lingens estimates that no more than 5 or 10 percent of the Auschwitz guards were instinctual criminals in the clinical sense. The others were entirely normal people who certainly knew the distinction between good and evil.

Benedikt Kautsky has corroborated this view. "Nothing would be more incorrect than to believe that the ss was a horde of sadists who tortured and abused thousands of people on their own initiative, out of passion and a desire to satisfy their lust. The individuals who acted that way were certainly in the minority. Their image is more indelible because it is more sharply delineated than that of the less colorful ruffian who meets his prescribed quota of brutalities bureaucratically, so to speak, without ever missing his lunch break."

If others, who as inmates were not able to obtain as good a perspective as Kautsky and Lingens, estimate a higher percentage of sadists, this may be due to the fact that ss men with sadistic tendencies were preferred for positions that brought them into direct contact with the prisoners; the majority of the ss men served as guards on the towers or as escorts of the labor details and thus remained anonymous as far as the inmates were concerned. Hans Schillhorn, a trainer of the guards, has pointed this out. "All the guards who came from the guard unit to the protective custody camp volunteered for this duty." According to Schillhorn, the "active types among the guard units" attempted to get assigned to the commandant's office and thus have direct contact with the camp. The lighter duty and the much greater opportunities to "organize" attracted these "active types," and the more intimate contact with the machinery of murder did not bother them.

This was confirmed by Friedrich Althaus, the chief accountant of a guard company, in his testimony before a court. "I know that participants in special operations received an extra ration of schnapps and cigarettes. I believe that ss men who volunteered for such actions did so not only because of the extra rations but presumably because they enjoyed them. In this respect the support system of the troops was good."

Nevertheless, Hannah Arendt has properly observed that the organization

of the mass extermination counted on neither fanatics nor serial killers and sadists. "It relied only on the normality of people like Herr Heinrich Himmler,"
writes Arendt.

■ Over the years the cadre of "old camp hands" was augmented more or
less accidentally by others. The case of Gerhard Neubert illuminates the role
played by chance. Like many other Sudeten Germans, this man, who was born
in 1909, became a member of Konrad Henlein's party and, like most of the
latter's adherents, joined the ss after Germany's absorption of the Sudetenland. After the outbreak of the war, he was placed in a frontline unit. Neubert testified about his further career as follows: "We suffered a considerable
number of casualties in the fighting. Our unit retreated to Cracow for reorganization. I was given home leave but was recalled after a short stay in Diepholz. Because of transportation problems I arrived in Cracow two days late
and together with other late returnees was informed that we were going to be
posted to Auschwitz. I was able to return to Diepholz and spend the rest of
my leave there. After that, in February or March 1943, I reported for duty in
Auschwitz." There Neubert incurred guilt and had to be sentenced in Frankfurt.

Franz Wunsch was sixteen when his Austrian homeland was forcibly annexed to the German Reich and volunteered for the ss before his eighteenth
birthday. More than three decades later, Wunsch explained this step to a Viennese court in these words: "I regarded it as an elite troop and adapted to the
general trend and the mood of the population at the time." According to him,
the recruitment offices were crowded and the unbroken chain of German victories created a "terrific atmosphere" among young people. He and eighty
others were examined together, but such high standards were applied that
only four of them were accepted. Wunsch was not transferred to Auschwitz
until he had been wounded at the front and was no longer fit for frontline
service.

The infamous ss roll call leader Oswald Kaduk also began his military career in a frontline unit of the ss. After falling ill he was transferred to Auschwitz. Kaduk was an ethnic German from Upper Silesia; when the expansion
of the camp required more troops, an increasing number of ethnic Germans
were added to the Auschwitz guard unit.

In a report addressed to Himmler and dated October 10, 1943, Gottlob
Berger, the ss lieutenant general (*Obergruppenführer*) who was responsible for
the staffing of the ss units, cautiously stated that "recruitment in the labor
camps (of ethnic German resettlers) had been somewhat forcible." That this
"somewhat forcible" recruitment was a common practice before that time is

demonstrated by the way in which Wladimir Bilan and Stefan Baretzki joined the SS.

These two men were resettled from the Bukovina to Germany along with numerous other ethnic Germans. According to Baretzki, an announcement in his church invited all ethnic Germans to report for resettlement. He accepted the invitation and was sent to Breslau. There the young fellows were examined but not told that they were being considered for a voluntary unit (the SS) rather than the Wehrmacht. At that time Wladimir Bilan and his family were sent to Hirschberg. He recalls that in the fall of 1941 a commission there examined all men between thirty and forty years of age, including him. Without having to incur any special obligation or sign anything, they were ordered to report at the KL Auschwitz on October 21. According to him, resettled ethnic Germans of near-company strength were added to the guard. He had to ask what KL meant because he had never encountered the abbreviation before.

Many of those who proudly wore the SS uniform in Auschwitz had worn a different one at the beginning of the war. Peter Weingartner fought in the Yugoslav army when Germany attacked that country. As a prisoner of war he was recruited into the SS in October 1942 and assigned to Auschwitz. When Hitler invaded Poland, Perschel and Nierzwicki were in the Polish army; Perschel fought in the battles at Modlin, and Nierzwicki served in the Polish navy. Thanks to his German descent, Nierzwicki was released from captivity after just three days. All three men had the blood of many of their fellow human beings on their hands.

A young lad from the Banat region—unfortunately his name is not known—joined the SS because he could thus obtain a waiver of the required entrance examination for universities, the so-called *Matura*. He was among those who did not allow themselves to be infected by the indoctrination and milieu of Auschwitz. He joined prisoners who were trying to escape, and he was probably captured and shot.

"We had thousands of guards who knew hardly any German," said Höß in his testimony. This sometimes led to grotesque situations with the *Beutegermanen* [Germans obtained as spoils of war], the German SS men's disparaging term for the ethnic Germans. Racz, who guarded our detail in the SS infirmary, was from the Banat. This uneducated fellow had trouble with the German language, and so he sometimes asked me to compose love letters for him, and I agreed because this put him in my debt. Bara, another ethnic German on duty at the same place, was from the Auschwitz area and spoke Polish better than German. When no other SS man was around, Bara would converse with the Poles on our detail in their shared mother tongue. He used the personal contact to have the inmates "organize" things for him, and in this way they "bought" him. Johann Schindler, the top sergeant of the guard battalion and later adjutant of the commandant of Auschwitz, estimates that the guard was composed of 60 to 70 percent ethnic Germans from eastern Europe.

▋ In the final phase the ss had at its disposal too few members. A letter dated June 5, 1944, and signed by Oswald Pohl, the chief of the wvha, indicates that in those days 10,000 members of the Wehrmacht were integrated into the Waffen-ss and assigned to guard various camps, replacing ss guards who were sent to the front. At that time ss First Sergeant (*Stabsscharführer*) Detlef Nebbe was appointed sergeant major of the Wehrmacht's office in Auschwitz, which, according to his recollection, was established around April 1944. Approximately 1,200 to 1,500 members of the army were transferred there, though not all of them were assigned to guard duty. A letter from the resistance movement dated August 22, 1944, gives the number of members of the Wehrmacht on duty in Auschwitz in ss uniforms as slightly over 1,000. Most of them were older and sickly soldiers who could no longer bear the rigors of frontline service. Many were an agreeable contrast to ss men, but, to be sure, not all of them. Thus Olga Lengyel writes that the members of the Wehrmacht who came to her attention were just as brutal as the most rabid ss men.

Other units were also assigned to guard some small satellite camps in the final phase. Thus the labor camp Laurahütte, established in the spring of 1944, was guarded by a unit of the coastal flak artillery. Arnost Basch has testified that thanks to these guards the inmates were not treated as badly there as they were in other camps. The real camp administration, however, was in the hands of experienced ss men. In the subsidiary camp Althammer, the inmates were guarded at work by members of the navy who were no longer fit for action.

The recruitment of female wardens posed particular problems. Höß has described how most of these women came to Auschwitz. "Despite diligent recruiting by the Nazi women's organizations, very few candidates for duty in a KL came forward, and, in view of the ever increasing need for wardens, they had to be procured by force. Every arms factory to which female inmates were to be assigned had to make available a certain percentage of its female employees for duty as wardens. Considering the general war-related dearth of female workers, it is all too understandable that these firms did not give us their best material."

Of the sixteen female wardens who were transferred to Bergen-Belsen after the evacuation of Auschwitz and had to answer for their actions in the Lüneburg trial, eleven had been made available to the camp administration in 1944 by Upper Silesian armaments factories in the manner described by Höß, and five had already been wardens for some time. Herta Ehlert worked in a bakery before she arrived at the ss. Elisabeth Volkenrath was a hairdresser; she had to work in a munitions factory during the war and was "transferred" from there to the SS, as she told a British military court that sentenced her to death. Gertrude Liehr, born in 1921, was induced by her father to join the NSDAP. As a former official of a labor union, he was viewed with suspicion by the Nazis, and he hoped to safeguard his daughter, born in 1921, who was also sent to Auschwitz from an arms factory.

■ These people, who came to Auschwitz more or less by chance, were roughly speaking an average group, according to the SS physician Hans Münch, who worked in the Institute of Hygiene at Auschwitz. "The main contingent of the guard troops," he writes, "was comprised of people that we see and know almost daily from our everyday life, people who with their education, their background, and the German mentality of the time corresponded exactly with what was expected of them. In many respects they were bureaucratic types that may be observed with particular distinctness in Germany, people who did their duty and to this day are proud of having been good soldiers." Münch evidently got to know the men who worked in the administration better than anyone else.

All 7,000 of these people—old camp hands, ingenuous ethnic Germans who were wounded and no longer fit for service at the front, and girls sent by arms factories—were confronted in Auschwitz with the well-organized machinery of human extermination into which everyone was integrated directly or indirectly.

Their RFSS, who trained them to obey every Führer order "even if an individual believes that he cannot personally accept it," set the tone that those active in the extermination camp gratefully adopted. This is what Himmler told his SS leaders: "For the organization that had to implement the order (to kill as well Jewish women and children), it was the hardest we have had up to now. It has been carried out, without—I believe I can say—having done harm to the minds and souls of our men and our leaders. There was a very real danger that this might happen. The path between the two possibilities arising here—either to become too brutal, to become heartless and no longer respect human lives, or to become soft and crack up to the point of nervous breakdowns—the path between Scylla and Charybdis is dreadfully narrow."

When Himmler's SS leaders were later asked by judges why they had participated in the mass murders, all they said was this: "It probably crossed every SS man's mind that this (the extermination of Jews in Auschwitz) was not the right way, but there was no power to change it." "It simply did not occur to anyone not to execute an order. And if I hadn't done it, someone else would have." "If I had refused, I would have been in for a punishment, and the order would in any case have been carried out by others under the same compulsion." These were the answers of Adjutant Höcker, Commandant Höß, and the notorious camp physician Dr. Entress. One could just as well transpose the names of the speakers, given how alike their words are. Even the leaders who were well aware of their power regarded themselves afterward only as tiny cogs in an all-powerful machinery.

Himmler, who felt nauseous the first time he attended a mass execution, saw to it that the distance between deeds and doers was kept as great as possible—"the most dangerous constellation of acts and actors that is criminologically conceivable," as the jurist Herbert Jäger put it. Himmler ordered that the extermination of human beings be "humanized." Jäger correctly remarks that "what it (the SS leadership) meant by 'humanization' was evidently a distancing, deemed necessary in the long run, from situations that might arouse compassion. Thus the inhibiting effects of the mass shootings that caused even Himmler to feel weak were probably the reason for the subsequent murders in gas wagons and gas chambers."

Hannah Arendt has pointed out another trick that was capable of "liberating" SS men in extermination camps

> from the reactions of quasi-animal compassion that almost inevitably takes hold of normal people at the sight of physical suffering. The trick employed by Himmler, who appears to have been especially susceptible to such instinctive reactions, was very simple and quite effective. It consisted in reversing this nascent compassion and directing it not at others but at one's own self. As a result, whenever the horror of their deeds gripped the murderers, they no longer asked themselves, "What on earth am I doing?" but rather, "How I have to suffer when I do my terrible duty! What a heavy burden this task is to me!"

The uniform worn by the executioners made it appear that the killings had a quasi-military character and also offered them the chance to hide behind the Prussian ideal of blind obedience and to exonerate themselves from any personal responsibility.

Höß plays a different tune when he writes: "I wanted to be notorious for my hardness in order not to be regarded as soft." Gerhard Lachmann, the young SS sergeant of the Political Department, told me this at a hearing in which he included a lecture about the necessity of exterminating the Jews. "Yes, eradicating the Jews is cruel, but you have to be able to be hard if you want to take a great action. What makes a leader is his ability to be hard in pursuing a goal that he has recognized as the right one." His even younger colleague Hans Stark had this slogan affixed above his desk: "Mitleid ist Schwäche" [Compassion is weakness].

Herbert Jäger properly states that "hardness was, so to speak, the quality norm of the ss that had to be satisfied. Nothing was feared more than being regarded as soft." Hardness and self-pity were summoned up in order to deaden conscience.

But conscience was also lulled by the fact that both the murderers and their victims had been torn out of their normal societal surroundings. In the words of Hans Buchheim:

> The Jewish victims had at least been systematically socially isolated in the area of the "Greater German Reich" for years (and this isolation was accepted by the "Aryans" — the few exceptions only prove the rule — and the Gypsies had always been pushed away by the surrounding world), but the hangmen were also isolated while serving "somewhere in the East." Since the campaigns of murder were conducted with the strictest secrecy, there was considerable temptation to delude one's conscience into believing that the deeds committed outside any social control never happened. Who was going to ask at home at a later date what was done to an unknown Jew in a forest near Minsk or behind the barbed wire of Auschwitz?

Added to this was the belief that the reign of Nazism was going to last for a thousand years — an incalculable period of time. It was tempting to be counted among the elite in this Führer state, and it seemed dangerous to break away from it.

Finally, the hammering, monotonous, total propaganda of the Nazis did its bit. Himmler wrote that the life-and-death struggle against the Jews was as much of a natural law "as man's fight against some epidemic, as the contest between the plague bacillus and a healthy body." The ss general Erich von dem Bach-Zelewski said the following in a Nuremberg jail cell: "I am convinced that if it is taught for years and decades that the Slavic race is an inferior race and the Jews are not even human beings, such a result (that is, unresisting participation in mass murders) is inevitable."

"We were relieved of thinking, for others were doing it for us." This is what Hans Stark, who had been ordered to go to the Auschwitz mill at age nineteen, told his judges. "After all, every third phrase was 'The Jews are to blame for everything, the Jews are our misfortune.' This was drummed into us." The younger a person was when he was installed in the machinery of murder, the more effective was the total propaganda.

■ It would be wrong to look at the ss in isolation. Reinhard Henkys warns against failing to observe that "in the Germany of the Hitler years, an atmosphere had developed that did not give those who performed the task set by the Nazi leadership to eradicate 'inferior' races and peoples the feeling that they were behaving antisocially or placing themselves outside the basic norms of society."

The jurist Ernst-Walter Harnack has pointed out that the crimes committed in the name of Nazism were supported by an enormous cluster of governmental and government-related organizations

> in which there was a hierarchy of thousands of people ruled in accordance with superiority and subordination, orders, instructions, and obedience, influenced and guided by a fascinating ideology of far-reaching power, by feelings and pledges of loyalty, by belief in authority and some form of trust in the better judgment of the government—a government, moreover, that was waging a war, and was at least tolerated by the world until its outbreak, that the people with their universities and churches had on the whole approved of for years and that was headed by a Führer who was often almost religiously transfigured, particularly by more simple-minded and younger people.

Harnack is clearly attempting to exculpate the ss. For example, it could not have escaped his attention that those crimes had been committed in embryonic form before the outbreak of the war. However, one cannot make light of his reference to the connivance of "universities and churches." Viktor von Weizsäcker has aptly referred to collective crimes that were committed "with moral anesthesia."

Alexander Mitscherlich refutes the frequently voiced view that the murders were committed by some dregs of society who sullied the German name. He counters it by writing:

> But we know that the Hößes and Bormanns, the higher-ups and the lowly, were in agreement with virtually everyone. Everyone enjoyed seeing the Jews being herded away like cattle, just as everyone enjoyed it when the black slaves were crowded to death on vessels of the East India Company. The rear guard of history should note that it is a matter of unconscious enjoyment that paradoxically could fail to enter the consciousness even of those who choked others with their own hands, trampled on them with army boots, and shot them with guns belonging to our state. People were executed with a steely fulfillment of someone's duty. No pleasure, says Biedermann [in Max Frisch's play The Firebugs]. The grandeur of the genuine Marquis de Sade is not often encountered; Himmlers are more likely to be legion.

Helmut Gollwitzer goes even further when he says that the unimaginable atrocities were "largely committed by entirely normal persons whose sadistic opportunities were created by a historical constellation for which the entire people is to blame, which makes both the murderers and the murdered the victims of society." Even though it would be calamitous to intermingle guilt in the criminal sense with shared moral responsibility, this does not invalidate Gollwitzer's reference to shared moral guilt. Where parts of society became aware of their responsibility, they were able to inhibit the commission of crimes. The mass murder of mentally ill German nationals was stopped by Hitler in view of the negative reaction of wide circles of opinion, whose spokesmen were clerical dignitaries.

The murders of Jews, Gypsies, and Slavs somewhere "in the East" did not elicit comparable reactions. Thus it was possible to assure ss men that they were doing things one could not discuss but could be proud of, things that ordinary people could not be expected to do, whose value would be properly assessed only by future generations. Thus they were eventually capable of murdering Jews and Gypsies with the mentality of exterminators who kill vermin. This should be taken literally because the ss men who were trained in the use of poison gas were called "disinfectors."

■ Neither the Nazi propaganda nor the general attitude of the German people could exert as enduring an effect on ethnic Germans as they did on people who had grown up in the Third Reich. The ethnic Germans were influenced by simpler methods. Stefan Baretzki, who had been posted to Auschwitz at age twenty-two, gave the Frankfurt court a rather graphic picture of how these young, primitive fellows were molded in Auschwitz. During one of his spontaneous outbursts in the courtroom, Baretzki exclaimed: "In those days we were shown rabble-rousing films like *Jud Süß* and *Ohm Krüger*. I remember these two titles. And what consequences they had for the inmates! The films were screened for the ss staff—and how the inmates looked the next day!" Erich Kohlhagen remembers that he and other Jews in the penal colony at Sachsenhausen were beaten up after the ss had watched the film *Jud Süß* the evening before.

Baretzki also described to the Frankfurt court how the young ethnic Germans were induced to carry out all orders. Once he blurted out:

I was in Auschwitz. Thousands were killed there. We were told that this was a law and had to be done that way; that's what ss camp leader Schwarzhuber said at an instructional session. They said that there must be gassings. We were instructed by officers and civilians. We were told that it was necessary to exterminate the Jews. I'm not a good speaker, so you'll have to help me, Your Honor. Some of us did ask: "What did these people do?," and they answered that they poisoned the wells and committed sabotage.

When we asked, "The women and children, too?," the answer was, "When you are in the first grade, you use the book for that grade and not the one for the fifth grade."

In response to the presiding judge, who asked whether that meant he and the others did not understand the situation at that time, Baretzki replied: "Yes sir. They told us we would find out later. They also told us that everything Hitler did was law."

Baretzki's defense was anything but sophisticated, and thus he can be believed when he testified as follows at the preliminary hearing: "We were often told by SS officers and civilians that what happened in Auschwitz was legal because the inmates had acted as saboteurs. I personally held the view that all these things were an injustice. For example, what acts of sabotage could children have committed? When I was on leave in Romania in 1943, my mother told me it would be best if I did not return to Auschwitz and lived illegally in the mountains. On that occasion my brother also advised me to go to the mountains. But I thought that if I didn't go back, there might be reprisals against my mother."

■ The commandant of the ethnic German Baretzki never toyed with such thoughts. When Höß was asked in his prison cell at Nuremberg whether he could have refused to execute an order, this was his reply: "No. On the basis of our entire military training, the idea of disobeying an order, no matter what it was, simply did not cross our minds." Höß added: "I assume you are unable to understand our world. I had to obey orders, of course."

Höß returned to this subject when he was working on his memoirs in the Cracow prison: "Since my arrest, I have been told repeatedly that I could have refused that order (to expand Auschwitz into a place of mass exterminations) or that I could have gunned down Himmler. I don't think that even one of the thousands of SS leaders could ever have entertained such a thought. That sort of thing was simply impossible. Sure, many SS leaders grumbled and groused about many a hard order from the RFSS, but they did carry out every order. The SS indoctrination was deep seated, and the RFSS knew quite well what he could ask of the SS." Even in prison the awareness of being subject to higher command had not disappeared. Höß continued: "But outsiders can't understand that there was not one SS leader who refused to obey an order from the RFSS or did away with him because of a cruel or harsh order. What the Führer ordered, or what we were ordered to do by his second in command, the RFSS, was always right." Höß emphasized the word "always."

Josef Kramer, the commandant of Birkenau, gave this testimony before the British military tribunal in Lüneburg: "Himmler was my commander in chief, and his every order had to be executed, of course. There simply was no other view, and not to carry out a military order was utterly out of the question."

Adolf Eichmann asserted in Israeli captivity that only one thing could have given him a bad conscience: not carrying out the orders given him. In the courtroom he said that his guilt was obedience, but he immediately added that obedience is to be praised as a virtue. Like Höß he doubted that his judges would be able to understand him.

When the engineer Klaus Dylewski was asked by an examining magistrate why he did not refuse to carry out criminal commands in Auschwitz, he replied that this would have been "a reaction alien to the German national character."

In Nuremberg Höß admitted that he sometimes had doubts about carrying out mass murder. "The only decisive factor in dispelling these doubts was always the unconditional order and the accompanying rationale of RFSS Himmler." In Cracow Höß gave this pithy summary: "Having been raised in the strict discipline of the SS organization, I believed that everything that its head and Hitler ordered was right, and it was my view that it would be a disgrace and a sign of weakness if I tried to evade the execution of these orders in any way."

■ In these ex post facto attempts to explain their conduct, it is significant that neither Höß nor the others defended themselves by saying that they had executed the orders to commit murder out of a fear of punishment. Evidently such an excuse seemed too shameful and incredible to them. For example, when asked by an examining magistrate about what happened to SS members who declared that their nerves and emotions did not permit them to carry out certain assignments, Emanuel Schäfer, an SS lieutenant colonel and the first head of the Kattowitz Gestapo, responded: "Such people were transferred for their own best interests and were assigned duties that were not such a strain on their nerves and emotions. I can't name a specific case offhand, but I know that such transfers were made. I think it is absurd if people claim today that such people were under threat of being shot. Of course, those involved ran the risk of being regarded as 'Schleimscheißer' [pantywaists]. There also was the possibility that such persons had to wait longer for their promotion, but this too cannot be stated with certainty." Schäfer ought to know because he was the superior of the SS men who served in the Political Department at Auschwitz.

Richard Böck remembers a comrade named Lange, an "old fighter" who had been honored with the Blood Order and the Golden Party Badge. In the early period, when shootings of prisoners were still handled by execution squads, Lange managed to have only volunteers used for the purpose. He argued for his initiative by saying that as an old Nazi he had not fought for this sort of thing. This prompted the head of his company, ss First Lieutenant Josef Kollmer, to snap at him in front of his lined-up unit and tell him that he ought to be ashamed of himself. Thereupon Lange submitted a request for a transfer to Dachau, which was immediately approved. When I asked Böck whether Lange's initiative had not embarrassed the company chief, he replied: "More men volunteered for those executions than could be used." This has been confirmed by Wilhelm Brock, who was in Auschwitz from the beginning to the end and testified as follows: "On a number of occasions an ss man who had been assigned to an execution squad did not want to participate. Then there was a discussion among the men, and someone always came forward as a replacement. All the officers cared about was that the numbers were correct."

As is well known, despite thorough research and the expertise of their clients, not a single defense attorney in the numerous trials of Nazis was able to present even one case of an ss man having been punished as an example to others for refusing to obey an order to murder someone.

■ It is not the aim of this study to fathom the boundless authority that the pedantic-bureaucratic Himmler enjoyed among his ss; he was in no way akin to the ideal image in whose spirit his men were educated. But a few revealing episodes will be mentioned here. Himmler inspected Auschwitz on two occasions, on March 1, 1941, and on July 17 and 18, 1942. On the latter occasion the mechanism of mass destruction had recently been installed, and he inspected it closely, becoming "weak in the knees," as Höß put it to Eichmann. Despite this sign of weakness registered by Höß, Himmler ordered an expansion of the capacity for killing at that time. To Höß he served as an example of how a man must overcome his weaknesses and remain hard.

In Auschwitz Himmler observed with interest how corporal punishment was administered to a woman. Another episode is also characteristic of this man. Since Himmler had a special interest in anything connected with agriculture, he asked to see a cowshed. Teddy Pietrzykowski, a Polish prisoner, was working there at the time, and after he had reported in accordance with regulations, he was asked by Himmler whether there was anything to drink. Teddy answered: "Yes sir, regular milk, skim milk, and cream." Himmler took a glass of skim milk and gave Teddy a pack of cigarettes for it.

Himmler's effect on the Auschwitz ss is indicated by the following marginal statements at the Frankfurt trial. Twenty-two years later ss roll call leader Oswald Kaduk astonished the court with this minute description: "The visit (Himmler's) took place on July 17, 1942. At 2:20 P.M. the RFSS arrived at the main camp and stayed there until 3:00 P.M. The RFSS was not present at the roll call and was driven to Birkenau at 3:05." During his visit Himmler spoke to an ordinary SS man; when Baretzki asked him afterward what Himmler had told him, all he answered was: "Do you think I know? I was so afraid that I peed in my pants."

Höß's adjutant, the Hamburg export merchant Robert Mulka, who was in no way a primitive person, gave the Frankfurt court this recollection of Himmler's visit: "I had a discussion with the RFSS about the strange behavior of SS leaders. At the dinner table in the SS leadership home, an SS second lieutenant leaned on the table with both arms. I sent an orderly to him and asked whether he would not like a chaise longue. Himmler overheard this and said: 'Great! That's how I want my leaders to be! They shouldn't just be brave at the front but should be able to walk in patent-leather shoes in any salon.'" Two decades later Mulka remained proud that the RFSS, as he still respectfully called Himmler, honored him with two sentences. It was also characteristic of Himmler that even toward the end of the war he concerned himself with trivial matters while frequently leaving decisive problems unsolved. This reinforced the feeling in members of the SS that they were constantly under the direct control of the RFSS. This is illustrated by the following unusual episode.

Rudolf Friemel, a Viennese, fought in the ranks of the international brigades in Spain and married a Spanish woman. There was a civil wedding in accordance with the laws of the Republic. After the defeat of the Republic, Friemel, like most of his comrades, was interned in southern France and finally landed in Auschwitz. His wife, who had given birth to a son and also emigrated, moved in with his father in Vienna. Since the Franco regime did not recognize civil marriages contracted at the time of the Republic, the German authorities also regarded Friemel's marriage as invalid. For this reason Friemel's father and his wife tried very hard to enable Rudi Friemel to marry his wife again in accordance with German law, and their petition wound up on Himmler's desk. Himmler made a positive judgment; the father, the wife, and the little son received permission to travel to Auschwitz, and Rudi was permitted to let his hair grow. On March 18, 1944, he put on civilian clothes and went to the Auschwitz registry, which normally issued only death certificates, and the marriage was contracted in accordance with German law. Because Himmler had personally given permission for this, the camp administration granted Friemel unusual rights. The Identification Service, which took only photos that filled rogues' galleries, made a real wedding picture, and a room in the camp bordello was placed at the disposal of the couple for one night.

■ It is easy to demonstrate that it cannot have been just blind obedience that caused the SS men of Auschwitz to carry out all murderous commands instantly, for other orders were generally ignored. For example, sexual intercourse between members of the SS and *Fremdvölkische* (members of other nationalities) was forbidden. It was necessary to keep reminding the SS of this order, which was regularly circumvented. Orders from the commandant's office frequently began with these words: "For the last time I draw your attention to the prohibition . . ."

Any personal relationship with an inmate was forbidden with particular strictness. Nevertheless, many SS men took up intimate relations with female prisoners. Höß, who said that every order was sacred to him, was one of the first to transgress this prohibition.

Himmler put particular emphasis on prohibiting his men from appropriating the property of those murdered in extermination campaigns. The RFSS threatened that "anyone who takes even one mark is a dead man." Only a tiny number of SS members did not enrich themselves in the places of destruction. Konrad Morgen, who headed an SS commission charged with investigating cases of corruption, remembers that in several dozen cases SS members in Auschwitz were sentenced to prison terms (and, despite Himmler's threat, certainly not to death) for appropriating the property of murdered persons. This did not have a deterrent effect.

SS men misappropriated not only the gold of the murdered but also the food of the living. Baretzki, a block leader in Birkenau, has given a graphic description of this. "At nine o'clock the head of the Labor Service and the SS roll call leader went to breakfast in the inmate kitchen, followed by the SS camp leader at ten." From Höß on down, the prominent leaders went to Harmense to get fish, which were raised in ponds there. Pery Broad writes that every day vehicles with sausages and meat destined for the inmate kitchen were driven to the SS kitchen. "The SS cuisine worsened perceptibly after Egersdörfer, who administered the storeroom of the inmate kitchen, had a fight with SS Technical Sergeant Scheffler, the head of the SS kitchen, which meant that there no longer were any special allotments." Egersdörfer testified that SS members transferred large quantities of food from the inmate kitchen. He claims to have noticed that about 200 hundredweights of margarine that were part of the inmates' rations had been concealed in the cellar of the commandant's building.

Goods that were scarce in wartime were openly appropriated from Canada. The higher the rank of an SS man, the more uninhibited the method of appropriation. If an SS man had a bath prepared for himself in the SS infirmary, the inmate charged with that chore also had to provide soap and cologne. No one asked where he got those things, and it goes without saying that they disappeared after the bath.

In the SS Tailoring Detail, twenty-three female prisoners were occupied exclusively with sewing for the wives of SS leaders and female SS wardens. At a time when Himmler had repeatedly and very vigorously ordered that the greatest possible number of inmates be made available to the arms industry and that inmates could be used only for absolutely necessary work in the camp, this detail was enlarged. I need hardly mention that the material was obtained in Canada. In those days "Aryanizing" was not considered an insult to one's honor, and that is why despite all the threats of punishment most SS members had no compunctions about ignoring the prohibition.

If German society had actively opposed or tacitly rejected the aims pursued by the SS, the orders to kill would probably have been treated like the prohibitions of enrichment through the appropriation of Jewish property. Orders to murder confer an intoxicating power; they require a hardness one can be proud of and promote elitism because they cannot be given to everyone. This distinguishes them from other orders that were not carried out so zealously because those concerned counted themselves among an elite from which extraordinary things can be demanded. The following episode is characteristic.

When Auschwitz was built, the Poles living in the vicinity were resettled. Anyone who knows the SS can imagine the scenes that took place there. Richard Böck reports that some SS men in his company refused to participate. SS camp leader Schwarz did not call their attention to the consequences of refusing to obey orders but just lit into them: "What kind of men are you?" This sufficed to make the recalcitrant men cease their resistance.

However, as the following example shows, the pressure exerted on members of the SS should not be overestimated. The NSDAP expected its adherents to leave their religious denominations and designate themselves as *gottgläubig* [believers in God]. As an elite Nazi organization, the SS desired this even more strongly. The religious creed of thirty-nine of the forty defendants in the big Auschwitz trial at Cracow has become known. Eleven described themselves as believers in God and four as religiously unaffiliated. Seventeen stated that they were members of the Protestant denomination and seven of the Catholic. That trial primarily featured prominent members of the SS.

■ Himmler imitated the tactics of his master Hitler that had been so successful. He often left even decisive questions to the initiative of his subordinates, from whom he demanded independent actions. Eugen Kogon writes in this connection: "The SS expected subordinates to be at once obedient and independent, and both of these qualities had to be sensed by them, so to speak. Consequently, those who were considered the best members of the SS 'knew what was involved,' who did not wait long for explicit orders but acted in the spirit of the RFSS." Kogon aptly compares the typical SS member of the guard unit to "a bloodhound trained to attack people; he follows his instinct in a free chase but immediately heeds any remote whistle of his master, whether it means 'Down, boy' or 'Sic 'em.'"

Most SS leaders evidently regarded it as a distinction that they were entrusted with an assignment that was as important as it was secret: the extermination of human beings for the benefit of the "German race." They thought they understood their Führer well if they displayed initiatives beyond the explicit orders. This attitude is expressed in the description given by Adolf Eichmann in Israel of the conduct of the Auschwitz SS leaders when they escorted high-level visitors to the extermination facilities: "When someone came there, these people turned the whole thing into a spiteful spectacle, describing the matter as gruesomely as possible to a person who had a desk job, and presenting it as abruptly as possible; of course, they rejoiced every time if the visitor's nerves did not permit him to maintain the same *Haltung* [composure], as they called it, as they did."

This has been quoted verbatim from the tape that Eichmann made during the preliminary investigation. Eichmann also described how a person should behave "SS-like" if his nerves threatened to give out in the face of the mass gassings: "It would not have looked good if I had fainted (at the sight of piles of corpses on the grating where they were burned) because, after all, there was a little group of subordinates behind us, who would have interpreted it as a lapse, and word of it would immediately have spread like wildfire, and people would have personally revised their entire attitude—something that could not be allowed to happen." These sentences were taken from a tape that Eichmann made as a free man in Argentina.

Wanda von Baeyer-Katte has investigated the consequences of the feeling of belonging to a special elite within the elite of the SS. "The crimes that were committed," she writes, "constituted a kind of blood bond for the executors as well as the secondary participants in the line of duty. It bound them close together in that each person prompted in the other the consoling thought that it was possible to participate here without despairing."

A camaraderie comes into being, a variant of comradeship. People cover each other's transgressions, jointly circumvent unpleasant orders, and think they are above the norm. The camaraderie is preserved throughout the shared period in the camp; and if one has to testify in court, it resembles the solidarity of gangsters, each of whom knows that the other fellow could also tell tales.

At the same time the SS men of Auschwitz got to know and fear the unscrupulousness of their masters. When the SS judges Konrad Morgen and Gerhard Wiebeck visited the gas chambers in the course of their investigations, an SS noncommissioned officer asked them what would happen to them when the war came to an end. Broad has written about this subject more clearly: "Again and again, simple soldiers on guard duty said that they could not imagine ever being discharged and becoming free human beings again. Some surmised that to keep the secret they would probably be the last ones to march into the gas chambers. It is revealing that everyone regarded it as self-evident that Himmler would muster the necessary lack of character and the brutality required for such a step."

PEOPLE, NOT DEVILS
■ ■ ■

It is very tempting to force into patterns the people who wore an SS uniform in Auschwitz, particularly since several trials have made their deeds public knowledge. The German jurist Herbert Jäger has pointed to two variants: "On the one hand, there is a tendency to demonize the perpetrator and turn him into a 'monster' by projecting all that happened onto him without a closer examination of his concrete conduct, the situation in which the deeds were committed, and his personality. On the other, there is a tendency toward a complete depersonalization that turns the functionary into a particle of a machinery of terror operated by remote control, a person who did not act independently or on his own impetus." Jäger adds that both models seem equally improbable to him.

"The brutal, expressionless faces of the uniformed men with the symbol of death on their caps and collar patches, the hunting whips in their hands, the guns in their belts, and the high boots on their legs—all this made a frightening and indelible impression on the new arrivals." This is how Reimund Schnabel has described his first encounter with the SS on his arrival in Dachau. Yet Schnabel could have differentiated among SS men much more easily than most prisoners, for he spoke their language; and as a former Führer of the Hitler Youth, he was familiar with the barking, rasping tone of voice and the uniform behavior behind which an individual was hidden.

A statement made by a well-educated German Jewish woman who was asked to give her observations of the SS is typical: "To me they were all the same. If you ask me what they looked like, I can only say that all of them wore boots." For the nameless inmate who was tortured daily and did not dare raise his eyes, cudgels and boots were a substitute for his tormentors' faces. Schnabel writes that these seemed to be standardized as termites of terror and creatures bred in hell. Only prisoners who came into closer contact with individual members of the SS were able to get an idea of their personality.

Even Józef Kret, a Polish pedagogue who strives for objectivity in his descriptions, has given this characterization of the SS escort that took him and his fellow sufferers to the penal company in Birkenau: "These brutish, evil, obedient, and uncritical automata trained in the Himmler school of the art of murder would ply their shameful trade thoroughly and unfeelingly wherever a command placed them." Professor Robert Waitz, an inmate physician in Monowitz, did not make his observations on a brief march under excessive psychic pressure, as did Kret, but calmly and over a long period of time. However, he does not avoid the risk of making sweeping statements when he writes: "All SS officers regard themselves as outstanding, almost as supermen. All SS noncommissioned officers are crude fellows, sadists, and thieves who try to "organize" as much as possible for themselves. They are all really convinced that inmates are not human beings but personifications of the evil of this world. To them an inmate is a species of animal that must be punished and ought to be made to suffer by every means and as much as possible before it is finally exterminated. Generally speaking, feelings of compassion or human mercy are completely unknown to them."

Anyone who today, after the fact, wants to dispel the uniform anonymity of the jailers of Auschwitz is bound to encounter difficulties. Like many surviving prisoners, the jailers did not write their memoirs. The small number of those who did so had an ulterior motive, and this should be kept in mind when using their writings. Facing their judges, the jailers are usually taciturn and like to take refuge in memory gaps. As a rule, the depositions signed by them are meager.

■ In using accounts of former prisoners, memory displacements must be taken into account. If a member of the SS is repeatedly named in public in connection with especially monstrous deeds, it is possible that survivors will project their experiences onto him. This could be observed in the case of the camp physician Josef Mengele. More than once I heard survivors say that Mengele did this or that to them, even though Mengele had not yet arrived in Auschwitz at the time. Olga Lengyel has described him as a blond angel, even though Mengele was a markedly dark-haired type. In short, crimes of an anonymous SS physician were imputed to Mengele, about whom people had read so many bad things. On one occasion Stefan Baretzki blurted out in the Frankfurt courtroom: "Today everything is blamed on Dr. Mengele. He was interested in very different things."

Other memory transfers can also be observed. Many victims remember their tormentors in a visually far more pleasant form than was actually the case. If one looks at those who populated the docks in the Nazi trials, one soon notices that years earlier only a few SS men could have corresponded to the blond, blue-eyed, athletically trained type. Nevertheless, in their book Simon Laks and René Coudy confer on about fifty SS men whom they observed escorting a column of prisoners this blanket attribute: "All handsome, young."

Such memory shifts were probably caused in part by the glaring contrast between the filthy prisoners in their patched garb and the neat SS uniforms, along with the self-confidence of an SS man that was expressed in his bearing and appearance and identified him as a being from a world quite different from that of a cringing, harassed inmate who was always on the lookout for possible perils.

Some well-known SS men have been positively idealized after the fact. Thus Fania Fénelon has called Mengele a "handsome Siegfried," and Thérèse Chassaing writes: "Mengele is immaculate in his belted uniform, tall, with shiny black boots that bespeak cleanliness, prosperity, and human dignity. He does not move a muscle. He is insensitive." Elie Wiesel mentions as Mengele's characteristic attributes "white gloves, a monocle, and the rest"; Jiri Steiner, a twin used by Mengele in his series of experiments, speaks of his "angelic smile," and Siegfried van den Bergh believes that in a film Mengele should be portrayed by no less than the famous lady-killer Ramon Novarro. Carl Laszlo describes Mengele as a "strikingly handsome man who had a fascinating, spellbinding effect even on female prisoners" and continues: "Mengele came with a motionless face, and his beautiful, regular, cold features that seemed to be carved out of stone appeared to be the mark of death itself. In his shiny boots he walked rhythmically on the camp road."

I saw Mengele almost every day in the office of the SS infirmary where he was doing routine bureaucratic work, and he struck me as neither particularly attractive nor elegant. I never saw him wear a monocle.

Dounia Ourisson-Wasserstrom, who frequently encountered Maximilian Grabner as interpreter for the Political Department, has described the department head as tall and very elegant. Grabner, however, was on the short side; and while his appearance was indicative of overwrought self-confidence, it did not bespeak elegance.

Alina Brewda, a physician who frequently saw the SS garrison physician in the experimental block, approaches the SS ideal in her description of his appearance. She speaks of his "piercing blue eyes, hard as steel." Dr. Wirths did have light eyes, but they were not blue. A Greek Jew who was sterilized by Horst Schumann described that physician twenty-four years later as having had the beauty of a woman. Photos of Schumann in his Auschwitz period refute that exalted description.

Such memory shifts cannot be generalized either. Thus Grete Salus was able to avoid any demonization though she was in Auschwitz for only a short time and therefore did not become closely acquainted with the SS. She writes: "I am afraid of people. I fear nothing as much as people. How good and how bad can they become? There is no measurement, no foundation, no certainty for that. A person's living conditions and education usually ensure that neither the good nor the bad side can assume boundless dimensions. Here there were petty officials, craftsmen, young girls and women. Under different circumstances all the malice inside them could at most have expressed itself in gossip, cheating, tyranny in the family circle, and the like." Those who kept the machinery of murder going in Auschwitz were not devils; they were humans.

Another point should be considered when one draws on former prisoners' characterizations of their guards. Experience has shown that they remember the good acts of individuals much better than all the bad things that they had to suffer at the hands of largely anonymous guards.

■ Before we attempt to draw a picture of individuals who played a special role outside the barbed wire of Auschwitz, it is useful to consider the effects of the demoralization that no guard in an extermination camp could escape. It emanated from the places of extermination, and the ss judge Konrad Morgen gave a vivid description of them in his account of an inspection of the crematoriums.

> The crematoriums did not attract special attention. Through a big gate we proceeded to the so-called undressing rooms. There were numbered spaces and even coatroom checks. Arrows on the wall indicated the way to the shower rooms, and there were inscriptions in six or seven languages. In the huge crematorium everything was smooth as glass, and there was nothing to indicate that in the preceding night thousands of people had been gassed and burned there. Nothing has remained of them, not even a speck of dust on the fittings of the ovens.
>
> I wanted to get to know the ss men, and so I went to the ss guardroom in Birkenau. There I suffered my first real shock. Whereas guardrooms generally were Spartan in their simplicity, here ss men were lying on couches and dozing with glassy eyes. Instead of a desk there was a hotel-type oven; four or five young Jewish women of oriental beauty were making potato pancakes and feeding them to the men, who were served like pashas. The ss men and the female prisoners addressed one another as if they were relatives or friends.
>
> In response to the horrified question in my eyes, my escort only shrugged his shoulders and said: "The men have had a hard night. They had to handle several transports." During the ensuing check of the lockers, it turned out that in some a fortune in gold, pearls, rings, and all kinds of foreign currency was stored. In one or two lockers we found genitals of freshly slaughtered bulls that were supposed to enhance a man's sexual potency. I have never seen anything like it.

Leon—an inmate on the Sonderkommando who was born in Poland, emigrated to France, and was deported from there—cooked exclusively for the ss men working at the crematoriums, for they spurned the cuisine of the ss kitchen. Leon had to procure the food himself.

Another example can serve to illustrate how quickly a person became infected by the general demoralization. A great deal of the gold broken out of the teeth of corpses was skimmed off before it was sent to Berlin. The Central Office found out about this and sent a special agent to Auschwitz. Zdzislaw Mikolajski was able to observe him and reported as follows: "A man named Kerper came from Berlin to take charge of the dental gold, and he ordered that it be melted and turned into ingots here. One day he left for Berlin with the gold, which he always had to deliver personally. Some time later Berlin inquired what had happened to Kerper and the gold, and the dental clinic replied that Kerper had left two or three days earlier. A week later I learned from an ss man that Kerper had been arrested with the gold in Düsseldorf, where he lived."

The ss offered its men alcohol as an outlet, and participants in *Sonderaktionen* [special operations] were also offered schnapps. ss men who were drunk on duty were not a rarity. This story is told about the Birkenau block leader Weiß: "He liked to drink. One time, when he was intoxicated, he said, 'Mother, if you knew that your son has become a murderer!'" ss roll call leader Oswald Kaduk, whose name became synonymous with sadistic excesses after what was revealed at the Frankfurt trial, testified: "At ten o'clock I was already loaded." Witnesses confirmed this and emphasized that Kaduk was much more dangerous drunk than sober.

Hans Spicker, an inmate who worked in the camp's print shop, indicated the ways in which ss men who had no direct access to Canada obtained alcohol: "It was probably before the end of 1943 that an ss sergeant ordered me to act as a forger and print post-exchange vouchers for schnapps, cigarettes, and other things. I did print these, and the sergeant gave me margarine, bread, sausage, and cigarettes."

It was in the prisoners' interest to support the corruption of the ss. What the block elder of the Gypsy camp, Anton van Velsen, said has general validity: "We systematically attempted to soften up the ss men and gave them watches, rings, and money. If they were on the take, they no longer were as dangerous. In the end they were demoralized to point zero."

Bernhard Rakers, the ss roll call leader of Monowitz, is an example of such severe demoralization. When inmates who held a certain position committed some offense, he would not report them but blackmail them, instead. According to Felix Rausch, Rakers took some food he had found while searching an inmate and then yelled at the prisoner: "Next week bring me eggs!" It goes without saying that the frightened inmate endeavored to "organize" eggs for Rakers within that time period. In this way he escaped punishment, and Rakers saved himself the trouble of turning in the confiscated food.

Erich Kohlhagen has drastically characterized Rakers: "In the whole factory there was no article that he could not use—from pins and padlocks, electric appliances, suitcases, and pictures to bicycles, beds, furniture, and any kind of clothing. He had a use for everything, and he made inmates, who had no other choice if they wanted to have a little peace, steal everything for him. He sent whole wagon loads of things that he wished to use himself to his wife, but he expended a considerable portion on the sustenance of his numerous mistresses."

One day Rakers got hold of a letter written by prisoners on a typewriter in the inmate infirmary and addressed to French forced laborers who were also employed in the Buna Works. Contact between prisoners and foreign workers was subject to the most severe punishment, but Rakers did not report his discovery. Instead, he blackmailed the functionaries in the infirmary, who finally "bought" the incriminating document from him with food and medications.

◼ The demoralization of the female wardens was especially great—or else they were not as good at covering themselves as their male colleagues. This is what Höß had to say on the subject:

> Many female wardens had to appear before an SS court because of theft, but they were only the few who had been caught. Even severe punishment did not deter them from continuing to steal and use inmates as intermediaries. There is a striking case of this. One female warden let herself go to such an extent that she took up with male inmates, mostly Green capos, and as payment for her readily granted sexual favors took jewelry, gold, and other things. As a cover for her indecent activities, she had an affair with an SS first sergeant of the garrison in whose place she stored her hard-earned property, wrapped and under lock and key. This idiot had no idea of his sweetheart's activities and was very surprised when those nice things were found in his quarters.

As legal officer Robert Mulka had ordered searches of female wardens that turned up jewelry of considerable value. He writes: "They also had underclothes that originally were the property of prisoners. I saw to it that such cases were reported to the SS and police appeals court in Breslau. I remember prison sentences of two or three years." Wilhelm Boger confirms that he conducted numerous investigations of female wardens. Dorothea Becker recalls proceedings against her colleague Buchalla: "It was said that she had two or three suitcases full of things. Her trial took place in the canteen of the staff building, and we, the other wardens, had to be present as a deterrent." Becker does not remember what punishment Buchalla received.

As happens so often, it was the minor offenders who got caught. According to SS roll call leader Wilhelm Claussen's testimony in American captivity, when the commission headed by the SS judge Morgen came to Auschwitz to investigate cases of corruption that could no longer be covered up, only the rooms and lockers of the rank and file up to the rank of SS master sergeant were searched. "One thing was missed: searches of SS leaders and those holding responsible positions in the camp generally. They had a lot of time to hide their treasures or send them out of the camp. After all, there was no doubt that such searches would have had the greatest yield." Nevertheless, the searches that were conducted disquieted the SS leaders not only in Auschwitz but also in the Central Office, for the stream that had been diverted from Canada also flowed there.

The investigating commission stored the confiscated valuables in a barracks, and one night it burned down. Two decades later Morgen responded to my question by saying that an investigation had turned up two sources of the fire. "It was not possible to identify the perpetrators of the obvious arson. Every member of the SS kept silent." Claussen writes in his report that the cause of the fire could not be determined, but he mentions rumors that SS First Lieutenant Reimers, a member of the commission, was himself the arsonist. He had been summoned to Berlin on suspicion of having helped himself to the treasures of Canada, and he might have wanted to obliterate all traces by means of the fire. Reimers was arrested, but he later claimed that his rigorous investigation had caused him to fall out of favor and to be placed under arrest temporarily. Reimers testified that he had ordered searches of about thirty members of the SS. "The result of this action," he said, "led to the arrest of eight to fourteen SS men in whose homes valuables had been found that were demonstrably the stolen property of inmates."

His colleague Helmut Bartsch seems to remember more clearly: "Between October 1943 and my departure in late April 1944 the investigating commission conducted 123 investigations of members of the SS. On the basis of its findings twenty-three lower-ranking and two higher-ranking SS leaders were arrested. The former were immediately turned over to the SS court. Soon thereafter charges were filed, and sentences were regularly passed down. I know that these ranged from two to four years in prison, and in most cases the convicted men were discharged from the Waffen-SS."

Bartsch points out that the swamp of corruption extended beyond the guards of Auschwitz. "Thus SS Captain Eisenreich, the head of the Volksdeutsche Mittelstelle (Ethnic German Liaison Office) in Kattowitz, was arrested by the special commission and turned over to the SS court after it had been proved that he had committed extensive thefts and misappropriated property of inmates." This court, however, does not seem to have acted so promptly in the case of higher-ranking SS leaders. Bartsch testified that he did not know the outcome of the proceedings. Many cases did not even come before an SS court. For example, although Wilhelm Emmerich, the head of the Labor Service, was detained in the bunker because gold had been found in his possession, he was discharged without a judgment.

These cases demonstrate that the SS did not have to take all that seriously the threat of its RFSS that anyone who took even one mark from the property of murdered Jews would be a dead man.

When the SS judge Morgen was in American captivity and attempted to describe the dilemma he faced in his dual capacity as jurist and SS leader, he pointed to a factor that he deemed responsible for the frequent infringements of the law by members of the SS. "It was an additional special cancer sore of the SS that it had developed in an illegal mode against the party, the state, and the army and basically never abandoned this illegality. Consequently an SS judge repeatedly encountered actions that were prohibited by law but from an SS viewpoint were appropriate and in compliance with orders. A judge could act only indirectly in such instances by convicting the perpetrators of other offenses that were outside this conflict. This was not so difficult because people who live and act in unlawfulness soon lose all inhibitions and do pretty much what suits them."

Wilhelm Boger, who had acquired a great deal of experience in investigating property offenses, claims that he told Dr. Morgen at the time: "If the transports of Jews are not stopped, you can change the entire guard every four weeks."

The following chapters will take a close look at those who were placed in this milieu.

THE COMMANDANT
■ ■ ■

No one influenced the character of the Auschwitz extermination camp so strongly and had such an enduring influence on its guards as Rudolf Höß. Even though he was relieved of the position as head of the camp in November 1943, he is generally regarded as the commandant of Auschwitz. He organized the mass extermination, which continued unchanged after his departure. Höß returned to Auschwitz in the spring of 1944 to supervise the largest extermination campaign, the one against the Hungarian Jews, and temporarily held the position of ss senior garrison commander.

The detailed notes he made in the Cracow prison and his volubility at his interrogations make it possible to draw a more precise portrait of him than of other ss leaders in Auschwitz.

Even his earlier life has been revealed in that way. He was born in the Baden region in 1900, received an authoritarian and religious education, and at the tender age of sixteen volunteered for military duty in World War I. Despite his youth he became a noncommissioned officer. After the end of the war he did not apply for professional training but joined the Free Corps that was fighting in the Baltic area. Höß later idealized this step in the language of his generation. "I always felt drawn to a camaraderie in which a man could always unconditionally rely on another in times of need and danger." He characterized the types of people who had gathered in these units as follows: "This Free Corps comprised officers and soldiers who had returned from the World War but could no longer connect with civil life, adventurers who wanted to try their luck in this way, unemployed men who wanted to escape idleness and public welfare, and young enthusiastic volunteers who rushed to arms because they loved their fatherland."

He presumably counted himself among the "young, enthusiastic volunteers," and his case clearly shows the use to which such enthusiasm was put. At barely twenty-three years of age, he participated in the murder of a "traitor," was sentenced to ten years in the penitentiary, and served slightly more than half of that sentence. Höß writes that he was a model prisoner, and this is credible because he behaved in disciplined fashion in Polish captivity as well. The clear relationship between authority and subordination in a prison accommodated Höß's need to integrate himself into a distinct system of command and obedience.

After he was paroled, Höß joined the Artaman League, which preached

"Germanic tradition" and love of agriculture. Testifying in a Nuremberg court-room, the usually verbose Höß gave a notably concise account of his progression from there to the guard rooms of concentration camps. "When Himmler inspected the SS in Stettin [where Höß had organized an SS equestrian group], I came to his attention. We knew each other from the Artaman League, and he persuaded me to join the administration of a KL. Thus I went to Dachau in November 1934." He was integrated into the SS with the rank of sergeant, began his service as a block leader, was quickly promoted to SS roll call leader, wore the insignia of an SS second lieutenant in September 1936, and became adjutant and SS camp leader in Sachsenhausen. In May 1940 he was appointed as commandant of the camp near Auschwitz [Oswiecim] that was under construction.

■ In his Cracow prison cell Höß wrote: "From the very beginning my task, my assignment completely filled me, even possessed me, and all the difficulties that arose only spurred me to increased zeal. I refused to let anything get me down because my ambition would not permit it. All I saw was my work."

In a document that he gave to his Polish examining magistrate, Höß described his feelings at the first trial gassing in Auschwitz. "(I saw) for the first time a whole pile of gassed dead bodies. I felt uncomfortable and shuddered, though I had imagined death by gassing as worse. I had always thought it was painful suffocation, but none of the bodies indicated any convulsions. As the physicians told me, prussic acid has a paralyzing effect on the lungs, but it is so sudden and so strong that there is no evidence of suffocation, as there is, for example, with carbureted hydrogen or the removal of oxygen." The uninhibited Höß continued: "At that time I did not worry about the killing of the Russian prisoners of war (the victims of these trial gassings); it had been ordered, and I had to obey. But I must confess that this gassing had a calming effect on me. After all, in the near future the mass extermination of Jews had to be started, and neither Eichmann nor I had any clear idea of the way in which the expected masses were to be killed. Now we had discovered the gas and the procedure."

This mood was not limited to Höß. SS camp leader Aumeier also testified that, even though they had suffered a shock, "everyone was joyfully excited."

In a conversation with the American psychiatrist G. M. Gilbert, who studied Höß in his Nuremberg cell before he was sent to Poland, he said the following: "Believe me, it was not always a pleasure to see those mountains of corpses and to smell the constant burning. But Hitler had ordered it and even explained its necessity. And I really never wasted much thought on whether it was wrong. It simply seemed necessary."

In his Cracow notes, however, Höß stated: "This mass extermination with all its side effects did not simply pass over those who participated in it. I suppose that with few exceptions these events gave pause to all those who had been ordered to do this monstrous 'work' and 'duty,' including myself, and left deep impressions on them."

The contradiction between these statements cannot be explained by the fact that Höß made the one just cited with a view to offering extenuating circumstances in his forthcoming trial, for he also gave the earlier statement to his examining magistrate. Rather, in both instances Höß appears to be endeavoring to paint a self-portrait that resembles the ideal type of the ss. On the one hand he sees himself as a man of blind obedience who "never really wasted much thought" on the substance of the Führer's orders, and on the other hand he endeavors to resemble the model of an officer who has to set an example for his troops, especially in carrying out "hard" orders even if those procedures give him pause.

This endeavor is also expressed in the following paragraph from his notes: "During my inspections of the extermination facilities many of those involved often came up to me and used me as an outlet for their impressions and depressions, to have me reassure them. In their confidential conversations I kept hearing this question: Is it necessary to annihilate hundreds of thousands of women and children? And I, who deep inside me posed this question to myself countless times, had to put them off with the Führer's orders, had to tell them that the extermination of the Jews was necessary to rid Germany and our descendants of our toughest adversaries for all time."

Faithfully following Himmler, Höß took refuge in comfortable self-pity as he continued.

The Führer's order was unalterable for all of us, and the ss had to obey it. Yet secret doubts gnawed at everyone, and I could not acknowledge mine under any circumstances. To compel those involved to persevere emotionally, I had to show that I was firmly convinced of the necessity to carry out this cruelly hard order. All eyes were on me. What impression did the scenes I have described make on me and how did I react to them? I was closely observed in that regard, and my every statement was discussed. I had to keep myself under strict control to avoid revealing my inner doubts and depressions in my agitation about something I had just experienced. I had to appear cold and heartless at procedures that wrenched the heart of anyone who still had human feelings. I could not even turn around when all too human emotions welled up in me but had to look on coldly as mothers went to the gas chambers with their laughing or crying children.

I had to watch everything that went on. Day or night I had to watch the corpses being carried and burned; for hours on end I had to watch how teeth were broken out and hair was cut off; all those horrible things. I even had to stand there for hours when bodies were exhumed from the mass graves and burned—a ghastly process that produced a dreadful smell. Because the physicians drew my attention to it I even had to look at death itself through a peephole in the gas chamber. I had to do all this because I was the one that everyone looked to, because I had to show everybody that I not only gave the orders and made the arrangements but also was prepared to be present everywhere, as I required of those under my command.

A person who might under different circumstances have become a conscientious postmaster was enabled by a perverted sense of duty and an equally perverse self-pity, developed according to Himmler's prescription, to be the commandant of an extermination camp. And one has to say that what Höß said is true: he really was always on the move in Auschwitz, and the camps occupied him far less than the killing facilities.

■ One should not view Höß merely as a highly placed executive agent. In a Führer state the head of an extermination camp is authorized to make decisions. Höß himself said that Himmler delegated important decisions to his subordinates. Here is Höß's account, in bureaucratic language, of the dilemma he faced because of conflicting orders. The initials stand for the following: RFSS, Reichsführer SS, that is, Himmler; RSHA, Reichssicherheitshauptamt (Reich Security Central Office), which was responsible for deportations to the extermination camps; WVHA, Wirtschafts- und Verwaltungshauptamt (SS Economic and Administrative Central Office). Höß writes:

In accordance with the RFSS order of summer 1941, all Jews were to be exterminated. The RSHA raised serious objections when the RFSS at Pohl's suggestion ordered that those fit for work be exempted. The RSHA has always been in favor of the complete elimination of all Jews and regarded every thousand newly arrived able-bodied Jews as a danger, fearing that some circumstances might keep them alive and eventually liberate them. There probably was no office that was more interested in seeing a rise in the death rate of Jews than the Jewish section of the RSHA. On the other hand, Pohl had been ordered by the RFSS to have as many inmates as possible work in arms factories. Hence he regarded it as imperative that the greatest possible number of inmates be provided, including Jews fit for work taken from the transports destined for extermination. He also attached the greatest importance to the preservation of these laborers, though he had little success in that regard. Thus the RSHA and WVHA held diametrically opposed views. Pohl seemed to be stronger, for the RFSS stood behind him, and, compelled by his promises to the Führer, Himmler demanded ever more urgently inmates for the armament industry. On the other hand, the RFSS also wanted to have as many Jews as possible destroyed. . . .

The concentration camps were midway between the RSHA and the WVHA. The RSHA supplied inmates with the ultimate aim of having them annihilated; it did not care whether this was done immediately through executions or gas chambers, or somewhat more slowly through epidemics (caused by the untenable conditions in the camps, which were deliberately left unaddressed). The WVHA, on the other hand, wanted to preserve the inmates for the arms factories.

Elsewhere Höß wrote as follows about SS Lieutenant General Heinrich Müller, Eichmann's boss in the RSHA: "My personal interventions with him to put the brakes on the campaigns (deportations to the extermination camps) so that bad conditions could be rectified were never successful because he always hid behind the strict orders of the RFSS: "The campaigns ordered must be carried out relentlessly!" I tried everything in this regard, but in vain, even though in many matters I got through to him in ways others could never have done. Today (November 1946) I believe that they did not want to improve conditions in Auschwitz in order to maximize the effect of those campaigns in a cold way."

It is plausible that Höß attempted to get Müller to ease up on the extermination campaigns, and there are documents that confirm his account of the RSHA's policy. However, while others, such as Dr. Eduard Wirths, the SS garrison physician, used the conflicting orders to put the brakes on the machinery of destruction, Höß was only put off by the clash of authorities. He continued his account as follows:

The selection of Jews fit for work had to be done by SS physicians. On a number of occasions, however, this was done also by leaders of the protective custody camp or the Labor Assignment Office without my knowledge or permission. This always caused friction between SS physicians and the heads of the Labor Assignment Office. A conflict arose between the views of the leaders of Auschwitz, and it was always fed by the conflicting interpretation of the RFSS's order by the highest authorities in Berlin. For reasons of security the RSHA (Müller, Eichmann) had the greatest interest in destroying as many Jews as possible. The Reich physician SS, who gave the SS physicians guidelines for the selections, was of the opinion that only fully able-bodied Jews should be selected for work because weaker, elderly, and only partially able Jews would in a short time become unfit for work, worsen the already overstrained state of health, cause an unnecessary proliferation of infirmaries that would require additional medical personnel and medicines, and would in any case have to be killed eventually. The

WVHA (Pohl, Maurer) had an interest in preserving the greatest possible number of workers for the arms industry even if they later became unfit for work. These conflicting interests were exacerbated by the immeasurably rising demand of the Ministry of Armaments or the Organisation Todt for inmate labor. The RFSS kept making these organizations promises of numbers of workers that could never be fulfilled. SS Colonel (*Standartenführer*) Maurer now had the difficult task of meeting the constant demands of these offices in some fashion, and he goaded the heads of the Labor Assignment Office into preserving as many workers as possible. It was not possible to obtain a clear decision from the RFSS.

The confused situation was exploited by each person in line with his attitude. The SS garrison physician did what he could to put the brakes on the extermination; despite the urging of his superior, Hermann Maurer, Max Sell, the head of the Labor Assignment Office, did his best to accelerate the machinery of destruction; and when technical difficulties threatened the program of extermination, Höß improvised and staked his whole authority on getting his subordinates to act in his spirit, whereas Liebehenschel limited himself to carrying out orders.

Despite Himmler's silence Höß received unmistakable signals. Only three SS men in Auschwitz received the wartime Distinguished Service Cross with Swords, a decoration for special bravery in the face of the enemy. The recipients were Otto Moll, who was in charge of the gas chambers; Josef Klehr, who administered the largest number of poison injections and later became chief of the "disinfectors," who had to insert the poison gas; and Höß himself. These decorations were an unmistakable indication that Himmler approved of the three men's zeal, and at the same time it underscored the fiction that mass murder in Auschwitz was the equivalent of frontline service.

■ When Eichmann recorded the story of his life in Argentina, he talked about Höß and Himmler:

I learned from Höß that his work, part of which was the extermination of adversaries, made him suffer as a human being. One time, when we were sitting in his home (with SS natural wood furniture, clean and simple, homey and nice, as Eichmann described it elsewhere), Höß told me that the RFSS had visited the KZ Auschwitz a few days previously and had looked at everything, including the physical destruction of our adversaries from gassing to burning. Höß was also present when Himmler told the SS men: "These are battles that our coming generations will no longer have to fight." Höß told me that these words assured not only his men but also him that this intrinsically hard and burdensome work was necessary for his race and must be done. From this I gathered that Höß was not a bulldog-like, un-complicated, brutal κz commandant but a man who was used to sitting in judgment over himself and giving himself an accounting of what he was doing.

When his Führer Himmler spoke of battles that coming generations would be spared, Höß was able to feel himself to be an upright warrior as he orga-nized the stages of the most extensive mass murder. He wrote about "human inhibitions" that he had to bury deep down inside, of "human stirrings" that almost seemed like a betrayal of the Führer after conversations with Eich-mann, and of "gloomy moods." Eichmann, for his part said that he had to control himself to keep from fainting and thereby setting a bad example for others. None of the organizers of the extermination wanted to appear "weak" or "soft" in front of others. One attested to another that his task made him suffer, but they forced themselves and heroically made the sacrifice that their Führer demanded of them, and they repeated his statement about "the de-struction of our adversaries," though a simple man like Baretzki asked himself whether women and children were enemies.

Höß received an impressive reward from Himmler. The inmate Stanislaw Dubiel, a gardener and handyman in Höß's villa, has described Himmler's visit to the commandant's house. Himmler spoke "very cordially with Höß and his wife, had their children sit on his knees and call him 'Uncle Heini.' Such scenes were memorialized through enlarged photographs that hung on the walls of Höß's home." Höß apparently did not use this personal relation-ship to get Himmler to decide the authority conflict between Pohl and Eich-mann; perhaps he was proud of being able to decide such an important matter himself.

When Höß wrote, "Since the beginning of the mass extermination I was no longer happy in Auschwitz; I became dissatisfied with myself," this was one of the lies with which he tried to make himself look better in his own eyes. In his report about his transfer from Auschwitz, officially because of the expansion of the camp that made a tripartition necessary, Höß gave himself away: "When Auschwitz was divided at Pohl's suggestion, he gave me a choice between becoming commandant of Sachsenhausen or head of the D I office (that is, department head in the central administration of all concentration camps). It was very unusual for Pohl to let a leader choose his assignment, and he also gave me twenty-four hours to think it over. However, it was only a benevolent gesture intended to console me for the loss of Auschwitz, as he saw it." The following statement confirms that Pohl was not mistaken in his opinion that Höß was in need of consolation: "At first tearing myself away was painful, especially because of the difficulties, the shortcomings, the many difficult tasks that had bound me closely to Auschwitz, but then I was glad to be freed from all that in this way."

His future behavior showed how false all this was. He had his family stay on in Auschwitz for an extended period after his transfer and used every opportunity to visit them. At a later date he could have avoided a (temporary) transfer to Auschwitz by pointing to his ever growing responsibilities as head of a department. However, he went there and worked very hard to eliminate problems of transportation so as to increase the capacity of the machinery of destruction in Auschwitz toward the end of the war.

The testimony of the secretary of Hermann Krumey, Eichmann's deputy in Hungary, does indicate that Höß's conflicted attitude was not something he later fashioned for himself. In the Krumey trial at Frankfurt, Frau Ferchow testified on January 17, 1969, that Höß once asked her in Budapest to write several telegrams to the RSHA for him. On that occasion Höß is supposed to have told her that he could no longer stand it up there (evidently in Auschwitz). Even though such a frank confession to a secretary hardly known to him does not fit the image of a self-confident SS lieutenant colonel who was always striving for composure, there is no apparent reason why Frau Ferchow should have fabricated this statement.

On the other hand, Höß boasted about his deeds. In October 1944, after his alleged statement in Budapest, Grabner was called before an SS tribunal to answer for killings concealed from his superiors, and Höß was among the witnesses. Dr. Werner Hansen, who presided, has given this vivid description of his behavior: "Höß attempted to exonerate Grabner. He swept into the courtroom in a very haughty manner and said: 'You have no idea of what is happening. In Auschwitz entire transports are being liquidated.' I recall that he stood next to Grabner during a break and made derogatory remarks about the court."

■ Even though Höß spent his entire life in a strictly regulated relationship between orders and obedience and felt good in it, his deeds in Auschwitz cannot be explained by subjection to authority alone, for not all of Himmler's orders were equally sacred to him.

As the commandant he frequently reiterated to his subordinates Himmler's strict prohibition on appropriating the property of others. Höß's own actions have been described by Stanislaw Dubiel. When the commandant gave a party, Frau Höß told Dubiel what foods she needed. At a later date Dubiel told a Polish court how he had to procure these:

In the beginning I took the goods from the inmates' storeroom, which was administered by SS Sergeant Schebeck, and carried them in a basket; later

I used a car. From the storeroom I took for Höß's household sugar, flour, margarine, cinnamon, semolina, peas, and other products. Frau Höß was never satisfied and constantly talked to me about what she lacked in her household. With these foods she not only took care of her own home but also sent some to her relatives in Germany. I also had to supply the Höß kitchen with meat from the slaughterhouse and milk. Höß never paid anything for all of the food that came to his household from the storeroom and the camp slaughterhouse.

Every day Dubiel took five liters of milk from the camp dairy to the Höß villa. Based on the ration cards for milk, the Höß family was entitled to only one liter and a quarter per day. In the course of a year Dubiel had to "organize" three bags of sugar weighing eighty-five kilos each. In the villa he saw cases that had in each 10,000 Yugoslavian cigarettes of the Ibar brand. Frau Höß used these cigarettes, which were officially intended for the inmate canteen, to pay for illicit work done by prisoners. She impressed upon Dubiel that no SS man must ever find out about any of this because Höß had forbidden both "organizing" and illicit work and threatened the most severe punishment.

Marta Fuchs, a seamstress from Bratislava who had been deported for racial reasons, worked for many months in the Höß villa, along with some assistants. An attic room was fixed up as a workshop. The fabric was evidently obtained from Canada. Manza, another Jewish woman, worked for Frau Höß as a hairdresser. She skillfully exploited the latter's penchant for having prisoners work for her and induced Frau Höß to request a woman to do knitting for her children. Thus another prisoner obtained a good, protected position and Frau Höß an additional personal slave.

When there was already too much talk about the illicit work in the commandant's villa, Frau Höß established a tailor's workshop in the staff building, which gave the wives of other SS leaders a chance to profit from it as well. However, even then Marta Fuchs and another seamstress were still ordered to do smaller jobs in the Höß villa. Two Jehovah's Witnesses were also employed there, one as a cook and the other as a maid. The name of one of these is known: Sophie Stipel from Mannheim.

At that time Höß repeatedly issued orders to employ as many inmates as possible in arms factories and to subject all other positions to a rigorous examination, so that every worker who was not absolutely essential could be placed at the disposal of the arms industry.

The peculiar relationship that developed between Höß and Erich Grönke is especially revealing. Grönke, who had a criminal record of thefts, rape, and unnatural acts and had been sent to the concentration camps as a so-called career criminal, was among the first thirty German inmates who had been sent to Auschwitz from Sachsenhausen. He became a capo in a leather factory. There he had many opportunities to get his hands on leather goods and later, when all leather items taken from the deportees at the ramp were sent to that factory, on valuables hidden in them as well. Höß managed to get Grönke released in 1941 and appointed head of the leather factory. He was given a chance to take an exam in Bielitz and become a master shoemaker.

Grönke, who was charged with murdering inmates, gave the following testimony about his relationship with Höß before the examining magistrate in Frankfurt: "I frequently went to Höß's villa, sometimes twice a day. Höß always had special requests, and this is what I had to do for him: care for the saddlery of his horses and the family shoes, and obtain things that were needed every day. The leather factory housed not only the shoemaker's workshop but also the smithy, the locksmith's shop, the wheelwright's workshop, and eventually also the tailor's shop. Höß wanted something from all these workshops, and he used me as an intermediary." Grönke added that he often gave Frau Höß a ride in a carriage. Stanislaw Dubiel remembers that Grönke drove up to the Höß villa every day and brought not only clothes and shoes for the entire family but also fashion accessories and fabrics.

Eventually Höß and this career criminal became such good friends that the commandant went hunting with him and used the familiar *du* in their conversations. ss camp leader Hofmann recalls that one of Höß's sons would not go to sleep until Grönke had said "good night" to him.

Grönke was Höß's main supplier, but not the only one. The former ss technical sergeant Robert Sierek testified that he got into trouble because he had been too friendly to inmates. "There were no serious consequences for me; I only got a warning from commandant Höß. The main reason that Höß took no action against me was that he was dependent on my help and support, for I always had to get something for him, mainly fabrics. I was able to obtain such things because I often traveled as a buyer for the camp administration."

When the Höß family finally left Auschwitz, the ss garrison physician wrote to his family on November 26, 1944: "With reference to Höß's house and garden, he (commandant Baer) told me that it was a disgrace—and irresponsible—how everything was fitted out there. He said the move was accomplished with two railway carriages and a huge number of wooden boxes! Unpleasant . . ."

■ What everyone knew could not remain hidden from Eichmann, and yet he said that "Höß was modesty personified." Eichmann's idealization is, if anything, even more mendacious in this statement: "Höß was a model family man." Yet Eichmann must have known that one reason for Höß's transfer was the affair he had with a female inmate named Eleonore Hodys. Here is a statement made by the SS judge Morgen, who headed the investigating committee that had uncovered the situation: "I am certain that Höß's transfer to Berlin had something to do with the proceedings started by me. Evidently this was done so Pohl could get jurisdiction and protect Höß."

Dr. Morgen confirms that Pohl was informed of Hodys's testimony about the relationship and Höß's attempt, after it had been revealed, to have her starve to death in a stand-up cell of the bunker. Pohl trivialized these facts and promoted Höß. Stanislaw Dubiel hints at the reason for this when he says that there was a very cordial atmosphere when Pohl visited Höß, that there always was a big reception in his honor, and that Höß gave Pohl presents.

Höß, who in captivity wrote frankly about his participation in the mass killings, avoided any subject that could have led to his affair with Hodys. All he said to Gilbert, the psychiatrist, was this: "Even when I was carrying out the task of extermination, I led a normal family life and so on." To questions prompted by the telltale "and so on," he replied only that his sexual relations with his wife were normal in Auschwitz, "but after my wife found out what I was doing we seldom desired sexual intercourse." Höß added that sex had never played a big role in his life and he had never felt the urge to start or continue an affair. Höß was not specifically questioned about his affair with Hodys; evidently the examiner did not know about it.

Höß heedlessly disregarded the orders not to appropriate the property of inmates or start affairs with female prisoners, but he took the order to keep the extermination secret quite seriously. This is from his testimony in Nuremberg: "In late 1942 remarks by the then *Gauleiter* (NSDAP regional leader) of Upper Silesia drew my wife's attention to what was going on in my camp. She later asked me whether this was the truth, and I admitted that it was. This was my only breach of the promise I had given to the RFSS (about keeping the mass destruction secret); I never spoke to anyone else about it."

Höß was feared by the SS as well. Thus the former SS technical sergeant Hans Schillhorn testified as follows: "Höß proceeded rigorously against the inmates as well as the SS."

This is what the SS judge Konrad Morgen thought of Höß: "I do not maintain that Höß was basically a bad person. In my opinion he was a typical *Kommisknopf* [a man with the mentality of a little clerk]. The conditions in the KL Auschwitz and elsewhere demoralized him, too. No human being can bear being an unlimited master over life and death who can turn a person into ashes from one minute to the next."

When Eichmann described his life and work in Argentina, he called Höß a lovable comrade and friend: "Höß was the personification of punctuality and accuracy. He was his own registrar as far as his meticulous bureaucratic activities were concerned. In the end his horizon may have been too narrow to handle the enormous KZ area of Auschwitz."

▪ After Höß had been arrested on March 11, 1946, in Schleswig-Holstein, where he had lived as a farm worker under an assumed name, and his testimony about Auschwitz had agitated the public, he was examined by psychiatrists. This is what the Polish professor Stanislaw Batawia wrote in his assessment:

> Rudolf Höß is neither an abnormal person of the "moral insanity" type or an unfeeling psychopath nor a person who displays any criminal inclinations or sadistic tendencies. He is a man of average intelligence . . . an extremely reserved, autistic, and undoubtedly sensitive person (with the peculiar sensitivity of the schizothymic type), though he does not reveal his emotional reactions. . . . He is a man who since his early youth has been used to taking his duties seriously and performing them with great conscientiousness and zeal. He is also an individual of the type that one usually calls a strong man with a willpower not encountered every day.

On the basis of his earlier investigations in Nuremberg, the American psychiatrist G. M. Gilbert came to the conclusion that Höß impressed one as being mentally normal "but with a schizoid apathy and the kind of extreme lack of empathy that is found in real schizophrenics." When Prince Schaumburg-Lippe, who is not a trained psychologist, encountered Höß in the Nuremberg prison, he asked who that flower-picking village schoolteacher type was.

Gilbert wanted to fathom what went on inside Höß when he was carrying out the orders to murder given him by Himmler in private:

> I asked him if he had ever considered whether the Jews he was murdering were guilty or deserved such a fate in any way. He again tried to explain to me patiently that such questions were unrealistic, because he had lived in an entirely different world. "Don't you understand that we SS men were not supposed to think about such things? It never occurred to us to do so. And besides, it had become, so to speak, a self-evident truth that the Jews were to blame for everything." I pressed him to explain why that had become self-evident. "Well, we never heard anything different. It could be read in newspapers like Der Stürmer, and we heard it everywhere. Even in our military and ideological training it was taken for granted that we had to protect Germany from the Jews. . . . Only after the collapse, when I heard what everyone was saying, did I realize that perhaps it was not quite true after

all. But earlier no one said anything like that; in any case we heard nothing about it."

Höß came to think about the matter not because of his conscience, but only when he was a prisoner subject to the authority of others. It is also characteristic that in the Cracow jail Höß zealously put on paper what his superior in that place, the Polish examining magistrate Jan Sehn, needed for the hearings, even though he had properly drawn Höß's attention to the fact that his notes could be used against him in the trial. Höß named another factor that might have induced him to write so frankly about the extermination camp and himself: "Only in these Polish prisons did I learn what humaneness is. I, who as commandant of Auschwitz did so much damage and caused so much suffering to the Polish people, though not personally and on my own initiative, encountered a human understanding that often made me feel profoundly ashamed—not only from the top officials but also from the simplest guards. Many of them were former inmates of Auschwitz or other camps."

It cannot be assumed that Höß wrote this in hopes of being pardoned shortly before the execution of the death sentence. He was under no illusions about that.

■ After the death sentence had been pronounced, Höß wrote the following about himself:

It is tragic. I, who was by nature, soft, good natured, and always ready to help, became the greatest exterminator of human beings, someone who coldly and resolutely obeyed every order to destroy them. The years of rigorous training in the SS that aimed at turning every SS man into a spineless tool for the execution of all plans of the RFSS had made me, too, an automaton that blindly obeyed every order. My fanatical love of my fatherland and my greatly exaggerated sense of duty provided a good basis for this indoctrination. It is hard to have to admit at the end that one has taken the wrong road and thus is responsible for this end.

Even in this farewell letter, which Höß wrote to his wife shortly before his execution, he cannot free himself from the mendacious heroic pathos of Nazi jargon. "All my life I was a reserved fellow, never liked to give anyone an insight into what moved me deep down inside, and came to terms with everything myself. How often, dearest, you were painfully aware that even you, who have been closest to me, could not participate in my inner life. Thus I dragged around for years all my doubts and depressions about the rightness of my activities and the necessity of the harsh orders that I had been given. I was not permitted or able to talk with anyone about that."

Like many other Nazis, Höß returned to religious reflections. After a strict Catholic education, he had turned away from the church under Nazi influence. He wrote his wife that his long incarceration had given him the insight that his actions in the service of Nazi ideology were completely wrong: "Now it was quite logical that strong doubts arose in me as to whether my abandonment of my faith in God wasn't also based on completely false premises. It was a difficult struggle, but I have regained my belief in my God."

In his farewell letters the commandant of the extermination camp Auschwitz summed up his feelings. He wrote to his wife: "My misspent life imposes on you, my dearest, the sacred obligation to educate our children in a true humanitarianism coming from the bottom of their hearts. All our dear children have a good nature. Nurture all these good stirrings of the heart in every way and make them sensitive to all human suffering."

To his oldest son Klaus he addressed the following last words. "Become a human being who is guided primarily by a warmly sensitive humanity. Learn to think and judge independently. Do not uncritically consider everything that comes your way as the absolute truth. Learn from my life. The biggest mistake of my life was that I trusted and believed everything that came from above and did not dare to have the least doubt of the truth of what was given. Go through your life with your eyes open. Do not become one-sided, but consider the pros and cons of all things."

Remorse? Soul searching? Empty phrases?

If the war and the Free Corps had not thrown the commandant of Auschwitz off course, and if he had not eagerly and willingly absorbed the training of the ss, he would not have been very different from others who do their duty wherever they are placed. Morgen was right: "No human being can bear being an unlimited master over life and death."

SS LEADERS

■ ■ ■

Anyone who knew how to adapt to the mentality of the SS was able to climb the ladder quickly. The Nazi system liked to put young and dedicated people in high positions and thereby bound them even more strongly to itself. Most of the leading SS men in Auschwitz were young.

Möckel, Liebehenschel, and Caesar were born in 1901 and thus were one year younger than Höß. All three attained the rank of SS lieutenant colonel. Ernst Möckel, the head of the administration, had never had a normal occupation. Even before Hitler's assumption of power in 1933, he worked chiefly for the SS. His successor Wilhelm Burger, who was born in 1904, was trained as a teacher but never practiced that profession; he became an insurance agent, but the economic crisis caused him to lose his job. In Auschwitz it was his task to see to it that despite transportation problems there was always a sufficient supply of poison gas to let the extermination process proceed without interruption. At the age of twenty-four, Burger had married a Jewish woman, the daughter of the general manager of a cellulose factory in Aschaffenburg. That relationship may have been useful in 1928, but when Hitler became the head of the German government, it was an impediment. Thus he divorced his wife in 1935 because, as he put it, he had not recognized the worthlessness of the Jewish race at the time of his marriage. Now there was nothing to impede his rapid career in the SS. At a later date Burger tried to use the Jewish connection to demonstrate to his judges that he had never been an anti-Semite.

Arthur Liebehenschel and Dr. Joachim Caesar had been members of the SS cadre since Hitler's assumption of power, but they did not pass through the Dachau school, something that was noticeable in Auschwitz. Liebehenschel served in the army for twelve years before transferring to the SS, which soon placed him in the Central Office. Caesar, a trained agriculturist, gave up his profession in 1933 and became a mayor. A year later he was assigned to the training office of the SS and put in charge of the training manuals. Finally, he became the head of the agricultural enterprises in Auschwitz, whose leadership was a special concern of Himmler.

Friedrich Hartjenstein, the commander of the guard unit and the first commandant of Birkenau after the tripartition, and Maximilian Grabner, the head of the Political Department, were both born in 1905 and Heinrich Schwarz, the head of the Labor Assignment Office and commandant of Auschwitz III, one year later. With the exception of Max Sell (born in 1893), Schwarz's successor in the Labor Assignment Office, and Karl Bischoff (born in 1897), who headed the central construction office of the Waffen-SS, those holding top positions in Auschwitz were strikingly young for their high ranks. Hartjenstein, Schwarz, and Sell did not join the SS until the beginning of the war, and the Austrian Grabner joined after the occupation of his country. Of the top functionaries, only Bischoff, Hartjenstein, Baer, and the physicians Dr. Wirths and Dr. Mengele ever served at the front. Bischoff served with the Luftwaffe as a construction specialist and was posted to Auschwitz in October 1941.

SS camp leader Schwarzhuber was born in 1904, and his colleagues Aumeier, Hössler, and Franz Hofmann were two years younger. Baer became the head of the largest Nazi concentration camp at the age of thirty-three.

■ It is regrettable that Arthur Liebehenschel, who succeeded Höß as commandant of Auschwitz, did not produce a similar written confession during his imprisonment. It would have been interesting to learn about the feelings of this head of the extermination camp, whose work was so strikingly different from that of his predecessor. Thus we are dependent on statements of others. Not many former inmates got to know him well during his six months as the head of the Auschwitz SS, but we do have some revealing reports.

Thus Dr. Erwin Valentin testified on May 16, 1945, when his memories were still quite fresh: "Under Liebehenschel life in Auschwitz changed to such an extent that it can almost be described as relatively bearable. Liebehenschel was especially favorably disposed toward the Jews. He prohibited the beating of Jews in workplaces, dismissed capos and foremen who had administered such beatings, and also accepted complaints from Jews." This testimony carries weight because Valentin wore a Star of David himself.

When Rudolf Steiner was caught "organizing" shoes, he was sentenced to ten blows on his buttocks. This punishment was administered in Block 11 in Liebehenschel's presence. Experienced inmates advised Steiner to cry out loudly, for Liebehenschel could not stand this sort of thing. Steiner screamed at the top of his lungs after the first blows, and the commandant did stop the whipping before all ten blows had been dealt.

Here is a written statement by Jenny Spritzer: "While Höß was seldom seen, and then only as he whizzed by in an elegant car, Liebehenschel personally inspected the camp and observed the inmates at work outside it. On a few occasions Liebehenschel came to our office (the Political Department), opened every door, motioned to us to sit down after we had (as usual) jumped up, asked me (among other questions) to tell him about my work, and attended some interrogations. He reduced every punitive stay in the bunker that our department had decreed by half, for the commandant had to sign off on all these punishments."

Spritzer's description proves that the jealous Höß's characterization of his successor was anything but objective: "L. was more in his office in Auschwitz, too, where he dictated one order after another as well as reports, and held hour-long discussions of senior garrison officers while the general condition of the camp kept deteriorating."

In the Frankfurt courtroom Franz Hofmann, the ss camp leader of the main camp, testified about the difference between the two commandants: "I believe that under Liebehenschel only actions ordered by Berlin were carried out; this was not the case when Höß was the commandant."

In the Cracow prison Höß provided characterizations of numerous ss leaders, including one of Liebehenschel that illuminates his attitude toward his successor. The two men had already been neighbors in the ss colony at Sachsenhausen. With reference to that period, Höß described Liebehenschel as follows: "L. was a quiet and very good-natured person who always had to be aware of his serious heart condition. . . . We frequently got together, but we did not get closer to each other, for our personalities were probably too different and our interests too divergent." Both Höß's dislike of Liebehenschel and his view of the proper conduct of a KZ commandant are expressed in the following statement: "In his opinion I had always done everything wrong in Auschwitz, and he started to change everything." Höß continued: "In a short time he was 'outmaneuvered' and did what the inmates wanted. . . . He also made speeches to the inmates and promised them that everything would be better now, for he was going to turn the murder camp into a real KL."

Eichmann had the same opinion of Liebehenschel, and he summed it up in these words: "In Auschwitz he behaved like an *enfant terrible*, so to speak, and in the end he winked at everything."

At the big Auschwitz trial in Cracow, Liebehenschel was sentenced to death. Here is an excerpt from the court's opinion: "There is no doubt that after his arrival at the camp the defendant introduced a number of changes in the treatment of the inmates that significantly improved their fate." After stating that such arrangements by Liebehenschel were in line with the Berlin Central Office's interest in a more thorough utilization of the inmates' labor, the court emphasized this point: "Nevertheless, the issuance of this order must be counted in the defendant's favor because he supervised its execution and interpreted the orders he received from his superiors in a liberal rather than a narrow fashion."

That Liebehenschel still received the same punishment as Höß may have been legally inevitable, but it does indicate the inadequacy of measuring such atrocious deeds with normal standards of justice.

■ When Auschwitz was to be prepared for the greatest campaign of exter-mination in May 1944, "soft" Liebehenschel was in the way. Höß hints at intrigues when he writes: "For years he had not been on good terms with his wife, who was very cantankerous and petty. In the receptionist of Glücks (Liebehenschel's boss in Oranienburg) he had now found a woman who understood him and appreciated his special qualities. He divorced his wife, which meant that he could no longer stay in the inspector's office (dealing with all concentration camps) and was transferred to Auschwitz." The discre-tion with which Höß passed over his relationships and those of his friends is not in evidence in this case. "In the meantime he had married again, and it turned out that his second wife had been accused by the SD (Sicherheits-dienst [SS Security Service]) of having associated with Jews for a long time, even when the Nuremberg laws were already in force. This fact soon became known in Auschwitz, and then L. could no longer stay there."

At an interrogation in Frankfurt, Richard Baer, who was Pohl's adjutant before he succeeded Liebehenschel as the third commandant of Auschwitz, vigorously denied having participated in this intrigue:

> I deny that I behaved tactlessly toward the outgoing commandant Liebehen-schel and his wife when I assumed my post. I did not even meet the couple when I started there. It is true that six or nine months before that Pohl had asked me to take a personal letter to Liebehenschel. This letter dealt with Liebehenschel's forthcoming marriage and expressed misgivings about his intended, who was reputed to have had an affair with a Jew. When I brought him that letter, I sat down with Liebehenschel and in comradely fashion interpreted the contents of the letter for him—that is, I prepared him for what it contained. Pohl had ordered me to have this comradely conversation with Liebehenschel.

A memorandum that Baer gave to his superiors on July 3, 1944, contains a clearer indication of his behavior toward Liebehenschel:

> I sat down with L. in a room at the SS leadership home. After a detailed discussion of professional matters, I handed him the letter and told him that SS Lieutenant General Pohl had given me the special assignment to help him in his fate. . . . When I explained to him in the course of the conversation that it was impossible for an SS leader to marry or associate with a woman who at the age of nineteen still associated with Jews in 1935, he told me that this had already happened and had not remained without consequences. I told her (Fräulein Hüttemann) that it was our intention to procure an apartment and employment for her and her mother in Posen and continued: "The information obtained by the SD makes it impossible

for you to marry an SS man in the future. You are free to marry any other man, even a director general, but not an SS private (SS-*Schütze*)."

Baer describes Liebehenschel's appearance on April 21: "He could barely see because his eyes were quite swollen from days of weeping. His bearing was anything but manly. When I indicated that there now were two conflicting records concerning Fräulein Hüttemann, he told me that in his long activity as an SS leader he had become sufficiently acquainted with the OGPU methods of the SD of the RFSS. When I said that his accusations were extremely bold and that he would have to prove them, he indicated that he would be able to do so in countless cases."

Höß devoted only one sentence to this affair: "Incidentally, when Liebehenschel was transferred, Baer behaved in an extremely tactless way toward him and his second wife."

This look behind the scenes puts the moral principles that were prevalent among the SS into focus. Trivializing the fact that Höß had made an inmate of Auschwitz his mistress and wanted to eliminate her after this became known, Pohl allowed Höß to be promoted. On the other hand, Liebehenschel's legal union with a woman said to have had an affair with a Jew years earlier constituted such a misalliance in Pohl's eyes that Liebehenschel could not remain the commandant of Auschwitz, even though his wife had held a position of trust with a high-ranking SS leader.

▪ Richard Baer, the third commandant of Auschwitz, was not as colorful as his two predecessors. He had had the typical career of SS bigwigs. Having been trained as a pastry chef, he was laid off in 1931, when he was twenty, and was already in April 1933 a member of the guard unit at Dachau. After his arrest he told the prosecutor in Frankfurt: "If I am asked why I joined the General SS, I would like to answer that I had no special political reasons, and today I can't really say what attracted me to it. I particularly liked the military discipline and enjoyed playing soldier. We met every Monday or Tuesday in the Protestant clubhouse (in Welden), which had a hall where we exercised and engaged in sports. Martin Weiß, later the commandant of the concentration camps Neuengamme and Dachau, was a member of this group. I remember that he was once ordered to take a training course in Amberg. When he returned, he taught us the goose step and similar things. It was fun."

Baer testified as follows about his training period: "Our duties were very rigorous. The district police (which had jurisdiction over Dachau in its early period) really put us through our paces, and the harder we were drilled, the prouder we were of it." As early as September 1938 Baer was promoted to the rank of SS second lieutenant, and his mind-set predestined him for a rapid career.

SS Corporal Oskar Kieselbach has made the following comparison of the commandants: "Baer was stricter than his predecessor, Liebehenschel, who was popular with both the SS and the inmates. This can hardly be said about Baer." Franz Targosz, a Pole, describes Baer as "arrogant and flippant. His weaknesses were hunting, women, and wine." That this commandant also succumbed to the general mania for appropriating things is indicated by this remark: "I saw in his possession stamp albums of a well-known Belgian collector."

Höß wrote: "Baer was adroit and well spoken, a man who knew how to get ahead." Höß describes the position of trust that Baer was able to achieve as the adjutant of the powerful Pohl. Everyone who wanted something from Pohl endeavored to get into Baer's good graces. "This spoiled Baer immeasurably and made him power-hungry and overwrought," Höß said.

When Baer was appointed as Liebehenschel's successor, he should have been briefed by Höß rather than his immediate predecessor. "However, in his view this was not necessary," Höß sneered in a Cracow prison. "He had other interests, went hunting and fishing, and took rides for pleasure. Baer believed that he had done enough work as Pohl's adjutant and now needed a rest." Finally, Höß blamed him for clearing out "in good time and in the biggest and best vehicles" at the evacuation of Auschwitz. In the final phase Baer was installed as the commandant of Mittelbau. This is how Höß concludes his characterization, which is as revealing about the characterizer as it is about the person characterized: "When things got hairy in Mittelbau and the air raids became more severe, Baer sprained his foot and retreated to Styria to let it heal."

■ The commandants of Birkenau and Auschwitz III, Josef Kramer and Heinrich Schwarz, became notorious for personally mistreating inmates. Kramer, who had only an elementary school education, had worked in a factory, lost his job, and been unemployed for years before he joined the SS. Höß characterized Schwarz, who was a printer by trade, as "the choleric type, easily aroused and irascible."

Olga Lengyel has described Kramer's conduct at a selection in the infirmary of the women's camp. When the victims were being loaded on a truck, the SS was gripped by a kind of collective madness. Kramer, who staged this scene, lost his appearance of a motionless Buddha. His small eyes shone strangely, and he behaved like a madman. On another occasion Lengyel observed him attacking an unfortunate inmate and smashing her skull with his cudgel. Kramer's portrait is filled out by his wife's statement before a British military court. She testified: "The children have been everything to my husband. He is such a music lover."

When I think of Schwarz, the following image always appears before my eyes. In the fall of 1942, we were once again lined up at an evening roll call. Schwarz, at that time the SS camp leader of the main camp, ordered an inmate who had evidently been reported to come forward. An elderly, emaciated, completely run-down man stood trembling in his shabby inmate's uniform before the fat Führer, who exuded power. With all his strength Schwarz beat the *Muselmann* and stepped on him after he had fallen to the ground. I shall never forget how he foamed at the mouth, his eyes popped out, and his face became flushed.

Höß, who was usually quite sparing with praise of lower-ranking SS leaders, expressly emphasized that "Schwarz was a loyal helper who relieved me of much important work. In the extermination campaign against the Jews, too. When Schwarz was on duty there, I could rest easy." Elsewhere Höß wrote: "Schwarz was a tireless worker, and no task was too much for him. He was always fresh and ready for action. I could entrust even the most difficult tasks to Schwarz without any hesitation because he carried everything out conscientiously and circumspectly."

Schwarz's successor, SS camp leader Franz Hofmann, has provided a clearer description: "Schwarz's watchword was always 'Destroy, destroy!'" In Hofmann's view Schwarz, together with Höß, Grabner, and Aumeier, was among those who moved the program of extermination forward. "If no transport arrived, there was the devil to pay. 'What are those people in Berlin doing?' they groused. They didn't like it when nothing was going on."

Hans Aumeier went to school for six years, was trained as a metal lathe operator, and became unemployed for the first time at the age of eighteen. In February 1931 he received a full-time position with the SA and the following year transferred to the SS. He was among the first SS men to be posted to Dachau. After a short time he was put in charge of the *Sonderausbildung* (special training), where Höß also was trained. The latter has characterized Aumeier as follows: "He was not independent and also lacked initiative. He always had to be pushed. 'He has too small a brain,' said the RFSS on a visit in 1942."

According to Höß, Aumeier "stuck with Eicke's antiquated views about the treatment of inmates." The expansion of the camp was too big for his range of vision. Höß continued: "He became nervous and more distracted, also drank more and more." Under Aumeier, "the worst creatures" were made block elders and capos, and Höß observed that "anyone with a dashing appearance could gain Aumeier's favor." This may have been true of Green capos; the nameless inmates feared him more than other leaders. When Aumeier was interrogated in August 1945, the examining officer gained the impression that he was an utterly uneducated man.

■ There are more numerous reports about the ss camp leader of the Birkenau men's camp, Johann Schwarzhuber, than about others; he evidently stood out. Like Baer, Schwarz, Aumeier, and many others who passed through the Dachau school, Schwarzhuber was a Bavarian. In 1935 he was trained as a block leader in Dachau. According to Höß, who at that time held the same position there, Schwarzhuber, like Höß, tried to absent himself when punishments were being administered, although many others were eager to be present. It was part of Eicke's education in "hardness" to have a company of guards witness the whipping of inmates.

The block leader Stefan Baretzki, the only defendant in the Auschwitz trial at Frankfurt who described the atmosphere in Birkenau, also spoke about Schwarzhuber, who evidently did not prove "soft" enough to jeopardize his career (which also was the case with Höß). "My superior, ss camp leader Schwarzhuber, was in the camp every day. At 5:30 every morning, orders were issued, and he told us what had been done wrong the preceding day. During the day it was impossible to speak with the ss camp leader, but in the morning he would say, 'Who has another question?' He knew about everything that went on in the camp. When one of the bigwigs was in the camp, there was the devil to pay." When he was asked whether Schwarzhuber reprimanded him when he heard that Baretzki had mistreated inmates, the defendant replied: "All I was told was that if something was wrong, I should intervene. It wasn't possible to get anywhere in the camp with kindness." Baretzki described to the court how he tried (unsuccessfully) to alleviate the water shortage in Mexico, a newly established section of Birkenau. "When I talked about it with ss camp leader Schwarzhuber, he always told me, 'But that's none of your business! It's high time for you to comprehend that these are Jews!'"

Lucie Adelsberger, an inmate physician, has recorded her memories of Schwarzhuber. One day, when she was taking a shower together with some nurses (the infirmary personnel was permitted to bathe more frequently), "Herr Schwarzhuber of the camp administration was making an inspection and found us. And inspect the ss chief did—as a man, condescendingly and appraisingly, curtly and yet graciously, a smirking lecher. He checked each of the naked women for her origin and number, her work in the camp, her curves on top and on the bottom, her breasts and her hips."

Czeslaw Mordowicz has rendered this pithy judgment: "It was possible to imagine worse people than him. Personally, Schwarzhuber was not as brutal as others." This is confirmed by Ota Kraus and Erich Kulka, who write: "He never committed brutal or violent acts against an inmate; for such things he always found suitable people, ss men or inmates. He also knew how to play the role of caring commandant who always had only the welfare of those under his 'protection' in mind. Yet a handful of ss men subjugated tens of thousands under his direction."

Schwarzhuber is to blame for the fact that even when the Greens had already been replaced by Reds in the main camp, Danisch as camp elder and other criminals as block elders were able to continue their nefarious rule in the Birkenau men's camp. As long as Schwarzhuber used such types as tools, he was able to practice personal restraint. To be sure, Baretzki also described for the Frankfurt court an episode in which Schwarzhuber played a different role. In his ponderous speaking style, this defendant gasped out the following: "There was the Theresienstadt family camp, and it was common knowledge that this camp was to be gassed. There were children, too; they established a children's theater, and we had already gotten used to these children. When the camp was supposed to be gassed, we (evidently, several block leaders) went to see the ss camp leader and said, 'But not the children, too?' It was a group of sixty-eight or seventy children. ss camp leader Schwarzhuber saved the boys by putting them in the men's camp." One of those spared was Otto Dov Kulka. He remembers that in those days there was a spirited discussion among the ss camp leaders, other ss men, and inmates who taught the inhabitants of the children's block before he and the others received the life-saving order to move to the other camp.

Hofmann, who had been a friend of his colleague Schwarzhuber since their service in Dachau, told me that Schwarzhuber was the only person who told Höß straight to his face that he had not joined the ss to kill Jews. When I asked Hofmann whether Schwarzhuber was drunk when he said that, he denied it. While Höß does not mention this incident, he does give the following report in connection with the inmates of the Gypsy camp: "It was not easy to get them into the chambers. I did not see it myself, but Schwarzhuber told me that no extermination of the Jews had been so difficult, and he had a particular hard time of it because he knew almost all of those inmates well and had a good relationship with them."

Like all the others, Schwarzhuber freely helped himself to property whenever he had a chance. Viennese-born Franz Kejmar, one of the few Birkenau capos with a red triangle and a good reputation, knew on the basis of his ample camp experience how to "buy" an ss leader. One day he reported to Schwarzhuber that he had found gold and jewelry in Canada. As a matter of course, he imparted this information in such a way that no one was able to overhear it, and he showed the ss camp leader valuables that he had "organized" for that purpose. Schwarzhuber understood immediately and told the capo: "Fine, you are all right. Don't talk with anyone about it." And he added: "Any time you need schnapps, come and see me."

On one occasion Kejmar observed Schwarzhuber while inmates were once again being led to the crematorium. As so often, he was drunk and weeping.

Alex Rosenstock worked in the inmates' dental clinic, which was located in a section of the camp that was under Schwarzhuber's jurisdiction. Like many others, Schwarzhuber preferred not to be treated by SS dentists but by this inmate. One day Rosenstock learned that his brother, an inmate of the main camp, had been chosen for gassing at a selection. Since the dental treatment had created a certain personal contact between them, Rosenstock in his desperation ventured to ask the SS camp leader to save his brother. Schwarzhuber took his number and actually managed to have him pulled out of the group of selectees, even though he had no jurisdiction over the main camp.

Dawid Szmulewski recollects that Schwarzhuber regularly visited the block elder of the Sonderkommando, a Jew whose first name was Georges. Schwarzhuber brought him schnapps and in return received gold and jewelry that had been "organized" by members of the Sonderkommando. SS roll call leader Wilhelm Polotschek, whose home was nearby, followed the same practice. Szmulewski presumes that Polotschek illegally sold the jewelry in his hometown for the benefit of his boss and for his own pocket.

▨ As a block elder, Emil Bednarek observed folk dances performed at the camp fence by Russian prisoners of war at Schwarzhuber's behest while his family watched outside the wire fence. "He always meant well in his dealings with the Russians," says Bednarek at the end of his account.

Like many others, Schwarzhuber liked music, and therefore the camp orchestra, which he sponsored, played a special role at his birthday celebration. Simon Laks and René Coudy have reported that on that day, when the SS camp leader's automobile arrived, the band stopped the march that it customarily played as the inmates' columns marched off to work. A fanfare composed for this occasion resounded, and the SS camp leader snapped to attention. When the trumpets were silent and the orchestra began to play its festive program, Schwarzhuber's wife and two children got out of the car. The wife, who radiated freshness, good health, and beauty, lovingly took the arm of her husband, and the two blond children completed the idyllic picture. Pointing at the camp, Schwarzhuber spoke to his family, and finally ordered his favorite song, "Heimat, deine Sterne" (Homeland, your stars), to be played.

Laks and Coudy have described another episode. One evening, when the details had marched back to the camp and the orchestra had completed the last march, Schwarzhuber came tottering along, walking all over the place and stumbling over invisible obstacles—in short, he was stinking drunk. With the impatience of a spoiled child he motioned to some low-ranking SS officers and privates who had followed him at a respectful distance to go and handle the evening roll call. He walked up to the band, took a baton, and with a broad smile ordered it to play his favorite song. He conducted as well as a drunken man could.

Laks and Coudy report:

> We played as usual and reached the end of the piece without any incident. But we certainly were astonished when Schwarzhuber asked us out of the blue whether we could play the "Internationale" for him. Everyone got frightened, and nobody knew how to react to this question. Lucien was the first to recover his balance, sat up straight, and said: "Herr Lagerführer, we don't have the music." "And why don't you have it yet?" asked Schwarzhuber with the obstinacy of a lush. Then he added calmly, "It's okay, you'll get it soon," and went into the camp. After the roll call, he made a speech in which he urged the inmates not to believe false rumors or let bombardments and the roar of cannons demoralize them. He said that victory was assured and that the inmates were perfectly safe in the camp.

In the Frankfurt courtroom Baretzki described a scene that no one could have imagined. When he was asked whether children of SS men were permitted inside the camp, he answered in his clipped, harsh speaking style: "What's meant by children of members of SS in the camp? A child is a child, and children, that's many children. There was Schwarzhuber's boy, he was six years old, and when he went to the camp to look for his father, he had a sign around his neck that said he was the son of SS camp leader Schwarzhuber so they wouldn't grab him and send him to the gas chamber. He was only looking for his father." When I referred to this episode in a conversation with Baretzki in the prison, he explained why the child wore this sign. Once Schwarzhuber's son disappeared, and since he frequently came into the camp, they frantically looked for him there. "Because no transport had arrived on that day," said Baretzki, "he could not be in the gas chamber." After the roll call the boy came running along. From that time on, he wore the sign whenever he came into the camp.

■ Franz Hofmann pointed out to his Frankfurt judges that as an SS camp leader he was more humane than Aumeier and Schwarz. This has been confirmed but does not mean much. Hofmann was from Bavaria like the other men and was trained as a decorator, but he could not find a job in this field; and when he was not unemployed, he kept afloat as a waiter, hotel porter, and sales clerk. In 1933 he already was a member of the guard unit at Dachau, where he rose through the ranks. In his own defense Hofmann told the court how hard it was for an ss camp leader to stand up for inmates: "One time, when I was still in Dachau (as ss camp leader), there were some problems with clothing and food, and I reported these. Himmler himself sent for me and told me that if I could not manage things, he would send me to a KZ for a year. Another time a firm offered us a thousand pairs of shoes, and I had the money to buy them. Everything was set, but I could not get the shoes without a miserable scrap of paper, and Pohl refused to give me this paper." Hofmann excitedly added: "Those were the guilty ones who sat at their desks and talked on the phone! They simply told us to shift for ourselves."

I don't believe that this was one of the usual attempts by a defendant to talk his way out of a conviction at the expense of people no longer alive. Hofmann seemed too simple minded, and his account of Pohl was too characteristic for that.

Some Poles who were interned in Auschwitz from the beginning and hence had a better basis for comparisons than others have called Franz Hössler the best Auschwitz ss camp leader. For a time he worked in the women's camp. Before the British military court to which Hössler had to answer after the end of the war, he declared that he had improvised a great deal in that camp, which was in a catastrophic condition even by Auschwitz standards: "Since this construction was not part of the official plan, as the ss women's camp leader I built by taking the material from other construction sites with the help of capos and other inmate functionaries and smuggling it into my camp." Up to a point Anna Palarczyk, a former block elder, confirmed this defense when she told me this: "He was a stove fitter by trade and could not stand it if something did not work. It was characteristic of him that he made sure the stoves in the barracks were in order."

A transcript of Grabner's testimony in September 1945 indicates that Hössler "organized" not only for the camp that he was in charge of. "I remember," said Grabner, "that early in 1943 I received a report that said that at night a motor vehicle under the direction of the ss camp leader (Hössler) was in the Canada section, where the confiscated and stolen possessions of the executed Jews were stored. The vehicle was loaded, and the objects were distributed among the participants. This report bore the notation 'Confidential.' Even though I passed this confidential report on to the proper court, I never heard anything about it." Grabner was at loggerheads with Hössler, as with all ss leaders who were regarded as "soft." His attempts to defame his erstwhile enemies can be demonstrated in other cases as well.

Alica Jakubovic, who was deported from Slovakia, emphasizes that it was possible to speak with Hössler, something that was generally impossible with SS leaders. "He was not as bad as the others," she writes, though she admits that he made many promises but often forgot to keep his word. At a selection in March or April 1944, Hössler said that enough Slovak women had already been selected, and so they were exempted at that time.

An episode described by Judith Sternberg-Newman corroborates Jakubovic's characterization. One day a Jewish woman named Frieda became the victim of a selection even though she did not yet look like a *Muselmann*. In her despair she begged SS camp leader Franz Hössler for her life. He replied that he could not help her and that it would make no difference to her whether she died sooner or later. In her mortal fear Frieda continued to implore him, assured him that she was willing to work, and emphasized that her husband had served at the front in World War I. Hössler now asked her where she was from, and she replied, "From Osnabrück." At length he promised that he would save her. However, when the selected women were loaded on trucks, Frieda also had to board one; evidently Hössler had forgotten his promise. When the trucks from the women's camp drove by the SS camp leader, Frieda cried as loudly as she could, "Herr Lagerführer!" This attracted Hössler's attention and he asked: "Are you the woman from Osnabrück?" When she answered in the affirmative, Hössler took her out of the vehicle. She never found out what Hössler associated with Osnabrück.

Eva Landstofova-Neumanova has described a similar incident. At a selection in the inmate infirmary, two healthy nurses were put on the list of those to be gassed. Bozena Teichnerova, the block elder, was bold enough to ask Hössler to help those two women. "This was an extremely inopportune moment because Hössler had just applied his boots to the necks of a few women who were kneeling before him, begging for their lives." Nevertheless, Hössler granted the request of the courageous block elder. This happened in the middle of 1943.

Krystyna Zywulska reports that Hössler took a liking to a five-year-old Russian boy and always asked about him when he visited the Russian block. While other children shyly hid from the SS, Wolodja ran up to Hössler right away, called him "Uncle," and asked him how he was doing. This is what attracted Hössler's attention; and when Wolodja died, he seemed shaken.

Witnesses at the first Auschwitz trial in Vienna who had been able to observe Hössler closely—because they had greater freedom of movement as capos—unanimously testified that Hössler had displayed great zeal in supervising the construction of the extermination facilities. It was probably due to this initiative that he was promoted to the position of SS camp leader with unusual rapidity. Tadeusz Paczula describes Hössler as a man who changed completely when he had advanced to the rank of a Führer. "In the beginning he made the worst impression; nobody was worse than he. But as a Führer he was quite different; for us inmates he was really the best SS camp leader."

Must it be pointed out yet again that former prisoners tend to remember exceptions well and that to them it often no longer seems worth mentioning the rule that every SS camp leader ordered and implemented selections?

Like most of his colleagues, Hössler, who was born in Swabia in 1906, belonged to the old guard of the concentration camp guards. He and Schwarzhuber received the same sentence as Aumeier and Schwarz: death. What has been said about the same sentence for Höß and Liebehenschel applies here as well.

■ "Everyone who was there," writes Ella Lingens, "did something good at some time, and that was the worst thing. If the SS men in Auschwitz had always committed only evil deeds, I would have told myself that they were pathological sadists and could not act differently. However, these people were able to distinguish between good and evil. They decided in favor of good once and in favor of evil 999 times."

One exception from this rule was Maximilian Grabner, the head of the Political Department, who, except for Höß, was the most vigorous exterminator of human beings. No report indicates that he decided in favor of good even a single time. This is what I wrote about him in my notes:

Today I met Grabner, the dreaded head of the Political Department, for the first time.

Ernst told me his story. He was an Austrian from the Waldviertel, a former policemen. Under [Chancellor Kurt] Schuschnigg he worked in the Communist Department. After the Anschluß, he was integrated into the Gestapo. Since the construction of the Auschwitz camp, he has been head of the Political Department. The periodic shootings in the bunker are his work. No one, not even the commandant, is as feared as Grabner.

"Hey you, come down!"

From below me in the stairwell of the SS infirmary, I hear a voice — soft, terse, eerie. The person addressed, a member of our detail who has been standing at the window in the hallway, runs down the stairs. I can hear him click his heels.

"What were you doing at the window? Come with me."

Once again a truck had arrived at the yard of the crematorium, and our comrade had been watching the unloading of the victims. That inmate did not return to our detail, and the next day his number arrived at the office. Pneumonia was given as the cause of death.

The voice I heard was Grabner's.

Just a few words spoken by him may characterize his mind-set. When Albert Matz, a German civilian worker, requested additional food for inmates who were doing forced labor in his plant near Auschwitz, this was Grabner's response: "Take a stick and kill those bedbugs."

His subordinate Pery Broad, who got a taste of Grabner's hatred of anything intellectual, has given this drastic description of his boss: "In the office of the director of Department II of the commandant's office, all of the officials and clerks are assembled. The boss, ss Second Lieutenant Max Grabner, is conducting a staff meeting. Grabner, a man of average height, prattles pompously behind his desk. His incoherent sentences and faulty German reveal that despite his silver epaulets this is an utterly uneducated person. Insiders know that in civilian life he was a cowherd on some alpine pasture."

An account composed by Grabner in his own defense at the Cracow prison shows that Broad was not exaggerating. Here is an excerpt, quoted verbatim: "*So konnte ich doch nicht gegen dieses unheimliche und rücksichtslose Regim, schon war ich doch schwarz über schwarz beschrieben. Drohung über Drohung mit dem ss und pol. Gericht wegen Befehlsverweigerung, Militärischen Ungehorsam, Sapotage usw. und wie man die Leute einfach verschwinden lies, zwang mich Folge zuleisten.*" (Well, I couldn't against this uncanny and ruthless regime, I was already marked black on black. Threat after threat with the ss and political court on account of refusal to obey orders, military disobedience, sabotage etc. and how they simply made the people disappear, forced me to toe the line.)

That Grabner was also feared by the guards is indicated by the testimony of ss Sergeant Horst Czerwinski. "Grabner was very arrogant toward us ss men and constantly yelled at us."

It was one of Grabner's duties as head of the Auschwitz Gestapo to fight corruption among the guards. The testimony of Feliks Mylyk, a former inmate who occupied a position of trust on the Political Department Commando, documents Grabner's qualifications for this task: "At Grabner's request I had to 'organize' various things for him. In his Auschwitz apartment I saw many suitcases, coats, and other items from 'Canada.' The suitcases still bore the names of their former rightful owners." At Grabner's trial in a Cracow courtroom, Mylyk testified that the defendant had ordered him to put together some parcels and send them to Vienna, where Grabner's family lived. These packages contained items from Canada. The testimony of Grabner's orderly, ss Corporal Heinrich Pyschny, sounds relatively harmless: "One time I had to shoot foxes so a fur coat could be made for his wife."

Pery Broad reports that Grabner had capos of the leather and equipment factories, the slaughterhouse, the dairy, and the garden center provide him with commodities of all kinds, including furniture and food. In return, he wrote favorable reports about these capos.

■ When a confiscated overweight package that contained dental gold made it impossible to cover up this corruption any longer, SS judges were sent to Auschwitz for an investigation, and they discovered the source of all offenses against property: the extermination of the Jews and Canada. (This has already been discussed elsewhere.) At first the commission received "full support from all sides, including Himmler," as Dr. Morgen put it, but this changed when the investigation was extended beyond cases of corruption. As it was, no SS judge dared to include the mass destruction of the Jews in the legal process; a reference to Hitler's order sufficed to close the eyes of these jurists and tie their hands. However, they also encountered Grabner and the executions at the Black Wall that he supervised. Unlike prisoners who were gassed on their arrival on RSHA transports and reported to the Central Office as SB— that is, *sonderbehandelt* (given special treatment), the common euphemism for killing—the inmates who had been shot were reported to the Central Office as having died of fictitious illnesses. For this reason the SS judges felt authorized to regard these killings as arbitrary and include them in their investigation, especially because the great majority of the victims were Poles and thus "Aryans." Proceedings against Grabner were started.

After the war Kurt Mittelstädt, the former director of the Central Office of the SS Court, called it a success on Dr. Morgen's part that the investigation, which had originally been started on account of corruption, was extended to crimes against the bodies and lives of prisoners. However, he confirms that "certain forces opposed these investigations." Helmut Bartsch remembers that the proceedings were not limited to arbitrary killings: "SS Second Lieutenant Grabner, the head of the Political Department at that time, was also accused of having appropriated the property of inmates, and preliminary proceedings were started against him for theft."

Such proceedings were started against Höß, Schwarz, and Aumeier as well, but they petered out. Liebehenschel did support the work of the SS judges, but when SS judge Dr. Gerhard Wiebeck reported that he had found a female inmate with whom Höß had had an affair, Commandant Baer's only reaction was this: "Through the chimney with her!" Wiebeck remembers that Baer said this "in a very sharp tone of voice."

At a later date Reinecke, the deputy director of the Central Office of the SS Court, testified in Nuremberg that the criminal proceedings against Höß were stopped at the preliminary examination stage.

This left, apart from some judgments against low-ranking SS men for corruption, only the proceedings against Grabner. According to Boger, who was a witness, his trial began in Weimar on October 13, 1944. Boger believes that Grabner was supposed to take the blame "for the bigwigs." "Höß and Dr. Mildner disappeared, and Grabner was to be hanged." On another occasion

Boger said, "To me Dr. Morgen is a henchman of the top leaders in the wrangling among the various departments."

Dr. Werner Hansen, the ss judge who presided at the Grabner trial, later described the course it took:

> Grabner was accused of having murdered 2,000 inmates. They were said to have been shot when the Auschwitz jail was overcrowded. The deaths were said to have been camouflaged with fictitious medical histories and causes of death. Grabner testified that he had received special orders for these 2,000 killings from the RSHA with instructions to destroy these orders immediately after they had been carried out. To be sure, Grabner did not say this until I had pushed him into a corner. We asked the Central Office whether there had been such orders but received no answer. As a witness, Höß tried to exonerate Grabner, but he certainly took no responsibility for what had been done.

Franz Hofmann has described the atmosphere of the trial. He said that before testifying as a witness in Weimar, he had met with Wirths, the ss garrison physician, and ss camp leader Schwarz, who had also been called as witnesses. Even though both of them were against Grabner and Wirths had seriously incriminated him in the preliminary examination, they agreed at that meeting to exonerate Grabner. Neither Wirths nor Hofmann dared to express to Schwarz their intention not to minimize Grabner's guilt. Dr. Wiebeck recalls Boger's theatrical proclamation in a courtroom: "We don't kill nearly enough of them! Everything was done for the Führer and for the Reich!"

The prosecutor requested that Grabner be sentenced to twelve years in the penitentiary. The court was adjourned. ss Second Lieutenant Kaiser was sent to the Central Office of the Gestapo to ascertain whether Grabner had actually been given the orders he claimed he had received. Heinrich Müller, the head of the Gestapo, thwarted an examination, and therefore the proceedings were never completed.

Grabner later described his future fate as follows: "Afterward (that is, after the interrupted trial) I went to Berlin again and from there to Kattowitz. Another investigation was started. From Kattowitz I went to Breslau, and then I was supposed to be accompanied to Berlin by an officer and report to the Reich Criminal Investigation Office, but this never happened because the two of us went our own ways."

"The bigwigs of the WVHA were at loggerheads with the RSHA." This is how Boger summed up the proceedings, and he was probably right.

PHYSICIANS IN THE SS

■ ■ ■

The physicians attached to the guard unit in Auschwitz were different from the other ss leaders. They were academics, whereas the others usually had only an inadequate education, and they were not conscripted until the beginning of the war, whereas many others had already been molded in Eicke's school for years. Even though this meant that these physicians were less prepared for the program of extermination than the others, they were assigned a special role in it. As a rule, they had to decide at selections who had to die in the gas chambers. It is not clear whether the highest leadership had ordered this in order to keep up the fiction that such decisions were made on the basis of a physical examination. Already at the very first Nazi mass murder operation against mental patients, only physicians in the "euthanasia" institutions were permitted to turn on the gas.

The task assigned to the physicians in the mechanism of killing completely ran counter to their professional training, and it created conflicts in many of them, most severely among those who took their medical profession seriously and were not true believers in Nazism.

Because of their key positions, the ss physicians were watched very carefully by the prisoners, for it was extremely important to find out who had moral conflicts and how these might be put to use. Inmate physicians and clerks were in the most favorable position to make such observations because their work brought them into contact with the ss physicians. Added to this was the fact that many ss physicians were young and inexperienced, and they attempted to make their service in a kz count toward their professional advancement. For this reason many of them sought to have medical discussions with inmate physicians, and frequently they did not hesitate to learn quite openly from them. The professional contact led to a personal one, and this was promoted by the fact that the intellectual level of the other ss leaders was in glaring contrast to the level of the physicians, who experienced the contempt for education and intellect that was widespread among the ss. Thus the intelligence of the inmate physicians and clerks was capable of tempting them to engage in conversations that went beyond what was necessary in the line of duty.

Having been a clerk in the inmate infirmary of Dachau, I brought to Auschwitz experience in associating with ss physicians. In Dachau I had learned not to address them as "Herr Hauptsturmführer" or "Herr Obersturmführer," as regulations would have required, but always as "Herr Doktor." No physician in Dachau or Auschwitz ever told me not to do so. I did this because I had observed that this form of address, which was unusual in the camp, replaced the customary curt military tone with an informal civilian one that could more easily be given a personal note. Many a conversation that went beyond daily duties was eased by such an unmilitary address and an avoidance of the required snappy "*Jawohl!*" (Yes sir!) in favor of a gentle Austrian "*Bitte schön*" (Gladly). My work as the inmate clerk of the SS garrison physician of Auschwitz brought me in close contact not only with that physician but with all other SS physicians, who depended on me in their expanded bureaucratic activities. Besides, I attentively registered everything that I could learn from friends about the conduct of the physicians in the camp.

From the only point of view that interested us, three types of SS physicians could be distinguished, though with the caution necessary in making any classification by type: those who reluctantly participated in the machinery of destruction, those who executed all orders impassively and stolidly, and those who added to the murderous orders "for extra credit."

■ Of the SS physicians I was able to observe—that is, those who were in Auschwitz after August 1942—Dr. Friedrich Entress was the most striking embodiment of the type that took the initiative in acting "for extra credit." He was born in 1914, came from Posen, where his father worked in the university library, and had just completed his medical studies when he was sent to the Groß-Rosen camp at the beginning of 1941 and from there to Auschwitz in December of that year. He received the title of physician in 1942 without having had to submit a dissertation; this was made possible by a decree that gave preferential treatment to Germans from the eastern region.

Entress interpreted an order from the Central Office as a license to kill and introduced lethal injections in the infirmary, organizing it in such a way that any of the SS medics to whom Entress soon entrusted this dirty work could easily and without a hitch kill a hundred or more patients by means of phenol injections. Entress limited himself to determining who would be murdered and supervising the injections.

He did not hesitate to learn from inmate physicians. Together with the Polish lung specialist Wladyslaw Tondos, Entress and his colleagues Dr. Jäger and Dr. Vetter practiced for about three months treating TB patients with pneumothorax. He arranged for the patients to receive double food rations during this treatment, for otherwise the results could not have been observed without distractions and the patients would have died. When Entress and his colleagues lost interest in this treatment, their patients were murdered by injecting them with phenol, something that only Entress could have ordered. This probably happened toward the end of 1942.

Entress also studied surgery with another Polish physician, Dr. Wladyslaw Dering. At one time he ordered that healthy prisoners be infected with the blood of typhus patients, for he wanted to study the consequences of such an infection.

Entress directed the biggest campaign of extermination that was ever conducted in an Auschwitz infirmary: the selection of the typhus patients, the convalescents, and even several nurses in late August of 1942. Among those who had already recovered was the former head of the Polish ministry of health, Dr. Bujalski. He asked Dr. Entress to be allowed to stay in the infirmary because he felt well and was able to work. Entress replied that he would be sent to a convalescent home where he would have rewarding work as a physician. Dr. Bujalski believed the ss physician, and when he had already boarded the truck that was to take him with all the others to a gas chamber, he asked Entress for permission to get off and fetch his stethoscope. Entress told him he would be given a stethoscope in the sanatorium and need not take his along. He cynically played this scene to the very end.

His zeal brought Entress in close contact with the office that was most radically instrumental in the extermination. He established a close connection with the Political Department, one that he kept up even when Dr. Wirths became the ss garrison physician and thereby his superior. He did so even though he must have known that Wirths's attitude ran counter to that of the Political Department and that this quickly produced an ever increasing conflict between Wirths and Grabner.

This conflict was caused by the vague and frequently contradictory orders of the Central Office and the different interpretations of them by Grabner and Wirths. The ss garrison physician followed an order from his superior to the letter: patients with pulmonary tuberculosis were to be given "special treatment" because they could not be cured in Auschwitz but constituted a focus of infection for as long as they were alive. But he also relied on another directive that called for a decrease in the number of deaths. In his view, only sufferers from tuberculosis and no other inmates were to be killed. Grabner and Entress, however, interpreted the order from Berlin as a license to inject all Muselmänner and patients who were not likely to become fit for work again in the near future. Wirths's predecessors had introduced this practice, and their initiative was clearly appreciated. In line with this attitude, Entress contented himself with just glancing at the naked patients presented to him in the clinic before he made his decision. However, he reported to Wirths that all those he had destined for death had tuberculosis. I have already described how it was possible to provide the ss garrison physician with evidence that Entress was deceiving him.

After that, the daily killings by means of phenol injections were stopped, and Entress was transferred to Monowitz as the camp physician. This brought about a clear improvement for the inmate infirmary in the main camp but worsened the situation in Monowitz. Oszkár Betlen has testified that Dr. Entress was particularly radical in categorizing inmates, and Stefan Budziaszek, the camp elder of the Monowitz infirmary, has characterized Entress as a man who was "imbued with the will to kill." However, Entress did not introduce injections in Monowitz.

Because of their permanent conflict, Wirths never proposed that Entress be promoted. Only when Wirths used the favorable situation that had been created by the transfer of Höß and the arrest of Grabner to remove Entress from his post was Entress able to advance. SS Colonel Dr. Enno Lolling, the physician in charge of all concentration camps, knew about the cause of the conflict between Wirths and Entress, and he encouraged Entress as well as like-minded physicians by appointing him as SS garrison physician of Mauthausen and promoting him to the rank of SS captain.

Was it his markedly unathletic appearance and his sickly disposition that prompted Entress to be "harder" and more cruel than others? Did he feel that as an "ethnic German" he was inferior, and did he want to compensate for this lack by displaying murderous overeagerness?

■ Dr. Franz von Bodman also developed initiatives in murdering. He was in Auschwitz for only a short time and therefore became less well known. After contracting typhus, he never returned. In the summer of 1942 he temporarily served as SS garrison physician and had no superior in the camp who could have ordered him to do what he did. It was quite a bit. Unlike Entress, who ordered his underlings to give phenol injections, Bodman personally killed inmates with such injections. The former camp elder of the inmate infirmary in the women's camp, which was then still located in a separate section of the main camp, remembers that he "injected a great many people." He injected into a vein rather than the heart, which prolonged the agony.

One day a Jewish woman from Slovakia refused to work and called on her comrades to stop working as well, whereupon a guard shot her. Manca Svalbova remembers how this girl was taken to the infirmary with chest and stomach injuries and how Bodman prohibited the bandaging of her wounds. At his behest she had to bleed to death as a deterrent. According to Svalbova, on another occasion two girls who had been shot (one in the stomach and the other in the thigh) were brought to the infirmary. Bodman again barred any help and killed both of them with injections of poison.

■ Of the camp physicians who killed in excess of their orders, Dr. Josef Mengele became the best known because, in contrast to most of his colleagues, he was a workaholic. For a time he was in charge of the women's camp. Olga Lengyel reports: "Whenever there was an opportunity, Dr. Mengele never neglected asking women embarrassing and offensive questions. When he learned one day that a pregnant prisoner had not seen her husband, a soldier, for many months, he could not hide his amusement. Another time he discovered a fifteen-year-old girl who had evidently been impregnated in the camp. He subjected her to a long interrogation and wanted to learn even the most intimate details of her affair. When this curiosity was satisfied, he did not hesitate to earmark his victim for the next selection."

Manca Svalbova remembers a young girl who begged Mengele to spare the life of her mother, whom he had just selected. "Mengele's response was to send the child to the gas as well," said Svalbova tersely.

Mengele can be most clearly characterized by what Anna Sussmann was forced to experience because of him. When she was deported to Auschwitz in August 1944, she was pregnant, but this was not noticed at the entrance selection. At that time the camp administration had heard that pregnant women were concealing their condition, and in order to avoid the bother of an examination it was announced that all pregnant women would receive a quarter liter of milk every day. A Polish physician who had befriended Sussmann advised her not to come forward under any circumstances. "That was a hard test," recalls Anna Sussmann, "because each day we were given about two ladlefuls of soup for six persons." One expectant woman came forward and actually received the promised milk for a few days. This prompted others to follow suit, but Sussmann did not. All the women were taken out of the camp and never seen again.

The heavy lifting she had to do at work caused Anna Sussmann to give birth prematurely. "The labor pains started at the roll call," she writes, "but I still had to stand at attention. When the roll call was finally finished, I sneaked into the block and had to deliver under some blankets. It was a live boy. I tried very hard to restrain myself, but I did emit one scream. Mengele heard it, took the child, and threw it into the open fire. At that moment, I hadn't even expelled the afterbirth yet." Twenty years later Anna Sussmann still turns pale when she hears Mengele's name. She is not the only one.

Ella Lingens describes how this "merciless cynic" with organizational talent and initiative combated the typhus in the women's camp that other ss physicians had not managed to keep under control. He first sent 1,500 sick Jewish women to the gas chamber, thereby emptying barracks in the overcrowded camp, which he had disinfected and provided with fresh pallets and clean blankets. Then patients from another barracks were carefully deloused and taken to the cleaned barracks without their clothes. At that point Mengele had the free barracks disinfected, occupied, and so on. This actually stopped the epidemic. That the same thing could have been accomplished without sending human beings to their death, perhaps by building a new barracks, does not seem to have crossed Mengele's mind. In January 1944 typhus was combated with similar methods in the infirmary of the men's camp. Alfred Fiderkiewicz writes that "the epidemic in the infirmary was controlled at the cost of a few hundred human lives." Mengele's example probably found some imitators. That Mengele was satisfied with his success in fighting an epidemic is shown by stories of Felix Amann, the capo of the disinfecting detail, who successfully accomplished the delousing of the Gypsy camp. As a reward Mengele gave him cans of sardines, and once even a bottle of schnapps with these words: "*Du sollst auch leben*" (Live a little).

At that time noma, an illness rarely encountered in Europe, was going around in the Gypsy camp. This deficiency disease bores holes in children's cheeks. Czelny, at that time a corpse carrier in that section of the camp, had to drag the bodies of children who had died of noma from the shed where the corpses were stored until they were transported to the crematorium. He had to separate their heads from their bodies under Mengele's supervision, and the physician had the heads placed in glass vessels filled with chemicals.

Dr. Berthold Epstein was the inmate physician in the Gypsy camp. Before his deportation he had lectured on pediatrics at the German university in Prague. Mengele told him that though he would certainly never get out of the camp, he could make his life more bearable if he wrote a scientific paper for him. Epstein decided to write a treatise about noma and help the patients in this way. This was fine in Mengele's opinion, and a noma section was established in the infirmary. Forty-five Gypsy children were sent there, and Mengele saw to it that they received medicines and better food. He took photos of the children before their arrival and after treatment. One case became the showpiece and pride of the noma clinic. After treatment a Gypsy girl named Zdenka Ruzyczka, about ten years old, whose cheek had already been pierced, exposing her teeth, was healed as her skin closed up and a scar formed.

■ At that time research on twins was actively promoted. A scientist who could find a way to accelerate the growth of the "master race" could count on the greatest support and recognition. Mengele had specialized in this field and had worked at the Institute of Hereditary Biology before he was sent to the front.

All ss physicians took turns working at the ramp, where they had to make selections. Mengele showed up at the ramp even when it was not his turn because he was picking out pairs of twins who at his behest were housed in a special barracks, given better food, and according to all the rules tested and measured. Lucie Adelsberger, who for some time supervised the children's block, which was part of the Gypsy camp, has described Mengele's visits. "His pockets were full of candies, and he distributed them by playfully tossing them at the children. There was not enough for everybody, but every child got something—if not on that day, then on the next or the day after that. The children beamed when the camp physician appeared. One piece of candy made them forget their troubles."

And it was with candy that Mengele accompanied the twins to his car upon the completion of his examinations, invited them to come for a drive, and took them to the crematorium. Nowhere else in the world was a scientist doing research on twins able to autopsy his test subjects and compare their vital organs on the same day. Mengele saw to it that his twins died at the same time and of the same cause. He established a pathological-anatomical section in a crematorium, pulled the pathologist Dr. Miklos Nyiszli out of a transport of Hungarian Jews and put him to work in that section. Nyiszli, who survived Auschwitz, has reported how the corpses of a pair of twins were put on his table together with the results of all kinds of clinical tests and X rays. "All that was missing," he writes, "were the autopsy findings, which I had to prepare. Mengele sat next to me for hours surrounded by microscopes and test tubes, or else he stood for hours at the autopsy table in a blood-stained coat and with blood-spattered hands, searching and researching like a man possessed."

The cause of death of the test subjects did not remain hidden from Nyiszli:

> When I examine the heart, I find on the outside of the left ventricle a small, roundish, pink spot that was caused by the sting of a hypodermic syringe aimed at the heart. I open the left ventricle. As a rule, blood is taken from it with a spoon and then weighed. That cannot be done in this case, for the blood has congealed and become a solid mass. I remove the clotted blood with a forceps and smell it. I notice the characteristic strong smell of chloroform. The body parts, which might also be of interest to the Institute of Hereditary Biology and Genetics in Berlin-Dahlem, have to be preserved and expertly packed in accordance with the postal regulations for such material. For faster delivery the packages are stamped "Rush. Important war material."

The writer of that report remembers a total of more than sixty pairs of twins, ranging in age from two to fourteen, in the Gypsy camp. When the inhabitants of that section of the camp were murdered on August 1, 1944, only seven of these pairs were still alive.

An inmate physician, Rudolf Vitek, who had to examine these children on orders from Mengele, mentions the twins Dieter and Hans Schmidt, German

Gypsies who were three-and-a-half years old. Mengele invited them one time to go for a ride with him in his car. On his return he asked which internist had examined the two children, and Dr. Benno Heller, a Berliner, came forward. Mengele was annoyed and yelled at him: "You are a bad internist. You wrote down that neither of them had any pulmonary disease, but during the autopsy I noticed that Dieter had diseased apexes of the lungs."

Deformed people, dwarfs, and other persons with anomalies shared the fate of the twins. Mengele fished them out of the stream of deportees at the ramp and had them thoroughly examined, killed, and dissected.

Mengele also conducted experiments in other areas in which laurels seemed attainable at the time. Here is a report by Ella Lingens: "I remember little Dagmar. She was born in Auschwitz (in 1944 as the child of an Austrian woman), and I assisted at her birth. She died after Mengele had given her injections in her eyes in an attempt to alter their color. Little Dagmar was supposed to get blue eyes." Dagmar was not the only child that Mengele misused for such experiments. Romualda Ciesielska, a former block elder who was in charge of a children's block in Birkenau, reports that Mengele chose thirty-six children from this block for experiments with eye colors. They were in pain, and their eyes suppurated but slowly became normal again. According to Ciesielska, one child became almost blind in one eye.

Mengele was generally interested in anomalies of eye color. Years later his teacher, Professor Freiherr von Verschuer of the Kaiser Wilhelm Institute, admitted in a conversation with me that Mengele sent this institute extremely interesting specimens of pairs of eyes with different colors. These were the eyes of Gypsies whom Mengele had ordered to be killed because of this anomaly. When I informed the professor of this, he appeared to be surprised and upset. Did he never wonder where his pupil had obtained these specimens?

▣ It is not surprising that false rumors circulated about this unscrupulous, work-possessed physician. Thus Olga Lengyel heard that the only reason Mengele carried on his horrible experiments was to escape frontline service. This is true of some other physicians who conducted experiments on human beings in Auschwitz, but not of Mengele. I examined his health record in the SS infirmary, and it indicates that he was with an SS unit on the eastern front and was transferred to Auschwitz in the spring of 1943 after he had been declared unfit for service at the front. I remember that he proudly wore the Iron Cross First Class and liked to remind his colleagues who had never seen a front that he had already been in combat. Later I learned that after he had been found unfit for duty at the front, he applied for a transfer to Auschwitz because he would find sufficient human material for his scientific work in that camp.

People who were rather closely acquainted with Mengele have not described him as a brute with a sadistic disposition. Czelny emphasizes that he always spoke with inmates politely and calmly, eschewing the customary rudeness of the SS. Robert Lévy, a former inmate physician in Birkenau, writes that he sometimes managed to get Mengele to remove an inmate from the death list after a selection by pointing out that he might soon be fit for work again. However, if he spoke on behalf of inmates who were clearly too weak, Mengele threatened to have him share the fate of the selectees.

A Polish pathologist who had to do research for Mengele was released from Auschwitz with his help because she was pregnant. Living in freedom in Cracow, she had to continue to prepare tissue samples for Mengele. After she had given birth Mengele sent her a bouquet of flowers.

The background of this physician, who is so infamous that he is regarded as *the* SS physician in extermination camps, is revealing. Mengele was born in 1911 in Günzburg and received a "good Catholic" education from his well-to-do parents. His fellow students describe him as a man who was popular, friendly, and enjoyed life. Apart from his pronounced ambition, they do not recall anything that might have indicated his later development, nor do they describe him as a fanatical Nazi. In a questionnaire that he filled out in 1939, Mengele stated that he had joined the NSDAP on May 1, 1937, but had held no office in the party or in the SS.

In a letter dated March 12, 1940, his teacher, Professor Freiherr von Verschuer, the head of the Institute of Hereditary Biology, says that Mengele is absolutely reliable and adds: "His special training in anthropology in addition to his general medical training is of great use to him in his work at my institute, particularly for the hereditary and racial examinations to determine an individual's heritage." Verschuer adds that lectures given by Mengele in Verschuer's absence demonstrated his ability to present even difficult intellectual subject matters and his suitability for an academic career. In addition to medicine, Mengele studied law and obtained degrees in both subjects.

The physicians Tadeusz Szymanski and Rudolf Vitek got to know Mengele as inmates. Szymanski describes him as very intelligent, and Vitek portrays him as a fanatical Nazi and a cynical, cold, devious, sly, and keen-witted person. Vitek also says that Mengele had great medical knowledge and was ambitious in the scientific field.

Many years later, I asked the SS physician Hans Münch, who had been acquitted in Cracow and clearly had a good regard for Mengele, how he was able to commit the deeds described above. Münch replied: "Mengele was convinced that a life-and-death struggle between Germans and Jews was being carried on and that the Germans consequently had to eradicate the Jews, whom he considered an intelligent and therefore all the more dangerous race. He had a different view of the Slavs, and there Mengele made distinctions."

■ Mengele is regarded as the prototype of an ss physician who misused prisoners in the extermination camps for his experiments. However, he was certainly not the only one to do so. Physicians who were not members of the ss also applied to conduct experiments on human beings in Auschwitz.

The most prominent among these is Professor Carl Clauberg, who was born in 1898. He made a name for himself as a gynecologist specializing in research on female sexual hormones. At international conferences of gynecologists, he was regarded as an esteemed expert. No one could have forced this respected scientist to work in an extermination camp. The correspondence that has been preserved indicates that he personally asked Himmler for permission to experiment with women interned in Auschwitz. He was searching for a method of sterilizing women quickly and inexpensively, without an operation. Himmler was interested in experiments of that kind and granted Clauberg whatever he wanted.

Clauberg's experiments were criminal, but that is not the whole story. Their aim was to support the "negative population policy," as Himmler liked to describe the most extensive crime organized by the Nazis. Clauberg was to find an answer to a question that occupied the heads of all concentration and extermination camps: how can offensive peoples be eradicated while still making use of their labor for the arms industry? Block 10 in the main camp was furnished in accordance with Clauberg's wishes, and the women that he required were placed at his disposal. In the camp lingo these women were called "rabbits."

Clauberg was ruthless in conducting his experiments, but some women have testified that he shielded them from brutalities of the ss. Because he was the director of a clinic in Königshütte, he came to Auschwitz only occasionally and used assistants. Thus he induced Dr. Johannes Goebel—an employee of the Schering Works who had to obtain material for Clauberg's injections— to move to Auschwitz. Clauberg procured a house for him in the vicinity of the camp, and, even though Goebel was not a medical man, he entrusted him with independently giving intrauterine injections.

Goebel boasted about what he was doing so loudly that the Schering Works dissociated itself from him. Eduard de Wind has characterized him as follows: "He stuck his nose into everything and mercilessly forced all women to subject themselves to his experiments, whereas Clauberg was occasionally quite decent and spared a woman if she asked not to be injected for one reason or another. Goebel was crude and sarcastic. He displayed the typical pettiness of people who have not learned how to occupy a leading position but are suddenly given great power." De Wind has given this description of his appearance: "He wore civilian clothes, and his riding breeches were ill suited to his spidery legs. In his light sports jacket he looked like a minor official who had grabbed something at a sale."

Clauberg recruited assistants among the prisoners as well. I have already described how he induced the Polish inmate physician Wladyslaw Dering to participate in the human experiments with his full ability and great ambition. After Clauberg had secured Dering's release, he made sure that he could continue to avail himself of Dering's expertise by putting him to work at his clinic in Königshütte.

He granted a young Slovak Jew named Sylvia Friedmann privileges in the experimental block in order to have a willing servant. She was given considerable power over the other inmates of the block, and in return she had to be Clauberg's personal servant—for example, "organize" coffee and cigarettes or knit pullovers for him. Once he even brought his three-year-old daughter to the experimental block so his "rabbits" could take her measurements and knit for her as well.

When the end of the war was in sight, Clauberg lost interest in his experiments; he had evidently grasped that Himmler could no longer further his career, and he increasingly reached for the bottle. After the end of the war, Clauberg was arrested and extradited to Russia, and after summary proceedings sentenced to a prison term of twenty-five years, which was obligatory at the time. He was released with others in 1955. Proceedings were brought against him in Germany, and in the court records may be found an answer to the question as to what induced this respected gynecologist to push to commit such crimes.

Clauberg testified that he had since his youth suffered from constant discrimination because he was so short (154 centimeters) and had always felt a need to fight back when he was mocked. In point of fact, his appearance was ridiculous; he was short and stocky and wore civilian clothes having a military tone. It was characteristic of him that in testimony before the examining magistrate in Kiel he gave a higher military rank and a higher salary at the Knappschaft Hospital in Königshütte than could be documented. A psychiatrist diagnosed a craving for power; his evaluation had been ordered because episodes had become known from Clauberg's life that indicated striking brutality. When he was a student, he was accused of murder, but later the proceedings were dropped because it was found that he had done the shooting in self-defense. He once threatened his wife with a loaded hunting rifle and injured his mistress by throwing a knife at her. Four days after his return from Russian captivity, he wrote his wife that she should "recommend to your pimps and housekeepers (Zu- und Haushälter) that they hang themselves." Otherwise, he would appear in person, and then "they will not die a relatively gentle death with a rope around their necks but a much more painful one."

His inflated self-assurance triggered the proceedings that were brought against him in Germany. On his return from Russia, he had himself celebrated as a martyr on German television, and this drew attention to him for the first time. He also advertised in newspapers that he was looking for a secretary "for the continuation of my scientific work."

■ Dr. Horst Schumann was Clauberg's rival in conducting experiments in Auschwitz. Like Clauberg, he was not a member of the ss but a Luftwaffe physician who had so proven himself at the first Nazi campaign of mass murders (under the cover name "Euthanasia," for its victims were primarily mentally ill) that he was entrusted with sterilization experiments, even though he had no specialized knowledge in this field. While Clauberg tried to make women sterile by means of injections, Schumann attempted to do so by radiating their genitals; and he also experimented on men. After radiation he had the uterus or the testicles of his victims removed, and he used these organs to determine the degree of destruction after radiation treatments of different durations. Like Clauberg, he did not care what happened to his "rabbits" afterward. Schumann's experiments and surgical procedures weakened his victims more than Clauberg's did, and thus their chances of staying alive were even slighter.

Schumann was born in 1906 and grew up in what he characterized as a "nationalistic-conservative" home. At the age of fourteen he volunteered for messenger duty at the civil war–like clashes in Saxony; then he became a "tradition-bound" member of a dueling fraternity and early in 1930 joined the NSDAP. He met the organizers of "Operation Euthanasia" by chance. A former fellow student, also a physician, did not wish to participate in this killing operation and suggested that those in charge contact Schumann, whom he knew as a staunch Nazi. Schumann had no scruples.

As the director of the killing facilities in Grafeneck and Sonnenstein, Schumann had to turn on the gas after the patients had been taken to the gas chamber and watch them die. He asked the mental patients who were scheduled to die questions — "in order to further my knowledge; after all, there were things to learn," as he assured his judges in 1970. He freely admitted to the court that he had no psychiatric training that would have enabled him to judge mental illnesses; and when he began his series of experiments in Auschwitz, he did not know any more than that about radiation treatment. For this reason Clauberg, the expert, described Schumann to his examining magistrate as a criminal while not displaying any guilt feelings himself.

Schumann treated the inmates whom he employed as assistants well. Thus he assured himself of the willing participation of Staszek Slezak, who took care of his X-ray equipment, by promising to recommend his release. However, he did not take this promise as seriously as Clauberg did the promise he gave to Dering, or else his influence was not as great as the professor's. Slezak remained in the camp, and after the completion of the experiments he suffered the fate of bearers of secrets.

Emil Kaschub, who also conducted experiments on human beings in Auschwitz, was not a member of the ss either. He came from Upper Silesia and served in the Wehrmacht as an ensign (*Fahnenjunker*). Stern, a French lawyer who was a nurse in the dormitory that housed Kaschub's "rabbits," has described him as a twenty-seven-year-old medical student with an "attractive appearance" who had been assigned to medical duty in Breslau. Kaschub was not on the level of Schumann or Clauberg, and he did not stay in Auschwitz as long as they did. His experiments lasted for only a few weeks. By means of subcutaneous injections and ointments—Fejkiel remembers pus, sewage, and unknown chemicals—Kaschub gave his test subjects cellulitis, which he repeatedly photographed and lanced. The liquid drawn from the wound was sent to Breslau. Fejkiel believes that these experiments were intended to find out how slackers managed to make themselves sick to escape service in the Wehrmacht.

After Kaschub had once again photographed a victim and plainly put the patient, who had a high fever, in agony, he said to his assistant Stern, "Believe me, I felt as lousy as you did, but I had to do it." That also differentiated the little ensign from the professor and the Luftwaffe officer, who certainly did not have to do "it" and who were never overheard making similar remarks.

▨ A medical man who differed from other camp physicians in many respects also used his stay in Auschwitz for experiments with the "available human material." Johann Paul Kremer was fifty-nine years old when he was ordered in 1942 to go to Auschwitz during the break between semesters, and thus he was of a different generation than most other ss physicians. Since 1935 he had been a professor of anatomy at the University of Münster, and he was the only university professor who worked in an extermination camp. Kremer's diary contains his reactions to what went on in Auschwitz.

According to this diary, Kremer participated in fourteen selections at the ramp and the subsequent gassings. When he was assigned to a "special action" for the first time (on September 2, his third day in Auschwitz), he noted in his diary: "By comparison, Dante's *Inferno* almost seems like a comedy to me." Three days later he called a selection in the women's camp "the most horrible of all horrors" and agreed with his colleague Thilo, who characterized Auschwitz as the "*anus mundi.*" On October 12, after he had attended his tenth selection and gassing, Kremer wrote: "A horrendous scene in front of the last bunker (Hössler)." Almost five years later Kremer interpreted this terse note for an examining magistrate in Cracow: "I remember that Hössler tried to squeeze the entire group (of 600 Dutchmen) into one bunker. He managed to do so, with the exception of one man, and Hössler shot that man with his pistol." Six days later Kremer again noted "horrendous scenes" in his diary. Three young, healthy Dutchwomen who begged for their lives outside the bunker were shot on the spot.

Kremer's diary affords us an insight into the conduct of a university professor on the threshold of old age who obviously did not feel good about the mass murders. However, his feelings of disgust could not have been that great, for right after Kremer's terse reports about extermination campaigns he gave detailed descriptions of various meals.

Kremer qualified for a university lectureship with a postdoctoral thesis titled "Über die Veränderungen des Muskelgewebes im Hungerzustande" (Changes in the muscular tissues of starving people). In another treatise that was published shortly before his posting to Auschwitz, he described changes in the cells of cold-blooded animals after experimental starvation. The SS garrison physician learned of this research, and "he said that I could use for my investigations fresh, living material from inmates who were being killed by injections of phenol," according to Kremer's testimony years later. One can imagine that Kremer did not have to be urged to do so.

This is Kremer's testimony given in Polish captivity:

If I was interested in someone because of an advanced process of starvation, I ordered the medic to reserve the patient for me and notify me when he was going to be killed by means of a phenol injection. On that day the patient chosen by me was taken to the block and put on the dissecting table while he was still alive. I stepped up to him and asked him about details that were of interest for my investigation—for example, his weight before his imprisonment, the weight loss in the camp, any medicine taken recently, and so on. After I had obtained this information, the medic came and killed the patient by injecting him in the cardiac area. I never gave lethal injections myself. I waited at a certain distance from the dissecting table with prepared containers. Right after the patient had died from the injection, inmate physicians removed parts of his liver and pancreas. I put these in the receptacles, which contained a preservative liquid. In some cases I had photographs made of the patients who were going to be killed so specimens could be taken from their bodies for me. I took the specimens and the photos to my apartment in Münster.

A laconic entry in Kremer's diary refers to this practice: "Today I fixed fresh, living material from a human liver, spleen, and pancreas." There are a number of similar entries.

The Polish inmate physician Wladyslaw Fejkiel reports that one day Kremer requested two starving inmates for research purposes. Fejkiel did not hesitate to pick out two patients, for Kremer's academic rank was known in the camp and Fejkiel did not believe that a university professor was capable of a criminal initiative. Later he learned that the women were killed and dissected.

Kremer did not use his brief stay in Auschwitz only for his scientific work. This pedantic entry in his diary is dated October 16: "At noon today I sent off the second package with a value of 300 Reichsmarks to Frau Wizemann (an acquaintance in Münster) for safekeeping." On the margin he added: "Soap, soap flakes, food." In an entry of November 17 Kremer listed the more substantial contents of the fifth package: "2 bottles of brandy from the co-op, vitamin tablets and tonics, razor blades, soaps for washing and shaving, thermometers, clippers, bottles of iodine, specimens in 96 percent alcohol, X-ray pictures, cod-liver oil, writing utensils, compresses, perfumes, darning wool, needles, toothpowder, etc. etc." At a later date Kremer was asked where all those items were from, and he glossed over his theft of possessions of murdered inmates by saying: "The inmates stuffed my pockets. I could not ward them off."

Nevertheless, Kremer was not among those who enjoyed staying in Auschwitz because of the unexpectedly great chances to enrich themselves. "I hope to be in Prague soon. Here there is nothing to tempt me," he wrote in a letter from Auschwitz dated September 5, 1942.

Toward prisoners Kremer was neither imperious nor rude. He used the formal *Sie* in addressing inmates—a rare exception. When he was doing selections in the infirmary, the number of victims was usually smaller than when Entress was selecting.

At the end of the semester break, Kremer returned to his university. "I am almost ashamed of being a German," he wrote in his diary a scant two months after leaving Auschwitz. The reason for this remark was that Kremer had not received the coveted chair for genetics. "Is there still an eternal justice, a providence, and a God without whose will not one hair falls from our heads?" Kremer did not write this question down because of the gas chambers that he had seen; it was prompted by a bombardment of Münster in 1943.

The Americans marched into Münster, and the war was coming to an end. Kremer conscientiously continued his diary; his last entry bears the date August 11, 1945. Five days earlier he had been ordered to clear debris in Münster, and he wrote indignantly: "A man has to endure this sort of thing because he was an SS physician." He evidently had completely repressed the "horrendous scenes" of Auschwitz. Not a single remark after his departure from Auschwitz refers to the camp and the mass murders in which Kremer participated. In fact, Kremer evidently did not even realize what he had recorded about his actions in this diary. When he was informed in a British internment camp that his diary had been found, he rejoiced because he believed that it contained proof that he had been treated badly by the Nazi regime and could therefore not be regarded as having been loyal to that regime.

The case of Kremer proves that even intellectually trained people are able to repress guilt feelings completely. After he had been pardoned in Poland, Kremer was sentenced in Münster to ten years in the penitentiary. The court's opinion was given by the presiding judge: "Kremer would be free of guilt even today if circumstances over which he had no control had not placed him in a situation that ultimately gave rise to these criminal acts. He became liable to punishment because he did not resist and refuse." He might have added: because Kremer did not hesitate to participate even though he regarded mass murder as something horrible—one need only consider the "fresh, living material" and the packages of stolen property.

At the age of eighty-one, when he had already served his sentences, Kremer was hauled into court once more. In Frankfurt he was supposed to testify, this time as a witness, about a diary entry that said that many SS men were keen to participate in campaigns of gassing because they received extra food rations for it. The old man said with a gentle smile: "Oh, but this is humanly quite understandable; it was wartime, and there was a shortage of cigarettes and schnapps. If someone was addicted to tobacco . . ."

■ Dr. Hellmuth Vetter was another physician who used his stay in Auschwitz to experiment on humans. Before he was posted to concentration camps as an SS physician, he had been in the employ of the IG Works in Leverkusen. He kept up that connection, and the Bayer Works regularly sent him new preparations that he was to test for their effectiveness on inmates. The physician, who was born in 1910 in Thuringia, supervised these experiments, which he had not been ordered to make, with great zeal and prohibited the administration of other medicines to the patients in his series of experiments. He even returned to Auschwitz after he had been transferred to Mauthausen-Gusen in order to learn about the further results of his experiments. "After the completion of his experiments he was not interested in the fate of these patients," said the nurse Stanislaw Klodzinski. Vetter also conducted human experiments in Gusen. When he had to answer for his actions before a military court in Nuremberg, documents were presented that indicated forty deaths among seventy-five persons who were treated with a new experimental drug in one of his series of experiments.

After Vetter had been sentenced to death, he wrote his brother and asked him to locate me: "Herr Langbein can confirm that I tried to save people wherever I could. I regarded Jews as human beings and patients, and I treated them accordingly." He counted on my advocacy because he remembered that he had fulfilled many of my requests concerning patients in Dachau, where we first met, and that he had sought conversations with me that did not relate to duty. He seemed to have repressed the fact that I knew that most of his "rabbits" in Auschwitz were Jews. According to Sonja Fischmann, when Vetter was once shown moldy bread that had been distributed, he responded that "mold is healthy."

The self-assured and corpulent Dr. Viktor Capesius, a pharmacist, is hard to classify. He, too, did more than merely carry out orders. He came from Siebenbürgen, where he was born in 1907. His schoolmate Karlheinz Schulery, who became a clergyman and whom Capesius sent for as a witness for the defense at the Frankfurt trial, testified verbosely that Capesius came from a very religious and social-minded family that had done much good. Like many other ethnic Germans from Romania, Capesius joined the ss in 1943. Since he had been a representative of the Bayer Works in Romania, the ss employed him as a pharmacist.

The defense attorneys assured the Frankfurt court that Capesius was not a convinced Nazi, and they were believable. They tried to prove their case by pointing out that the defendant's wife was Jewish. Evidently Capesius managed to conceal this "defect" from the leadership of the ss in distant Siebenbürgen.

After the death of his predecessor, Capesius became the manager of the ss pharmacy in Auschwitz in early 1944. Like every other ss leader in the office of the ss garrison physician, Capesius was from time to time assigned to ramp duty when the transports from Hungary were selected. This put him into an unprecedented situation. As a representative of the Bayer Works, he was personally acquainted with the physicians and pharmacists of Siebenbürgen, which was part of Hungary at that time. Many of them were Jews; and when they saw him again at the ramp, these perplexed people begged him for help. Capesius spoke Hungarian with them: "He was extraordinarily gemütlich, very amiable and jovial. He said that anyone who was tired should go to the other side; they would be sent to a rest camp where everything would be fine and dandy, and they would be reunited with the relatives from whom they had been separated at the first selection in Auschwitz. Many people voluntarily went to the other side, entire columns of five went there." This is how Marianna Adam remembers Capesius. With his friendly persuasion, Capesius facilitated the selection; the victims voluntarily joined the group of those destined to die.

However, the selection was not the most important thing for Capesius at the ramp. Tadeusz Szewczyk, who worked in the SS pharmacy, has described his boss's return from the ramp.

> One day at noon Dr. Capesius drove up in the Sanka (*Sanitätskraftwagen*, ambulance) and ordered us to take some suitcases out of the vehicle. There were about fifteen leather suitcases of different sizes. I was assigned to sort the contents, and Dr. Capesius stayed with me. The suitcases contained clothes, shirts, cosmetics, money, razors, and similar items. Dr. Capesius put the better clothes and all the money in the better suitcases. The other things were taken to the attic for general sorting. He immediately put the foreign money in his cashbox but left the German money in the suitcase. Jewelry, watches, and the like he also put there and in his pockets.

Szewczyk confirms that Capesius was not stingy at this sorting: "He distributed food among the inmates."

The storeroom of the SS pharmacy was located in the attic. Wilhelm Prokop describes what he had to witness there:

> One time Dr. Capesius inspected the attic and I had to be his guide. I showed him all the suitcases containing medications. On the way back Capesius noticed on the right side cases filled with dental prostheses, dentures, and the like. Bone fragments and gums were still attached to some of them; everything was already decaying, and there was a terrible stench. Capesius asked me what that was, and I told him that those cases belonged to the dental clinic. Capesius walked up to the suitcases, squatted next to them, and rummaged around in the stinking stuff. He pulled out a prosthesis and held it up as if he were assessing its value.

Prokop noticed how the contents of these suitcases diminished daily. Capesius threatened him with death if he talked about this.

The Pole Jan Sikorski, who as a camp-wise foreman in the SS pharmacy had the best opportunities to get at all the valuable things that wound up there, testified as follows before the Frankfurt judges: "Dr. Capesius was no friend of the inmates, but he was not as much of a bandit as the others. He did not care about supplying the camp with medications. But because the war was coming to an end, he protected himself by being friendly to many inmates. Once he said to me: 'Now I am an officer, and you are inmates. In two months this may already be reversed.'"

Sikorsky told me about the lengths to which Capesius went to gratify his desires. One time he was looking for a diamond brooch and promised Sikorski twelve bottles of schnapps if he "organized" one for him. Sikorski gave Capesius the desired brooch within the time they had agreed on, and Capesius handed him the schnapps. Because Sikorski did not want to take the risk of smuggling twelve bottles into the camp, he induced his boss to carry the schnapps into the camp for him. Capesius, who held the rank of SS major (Sturmbannführer), was of course not checked when he entered the camp. Once inside, he turned the bottles over to his business partner.

Capesius knew how to get along. His subordinate Kurt Jurasek, who frequently traveled to Oranienburg as a courier, brought "little gifts" from Capesius to his superiors. I have never been able to see any evidence of friendliness in this manager of the SS pharmacy; all I saw was arrogance. To be sure, I was not able to be of use to him in "organizing."

The Frankfurt judges, who were very careful in the formulation of their opinion, summed up by stating that Capesius "enriched himself to an extent that was bound to attract attention even in Auschwitz, where people did not exactly act conscientiously in that regard."

■ Capesius's compatriot Dr. Fritz Klein must also be numbered among the type of physician who developed initiatives of his own in the extermination, although Klein was different from those discussed above. There was an age difference, Klein was born in 1888, and until age fifty-four he was a general practitioner in a small town in Siebenbürgen. While his colleagues gave one the impression that the SS uniform made them feel exalted and validated, Klein did not fit into his uniform.

He was a convinced anti-Semite. Ella Lingens remembers a conversation with him that she was able to have because as the only German inmate physician she had more privileges than others. Once she pointed to the obligation of every physician to protect the life of every human being. Klein responded that it was reverence for human life that prompted him to remove an inflamed appendix from a diseased body. Klein concluded this comparison by saying that the Jews constituted an inflamed appendix in Europe.

Manca Svalbova has not forgotten Klein's order to replace Jewish nurses in the infirmary of the women's camp with "Aryan" women. Only Jewish female physicians were allowed to stay. When on one occasion a German Jewish woman who had been selected begged him for her life, Klein replied: "You are old enough to die. What the others can do, you can do, too." Judith Sternberg-Newman remembers this response.

His behavior at campaigns of murder was not like the customary behavior of others. The nurse Janusz Mlynarski heard in the main camp that Klein yelled at the supervising SS man when physically feeble prisoners were once again being loaded on trucks on their way to the gas chambers: "How can you pack the trucks like this? These are human beings and not sardines!" Of course, Klein could have no doubts about the destination of this ride.

During a visit to the HKB of the women's camp, an inmate physician called Klein's attention to the fact that some patients needed another two or three days' rest, whereupon Klein very politely ordered five to eight days of bed rest for these convalescents. Two days later trucks appeared in front of the HKB and all patients who had been laid up for more than five days had to board the trucks that followed the familiar route to the gas chambers. This happened in October 1944, when the end of the war was already clearly in sight.

Igor Bistric, a clerk in the HKB of the main camp, once asked Dr. Klein to remove the name of a Hungarian Jew from the selection list. Klein refused, and the selected man, a deputy in the Hungarian parliament whose name was also Klein, had to go to the gas chamber. Bistric remembers that "afterward Dr. Klein did not dare to look me in the eye."

On May 15, 1945, Dr. Erwin Valentin, who worked in the same HKB as Bistric, testified on the basis of his fresh memory that Klein selected a fourteen-year-old Jewish lad even though there was nothing wrong with him. Valentin had operated on a carbuncle on his neck but had already certified that he was fit for work. When the boy screamed and moaned that he was quite healthy and wanted to live, Klein is reported to have declared amid hand-rubbing and stroking that the boy would not go to the chimney but be taken to another infirmary, where things would be much nicer.

Some Jews, to be sure, got to know another side of Klein. Olga Lengyel describes him as the only SS man whom she never heard raise his voice. Once the senior camp warden selected 315 women and locked them up in a barracks where they had to wait for the SS physician's final decision as to who would be sent to the gas chamber. Lengyel, a medical student who worked as a nurse, had to accompany the camp physician on his way to this barracks. She attempted to explain to Klein that among those selected there were some who were still able to work, but Klein did not react to her requests. When he reached the camp, he looked at the unfortunate women and chased some of them out with the remark that they were quite healthy and only malingerers. He thereby reduced by thirty-one the number of those who were soon to be forced to board the trucks.

One time Lengyel was supposed to kneel by way of punishment. Klein sent for her under some pretext and thus spared her this punishment. When, on another occasion, she called Klein's attention to the inhabitants of one block who had to stand lined up outside in the rain for hours, Klein did not answer but immediately went there and ordered the women to go inside. That Lengyel had such experiences with Klein may be due to the fact that she was from the same area of Siebenbürgen as the SS physician and that they spoke Hungarian with each other. More than once Lengyel observed Klein at selections when he sent hundreds to the gas chamber. She came up with the designation "civil murderer" for him.

Eduard de Wind has not forgotten that Klein once removed his name from a list of inmates who were to be assigned to the penal company. He did this at the request of de Wind's wife, who was also in the camp. To be sure, shortly before this Klein had not only given de Wind's block elder a whipping but also removed him from his post because he had refused to beat a sick Jew. De Wind and his wife were from Holland, and so they did not share a homeland with Klein.

Jehuda Bacon, who was laid up in the children's block of the Theresienstadt family camp, testified that Klein was interested in the children housed there and sometimes came close to playing with them. He got them a soccer ball and behaved "almost like an uncle."

Klein once asked me to type up a play that he had written, to do this in my free time and make some carbon copies. I have forgotten the details of this play, but I do remember that it was a very ineptly written blood-and-soil drama set in Klein's homeland, one in which the Germans were depicted as an elite with a mysterious connection to their people. Pawek Reinke, the manager of the inmate office in the main camp, had to find rhymes for Klein's poems, in which he extolled the good things the Nazis were doing for his homeland. Dr. Fejkiel observed that Klein always had a picture of Hitler with him.

According to Olga Lengyel, Klein was under no illusions about the outcome of the war. Once he rode his bicycle to the women's camp and complained that he had been deprived of his service car because of a gasoline shortage. He concluded by saying that the war would soon be over and that he was sure that neither those women nor any other inmates were going to do anything for him after the end of the war.

Like many others in Auschwitz, Klein liked to indulge in alcohol. His compatriot Capesius, who was at the source, claimed that he provided him with plenty of alcohol. In the final phase Klein was transferred to the Bergen-Belsen camp, where he was arrested by the British and with others brought before their military court in Lüneburg. When he was asked about the methods of extermination, all he said was this: "Of course, I did not approve of the gassings, but I did not protest, either, for that would have been senseless. You can't protest when you're in the army. Participating in the selection was no pleasure."

■ Physicians who stolidly carried out orders without doing more than that but did not help the prisoners, either, remained colorless; there is relatively little to report about them. The following are some of the medical men who belonged to this group.

Dr. Bruno Weber, born in 1915, was the director of the Hygiene Institute of the Waffen-ss in Auschwitz. Marc Klein, an inmate who worked in that institute, has described him as follows: "As a medical man he appeared to have had a good biological training; his special field was microbiology. He was a man of impeccable elegance, an arrogant manner, and cool irony. He kept away from the inmates but always acted correctly." Dr. Hans Münch, who worked under Weber, reports that Weber kept his distance from other ss leaders as well. He remembers that before the war Weber studied in the United States on a scholarship. I had the impression that Weber was nauseated by the goings-on in Auschwitz but still preferred serving in the extermination camp rather than on the front line. He always strove to emphasize the importance of his institute and devoted his entire energy to its expansion. Because the inmates who were skilled workers there enjoyed far more favorable conditions than could be found on most other details, they supported Weber to the best of their ability.

It is difficult to place Dr. Hans Wilhelm König, born in 1912, in one of the previously mentioned three groups, but perhaps he fits best into the one under discussion. On the other hand, König attempted to learn at the expense of the prisoners. Dr. Samuel Steinberg observed in the main camp how Dr. König performed amputations on cellulitis sufferers, although, in Steinberg's opinion, a simple incision would have sufficed. In those days, however, König wanted to learn different methods of amputation. Afterward the amputees were classified as unfit for work and sent to the gas chambers.

Ella Lingens writes that König used his stay in the camp to get further training and did not hesitate to learn from Jewish inmate physicians. If a patient's ailment interested him, he had that patient given good care and every day asked how he was doing. However, when he was no longer interested in the course of the disease, he sent the patient to the gas chamber. Lingens describes König as intelligent, industrious, and "not inhumane with regard to details." Whenever he had to make selections in the women's camp, he got drunk.

Georges Wellers emphasizes that König always treated him and his fellow prisoners in the laboratory of the HKB in Monowitz courteously and addressed him as "Herr Professor" when they were alone, even though Wellers had to wear a Star of David. On one occasion he shielded the inmates when they were in danger of being caught cheating by the ss camp leader.

Lingens recalls that König had a lot of respect for Enna Weiß, the young Jewish senior physician, and he said to her, "Perhaps the English way of life isn't so bad." Dr. Fritz Berl reports that in the Birkenau dissection facilities

König happened to recognize a Jewish dentist who had been a fellow student in Prague. He brought him food and had him assigned to a better detail. On other occasions, however, he acted more fanatically than many others.

Once Dr. König made this proposal to Manca Svalbova: "Let's put our cards on the table. I know that you are hiding patients with typhus and scarlet fever. You can keep on doing this, but show me the patients and the diagnoses that you enter in place of these infectious diseases." König gave as the reason for this strange offer his fear of the higher-ranking Dr. Mengele. Svalbova acted in accordance with this proposal, and König never did anything to the detriment of the sick women who were registered with false diagnoses. This happened in 1944.

There are varied reports about Dr. Werner Rohde as well. That physician, who was born in Marburg in 1904, could not resist the temptation to misuse inmates for experimental purposes. On only one occasion he forced four inmates to drink a liquid that did not have a lethal effect on every one of them—an insignificant incident by Auschwitz standards—but his initiative in this particular murder has been documented. On the other hand, Edward Pys, an attentive observer who was in Auschwitz from the beginning and got to know all SS physicians, describes him as one of the most humane, although he admits that he does not know whether people had the same impression in all infirmaries. Dr. Erwin Valentin reports that Rohde sometimes exempted people from a selection on the basis of objective considerations.

The camp elder Wladyslaw Fejkiel describes Rohde as "a typical German fraternity member" who often came to the infirmary "slightly inebriated." At such times he was "soft" and could be talked into many things. He signed any paper without reading it, was not interested in anything, and "behaved more decently than all the others." Fejkiel concludes this characterization by saying that "we were able to save comrades from all kinds of dire straits" on several occasions. Tadeusz Paczula confirms that Rohde earmarked fewer prisoners for death than the medic Klehr proposed. Paczula remembers this statement by Rohde: "You can save whomever you want, but not Jews."

The most positive statements about Rohde were made by women; evidently Rohde was most accessible to requests by female inmates. Izabella Sosnowska testifies that "at selections he showed human emotions, was off balance, and had drunk a lot." Lilly Meitner and Margit Teitelbaum wrote that Rohde worked toward the improvement of hygienic conditions in the women's camp and ordered that packages addressed to people who had died be distributed among the inmates. Before this, the SS had appropriated these parcels.

Ella Lingens knew that camp physician best; the two had been medical students at the University of Marburg an der Lahn at the same time. Lingens describes him as a scatterbrain who made one wonder how he managed to get into the SS. On one occasion he told her that after the war they would get together over a glass of wine. Lingens remembers that Rohde endeavored to improve conditions in the women's camp, but in the end he did have the typhus patients taken to the gas chamber. After this action he was no longer given the names of women suffering from typhus. Rohde seemed to be grateful for this because he evidently feared that if any more epidemics became known he would be unable to stave off the customary method of fighting epidemics in Auschwitz.

Rohde acted courteously when he had inmates "organize" for him. Once he asked a Polish inmate to get him a nice present for his wife, and the inmate obtained a pigskin toilet case for him. Later Rohde told the Pole that his wife had liked the present and thanked him for it. It goes without saying that the inmates tried to corrupt him completely by means of gifts, and they largely succeeded.

Rohde was transferred from Auschwitz to Natzweiler. When he had to answer to a French military court for his activities there, Verse, one of his professors in Marburg, testified that Rohde was "a good student in the best sense of the word. I never noticed in him an active or propagandistic participation in favor of the NSDAP." The positive testimony of Professor Paulsen, who was an inmate at Natzweiler, carried greater weight than Verse's.

■ One could see that several SS physicians obeyed orders to murder with reluctance. They could be induced, to varying degrees, to help prisoners here and there.

This third type, which was the most important for the inmates, included a medical man who had become a Nazi earlier than all the others. Dr. Willi Frank, a dentist, became a founding member of the NSDAP in Regensburg in 1922 at the age of nineteen. He participated in the march to the Feldherrenhalle and was permitted to wear the insignia of an "old fighter." Inmates who worked under him at the dental clinic in Auschwitz gave him good marks—for example, his *Kalfaktor* (handyman) Männe Kratz, a German Jew. "Frank went to bat for me, and I was given an easy privileged position." Thanks to Frank, Fenny Herrmann was able to work in the dental clinic of the women's camp; she testified that "Frank was very kind to all women at the dental clinic and helped wherever he could." In her case, too, the Star of David was no impediment. Frank brought white bread and margarine to Jewish dental technicians who had to melt dental gold in the crematorium, although he could not save them from being eventually killed as bearers of secrets. I never heard Frank address a harsh or angry word to an inmate.

In the final plea that Frank was entitled to make in the Frankfurt courtroom, he said: "The former inmates with whom I dealt in Auschwitz have borne witness to my behavior there. None of them has incriminated me. On the contrary, all have said that I treated them humanely, and several have testified that they owe their life to me." This is what he told his judges about the mass extermination: "All I can say is that I regarded what happened in those years as monstrous." Nevertheless, Frank made selections at the ramp without protesting when it was his turn, and he was sentenced for this in Frankfurt.

■ Dr. Franz Lucas sat in the dock next to Frank in Frankfurt. Former inmate physicians testified on his behalf. One of them was Dr. Wladyslaw Fejkiel: "Lucas always acted correctly toward the patients and treated us well." Dr. Aron Bejlin testified under oath as follows: Once Lucas had a lengthy conversation in the Gypsy camp with Professor Berthold Epstein, an inmate physician from Prague. That was a rarity. I did not hear what was said, but afterward Epstein told us: 'Fellows, that's a decent man.' Later Dr. Lucas worked in the infirmary at Birkenau as a substitute for Dr. Thilo. At that time selections stopped there. Lucas performed operations together with Jewish physicians from whom he apparently wanted to learn. Sometimes he brought those physicians something to eat.

Epstein could not be questioned about this because he was no longer alive at the start of the trial. Dr. Tadeusz Snieszko gave this testimony in Frankfurt: "One time all of the inmate physicians in the Gypsy camp were called to a conference. To our great surprise Dr. Lucas made a speech. He told us that he wanted to discuss our work with us, that he realized we were in a difficult situation but could not do anything about it. He said he was convinced that we were not criminals; as a physician, he regarded us as his colleagues and was going to do whatever he could to help the patients and the medical staff. And he did do whatever he could." Dr. Tadeusz Szymanski also testified in his favor: "Dr. Lucas was a mensch. He restored my faith in the Germans."

Emil Panovec happened to run into Dr. Lucas on a staircase in the ss infirmary on the day when rumors about the attempt on Hitler's life started to circulate. At first it was believed that the attempt had succeeded. According to Panovec, Lucas welcomed the attempted assassination and announced that all inmates would be able to go home soon.

No witness has accused Lucas of cruelty, but a few did say that he was indifferent to the lot of the prisoners. The most serious accusation was made by a fellow defendant, the block leader Stefan Baretzki, who said, among other things, that Lucas had made selections like all other ss physicians. After denying this for a long time and with a great deal of pathos, he finally admitted it. An episode graphically described by Baretzki casts an unfavorable light on

Lucas. At the "liquidation" of the Theresienstadt family camp, Baretzki and a few of his colleagues urged that children not be forced to go to the gas chambers together with grown-ups. At that time SS camp leader Schwarzhuber saved the boys, as described above, but "he could not save the girls" because he had no jurisdiction over the women's camp, where they would have had to be sheltered—"and they had such nice long hair. So we went to see Dr. Lucas, but he did nothing about it." When Baretzki was asked if Lucas could have saved the girls, he replied: "Easily. He could have taken the girls to the women's camp."

In a curriculum vitae prepared in 1937, Lucas stated that even at the *Gymnasium* he had made no secret of his Nazi orientation. He joined the SA as a student in June 1933 but then left it, stating as a reason that the spirit of many members of the SA's student units was anything but ideal. That is when Lucas joined the SS and left the church, though without inwardly breaking with it. He later maintained that he had done this only to please the SS.

Lucas told his judges that when the confrontation with the mass murder in Auschwitz produced a spiritual crisis in him, he confided in Bishop Dr. Berning, a classmate of his father: "The bishop told me that immoral orders must not be carried out, but a person should not go to the point of endangering his own life." Lucas asserted that orders must be obeyed to avoid becoming a victim of a rigorous system of justice or a liquidation without due process, and he added: "I did not receive any special advice from a high-level jurist either." According to Lucas, this presiding district court judge said that "we were in the fifth year of the war and many things were happening." These statements could not be confirmed.

There are many indications that Lucas "bought a return ticket in time," as Baretzki put it at the trial, for most of the testimony in his favor refers to events in 1944 or early 1945, when Lucas was helping inmates in Ravensbrück. His devious defense in the courtroom, which he changed more frequently than any of his codefendants, reinforced that impression. In his closing statement he grandiloquently assured the court that he would never get over Auschwitz and then said: "Even today I do not see how I could have done things differently at that time."

■ Dr. Hans Münch, already mentioned several times, could do things differently. To be sure, this physician, born in 1911, was in a particularly favorable situation in Auschwitz because the Hygiene Institute, where he worked, was under the direct supervision of Professor Joachim Mrugowski, the chief hygienist in Oranienburg. He once described how he used this affiliation to get out of being assigned to selections:

At first I did not refuse outright, which seemed impossible to me in the realm of such a bureaucratized, pseudomilitary entity as Auschwitz, but I simply said: I cannot do it. Then I went to see my immediate superior (Dr. Weber), presented the matter to him in simple terms, and told him about all my troubles. He understood, of course, and recommended that I make the same presentations to the authorities on the next level. There, too, I met with understanding; and after I was able to demonstrate that I was fully occupied with very important other work, I was left in peace for the next six months and was able to avoid selections. Later, when I was accustomed to Auschwitz, people found other loopholes and dodges to escape such things.

Marc Klein has this to say about Münch: "He was relatively friendly toward the inmates, which was rare though not unique." Dr. Vilo Jurkovic said that Münch was proof that Germans could behave humanely even in ss uniforms. Münch was the only one of forty defendants in the big Auschwitz trial in Cracow to be acquitted. In its opinion the court pointed out that he had been able to keep clear of the machinery of murder and that witnesses had confirmed that he helped prisoners establish contact with their families and provided them with medications, that he once got two women released from the penal company, and that he got into trouble because of his friendly attitude toward the inmates.

However, neither Münch nor his superior Weber objected to a certain practice that had become customary in the Hygiene Institute. Originally beef was used there as a culture medium. One day the leaders of this institute had the idea of eating the beef allotted for that purpose themselves. When there were shootings at the Black Wall, they had flesh cut from the corpses of those not yet completely emaciated and used this flesh for the cultures, while the beef that continued to be requisitioned made its way to the cooking pot.

After the war I asked Münch, who had settled in a small Bavarian town as a general practitioner, how he had joined the ss. He told me that he had chosen problems of hygiene as his specialty and investigated living conditions of the population in the Bavarian forest for the Nazi students organization. For this work he received a prize and attracted the attention of Dr. Weber, who was already in the ss. Weber persuaded Münch to join the ss as well, for this would give him the most favorable opportunities to continue his research in his special field, whereas there were few other opportunities for work. This is how Münch, who had not been raised in the Nazi spirit, became a member of the ss; and when Weber was posted to Auschwitz, he went there as well.

■ For a short time a young physician named Hans Delmotte, a recent graduate of the *Junkerschule* (SS officers school), worked at the Hygiene Institute. His family was well established in industry, and some of his relatives occupied high positions in the Nazi hierarchy.

Like any other physician who was transferred to Auschwitz, Delmotte initially had to accompany a colleague on his rounds in order to become acquainted with all his duties. Thus Delmotte encountered a selection at the ramp on his first days in the camp. Münch has described what followed:

> He came back completely distraught, brought by an SS man because he was in no position to drive. He lived in the room next to mine. When he came in and noisily rumbled down the creaking stairs, I thought he had not tolerated the schnapps that was usually available at the selections. He vomited and was unable to speak. It was not until the next morning that I noticed that alcohol had not been the most important factor. Even in the morning we could not have a proper conversation because he was completely shattered. He put on his dress uniform, marched briskly to the commandant's office, and declared that he refused to perform such a duty, that he simply could not do it. As he told us later, he did this in a diplomatically maladroit fashion, officially refusing the duty and asking to either be sent to the front or be gassed. But he simply could not do this.

The commandant referred Delmotte to the SS garrison physician, and the young physician told him the same thing. The result was that Delmotte was instructed to accompany Dr. Mengele for an extended period and let Mengele convince him of the necessity of exterminating the Jews. Münch remembers the argument with which Mengele finally succeeded in doing so. He is said to have pointed out to the young physician that in exceptional situations a physician must take the responsibility for selections; every medic in the army has to make selections at the front because after a battle he cannot possibly treat all urgent cases simultaneously. For this reason he must decide whom he will treat first, thereby deferring the treatment of others at the risk that later they cannot be saved anymore. Another of Mengele's arguments was that at the ramp it was, after all, only decided who was still fit to work. Since a firm decision had been made to eradicate all Jews, deciding who would first be admitted to the camp was not such a momentous matter.

Young Delmotte eventually let Mengele persuade him and made selections like any other SS physician. According to Münch, Delmotte did so with revulsion and was a completely changed man—"a broken man in the truest sense of the word." Only after the selections were discontinued in the fall of 1944 did he seem to be emotionally more relaxed.

Dr. André Lettich remembers that Delmotte immediately came into the camp when he heard about the selection of an inmate named Burstein who was working at the Hygiene Institute. By claiming him as an indispensable expert, Delmotte pulled him out of the group of those doomed to die.

When Delmotte had to expect to be arrested after the end of the war, he committed suicide.

▪ In three physicians who were in Auschwitz for a long time, I most clearly noticed inhibitions about obeying commands to murder, and not just in the final phase of the war. They were Dr. Bruno Kitt, Dr. Horst Fischer, and especially Dr. Eduard Wirths.

The oldest was Kitt, who was born in Hamm in 1906 but appeared older and almost studiedly unmilitary. He did not conceal the fact that he was not a fanatical Nazi. I had the impression that he had had a better professional training than most of his younger colleagues. Edward Pys considers him the most intelligent SS physician he encountered in Auschwitz. Ludwig Wörl met Kitt in the winter of 1942–43 in Monowitz, when he was camp elder in the HKB and Kitt was the camp physician. Wörl confirms that it was sometimes possible to talk with him, and Wörl's successor as camp elder, Heinrich Schuster, also says that Kitt was "open to some of our suggestions." Sonja Fischmann puts it concisely: "We were not afraid of Kitt."

On one occasion Kitt described to his superior, Dr. Wirths, his distress when he had to make periodic selections in the inmate infirmaries under his supervision and asked him to relieve him of his duties as a camp physician. Wirths gave him a temporary appointment as physician for the SS troops, which meant a normal medical activity. To be sure, even such a medic was not exempted from duty at the ramp.

Like many others, Kitt joined the SS in the year of Hitler's assumption of power. Many years later, when I asked Kitt's wife why he took this step, she replied that he wanted to escape the pesky Sunday exercises in which he, as a student member of the SA, would have had to participate. On the basis of my knowledge, I believe that if Kitt had, like Lucas, been tried in Frankfurt, more witnesses for the defense could have been found for him than for Lucas. However, Kitt was transferred from Auschwitz to Neuengamme, and for the crimes he committed there he was sentenced to death by a British military tribunal.

According to my observations, Dr. Horst Fischer seemed to contend with even stronger inhibitions. After the war this physician was able to practice undisturbed in the German Democratic Republic, but in March 1966 he was put on trial for his actions as an Auschwitz camp physician; so there is some personal information about him. He was born in Dresden in 1912, lost his parents at an early age, was raised by relatives, and studied medicine. He joined the ss on November 1, 1933, and he gave the court these reasons:

I was an orphan, and so I had to apply for an exemption from paying tuition. In order to receive this exemption, a student had to provide proof of Nazi activities, and at that time I joined the ss for various reasons. For one thing, a lot of my colleagues already were in the ss. For another, it may have been the uniform that impressed and enticed me at the time. Besides, I was under the impression that I was somewhat unmanly and soft, and perhaps I wanted to compensate for this by joining a particularly tough organization.

Fischer also gave an account of his road to Auschwitz. Because of an illness he had to be transferred from frontline service. If I remember correctly, his medical records indicate that he had pulmonary tuberculosis. In an ss convalescent home he met the physician in charge of all concentration camps, Dr. Enno Lolling, and expressed to him his desire to continue his surgical training. Lolling advised him to apply for a transfer to a concentration camp and added that he could easily perfect his surgical skills there. Fischer agreed to this.

This route took him to Auschwitz in November 1942. In the courtroom Fischer described how Dr. Wirths, the ss garrison physician and a friend since their shared training period, wanted to help him get over the shock that he suffered on his first assignment to selections. According to Fischer, this is what Wirths told him: "We are all serving at the inner front, so to speak. If you consider how many young soldiers give their lives every day and every hour, you will get over it more easily." To me Fischer admitted that his duties in Auschwitz disgusted him. He was always friendly and frank in our conversations in the inmate office at the ss infirmary—probably because Wirths had told him that he could safely do this.

Inmates who were able to assess his activity in the infirmaries have testified that we were not the only ones with whom he talked that way. Robert Waitz writes that "sometimes human emotions" could be observed in him and emphasizes that this distinguished him favorably from Dr. König and Dr. Entress. Siegfried Halbreich, who also met Fischer in Monowitz, confirms this. The camp elder in that infirmary, Stefan Budziaszek, states that Fischer "proceeded from human considerations," was open to requests, and once told him, "I've been fed up with all this for a long time, but I can't resign." In my characterization of camp elder Budziaszek I have already mentioned the testimony of both Waitz and Oszkár Betlen that Fischer reduced the number of victims at selections.

In my *Bericht* I recorded a conversation with Fischer that is characteristic not only of him but also of conditions in the satellite camps:

"Do you have some time, Langbein?" Dr. Fischer, Wirths's deputy, is standing in the doorway.

"Yes sir. A small sheet or a big one, Herr Doktor?"

"A big one with a carbon copy. Wait—no, come with me, I'll dictate in the boss's room."

Fischer evidently does not want to speak within earshot of Zbyszek and Emil (who were sitting in the clerk's office with me). It must be something special. He sits down behind Wirths's desk.

"Take a letter: To the ss garrison physician. Make several copies, I've already spoken with the chief, and he wants to send this report to Berlin with a covering letter."

"Concerning . . . ?"

"Sanitary conditions in the Jawischowitz labor camp."

Dr. Fischer's assignment is to be the physician for all satellite camps. Only recently I called his attention to the fact that the mortality rate in Jawischowitz has sharply increased in recent months, while it decreases in springtime in most other camps. (That conversation took place in the spring of 1944.) He has probably tried to find the reasons for this. His letter is a complaint about Otto Heine, the director of the mine, which is part of the Hermann Göring Works.

Heine is demanding that the working day be extended, that the inmates get no lunch because the distribution of food takes so much time, and that the inmates who are not fully fit for work be routinely removed from the camp (that is, gassed) and replaced with fresh laborers.

During the dictation Fischer has become enraged. "People always call us ss men bad, but they don't take a look at these gentlemen! They're always pressuring us! And this is not the first time!"

At that time I availed myself of the opportunity to send a reliable nurse to Jawischowitz as camp elder of the infirmary. From then on, the resistance organization had a connection with that satellite camp as well.

Wirths trusted Fischer, to whom he felt close because of their shared training period and similar attitude toward the mass murders in the extermination camp, but he was reserved and formal to the other physicians under his supervision. He rapidly promoted Fischer, who became his deputy as the highest-ranking physician. In a letter to his wife written in August 1943, Wirths characterizes Fischer in these words: "He is such a decent and dear fellow, but he bellyaches too much and sees too much of what one shouldn't or mustn't see or would sometimes do better to overlook. . . . Horst is the type of person who is always forthright and honest but thereby makes difficult many things for himself and for me."

I gained the impression that Fischer lacked not only the caution that was indicated but also the persistence that I learned to appreciate in Wirths. If he saw no way out, he resigned and did his duty in the machinery of murder, albeit with inner repugnance. For the rest, he wanted to augment his specialized medical knowledge. It was not a later invention of his when he testified as follows on February 22, 1966: "The inmate physicians were real medical luminaries whom ss garrison physician Wirths recommended to me for my further professional training."

Unlike almost all the others, Fischer at his trial did not resort to denials, whitewashing, and memory lapses but was ready to tell all. For this reason it was regrettable that his trial in East Berlin was not conducted as painstakingly as the subject required. At least in one respect, Fischer's testimony can clarify what all other ss physicians left unsaid in the courtroom: the criteria for selections in the infirmaries. This is what Fischer had to say on that subject:

> There were a number of conferences of all ss physicians in Auschwitz for the purpose of working out firm criteria for the selections. These discussions produced essentially the following characteristics as prerequisites for selections: starvation edemas; the complete lack of fatty tissue in the buttocks (to diagnose this the physicians had the naked inmates turn around); the suspicion of TB (because of the deficient medical equipment actual TB was difficult to diagnose, and it evidently seemed too bothersome to perform X rays in the main camp); accidents that caused broken bones; and severe suppuration. Roughly speaking, these were the cases in which selections appeared to be indicated.

Fischer also gave this frank description of the mind-set of the ss physicians: "We hardly discussed the fact that inmates with these characteristics were being killed. As for me, I viewed this as the fulfillment, so to speak, of one of the purposes of Auschwitz."

DR. WIRTHS

■ ■ ■

The most important of the physicians in uniform who reluctantly served in the machinery of destruction was Dr. Eduard Wirths. His reluctance was of the greatest practical importance to the prisoners, for he held the office of SS garrison physician from early September 1942 until the evacuation of Auschwitz—that is, during virtually the entire period in which masses of human beings were murdered—and he accepted the consequences of his attitude as no other physician did.

I already knew him from Dachau. In my *Bericht* I described my first encounter with him in the Inpatient Department of the inmate infirmary where I was serving as a clerk.

A new ward physician has arrived. His name is Dr. Eduard Wirths. Tall, thin, dark hair, very bright eyes, resolute bearing. In the buttonhole of his uniform coat, there is a medal ribbon that I have not seen on anyone else. "That is the EK II [Iron Cross second class]; he must have served at the front," says Valentin, a German nurse. Later I learned that Wirths was rendered unfit for further frontline service during an action of his SS unit in Lapland and that Dachau was the first KZ that he encountered.

On the second day I already notice something else that distinguishes him from the other SS physicians. He is standing in the outpatient section, the veins on his neck are swollen and his voice is menacingly sharp. In front of him stands Heini (the young senior nurse in the inpatient section who has all too often irresponsibly neglected the patients entrusted to his care) with his hands on the seams of his trousers.

"Why didn't you administer the injection yesterday, as I had ordered?"

"Herr Obersturmführer, I didn't get a chance to do it; there was so much work in the ward." Heini wants to talk his head off, but Dr. Wirths interrupts him: "Don't you know that this person could have died. Have you no sense of responsibility?"

This is something new. He also makes rounds differently from the other physicians. Every day he walks from bed to bed, sometimes addresses a few friendly words to a patient, and once I even caught him trying to communicate with an old Pole in Polish, something that would never have occurred to any other arrogant SS man.

I accompanied Wirths on these rounds, which were so unusual in our experience, conscientiously wrote down his instructions, and in front of every bed briefly summed up what he had previously ordered. In this way I forced senior nurse Heini, who was as high handed as he was indolent, really to follow the instructions. Wirths could not have known what motivated me, but he learned to appreciate me as a conscientious clerk. He remained on our ward for only a short time. This is what I wrote in my *Bericht*:

> Dr. Wirths is taking over another ward. Once I ran into him in the corridor. We are alone, and I stand to attention.
> "Well, how are things in the inpatient section, Langbein?"
> "Not as good as when you were with us, Herr Doktor." When Wirths has already passed me, I notice that he has blushed. It is quite noticeable on his neck and ears. Does he rejoice when an inmate praises him? Strange. He isn't like the others.
> Later Dr. Wirths is transferred—to Neuengamme, according to office gossip.

I had been in Auschwitz for less than three weeks when I learned that a new SS garrison physician had arrived who was looking for German inmates to serve as clerks. Karl Lill, who had been transferred to Auschwitz together with me, and I were the only clerks in the HKB who were listed as Germans; most of the others were young German-speaking Poles. The two of us were ordered to go to the SS infirmary and had to wait in the office where a few SS men were sitting around idly. In my *Bericht* I described what followed:

> The door opens. The two SS men jump up and click their heels. A tall man wearing an officer's cap comes in. But that's Dr. Wirths from Dachau! He has already recognized me. Before his orderly, who is accompanying him, has a chance to say anything, Wirths calls out loudly: "Langbein— it can't be! I'll be darned! How did you get here?" And then he asks me about the condition of the patient who was laid up with chronic gastritis at the Dachau infirmary and of one who had articular rheumatism, whom he treated. Finally he turns to his top sergeant and says, "Langbein is going to be my clerk." Then he leaves. One of the SS men is offended, sits down, and says: "Since his arrival the SS garrison physician hasn't spoken with me as much as he has with these inmates."

This is how my employment by the SS garrison physician began, and it continued for almost two years until my transfer to Neuengamme on August 25, 1944, with two interruptions caused by typhus and detainment in the bunker.

■ The following description of Dr. Wirths was produced by Höß in the Cracow prison:

Before the war Wirths had an extensive rural practice as a general practitioner in the Baden hinterland. (His family's address, which I often wrote down, was Merchingen, postal district Osterburken). At the beginning of the war he was conscripted into the Waffen-ss as a physician and served at the front with various units. His indifference to personal risk caused him to develop a serious heart condition in Finland, and he could not be used at the front any more. Thus he served in the office of the inspector of concentration camps and then in the KL Auschwitz.

Wirths was a capable physician with a pronounced sense of duty, extremely conscientious and cautious. He had a comprehensive knowledge in all medical fields and always strove to expand his medical knowledge and ability. Yet he was very gentle and good natured and definitely needed strong support. He carried out all orders that he was given with painstaking care, and in cases of doubt he always made sure that they were correct.

Thus he always had the orders of Grabner's Polit. Dept. relating to camouflaged executions confirmed by me as a matter of principle before carrying them out. Grabner took this very amiss, and it was a permanent source of annoyance for him. Wirths often complained to me that he could not reconcile the killings demanded of him with his conscience as a physician and that this caused him a lot of suffering. He repeatedly requested another medical assignment from Lolling and the Reich physician, but to no avail. I had to keep getting him back on his feet by pointing to the harsh necessity of the orders issued by the RFSS. He also had scruples about the entire extermination of the Jews, and he often revealed these to me in confidence.

Höß made the following addition to this characterization: "W. was in a running fight with those in charge of construction because he constantly urged the improvement or replacement of the hygienic facilities, and if defects came to his attention, he did not relent until these were eliminated."

The permanent wrangling with the Construction Department was conducted in writing, and I remember it well. I repeatedly informed Wirths of bad conditions in buildings and reminded him of promises not kept by those in charge. Eventually Wirths requested a construction expert for our detail so that smaller jobs in the various inmate infirmaries might be prepared directly by his office. Thus Hanus Majer, a Jewish engineer from Czechoslovakia, joined us. He survived the camp.

To continue with Höß's characterization of Wirths: "Even Lolling admitted that W. was the best physician in any concentration camp, an admission he did not like to make. In my ten years of service in the concentration camp system, I never encountered a better one. In associating with the inmates, he was proper and attempted to do justice to them. In my opinion, he often was too good natured and above all too credulous. Also, his good nature frequently was exploited by the inmates, especially the female ones, to his detriment. He particularly favored the inmate physicians. In fact, I often had the impression that he treated them as colleagues. This caused considerable problems for the camp."

Höß concludes his description with these words: "W. was very companionable and very popular with his comrades. He helped everyone who came to see him and gave much medical assistance to the families of ss men as well. Everyone trusted him." In his characterizations of other ss leaders in Auschwitz, Höß used praise quite sparingly.

Even Maximilian Grabner, the director of the Political Department, with whom Wirths carried on a permanent feud and who tried to disparage Wirths in another context, had to make this admission in notes he prepared in Polish captivity: "Wirths was regarded as the only physician who got his camp epidemic-free and as the best physician in any of the camps."

There are testimonies by others as well. Thus ss camp leader Franz Hofmann made this statement: "When the physicians made selections in the camp, they had received orders from higher-ups. I have proof of this; I know it from a conversation with ss garrison physician Wirths, my good friend from our days in Dachau. We often had heart-to-heart talks. One day he came to me and said: 'Franz, I had another adventure today. I had to go up and see Höß, but before that I had a conversation with Aumeier and Grabner.' Wirths opposed the selection of inmates, saying that physicians were not there to make selections but to treat patients. The upshot of the matter was that Wirths told me a few days later: 'An order has come directly from Berlin, and now I have to do it.'"

At the Höß trial in Warsaw, Maria Stromberger, a nurse who worked in the ss infirmary, testified as a witness that someone reported her in early 1943. Wirths reproached her for treating the inmates too maternally and humanely, saying that he had heard this from several sources. Then he ended his admonishment: "I would not want you to be put behind the wire, and so I am warning you." She responded that she was neither an ss man nor a guard, and if her conduct was cause for criticism, she would ask for a transfer. Thereupon Wirths patted her on the shoulder and said: "Nurse Maria, you stay here, and I will protect you from any further slander."

▪ In the two years that we worked together, I got to know Wirths better than any other wearer of an ss uniform. Single-mindedly I worked toward gaining influence over him, and in this I was aided by the situation created by my employment.

If a physician in an ss uniform is not lazy and uninterested, he looks for a secretary who will think along with him; if a clerk wearing an inmate's garb is not egotistical and heartless, he will use the opportunities that this offers. Any intellectually active prisoner is superior to his guard because he constantly concerns himself with the problems that arise from his situation, whereas those who guard him are distracted by other issues. In the long run neither instructions nor warnings could keep a daily contact at work from deepening and becoming a personal relationship if that is what the inmate was aiming for. The relationship between Wirths and me is not an isolated exception. Thus Kogon writes: "Occasionally it was possible to turn higher-ranking ss leaders into tools of the inmates' self-government not only by corruption but also by direct political influence. These cases were extremely rare and involved a great risk. Such attempts were most likely to succeed with a certain kind of ss physician." Kogon was himself the secretary of an ss physician in Buchenwald, and thus he speaks from personal experience. Similar experiences were had by Walter Poller as the clerk of the physicians in Buchenwald and Ernst Martin as the clerk of the ss garrison physician of Mauthausen. However, to my knowledge no other ss physician went as far as Wirths did.

Several factors combined to produce this: Wirths's attitude toward the crimes committed in the concentration camps, which I was able to study in Dachau; his diligence, which made him look for a secretary who could also handle confidential messages and who had neither the dull indifference nor the limited intelligence of ss Sergeant Richter, the official clerk in his office; the attacks of other ss leaders to which he as an intellectual was subject (he once wrote that he often heard statements like this one: "You're one of those international eggheads, too!") — all this combined to further my aim to create a personal relationship between us and then use it for the benefit of the camp. By strictly adhering to two principles, I endeavored to make sure that I remained the active partner. As a matter of principle I never used my chances to secure something for myself; in that way I kept from being corrupted, and this impressed Wirths. I discussed every important step with Ernst Burger and later with the leadership of the resistance movement, and this protected me from becoming a privileged tool in the machinery of extermination. A conversation I had with Wirths in the early weeks bears witness to that. In my *Bericht* I wrote:

Wirths goes up to the desk again and sits down. He gives me a quizzical look: "Langbein, can I rely on you?"

"Herr Doktor, I shall help you to the best of my ability with anything that is useful for the inmates of this camp. You won't demand anything else of me. I'd like to leave the camp some day, but in such a way that I don't have to lose respect for myself."

We have never talked with each other like this. Wirths dictates a few more trivial things and then he is finished. I have taken a step on a very dangerous path. That evening I tell Ernstl about this conversation.

In another context I have outlined what could be achieved for the infirmaries in this way.

In an effort to avoid giving a one-sided picture of the man who probably was the most interesting personality in the ranks of the Auschwitz ss, I shall draw on the descriptions of others who got to know Wirths as inmates.

This is what Wladyslaw Fejkiel wrote about him:

In the inmate infirmary the changes began with the arrival of a new ss garrison physician. This position was taken over by ss Major Dr. E. Wirths, who came from Dachau. A few dozen Austrian and German communists who had worked as nurses in that camp arrived together with him. (Fejkiel made some minor mistakes. It is true that we knew Wirths from Dachau, but we did not come with him; he had served in Neuengamme for some time. There were only seventeen of us, and only the better-known men were communists.) It was a group of inmates who had a lot of experience in conspiracy and camp life and who worked well together. These inmates were favored by the ss garrison physician, who was a Nazi but hated criminals with an elemental passion. The new arrivals quickly familiarized themselves with the Auschwitz atmosphere, established contact with the group of Polish democrats, and with the aid of the ss garrison physician produced a sort of revolt in the infirmaries.

Fejkiel's statement confirms the following passage from the apologia composed by Wirths after the war: "It is all but unimaginable that the innocent political prisoners, irrespective of their persuasion, were supervised in the camp by men who had committed serious crimes. At all times and in all places, I proposed that these felons be replaced with the so-called politicals, innocent men of good character whose ranks included the Jews. The reason this proposal met with opposition was that the leaders viewed this as a strengthening of their political opponents. In the infirmaries I did not tolerate having imprisoned criminals in leading positions."

Fejkiel has provided a description of his first encounter with the ss garrison physician shortly after his transfer to Auschwitz; it took place when Wirths was inspecting the inmate infirmary.

He gained an insight into the organization and order, conversed with patients, and asked the physicians about their methods of treatment. The impression he made on me was different from that of the other ss men. After inspecting the infection section, he called me and arranged to have the section receive several hundred cans of meat as a one-time gift, which one would not have expected from an ss man. In the evening we picked up the canned meat, took it to the block, and pondered the significance of this occurrence. After all, the whole thing looked suspicious.

I had never trusted the ss, never believed in its good will and benevolence. After our experiences with phenol and gas, we could hardly believe that the ss garrison physician had sent those cans for the nourishment of the patients. I suspected that this was a new method of getting rid of the sick, and this assumption was reinforced by the fact that Wirths had expressly stated that the canned meat was for the exclusive use of typhus patients and could not be given to other patients or nurses.

Doubts gnawed at me. Together with my friends Stanislaw Glowa, Stanislaw Klodzinski, and Tadeusz Szymanski, I considered what was to be done. Caution prevailed, and we retained the cans with the intention of secretly throwing them away. However, during the night some patients pounced on the cans and ate the meat. In the morning they felt all right. We waited until evening to see whether symptoms of poisoning would show up. Nothing of the kind happened, and so we were finally able to distribute the cans.

Testifying before the Frankfurt judges, Fejkiel characterized Wirths as "an intelligent physician and not a bad person. He brought medicines and knew how to combat typhus." Dr. Kurt Uhlenbrook, Wirths's immediate predecessor as ss garrison physician, had fought typhus by having the lice gassed together with the patients. Fejkiel added that in the fall of 1943 Wirths got him released from the bunker, where he had been detained under suspicion of belonging to an underground organization.

Dr. Alina Brewda reminded me of an action that we took together and that had slipped my mind. She was a physician at the experimental Block 10, where a block elder named Margit was misusing her power and beating patients. After Brewda had called this to my attention, I induced Wirths to send for Brewda and have her describe the situation to him. He relieved the block elder of her duties; but he felt constrained about appointing Dr. Brewda as her successor because Dr. Brewda was a Jew. Thus he ordered, without further ado, that the position of block elder remain vacant and that the deputy block elder report to the physician in charge—that is, Dr. Brewda.

I have already reported that Dr. Wirths broke with the taboo and appointed inmate physicians to key positions, including camp elders, in the infirmaries.

Teddy Pietrzykowski, a Pole who worked in the SS infirmary, was once whipped by Irma Grese, an SS warden, because he had not taken off his cap to her. Wirths, who observed this, warned the warden in front of the inmate: "Don't beat my people!"

The Pole Irena Idkowiak came to Auschwitz with her parents at the age of nineteen. After the death of her parents, Wirths pulled her out of the camp by requisitioning her as a maid. After the end of the war, she stayed on in the home of the Wirths family for a few months and in the fall of 1945 testified as follows: "I declare herewith (with reference to an oath taken) that Dr. Wirths always stood up for the inmates in a humane fashion and that thanks to his vigorous fight against epidemics and his self-sacrificing care thousands of inmates were kept alive. His care was so great that wives of SS complained that Herr Doktor Wirths preferred the inmates to them. I emphasize again that I heard only good things about Dr. Wirths from my fellow inmates."

When Karl Lill, a communist who had been transferred from Dachau to Auschwitz along with me and replaced me as the SS garrison physician's clerk after my transfer, was asked about Wirths by the presiding judge at the Frankfurt trial, he testified as follows:

> Lill: "I knew Dr. Wirths from Dachau. He was a man who treated the patients there like a real physician would, and he endeavored to do good work."
>
> Judge: "Did he effect improvements in Dachau? Did he stop the capricious injections of sick inmates?"
>
> Lill: "There is no doubt that this happened because of him."
>
> Judge: "Was there a conflict between him and Dr. Entress?"
>
> Lill: "Sure. Entress was a medical monster."
>
> Judge: "Some witnesses here have described Dr. Wirths as arrogant. Is it your impression that such an arrogance might perhaps have been just a pose?"
>
> Lill: "Yes, that is how I perceived it."

Despite frequent disappointments Wirths constantly strove to stir up his superiors. From time to time he had to write reports for Berlin, and this is what Höß, who had to initial these reports, said about them:

> In his monthly medical reports to D III and the Reich physician SS, Wirths described in minute detail, in a clear style, and with the most unsparing

frankness the exact health conditions, the state of all the hygienic and sanitary facilities, and the defects that had developed. In each of these reports Wirths begged for help in eliminating this rough and subsequently horrendous general condition of the camp. Everyone who read these reports could gain a realistic insight into these conditions. In his oral reports to D III and the Reich physician SS, Wirths did not pull his punches and gave unsparing accounts. When Pohl requested, via D III, special reports about epidemics — for example, when the high death rate gave him pause — Wirths's presentation was so blunt and, above all, emphasized the causes of all these bad conditions so unambiguously that his reports often seemed too overstated even to me. However, I did not rein Wirths in. These medical reports never produced any perceptible help for Auschwitz, but no responsible higher authority could remain in the dark about the catastrophic conditions in the KL Auschwitz and no leader, not even the RSHA, could ever claim to have heard nothing about them.

Wirths dictated his monthly reports to me and also had me collect the documentation for them. I drew the SS garrison physician's attention to inaccuracies and whitewashings in the reports from the individual camps, and I frequently pointed out problems that he then included in his reports. Our collaboration was so smooth that on one occasion, when the deadline for submitting the monthly report was near and he was busy with other things, he told me to work up a report by myself "as usual" on the basis of documents and present it to him for his signature. He sent this report off unchanged even though it was a bit more pointed than usual.

At a later date Wirths wrote about this collaboration that "from the beginning of my work I dictated to a prisoner whom I knew well all reports with figures in the silent hope that this would make these figures known. Also, in my monthly reports I described conditions in the camp in accordance with the actual situation."

I had to overcome doubts about whether the Central Office should be informed so openly. There might be a negative reaction — for example, something like this: if the overcrowding of the camp produces such atrocious conditions, then we have to step up the gassing of the inmates in order to gain some space. The leadership of our organization discussed this, and we concluded that prettifying reports might have more deleterious consequences than realistic ones. We were under no illusions about the effectiveness of even completely unvarnished reports because I knew the noncommittal responses to Wirths's pleas for help that kept coming from Berlin. Hence I must agree with Höß when he writes: "He (Dr. Lolling, the SS garrison physician's superior) probably visited Auschwitz most often, but I never saw him take any action on the basis of his extensive inspections. Any sanitary or medical improvements made in Auschwitz were the work of the camp physicians themselves. Dr. Wirths often bitterly complained to me that he received absolutely no help and understanding from Lolling."

Nevertheless, these reports probably had a certain effect when the war situation worsened for the Germans, which made them more sensitive to news about the extermination system of Auschwitz that was disseminated by the Allies.

■ The most terrible burden that was imposed on every physician in the extermination camp by the SS leadership was to decide who would be gassed at selections. Several witnesses have testified about Wirths's conduct as the chief of all SS physicians in Auschwitz.

His friend Dr. Horst Fischer told the court that in the spring of 1943 Wirths managed to have the selections of arriving transports made by responsible SS physicians rather than the SS camp leader and his subordinates. According to Fischer, Wirths effected this change because he observed the leaders making selections too rigorously and sending even able-bodied prisoners to the gas. Wirths used the same arguments in explaining his initiative to his brother. In his apologia he wrote: "I had to burden the physicians serving under me with this terrible reality by asking the camp leadership to consult the physicians on decisions about fitness for work."

Wirths did not impose this burden only on his subordinates but insisted that he himself be periodically assigned to ramp duty, just like any other SS physician. If he was ever unable to perform it, he made up for it later.

His attitude toward selections may be gleaned from a letter he addressed to the SDG of the satellite camp Golleschau on November 16, 1943. Wirths points out that "the inmates who arrived on the latest transport of patients were horrendously uncared for . . . in particular, inmates with injuries wore exceptionally filthy bandages. Their wounds were neglected and soiled. When asked, the inmates stated that some of the bandages had not been changed in ten days." The SS garrison physician concluded his letter with these words: "I hold you fully responsible for these occurrences; and if this happens again, I may mete out the most severe punishments." Both this kind of threat on such an occasion and the reference to statements of prisoners are unusual. This letter proves that Wirths wanted to prevent the killing of the patients who were transferred from satellite camps because otherwise he would not even have been informed about their condition. I remember that Wirths dictated to me similar letters on a number of occasions.

Years later I became acquainted with letters written by Wirths from Auschwitz to his family. Here are some excerpts that shed light on his personality.

Auschwitz, Sept. 9, 1943—to his wife. Möckel (ss first lieutenant and chief of administration) has returned from Berlin and is very happy to be here again. He says that he does not want to go away again. So such creatures exist, too!

Auschwitz, Nov. 29, 1944—to his wife. You can imagine, my love, how beautiful it is for me that I won't have to do this terrible work again—in fact, that it no longer exists. (At that time the gassings were discontinued.)

Auschwitz, December 13, 1944. Dear Parents, you are wrong if you believe that it was I who produced the present great changes in Auschwitz. No, the order came from the very top. My arm still does not reach that far. The only credit that I might be entitled to is perhaps that I started the ball rolling by using every opportunity to pressure all the high-ranking people who were accessible to me, pointing out to them that the whole process is inhumane, impossible, and truly shameful, that I have attempted in every way to paint this terrible burden in the most glaring colors in order to show those persons what they have saddled our whole people with and continue to encumber it with for as long as there is no change, particularly during such a terrible war.

It is a wonderful satisfaction for me that I was able to hear, after my return, this clear, unambiguous decision made in Berlin and to take along the complete rejection and even prohibition of such things. We breathed a sigh of relief that I can't even describe to you. You, dear father, know what my thoughts are. There is no denying the guilt.

This letter bears the notation: "Please don't preserve this letter." Nonetheless, it was preserved twice: by Wirths's father and by the resistance organization in Cracow, for Wirths dictated it to his clerk Karl Lill, who gave a carbon copy to that organization.

■ On other occasions, too, Wirths shouldered the burden of responsibility when he had a chance to take some helpful action. He mentioned such an initiative in his apologia:

The Gestapo frequently staged courts-martial, and after the verdict almost 100 percent of those sentenced were shot. When prisoners drew my attention to those sessions, I requested permission to participate in them as a physician to decide psychiatric cases. These sessions involved exclusively Polish citizens who were accused of sabotage. In many cases my medical judgment prevented a death sentence; I was often able to accomplish this by pointing out that the defendant's physical condition enabled him to work.

In this way the men who had been sentenced were admitted to the camp as prisoners and preserved from death.

One such rescue can be verified. Jan Pilecki, the Polish clerk of Block 11, where the prisoners of the Gestapo waited for the court-martial, had observed that in sessions in which Dr. Wirths participated fewer defendants were sentenced to be shot. Since Pilecki had to call the prisoners in, he was able to observe Wirths's favorable influence. One day, when the Gestapo got its hands on Pilecki's fiancée, he asked me to induce Wirths to attend the next session of the tribunal. Wirths did so, and Pilecki instructed his fiancée how to behave; according to his observations, those prisoners had the best chance who looked the ss men in the eye as they answered their questions loudly and in good German. As a matter of fact, the woman was not shot, survived the camp, and married Pilecki after the liberation. Of his own accord Wirths assumed joint responsibility for the courts-martial in order to avert at least some death sentences.

There are some negative judgments on Wirths as well. Most of those that came to my attention are either by prisoners who did not know him personally but were only familiar with his uniform and function or by ss men who as usual attempted to whitewash themselves in a courtroom at the expense of people no longer alive.

■ I have often asked myself how that man had come to wear an ss uniform. On one occasion Wirths told me this: "I am not a Nazi, for I am a physician and as such an individualist." From his personal papers I learned that he was born in Würzburg in 1909 and joined the ss on May 1, 1933. That he was not raised in the spirit of Nazism at home I learned from his private letters. In his apologia Wirths wrote:

> In the summer of 1930 I started my medical studies and passed my *Physikum* in Würzburg in the academic year 1932–33. For further studies a certificate of political reliability was required, and I was described as unreliable because I sympathized with the SPD. In an effort to avoid the threat of expulsion from the university and interruption of my studies, I applied for admission to the SA. I served for only abut four weeks in June and July, but I was not admitted. Service in the SA had to be accomplished in my parents' place of residence, Geroldshausen near Würzburg. To enable me to continue my studies, I applied in October 1934 for admission to an ss medical unit in Würzburg. As a candidate for the ss, I served in that unit until January 1935 and then went on leave to prepare for the *Staatsexamen* and get more professional training. As a consequence I always remained a candidate for the ss.

The dates in this statement are at variance with the ones I remember from Wirths's personal papers, and so this apologia stirred doubts in me. I therefore later asked his brother, and he told me that it was the fine uniform that had prompted Eduard Wirths to join the SS. If a man wanted to study and advance in those days, he had to be a member of an organization of the NSDAP, but the SA was too plebeian and disagreeable.

Wirths owed his appointment as SS garrison physician of Auschwitz to his good reputation as a physician. All the previous SS garrison physicians had failed to combat the typhus epidemic, which gave the physician in charge of all concentration camps headaches because it spread to the SS contingent and the civilian population, or else they had taken sick themselves and dropped out. Wirths wrote that when he was appointed SS garrison physician, Lolling told him that his exclusive task would be the combating of the typhus and typhoid fever epidemic among the SS garrison. Other duties would not be his concern. According to Johann Schindler, who had a good overview of the general picture as the top sergeant of the guard unit, there were about fifty cases of typhoid among the SS.

After the war Wirths asserted that when he was confronted with the system of extermination, he turned to Höß in despair. The commandant pointed out that Auschwitz was an extermination camp and medical help did not matter. According to Wirths, the numbers of deaths and the chaotic hygienic conditions brought him to the verge of suicide.

When Wirths was confronted with the system of the Nazi concentration camps for the first time in Dachau, he turned to a clergyman of his acquaintance, Father Wolfram Denser of Munich, for counsel. After the War Denser confirmed that he had told Wirths that it was his duty to continue working in the KZ and to do as much good in the medical field as he could. In view of the daily mass murder in Auschwitz, Wirths again sought counsel, this time from his father, and again the response was that he ought to stay and help wherever this was possible. Years later the aged father repeatedly urged me to respond to the tormenting question of whether he had given his son the right advice.

In my Bericht, which I wrote when I knew neither Father Denser's testimony nor the answer of Wirths's father, I have described a critical moment. On the basis of my information about the shootings at the Black Wall, Wirths complained to the head of the Political Department. The formal occasion was the fact that in the reports sent to Berlin the murdered inmates were listed as having died of some fictitious illness rather than as having been executed. At that time Wirths strove to reduce the death rate, and in this endeavor he was able to refer to an order from the Central Office. This is what I wrote in my Bericht:

Yesterday Wirths was very nervous and curt. Today he dictates to me a letter to Lolling, his boss, in which he applies for a transfer from Auschwitz. As his reason for doing so, he states that ss Second Lieutenant Grabner, the director of the Political Department, describes his conduct to the commandant as unworthy of an ss leader—surely in connection with the reports of deaths in Block II.

While I am tapping this letter out on my typewriter, I must do some thinking. Did Wirths deliberately dictate this letter to me rather than to ss Sergeant Richter, who always has to write letters dealing with internal matters of the ss? Does Wirths want us inmates to know about this? Does he really still believe in Hitler's victory? Also, his transfer would be a great blow to our organization. Who knows who will succeed him. Surely it won't be someone who can be as effectively influenced as Wirths. By now I know at least two dozen ss physicians from Dachau and Auschwitz; none of them is like Wirths, and I have not been able to achieve as much with any of them.

I wait until he is alone in his room and then take the letter to him. He looks at me quizzically.

"Here is the letter to D III, Herr Doktor." He nods and reads the letter with his fountain pen in his hand. Then he signs it with his big slanted letters. He looks up again and seems surprised that I am still here. "I don't have anything more to write, thank you."

"May I speak quite openly with you, Herr Doktor?" He leans back, and I stand before him. "I wanted to ask you not to send this letter."

"Well, I can't possibly put up with this."

"In making this request I have primarily us inmates in mind."

We look at each other for a long time. I'd like to know whether he desired or expected it, but I can't make it out. "It's all right, Langbein. You can always speak frankly with me; you don't need to ask."

I never found out whether Wirths sent that letter off. In any case, he stayed. He was obviously referring to that letter when he wrote this in his apologia: "On many occasions the inmates of the camp urged me so ardently not to give up my work and leave my post—because otherwise there would be no one to protect their lives—that I could not evade this task of preserving the lives of many tens of thousands of human beings for reasons of egotism and my own health without causing the most serious moral dilemmas."

When I spoke to Wirths in that vein, I was not thinking of burdening him morally but only of us inmates.

Wirths received the same advice from all sides. With his willpower and intelligence, he would surely have found a way of leaving Auschwitz on one pretext or another, but he stayed and was able to achieve positive things:

The lethal injections in the infirmaries were stopped; the most dangerous murderers in his department, Entress and Klehr, were removed from their key positions in the main camp; epidemics were brought under control; the supervision of nutrition was improved; responsible prisoners were given influential positions in the inmate infirmary, and inmate physicians were entrusted with medical tasks; steps were taken against the mistreatment of inmates if this was discovered at their admission to the infirmary; and, finally, Wirths was able to influence the second commandant, Liebehenschel, whose reforms eliminated or alleviated many bad conditions. All this gave meaning to Wirths's continued presence in the camp.

■ During the entire period, however, the SS garrison physician of Auschwitz performed the tasks assigned to the physicians in the program of destruction. Even he was not able to evade the influence of the murderous atmosphere exuded by Auschwitz. I sensed that he might become disheartened, and in an effort to encourage him I asked Zbyszek at Christmastime 1943 to prepare a card with fancy lettering that said that 93,000 prisoners owed their lives to his activities. There also was a quotation from Grillparzer: "*Ein Menschenleben, ach, es ist so wenig, ein Menschenschicksal aber ist so viel!*" (One human life, alas, it is so little, but one human fate is so much!). The messenger Emil, who had access to Wirths's apartment, put this card on a table. This was the thinking that led me to the number given above: if the mortality rate in 1943 had remained as high as it was in the summer of 1942, before Wirths came to Auschwitz, it would have been necessary to register 93,000 more deaths. It was a rather theoretical calculation, but it was perceptibly effective. Wirths gave the card to his father, and after the war, when he was waiting in Hamburg to be interrogated by British officers, he wrote his wife on May 24, 1945. "If only my father could help us! I gave him two additional documents. We received a Christmas card in 1943, didn't we?"

I soon took another step. The occasion was the agitation among the SS that was caused by a London broadcast inspired by us. It gave the names and exact personal data of members of the SS who occupied key positions in the machinery of death. They were threatened with the death penalty. As I knew from personal papers, Frau Wirths was celebrating her birthday at that time. This is what I wrote in my *Bericht*:

We obtained flowers from inmates who worked in the Garden Center and had an artist who was laid up in the infirmary paint a picture of her and the children on the basis of a photo (Fejkiel remembers the artist's name:

Mieczyslaw Koscielnak), and we sent everything to Wirths's home via our Czech runner Emil.

Early the next morning Wirths rings for me. "Please write . . . ," and then he dictates the results of his examination of a female warden whom he saw at the clinic. He dictates the last sentences fast, and I am still writing when he has finished. Okay, now I have got it down, and I want to get up, but he bends across the desk. "Tell me, Langbein, do you know about the picture and the flowers?" "Yes." "Why did you do it? This puts me to shame." "The painting has its significance, Herr Doktor."

His face is flushed, and he gives me a quizzical look. "You know, Herr Doktor, that a death sentence has been pronounced on you and your family, too." I pause, and he is silent. I sense that he knows about it, and he does not show any surprise. "The picture is meant to indicate that the death sentence has been revoked." "Yes, but how—I mean, where do you know that from?"

"I have the right to inform you. I am not saying this in my name."

It's quiet. The statistics on the wall show, in red and black zigzag, the number of inmates in the camp and the decline of the death rate. I can hear him breathe.

"That's good. But are my children to blame? And my wife?"

Quiet again. "I have to thank you, Langbein."

"Not me, Herr Doktor."

When I walk out the door, I snap to military attention, as I always do. Now, this is no more than a formality.

This was our plan: Wirths should know that he is dealing with an organization and not just with me. He can take no action against us because he learned about us at the same time as he was informed of the fact that we want to save him and his family. He loves his family and wants them to live. You are our tool now, ss garrison physician!

Wirths does not mention this episode in his apologia; he only writes that he "always cooperated closely with inmates I knew well, particularly Hermann Langbein, who informed me about bad conditions and the undermining of my activities by the leadership of the camp."

It is part of Wirths's personality profile that he and his family lived on his food ration coupons. We learned this from the female Jehovah's Witness who worked in his household. In this he was a lone exception in the jungle of corruption.

■ However, even Wirths could not resist the temptation of misusing for experimental purposes the "human material" of Auschwitz that was destined to die. He had been ordered to satisfy Professor Clauberg's and Dr. Schumann's needs for guinea pigs. Many women were transferred to Block 10 to be at the disposal of those two as "rabbits." In cooperation with his brother, a gynecologist in Hamburg, Wirths wanted to find a method of diagnosing uterine cancer early. At a later date the brother testified that Eduard Wirths had started colposcopic experiments "on his own initiative": "The specimens—a small number, in my estimation—were sent to the laboratory at our clinic in Altona, where they were examined by Dr. Hanselmann." In a conversation the brother assured me that these experiments were absolutely harmless. Physicians who were not themselves involved in these experiments also stated that taking tissue samples from the uterine orifice was not medically injurious. However, apart from the fact that the procedures were painful, as attested to by the nurses on the block, Wirths must have realized that the very undertaking of an experiment in the KZ constituted an extraordinary emotional burden for any woman. Was there anyone in that place who could believe assurances that these were brief and harmless surgical procedures when those who performed experiments intended to produce permanent sterility also said, if they said anything at all, that everything was completely harmless?

In the experimental block Wirths met Maximilian Samuel, an inmate physician, and involved him in his experiments. When Samuel was killed, Wirths must have known about it. In that block the SS garrison physician also met the French physician Adelaide Hautval, who had refused to participate in human experiments. As I have already mentioned, Wirths used anti-Semitic arguments to convince her that experiments on Jewish women were permissible, but she stood firm and was not punished.

In my view, the darkest chapter in his activity as the SS garrison physician of Auschwitz is an episode in which "only" two human beings had to die (by Auschwitz dimensions, a bagatelle) but that incriminates Wirths more than anything else. After I had assured Wirths by means of the family picture that we were prepared to protect him, this is what happened (as recorded in my Bericht):

> In the infection block 20, two small rooms on the ground floor are being cleared—"for experiments," says Hans (Sauer), and as the block elder he ought to know. Experiments? Wirths told me nothing about experiments. Every evening I look at the rooms. It is strictly forbidden to enter them. I pass the doorkeeper and the nurse as though it were the most natural thing, and neither man dares to keep the clerk of the SS garrison physician from entering the rooms. On this evening the rooms are occupied. Four Jews, all of them healthy, are lying in them. I go to see the camp elder of the infirmary (Fejkiel).

"Say, what's happening with the Jews in the two rooms in Block 20?" "I mustn't tell you." "It's all right to tell me." "The ss garrison physician expressly ordered me not to discuss it with anyone, including you. So you mustn't report me. Those four Jews are being given typhus artificially. The ss garrison physician wants to try out a new remedy, but we no longer have patients with typhus in the camp. He sent me to Birkenau, but there I didn't find anyone suffering from typhus in the whole infirmary."

"Have they already been infected?" "Yes, they were yesterday. Wirths himself was here."

I am thinking: should I speak with Wirths about it? Yes, I have to talk with him; such a step might be followed by others. I must keep him in check. I wait for a moment when I am alone with him and he has time.

"Herr Doktor, may I say something?" "Yes."

A familiar opening, but what follows has never before been discussed by us.

"Yesterday I was in Block 20 in the two rooms that you filled with four Jews." "How come you know abut this?" His voice is unpleasantly harsh.

"Herr Doktor, there are few things in the camp that we don't hear about." I emphasize the word "we." "So?" "The four now have typhus, but they were healthy when they came to the infirmary." "I have received a new medicine for typhus, and it is probably very effective. It benefits science and also the inmates when an effective remedy against typhus is available."

"Four human beings are lying in the two rooms. Last night they had a high fever."

Wirths's face is quite red. "Am I the ss garrison physician or are you?" He pounds the table with his fist in a real rage. He has never spoken to me like this.

"You are, Herr Doktor." I ready my shorthand pad and remain silent, waiting for him to dictate.

"I don't need you any more." Have I gone too far? Can he be a danger to me? Can he still be a danger to anyone?

The next day I respond to all his orders with a strictly military "Jawohl." Once, as he dictates, he makes a remark that is supposed to lead to a conversation, but I don't take the bait. Between two letters he pauses for a long time; I have the impression that he wants me to start a conversation, but I bend mutely over my shorthand pad. I mustn't display any weakness on my side. He has to take the initiative. As I leave the room I stand at attention more snappily than usual.

In the afternoon the time has come. "Did you see those four yesterday? How are they doing?" He asks this question suddenly while dictating a letter to the Construction Department concerning the installation of water pipes in the new buildings of Birkenau that are to be populated in the near future.

"*Jawohl*. They are not doing well." "Are they getting enough to eat?" "Typhus patients have no appetite." He avoids eye contact with me. Is he ashamed?

"Herr Doktor, you shouldn't make it so hard for me to help you." "Why? What do you mean?" "I am referring to that picture. I stood up for you."

His fingers play on the glass top of the desk. "This will be the last time, Langbein, that this sort of thing has happened in the camp. Does that suffice for you?"

"Yes." So he can't step out of line anymore. If the Red Army were still fighting in Stalingrad and had not reached the Polish border, this conversation would have ended differently. Two of the four infected Jews have died, and I have informed Wirths of this.

In my view, this experiment, which resulted in two murders, is weightier than all the things he did in the machinery of killing on orders. Every experiment on human beings must be debited to his personal account as guilt. Wirths failed most spectacularly at experiments. It is no accident that most damning judgments have come from female occupants of the experimental block. For example, Jeanne Salomon has described Wirths as "a man of exceptional courtesy but a real sadist of the worst kind."

My *Bericht* also includes this account of my last conversation with Wirths:

This morning a very excited Emil takes me to the radio in the SS garrison physician's office (where we regularly listened to the BBC from London before the SS reported for duty). The SS is still asleep. The speaker makes this clear and unmistakable statement: "Romania has capitulated and the southern front is open." We stand behind Wirths's desk and look at each other. I have to think of Austria.

The weather is fine. The SS men come along at a leisurely pace. They don't know yet. Wirths rings; he, too, is clueless. How he reacts to this news will enable me to gauge his true political orientation better than before.

"Herr Doktor, have you heard that Romania has declared war on Germany?"

"Yes, it has gone over to the Russian side."

"You don't say! Where did you hear that?"

"We in the camp always know everything a bit sooner."

"That's bad news."

"It means that the war is definitely lost now." I almost said "definitely won."

"Do you really mean that?"

"Of course."

"But we stopped the Russians conclusively at the Vistula."

"How often have you stopped the Russians conclusively in the past two years? With their next offensive they are going to be here in Auschwitz, and that means in Upper Silesia as well. There is no firm front in the East or the West. Herr Doktor, the war is definitely lost."

"But that's terrible."

"It is good, Herr Doktor."

"How can you say such a thing? After all, you are a German, too."

"I am thinking of the drawing you once showed me. The projected expansion of Auschwitz. The enlargement of the camp after the victory. Both of us know Auschwitz. Isn't it good that it can no longer be expanded?"

Wirths once showed me this blueprint, and when I asked him when this expansion of the camp was to be accomplished, he replied: "After the war, when we shall need even bigger camps." Now he doesn't answer for a time, and his head is lowered.

"Then all my work for the military hospital would come to naught."

"Of course." In recent months Wirths has concerned himself particularly with establishing an ss military hospital. It is a source of pride to him and is to be opened in a few weeks; Pohl and Lolling are coming for the festive inauguration, and Wirths is counting on being promoted to the rank of ss major on that day. He stops talking, and his hand lies feebly on the table.

"Only one thing has not come to naught: our work here in the camp and our help for the people here." Wirths does not respond. No, he has not reached the point where I can include him in plans to escape.

On the next morning I was, at the behest of the commandant and to my surprise, assigned to a transport that left the camp. Karl Lill took over my duties as Wirths's clerk.

This, too, is part of Wirths's picture: he feared a defeat of Nazism even though he had become acquainted with its true face more distinctly than anyone else. As I gathered from another conversation, he clung to the very end to the insane notion that the Führer did not know about all the things that were happening in the places of extermination. He probably needed this idea to justify his membership in the Nazi movement to himself.

■ When the Russian front was approaching Auschwitz, the resistance organization learned about a plan to kill the sick inmates and those unable to march at the evacuation. Lill spoke about this with Wirths, who confirmed the existence of such a plan but also said that he had managed to have the inmates who could not be transported left behind alive. This actually happened. True, after the evacuation there were several instances in which inmates were killed by returning SS units, but most of those who had been left behind in the camp were liberated by Russian troops on January 27, 1945.

In his apologia Wirths wrote: "I succeeded in saving numerous sick prisoners from the intended killing to be done at the eventual clearance of the concentration camp Auschwitz."

Wirths was transferred to other camps and at the end of the war was able to make his way to Hamburg, where his brother lived. From there he wrote to his wife on May 24, 1945: "If due to human inadequacy and a lack of mental clarity I was unable to recognize in time the true face of this period, this may also have been God's will, because later, when I was given superhumanly difficult tasks, I applied my strength to helping and saving whatever I could in order to snatch it from destruction."

In another letter Wirths wrote: "In the meantime we have arranged for me to speak with the English, but I shall have to wait for a decision until Monday. And then there is no telling how everything will develop. Oh, what wouldn't I give if I had one of my familiar prisoners from A. here who could bear witness for me in this terribly difficult undertaking! With the best conscience it is a difficult step because it is hardly possible to foresee to what extent the other side will understand the difficulty of my task, whether it will be able to appreciate how heavily the hard pressure weighed on me, and all the things that caused, and still cause, so many headaches."

Wirths was arrested by the British. Years later Colonel Draper, who interrogated him, described to me what followed. He had Wirths brought before him, extended his hand, and said: "Now I have shaken hands with the person who as the physician in charge at Auschwitz is responsible for the deaths of four million human beings. Tomorrow I shall interrogate you about this. Reflect during the night about your responsibility and look at your hands."

During that night Wirths hanged himself. He was cut down before he was dead and did not die until a few days later, on September 20, 1945.

When I told Colonel Draper almost twenty years later what role Wirths had played in Auschwitz, he asked me whether he had acted incorrectly then. I said that he had not. Draper was familiar with Auschwitz and Wirths's function there, but did not know any details. Around the same time I spoke with Wirths's widow, and she said that it was probably best for her husband that he had ended his life. I agreed.

SUBORDINATES OF
THE SS LEADERS
■ ■ ■

The vast majority of the thousands of ss members who served under the leaders of Auschwitz have remained unknown. Only those who stood out from the mass by virtue of their special functions or striking behavior were remembered by the inmates. In the case of persons who had to answer to a court, the testimonies of witnesses have been collected. I shall present portraits of some of these ss men here.

The members of the ss who served in the dreaded Political Department were different from those who served as sentries.

The most feared man was ss Technical Sergeant Wilhelm Boger. He was born in Württemberg in 1906 and at the age of sixteen joined the Nazi youth movement, which was largely unknown at that time. When Hitler came to power, this loyal vassal was made a member of the auxiliary police.

"Boger loved his profession—he was a criminologist. He had to work. If he had no interrogation scheduled, he rode his bicycle to the camp and looked for something. He always found something." This statement was made by Dounia Ourisson-Wasserstrom, who served Boger as an interpreter. He enjoyed spreading fear and terror. The most dreaded instrument of torture was called the Boger swing. Grabner later testified that Boger had learned this torture from a Gestapo official who had come to Auschwitz for interrogations and introduced right then and there the swing, which involved having the unprotected genitals of the victim bared for directed blows. When Liebehenschel prohibited its use, Boger said: "How can these pigs be made to talk if they can't be hit?"

One could observe in Boger a general phenomenon: if an ss man had become personally acquainted with an inmate, thereby detaching him from the gray, anonymous mass, human feelings came to the fore that were otherwise totally lacking.

Witold Dowgint-Nieciunski saw Boger daily because he was a cleaner in the commandant's building, where Boger had an office. There he had good opportunities to observe what went on, and later he testified in detail in court about Boger's crimes. "I have to remark," he said, "that Boger acted very properly toward me. He interrogated me once and did not beat me. He also cared a great deal about flowers and saw to it that they were watered." Nieciunski was a Pole, and Boger, who hated that nation with a passion, primarily hunted Polish inmates.

Boger also took care of the Jewish women who had to work for him. "He made sure that we received an additional kettle of food," said Regina Steinberg-Lebensfeld. And Maryla Rosenthal testified as follows: "I was Boger's clerk, and Boger treated me very decently. He would leave some food in his mess kit and say, 'Maryla, this is to be cleaned.' He really was not allowed to do this. In winter he got me warm clothes and shoes."

In his own way he occasionally "consoled" girls who worked for him. This is what Lilly Majerczyk remembered. "As bearers of secrets we had to expect to be gassed. On one occasion, after Boger had made a remark about the threatening defeat of Germany, I asked him, 'Herr Oberscharführer, what will happen to us then?' He answered, 'That's not so bad; three minutes and you're gone.'"

Boger spread terror even among the guards. ss Sergeant Karl Hykes testified that Boger was almost as dangerous to the ss people as to the inmates. "If he found that an ss man had some contact with an inmate, he also proceeded against the ss man."

Boger frequently had to conduct investigations of ss men because they had appropriated the property of inmates, but this did not keep him from taking whatever he needed, just like his boss Grabner. In this pursuit he fully exploited his position. One day Jiri Beranovsky was locked up in the bunker. His friend, the capo on the Installations Center Detail, intervened with Boger, who happened to be looking for an enamel bathtub for an apartment he was furnishing in Auschwitz. An official request would have brought him only a stone tub, but the capo supplied the desired kind and Beranovsky was released from the bunker.

On another occasion Boger needed a five-liter kettle for boiling his laundry, and he asked for one from Tadeusz Jakubowski, who was working in the storeroom; but that inmate saw no way of fulfilling Boger's wish. As a consequence he was arrested for smuggling and so severely tortured in the Political Department that he died. Then Boger expressed the same wish to Stanislaw Pawliczek, the clerk in the storeroom. Since the latter was prohibited from supplying anything without an order form, he requested one. Boger said that he did not have one, but he could invite Pawliczek for a brief conversation, as he had recently done with Jakubowski. Thereupon the clerk asked only when and where he should take the desired kettle. Boger's wife accepted it, and Boger left Pawliczek in peace.

It is typical of Boger and many of his colleagues that they defended themselves against this kind of testimony much more vigorously than against accusations of murder, even though they could no longer be charged with appropriations, blackmail, and similar crimes. According to the SS code of ethics, these were regarded as dishonorable, but tortures and killings were not.

Boger's depredations did not remain hidden from his superiors. In an effort to undermine his position, the resistance movement in the camp once arranged to have an anonymous letter to the commandant sent from the outside that listed the valuables unlawfully appropriated by Boger and stated where they could be found. We watched for the consequences of this report, but neither Boger's zeal nor his position were affected.

Boger, who enjoyed making everyone tremble, was himself beset by fears and was repeatedly laid up as a patient in the SS infirmary. Edward Pys, who had to clean the sickrooms and serve the patients, thinks that Boger suffered from a nervous disorder. "Once I had to bring him a bottle of apple juice," Pys said. "When I entered his room, I saw that the bottle had already been opened. Boger screamed at me, and I had to bring him another bottle, which I had to open in his presence."

■ The most distinctive personality among the members of the Political Department was Pery Broad. The course of his life is itself out of the ordinary. He was born in 1921 in Rio de Janeiro, and his father, whose family had come from England, was a Brazilian citizen. At age four Broad and his German mother moved to Berlin, where he joined the Hitler Youth and began his studies at the Technical Institute.

Anton van Velsen states that "Broad was much more intelligent than Boger; he did not fit into the general picture of the SS." Jenny Spritzer remembers that "we never knew what to expect from Broad. He was friendly and intelligent, but he often asked us catch questions." Dounia Ourisson-Wasserstrom describes Broad as follows: "He was young, smart, and crafty. I never knew what he was thinking, whether he felt compassion for us or hated us. It seemed as if he did not take the occurrences in Auschwitz seriously." This is indirectly confirmed by van Velsen, who as a block elder in the Gypsy camp had close contact with Broad. "He was always in my room; I had a map on the wall there, and we checked the progress of the front on it. That was our hope. Broad took no action against it. Once it was rumored that I had money, and Broad found Polish zlotys. He confiscated the money but took no further action."

This idiosyncratic SS man, who only achieved the rank of corporal, had books by Molière and Racine on his desk, took Russian lessons from female inmates in his department, and was exceptionally musical—something that has been confirmed by the French musicians Simon Laks and René Coudy. He regularly visited the orchestra of which these two were members and occasionally played with it. Laks and Coudy believe that he could have played his accordion in a first-rate orchestra, and they describe him in these words: "He is very cultivated and speaks several languages fluently." Van Velsen reports that Broad formed an orchestra in the Gypsy camp. The Dutchman remembers that "he loved jazz, which the SS decried as decadent." "Once, when I was standing behind the door in the barracks of the Political Department," writes Raya Kagan, "I heard him play a Bach concerto on his accordion."

Broad regularly participated in executions in the bunker. On one occasion Fritz Hirsch was locked up in a bunker cell, the vent of which faced the yard next to the Black Wall. "During the executions in the yard, this shaft, which went to the window in our cell, was covered up. Then the cover was removed, and Broad was standing before us. With a friendly smile he gave us a cigarette butt." Hirsch concludes his report as follows: "At that time I counted thirty-four shots."

Regina Steinberg-Lebensfeld, who was assigned to Broad as a clerk, remembers a conversation he once had on his return from the Black Wall: "He was with Lachmann, whose door to our room was open. Standing in the doorway Broad said to him: 'You know, Gerhard, it spurted out again today as from a beast.' He said this with a laugh. Then he gave me his coat for cleaning. It was spattered with fresh blood." When the defendant Broad was asked in court to respond to this testimony, all he said was this: "I always stood so far from the Black Wall that I could not be spattered." Steinberg also remembers that once Broad and Wilhelm Hoyer beat a prisoner on the swing until he fell off, all bloody and groaning. The prisoner was doused and taken out of the room, whereupon Steinberg had to remove the trail of blood from the floor.

Broad was transferred to the Gypsy camp and took Steinberg along as his secretary. She testified that once a boy of ten or twelve was brought to Broad's office. The child had arrived in Auschwitz on a transport of Hungarians and apparently had been able to escape selection by hiding. Amid tears the boy assured Broad, displaying his childlike hands, that he was strong and able to work. Broad just laughed, told the guard who had escorted the boy to take him to the others, and pointed in the direction of the gas chamber. Steinberg-Lebensfeld sums up her opinion in these words: "I have the impression that doing his duty gave him great satisfaction."

Other statements by witnesses conflict with that view. Edward Burakowski, a Pole, served in the Political Department as a cleaner. One day the Kattowitz Gestapo conducted interrogations in Auschwitz. "The inmates were flogged unmercifully," wrote Burakowski, "and Broad told me this: 'When the SS men of the Gestapo leave, bring some water for the people here.'" Broad called the Gestapo officials butchers and murderers. The same witness has also reported another incident: "Family members from the Jewish communities of the area were to be gassed. The people were escorted by German policemen, and an SS man from the commandant's office was at the head of the procession to show them the way. A high-ranking SS man walked up to Broad and said to him: 'Come along, quickly!' Broad pointed to his leg and acted like a sick man, whereupon the SS man laid off and took someone else. I had the impression that Broad only feigned his foot trouble. On that occasion Broad said to me: 'My hands are clean, and I don't want to have anything to do with this.'" At length he told Burakowski that he was going to absent himself as soon as he looked out the window and saw transports arriving. Burakowski was instructed to say that his boss was not there. To the best of the Polish witness's recollection, this transpired in the middle of 1943, when others did not yet impose restraints on themselves.

In British captivity this shady, intelligent man tried to curry favor with the victors and wrote a report about Auschwitz that is repeatedly quoted. Could someone who did not actually feel revulsion at the mass murders have composed it in this form? To be sure, at the Auschwitz trial in Frankfurt Broad's behavior was no different from that of the others. He denied whenever he could, was careful not to say anything bad about a codefendant, and took refuge in memory gaps where an outright denial would have been too implausible. At best he did all this somewhat more intelligently than his colleagues.

■ Two female inmates who worked in the Political Department have painted a vivid picture of one of these colleagues, SS Sergeant Bernhard Kristan, the director of the registry that was part of that department. Raya Kagan testified as follows: "He was from Königsberg and twenty-two years old at that time. I remember him as an especially convinced Nazi. We knew that he had been a high-ranking leader in the HJ (Hitler Youth) in East Prussia. He despised all Jews and strove almost frantically not to come into contact with us or with objects that we touched. For example, I still remember that he pressed the doorknobs of our rooms with his elbow rather than his hand." Julia Skodova writes this about Kristan: "He is a typical product of the HJ—cruel, bloodthirsty, and firmly convinced of Hitler's divinity. He does not have the slightest doubt that the Third Reich will rule all of Europe (this is still so in the spring of 1944), and he is equally convinced of his own importance and the important role that he will play in the historic events. He does not care that his actions make him hated. On the contrary, this hatred of the hounded is proof that the superiority of the 'masters' is recognized." The fact that Kristan, like so many other "high masters" of Auschwitz, had trouble with his writing completes this portrait.

Wilhelm Claussen also worked in the Political Department before he became an SS roll call leader. It sounded implausible when he asserted in American captivity that he was expelled from the SS "because of desertion and other things" and became an inmate of Buchenwald. He claimed that he had been transferred to Auschwitz from there, but as an SS man rather than as a prisoner. He said that his brother died as an inmate of the concentration camp Natzweiler in March 1943, when he already was a junior officer in Auschwitz. However, documents have been preserved that verify these statements.

It has been established that Wilhelm Claussen was interned in the Buchenwald camp as a political prisoner from November 21, 1940, to February 19, 1941. His brother Egon was taken to the KZ on April 1, 1941, and died there. The documents do not give the reasons for this internment. Grabner has described Claussen as a confidant of Höß who also had to report to the commandant about Grabner. Höß probably used Claussen's past to gain an informer.

■ Particulars about other defendants at the Frankfurt trial permit us to draw conclusions about the character of individuals who personify the inhumanity of the SS.

One of these figures is SS roll call leader Oswald Kaduk. He grew up in the part of Upper Silesia that was given to Poland after World War I and was twelve when Germany lost that war. "About my political development I can say that I have had a nationalistic orientation since my youth. This thinking along nationalistic lines was determined by the milieu at home and by the fact that I lived in an area where there were conflicts between Germans and Poles." In these words, which he spoke not nearly as fluently as they read here, Kaduk described his youth to the court with his harsh accent. The last camp elder of the main camp, Heinrich Dürmeyer, believes that Kaduk became a particularly "hard" SS roll call leader because as an ethnic German he wanted to prove that "he was an especially good German and a 150 percent SS man. The SS people called him a *Wasserpolak* [disrespectful term for a Polish-speaking Upper Silesian]." Jerzy Pozimski of the Labor Service, who was able to observe Kaduk rather closely, believes that feelings of inferiority vis-à-vis the "real" Germans prompted Kaduk to be, whenever he could, harsher, more brutal, and "harder" than they. Pozimski rounds off his characterization by saying that "schnapps was everything to him."

Kaduk was the most unpredictable SS roll call leader; but there was even more blood on the hands of his colleague Gerhard Palitzsch. This Saxon entered Eicke's school in Dachau at the age of twenty and proved to be an apt pupil. As an experienced and energetic SS roll call leader, he largely determined the atmosphere in Auschwitz from the beginning. This is what Höß wrote about him:

P. was always present at the executions, and he probably also killed the greatest number of inmates by shooting them in the neck. I often observed him but never noticed the slightest stirring of an emotion in him. He performed his horrifying tasks nonchalantly, with an even temper and a straight face, and without any haste. Even when he was on duty at the gas chambers, I could not detect any trace of sadism in him. His face was always expressionless and immobile. He was probably so hardened emotionally that he was capable of killing constantly without thinking about it. P. was also the only one of those directly involved in the exterminations who never spoke to me in a quiet hour and poured his heart out concerning the cruel doings.

Pery Broad has given a graphic description of Palitzsch's behavior at executions: "The executioner mechanically reloads his gun and performs one execution after another. If there is a delay, he puts his weapon down, whistles a little tune, or converses with those around him about studiedly unimportant subjects. With this cynical attitude he wants to demonstrate how little it matters to him 'to bump this riffraff off' and how 'hard' he is. He is proud of killing these innocent people without any stirring of his conscience. If someone moves his head, he presses the muzzle of his gun against the inmate's neck and his face to the wall." In a letter from the resistance movement, Palitzsch is succinctly characterized as "the biggest bastard in Auschwitz." The inmates called him "William Tell" because he was often seen walking to the bunker block with his rifle. Elsewhere, Höß characterized his ss roll call leader in these words: "Palitzsch was the shrewdest and craftiest creature that I met and experienced in my long and varied service in various concentration camps. He literally walked over dead bodies in order to satisfy his lust for power!"

The ss man Johann Becker remembers that the same Palitzsch once took exception in the slaughterhouse to the inmates' slaughtering the cows in too rough a manner.

■ The harshest judgment in Frankfurt was passed on the ss medic Josef Klehr, who was sentenced to 475 life terms in the penitentiary for that number of murders committed "on his own initiative and with special malice," not to mention an additional sentence for aiding and abetting thousands of murders. Every court must base its judgment on minimal numbers, and the presiding judge repeatedly pointed out that in all likelihood the number of victims was considerably higher.

Like Kaduk, Klehr was from Upper Silesia and two years older than his colleague. After attending an elementary school, he learned carpentry, but he did not work at this trade for long. At the age of thirty he became a nurse in a sanatorium and two years later worked as an assistant guard in a prison. In 1932 Klehr joined the ss and was made a medic in Dachau and later in Auschwitz, presumably on the strength of his earlier work in a sanatorium.

Klehr's nickname was "Professor" because he loved being in the limelight. When he went to Block 20 to administer poisonous injections, he put on a white physician's coat. Czeslaw Glowacki, a corpse carrier who frequently observed him, asserted that "killing was a pleasure for him." Evidently he wanted to enhance this pleasure for himself because he killed not only those whom an SS physician had selected but chose additional victims. One arbitrary selection has particularly stuck in the memory of Tadeusz Paczula, a Polish roll call clerk: "On Christmas eve (1942) the SS physician scheduled to be on duty telephoned to say that he was unable to come. I notified Klehr, and he said, 'Today I am the camp physician.' On that day the number of victims, including the medical presenters, probably was around 200." Paczula has also described how Klehr made his selections: "Klehr usually sat on the table (in the ward). He kept his headgear on, and the inmates had to approach him with their temperature charts. All the patients in the ward had to pass by him. Klehr took the charts and put some on each side. While he was doing this, he kept his pipe in his mouth." The clerk of Block 20 remembers that on one or two occasions Klehr had to cut a selection short because he was too drunk.

Karl Lill was able to overhear many conversations among SS men in the office of the SS infirmary. "I was never able to perceive any human feelings in Klehr," he said. "Others would say when they were just back from a leave that they would now have to return to this murderers' den. Klehr was capable of killing a few hundred human beings the way a cobbler rips a frayed sole from a shoe." Jan Weiß recalls that for Klehr there was only one reason for expediting the daily murders. "Often two inmates were taken to the room at the same time. I believe this happened when Klehr was in a hurry. You see, he raised rabbits in the yard. When he wanted to go there, he injected faster." Weiß had to present the doomed men to Klehr.

I have met no member of the SS who savored his feeling of power as much as this utterly uneducated man, who needed a lot of time to write his short name and was described as semiliterate by the Frankfurt court.

Tadeusz Paczula has vividly described the way in which Klehr wanted to be received in the HKB:

First of all, an inmate had to clean the motorcycle on which he always arrived. Then he went into the physicians' room and had an inmate take off his boots and wash his feet. At the same time another inmate had to brush and polish his fingernails. After that, he would sit in the middle of the room with a pipe in his mouth and his feet in a bucket. Sometimes he made eight inmates dance attendance on him, and they had to anticipate his very wish. He behaved just like a pasha. For example, an inmate tailor had to come and take his measurements, and he dictated some letters to another inmate. At the same time the camp elder of the inmate infirmary had to appear and give him a report about what happened in the HKB. The inmate pharmacist had to bring him medicines, which he took along. However, he did all this only when the camp physician was not present.

When he was being interrogated by an examining magistrate, Klehr denied ever having beaten prisoners and gave this rationale for it: "I was so highly respected that as a rule I did not even need to give any beatings."

Klehr was ambitious enough to try to play physician. Jan Weiß has described this as follows: "One time I had to carry two corpses out of Block 20 on a stretcher. On the steps the bodies fell off, and at that very moment a female SS warden walked by with two inmates. She thought that we had done this deliberately, slapped our faces, and took down our numbers. This is why Klehr assigned me to the experiments." Weiß was referring to Klehr's attempts to drain fluid from the spinal cord by means of a long hypodermic needle—that is, to perform spinal taps. He selected as the victims of these experiments mostly those who were destined to die, and they had to endure this procedure before he killed them with an injection of phenol. It is rumored that if an inmate cried out when Klehr did not apply the needle between the dorsal vertebrae expertly, causing great pain, he beat this victim before killing him.

Klehr also loved practical jokes. He liked to sit on one half of the desk at which the clerk Paczula had to work. More than once he lifted one of his buttocks, emitted a pleasurable loud fart, and ordered Paczula to "inhale deeply." The seventeen-year-old Bartosz Oziemkowski was gatekeeper in Block 21, where Klehr regularly came and went. He testified that

> it was the rule that Klehr manhandled me whenever he passed me. His blows were not always painful. Often he hit me in the face with his gloves or ordered me to stand in a corner. Then I got a blow in the pit of my stomach; and when I writhed with pain, he slapped my face. Once he made a typical SS joke. He gave me a friendly pat on the shoulder and asked me, "Are you afraid of me?" He was smiling, and so I said, "No." Then he ordered me to go to the room and drop my pants. I had to bend over a stool, and he took a broom and beat me, all the while smiling. He beat me until I screamed, whereupon he stopped. Finally he said, "You see, that comes from not being afraid of me."

Once Klehr was jailed because, as he told his judges in Frankfurt, he had given his superior a piece of his mind while intoxicated. Klehr gave the following reason for his little rebellion. "I complained that the SS leaders had inmates make new uniforms for them, even though this was strictly prohibited.

We noncommissioned officers would have liked to have had new uniforms, too." Evidently this was what depressed him most. Later he found ways of matching the actions of his superiors.

Even this man's inhumanity was not clear-cut, for there was another side to him. In the latter half of 1942, the inmate Josef Farber was a medic in the satellite camp Gleiwitz. Klehr was there at the same time, and his family lived nearby. "One time his wife and two children visited him in Gleiwitz," wrote Farber. "This wife was a nice, decent woman. I overheard a conversation in which she said: 'I've heard that you people are gassing women and children here. I hope you don't have anything to do with that.' Klehr answered: 'I am an SDG here. I don't kill, I heal.' Afterward he told me that I should not dare to blab about it. When the wife talked to me, she always did so out of compassion. The children were also nice and really well brought up."

Klehr's wife Frieda, who married him in 1933, was called to Frankfurt as a witness for the defense. She was supposed to confirm that Klehr was at home at Christmastime 1942 and therefore could not have conducted an arbitrary selection at that time, which is what Paczula and other witnesses claimed. She readily admitted that she knew about these accusations. Frieda Klehr, who was ten years younger than her husband, was a likable woman dressed in black. At first she wanted to be excused from testifying, but at the urging of her husband she changed her mind. To the key question as to whether she could remember that her husband was home for Christmas in 1942, she replied: "I am not 100 percent certain." After she had been excused, she shyly bid her husband farewell with her eyes. It remains an open question how such different people were able to live together for such a long time, how they influenced each other so little in all those years.

■ The records of the Frankfurt trial illuminate like a flash of lightning the common attitude regarding the lives of the prisoners.

Hermann Kleemann, who headed the satellite camp Janinagrube, was forty-five years old when he testified as follows on January 31, 1961: "I still remember injuring an inmate's hand when I wanted to shoot some object out of his hand. However, this inmate did this on his own. I assume that it was a playing card. I did not hurt this inmate intentionally, of course." Kleemann, who was trying to present himself in as favorable a light as possible, immediately added this: "It could only have been on a bet that I did this. In any case, the inmate was a German. I believe the bullet went between the inmate's fingers, for he only had a flesh wound." How, one wonders, did this absolute sovereign of Janinagrube deal with non-German prisoners?

The infamous head of the crematoriums, SS Technical Sergeant Otto Moll, was the top man in the camp Fürstengrube in its final phase. One day he escorted several inmates to the camp in Birkenau where they "organized" under his supervision 600 quilts for his camp. Joseph Hermann, who was part of that group, reports as follows: "The theft was successful, and Moll was very pleased about it and in high spirits. As we were leaving the camp, he saw a two- or three-year-old girl and said to us that this child was going to be gassed and we wanted to spare her this fate. He lifted the child up by her hair, shot her in the neck, and threw her in front of a woman's feet."

As for the female wardens, one is tempted to say that they were even more demoralized than the male guards. Their health records, which we were able to examine, indicate that there was hardly any warden who was not treated for a venereal disease during her service in Auschwitz.

The head of the female wardens was SS women's camp leader Maria Mandel, who was born in 1912 in Upper Austria. On the basis of the "credits" that she earned in Ravensbrück, she was appointed to her top position. Her appearance was largely in keeping with the picture that Nazi propaganda painted of a blonde German woman; it was marred only by a brutal line around her mouth. Mandel ordered beatings and did some flogging herself. Once I heard her complain to Dr. Kitt, at that time the camp physician in the women's camp, that there had been no selections in her camp for a long time. She said that because of its overpopulation she could hardly keep order, and she urged him to reduce it by means of a selection.

Mandel had her "weak" sides, too. She loved music and therefore sponsored the orchestra in the women's camp and its conductor, the violin virtuoso Alma Rosé. When Rosé fell ill, Mandel arranged for her to be nursed in a single room even though she was Jewish. Once she assured her protégée Rosé that she would surely be the last to be sent to the gas chamber.

Wladimir Bilan, an SS sergeant who worked in the women's camp, has described Mandel as highly intelligent. In his opinion Mandel was convinced that what she did was good for the Reich.

Another "weakness" could be observed in Mandel. She loved children. This did not deter her from executing all orders to exterminate inmates, including children, but sometimes she let her feelings be expressed in a gesture. Ella Lingens once observed that she invited two children to see her in the block leader's room. When they came out, they had cookies and chocolate in their hands. Lingens also heard the all-powerful SS camp leader ask a pregnant German prisoner to let her have the baby after the prisoner gave birth because she was unable to have children. Her request was denied.

■ Courts made detailed examination of the background of two men who put on the SS uniform at a very early age and were posted to Auschwitz. Thus we are able to become acquainted with them retrospectively.

The expert witness, Dr. Helmut Lechler, reported to the Frankfurt judges on whether Hans Stark could be regarded as having been of age when he committed the crimes in Auschwitz of which he was accused. "Defendant Stark was born in Darmstadt on June 14, 1921," he testified.

His father was the police chief there. He had a typically Prussian education based on the principle "Someone who cannot obey can never command." After attending elementary school Stark became a pupil in a *Realgymnasium* in Darmstadt, where he was an average student. Later his achievements declined, and this caused vehement arguments with his father, who deemed it necessary to instill some real discipline into his son. He wanted to send him to the Labor Service or the armed services, but neither was possible because Stark was not much more than sixteen. At that time the father received a leaflet of the ss *Totenkopfverbände* (death's head units). He thought that this kind of unit was suitable for his son's education, and on December 1, 1937, he gave his written permission for his son, then aged sixteen and a half, to join one. Stark was sent to Oranienburg as the youngest recruit of his unit. The ss gave him intensive indoctrination in Nazi ideology. Stark spent the first six months of his basic training with this unit without any leave. As early as January 1938 he was assigned guard duty in the Oranienburg concentration camp (Lechler probably meant the nearby Sachsenhausen concentration camp). He was strictly forbidden to say anything about the goings-on in the KZ on his first home visit. At home he seemed depressed, and for this reason his father tried to get his son out of the ss. From June 1938 to September 1939 Stark received further training in the ss unit at the Buchenwald concentration camp and later in Dachau. In August 1940 Stark had a riding accident near Munich and was classified as fit only for service in a garrison in the homeland. Stark was assigned to outside guard duty in Dachau and later transferred to Auschwitz.

The report given above was based on information supplied by Stark, but it was impossible to verify every detail.

Stark's father continued his efforts to get his son out of service in the ss, and he was advised to have his son apply to continue his education: that was the only way. Stark did so, passed his *Abitur* [the qualifying exam for entering higher education] during a leave, and on another leave attended courses at the law school of the University of Frankfurt. After that he applied for frontline duty. In Auschwitz Stark was soon entrusted with the leadership of the admissions detail of the Political Department. Several Polish inmates who spoke German and as students were qualified for office work were his subordinates there.

Stark participated in the shootings that members of the Political Department had to attend regularly. Kazimierz Smolen, one of the students, gave the following account: "When Stark returned from such a duty, he was always nervous, washed his hands, took off his coat, and ordered his *Kalfaktor* (handyman) to shine his boots. Stark was not a heavy smoker, but at such times he did smoke." The *Kalfaktor* was Erwin Bartel, a Pole two years younger than Stark. This is how he described the behavior of his boss to the Frankfurt judges: "When he returned from shootings, he said, 'Bartel, a bowl and water—I would like to wash my innocent hands.'" When Stark was expected to return from a shooting, the inmates in the admissions section tried to catch all of the flies in the room because at such times Stark was capable of becoming enraged if he was bothered by a fly.

Bartel reported this revealing episode to the court: "I remember exactly that one time ss roll call leader Palitzsch told Stark to go to Block 11. On that occasion two or three inmates may have been shot there. When Stark came back, he said: 'Now an inmate has been shot who should not have been shot. My God, what is Grabner going to say about this?'"

Stark loved testing the inmates working for him while he was preparing for his *Abitur*. The Dutchman Johann Beckmann said, "It was typical of him that he wanted to show that German schools were better than schools in other countries. He repeatedly gave us a kind of test and was proud when he knew something better." Kazimierz Smolen expanded on this when he wrote:

> Stark always found a pretext for asking us questions about history, mathematics, physics, or German literature. These questions were directed primarily at inmates who had passed their *Abitur*. Posing as a conceited teacher, he tested their knowledge of the teachings of Thales, the axioms of Euclid, and the laws of Archimedes. Then he started analyzing works of Schiller, Goethe, and Eichendorff. Since he was a German, it was only natural that he had a superior knowledge of German literature and history. That marked the end of the examination, and Stark began his ironic criticism of the level of the Polish educational system.

He developed a rather peculiar relationship with his *Kalfaktor* Bartel. On the one hand, he wanted to make him "hard" because he evidently regarded this method as ideal; on the other hand, he sometimes sent good things his way. On their return from Birkenau one day, where they had done some work, Stark said to Bartel at the camp gate: "Look at all the bricks here! At the end of the war each brick will bear the name of an inmate who has been killed. Perhaps there won't be enough bricks then. There are lots of bricks here for your family, too."

When Stark was transferred to a frontline unit in 1943, he visited Auschwitz on his way to the eastern front. "He came into his office," writes Smolen about their meeting, "but he was no longer the same man. His arrogance and presumptuousness were completely gone. He feared the 'Russkies,' as he called the Russians. He had some questions for us, but these had nothing to do with literature or history. It was a matter of getting warm gloves, socks, and soap. He got these things from some storeroom."

In the Frankfurt courtroom the Polish pedagogue József Kret, who had come into contact with Stark as an inmate, testified as follows: "He was young and had an attractive appearance. I could not understand why he was so cruel. A comrade who worked on his detail once told me: 'I don't know what's the matter with Stark. He is basically a decent man.' It seems to be that he came under the influence of a bad ideology too early. This saying was affixed over his desk: 'Compassion is weakness.'"

The previously mentioned expert, Dr. Lechler, has summed up his findings in these words: "Defendant Stark is an example of how a young man with average talents and an entirely normal, inconspicuous disposition readily submits to what may be called a reversal of conscience. He is an example of a person's vulnerability to letting himself be perverted and turned into a tool of totalitarian potentates. As a result his moral control is replaced with the mind-set of a Führer. The final consequence is the development of functionaries without a conscience."

Stark's father committed suicide after the end of the war, reportedly because he could no longer bear the guilt he had incurred by sending his son to the SS. Stark himself received a prison term of ten years, the maximum sentence that could be imposed under the criminal law governing minors.

■ The case of the warden Irma Grese constitutes a parallel case. She was barely ten years of age when Hitler became chancellor, and Nazi propaganda reached even the village school in Mecklenburg that Grese attended. As a child she never participated in brawls but preferred to run away. Her father, a conservative farmer, prohibited his daughters from joining the Nazi organization. After leaving elementary school at the age of fourteen, Irma Grese did farm work for a year; then she left her parental home and studied nursing. She was sent to a sanatorium for Nazi VIPs at Hohenlychen, where she was indoctrinated and joined the SS at the age of eighteen. This caused such vehement quarrels with her father during a leave that she never went home again.

She was trained as a warden in the Ravensbrück camp and transferred to Auschwitz when she was a little over nineteen. Gisella Perl has provided this description of her: "One of the most beautiful women I have ever seen. Her face had an angelic clarity, and her blue eyes were the liveliest and most innocent eyes imaginable." Perl adds to this by stating that Grese was the cruelest warden she encountered. Olga Lengyel also writes that it defied belief that such a pretty girl could be so cruel. When she walked through the camp with a whip in her hand, she was surrounded by a cloud of choice perfume.

A woman who had once run a respected salon in Budapest had to be Grese's seamstress. She was always fully occupied, and Grese "organized" the costliest fabrics. It was Grese's ambition to become a film star, and she often posed in front of a mirror for a long time. She also beat women on the breast with her whip and made selections without displaying any emotion. In that way she rapidly advanced and became ss roll call leader and eventually ss camp leader in Birkenau, where the able-bodied women who were waiting for a transport to a labor camp were taken in the summer of 1944. Once Gisella Perl, a physician, had to perform an abortion on Grese, who threatened to kill her if she talked about it but promised to pay her with a coat (which Perl never received). Grese made amorous advances toward Iris Langer. When the latter tried to fend off the warden by pointing to her Star of David, Grese said that Iris was a Jew who was different from the other Jews.

I have heard something good about Grese from only one woman. On one occasion Ruth Kersting was caught conversing with a male inmate. Grese lit into her: "Don't you know that this is forbidden?" When Kersting replied that she did know, Grese let her go.

After the evacuation of Auschwitz, Grese was transferred to the kz Bergen-Belsen along with other female wardens. She was called to account in the first kz trial before a British military court in Lüneburg. Journalists who observed this sensational trial described the beauty of the very young Grese, who attracted attention with her blonde hair and blue eyes. Her behavior was also striking. When a codefendant tried to wiggle out with dumb excuses, she had to cover her face with her hand because she was unable to stifle her laughter. She herself admitted that she had always carried a whip and used it for beatings even after the commandant had forbidden the use of whips. When she was asked whether she had ordered others to flog inmates, she answered only, "Yes," and when asked if she was authorized to give such orders, all she said was "No."

Because of her unreserved confession, other statements by her are credible. Once she mentioned that Himmler personally gave a female warden twenty-five blows on her buttocks because she had helped inmates. The other wardens were forced to watch the administration of this punishment, and Höß ordered Grese to deal the last two blows. In this way, which Eicke had taught him, he wanted to make the warden, who was less than twenty at the time, "hard."

Grese said this about the difficulties she encountered as the ss camp leader in the c-camp: "When the hunger was great, the distribution of food was difficult. At every corner twenty to thirty women were waiting to attack the transport (of the food pails from the kitchen to the barracks)." The only expedient she could think of was to use her whip to restore order.

Grese was sentenced to death. She is said to have sung in her cell on the eve of her execution.

SEXUALITY

■ ■ ■

Since there were sexual relations between prisoners and guards, this chapter about sexuality in Auschwitz does not appear in the part of the book that deals only with the inmates and their problems, for it presupposes some knowledge of the problems faced by ss members. The second part of this chapter will deal with people who have already been introduced in earlier chapters.

Did the prisoners have sexual problems? "My estimate surely is not too high," writes Benedikt Kautsky, "when I say that 90 percent of the inmates did not have a sexual problem." This estimate is valid for Auschwitz as well, even though men's and women's camps existed next to one another there.

Chronic undernourishment was not the only reason for this. Elie A. Cohen observed that even normally nourished new arrivals immediately lost any sexual urge, and he attributes this to the shock caused by contact with the mass murders. Jews experienced this shock most strongly. Primo Levi confirms that sexual abstinence did not cause them any suffering.

Désiré Haffner observed in Birkenau that even after years of imprisonment inmates had neither erections nor nocturnal emissions. To be sure, he excepts Green VIPs, among whom the sex drive did play a role. Haffner also learned that women no longer had their periods and that those who were having their period when they arrived in Auschwitz abruptly stopped bleeding and did not bleed in the camp. The physician Janina Kowalczykowa confirms the stoppage of menstruation. She agrees that in addition to malnutrition there was a psychic component, namely constant fear. Even women who received above-average nourishment lost their period. Professor Carl Clauberg confirmed this: as soon as they arrived at the camp, "almost 100 percent promptly lost their menstruation." The Russian commission that examined the inmates remaining in the camp after the liberation came to the conclusion that 97 percent of the women examined had no period during their imprisonment. When female corpses were autopsied after the liberation, it was observed that their genitals were reduced in size. It should be borne in mind, however, that only sick people and those unable to march had been left behind.

Along with the reproductive instinct, the sense of shame was eliminated; the camp administration saw to that. Again and again inmates had to line up without clothes, whether they were headed for the bath, the disinfection, or a selection. "Thousands of naked people next to one another—this is nothing human but a herd. Then any sensitivity is as ludicrous as it is futile." This statement by Ana Novac has general validity.

Zofia Posmysz has described the washing facilities in the penal company: "One liter of water in the bowl used for eating had to suffice for everyone. Inmates poured water in the hollow of their hands and washed their genitals. A guard was strolling up and down behind the wire. The sight of the figures with their legs apart did not bother him any more than his presence bothered us."

Everyone had become accustomed to the sight of naked inmates. However, if men encountered naked women, the sight was very depressing. Grajan Fijalkowski has described it in these words: "A few hundred women were waiting their turn to take a bath. A compressed heap of naked hairless skeletons looked at us with dim, completely expressionless eyes, and only dry flaps of skin hanging from their chests indicated that these had once been women full of life."

An encounter with dressed female *Muselmänner* stirred men more than the accustomed sight of run-down members of their own sex. Józef Kret writes: "A procession of female inmates came from the women's camp. A few hundred women with shaved heads passed us, wearing, as we did, the uniforms of Soviet prisoners. The lack of water for washing, underwear, and even the most primitive facilities had caused their indescribable condition. These were no longer human beings but only some apathetic humanoid automata, masks without life and expression. When we passed their column, we got a whiff of a stench that took our breath away."

I still have before my eyes the image of a column of women who were being taken to the main camp—to be disinfected, I believe. Since we were not allowed to approach the women, we tossed them some bread, but we soon stopped because they pounced on it, hit one another, and were then beaten by the guards. Instead of helping, we had only worsened their situation. Gizela Strebinger remembers a similar scene. When a group of women threw bread to half-starved men, they rushed to it like hyenas, whereupon the guards sicced their dogs on the wranglers, which made the women reproach themselves for their well-intended deed.

Thoughts of sex were precluded in human beings in that condition. They played a role only in the thin stratum of well-nourished prisoners who did not have to fear the machinery of destruction directly. These were primarily inmates with functions, particularly Germans—not only because German prisoners hardly needed to be afraid of the gas chamber but also because most of them got to see women again for the first time after years of imprisonment. In this regard there was no difference between criminals and political prisoners. The atmosphere of the extermination camp frequently removed all inhibitions. The principle that many VIPs lived by was to reach unhesitatingly for any pleasure without thinking of tomorrow. German criminals set the tone in this by virtue of their privileged position, their lesser moral inhibitions, and their ample experience with incarceration. However, in this respect a considerable number of other VIPs were hardly different from German career criminals.

In defiance of all prohibitions and punishments, this group of privileged prisoners found ways of coming in contact with inmates of the women's camp. According to Ella Lingens, every girl who, because of her position, was able to feed and groom herself to some extent had a lover, and quite a few children were fathered in the camp. A relationship was a lifesaver for many because men who were able to gain access to the women's camp also had a chance to "organize." As Krystyna Zywulska reports, the role played by flowers in normal life was taken by margarine; when a man came to see his girlfriend, he brought her a stick of margarine.

Olga Lengyel says that buxom women were regarded as the ideal of beauty, which is understandable in the Auschwitz milieu. She has also made this pithy statement about prostitution: "Often a potato sufficed." According to the experiences gathered in 1944 by Gisella Perl in the section of Birkenau where the able-bodied women deported from Hungary were waiting for a transfer, menstruation had ceased but "sexual desire was still one of the strongest drives." Men came to this camp for various chores, including the cleaning of the latrine. Perl writes that "the latrine was used as a love nest" where the women showed their appreciation for the food the men had brought along.

The experimental Block 11 in the main camp was strictly isolated; its gate was always locked, and there always was a female warden on duty. However, functionaries found pretexts to enter the block, or else they bribed the warden. According to Sara Spanjaard van Esso, the men brought their women parcels. Since there was no privacy in the big living quarters and only the block elder had her own room, she was also given a present, whereupon she permitted the couple to use her room for a short time. In the final six months Spanjaard's compatriots — that is, deportees from Holland — had so acclimated themselves that "everyone had her *kochany*." She used the Polish word for "lover" that was customary in the camp lingo, and this also indicates the nationality of most of the *kochanys*.

Rudolf Vrba has described the methods that were used. One room in the camp area was always kept locked because the poison gas Zyklon B was stored there. Otto Graf, an SS sergeant, had the key to this room, and for a bribe he occasionally let a pair of inmates use it. They made love next to the containers of poison gas.

A remedy for sexual distress that was customary in other concentration camps, in which no women were interned next to men, was frequently used in Auschwitz as well. Capos kept *Pipel*, young fellows who in return for personal services were exempted from hard labor and enjoyed other privileges. Quite a number of capos abused their boys sexually. Thomas Geve, who was in Auschwitz as a young man, was told by an acquaintance of the same age that his capo was exploiting him sexually. "What else could have protected me from heavy labor, hunger, and disease?" With this question the lad gave the reason for submitting to the capo. Elie Wiesel, like Geve an inmate of Monowitz at an early age, mentions a Green capo who procured bread, soup, and margarine for boys, though of course not altruistically. Abraham Matuszak reports that what functionaries in Auschwitz did with their *Pipel* cried to high heaven. If the boys were not willing, they were sent the way of all flesh.

H. G. Adler has described one *Pipel* in Birkenau. "With the barracks assistant comes the runner of the block elder, his fourteen-year-old darling. He is fat and has rosy cheeks. He does not even come up to the shoulders of most inmates but is a strong lout who can do whatever he likes, an aggressive, cantankerous creature. His slaps in the face are well aimed; he is permitted to flog the strongest men, and they cannot defend themselves because the young rascal is under the protection of the block elder, who might kill anyone his darling complains about."

Thomas Geve sums it up when he writes that "homosexuality was an open secret despite all efforts to eradicate it." Even though a capo had opportunities to bribe those who knew about it, a homosexual affair was sometimes busted. In the intrigues of the privileged prisoners, this weapon was also used. If a homosexual relationship was exposed, the SS locked the capo, usually a German, and his *Pipel*, most of the time a young Pole or Jew, in the bunker. The German had to sign a declaration that pledged him to have himself castrated. After the surgical procedure he was released and usually given his job back. The young fellow who had done his bidding to safeguard his life was shot at the Black Wall. During my detention in the bunker, I overheard in quiet evening hours many a conversation from one cell door to another across the echoing corridor. Often the lads desperately begged for help, and the capos answered them with sentimental phrases.

If a German inmate was castrated because of homosexual activities, this had to be reported to the Central Office, and thus Himmler was informed of the number of sterilized Germans. Since the German prisoners were the only ones whose release was expected and the infertility of many of the men released from the camp might inhibit the desired rapid proliferation of the "master race," Himmler ordered the establishment of bordellos in the concentration camps. This was intended to combat homosexuality. On one occasion Himmler said that these brothels also were supposed to constitute an "incentive for greater achievements"; an inmate had to pay for visits to the brothel with bonus coupons that were awarded for good work. However, the first reason mentioned above was probably the decisive one. Wirths once told me this in a conversation, and Franz Ziereis, the commandant of Mauthausen, also reported that the combating of rampant homosexuality was the reason for the establishment of bordellos. In the literature other reasons are given, such as the breaking of the political prisoners' will to offer resistance and the undermining of their morale, but this cannot be documented.

The fact that the order to establish brothels was issued around the time when German career criminals began to be recruited for the special Dirlewanger Unit also speaks for the version confirmed by Wirths and Ziereis. On June 30, 1943, a brothel was opened in Block 24 of the main camp, and a second brothel followed in Monowitz. The central order must have been issued earlier because in a letter dated March 5 Himmler expressed his surprise that he had not been able to inspect a bordello on a visit to Buchenwald.

SS camp leader Mandel took great care to have women assigned to this duty on a voluntary basis. We have a description of the recruitment from Ella Lingers. SS camp leader Hössler had young girls line up who were forced to work hard under the open sky, sleep in crowded quarters without facilities for washing and changing their underwear, and live in constant fear of floggings. He announced that anyone who volunteered as a *fille de joie* would be given her own room, clean clothes, sufficient food and cigarettes, and the opportunity to bathe every day. He also intimated that occupants of the brothel might be released "on good behavior." It went without saying that only "Aryans" were acceptable and that Jews were not permitted to visit the brothel.

The volunteers were presented to the camp physician. "It was one of my duties to select women for the brothel," said Dr. Fritz Klein. "Fifteen were brought to me, and I picked out the ten who were most qualified." The records of those who had come forward were checked because there had to be order. SS Corporal Pery Broad performed this task with pleasure. Dounia Ourisson-Wasserstrom heard him shout gleefully when a woman's personal record listed her profession as prostitute: "In our camp every inmate can practice his or her profession! Isn't this a model camp?" Alina Brewda, who as the physician in charge in the experimental block had to examine the occupants of the bordello regularly, remembers that most of them were Germans and that there also were a few Poles and Russians.

■ Tadeusz Borowski has described the brothel on the first floor of Block 24 in this satirical fashion:

There are windows that are half open even in winter. After the roll call one sees women's heads of all colors and shades in the windows, and from the blue, rose-colored, and light green robes emerge arms that are whiter than sea foam. Fifteen heads, I believe, and thirty arms, not counting the old madam, whose heavy, epic, legendary bosom watches over the heads, necks, arms, and so on. Madam usually does not stand by the windows but acts like a Cerbera at the cathouse door.

The camp VIPs crowd around the bawdy house. If there are ten Juliets, there are at least a thousand Romeos, and, by God, they are not the worst. There is pushing and shoving and keen competition for every Juliet. The Romeos stand by the windows of the opposite block, shouting, signaling with their arms, and beckoning. The camp elder is among them, and so are the camp capo, the physicians from the infirmary, and the capos of various details. Many a Juliet has a regular swain, and in addition to vows of eternal love and promises of a better and happier life together after the camp, in addition to disputes and reproaches one can hear conversations that primarily concern soap, perfume, silk panties, and cigarettes. This is how the cathouse looks from the outside. One can enter it only by way of the office and with a card that one receives as a reward for good, industrious work.

Borowski describes how a camp-wise Pole from the first transport—"his number is smaller by a third than the last digits of my number"—gained admittance to the brothel.

He gallops into the office, stops, and as soon as one of the approved numbers is called and not claimed, he cries, "Here," grabs the pass, and trots over to the madam. He presses a pack of cigarettes into her fat paws, she gives him a whole series of mainly hygienic treatments, and the freshly sprayed young man rushes up the stairs with big leaps. In the corridor the Juliets from the windows are walking around with their robes nonchalantly wrapped around their bodies. From time to time one of them approaches him and asks *en passant*, "What number do you have?" "Eight," he says and looks at his card to make sure. "Oh, that's not me, that's Irma, the little blonde," she whispers a bit disappointed and flits off in the direction of the window. The young man walks up to door number eight. He quickly reads a posted notice that says that one pleasure or another is forbidden on pain of internment in the bunker, specifies the things that are permitted, and gives the number of minutes one can stay. He heaves a deep sigh in the direction of the spy (the peephole in the door) through which the female colleagues sometimes look, occasionally the madam, the leader of the Whorehouse Commando, or even the SS camp leader himself.

Robert Waitz has given a more sober description of the Monowitz brothel:

The bordello is reserved exclusively for Aryan VIPs, but the German Reds make no use of it. The institution itself is located in a block that is fenced off with barbed wire. There the Green gentlemen and the Poles vie for the favors of the ladies, who lack nothing. In the bordello there are alcohol, food, wine, clothes, and perfume. The SS roll call leader, who is in charge of it, attaches great importance to its good functioning. Every day he takes his ladies for a walk outside the camp and has them call him "*Papi*" (Daddy). On three evenings each week, the lovers come at intervals of twenty minutes in accordance with a prearranged timetable, and an Aryan physician is available for prophylactic measures.

The political prisoners generally did not visit the brothel in the main camp either. Exceptions became the subjects of conversation and sometimes provided merriment. Once, a Red capo who shunned the brothel during official visiting hour because he would be embarrassed in front of his friends tried to get in with the aid of a ladder. He fell off and sustained broken bones. His adventure could not be kept secret. A young Austrian who had been arrested for resisting the Nazi regime before he had met any women experienced his first great love in the Auschwitz bordello. For me it was no temptation; the other problems were too great, and the facility was too grotesque for that.

When a young and exceptionally thin inmate passed the brothel windows, the women threw some bread down. Geve, who reported this, wrote: "A woman's heart remains motherly despite everything."

■ Anyone who knows how little attention members of the SS paid to prohibitions will not be surprised to learn that despite all those strict prohibitions many of them started sexual relationships with prisoners. It is understandable that this gave rise to numerous rumors in the camp, but some of these relationships can be documented.

Willi Wildermuth remembers a colleague in the motor pool named Fritz Schramme who was given a punitive transfer in 1943 because it became known that he had impregnated a prisoner. A female warden who had exchanged love letters with an inmate was personally punished by Himmler when the relationship was detected. He ordered that the warden, whose name is said to have been Buchhalter, be given twenty-five strokes on her buttocks, after which she was probably admitted to the camp as an inmate.

The case of the notorious SS roll call leader Gerhard Palitzsch caused a great sensation. He was one of the few who looked the way Nazi propaganda loved to present SS men: athletic, blond, well built. His wife, with whom he lived in the camp area, died of typhus in the fall of 1942. This was an indication that Palitzsch had "organized" clothes for her in Canada because this was the only way the woman could have come in contact with an infected louse. "The death of his wife," wrote Höß, "made him lose his last inner firmness and his last inhibitions. He began to drink to excess and constantly had affairs with women. In his apartment there was a steady stream of women coming and going."

Palitzsch did not content himself with that. There were many rumors about his various relationships with prisoners. One day he was caught in an unmistakable situation in the Gypsy camp. There are various versions of this affair. According to Tadeusz Joachimowski, the roll call clerk of the camp, Palitzsch fell in love with a woman named Wera Luca and made her the elder of the children's block. The camp elder, a German criminal who was reputed to have had an earlier affair with the beautiful Wera, is said to have informed on Palitzsch, who was caught in a compromising situation by members of the Political Department and taken away. Broad gives a similar report of this incident but calls the woman Vera Lukans. Felix Amann recalls that Wera Luca was from Riga. Deviating from these accounts, Höß wrote that Palitzsch had an affair with a Jewish inmate from Latvia. Jan Pilecki, the clerk of the bunker block, also learned that Palitzsch was arrested because of intimate relations with a Jewish woman; he heard that she was Katja Singer, the roll call clerk of the women's camp. It is entirely conceivable that in the course of the investigation several affairs with women were uncovered.

It is certain that it was this *Rassenschande* (race defilement) that brought the all-powerful ss roll call leader down. At first there was an attempt to hush the case up. On October 1, 1943, Palitzsch was transferred to Brno, the satellite camp situated at the greatest distance from Auschwitz, as the ss camp leader. This attempted cover-up failed; it may have been foiled by Höß, who was not on good terms with Palitzsch. Soon Palitzsch was arrested and taken to the bunker that he knew well from selections and subsequent shootings. The fact that he was not immediately arrested permits one to conclude that serious crimes were uncovered in the course of the investigation.

When Palitzsch was locked up in a cell of the bunker, a Pole with a low inmate number was being detained there. He has reported that "in private," as he put it, Palitzsch was a completely different person. At that time Palitzsch begged inmates who used to tremble before him for bread. He told the Pole that he was locked up because of an affair with a Jewish inmate. Otto Küsel, who as inmate number two knew Palitzsch very well and also was in the bunker at that time, having been arrested in Warsaw after his escape, reported that as a matter of course Palitzsch used the familiar address *du* that was customary among the inmates.

Various rumors about Palitzsch's further fate circulated as well. According to camp gossip, he was sentenced to death for *Rassenschande* and appropriation of other people's property, but Broad, who ought to know, writes that Palitzsch was sentenced to several years in prison. Documents indicate that Palitzsch was expelled from the ss on June 1, 1944. His sentence is said to have been finally suspended, as was usual at the time, and he is supposed to have been assigned to a probationary unit and to have fallen in the fight for Budapest in December 1944.

Other ss men had less trouble because of their affairs with female prisoners. Physician Franz von Bodman had an affair with such an inmate. In order to be with her undisturbed, he ordered a very strict camp rest in the infirmary of the women's camp between one o'clock and two o'clock in the afternoon, during which time no one was permitted to go from one room to another. Adjutant Robert Mulka remembers an argument he once had with the physician because of this affair, but no proceedings against him ever became known.

Both Max Sell, the Labor Service leader, and Viktor Capesius, the pharmacist in charge, are said to have had affairs with prisoners that had no untoward consequences for them. Sometimes, however, there were severe consequences, though not for the ss men. A man named Storch, the women's Klesgrube Commando leader, impregnated his forewoman. When this became known, he simply shot her, but he was still relieved of his duties. Richard Böck, who reported this murder, writes that after three weeks Storch resumed his position as though nothing had happened. Böck knows only that the victim's first name was Rosa and that she was from Rosenheim. Karl Hölblinger remembers a colleague named Koch who had an affair with a female inmate and also shot her. He was sent to the bunker, but his further fate is not known.

Grabner, who dealt with such matters as head of the camp Gestapo, confirmed that many ss men did not hesitate to kill their lovers as soon as their relationship put them at risk. According to him, his subordinate Wilhelm Boger killed a Polish woman for the same reason. Grabner did not say why Boger remained unpunished even though he evidently knew about his misconduct.

I have already reported about the bloody consequences of the intimate relations that a guard of the penal company in Budy had with a German prostitute, an incident that has become known as the Budy Revolt.

The reverse of these murderous episodes occurred as well. Thus Krystyna Zywulska tells about an ss man who came every day to see a Jewish woman from the Canada Detail with whom he had fallen in love and whom he assured that he was not to blame for what was happening in Auschwitz. Ernst Müller recalls Franz Wunsch, who was in charge of the property depot in Birkenau and whom he at first experienced as a brutal Jew-baiter. "He beat prisoners, including women, hard," writes Müller. Others have severely incriminated that man. Wunsch soon fell in love with a young woman from Slovakia, and her influence on him was so great that he became a changed man. Müller observed that Wunsch thereafter got out of duty at the ramp whenever he could and helped prisoners. On one occasion, when he had to escort selected inmates to the crematorium, he vomited. It cannot be established whether Zywulska and Müller were reporting about the same man or whether two SS men underwent a similar development.

When Wunsch was a defendant in a Vienna trial in the spring of 1972, he described this episode from his point of view and in his defense. He said that the girl was more helpless than the others on the detail that he was in charge of. When she came down with typhus, she asked him to help her because she had to expect to be selected if she was admitted to the infirmary. After inner struggles ("I had been raised differently," said Wunsch) he decided to help her; he concealed her in the property depot and cared for her in that hiding place. Wunsch concluded his testimony by saying that "we grew fond of each other." He emphasized that Helene did not betray him when she was interrogated by the Political Department and faced the threat of being shot. Rumors about this relationship had reached that department.

▪ Even though the best documentation is of Commandant Höß's affair with the prisoner Nora Mattaliano-Hodys, what became known about it sounds more improbable than other relationships. When an SS investigating commission commenced its work in Auschwitz, it also came upon the Hodys affair. Dr. Gerhard Wiebeck, a member of that commission, seems to recall that it was brought to the judges' attention by an SS man who was awaiting trial in a Weimar jail. Wiebeck presumes that this was Palitzsch. SS camp leader Hofmann has confirmed that Palitzsch had testified in the Grabner trial in Weimar and had been demoted. The theory that Palitzsch was the informer is buttressed by the assumption that he wanted to get even with Höß, who had probably seen to it that the charges against him were not dismissed.

At a later date, Dr. Konrad Morgen, who headed the commission, described the case as the most flagrant abuse of power that he had encountered. After Höß's affair with Hodys had resulted in repercussions, Höß "attempted to murder this female inmate in conspicuous fashion—for example, by having her locked up, completely naked and in utter darkness, in a so-called stand-up bunker in the cellar and depriving her of most of her food ration. I was able to save this woman in the nick of time and have her sent to a Munich clinic. . . . After she had recovered there, I interrogated her. She trusted me and fully revealed the whole state of affairs to me."

The transcript covers twenty-four pages. Hodys was born in Vienna in 1903 and, according to statements she made after the war, was sentenced in 1930 (in Hamm, Westphalia) to a prison term of two-and-a-half years for breaking the Heimtückegesetz (law against defamation of the state) and preparing to commit high treason. After she had served her prison term, she was sent to the Ravensbrück concentration camp and from there transferred to Auschwitz. Dr. Wiebeck seems to remember that Hodys was sent to a KZ because of fraud involving the misuse of an NSDAP badge. His recollection may be correct because after the war she was sought by the police for minor fraud.

Here is an excerpt from Hodys's transcript: "SS Lieutenant Colonel Höß had a warden named Langenfeld assign a private room to me in Block 4. A few days later I was ordered to see the commandant because an embroiderer was needed. In the commandant's house I was received by Frau Höß, who showed me a carpet in the hall and asked whether I could mend it. I took the job." She then made two Gobelin tapestries as well as silken Gobelin pillows, bedside rugs, and blankets there. Hodys testified: "I sat in a room all by myself and received the same food as the commandant. This consisted of soup, appetizer, meat, vegetables, pastry or cookies, fruit salad, and coffee."

One day, when his wife was not at home, Höß is supposed to have approached her in the villa. Hodys asserted that she was permitted to leave the camp over the weekend on the honor system and slept outside the camp; she was even invited to the Höß villa on her birthday. She said that she was locked up in the bunker in October 1942 but initially received preferential treatment. In her transcript we read: "I usually had a cell that was furnished with a good bed and a good mattress. I had a table and a chair and was able to read, write, and smoke." Normally the furnishings of a bunker cell consisted only of a bunk bed without a straw pallet, blankets, and a pail.

Höß is said to have visited her stealthily at night and impregnated her. After a futile attempt on her part to end her pregnancy, an abortion was performed, after which she was incarcerated in the stand-up bunker, fell ill, and was released and taken to Munich. In Nora Hodys's transcript, recollections seem to be intermingled with a sick person's fantasies. On the one hand, names are named and incidents are described that are correct and could not have been known by anyone who was not an eyewitness. Other details are incorrect, particularly demonstrable errors in the chronology. This is the least surprising thing, for experience has shown that former prisoners are most likely to err in specifying the times when events occurred. Thus this testimony must be critically examined. To be sure, there is no reason to make it inaccessible to historians. The Institut für Zeitgeschichte, where the document is preserved, informed Rolf Hochhuth that it must be treated confidentially because of its explicit erotic content. For this reason he was not able to examine the document and refers to Hodys as Höß's "Jewish mistress," even though she had been interned in the camp as an "Aryan." It is not likely that *Rassenschande* on

Höß's part would have been condoned. I was able to obtain the transcript in another way and found no explicit erotic content in it.

I made an effort to check the statements in this document. Hodys was originally employed in the property depot. Hugo Breiden, a capo in Birkenau, remembers that "she was in charge of the jewelry in Birkenau." This is also indicated by the nickname by which she was known in the camp: "Diamond Nora." According to Grabner, Hodys had to bring the commandant jewelry; when this smuggling became known, he had her locked up and tried to eliminate her. Grabner does not suggest that the two had intimate relations.

Since Hodys reports in her testimony about the Jewish seamstresses who worked with her in the Höß villa, she must really have been employed there, for otherwise she could hardly have learned details about these seamstresses. Both her detention in the bunker and her privileged treatment during her early period there are documented. She was even allowed to keep a cat in her cell. Dr. Alina Brewda confirms that in the spring of 1944 Hodys was transferred from the bunker to the experimental block, where she occupied a single room. She remembers that Höß came to that room one night and that she was ordered to perform an abortion on Hodys. Ruth Friedhoff, who was in the same block, knows about a woman who came to the block in winter 1943–44, someone "whom no one really knew anything about. She was regarded as somewhat mysterious and had her own room. She had a bad foot and was bedridden." Ella Lingens, for her part, remembers that one day a very ill looking woman was brought into the infirmary of the women's camp on a stretcher and that an ss leader (evidently Wiebeck) was especially interested in her. The woman claimed that the commandant had had an affair with her, but Lingens did not believe her.

At the Frankfurt trial Wiebeck testified that "Höß wanted to kill this inmate" by letting her starve to death in the bunker. Wiebeck, however, took her out of there. "She was placed on a stretcher; I believe she had bone tuberculosis. I had Hodys put in a private room." It can be shown that Hodys was in Munich from July 22, 1944, onward.

Finally, the ss judges confirm that this affair prompted them to start proceedings against Höß. However, his superior, Pohl, trivialized the case by saying, "What of it?" The case was dismissed.

REACTIONS OF
HUMAN NATURE
■ ■ ■

Otto Moll advanced rapidly in the extermination camp. As the leader of the penal company he did so well in the eyes of his superiors that he was appointed chief of the four crematoriums. He was in charge of the Sonderkommandos and had to see to it that the extermination of human beings proceeded quickly and smoothly. For his success the top leadership of the ss rewarded him with the highest decoration that members of the ss could achieve in Auschwitz, the Distinguished Service Cross with Swords, which he received together with Commandant Höß and medic Klehr.

Filip Müller, a survivor of the Sonderkommando, describes Moll as a possessed fanatic who neither smoked nor drank. "When there was a lot of work, he helped us toss the corpses (into the burning pits); he rolled up his sleeves and did the work of two men." Müller reports an episode that was characteristic of this man. "Moll, the chief of the crematoriums, once took a child from its mother; I observed this at Crematorium IV. There were two big pits in which corpses were burned. He threw the child into the boiling human fat that had collected in the ditches around the pit and then said to his *Kalfaktor* (handyman): 'Now I shall eat my fill, now I have fulfilled my duty!'"

The leadership also assigned Erich Muhsfeld to the center of extermination, the gas chambers and crematoriums where smaller groups also were shot. Another survivor of the Sonderkommando, Milton Buki, testified about him shortly after the liberation: "Once he ordered a man to sing a waltz tune during the shootings and promised him to let him live in return, but he eventually shot him as well. The shootings did not always kill all of the victims, but they all went into the ovens. Muhsfeld had a steel rod with which he beat us and the victims."

Moll probably inspired in Muhsfeld a predilection for music while he worked. Alter Fajnzylberg, who also survived the Sonderkommando, reports that "Moll ordered a naked woman to sit on the corpses near a pit and jump and sing while he was shooting the inmates and pushing them into the fiery pit. She did this, of course, in hopes of possibly saving her life in that way. After shooting everyone Moll shot the woman as well."

Mikos Nyiszli, an inmate physician in a crematorium, describes how Muhsfeld once asked him for an examination, complaining of heart trouble and a severe headache. Since Nyiszli had just observed Muhsfeld killing eighty men by shooting them in the neck, he pointed out that this activity had probably caused his complaints. Muhsfeld angrily denied this and asserted that it did not matter to him whether he shot five people or a hundred. He said the reason he did not feel well was that he had drunk too much.

The men who devised methods of torture in the Political Department—and, like Boger or Lachmann, developed a real hunter's passion—owed their positions to their murderous initiatives, as did Moll or Muhsfeld. Anyone who reads or hears about the actions of a Moll or a Boger, a Muhsfeld or a Lachmann, is inclined to dismiss the actors as monsters, devils, or deviants.

One should beware of such facile conclusions. Under different conditions Moll, Boger, and all the others whose names are today mentioned with disgust would hardly have stood out from the mass of the unknown. This also applies to the many people whose names have remained unknown to the public even though their monstrous deeds did not differ too much from those who became known through trials.

The inner nature of these people reacted to its permanent violation, even if only in sleep. A seamstress who worked in the Höß villa once overheard Frau Moll complain to the commandant's wife that her husband frequently cried out in his sleep.

Nyiszli has recorded the following incident involving Muhsfeld. When the inmates on the Sonderkommando were once again clearing the full gas chamber, they found among the dead bodies a girl of about sixteen who was still breathing. They sent for Dr. Nyiszli and he was able to restore the girl to full consciousness. Meanwhile Muhsfeld had come on the scene, and Nyiszli, who had a certain personal relationship with this ss technical sergeant, managed to have a private conversation with Muhsfeld. He urged him to save this young girl's life. Since she could not remain in the crematorium, perhaps it would be possible to smuggle her onto a female detail that was working in the vicinity. Muhsfeld visibly mulled this proposal over, but he finally rejected it by saying that this would be possible if the girl were older and more sensible. In the case of a sixteen-year-old, there was a risk that she would talk about her experiences in the gas chamber, and this would have unpleasant consequences. That is why the girl had to die. However, departing from his custom he did not shoot the girl himself but ordered a lower-ranking ss man to kill her with the customary shot in the neck.

Concerning Wilhelm Boger, Karl Lill, who as the inmate clerk of the ss garrison physician was able to examine the health records of the ss guards, wrote me as follows: "In the spring or summer of 1944 Boger, and around the same time Lachmann as well, came to see the ss garrison physician and told him that they were unable to sleep at night and had 'apparitions.' Both were diagnosed with thyrotoxicosis [Graves' disease], were given sedatives and, if I remember correctly, leave." In American captivity Boger testified in July 1945: "In November 1943 I was ordered to attend the administrative officers' training school in Arolsen even though my state of health had declined considerably because of complete nervous exhaustion." At that very time the investigating commission of the ss had begun its work in Auschwitz that led to the arrest of Boger's boss Grabner and also directly affected Boger. His wife Marianne testified that "at times his nerves were completely shot" and that she had requested his transfer for that reason. Boger once received convalescent leave of several weeks, along with his family, because of his nervous exhaustion. This happened before the critical period, the fall of 1943.

Numerous witnesses described to the court the tortures administered by the Political Department. One of them reported that after a long period of starvation he was forced to eat heavily salted fish. When he could not get it down anymore, the fish was stuffed into his mouth, and when he threw up, he had to eat the vomit off the floor. The prosecutor asked Boger, "Is it correct that Kral (the witness) was forced to eat herring?" The response was, "Unfortunately yes. I still get nauseated when I have to think of it. I have always had an aversion to fish. Please spare me having to go into details." He said that this torture was ordered by his boss Grabner. The latter, for his part, stated in Polish captivity that he had "suffered a complete nervous breakdown and a mental disturbance" in Auschwitz.

As for Gerhard Lachmann, Boger's zealous colleague, there is a medical report dated June 18, 1943, that documents that Lachmann, who was twenty-three at the time, complained of great nervousness, pain in the stomach area that spread to the heart, insomnia, and a feeling of anxiety that often befell him while he was speaking. Treatment in the ss military hospital at Bad Nauheim produced no improvement, and Lachmann lost weight (he weighed 59 kilograms). The physicians came to this conclusion: "The complaints indicate a psychogenic cause." This judgment is toned down by the handwritten addition "in part."

For years Klaus Dylewski was also involved in interrogations, tortures, and shootings in the Political Department. Later as a defendant he testified as follows: "Six weeks after my arrival in Auschwitz I received a mental shock from which I have suffered to this day." His first wife confirmed this: "He often had attacks at night. Before this he had been in excellent health." When she was asked about the kind of attack, Ruth Dylewski said: "When he lay down, he became completely immobile and had to be lifted up." A physician confirmed that the circulatory instability from which Dylewski suffered probably had psychological causes.

■ When the former Austrian government minister Eduard Baar von Baarenfels was an inmate at Dachau, he met ss roll call leader Josef Remmele, who had been trained in that model camp to be "hard." In Monowitz he encountered him again, this time as a released prisoner doing assigned civilian labor at the IG Works. At Nuremberg in 1947 Baar von Baarenfels testified that Remmele once told him: "It is terrible. This morning 7,000 Jews arrived, and 600 of them are still alive."

Julia Skodova once observed Walter Quackernack, the chief of the registry of vital statistics, standing by the window and muttering, "*Diese Schweinerei*" (This dirty shame). He had seen inmates being mistreated outside the barracks. Skodova assesses him as "good" for other reasons as well; for example, he sometimes left his newspaper so that inmates working for him could read it. However, many former prisoners remember both Remmele and Quackernack only with fright and abhorrence.

Klaus Dylewski had the following episode presented to the Frankfurt court in his defense. His wife, who had in the meantime divorced him, testified:

One time my mother-in-law and my husband were in the kitchen (of their apartment in Upper Silesia, not far from Auschwitz). I went into the kitchen and overheard a conversation. My mother-in-law said that a local barber had been arrested and taken to Auschwitz. She asked: "Can't you look after him? He is a nice man." My former husband replied: "If you ever hear that someone has been taken to Auschwitz, just give me his name. If there is anything I can do, I'll do it." My mother-in-law asked him whether that was not risky for him, but he only made a dismissive gesture. Later he mentioned in passing that the man was now a barber in Auschwitz, was doing well, and always cut his hair.

The relationship between Wilhelm Boger, the ss technical sergeant of the Political Department, and Hermann Diamanski, a German political prisoner, developed in a very peculiar way. This is what Diamanski said as a witness at the Frankfurt trial: "I was detained in a communal cell in Berlin, in the Prinz Albrecht-Straße (before his deportation to the KZ). There was one other political prisoner in the cell; the rest were ss people. On the bunk bed next to mine was Boger, an ss officer (later demoted). He was the Gestapo leader in Ostrolenka and was called the 'Hangman of Ostrolenka.'" Diamanski encountered Boger again in Auschwitz, but this time in an entirely different situation. "At first I was afraid of him when I saw him again in Auschwitz," said Diamanski in the courtroom, "but he never did anything to me, and I cannot say that he acted badly toward me." When he was asked whether Boger shared his parcels in their joint captivity in Berlin, Diamanski replied: "Yes, our beds were next to each other." Diamanski incriminated Boger considerably. When the latter was asked to respond to the accusations in Diamanski's testimony, all he said was this: "I know the witness very well from Berlin. I could point out many misconceptions, but I would like to be as comradely as he used to be."

There were also other members of the Political Department who did not react in their accustomed way when they encountered compatriots. One day the German foreman Paul Scheidel was escorted from Birkenau to the Political Department in the main camp because inmates had escaped from his detail. In a conversation en route, it turned out that relatives of his escort, Wilhelm Hoyer, an SS staff sergeant in the Political Department, had worked in a factory owned by Scheidel. Evidently as a result of this conversation, Hoyer spared Scheidel the tortures that were customary in interrogations dealing with escapes.

In the Indoctrination Section of Monowitz, where he was a camp elder, Siegfried Halbreich encountered Gustav Wieczorek, the SS technical sergeant in the Political Department. Wieczorek had been a journeyman baker in Tarnowitz (Upper Silesia), where Halbreich had gone to school. Halbreich told the SS man that he had bought something from that bakery every day. Eventually a relationship developed between the two men that Halbreich later described as amicable. Wieczorek not only came to see the camp elder daily in order to eat with him but also called his attention to measures being prepared by his department and informed him about general developments. Halbreich was not sufficiently acquainted with these because only "Aryan" inmates in the main camp, not prisoners in Monowitz, were allowed to subscribe to newspapers.

Once Heinrich Pyschny, an orderly of the chief of the Political Department, was punished with two weeks' detention because he had been observed shaking hands with a capo and giving him cigarettes. Pyschny was from Myslowitz, a small town near Auschwitz, and the capo was an old friend of his.

Hans Pichler of the Political Department, was *gefühlsbetont* (emotional), as a former prisoner of that department put it. For this reason his superiors did not take him seriously and did not assign him to campaigns of murder. On one occasion, when his colleagues had gone to Bedzin and Sosnowitz, Pichler told the prisoners: "That's a *Scheißerei* (shitty business). They've gone there to liquidate the Jews."

Kazimierz Smolen has not forgotten how outraged SS Sergeant Otto Klaus was when he saw his colleague Stark take a woman with two small children to be shot. Klaus came from Laufen am Neckar and was also a member of the Political Department.

■ If memories of their hometowns were capable of momentarily suppressing in members of the SS the "hardness" that had been drilled into them, human points of contact had an even stronger effect on SS men who were not among the elite within an elite. Renée Jellinek, a Jew who had been deported at age twenty, was asked by an SS man in Auschwitz where she was from. When she answered, "From Brno," the SS man said "I'm from there, too." He arranged for Jellinek to be transferred to the nursing staff, which was tantamount to saving her life. Jellinek never saw the man again and does not even know his name. All she knows is that he was young, tall, and feared by everyone.

Dr. Otto Wolken's life was saved in a similar fashion, as he testified at the Frankfurt trial: "I was at the selection (of new arrivals), and a movement of the SS physician's thumb had already put me on the side of those who were to be gassed immediately when an SS man came up to me. He had heard me speak and now asked me, 'Where are you from?' 'From Vienna,' I said. 'So you are a fellow countryman. You see, I'm from Linz. What is your profession?' 'Physician.' The man promised to get me out, and he did." Wolken, too, never saw that SS man again and does not know his name.

The Frankfurt judges had to learn about many heinous deeds of the ethnic German Stefan Baretzki, a flogger and murderer. However, a very special relationship developed between him and Henryk Porebski, a camp-wise Pole, who gave this testimony at the trial: "I know block leader Baretzki and frequently spoke with him. His Polish is fluent. He asked me where I was born and whether I was from Bukovina (Baretzki's homeland). I had many subsequent conversations with him. He always treated me properly." When the presiding judge asked him whether Porebski ever saw Baretzki mistreat inmates, this was his revealing reply: "He did not do so in my presence. I believe he felt embarrassed in front of me." The following dialogue developed between Porebski and the defendant, who usually attacked witnesses. Baretzki: "I know this witness. You came to see us at four o'clock every day, didn't you?" (As an electrician Porebski had to make regular examinations of the electrified fences and on his way enter the room of the block leader.) Porebski: "Yes, I remember. We spoke Polish with each other. One time, when I brought forbidden items into the camp, you checked me. You took me behind the kitchen and then permitted me to bring those things in. Don't you remember our conversation on that day? I brought a lot of medicines into the camp, and we often spoke."

In some cases a shared homeland produced a lasting bond with a prisoner. In their report Simon Laks and René Coudy mention SS Sergeant Joachim Wolff, who often attended the rehearsals of the Birkenau band. When Wolff learned that the Jewish musician Heinz Lewin was, like him, from Halle an der Saale, a real friendship developed between Lewin and this proper SS man who had a friendly manner about him. When Wolff returned from a leave, Heinz always asked him for news from their hometown. Wolff gave his report as if he were talking to a family member and also described the effect of the bomb-ings, mentioning streets and buildings that had been particularly affected.

Wolff had a good reputation. He is surely identical to the ss roll call leader whose name was spelled with one "f" by Józef Mikusz, a Pole employed by the Labor Assignment Office in Birkenau. He remembers that his first name was Joachim and says that "he was never at the ramp and never beat inmates. Of course, he came to Auschwitz as an ss sergeant and left the camp with the same rank." Alex Rosenstock, who worked in the dental clinic of the Birkenau men's camp and also got to know Wolff, remembers that he once told him this: "If you're smart, you'll be on the lam. No one will get out of here—you won't and I won't."

On the Accommodations Commando, Katarina Princz met Nagel, an ss man who was, like her, from Bratislava and conversed with her and her com-rades in Hungarian. This netted him the nickname "Nagel-Bacsi" (bacsi is Hun-garian for "uncle"). Once, when Nagel was about to go on leave, he offered to take letters from Princz with him. She trusted him, and so she accepted his offer. He gave her some fabric from which she made a shirt, and she sewed in its collar a letter in which she described the goings-on in the extermination camp. Nagel brought back an answer to this letter, and subsequently Katarina received cards and even parcels through him. Katarina's future husband met the ss man in the leather factory where Nagel lived and Princz had to clean his room. Nagel frequently left some food for him and discreetly enabled Princz to listen to BBC broadcasts from London on his radio. Both Princz and her future husband have described Nagel as a man of fifty or fifty-five. His son, who had also been a member of the ss, died in the war. The two do not believe that the only reason Nagel helped them was that the inmates "organized" for him in return.

It became known that two Austrian ss men continually, though not self-lessly, helped their compatriots. They were Sepp Spanner, an ss corporal from Lower Austria, and Karl Hölblinger, a Viennese employed at the motor pool with the same rank. Spanner told me later that whenever he heard inmates speak in an Austrian dialect, he spoke to them and helped them. This has been confirmed by two other Austrians. Hölblinger maintained such a close con-tact with the Viennese Rudi Friemel, an inmate who worked in the motor pool, that he not only smuggled mail and parcels for him but also visited Friemel's father in Vienna during a leave.

Hölblinger had no hesitation about taking selected victims to the gas cham-bers in his LKW (Lastkraftwagen, truck) and unloading them there if these were his orders. Before the Anschluß in March 1938, when the NSDAP was still for-bidden, he was an illegal member of it. At a later date he assured me that he was an idealist who was proud of his Germanness. He explained to me: "I used to be so indoctrinated that I said all Jews should have their heads cut off." In the face of the gas chambers, however, he condemned the extermination of the Jews. In August 1944 he was arrested for favoring inmates, and only luck spared him severe punishment. At that time there were in his locker ten letters from prisoners that he had promised to transmit as well as eight bottles of schnapps and 3,000 cigarettes that the letter writers had evidently given him as a reward. It was only because a friend, who was in on the secret, had removed the incriminating contents of this locker before a search was carried out that Spanner succeeded in denying everything. Franz Kejmar, one of the most successful "organizers" in Auschwitz, has confirmed that Spanner visited his father in Vienna and told him about the extermination of human beings. Even though Spanner gladly accepted payment for his help, everyone he helped at that time and whom I questioned after the war had the impression that this was not the only reason for his assistance.

▦ The feelings in which the organizer of the human extermination, Adolf Eichmann, indulged constitute a grotesque counterpoint to these traits. I shall here reproduce verbatim what Eichmann recorded on tape during the preliminary investigation in Israel and what he verified on the transcript. When Eichmann was organizing the resettlement of the Jews after the German annexation of Austria, he met Berthold Storfer, a Jewish businessman whom the government had honored with the title counselor of commerce (*Kommerzialrat*). He said this about himself and that man:

> . . . then I had again found in Berlin a telex from Höß that said that Storfer had urgently asked to speak with me. I told myself: All right, the man has always been decent; after all, each of us pulled some strings over the years — he by himself and I in my Central Office. This is worthwhile for me, and I shall go there to see what's going on. I went to see Gregor Ebner (the head of the Gestapo in Vienna). I remember it only dimly, but he said to me: Well, if only he hadn't behaved so imprudently, he hid out there and wanted to flee, and something happened there. The officials acted and locked him up, sent him to a concentration camp on orders from the RFSS [Himmler]; anyone who was in there was not permitted to get out. No one could do anything about it, neither Dr. Ebner nor I nor anyone else. Couldn't get out. I went to Auschwitz, called on Höß, and said to him, "Storfer is imprisoned here." "Oh yes, he was assigned to a labor block." Then Storfer was sent for; it was a normal human encounter. He told me about his troubles, and I said, "My dear Storfer, what bad luck we've had! Look, I really can't help you. On orders of the RFSS, no one can get you out. I can't get you out. Dr. Ebner can't get you out. I heard that you've done a stupid thing

here, that you hid out or wanted to flee, which really wasn't necessary."
Then I asked him how he was and he said he would request to be exempted
from work because it was hard labor. Whereupon I said to Höß, "Storfer
doesn't need to work." Höß replied, "But everybody has to work here." "All
right," I said, "I shall put a note in the files saying that Storfer is keeping
the gravel paths in order with a broom here (in front of the commandant's
office there were green gardens). There are small gravel paths, and he has
the right to rest on one of the benches with his broom at any time. Is that
all right, Herr Storfer? Does that suit you?" He was very pleased, we shook
hands, and then he got a broom and sat down on a bench. It was a great
inner joy for me that I at least saw the man with whom for such long years
. . . whom I at least saw in all those years—and we spoke. With no word
did this man, let us say, betray Judaism. Storfer didn't do that. In World
War I Storfer was a major in the Austro-Hungarian army, though he served
in the financial office—the administration, I would say, and unfortunately,
the way things go, I wasn't the commandant of the Auschwitz camp. When
I got back from Hungary one day, I heard that Storfer had been shot.

That was a verbatim transcription of the tape. Dr. Albert Wenger recalls that
in October 1944 Berthold Storfer was taken to Block 11 and never came back.
When Wenger later inquired about Storfer in the office, his file card contained
a date of death.

That explanation is typical of Eichmann. It demonstrates that lower-
ranking SS officers like Spanner could help their protégés more effectively
than the all-powerful SS lieutenant colonel, for to them orders to exterminate
prisoners were not as sacred as they were to Eichmann; they did not confine
themselves to putting notes in the files of their acquaintances for their benefit.

■ Among the guards there were some individuals who suffered nervous breakdowns in the face of the mass murders. Jan Pilecki heard about an SS man who
was evidently rendered insane by a campaign in which primarily Jewish children were gassed. He is said to have been gassed together with the children
when he began to rave. A guard told Thomas Geve that many SS men became
mad, and Edward Pys once read a news item about the suicide of an SS man
by hanging, though no reason was given.

At the time of the Hungarian campaign Alfred Woycicki, who worked in the
Identification Service, observed a block leader who came to the office. He was
inebriated and had suffered a nervous breakdown. He told the inmates what
he had had to witness. (In those days human beings were thrown alive into
the fire that had been built next to the crematoriums because their capacity
was insufficient.) Woycicki writes that this man suffered "a kind of hysterical

attack, and so we had to use various means of calming him down, for we could not let him go to the SS men in that condition." The block leader said that most of the SS men were incapable of participating in these campaigns without schnapps or rum. Woycicki continues: "When he had regained his balance somewhat, we asked him why he did not try to get out of this function and whether these special rations (of alcohol) were really so valuable for him. He replied that here they were protected from serving at the front."

Riegenhagen, an SS medic trained as a "disinfector," also suffered a nervous breakdown during a gassing campaign. Edward Pys reports that he was thereafter not ordered to participate in such campaigns. Nurse Maria learned that Riegenhagen complained to Mandel, the SS camp leader, about a particularly cruel selection in the women's camp, using the argument that came closest to justifying such a step in the eyes of the SS leadership—namely, that this meant sabotaging the workforce. Nurse Maria describes Riegenhagen, a physical education teacher by profession, as an intelligent man. I remember him as an accessible SS man who liked to "organize." He was later relieved of his duties as a medic and transferred to a guard company. Pys remembers another SDG named Josef Schmucker, who had already served in World War I and who, in front of Pys and other inmates, once cursed the Hitler regime and his fate.

Tadeusz Szewczyk has vivid memories of Boleslaw Frymark, a noncommissioned officer and one of the men unfit for frontline service who were integrated into the Auschwitz SS in 1944. He was assigned to the SS pharmacy, which is where Szewczyk met him. "He spoke Polish with us. It was in the summer of 1944 that Frymark told us he had been assigned ramp duty as a replacement for another SS man. He left with his helmet and pistol in the morning and returned at noon. He had a nervous breakdown in our room and said, 'Let them do with me what they want, let them send me to the front, but I will not go to the ramp again.' In point of fact, Frymark was never assigned ramp duty again."

One time Simon, of the SS dental clinic, returned from ramp duty in an agitated state and said to a prisoner who had worked for him for a long time, "My God, what goes on there! They aren't SS men any longer—they are bandits, they are murderers!" Like his colleague Franz Mang, he was able to get out of further service at the ramp. I have another memory of Simon: His family must have lived in the Munich area because I noticed that he made particularly frequent trips to the KZ Dachau on official business. At my request he took some information to a friend of mine who was an inmate working in the Dachau dental clinic, and he also conveyed my friend's reply to me. I did not have to "pay" Simon for this.

Alois Lorenczyk, like Frymark an ethnic German of an advanced age, had a low-level position in the Political Department. Once he observed a young colleague beat an older woman at an interrogation and screamed at him, "What are you doing, you snot-nosed kid? Don't you have a mother? Have you no shame?" After this incident Lorenczyk was transferred.

The younger a person was, the easier it was to violate his inner nature. Survivors of the women's camp tell about a young thing who had recently arrived as a warden. After seeing what everyone saw in Birkenau, she broke down in the inmate office and kept repeating that she could not stand this, that she was going to run away, that she would kill herself. The prisoners tried to calm her down and urged her to stay, for the inmates needed people with compassionate hearts. The warden stayed and in a short time yelled and beat people just like her colleagues.

■ If a prisoner had a good experience with a guard, this made a deep impression on him. A story told by Stefan Boratynski proves how relative the concept of good was. He was once locked up in the stand-up bunker with his hands tied behind his back. They remained tied even when food was placed in his narrow cell, and thus he had to kneel and bend over the bowl in order to eat. "The block leader Hugo Müller displayed some heart," said Boratynski. "He held his boot under my chin when I fell on the food face down." This movement of his foot qualified Müller as "good" in Boratynski's eyes.

Even among the guards of the Sonderkommando there were "good" men. The strictly isolated inmates on this detail had contact with the camp only when the food was picked up. Dov Paisikovic remembers a guard of about fifty who frequently escorted them to the kitchen. He was hard of hearing and therefore known as *der Taube* (the deaf man). When he was on duty, Paisikovic was able to throw bread to his comrades in the camp because the "deaf man" deliberately looked the other way. Paisikovic never saw this older ss man in the undressing room that adjoined the gas chamber or at executions. "He liked gold." With this remark Paisikovic intimates that the "deaf man" did not tolerate the smuggling of food out of pure humanitarianism. Others loved gold, too, but did not look the other way when help was needed.

Because of his brutality, ss roll call leader Fritz Buntrock was called "Bulldog." When the Theresienstadt family camp was closed, its inmates were murdered, and only some youths who appeared to be fit for work were spared. Otto Kulka, who was only eleven at the time, attempted to make his way to a group of bigger boys. Buntrock noticed this, summoned Kulka, and asked him his age. The camp-wise Kulka quickly made himself older and answered, "Twelve." The ss roll call leader lit into him: "Why are you lying?" But then right away he said, "Get lost!"—thereby permitting Kulka to return to the group of bigger boys and to stay alive.

On another occasion Buntrock's feelings also overcame his ss discipline. Before the gassing of the second transport housed in the Theresienstadt family camp, several able-bodied prisoners were pulled out and taken to other sections of the camp before the general annihilation. Among them was a woman who had recently given birth. She gave the three-month-old baby a sleeping potion and smuggled it through the gate in a handbag. When all the women had to undress in the sauna where they had been taken, the baby was discovered. A guard was so touched by the mother's deed that she wanted to let her keep the baby, but she did not dare not to report this incident to the ss roll call leader. Buntrock made the same decision as the guard. That the two were not able to save the baby boy was Boger's fault. While checking the number of those who had been gassed or transferred to other sections, he calculated that there was a deficit of one person. He found out who that person was and sent both the mother and her child to their deaths.

Buntrock did not always act that way. Before the gassing of the inmates at the Gypsy camp, the ss roll call leader of that camp, the ethnic German Paul Bonigut from Croatia, called in sick because he did not want to participate. Buntrock took his place and directed the transport of the Gypsies to the gas chamber. According to the clerk of the Gypsy camp, Tadeusz Joachimowski, Bonigut had at an earlier date delayed the liquidation of the camp, thereby saving many who were transferred before the final liquidation.

Oszkár Betlen characterizes ss Sergeant Swenty as "one of the most agreeable ss men I have met." On the evacuation march the same Swenty shot three inmates who had stayed behind in a shed—even though he was alone when he ferreted them out, no one had directly ordered him to commit this murder, and he did not need to fear any evidence that he had discovered the three men and let them live. One should remember this example when one learns about good deeds of a guard.

Even small gestures could become of great significance to the prisoners. Eva Korngold writes: "There was only one thing that gave us courage. Every time we passed our friend, the elderly soldier (on the march to the workplace), he whispered a few friendly words to us." The girls called this member of the Wehrmacht "Grandpa."

■ A noticeably small number of ss men availed themselves of the logical way of getting out of Auschwitz: volunteering for frontline duty. Only a few instances have become known.

Hans Bauernschmidt was posted to Auschwitz in October 1942, and he immediately explored possibilities of being transferred again. When he heard that it was possible to sign up for leadership training, he did so and was transferred after two or three months. When I questioned him about this, he replied that at that time only two other noncommissioned officers asked to be transferred, because it was known that those who completed the course were sent to the front.

Fritz Karl Ertl testified as follows about how he managed to get out of Auschwitz. "As early as the end of 1942 I saw how things were developing in the camp, and so I and a number of other comrades decided to apply for a transfer from Auschwitz. After the defeat at Stalingrad there was a favorable opportunity for this. Everybody was examined for his fitness for active service. We did not even wait for this examination but volunteered for such service, whereupon I was transferred to a reserve unit in Dresden on February 3, 1943." This transfer meant that Ertl lost his rank as an ss leader; as an architect he had held the rank of a specialized leader in the central construction office of the Waffen-ss and police, but now he was only an ss sergeant. Ertl did not name those who had joined him in taking that route out of Auschwitz. There could not have been many because otherwise these applications for a transfer would have become better known.

Kurt Leischow was asked by the presiding judge in Frankfurt why he had volunteered for frontline service to get away from Auschwitz. "Just imagine what you have to see every day," he replied. To be sure, Leischow did not take this route until the late spring of 1944, and he is reputed to have shown the inmates no mercy in the early period in Auschwitz.

Otto Graf, an ss sergeant and the head of the Canada Commando, where he incurred a lot of guilt, was sent to a frontline unit in September 1944. He had been classified as unfit for service at the front because of an injury suffered in the early phase of the war, but "after July 20 (the failed attempt on Hitler's life) it was possible to apply for a transfer, and everyone was accepted without a lengthy investigation," as Graf put it. Nevertheless, only two others joined him in making such an application.

More consequential behavior was displayed by a physician who was an ss leader and thus had greater opportunities than the rank and file. Dr. Otto Wolken has given the following account of this: "One time an ss physician by the name of Bartzel was transferred to Birkenau. In the Gypsy camp he encountered Professor Epstein, who was working there as an inmate physician, and said to him, 'But I know you! What's your name?' Epstein told him, and the ss physician said: 'Sure, you're Epstein the pediatrician! I studied under you in Prague. No, this here is no business for my mother's child.' Thereupon he left and was never seen in the camp again." Unfortunately there is no further information about this man, and Wolken is not even sure that he has remembered his name correctly.

Vera Foltynova describes a similar episode that occurred in the construction office. When Schosenow, an ss captain from Latvia who had recently been transferred to the construction office, looked out the window, saw the great processions of victims in the direction of the crematoriums, and learned about the fate that awaited them there, he said, "I am not a murderer, I am a soldier." According to Foltynova, he was sent to the front a few days later. From the very beginning this SS captain was different from all the others; he addressed the inmates with the polite "*Sie*," brought them clothes, and even introduced them to his wife and his son.

Dr. Roland Quästl (possibly Questel or something similar) applied to be transferred from Auschwitz to the front even though as the holder of a doctorate in biology he was employed in the agricultural experimental station at Rajsko and had no direct contact with the machinery of destruction. As Eva Gabanyi reports, Quästl at first kept away from the female inmates who were working in Rajsko. Later he told them that he had at first thought they were all criminals and murderers, which is what he had heard at the indoctrination sessions. After he had become acquainted with them and their fate he regularly brought them cigarettes, honey, and other foods. At Christmastime he used some pretext to have some women with whom he had a good contact detailed for duty at his apartment, where he had a Christmas tree and presents laid out for each one. Even when Quästl was already at the front, his mother sent these women parcels by way of SS Corporal Lettmann, who had served under Quästl in Auschwitz. Gabanyi knows that Quästl, who was born in 1915, came from Litomerice and had joined the SS to finance his studies.

▨ The establishment of contact with the outside world—above all, with relatives—was a particularly valuable help. True, "Aryan" inmates were permitted to write and receive mail regularly (every two weeks), but owing to the censorship these letters had to remain vague and constituted little more than a confirmation that the writer was still alive. As a rule, Jews had no legal opportunity to write. Decades later Gisl Holzer is for this reason still grateful to Sappe, an SS sergeant from Gablonz whom she met in the Labor Assignment Office, for smuggling her mail out of and into the camp. Others in the SS—for example, warden Gertrude Liehr—also accepted letters for mailing, and they were frequently paid for this.

In a very unusual way Eva Gabanyi was given a chance to establish contact with her family. In Rajsko, where she worked, a guard once addressed her in Slovakian, telling her that he was also from Slovakia and was very worried about his sick child. Gabanyi advised him, the next time he was on leave, to call on her brother, a physician who had not yet been arrested, and give him regards from his sister, for then he would surely help the child. The SS man did this and Gabanyi's brother was able to cure the child. From that day on, the grateful guard kept up the contact between Eva and her family for as long as he was in Rajsko. Gabanyi does not remember his name; her guess is that he was twenty-six years old. What struck her was that he spoke a primitive kind of German.

Some SS men helped with the procurement of what were often critically needed medicines. The corporal in the SS pharmacy, Tadeusz Dobrzanski—who, like many others whose humane conduct has been documented, was an ethnic German—insisted on good payment for supporting the smuggling of medications. The inmates working in the SS pharmacy gave him gold and dollars that they had found in the tubes and pastes brought from Canada. Martin Stocker, an SS man from Mannheim, regularly brought Felix Amann medications, and he did this without a quid pro quo. The two men met in the disinfection section of Birkenau. This is what Amann has said about Stocker: "He was so kind that later he was sent to Buchenwald as an inmate."

While serving as a guard in Harmense, a fish-farming pond, Helmut Pomreinke, an ethnic German from Romania, met the inmate Rudolf Rybka. The two men developed such a relationship of trust that Pomreinke visited Rybka's parents, who were living in Czechoslovakia, not far from Auschwitz, and brought Rybka food from them.

Artur Rablin remembers Kurt Fiebig, an SS technical sergeant from Zittau, who once called on the parents of an inmate at the inmate's request. Fiebig is said to have hanged himself in the building of the old crematorium after his connection with this inmate had been betrayed by other men.

All exceptions from the rule were carefully registered and not forgotten by the prisoners. Felix Amann recalls, in addition to Stocker, an ethnic German from Lithuania by the name of Viktor Cheimnis who was assigned to disinfections as well as gassings. Cheimnis openly displayed to Amann his disgust at what he had to do. Whenever he had an opportunity to do so, he aided inmates whom he knew. SS Master Sergeant Franz Xaver Dornacher of the SS canteen is described by Heinrich Dronia as "a person of rare kindness" who helped wherever he could and warned inmates against ill-disposed SS men. To be sure, in his position Dornacher came in contact with only a very small number of inmates. He openly cold-shouldered SS roll call leader Oswald Kaduk, a man feared because of his brutality, whom Dornacher outranked.

More than twenty-five years later, a former inmate recalled in court that members of the Luftwaffe slipped something into his and his comrades' hands when they were sorting fragments of destroyed planes in Birkenau. SS Technical Sergeant Friedrich Münkel, who was in charge of the shoemakers' and tailors' workshops in Birkenau, never gave beatings himself and did not permit others to do so in his presence. He sometimes gave inmates cigarettes.

In the winter of 1942–43, Erich Kohlhagen met Kuhn, an SS corporal in Monowitz who was, according to Kohlhagen, "anything but a Nazi" and neither gave beatings nor reported inmates. Kuhn once told him that he would never shoot at an inmate because he could not square that with his conscience.

Miriam Blits remembers a guard named Erika who secretly gave food to her and her comrades. Jehuda Bacon was fifteen when a female warden sent for him one day and served him a plate of noodles; he mentioned this episode in an interview fifteen years later. A long time afterward Alexander Princz also praised a young SS man in the canine corps who gave him something to eat. That SS man, whose dialect indicated a Bavarian background, intimated that he did not like serving in Auschwitz. When Princz met him again at the time of the evacuation, the SS man offered to help him escape, but Princz did not accept his offer.

■ There were some SS men who did not want to incur the risk of being sent to the front but shirked tasks directly connected with the mass murders.

When Hubert Christoph, an SS sergeant, was about to be transferred to the department that had to regulate the work assignments of the inmates, he resisted the move. When he was later asked why, Christoph, who had joined the SS in 1934, said: "When I joined the SS, I imagined something different. I did not want to work inside the camp." Christoph was harassed because of his attitude, but he was spared a transfer.

When a judge asked Horst Huley, an ethnic German from Romania who had served in Auschwitz as an SS private, why a person of his intelligence had not achieved a higher rank, he responded as follows: "I could have become a block leader if I had had the disposition for it. It was possible to behave in such a way that one did not become a block leader."

SS Sergeant Johann Piringer testified that on watchtowers there were graffiti like "Auschwitz, the murderer of my youth," which prompted a major investigation.

Richard Böck, who had been assigned to the motor pool, was once ordered to drive the selectees who were no longer ambulatory from the ramp to the gas chamber in his truck and to dump them there. After the first run he declared that he was incapable of taking this route again. He was excused and from then on had to transport only food. On such occasions he tried to help inmates, and once he was even locked up for aiding and abetting prisoners. Since this could not be proved, he escaped punishment.

Böck was the most consistent in shirking all transports to the gas chamber, but others also tried to do so. Knut Siebenlist, a German inmate with a position in the motor pool, states that SS drivers who had been assigned to transport victims from the ramp to the gas chamber repeatedly gave him food and said, "Tomorrow I'll fall apart. I can't go on." Siebenlist adds: "I was not surprised, given that our trucks always had to be cleaned after drives to the gas chamber. The condition of the trucks after such transports indicates what happened on these drives. The trucks were soiled with feces and draped with torn-out hair; I even saw chopped-off fingers."

Ruth Kersting drew my attention to Wladimir Bilan, an ethnic German who had to admit the new arrivals to the camp. He probably noticed her because of her then still well-groomed appearance and asked her the reason for her imprisonment. Kersting answered truthfully that she had been arrested because she had attempted to get in touch with her mother, a Jew who had been deported to Theresienstadt after the death of her "Aryan" husband. Bilan said that he was sorry for her and instructed the admissions clerk to register Kersting as a "German political prisoner from the Reich" even though as a Mischling (half-Jew) she should have been obliged to wear a Star of David. This probably saved Kersting's life.

Bilan touched her life on another occasion as well. Worn out and desperate after the first and hardest weeks, she happened to catch sight of Bilan in the camp. She ventured to accost him and asked him whether he had any work for her, a speaker of many languages, because she was anxious to get away from a detail that involved heavy physical labor. Bilan just took down her number. She was called that very evening, and Bilan took her to see his superior. At that time transports from Italy were expected, and since Italian was one of Kersting's languages, she was added to the Admissions Department, where she found much more favorable conditions.

When Kersting was quarantined prior to leaving the camp, she asked Bilan, with whom she had become better acquainted at work, how he could stand being in the camp. Bilan answered that as an ethnic German his only choice had been to join the Russians or the Germans, and that is how he had joined the SS. He would have liked to get out of Auschwitz, but he had been threatened and therefore had stayed.

I questioned other women who worked in the Admissions Department under Bilan and received answers that were unusually consistent. "During that entire period we never saw him beat an inmate, as others did," said Zofia Bratro. "He only helped us, and without prompting he suggested that we surreptitiously send letters to our families." Trude Guttmannova's answer was this: "He never beat us and only yelled when it was absolutely necessary—that is, when one of the high-level gentlemen was in sight. But he apologized immediately afterward, and we knew very well that he did not want to harm us. He brought us medications, books, and newspapers, all of which were forbidden."

In Monowitz, where Bilan was transferred, he behaved equally well. "He was always very, very decent and polite, almost comradely. We never heard an unfriendly tone from him. He never touched an inmate and believed everything that an inmate said during an interrogation." There, too, he brought the inmates books and newspapers. Unikower thinks that Bilan was not suited to the ss and the camp, and he presumes that he had been assigned to the Political Department on account of his knowledge of languages. (He was a native of Poland.)

I questioned this man, who constituted such a striking exception. He told me that at the beginning it had been impressed on them in Auschwitz that they had the honorable task of guarding the scum of the earth. Such phrases, he said, had lodged in the flesh and blood of many. "Most of them were of the opinion that this was the way it had to be. Many believed in the Thousand-Year Reich and thought they would not be called to account." This is how Bilan described the atmosphere in the garrison. And why did he not adopt this attitude? "When I saw a vehicle with corpses at the old crematorium, I thought to myself: this is being done by Germans whom we ethnic Germans admired so much. That was a signal for me, and I changed, because otherwise I might have done the same thing." This answer, to be sure, does not explain how he remained an exception, since probably everyone in Auschwitz saw mountains of dead bodies. The most convincing demonstration of Bilan's good conscience was his request for the addresses of surviving former prisoners with whom he had had contact in the camp. No other ss man whom I talked with afterward went to the trouble that Bilan did to establish contact with former inmates.

■ Fairly often one encountered members of the ss in Auschwitz who obediently executed the orders given them, even if murder was involved, yet who occasionally were incapable of following through because their inner nature rebelled. Many survivors remember an episode of this kind. In February 1943 Polish lads from Zamosc and environs were taken to the infirmary of the main camp. At that time the inhabitants of that region were evacuated and for simplicity's sake sent directly to the kz. The youths were to be injected because they did not seem strong enough to be assigned to labor. At a later date the medic Scherpe stated that these children were between ten and fourteen years of age, but inmates thought they were eight to twelve years old. Tadeusz Paczula says cautiously that none was older than fifteen. Stanislaw Klodzinski, a nurse in the block where the injections were given, still remembers the day on which those lads were taken there. "The children entered Block 20 through a side door. They had to undress and then line up in the corridor. Scherpe arrived. There was deathly silence in the block. The only thing one could hear was the sound of bodies falling on the floor of the washroom. After a few such dull thuds Scherpe emerged from the room. He said, 'I can't do it any more,' and left." On that day I saw a pale and upset Scherpe go to see the ss garrison physician. From later statements I gathered that he had declared himself incapable of killing children. He was excused, transferred to the satellite camp Golleschau, and promoted to the rank of SS technical sergeant shortly thereafter. The document recommending this promotion had probably been prepared earlier, but it was not canceled after Scherpe's refusal.

Emil Hantl killed the other children in Scherpe's stead. This is how Tadeusz Holuj described Hantl's behavior after these killings: "He was completely broken down, cursed the war, and talked about his earlier life." In other ways, too, Hantl stood out from the accustomed pattern. "He did not beat us and did not seem like a typical SS man to us," wrote Ota Fabian. "When Hantl came down to our cellar (Fabian was a corpse carrier), we did not even have to rise, nor did he say anything if he saw us eat potatoes." Tadeusz Paczula confirms that "he was quiet and polite, and sometimes he gave us a cigarette," and to a question from the Frankfurt judge he replied that the other inmates who knew Hantl well trusted him. Wladyslaw Dering testified that "Hantl gave us cigarettes and bread and never reported anyone." Hermann Reineck declared: "He made a good impression on me, and I was pleased that there were human beings even among the SS men." On one occasion Hantl evidently came out of his shell during the night shift and complained to Reineck, who was the block elder at the time, that he could barely stand service in Auschwitz. Ludwig Wörl, a camp elder, also testified that Hantl repeatedly complained to him that he had to give lethal injections and kept saying, "If only this stopped!" Wörl believes that Hantl was not brave enough to refuse the execution of orders to murder. From the office of the HKB, where he was employed, Igor Bistric was able to observe that even though Hantl killed people by injecting them with phenol, "he had retained a bit of humaneness." This SS man from the Sudetenland, who was forty-one at the time, sometimes conversed with Bistric in Czech.

The clerk of Block 20 particularly emphasizes one point: "The most important thing was that Scherpe and Hantl always said 'Good Morning' when they came into the block and 'Goodbye' when they left. For us, who had been so degraded, these were small signs of humaneness." Such favorable judgments about these two medics are due, among other things, to the fact that former inmates instinctively compared them with medic Klehr, who was active in the main camp at the same time. "By comparison with Klehr, Scherpe and Hantl seemed like angels." This remark by Glowa indicates the relativity of such judgments.

Twenty-five years later Max Kasner told me that he still felt respect for Ludwig, a medic who always acted humanely in the satellite camp Janinagrube. It has been reported that another medic, Neubert, on one occasion slapped a capo in the face because he had so mistreated an inmate that he broke his arm. Tadeusz Kosmider illuminates the relationship that developed between Neubert and inmate functionaries in the Monowitz infirmary when he tells of how they once gave Neubert a hundred marks and said, "Buy cigarettes—half for you, the other half for us."

Harmless-sounding episodes of this kind should not make people forget that these SS medics selected prisoners who were to be killed and then killed them with their own hands.

Even Klehr had his "weak" hours. The Pole Jerzy Tabeau owes his life to such a moment. In the summer of 1942 he was selected by Dr. Entress. Alfred Stössel, the Polish block elder, knew Tabeau and begged Klehr to take his name off the selection list. "Klehr ordered that I be brought before him," reports Tabeau. "He was sitting at a table in the small operating room, looked at me, and ordered me to get out. I was not sent to the gas." Stössel presumably was able to achieve this because he often did the injecting when Klehr was tired.

When Klehr was transferred as a medic to the satellite camps in Gleiwitz in the fall of 1944, he visibly changed. As Josef Farber testifies, "He committed no more brutal acts there and was in general decent. Moll, the SS camp leader (and former director of the crematoriums), was the only man who wanted to establish an Auschwitz-type regime in Gleiwitz. Klehr resisted this idea. I heard him yell at inmates who were beating other inmates." In those days Farber was even able to save the lives of two prisoners whom Klehr had selected by guaranteeing that they would be fit to work again in a short time. Farber attributes this transformation to the development at the fronts and also to the influence of Klehr's wife, who was able to visit him frequently in Gleiwitz.

An SS man named Flagge had the best reputation of all medics. He was probably around fifty when Ella Lingens met him in the satellite camp Babitz. She writes: "I encountered one island of peace in the concentration camp Auschwitz: the labor camp Babitz. It was to the credit of one man, SS Technical Sergeant Flagge. I don't know how he did it. It was clean there, and the food was correspondingly so. The women called him 'Daddy,' and he even procured eggs from the outside." In her book Lingens reports that Flagge shared his food with her and other inmates and made sure that the accommodations were heated when it rained so that the women could dry their clothes after returning from work. On one occasion, when he came into the camp unexpectedly, he surprised Lingens and the Polish nurse sleeping during working hours. He left without waking them. Lingens reproduced for the Frankfurt court a conversation she once had with this medic. "You know, Herr SDG, everything we do (in tending the sick) is so terrible and so senseless, because when this war comes to an end we shall all be killed anyway. They won't let any eyewitnesses survive." Flagge's response was this: "I hope there will be enough people among us who will prevent that." Dr. Otto Wolken met Flagge in the quarantine section of Birkenau where the latter liked to play with the children from the neighboring Theresienstadt family camp. Wolken observed Flagge when the inmates of that camp were being driven to the gas chambers; he stood by the window with tears in his eyes.

One time Lingens asked him how a man with his attitude could remain in Auschwitz. Flagge answered with a question: "Would you rather have an unfeeling man in my place?"

In the SS infirmary we encountered a type of man who was completely out of step with the others. Eduard Jambor was an aged teacher from the Sudetenland and a convinced Nazi. He had been assigned to the physician of the SS troops as a clerk, and the only prisoners he came in contact with were those who worked in the SS infirmary. However, what was happening in Auschwitz could not be concealed from him. Jambor, who realized that his ideals were being sullied, buried himself in his files and refused to acknowledge anything that was bound to shatter his conception of Nazism. He cautiously kept up a human contact with us. It was touching when he shared his bread with us, even though he was one of the very few who did not procure additional food in crooked ways and thus did not have much himself. He avoided conversations that might lead to the field of politics, but there was no overlooking his bad conscience. His frantic attempts to keep his hands clean seemed grotesque in that setting. As his wife wrote me at a later date, "He was always happy when he could spend a few days with his family and did not have to think of his experiences. He never gave us details." This last statement indicates that Jambor was disciplined even when he was with his family. His wife described him as "deeply religious," which stands in contradiction to his Nazi convictions.

■ Some SS men have remained nameless, but former prisoners do remember their conduct. An unknown SS man refused to shoot at female inmates. Helena Kopper testified before a British military court in Lüneburg that warden Irma Grese reported him for this. All she knows is that he was an ethnic German from Slovakia. Hermine Horvath met an SS man in the Gypsy camp who was so moved by the sight of children suffering from noma and the holes in their cheeks that he spontaneously brought them bread. Horvath concluded her testimony by saying, "The next day this SS man was no longer in the camp."

Josef Farber is also unable to name the SS man whom he met while engaged in disinfection work in Birkenau. The man was always friendly and often conversed with Farber. One day—Farber believes it was probably in the summer of 1943—the SS man told him, "I'm in trouble. I've been assigned to a gassing detail, and I will refuse to participate." Farber did not see this man for several months. When he encountered him again, he noticed how pale the man was and asked him if he was sick. The SS man told him that his refusal had caused him to be locked up and that he had now been ordered to go to the front as punishment. Farber remembers only that this man was from Romania, had a German-sounding name, reddish hair, and the lowest SS rank.

Teddy Pietrzykowski met an ethnic German from Croatia when he was cleaning a room in the staff building in which SS men with minor illnesses were laid up. That man was a recent arrival in Auschwitz; Pietrzykowski thinks that this probably happened in early 1943. At that time ethnic Germans from Croatia were taken to Auschwitz in a sealed cattle car. Pietrzykowski assumed that this was one of the usual transports to the gas chambers. To his surprise, however, the men put on SS uniforms after getting off the train. The SS man in the sickroom asked the Polish prisoner to get him some drug that would really make him sick, since he wanted to leave the camp at any cost. In point of fact, with Teddy's assistance he was such a skillful malingerer that he was released from the SS.

▉ There is documentation that some members of the SS were punished for favoring inmates. For example, Artur Breitwieser, who was in charge of the clothing depot, had to serve a prison term because he had given a female inmate three meters of fabric. Ladislaw Gura, an ethnic German from Bratislava, was incarcerated several times and finally sentenced to two years in jail by an SS tribunal in Kattowitz because he had been caught drinking schnapps with some inmates. The SS and police court in Breslau sentenced SS Private First Class Kurt Hartmann to four months in prison and expulsion from the SS, and Ludwig Karl Schmidt received a suspended sentence with a probationary period at the front. Schmidt had facilitated a meeting between a male and a female inmate, and Hartmann had given a prisoner some food. On November 30, 1944, Adolf Prem was sentenced for repeated military insubordination because he had bad-mouthed the SS leaders and talked politics with inmates. The indictment quoted this statement by Prem: "Life in Austria will never be as beautiful as it used to be." Prem belonged to the SS when it was illegal in Austria and was thus considered an "Old Fighter." At a later date Bogan Wnetrzewski characterized him as "a very decent and friendly Austrian and opponent of the NSDAP." On Prem's radio and with his knowledge, Wnetrzewski was able to listen to broadcasts of the BBC.

Another SS man from Austria is said to have treated the prisoners humanely. Oskar Gravogel, an SS corporal from Türnitz (Lower Austria), was court-martialed and shot in March 1945 for "insulting the Führer and doing crazy things." This information was supplied by Prem, who calls Gravogel "a good man."

An unusual incident has been described by Andrej Milar. In the summer of

1944 Vogel, a Wehrmacht soldier about fifty years of age, was transferred to Birkenau. Milar remembers that he was an artisan from Vienna. When those selected for the gas chambers were once again ordered to undress before they were forced to get on the trucks, Vogel, who was not yet familiar with SS practices in Auschwitz, asked a guard what was going to happen to the naked prisoners. He was given the official story that they were going to be taken to work in a factory. Since there was bad weather, Vogel vigorously demanded that the prisoners be clothed, and they were actually given blankets. After the trucks had left, Milar, who had been watching, took Vogel to the attic of a barracks from which it was possible to observe how the unfortunates were herded into the gas chamber, and he enlightened him about the extermination. The outraged Vogel rushed to the room of the camp physician, where Dr. Mengele happened to be. He is said to have told the physician that if such a thing was possible he was ashamed of being a German. When Mengele tried to calm him down by saying that death by poison gas was hardly painful, Vogel is said to have replied that Jews were human beings, too, and must be treated as human beings. He is supposed to have expressed his outrage to other members of the SS as well. One day he disappeared.

Ludwik Lawin has reported the following episode. When he was working in Porabka in the summer of 1942, he met an SS man, a pyrotechnist who had been posted there as a convalescent. Lawin heard snatches of a spirited argument between this young man and SS roll call leader Palitzsch. The former is said to have exclaimed, "What are you people doing to our thousand-year culture? What are you doing to our honor?" Whereupon Palitzsch is said to have replied, "Shit, this is the front, we're cleaning up here, the eastern area is being cleared." According to Lawin, the young SS man was taken away the next day, and there were rumors that he was assigned to an extermination detail and shot himself.

It remains uncertain to what extent the dwindling hopes for a victory of Hitler's Germany prompted some of those described in this chapter to treat the prisoners differently from the way they had been ordered to, but it cannot be overlooked that in 1944 there were more humane acts than before Hitler's defeat in Stalingrad.

"Demoralization" reached a new low when the end of Auschwitz was in sight, the Russian troops were approaching, and the bombardments of Germany had become a horrifying everyday affair. Igor Bistric, who served as clerk in Block 6 of the main camp at that time, reports that his block leader sometimes came to see him in the fall of 1944 in order to discuss the times before the KZ. "He did not spurn accepting a piece of inmate's bread with marmalade from a Jew," writes Bistric, and he emphasizes that in those days no one was beaten by a block leader any more. He explains this transformation by saying that "the dream of a Thousand-Year Reich was simply over."

Soon after the liberation Heinrich Dürmeyer testified that at Christmastime 1944 SS roll call leader Heinz Hertwig approached him in a completely drunken state, embraced him, and said: "Hey, if things ever change, you're gonna help me, aren't you? I'm already doing whatever you want."

FRANK AND PESTEK

■ ■ ■

Some members of the SS took the risk of helping inmates to escape. I have made an effort to reconstruct as accurately as possible the small number of cases that have become known.

German prisoners had the greatest chance of getting SS men to support their efforts to escape. Otto Küsel told me that an SS man aided his three Polish friends and him in their preparations for an escape and fulfilled Küsel's requests, one exception being the purchase of a revolver. They managed to escape on December 28, 1942, and this was due in large measure to this helpful SS man, whose name Küsel no longer remembers. All he knows is that he was an ethnic German from Upper Silesia.

The camp elder in the indoctrination section of Monowitz, a communist from the Cologne area named Rudi Kahn, was also helped by a guard in breaking out of the camp. In early 1943 Kahn chose for his undertaking a night from Saturday to Sunday because many SS men were on leave over the weekend. He escaped successfully from the camp in the vicinity of a watchtower that his friend had arranged to man.

Some SS men went even further. The camp-wise Birkenau capo Franz Kejmar was not merely helped by an SS man when he prepared to flee together with the Poles Zbigniew Pupalski and Edward Pasdor as well as the German Theodor Retzlof; the SS man joined them on November 3, 1943. After only three days of freedom the men were arrested. The lives of the inmates were saved by the fact that Commandant Höß had just been relieved of his duties and those caught while trying to escape were no longer executed under Höß's successor, Liebehenschel. However, Kejmar heard that the SS man, an ethnic German from Banat, was executed.

■ The "Combat Group Auschwitz" organized many successful escapes without the help of members of the SS. When it decided to send some of its leaders to partisans in the vicinity, it did not want to use the usual route because if the camp administration learned of the escape of several inmate functionaries known in the camp, including two who had been admitted as political opponents of Nazism, more intensive searches could be expected than the routinely ordered activation of the great cordon of guards for three nights.

First of all, we arranged with the partisans a place in the vicinity of the camp where we were to meet and receive arms from them. In order to reconnoiter the route to this meeting place, I prevailed on my boss to send me out of the camp—escorted by guards, of course—along with Zbyszek, who was also supposed to escape. This was prompted by the malaria that had spread to the ss guard. In an effort to destroy the carriers of this disease, Wirths had ordered the spraying of all bodies of water in the area, but this measure failed. When he complained about this, I told him that it was the fault of the ss men who were supposed to carry out this order; they preferred lying on the grass and sleeping to walking around and spraying all the waters. Wirths knew his men, and so he readily believed me. Then I found it easy to get him to send me out in order to mark on a map all ponds, marshes, and swampy places, so that these might be systematically sprayed, and to take along Zbyszek, who was a graphic artist and could therefore make the most precise markings. Thus we set out with two guards and a map that Zbyszek immediately copied so that it might be used for future escapes. We carefully committed the meeting place and the best route there to memory without our escorts suspecting anything.

An ss man was to take us safely out of the camp area and to the prearranged meeting place as if he were escorting an inmate detail. I have described how we tried to win him over:

Rudl's friend Karl, the capo of the clothing depot, has made an appointment for me with the block leader, whom we want to persuade to flee. At 9:00 in the evening, we are to meet in the capo's room on his block.

I am the first to arrive in his little attic room. I hear footsteps. The heavy nailed shoes of the ss man can be clearly heard.

When an ss man enters a room, inmates have to rise and snap to attention. However, I don't rise; after all, he is not an ss man now and I am not an inmate. I extend my hand from my seat, and he takes it. For a few moments I have a peculiar feeling, and it appears that he does, too. The two of us sit in the room opposite each other—he with a medal ribbon in his buttonhole, I with my inmate number on my chest. I purposely did not put on a different jacket. Anyone who wants to find me in the camp can easily do so. Let him see that I am not afraid of him.

"So, do you know what this is about?" I use the familiar address *du*, which is customary among comrades.

"No, not really."

"I am speaking with you in the name of our organization. You know that there is an organization here in the camp, don't you?"

"I could imagine it."

"Fine. First of all, no matter how you will feel about our proposal, I shall speak quite frankly and expect you to do the same. Your name and address are on the outside, both with the resistance organization in Poland and in London and Moscow. If something happens to me in the near future, you won't be alive much longer."

I look him firmly in the eye. His face doesn't change. His hands do not reveal anything either but rest calmly on his thighs.

"Shall I go on?" "Yes, keep talking." His voice sounds husky. He is impressed.

"Our organization is planning an escape. Do you want to flee with us?"

"I thought that something like this was going to happen."

"Then you have probably thought of a response." I give him a friendly smile. He asks a number of questions. Finally we agree that he will think the whole thing over and give me his answer in the clothing depot in two days.

"Don't forget what I told you at the beginning. It would only be unpleasant for both of us." We smile and shake hands.

We knew that this block leader came from an area in East Prussia that had become a battleground. Rudl had known him for a long time, and thus the conversation could take place in that form. His response was evasive. On principle he agreed to a joint escape because we had assured him of a good hiding place out there until the arrival of the Russians, but he hesitated when a timetable was to be established. I shall go on quoting from my *Bericht*:

We are again sitting together in the little room in the clothing depot. "Let's talk quite frankly. I am under the impression that you would like to postpone the escape, but we don't want to do this. Are you ready to flee now? It's all right for you to tell us if you're not ready; nothing will happen to you. But don't put us off any longer."

"Quite frankly, I'm not ready right now." He is visibly relieved.

"All right. Then help us escape without you. We need a pass and a uniform. What can you get for us without being suspected? That wouldn't be in our interest, since we want to organize more escapes later."

He liked that. He does not want to burn the bridges to us. "A pass is easy. I'll bring you an old one, and all you have to do is to put a false date on it. No guard will notice this if you do it skillfully. A uniform is harder to obtain. I can bring you pants. I have an extra pair. It's old, but you don't mind, do you?"

"No, we don't mind. We can get a jacket elsewhere, and a cap, too. Try to dig up a belt for us." Heinz is now working in the SS clothing depot as a capo. He has, relatively speaking, great freedom of movement and easy access to SS uniforms. He is getting us a jacket and a cap.

The block leader brought us the promised clothes. Everything was ready for the escape. The pass had been prepared, and a complete SS uniform was hanging in a locked closet in our office at the SS infirmary; it belonged to a medic who had been assigned to a satellite camp and came to the main camp only infrequently. Zbyszek had made a key for that closet. However, on the eve of the planned escape we were informed that the partisan group that we were supposed to meet had been attacked, and so we had to cancel our enterprise. Soon thereafter I was unexpectedly placed on a transport that had been under preparation for a few days. Thus I left Auschwitz and never heard what became of the young East Prussian block leader, whose name I have forgotten.

■ That happened in August 1944. The leadership of the Combat Group resumed its plans for escapes, and in October it was ready. This time Rudi Friemel and Vickerl Vesely induced two SS men from the motor pool to smuggle prisoners out of the camp in a chest on a truck that was taking dirty laundry to Bielsko. Since there was room for several people in this chest, five men were to participate in the escape. In addition to Ernst Burger and Zbyszek Raynoch, who had been scheduled to flee in August, there were three Poles from the resistance movement.

One of the previously mentioned SS men was named Frank. George Goiny-Grabowski has described him as an ethnic German from Romania or Slovakia who was about twenty years old. The other SS man, Corporal Johann Roth, an ethnic German from Romania, played a double game. He informed the Political Department about the plan. The men concealed in the chest, along with Friemel, Vesely, and Frank, were arrested, and the partisans were attacked at the agreed-upon meeting place. Roth was commended in a commandant's order of the day and received a photograph of Oswald Pohl, the chief of the WVHA, with a handwritten inscription.

Frank's fate is not clear. The SS judge Gerhard Wiebeck recalls that he once had to bring charges against an SS man who had been caught trying to smuggle a Jewish woman out of Auschwitz in a chest. At that time Wiebeck requested the death sentence. SS Captain Rohner was the presiding judge, but Wiebeck claims he no longer remembers the outcome. It is possible that Frank was involved in this trial. While Wiebeck correctly remembers the means of escape, the chest, he may be wrong about the person who was to be helped in making an escape, for no other case is known in which an SS man tried to smuggle one or more prisoners out of the camp with the aid of a chest. A Polish inmate who worked in the motor pool and knew Frank well claims to have seen him in Munich after the war.

■ There is better documentation of the fantastic story of another escape in which an SS man was a key figure.

SS Sergeant Viktor Pestek, a compatriot of Roth and Baretzki, stood out among the Birkenau block leaders. Josef Neumann describes him as "a decent person who never beat inmates," and Jehuda Bacon says that he was "more humane than the others." In the Theresienstadt family camp he was called Miláček, which is Czech for "darling." Vitezslav Lederer has researched the background of this remarkable man.

Pestek's father was a German-speaking smith in Bukovina and owner of a small farm. Viktor was also trained as a smith, but he joined the SS because his mother urged him to do so and he wanted to see the world. Baretzki has described how the SS recruited young lads after the resettlement of the Germans living in Bukovina. Pestek was sent to the Russian front. One day his unit was ordered to attack a village near Minsk in which partisans were said to be hidden, and to massacre the inhabitants. There was a fight in which two SS men were wounded. Pestek was shot in the arm and lower leg. When darkness fell, the SS retreated, but the two injured men had to spend the night in the destroyed village waiting for a rescue crew. Pestek's comrade died, and he kept his vigil in a barn. When the completely exhausted man finally heard footsteps in the morning, he cried out for help. A man with a rifle and woman with two children appeared, and Pestek identified them as Russians. Pestek indicated to them that he was thirsty; they dragged him to a fountain and then left.

Later Pestek was rescued by a unit and taken to a field infirmary. He could not forget that these people had let him live even though they had no reason to spare a man in an SS uniform whose unit had just mowed down all the villagers they could get their hands on. This experience reawakened religious convictions in Pestek, who had had a strict Catholic upbringing.

After this recovery Pestek was unfit for further frontline service, and thus he was posted to Auschwitz. He was shaken by the daily mass extermination and offended by the latent general contempt for an ethnic German *Beutegermane*. While serving as a block leader in the Theresienstadt family camp, Pestek fell in love with a tall, blonde Jewish prisoner named Renée Neumannova, for whom he obtained the position of a block clerk. These considerations brought about his decision not only to flee from the murderous atmosphere himself but also to help inmates to escape.

This was anything but easy for Pestek because at that time there was an incident that served as a warning to inmates with camp experience. An SS man by the name of Schneider persuaded two inmates on the Canada Detail to escape together. Since he was known as a "good" SS man, the two men accepted his suggestion. It was not hard for them to "organize" valuables from Canada that were intended to smooth their way once they were free. However, the two men were captured, taken back to the camp, and executed. The inmates on the Sonderkommando read the following words written in indelible ink on the chests of the dead bodies: "Schneider betrayed us." Evidently that ss man collected both the "organized" valuables and the camp administration's bonus for preventing an escape.

When shortly after this incident Pestek approached Josef Neumann, the capo of the Birkenau corpse carriers, regarding a joint escape, Neumann refused in light of what Schneider had done. Rudolf Vrba, at that time a block clerk in Birkenau, has provided the following report about subsequent efforts made by Pestek:

When I went over to his (Vrba's friend Alfred Wetzler's) room in the d-camp one evening in order to eat with him, I found him sharing a plate of potatoes with an ss man named Pestek, an uncommonly good-looking sergeant around twenty-six years of age. When I entered, Fred said to his guest, "I'd like to discuss this with Rudi. Would you excuse us for a moment?" The German nodded. Fred took me to another room and gave me the following explanation: "It's like this, Rudi. This fellow has a most unusual plan that might work. He is prepared to help me escape by dressing me as a higher-ranking officer and marching through the gate with me. All we need to do after that, he says, is to board a train to Prague." (Both Wetzler and Vrba were from Czechoslovakia.)

"You're crazy, Fred," I replied sharply. "Think of Fero Langer. Think of Unglick. (These two men had also been encouraged to flee by ss men a short time previously and had been betrayed.) It's a trap."

"I don't think so, Rudi," answered Fred. "I know these fellows. We have often eaten and gotten drunk together. Pestek is different from the others —one of the few decent ss people."

While I respected Fred's judgments about people, I still vividly remembered the photographs of Fero with half his face shot off and of Charles Unglick sitting on a stool and kept upright with spades.

"No, Fred," I replied, "it isn't worth the risk. Fero Langer and Dobrovolny (the ss man who had persuaded Langer to flee, an ethnic German from Slovakia who had attended the same school as Langer and smuggled his mail out of Auschwitz) were like brothers, and think of what happened!"

Fred thought about the matter for quite a while. Then he returned to his room and told the ss man. "Many thanks, Pestek, but I don't think that this can work. And if it fails, we're both goners."

The German shrugged his shoulders, glanced at me, and asked, "Did

Fred tell you about our plan, Rudi?" I nodded. "Then how about you? I'm sure we'll get through."

"Why do you want to do it, anyway? What's in it for you? Why do you want to risk your career and your life?"

"Because I hate all this rotten business," he answered calmly. "Because I hate having to witness the murder of women and children. I want to do something to forget this stench and be able to feel a bit cleaner."

"But how are we going to get through the gate? Let's assume that someone will ask some questions. There are hundreds of traps."

"If someone speaks to you, just nod in my direction. Don't forget that you are an ss lieutenant colonel and I am your adjutant. You don't associate with little people. You don't bark if you have a dog that does it for you."

"And what about the train? What happens if someone starts a conversation with me there? What about the conductor who asks to see the tickets? What about the military police and the border control?"

"You'll be asleep. An ss lieutenant colonel can't be disturbed. Your adjutant will deal with all those minor problems."

It was a daring plan, and it was so simple that it might be successful. I silently reflected for a while, looking for flaws in this web, but I couldn't find any. However, the specters of Fero and Charles were still too close to me. "Many thanks for your offer," I finally said, "but I believe the risk is too great."

A few days later Hugo Lenk, formerly of the International Brigade, who had arrived on the first transport of Czechs, said to me: "Do you know the ss man Pestek? He has a plan. He wants to smuggle me out of the camp in the uniform of an ss officer. It probably sounds crazy, but still . . ."

"I know all about it," I replied. "He first made this offer to Fred Wetzler and then to me. He appears to be trustworthy, if one can say this about an ss man, but there is something about the whole thing that stinks. If you want to listen to my advice, forget about the whole thing."

Lenk took my advice.

This is how Vrba, who soon thereafter escaped without the help of an ss man, described Pestek's futile efforts. Jehuda Bacon remembers that this peculiar ss man also maintained confidential contact with Fredy Hirsch, the head of the children's block in the family camp. On several occasions Hirsch asked Bacon to make sure that he was not caught conversing with Pestek.

■ One day Pestek had to escort Vitezslav Lederer, a block elder in the family camp, to the Political Department, which had summoned him for an interrogation. On that day he evidently was able to look at Lederer's file, which indicated that the inmate used to be an officer in the Czechoslovak army and had already been interrogated in Theresienstadt several times without revealing anything. En route Pestek asked Lederer whether he was from a wealthy home, and he replied that he had relatives in Pilsen. At length Pestek advised him about his conduct at the hearing and gave him a cigarette.

Soon thereafter Pestek proposed to Lederer as well the idea of escaping with him. Lederer had nothing to lose because he had been accused of sabotage and had to expect to be eliminated sooner or later. For that reason he accepted the offer and assured Pestek that acquaintances in Bohemia would help them if they managed to make their way there. Finally Pestek confided to him that he was in love with Renée and wanted to return to Auschwitz and liberate her. He procured material from which Lederer had tailors in the family camp make an ss uniform, supposedly for Pestek.

On April 5, 1944, they were ready. Pestek had obtained papers for his leave and said goodbye to his colleague in the room of the block leader, whom he had gotten drunk. In the meantime Lederer had put on the ss uniform and left the camp disguised as an inspection guard. Fearing that the guard might notice his condition, the inebriated block leader gave Lederer a wide berth. Pestek had taken the drunken man's pay book out of his coat pocket, and thus Lederer also had regular ss papers. They went right to the railway station. Everything worked. They evaded the Czech border control by breaking into a luggage car and staging an ss inspection in front of the intimidated postal workers. By noon on the following day they were in Prague.

The money and jewelry that Lederer had "organized" in Auschwitz helped them along; his acquaintances procured a hiding place for them and introduced them to a Czech engineer who forged documents. Pestek bought papers from him that identified him as an ss officer and empowered him to take three inmates out of Auschwitz for an interrogation—namely Renée, her mother (without whom Renée refused to flee), and a female acquaintance of the engineer, a condition for his cooperation. Meanwhile Lederer sneaked into the Theresienstadt camp, whose layout he was familiar with from his earlier incarceration there, in order to warn the camp administration against further transports to the gas chambers of Auschwitz. However, they would not believe him.

On May 23 Pestek and Lederer traveled to Auschwitz wearing the uniforms of ss leaders. There are different reports about what happened next. Lederer has stated that Pestek wanted to visit a Polish woman in neighboring Myslowice and pick up some jewelry that he had "organized" in Canada and given to her for safekeeping. That woman evidently revealed his return. According to Lederer, the ss lay in wait for Pestek and arrested him at the Auschwitz railroad station, while Lederer managed to get away.

The other reports, which are basically in agreement with one another, deviate from Lederer's account. Thus Josef Neumann, who by virtue of his function as a capo of the corpse carriers in Birkenau had relative freedom of movement, says that he was frisked by an unknown SS man on May 25.

He found something on me but returned the things to me and said, "Be glad that you weren't caught by someone else!" When I looked in my pocket, I found a slip on which was written "I am on Block X." (Neumann has forgotten the number.) That was the block in the as yet unfinished section B III (later called Mexico) where I used to meet Pestek. I went to the block, whistled, and Pestek responded. Hidden in the attic of the barracks, he helped me climb up and said, "Now you can believe that I won't betray you. Hurry and get ready, take everything you can get, and we'll leave at 11 o'clock." I still couldn't believe it, but I was prepared to take any risk.

When Neumann was on his way to the prearranged meeting place, he noticed from afar that the block was surrounded by SS men. He quickly returned to his section of the camp and slipped out of the civilian clothes that he was wearing under his inmate uniform. Before he was called to the gate, he hid everything that he had carried on him for his escape. Meanwhile Pestek had been arrested. "My hands were tied to Pestek's and we were driven to Block 11 of the main camp in Schwarzhuber's car. The inmates there were quite astonished that an SS man and a Jewish inmate were brought in tied to each other."

Block leader Stefan Baretzki, who had known Pestek since his childhood, confirmed that Pestek was arrested in Birkenau. He heard that Pestek was betrayed by a slip of paper that had not reached its addressee but had fallen into the hands of SS roll call leader Polotschek. Baretzki saw with his own eyes how SS men beat Pestek, who was tied up.

Pery Broad gave the following testimony about Pestek's arrest: "I can still remember that various capos in the Birkenau camp bragged about having ferreted this SS man out in the vicinity of the camp and beaten him half to death." According to him, a legal officer took charge of the case, and Pestek was executed.

Wilhelm Boger, who dealt with matters relating to escapes gave this testimony at the Frankfurt trial: "Pestek was duly sentenced by an SS and police court in Kattowitz and then executed. His trial took place in Auschwitz. SS Sergeant Heinrich Mertens, a clerk, was present there and in Miedzebrodze, where the sentence was carried out. Pestek was convicted of favoring inmates and desertion. He was nabbed when he returned to Auschwitz after his escape."

Wilhelm Zieg, a former SS man, testified before the court as follows: "I still remember the shooting of an ss man named Pestek. It took place outside the camp, near the Sola River. The entire company to which I belonged had to attend and witness Pestek's shooting as a deterrent. I was not part of the firing squad. From reports I learned that Pestek had helped an inmate to escape and later returned to the camp in the uniform of an ss second lieutenant in order to smuggle another inmate out of the camp. The shooting of Pestek took place on a Sunday morning in September 1944." Franz Wunsch also remembers that after a successful escape Pestek returned to the camp in the uniform of an ss second lieutenant and was caught and sentenced to death. Like Zieg, Wunsch had to be present at the shooting.

Neumann was severely beaten but survived. No one bothered Renée.

Many aspects of this unique event remain mysterious. There are, for example, the strikingly divergent versions of Pestek's arrest, and it is not clear why Pestek attempted to take Neumann out of the camp instead of the three women, as agreed upon and planned.

■ Other attempts by members of the ss to escape with inmates should be evaluated differently from the actions of Frank and Pestek, for they were undertaken at the evacuation of Auschwitz and thus were obviously intended to provide a last-minute alibi when the victorious powers swept through. An unarmed ss man who at that time had to escort thirty-two women enabled them to hide among the inhabitants of a village named Wilchwy. He delayed the march out of the camp until all of them had found a shelter, whereupon he also concealed himself in the village. Halina Wrobel, who has recorded this episode, emphasizes that the villagers helped not only Polish women but all women on an equal basis.

When his detail was evacuated, Anton Lukaschek, the ss camp leader of Bobrek, fled on a horse-drawn carriage together with his capo, a German criminal. He was probably inspired to do so by the nearness of his Upper Silesian homeland, which was on the evacuation route. Both men were captured. The capo was integrated into the evacuation process again, and so it is likely that nothing bad happened to Lukaschek either.

The ss men who tried to provide an alibi for themselves at the time of the evacuation were in the minority. Quite a few of them treated the inmates even more brutally than they had in the camp; evidently they had no hope of escaping punishment and thus enjoyed their power for as long as possible. They unmercifully shot anyone they suspected of trying to escape as well as those who were unable to march. And the ss men dispersed with gunfire the inhabitants of a town or a village who tried to give food to the inmates passing through.

In this chapter and the one preceding, I have named many guards who helped prisoners. An account of their actions may be impressive, but the following little statistic should put back into proportion what might have been skewed by such descriptions.

These two chapters contain a description of the conduct of members of the ss—from the block leader of the bunker, who supported the head of a bound prisoner so he could eat, to Pestek, who risked his life. There were sixty-eight of them, which is almost exactly 1 percent of the guards in Auschwitz. As already stated, prisoners have a good memory for aid rendered. All cases that have become known have been included in my account.

There was nothing positive to report about 99 percent of the guards.

CIVILIANS IN AUSCHWITZ
■ ■ ■

"We really did not know anything about Auschwitz and the extermination of the Jews." This is what many witnesses who occupied high positions in the government or the party when the Auschwitz crematoriums burned day and night told the Frankfurt judges. Such assurances can be heard not only in German courtrooms. Many people who had high rank and standing in the Third Reich afterward endeavored to demonstrate that the extermination of human beings had been a well-kept secret of the SS. Kaduk gave them a drastic response when he let loose one day during the Frankfurt Auschwitz trial: "When the ovens were burning, the leaping flame was five meters high and could be seen from the railroad station. That station was full of civilians. No one said anything. There also were furlough trains that often stopped in Auschwitz for a while. Sometimes the whole station was fogged in; then the Wehrmacht officers looked out the window and asked why there was such a sweet smell. But no one had the courage to ask, What's going on? There is no sugar refinery in this place. Why are these chimneys here?"

Pery Broad restrained himself during the trial, but at the preliminary examination he did not mince words. "The pitch-black smoke clouds could be seen and heard for kilometers. The stench was simply unbearable. The flames that came from the chimneys of the crematorium could also be seen from afar. In those days (1944) I had the impression that people were no longer trying to keep these things secret or to camouflage them." Adolf Bartelmes, a railroad official in Auschwitz, also confirmed that the flames could be seen from a distance of fifteen or twenty kilometers and that people knew that human beings were being burned there. From the busy railroad tracks it was possible to see columns of inmates escorted by SS men.

This study does not include an in-depth investigation of the number of Germans who must have known about the well-organized mass extermination. I shall merely point to some sources that could be plumbed for such knowledge or that can at least provide an impetus for well-founded assumptions.

It is true that the thousands of SS men assigned to the extermination camps were sworn to silence. However, it is only natural that such an obligation could not be strictly observed by so many people, especially when one considers the demoralization of the guards.

René Juvet, a Swiss, reports that during a train ride through Bavaria an SS man unknown to him spoke to him and, evidently under the influence, described the terrible conditions in the Mauthausen concentration camp, where he was stationed. Was Juvet the only person who happened to be informed in such a way about crimes committed in the camps?

How many people sent packages home from the extermination camps, like the university professor Kremer, who kept a record of this in his diary? Did none of the recipients wonder where these articles, which had become rare in wartime, came from?

ss men with higher-level positions lived in the camp area with their families. Can anyone believe that all their wives and children, who played a "gassing game" in Auschwitz, strictly observed their pledge of secrecy for years? Railroad workers came as far as the ramp and saw from close up what was going on. Every month employees of the Reichsbank took delivery of heavy containers of gold derived from prisoners' teeth. Alex Zink's felt factory at Roth near Nuremberg processed women's hair, which this firm regularly bought by the bagful from the commandant's office in Auschwitz at fifty pfennigs per kilogram. The machinery of the death organization extended far beyond the extermination camps.

Listening to broadcasts of enemy stations carried the most severe punishments, and all too often executions for this crime were publicized as a deterrent, but such broadcasts were listened to all the same. Goebbels knew this, and so he addressed the arguments of the broadcasts. We clearly noticed that the ss was also listening to the BBC from London. The radio stations of the Allies repeatedly reported about the organized mass murder in the East.

On March 1, 1943, Professor Kremer noted in his diary that he saw, at the workshop of a Münster tradesman of his acquaintance, a leaflet issued by the Socialist Party of Germany that said, "We have already liquidated two million Jews by shootings and poison gas." In the spring of 1944 a leaflet illegally distributed in Vienna contained detailed information about Auschwitz. My brother Otto gave the material to a communist group, which then produced the leaflets. No one should assume that there were only these two leaflets with information of this nature.

To be sure, the situation was as Ernest K. Bramsted has described it. "For many people the false atrocity stories of the Allies (during World War I) were a kind of protective curtain behind which their minds could hide so that they did not need to inform themselves about the real atrocities being committed by the Nazi regime." Anyone who did not want to have his tranquility disturbed by disastrous news found reasons to push all rumors away.

However, a considerable number of Germans who did not wear an ss uniform did not merely hear about the destruction of human beings; many of them had contact with Auschwitz as civilian employees and saw with their own eyes what happened there. The testimony of skilled workers of the Krupp Works, given under oath in Nuremberg, shows how they kept the silence to which they were pledged.

Erich Lutat testified as follows: "It was, of course, forbidden to talk about the things we learned about the KZ. However, we workers discussed it among ourselves, and I also mentioned it when I visited my family in Essen." His colleague Paul Ortmann said, "After about two weeks I went back to Essen (from Auschwitz) for a brief visit, and I know that at home I gave a horrified report about what I had learned in Auschwitz."

Civilians in Auschwitz learned details that were known only to a small number of people. On one occasion Georg Heydrich, the office manager of the IG Farben Works near Auschwitz, was told by an obviously shaken and tearful SS man how corpses were burned on pyres outside the crematoriums in Birkenau. The SS man said that he had witnessed living people being thrown on these pyres. This information is contained in a document submitted to the Allied courts in Nuremberg.

Those who did not want to learn the truth could pretend to be blind even in the face of the fiery glow of the crematoriums and the disgusting stench of burned human flesh. Hermann Hausmann, a metal worker who, like Heydrich, was employed at the IG Works, affirmed that the gassing of prisoners was in fact discussed at that time, but "we refused to believe it." Anyone who refused to believe it could assure people afterward that he did not know about all this.

The prisoners intently observed the reaction of civilians at the sight of their misery, since it told them whether the murderous attitude of the SS was shared by the German people.

The first time I encountered Germans without a uniform in the Third Reich was at the main railway station in Munich when I was escorted, together with sixteen comrades in the zebra-striped uniform of KZ inmates, from the track on which the local trains from Dachau arrived to another track where we would be put on a train going to Auschwitz. On that August day in 1942 the concourse of the station was full of life and movement. I could understand that no one dared to make a gesture of compassion, for the guards wearing the SS uniform surely acted as a deterrent. However, I found it revealing that I was unable to find even a trace of compassion in the faces of the people who were staring at us. I cannot believe that they gave us contemptuous looks because they regarded us as criminals. People in Munich must have known that human beings were being detained in Dachau for political reasons. Besides, we were clean and clean shaven, which means that we did not look the way criminals are popularly imagined. Pierre Petit, who was escorted through the same railroad station almost two years later, was reviled and physically attacked by people, and so the SS escorts had to protect him and his comrades.

Leo Vos, a Dutchman, was interned in Upper Silesian labor camps for twenty-seven months. Along with many others who also wore the Star of David, he was escorted past German civilians twice a day. Since he could not discern any signs of compassion on their part, he came to this conclusion: "Even those who did not actively participate in the horrors bear responsibility because of their halfheartedness and callousness."

In late 1944 Siegfried van den Bergh was ordered to load and unload railroad carriages in Gleiwitz, only a few dozen kilometers from Auschwitz. Since the carriages were supposed to be placed at the disposal of the railroad again as soon as possible, both the SS guards and the capos beat the inmates while they worked. "German citizens," as van den Bergh calls them, "watched the SS men flogging away. I then heard them say to the SS guards, 'I don't understand why you don't beat those dirty Jews to death.' This encouraged an SS man to throw another piece of coal at my head."

There was an entirely different reaction when inmates encountered non-Germans. Like all the others in the satellite camp Jaworzno, Karl Dubsky was every day escorted to work in a coal mine in chains. Polish civilians frequently put out packages of food for them. Most of the chained prisoners were marked as Jews. Jewish women who had to work in a foundry in the satellite camp Hindenburg were helped by Polish workers in that factory. Inmates who worked in a machine factory in Sosnowitz also report that Polish workers secretly slipped them food and left lit cigarettes for them. The Polish master Niklaszynski procured civilian clothes for Russian inmates working in the same camp and thereby helped them escape.

Charles Goldstein was transferred from Auschwitz to Warsaw with his detail for clearing operations, and their inmates' garb and run-down appearance attracted the attention of the civilian population. "On more than one occasion," writes Goldstein, "strangers declared their solidarity with us, cheered us up, and even greeted us with a kind of reverence. For us, who had for years known only curses, boots in the rear, and beatings as greetings, these manifestations of friendship were a great experience." Like his companions, he wore the Star of David on his inmate uniform.

■ In the years 1943 and 1944 Auschwitz was surrounded by an ever-growing ring of arms factories. "We are now swamped with factories that insist on getting inmates." This statement, made by the SS garrison physician to his friend Dr. Horst Fischer, refutes an assertion frequently heard after the war — namely, that inmates were forced on the armaments industry at that time. In those factories SS men were limited to guard duty, while German directors, engineers, and master craftsmen were in charge of the work and thus determined the atmosphere.

Höß sums up this situation by saying that he was aware that inmates were beaten not only by the SS and inmate functionaries but also by civilian employees.

IG Farben pioneered the building of a factory in the vicinity of the camp; as early as the first part of 1941, construction of a chemical factory for the production of Buna (synthetic rubber) was started near Monowitz. Because of the steadily growing need for inmates, the satellite camp that was built a year and a half later in the immediate vicinity of this factory soon became the biggest labor camp. For this reason, and also because soon after the end of the war the directors of IG Farben were called to account by an American military court, the behavior of the German employees of this factory has been the most thoroughly documented; numerous former inmates testified about this subject.

The judgment in this trial is accompanied by this laconic statement: "There were cases of inhumane treatment on this construction site (of the Buna Works) as well. Now and again the workers (that is, the inmates) were beaten by the plant's security force and the foremen, who were guarding the prisoners during working hours. On some occasions the workers suffered breakdowns."

As confirmation that the executives of this factory could not have remained ignorant of the character of the extermination camp, I shall quote only from the sworn testimony given in Nuremberg by Christian Schneider, a member of its board of directors: "The smokestacks of the KZ Auschwitz were visible from the IG Auschwitz. I heard that IG people who visited Auschwitz—for example, Walter Dürrfeld and other engineers—smelled the odor of burning bodies. Those gentlemen told me that it was a terrible stench."

Dr. Walter Dürrfeld was asked by an American court: "Were there inmates who had no shoes?" His answer was, "Yes, there were some." To further questions he replied that his superiors Dr. Otto Ambros and Dr. Heinrich Butefisch also knew about it. These gentlemen could easily have remedied this lack by pointing to the negative effects on the inmates' capacity for work. The top leaders did anything to step up the production of Buna.

Like his superiors, engineer Gustav Murr, IG Auschwitz's head of construction, endeavored to present his work and himself to the court in as good a light as possible. When he was asked about the employment of inmates, he responded, not without some pride, that "at first the inmates walked from Auschwitz to the Buna Works, but I urged that they go by train. I did this for humane reasons because if the inmates had to walk six kilometers every day, they could no longer do a full day's work." This selfless humanitarianism, coupled with fear of the infectious diseases raging in the main camp at that time, led to the establishment of a separate labor camp right next to the plant.

The following statements by Murr are even more revealing. "I knew that there were complaints when there were no longer enough workers. After such a complaint things usually improved. The SS sent us stronger people because a feeble inmate could not do much." When the presiding judge at the Auschwitz trial in Frankfurt asked Murr what concrete actions the camp administration took in response to such a complaint, all he said was, "I have no knowledge of that." The chimneys in the gas chambers that he could see were not within his authority, and so he was not interested in them.

Dr. Friedrich Entress, the camp physician of Monowitz for several months in 1943, was more specific in his testimony. "The turnover among the inmates in Monowitz was great. The inmates were weak and malnourished. It should be emphasized that the performance demanded of the inmates was not in accord with their living conditions and nutrition. Working with inmates of the concentration camp was beneficial to IG Farben in that this company would otherwise have had to employ civilian workers under far better conditions." Entress reported that at a conference in spring 1943 IG urged that the infirmary in Monowitz be kept small because it was particularly important to the plant to have as many able-bodied inmates in Monowitz as possible. The practical effect of this discussion was that while all sick patients were admitted to the Monowitz infirmary, they could only stay there for a limited time; and if their illness lasted too long (three or four weeks), they were taken back to the main camp, and most of them were sent to Birkenau for gassing. If more than 5 percent of the camp population were sick, the camp physician had to make selections.

Dürrfeld was evidently guided by commercial considerations. The IG had to pay the commandant's office a certain amount for each inmate of Monowitz. A prisoner not fit for work who was removed from Monowitz could be deducted from the IG's account.

The prisoners were made to feel this attitude of the top officials. Once Samuel Graumann was put in charge of a labor detail of a hundred youths between fourteen and seventeen years of age. A German engineer demanded that he spur the lads on by beating them because "we have to make every effort to be victorious." A German supervisor managed to get Graumann dismissed as a foreman because he had allowed his subordinates to wash during working hours. He said that he could not use any compassionate foremen. A civilian contractor who was commissioned by the IG leadership to do earth-moving work on the factory grounds was characterized by Graumann as an exploiter of the worst sort. "That man instructed the inmates to carry more bricks than before and sicced the guards on them."

Metzger Silber remembers that "the gentlemen stood there when beatings were being administered and were all smiles."

■ Primo Levi has provided a very vivid description of a certain Dr. Pannwitz of the Polymerization Department of the Buna Works. On one occasion the management requested more chemists, and, because Levi had studied chemistry, he was given a test along with others. The examiner was Dr. Pannwitz, "tall, skinny, and blond; his eyes, hair, and nose were of the type all Germans must have." Levi is standing in front of Pannwitz's desk.

> When he is finished with his writing, he raises his eyes and looks at me. There has never been such a look from one human being to another. If I could fully explain to myself the special nature of that gaze, which was exchanged as through the glass wall of an aquarium by two human beings inhabiting different elements, this would also explain the nature of the great madness in the Third Reich. What all of us thought and said about the Germans could be felt directly at that moment. This is what the intellect that ruled those blue eyes and well-manicured hands said: "This dingus in front of me belongs to a species whose eradication is of course appropriate. In this particular case it is a matter of determining whether it contains a usable aspect."

Primo Levi's imagination enabled him to describe how inmates must have appeared to German employees:

> To civilians we are untouchables. They believe, more or less undisguisedly and with all nuances of contempt and compassion, that, if we were condemned to such a life and had sunk to such a level, we must have incurred some mysterious, enormous guilt. They hear us converse in all kinds of languages that they do not understand and that appear to them grotesque and like the sounds of animals. They see that we are totally debased and enslaved—without hair and devoid of honor and names, the victims of daily beatings who become more depraved every day. Never do they find in our eyes even a flicker of rebellion, peace, or faith. They know us as predatory, unreliable, filthy, ragged, and starved. Confusing the effect with the cause, they think that we have deserved this depravity. Who could tell our faces apart? To them we are *das Kazet* (the KZ), which in German is a neuter noun in the singular.
>   To be sure, this does not keep many of them from occasionally tossing us a piece of bread or a potato and letting us scrape their bowls after the distribution of soup at the construction site; afterward we have to clean the

bowls and return them. They deign to do this in order to get rid of an insistent, greedy gaze or in a momentary surge of humaneness. Maybe they simply want to watch us come running from all directions to compete for a morsel, unrestrained and like animals, until the strongest inmate swallows it and the others limp off with their tails between their legs.

■ However, there also were Germans in the Buna Works who helped. Years later Heinz Galinski still talked about a foreman who gave him some food. Arthur Nedbal writes: "A fitter at IG Farben (like Nedbal, a Viennese) helped me. He smuggled mail out for me, and I received parcels through him." Arnos Tauber draws attention to a works manager named Thieme who expressed to him his disgust at the extermination of the prisoners. Thieme was a druggist from Breslau, and Tauber was a Jew.

"I have not forgotten anything," writes Jean Améry, "not even the few courageous people whom I encountered. They are with me: Herbert Karp, a disabled soldier from Danzig who shared his last cigarette with me in Auschwitz-Monowitz; Willy Schneider, a Catholic worker from Essen who addressed me by my first name, which I had already forgotten, and gave me bread; and the senior chemist Matthäus, who said to me with a pained sigh on June 6, 1944: 'Now they've finally landed! But will the two of us hold out until their final victory?'"

However, Améry had to get to know others, too. "Once a senior fitter by the name of Pfeiffer proudly appeared in a winter coat—he called it a 'Jewish coat'—which he had been efficient enough to procure." Améry sums up by pointing out that the positive exceptions "drowned in the mass of the indifferent, the malicious and the despicable, the shrews (whether they were old and fat or young and pretty), and those intoxicated with power who thought that communicating anything but rude commands to the likes of us was a crime not only against the state but also against their own selves. There were far too many of those, and they were not ss men but workers, file clerks, technicians, and female typists—and only a minority of them wore the badge of the NSDAP. . . . A victim was bound to believe, willy-nilly, that Hitler really was the German people. My Willy Schneider and Herbert Karp and Master Matthäus had no chance to prevail against the mass of the people."

At least two employees of IG Farben got into trouble because of their humaneness. Only after protracted negotiations did chief engineer Max Faust manage to free two masters who had been charged with favoring inmates. The same Faust wrote in his weekly report dated October 18, 1943: "Regarding the treatment of inmates, I was always against shooting inmates or beating them half to death on the construction site. However, it is my view that a moderate form of chastisement is absolutely essential for preserving the necessary discipline among the inmates."

When I was gathering material for this study, I met two highly qualified specialists of IG Farben who, as I learned, had already rejected Nazism inwardly when Hitler was still rushing from one triumph to another. Both became high-level employees of the Buna Works.

When the chemist Dr. Ferdinand Meyer was transferred to Auschwitz, his superiors instructed him to use the Jews at the disposal of the Buna Works only for the most menial tasks and warned him that compassion for them would not be tolerated. Levi has testified that Meyer helped them anyway. Dr. Meyer describes how instruction of this kind fell on fertile soil even in the final phase of the war.

> On my daily rounds (of the Buna Works) I observed a group of inmates who had to unload several carriages in the bitter cold (in the last phase of the war). I asked the German foreman to distribute the sheepskin jackets in our storeroom among the Jews. The German master immediately obliged, and all Jews worked in fur jackets. Half an hour later I tried to check on whether my instructions were still being followed, and to my consternation I noticed that this group of Jews was wearing their thin striped summer jackets. When I asked the foreman why the fur jackets had been collected again, he explained that a higher-ranking master had told him that a high-level directive prohibited the distribution of fur jackets among Jewish workers.

In the face of this "high-level directive," Dr. Meyer saw no alternative but to capitulate.

Reinhard Heidebroek, a graduate engineer, was the other IG Farben expert who had inwardly distanced himself from Nazism. He was gratified to note that in the department he headed in the Buna Works there were only two employees who were card-carrying members of the NSDAP. He described the shattering effect that the sight of inmates, particularly of columns of females, had on him and asserted that he had helped wherever he could by requesting warmer clothes for the prisoners and leaving some food for them. However, he shrank from establishing contact with inmates. "I had reason to fear that there were V-men (SS *Vertrauensmänner*) among them." To my question whether he had resisted a transfer to Auschwitz after learning what was going on there, he replied that he had not. He sent for his wife because the Auschwitz area seemed to be safe from bombardments at the time.

I asked both of the specialists who inwardly rejected Nazism whether in view of the permanent destruction of human beings they did not consider it appropriate and necessary to sabotage work in this plant, which was so important to the war effort; as senior engineers they could surely have found effective and undetectable ways of doing so. Heidebroek responded that the idea of sabotage never crossed his mind in Auschwitz. Meyer admitted that my question had made him think of this for the first time. When I expressed my surprise, he gave me this explanation: "It is probably a German characteristic not to reflect about instructions and to do one's duty." Evidently he still did not realize how perverted this conception of duty had become in the face of the Auschwitz reality.

■ No court has collected as many reports about the conduct of German employees in other plants that also used inmates of Auschwitz. However, what little has become known enables one to conclude that their behavior did not basically differ from that of the employees of the IG Works.

After the end of the war, masters of the Krupp Works testified that they were under instructions to treat inmates very strictly, and this surely does not apply only to them. Director Heine, the head of the coal mine in Jawischowitz, was at least as persistent as Dürrfeld in urging that prisoners who were no longer fully fit for work be replaced with newly arrived inmates even though he, like his colleague at the IG Works, knew the fate that awaited those who could not work. Rafal Dominik, who was from Poland, has testified that during inspections Heine beat inmates and instructed SS men to drive into the mine to check on inmates. "The Polish civilian workers behaved in different ways in the mine. Only a small number of them helped us." He also remembers the names of civilians who gave beatings: Apryjas, the Czuwa brothers, and Oberheuer Wojcik.

As an inmate physician in the satellite camp Janinagrube, Dr. Erich Orlik found out that Kröger, a man who spoke German with a Polish accent and was the director of the mine, tortured prisoners to death. There are other confirmations of Kröger's murderous rampages.

Henry Bulawko observed that most of the German masters in Jaworzno wore swastika pins, greeted each other with "Heil Hitler!," and beat people and yelled a lot. One of them, however, did not urge the prisoners on but fed them and permitted them to light a fire at their workplace in winter. Bulawko gives only the initial, L., of this master's name. He also entered into private conversations with prisoners, which indicated that he, like the inmates, yearned for the arrival of the Russian armies. Ethnic German civilian workers in that plant behaved in different ways; Karl Dubsky recalls that some gave beatings and others helped.

Franciszek Piper has collected all of the documents and statements about the satellite camp Jaworzno that were available at the State Museum of Auschwitz-Birkenau.

During working hours the inmates were under the control of the pit foremen, masters, civilian workers, and capos. The guards were usually Germans who were very prejudiced toward the inmates. Under one kind of pretext or another, they beat them unmercifully to the point of unconsciousness and murdered many of them. On one occasion pit foremen found inmates who had fallen asleep at work. Kazimierz Borowiec, who witnessed this incident, remembers that foremen rushed at these inmates and began to massacre them in beastly fashion. When the inmates no longer showed any signs of life, they kicked them to make sure that they were no longer alive. Most of those foremen belonged to the SA. At the party rallies they received pertinent instructions from their chief, Rempe.

Piper emphasizes that this mistreatment continued even after the SS camp administration had notified the plant managers in a letter dated January 29, 1944, that the beating of inmates by mine employees was forbidden. To be sure, there were also many mine workers who gave inmates food and medicines, transmitted messages, and even helped with preparations for escapes.

Arthur Schönberg, who was deported from Austria for "racial" reasons, points out that he owes his life to an engineer of the Union Works who confided in Schönberg that he would never have become a Nazi if he had known what was going on in the concentration camps. He smuggled mail from prisoners out of the camp.

If inmates were brought in as skilled workers, then the management had an interest in maintaining their ability to function, since they could not simply be replaced the way that unqualified workers were. At the Siemens Works in Auschwitz, specialists were employed for the most part. Chief engineer Kurt Bundzus, who built the works after the Berlin facility of this company was destroyed by air raids, described for the Frankfurt court his search for skilled workers: "When I arrived in Auschwitz, I gave 100 preselected inmates a competency exam. Fifty met the technical demands. I asked the commandant's office that these inmates be given additional food and preferential treatment until they were installed in our facility. These inmates were to be nurtured (aufgeforstet) with the greatest care.

However, neither Bundzus, whose use of the verb aufforsten (to cultivate a forest) gives one sufficient insight into his character, nor the uninterested camp administration checked on the way this preferential treatment worked in practice. In fact, the inmates picked out by Siemens received especially rough treatment while they had to wait in Birkenau for their transfer to the new factory. The reason may have been that the inmate functionaries who still ruled them envied the skilled workers their better future.

Erich Altmann, who also took a qualifying test at that time, confirms that chief engineer Georg Hanke requested him as a specialist even though he must have noticed that Altmann had falsified his profession at the test. Hanke addressed him as "Herr Altmann," which was so unusual that Altmann still emphasizes it years later. Hanke's help could only be effective because Altmann spoke German. Someone whose mother tongue Hanke did not understand would not have been able to win his favor so easily.

When a camp had been built near the Siemens Works in Bobrek, the chosen inmates were transferred there—that is, those who were still alive. Altmann has written the following about the conditions there:

> (I am to be) assigned to a detail of the Luftwaffe that has to operate a barrage balloon on the factory grounds. An ss private first class (*Obergefreiter*) gives us assignments. Inmates are in general very cautious in associating with soldiers. "Herr Obergefreiter" here, "Herr Obergefreiter" there. With every question one takes off one's cap. Then the private first class takes me aside and says: "You needn't call me Herr Obergefreiter; you can say *du* to me. We are comrades. If I didn't wear a military jacket, I would certainly have your garb on." He gave me his soup every day; and when he returned from leave, he even brought me an ointment for my scabies, which cured this unpleasant condition in a few days.

Altmann observed that the soldiers were afraid of one another. "Thus it happened that each of the four soldiers independently gave us food. None of them could be told about the others, since we could not trust our best friends." Altmann has also described how the demoralization emanating from Auschwitz took hold of the civilian employees of the Siemens Works: "All sorts of things were manufactured—rings, cigarette holders, etuis, combs, metal boxes, clock cases, tobacco pipes, lighters, bracelets, necklaces, and many other items. If a guard was looking for a present, he could find what he wanted inside the factory and obtain it for a little bread or margarine. More safety locks were secretly manufactured in Bobrek than were on sale in all of Upper Silesia. In the two weeks before Christmas 1944, not a single workpiece was shipped from the plant because everybody was busy manufacturing gifts. The foremen, the ss camp leaders, the guards—they had all placed their orders."

The most extensive construction project, the four big crematoriums, also employed Polish civilian workers. Adolf Weiß, an inmate who worked there, remembers two metal workers named Sonowicz and Boltys, from Königshütte and Rybnik respectively, who regularly brought the prisoners something to eat.

Others tried to get close to the gas chambers. According to Pery Broad, "Railroad workers liked to linger at the unloading ramp and pretended to be working on mechanical problems in order to steal things from the luggage left behind by the inmates." They were not the only civilians who misappropriated the property of deportees. At the Auschwitz railroad station, postal employees regularly stole things from parcels addressed to inmates. This practice did not stop until ss Sergeant Wladimir Bilan threatened them with dire consequences if packages continued to be brought into the camp half empty.

Not all postal employees had such an attitude. This is what the Pole Witold Dowgint-Nieciunski reported to the Frankfurt court: "I worked at the camp post office for some time. Almost every day we went to the post office in the town of Auschwitz, and so we were able to make contacts there—for example, with a German from Silesia who had been discharged from the Wehrmacht because he had lost an arm." I have already described the permanent, well-organized contact between prisoners and Polish civilians who were working in the camp area.

On the extensive grounds of the Buna Works, inmates encountered foreign laborers of various nationalities. Primo Levi writes:

An Italian civilian worker brought me a piece of bread and the leftovers from his meal every day for six months. He also gave me an undershirt full of patches, wrote a postcard to Italy for me, and saw to it that I got a reply. He did not ask for any reward for this and would not have accepted any, for he was good and simple and did not believe that a person should do good things for the sake of a reward. I believe that I owe it to Lorenzo that I am still among the living—not so much because of his material aid but because his presence, his quiet and simple way of being kind, constantly reminded me that there is a just world outside of ours. It is very hard to define this remote possibility of goodness that makes it worthwhile to preserve one's life.

However, Levi also met civilians who were not Germans, either, but behaved quite differently. When he was working in a laboratory, he came in contact with the Polish stockroom manager Liczba and other girls, whom he described as follows: "They don't talk with us and turn up their noses when they see us shuffle through the laboratory in our wooden shoes, miserable and dirty, sickly and shaky. Once I asked Miss Liczba for some information; she did not answer me but with a face that expressed disgust turned to Stawinoga (the Polish German head of the laboratory) and jabbered away at him. I could not understand what she was saying, but clearly heard the word Stinkjude (stinking Jew), and this made my blood boil."

English prisoners of war who had been assigned to labor in the Buna Works gave inmates a great deal of help even though any contact with them was strictly forbidden. Many grateful survivors have reported about this. The same applies to the coal mine at Jaworzno, where English prisoners of war established contact with inmates as well.

■ Women who were not employed by arms factories or personally involved with the KZ also came in contact with inmates. The wife of the IG engineer Heidebroek, who had moved to Auschwitz to be with her husband, still remembers that one day the wife of chief engineer Faust told her about a Jewish inmate who had accosted her on the factory grounds and stammered "Frau — Brot" (Woman — bread). When Frau Heidebroek asked her how she had reacted to that, Frau Faust replied, "I screamed and called the police." Frau Faust was the director of the Red Cross in Auschwitz.

The wife of SS roll call leader Gerhard Palitzsch complained to her husband that an inmate detail assigned to make repairs in her house had done shoddy work. The inmates were punished with *Baum* (tree) — that is, they were hung by their hands, which were tied behind their backs.

The wife of Wiegleb, the head of the property depot, behaved quite differently. According to Maurice Schellekes, when her husband, like Palitzsch and others, ordered inmates to work in his house or garden, Frau Wiegleb served them cake.

SS camp leader Hössler had Artur Rablin perform personal services for him, and so Rablin frequently came to Hössler's house. Frau Hössler not only gave him food and an occasional glass of liqueur but repeatedly asked him with a worried expression about her husband's reputation among the inmates. On one occasion, when Rablin was taking Hössler's children (two girls aged twelve and ten and a boy of six) for a walk, they passed an inmate detail. Evidently the children had talked at home about the way the inmates were treated at that workplace because Frau Hössler reproached Rablin for not having shielded the children from that impression and asked him to avoid making them eyewitnesses of such mistreatment in future. Here is Rablin's comment on his episode: "I could read a certain shame in her eyes."

In the Höß villa inmates came in contact with the commandant's wife. She was feared because she reported to her husband inmates who in her estimation were working too lackadaisically so that they would be punished. Marta Minarikova-Fuchs, who worked in the villa as a seamstress, confirms that Klaus, the oldest son, also made such reports. However, Frau Höß did not behave badly toward prisoners who worked for her directly, though she always kept her distance. She was visibly impressed with the nimble and skillful work of Frau Fuchs. This evidently did not jibe with her notion that Jews were not capable of working. When Teddy Pietrzykowski received an assignment from Frau Höß, he was regularly given bread, milk, and coffee.

Stanislaw Dubiel, the factotum in the Höß villa, once heard Frau Höß exclaim, "This is where I want to live and die!" When the inmate who was working as a gardener told her that a woman had given birth in the women's camp and that he was the father, she sent the young mother a pink baby jacket.

The wife of camp physician Werner Rohde occasionally came to the SS infirmary, and thus I met her. In my *Bericht* there is the following account of a conversation I overheard:

> The wife of SS Second Lieutenant Dr. Rohde is speaking with Richter, the SS sergeant from the office. I happen to be in the adjoining room that houses the file cabinets and pull something out. They have not noticed me.
>
> "Have you heard that there will finally be a Canada again?" That is the voice of Frau Rohde.
>
> "Oh yes, it's about time."
>
> "This time it will be Hungarian Jews, so far as I know."
>
> "I hope they'll bring enough."
>
> "Oh, my husband told me that there's loads of Jews down there."
>
> "What I meant was that I hope the Jews will bring along enough things."
>
> "Rest easy. These Jews still have whole mountains of treasures."
>
> Frau Rohde looks like a well-groomed, cultivated woman, and yet she can hardly wait for the flames in the crematoriums to be rekindled.

Dr. André Lettich also met that woman. When he was working at the Institute of Hygiene, he once had to check smears from her for bacteria because she had recently recovered from diphtheria. His first examination was positive, and Frau Rohde threatened him. "If the smear is again positive, I shall string you up with my own hands." She was eager to end the burdensome quarantine. Lettich thereupon certified that no bacteria could be detected.

▓ In the SS infirmary nurses tended to SS men with minor illnesses. A nurse with an outstanding personality was transferred there. Maria Stromberger was born in 1898 in a small town in Carinthia; her early years were hard. Not until she was more than thirty years of age could she train for the profession that she had dreamed about since her childhood. Then she became a nurse "body and soul," as her sister put it. At the Höß trial, Nurse Maria was a witness and testified as follows about her career, which finally took her to Auschwitz: "On July 1, 1942, I was transferred from Carinthia in Austria to an infirmary for infectious diseases in Königshütte. This was done at my request. In my homeland I had occasion to hear different things about what was going on in the East, and so I wanted to find out whether or not they were true. As some-one born in the days of the Habsburg Empire, I simply could not believe those stories. We have always been tolerant and humane. Thus I was transferred on July 1, 1942, and took a position as a nurse in the section for infectious diseases."

Others pretended to be blind and deaf when they heard something, but Maria Stromberger searched for the truth. In her section there were two typhus patients who had recently been released from Auschwitz — presumably Upper Silesians who had signed the German ethnic register, for at that time a number of *Volksdeutsche* (ethnic Germans) were released from the camp if they declared their loyalty to the German people, and the two patients spoke German. Maria Stromberger recalls that one was employed in the gasworks and the other man in a nitrogen factory. Nurse Maria testified that "both men shouted out terrible things in their deliriums. They were in the grip of unimaginable angst, and so we had to isolate them. Their feverish condition was such that one of the men became violent toward me." When Maria asked the men about what they were expressing in their feverish nightmares, "they folded their hands and begged me: 'Nurse, if you value your life and also our lives, you will never mention these things. They are based on the truth.'"

When the men told her that nurses in Auschwitz wore the same garb as she did, Maria asked to be transferred there. At a later date her sister wrote me: "I did not want her to go there, but she told me, 'I want to see how things really are; perhaps I can do some good there. Trust me.'"

The transfer occurred on October 1, 1942. Edek Pys was a Polish inmate who worked in the diet kitchen of the ss infirmary and thus had the most direct contact with Nurse Maria, the manager of that kitchen. Years later he wrote to me, saying that having had bad experiences with other nurses he did not trust Maria at first:

> Maria also kept her distance from us as far as professional relationships were concerned. She seemed to be rigorous, and so we only discussed matters relating to our duties in those days. She gave orders, and I carried them out to the letter. One day something surprising happened. It was already evening. We did not go into the camp because we were "under orders." Only Nurse Maria and I were in the kitchen. I was washing dishes when I heard a bang in the camp, not far from our kitchen window. I already knew what that meant. In those days inmates very often "went into the wire." At the same time I heard a soft cry behind me, where Nurse Maria was standing by the window. I turned around and saw that she had turned quite pale and feebly sank into a chair. She almost fainted. I got frightened and called Nurse Margarete. After a few minutes everything was all right again,

but Maria immediately went home. She did not come to work for two or three days. When she returned, she asked me what had happened that day. I explained it to the nurse and also told her the probable reason for that inmate's decision to go "into the wire." I noticed that she was unable to grasp this.

At that time Edek began to trust Nurse Maria and spoke frankly with her. He remembers that "she wanted to know all about the ramp." He told his comrades that Nurse Maria was trustworthy. On one occasion Staszek Baranski drew their attention to this when people were being gassed in the crematorium across the way (later called "the old crematorium"). From the window of the ss infirmary it was possible to observe the "disinfectors" as they poured poison gas into the shafts that had been affixed to the roof of the building, half of which was sunk into the ground.

At a later date Nurse Maria described her relationship with the prisoners in these words: "A detail consisting of Polish inmates was employed at the ss infirmary, and I established contact with these men. It was hard to gain the trust of these embittered young people, but I finally succeeded, and I must say that they offered me consolation."

Maria helped the prisoners wherever she could. She gave them food, regularly set aside for them some of the extra rations for ss men suffering from typhus (including chocolate, fruit, champagne, and the like), and procured medicines for them. She entrusted the key to the attic to Teddy Pietrzykowski so that he could pick out medications up there undisturbed. When inmates were caught smuggling food, she backed them up. Edek has described the lengths to which she went with her help:

One day in November 1942 I had a high fever and a very severe headache. However, I did not want to admit that I was sick because in those days there was a typhus epidemic. (To combat it, both the lice that carried this illness and the patients were sent to the gas.) Thus, as usual, I marched off to work every day. Nurse Maria recognized my condition. She took me to the bathroom of the ss infirmary, put me in the last stall on the left, gave me a few blankets and a pillow, and told me to lie there quietly. I had to be quiet because from time to time ss men came to the room to wash. This was hard, especially when I had to vomit. The nurse came in occasionally to give me injections and put compresses on my head.

At length Edek had to go to the infirmary after all, and Nurse Maria sent him medicines. "When the illness had run its course and I returned to the ss infirmary in a greatly weakened state, she made especially light meals for me. She was truly like a mother to me and to all of us."

Maria helped other inmates as well. Hunia Hecht, who worked in the SS tailoring workshop, reports that "Nurse Maria always brought us something when she came to see us." The foreman of this workshop, Marta Minarikova-Fuchs, told me that Nurse Maria tried to arrange her visits in such a way that no SS man was there at the same time, and so she was able to give them news about the situation at the front. The women on this detail first learned from her about the landing of the Allies in France in June 1944. Whenever Marta asked her for some medicine, Nurse Maria could always be relied on to bring it.

None of us ever thought of offering her a "payment" for her help, which was the usual thing to do if an inmate asked an SS man for a favor. Edek has reported an incident that is typical of Nurse Maria. Once he suggested that she pretend to start a fight with him, for people were already talking about her attitude toward the inmates, which differed so radically from the attitude of all the others. She replied only that she was not an SS man and would not even pretend to do anything that ran counter to her convictions.

She transmitted and received mail for many members of our detail, including myself. When I gave her a letter to my family in Vienna for the first time, I left it unsealed, but she sealed it in my presence without reading it. On another occasion, when she went home on leave, she offered to visit my relatives in Vienna on the way. At that time I gave her the material that my brother used for a flyer (I have reported about this in another context). In an effort to minimize the risk for Nurse Maria, Ernst procured a clothes brush whose wooden part had been hollowed out, and we concealed the papers in this cavity. The brush was screwed together in such a way that the screw heads were hidden among the bristles. Nurse Maria took the brush without asking any questions.

In the summer of 1944 I was preparing my escape. This is what I wrote in my Bericht: "I have also spoken with Nurse Maria and told her about our escape. This was necessary because she has been corresponding with my brother in Vienna. Now she can't write him anymore because after I leave Auschwitz the mail will surely be checked at home. She just looks at me with her brown eyes and says, 'If you think it's necessary, do it. But be careful and don't rush anything.' Before I leave the kitchen, she says, 'If I didn't know that you are an atheistic communist, I would now bless you with the sign of the cross.' 'Do it, nurse. And I thank you for everything.' "

After we had to discontinue our preparations for an escape and I was transferred to a satellite camp of Neuengamme, I wrote my friends in Auschwitz via Nurse Maria. The inexperience of the guards in that camp enabled me to send letters by regular mail, thus bypassing the camp censors. Nurse Maria addressed the reply to me in care of the camp, but she encoded news about my friends so skillfully that the censors could have no idea of what it was all about.

As Edek Pys reports, Nurse Maria took another step forward at that time: "When she had decided to work with the resistance movement, she went on leave to Bregenz (where her family lived). On her return she gave me two revolvers, a 9 mm caliber with three cartridges and a 6.35 mm caliber with thirteen cartridges. She said the guns belonged to her father and I should choose one. I took the 6.35 caliber, of course."

October 27, 1944, was a black day for the inmate detail in the SS infirmary. The attempted escape that the leadership of the resistance organization had planned and in which the artist Zbyszek from this detail was to participate was betrayed. Nurse Maria was one of the very few people who knew about the preparations for an escape. She did not let the shock caused by this failure disconcert her. On assignment from the resistance movement, she traveled to Königshütte and Kattowitz in the following weeks and transmitted not only letters but also fake IDs, Polish underground newspapers, and finally explosives. Edek remembers that Nurse Maria was once instructed to hand a small package to a man in an SS uniform at the Auschwitz railroad station at a pre-arranged time. To enable the man to identify her, she was supposed to wear a cape over her nurse's uniform. Neither Edek nor Nurse Maria knew what was in the package, but Maria carried out her assignment.

The reason for her transfer from Auschwitz in December 1944 can no longer be precisely reconstructed. She later told me indignantly that the SS garrison physician had her admitted to a sanatorium for morphine addicts even though she had never taken any narcotics. The only explanation I can give for Dr. Wirths's action is that he might have heard rumors about the help she gave inmates and wanted to put her out of the Political Department's reach.

After the end of the war Nurse Maria returned to Vorarlberg, where she was arrested by the French occupation forces. Edek Pys has preserved a letter that she addressed to him in Poland from her place of detention on July 18, 1946. Here is an excerpt from it:

At present I am in an internment camp! I am suspected of having treated inmates with phenol during my service in Auschwitz. Don't laugh, Edek! This is serious!—You know, I am surrounded by Nazis, SS, Gestapo! I, their greatest enemy! And I have to listen to the complaints about the injustice of what people are now doing with them. Then I see in my mind's eye the experiences of Auschwitz.

I can see the fiery glow of the pyres; I smell the stench of burned flesh; I see the miserable processions of returning details, followed by the dead; I feel the choking worry about you that I had every morning until I saw you before me again safe and sound; and I could scream into these people's faces and blindly lash out at them. The craziest thing about it is that I still have to keep quiet, for otherwise they might boycott me. But this time will pass, too, and I shall be free again. What I shall do then I don't know. I feel so empty and drained, and I have no joy. It seems to me that I have scattered my wealth of love in Auschwitz. I have reached my objective. What more can I do?

After she had finally been freed on the basis of interventions by survivors of Auschwitz, she never again practiced the profession that she had loved so much. Maria lived in seclusion in Bregenz and worked in a textile factory. Only once did she make a public appearance—when she was a witness in Warsaw and passionately and irately hurled her accusation at Commandant Höß.

In May 1957 her great heart stopped beating.

Afterward

INMATES AFTER LIBERATION
■ ■ ■

The advance of the Russian troops brought the history of the extermination camp Auschwitz to an end. In the wintry cold the inmates were driven away in miserable processions that have become known as death marches. Many of those who had been able to save their lives in the camp perished at that time; because they were not able to continue marching, some froze or starved to death, while others were shot. Those who managed to survive the marches and ensuing rides, frequently in open freight trains, experienced the final chapter in the history of the concentration camps in other camps. It was a phase of hunger beyond measure.

Dr. Georg Straka has described the condition in which the evacuees were delivered to other camps: "Driven by blows, they sometimes suddenly moved forward like a herd of cattle, with one pushing another. It was impossible to get their names out of them; even the kindest words were not powerful enough to make them speak. A long, expressionless stare was all. If they made an effort to answer, their tongues were unable to reach their palates to utter a sound. All one noticed was their poisonous breath, which seemed to come from innards already in a state of decomposition."

Some inmates met acquaintances in those camps and with their help and camp experience managed to escape the lowest rung of the hierarchy to which every new arrival was assigned. However, many did not, and their suffering did not end until the Allies reached the camps in central Germany—unless death had come as a surcease earlier.

Among the last camps to be liberated was Theresienstadt. Many prisoners were transferred there in the very last days after the advancing Allied armies had caused camps located farther west to be evacuated. A considerable number of inmates came from Auschwitz on long circuitous routes. H. G. Adler, the chronicler of Theresienstadt, has described the dissolution caused there by those transfers in the last days of the war:

Now no rules and regulations were in force anymore, not even camp regulations; the degraded inmates were no longer willing to observe them. If a human being has reached an end point that surrounds him as an unbridgeable abyss, a point where stark despair is coupled alternatively with indifference and furious aggressiveness, who would invoke even a modicum of law and order that might have redounded to the benefit of those unfortunates? How childish and hopeless such an enterprise must have appeared! These people no longer had any faith; they did not believe in anything or anyone; they did not believe in themselves anymore. Everything was extinguished and devalued. For them there no longer was a friend or breath of human warmth.

Here is an eyewitness report: "A few prisoners . . . are sitting on the ground impassively. They react only to food. The filth and the squalor make it impossible to make out their features. Those greedy expressions of brutish human animals. It is too horrible to describe. And it is impossible to help them."

Elsewhere Adler writes: "Any attempt at empathy is futile because every life gathered between the wires is strange and incomprehensible. Nothing of the existence of these lost souls can be translated into a language that anyone on the outside would understand. . . . It is not necessary to describe these human beings. It has frequently been done — all too frequently, I believe — and the horror of their outward appearance, which grips one only once but soon inspires only disgust and revulsion, has made commentators overlook the essential thing: the moral problem that will remain posed for humanity in the future as well." Adler concludes with this stern admonition: "Anyone who has not experienced this destruction himself does not know and will never know. He must keep silent. He has to listen and examine his mission in his own mind and as a human being living in the world."

■ Primo Levi was among the ill inmates who were left behind at the evacuation of Auschwitz; at that time he was in the Monowitz infirmary. He has given the following description of the last days of a patient in the anxious ten days between the evacuation and the liberation:

> Now it hit Somogyi, a Hungarian chemist of about fifty, thin, tall, and taciturn. He had recovered from typhus and scarlet fever, but now there was something new. He developed a high fever. Having said nothing for about five days, he opened his mouth today and said in a strong voice: "I have a bread ration under my straw pallet. Divide it among the three of you. I'm not eating any more."
>
> We did not know what to reply but did not touch the bread. Half of his face was swollen. When he was conscious, he morosely kept silent.
>
> However, that evening and night, and then continually for two days, his silence was broken by delirium. Following a last endless dream about submission and slavery, he murmured, "Jawohl," every time he exhaled. With every deflation of his pitiful chest, "Jawohl!" resounded, regularly and per-

sistently as from a machine, thousands of times, so that one was tempted to shake him, choke him, or at least get him to change the word.

Levi has described his feelings when the Russian troops finally reached Monowitz: "The news did not immediately excite me. For many months I had known no pain, joy, or fear, except for that uninvolved, remote way that is characteristic of the camp and that one could call conditional. I thought that if I now had my earlier faculty for feeling, this would be an extremely exciting moment."

A few months later Mira Honel, who had stayed behind to nurse ill inmates, also described her feelings on that historic January 27, 1945: "The Russians are here, and our torment is ended. Freedom, you are here! I've been expecting you for such a long time and with so much confidence. I was certain that you would come. It seems to me that I have been victorious. Even though I have no weapons in my hands, I feel as if I fought to attain you, as if I had devoted my entire life to this struggle. But why am I so sad now that I have won you and possess you? I always told myself that I might die of joy on this day. So why am I not happy now?"

According to Honel, because the patients had always been forced by blows to carry out all orders, they thought that everything was permitted after the departure of the SS. They relieved themselves next to their beds and refused to lift a finger to safeguard even minimal order. Only gradually could life be put on an orderly basis again.

The physician Eduard de Wind, who had, like Honel, remained with the patients, reports that after the departure of the SS the SS clothing depot, the property depot, and the pantries were plundered in the main camp. Vodka was found in a cellar, and in the evening some inmates had diarrhea and others were stinking drunk.

Primo Levi has described the first days after the liberation in the Monowitz infirmary:

Meanwhile the thaw that we had feared for so many days arrived, and as the snow gradually melted, the camp was transformed into a nauseating morass. Dead bodies and garbage polluted the air. And the grim reaper had not stopped mowing. The sick died in their cold beds by the dozen. Others dropped dead on the muddy paths as if hit by lightning; these included the greediest survivors who, blindly yielding to the imperious urge of our chronic hunger, had gorged themselves with the meat rations of the Russians, who were still involved in fighting at the nearby front and sent these gifts to the camp at irregular intervals—ranging from very little to enormous amounts.

Here is Levi's balance sheet: "About 800 of us remained behind in the infirmary of Buna-Monowitz. Of these, approximately 500 died of their illnesses or froze or starved to death before the arrival of the Russians, and another 200 died on the days that followed, despite all the help they received."

Tadeusz Chowaniec, a Polish physician who entered the camp three days after the Russian troops, has provided this report:

In a brick barracks we found several female prisoners, two or more to a bunk. Was it really the third day after the liberation? Had time stopped for these women — had nothing changed for them? Only the wild shooting of the SS men could no longer be heard, and the dogs did not yelp anymore, but the women still wore their striped garb. They had difficulty moving; it seemed as though every movement was carefully thought out and assessed. Their expressionless, mostly cold eyes aroused shame in us. Had they used up all their joy and enthusiasm on the first day, when all the prisoners rushed into the arms of the Soviet soldiers? They had the same bunks, but now they were free and knew that food was no longer a problem. I was sure that their apathy would fade and they would enjoy their freedom when their aching bones, slack muscles, and emaciated bodies had returned to their normal condition, when they had really and truly been restored to life.

The Russian medical commission diagnosed severe psychological illnesses in most of the liberated prisoners. Primo Levi has described a case of complete mental ruin. A boy of twelve, called Klein-Kiepura (Little Kiepura), was a protégé of the camp capo and widely known as "the little mascot of Buna-Monowitz." "Except for his patron no one loved him," writes Levi. "Well fed and well dressed, he led a dubious and frivolous favorite's life in the shade of power until the last day, an existence interwoven with gossip, informing, and twisted passions."

Klein-Kiepura remained in the camp as a convalescent and like all other patients was taken from Monowitz to the better-equipped main camp by the Russians. There Levi encountered him again:

For two days he was silent and lay in bed all doubled up and staring into space, with clenched fists on his chest. Then he suddenly started talking, and we yearned for his silence. The little Kiepura spoke as in a dream, and his dream was that he had been promoted and become a capo. We didn't know whether this was madness or a child's bit of black humor. Incessantly the boy sang and whistled in his bed the Buna marches, the brutal rhythms to which we marched with our tired feet every evening and morning. He screamed German commands to a nonexistent group of slaves. "Get up, you swine! Understand? Make your beds, but on the double! Shine your shoes! Line up for lice check, foot check! Let me see your feet, you bunch of pigs. Filthy again, you son of a bitch? You just watch out, I'm not joking. I'll catch you yet, and then you'll be off to the crematorium." He screamed like a German drill sergeant. "Line up, dress ranks, face right! Collars down! Forward march! Keep in step with the music! Stand at attention!" After a pause, he said in a shrill, arrogant voice: "We're not in a sanatorium here. This is a German camp by the name of Auschwitz, and the only way out is through the chimney; if that's okay with you, fine; and if you don't like it, all you have to do is go into the electric wire."

Elie Wiesel was transferred to Buchenwald, where he was liberated. "Our first action as free men," he writes, "was to storm the pantries. We didn't think of our parents or of taking revenge; our only thought was of bread." Wiesel was still a child when he was sent to the camp.

Because I was able to live under far more favorable conditions than the vast majority of the inmates, it is hard to compare my reaction with that of others. I escaped from an evacuation transport at the Salzwedel railroad station on April 11, 1945. Later I found out that those who remained on the train were loaded on boats that were sunk in Lübeck Bay shortly before the end of the war. I vividly remember the great joy with which the reencounter with nature filled me when I walked through a bright forest on a soft carpet of moss as well as on numerous subsequent occasions. On the other hand, the reunion with human society aroused only dull feelings in me. I avoided every conversation that was not absolutely necessary, but I did not shun conversations with former inmates or prisoners of war. In such circumstances, however, other inhibitions often arose. Former inmates regarded me, a German, as one of the privileged people in the camp whose domination had caused their suffering, and soon I came to sense this. On the first of May, the traditional holiday of the workers' movement, which I had not experienced in freedom since 1938, I was taking a solitary walk along a canal on the periphery of Hannover when I heard singing in the distance. Russian songs. Somewhere liberated people were celebrating. At first I wanted to join them, but then I did not have the nerve to do so. Would they accept me as one of them? Sadly and desolately I remained alone.

Since I knew that my family was in Vienna, a longing that crowded out all other feelings led me to disregard the regulation that barred civilians from using the highways and to set out for my homeland on a bicycle even before Germany's final surrender. I delegated my need for revenge to the English, who had taken me under their protection in Hannover. I gave them an account of my experiences and observations in the camps that I had written on a typewriter placed at my disposal by them. When I turned in my typescript, I experienced the first disappointment in this realm, which was to be followed by many more. My manuscript was accepted as if it were an unimportant document, and no supplementary questions were directed at me. I never heard about any reaction to this memorandum. I completed my trip in barely two weeks. I was home.

Again and again a former inmate remembers by day and during the night the other world that he experienced in the camps, just as a convalescent becomes aware of his feverish deliriums; he knows that this other world existed, but his memory of it remains unreal. Years later my brother claimed that I was still living as I did in the KZ. He was the best judge of that because he had known me best in the period before my internment. Yet my way back to normal human society was much simpler than that of the vast majority of former prisoners. I found my relatives and acquaintances again, and I had not physically deteriorated because there had been an adequate supply of food in the small labor camp where I had wound up.

"Just as a joint becomes stiff if it is not moved for a long time," writes the physician Max Mikorey, "a person's emotional life also becomes constricted and stiffens after such prolonged catastrophic burdens as years of detention in a KZ. Such psychological damage can frequently outlast the original oppressive situation for years and sometimes even become permanent. This applies particularly to young people, whose free personal development can be very seriously damaged by a lengthy internment."

Some young men have described how they experienced the liberation. Carl Laszlo is one of these. "A survivor found himself in a world in which he was nothing but a question mark. This world seemed alien to him and he felt like a guest in it. While he thought he was living like other people, he remained so intimately bound up with the realm of shades that it attracted him more than the world of life and noise. The great driving force, the desire to survive, became irrelevant, and suicide as a logical consequence and ultimate liberation could no longer be rejected out of hand."

Primo Levi has described his feelings on his journey to his Italian homeland:

> What would we find at home? How much of our selves had been consumed, extinguished? Were we returning richer or poorer? Stronger or weaker? We did not know, but we did know that a fresh trial, for good or evil, awaited us on the threshold of our houses, and we anticipated it with dread. Together with our tired blood the poison of Auschwitz coursed through our veins. Where were we to get the strength to start a new life, to break the barriers, the hedges that proliferate around a forsaken house and empty rooms dur-

ing every absence? Soon, on the very next day, we would have to do battle with as yet unknown enemies inside and outside us. With what weapons, with what energy, with what willpower? We felt as old as the hills, pressed to the ground by a year of the most horrible memories, worn out and defenseless.

Tadeusz Borowski has recorded his first thoughts in freedom. He would like to take a rest from his instincts, "but first, you know, I'd like to cut a throat or two, just to rid myself of the camp psychosis and get over my camp complex, the complex of eternally taking off my cap and having to watch defenseless human beings being beaten and murdered, the complex of angst. I fear that none of us will ever get rid of all that. I don't know whether we'll survive it, but I wish that some day we'll get to the point where we call things by their proper name, as brave people do." Borowski was twenty-three when he was released from the world of the extermination camps, one year older than Laszlo and three years younger than Levi. At age twenty-eight he ended his life, which was destroyed before it had a chance to develop.

Ernst Israel Bornstein, who is Borowski's age, draws not only on his own experience. On assignment from an American institute, he has recorded the biographies of companions in misfortune who are his age. With the detachment of more than a decade, he summarizes his findings as follows: "It is impossible to free oneself of the burden that one has borne for years as someone condemned to be exterminated, as a dehumanized creature. The years of angst and oppression have left in the psyche damage that is as irreparable as damage to the gray matter of the central nervous system. While a former inmate of a concentration camp may laugh and be merry with others, he aches and bleeds inside because the old wounds will not heal. Even though he has left the spatially limited concentration camp, the terrible atmosphere of the camp still encompasses him; it is as though the KZ were still inside him."

Elie Wiesel has characterized the survivors in these words: "These human beings have been amputated, but instead of lacking a leg or an eye, they lack the will to live and joie de vivre. They are no longer human beings. The shock caused a spring inside them to snap. Sooner or later the consequences become apparent."

Women have also described their feelings after the liberation. Ruth Kersting said: "After the liberation, I didn't want to see humans—only animals." People had caused her too great a disappointment. Charlotte Delbo writes about a French friend: "She too believes that the others don't understand her." The little word "too" indicates that Delbo frequently had similar experiences. Dora Lorska wrote in 1965: "The impression I had on my first day (in Auschwitz) was, so to speak, a mixture of hell and insane asylum, and I am still not entirely rid of this experience." Soon after making this statement, she died at the age of fifty-two. Grete Salus writes: "Most people have some physical defect, but the crack in the foundation of our human existence is far less curable." Elsewhere she writes: "Only now do we feel the wounds that have been inflicted on us. Suddenly our firm skin is no longer there; in fact, our innards have, as it were, been turned inside out and shrink from any contact with this world."

David Rousset has summed up his reflections in these words:

The world of the concentration camps is isolated and self-contained. It continues to exist on earth as a dead star that carries corpses. Normal people do not know that anything is possible. Even if the eyewitness reports compel their minds to admit it, their muscles do not believe it. The inmates of the concentration camps know it. A soldier who spent months under fire at the front has become acquainted with death. Every hour of their lives death dwelt with the inmates of the concentration camps and showed them all its faces. They have touched all its masks. They have experienced fear as an ever-present obsession. They have before their eyes the humiliation of the beatings, the weakness of the body under the whip. They have learned how devastating hunger can be. For years they moved through the fantastic scenery of every destroyed human dignity. They are separated from the others by an experience that is impossible to convey.

All of us have probably learned that even those close to us react with incomprehension, that a kind of jealousy can actually manifest itself when what has been experienced and lived through, what separates us from the others, once again asserts itself. "When you are with an Auschwitzer, you immediately behave quite differently." We frequently hear such statements.

A team of physicians at the psychiatric clinic of the Cracow Medical Academy found in an examination of seventy-seven survivors of Auschwitz that twenty-two of them have a stronger relationship with friends from the camp than with friends from normal life. The former are even closer to them than members of their immediate family. Auschwitzers were not even able to adapt fully to communities in which life was organized collectively. When I asked one of the leaders of an Israeli kibbutz especially rich in tradition whether the Auschwitzers in that community still differed from the others after two decades, he replied that "they all bear a burden."

The world around us promotes a group exclusivity of the Auschwitzers. We harbored the vague idea that after Auschwitz everything would have to change for the better, that mankind would learn a lesson from our experiences. Then we had to realize that people were not even interested in them. All too often the vapid, obtrusive pity that we experienced was like an escape to conventional feelings and, in fact, gave the impression of dishonesty.

German psychiatrists have reported about a Jewish woman who had been deported to Auschwitz from France at the age of eighteen and delayed her return home because she was afraid of what she would find there. She finally did return and described her feelings as follows: "I came back expecting a different reception after everything I had gone through. The indifference of people to the past hurt me. I no longer understood them, and they no longer understood me. This is how it has been to this day. I could not stand the superficial compassion of my coreligionists who had been spared."

Jenny Spritzer writes: "I correspond with most of my friends and colleagues (from Auschwitz) who lived to see the end of the war and thus their liberation. Strangely enough, they unanimously claim that they are actually disappointed with life in freedom. What is the reason for this? Did we imagine life as too beautiful?" Grete Salus has given an answer to this question: "We thought that we would find peace in the heart of a world that was beating for us and for our fate. That this is not so is a heavy blow for us that makes it difficult for us to find ourselves again. I am sure we are too demanding and during our imprisonment fashioned a world in our dreams that does not and cannot exist. We have experienced an extreme, real evil. We thought we would now experience the other extreme, real goodness. We have lost the proper sense of proportion and must first find the road between these two extremes."

Lucie Adelsberger writes: "It is not only the world around us that has changed; we ourselves have been reshaped. In fairy tales and legends we read that angels and messengers from heaven who are sent down to earth go astray and cannot find their way. Some of this also applies to those who return to earth from hell. Human ideas and standards dissolved. Everything there was oversized and excessive in its dynamics, and consequently our conceptions were changed and it is hard to get accustomed to normative paths again. After so much meanness and misfortune one expects a plethora of kindness and happiness that is not of this world." Adelsberger also points to another change: "Our sense of proportion has shifted in another respect as well, and perhaps this must be regarded as a defect. If one has experienced the dissolution of everything—money and property, honor and fame—which left only the inner bearing of a person, one develops a profound disdain for the externals of life."

This has been confirmed by many. Thus the team of Polish psychiatrists has documented this disdain by quoting such statements of survivors as "Material matters are now less important to me" or "In the struggle for existence I have become a minimalist; I am satisfied with food and a roof over my head."

Other reactions to the past in a KZ must be registered as well. Persons who had learned in the camps at a very early age that one can survive only if one disregards all regulations and prohibitions and observes "Never get caught" as one's only commandment have frequently become criminals. Moral scruples appear ludicrous to such people. They brush aside warnings of older people because those people failed miserably with their moral ideas in Auschwitz, while the younger ones, who had been forced to rely on their inner resources, coped with life far better.

The thick skin around our emotional world that protected us in the camp separates us from people with normal feelings in freedom. "For a long time I found it ridiculous when I saw people weep at funerals." The team of Polish psychiatrists cites such a statement as typical.

On my return to Vienna in May 1945, I learned that my Viennese friends Rudi Friemel, Vickerl Vesely, and Ernst Burger had been hanged shortly before the evacuation. The last-named was the person with whom I had the greatest mutual understanding and whom I esteemed the most. I reacted to this news, which was a great blow to me, in typical Auschwitz fashion: it has happened, and one has to come to terms with it. After I had given a lecture on Auschwitz, a woman came up to me and asked whether I had by any chance met a certain Rudi Friemel in the camp. I answered in the affirmative, and she wondered what had become of him. I replied briefly and soberly that Friemel was hanged in the roll call area on December 30, 1944. The woman broke down and wept uncontrollably. Afterward my brother, who had witnessed this incident, berated me for having given her this news so harshly and abruptly. My only response was this: "Well, who broke this news gently to me?" It took me a very long time to put my life back on a normal track. I have remained skeptical about public outbursts of emotion.

On one occasion Dov Paisikovic told me that he felt neither joy nor pain. Lord Russell of Liverpool discerned such an emotional emptiness in Kitty Hart, who had been deported to Auschwitz at the age of fourteen: "She believes that basically there is no limit to a human being's emotional endurance. At first a person feels impotent hatred, but then a point is suddenly reached where all feelings of love and hatred have been deadened and nothing is left but a kind of indifference. Even when she learned, at the end of the war, about the death of her father, whom she had loved very much, she felt no pain. She made every effort to mourn him, but she no longer had any feelings—no love, no hatred, no bitterness."

As a result of all this, strange habits become apparent. For a long time I did not like it when someone said, "After you," because in the camp an inmate always had to walk ahead of the escorting guard. Dr. Wanda Poltawska reports about a woman who was panic-stricken when someone walked behind her. This fear was incomprehensible to her. She had been sent to Auschwitz as a small child and had no conscious memory of her time in the camp. I am in the habit of transgressing against prohibitions even when this makes no sense at all. If, for example, there is a zebra stripe indicating a pedestrian crossing, I am tempted to walk just outside this stripe even if that is not a shortcut for me. An acquaintance of mine is reluctant to enter a telephone booth; he is evidently afraid of feeling locked in.

The same Frenchwoman who complained to the psychiatrists about the lack of comprehension and the superficial compassion that she perceived after her return married a former KZ inmate. "If I go to the country with my husband and see a freight train with cattle cars at a railway crossing, I nod and say nothing but have it in my head and heart again. It's the same when I see smoke rising somewhere, and that's the way it has been for eighteen years now."

There is another burden that we have to bear. Many years later I caught myself instinctively asking myself when I met a person, "How would he have behaved in Auschwitz? Would he have stood the test or failed?" Rudolf Vrba has described the same phenomenon: "We thought that we had become acclimated, but a barrier always remained. There was always something that reminded us of our recent past. Time and time again we noticed that we were relating everything to Auschwitz and judging everything by Auschwitz standards that no one else knew or understood. Every time we thought we were normal people, our past again rose before us and destroyed our illusions."

Grete Salus has described the same affliction: "Unfortunately I catch myself trying to read what is behind persons' faces and to imagine how they would behave in one situation or another. And when I view them in that way, I see almost nothing but failures. This is a heavy burden when it is added to all the other things that we KZ people continue to bear in life."

There are even heavier burdens. In Auschwitz Dounia Ourisson-Wasserstrom was compelled to watch Boger pick up a small child by his legs and kill him by beating his head against the wall. Then she had to wash off the blood. "Since then I haven't been able to look at a child without crying," she says. When she became pregnant after the liberation, she had an abortion.

Orli Reichert-Wald also avoided the sight of children after the liberation. As the camp elder in the infirmary, she had to watch all too often how SS medics killed babies and infants by injecting them with poison. Nor was she able to tolerate music, since it always reminded her of the camp orchestra that had to play during the transport of selectees from the infirmary in order to drown out the moans and screams of those who were being taken to the gas chamber. Although Orli was spared the fate of a *Muselmann* in Auschwitz and was able to lead a well-ordered life after the liberation, her nervous system was destroyed. I called on her in 1960, when witnesses were being sought for the Frankfurt trial of SS guards in Auschwitz. After all, by virtue of her position in the camp she had learned more than most others. When she checked a list of names that I had handed her, her hands trembled so much that I tried to take the list from her in order to end her obvious torment. However, she insisted on reading all of it, gave me a detailed account of her recollections, and refused to cut short a conversation that so visibly agitated her. Less than two years later, Orli was buried, and a friend said that her fourth attempt at committing suicide had been successful. According to her friend Jeanne Juda, "She was always distressed by the belief that she had not done even more for the inmates." Yet there was hardly anyone else who did his or her job at Auschwitz as selflessly as Orli.

■ Even if the life of many Auschwitzers is normal by day, it differs from that of the others; there are the nights, the dreams.

Edith Bruck was deported at the age of twelve. She has this to say about the early period of regained freedom: "I often dreamt about death, blood, and camps, and sometimes I dreaded falling asleep because the night was nothing but a nightmare."

Elisabeth Guttenberger was seventeen when she was deported to Auschwitz as a Gypsy. She lost thirty relatives there. Many years later she said: "I think it is an understatement when I say that I have dreamt of Auschwitz a thousand times, about that terrible time when hunger and death were dominant. I was a healthy girl when they sent me there. But I was sick when I left the camp, and I am still sick today."

Primo Levi was another person plagued by dreams:

> It took me many months (after returning home) to shed my habit of always looking down while walking, as if I were constantly in search of something to eat or of things that could quickly be pocketed and exchanged for bread. And I am still afflicted with a horrible dream that sometimes recurs frequently and at other times rarely. It is a dream within a dream; its details vary but its substance remains the same. I am sitting at the family table, am among friends, at work, or in a verdant landscape; at any rate, the environment is friendly, apparently relaxed and devoid of pain. Yet I am beset by a faint, yet deep feeling of apprehension, a clear presentiment of a threatening danger. And, as a matter of fact, either gradually or with brutal suddenness everything around me dissolves in the course of the dream;

the surroundings, the walls, and the people recede, and my feeling of oppression increases, becomes more urgent and more distinct. All around me is chaos; I am alone in the center of a gray, whirling void, and suddenly I know what it means, have always known it. I am in the camp again, nothing is real but the camp, everything else was a brief breather, a hallucination, a dream—the family, burgeoning nature, the home. The inner dream, the dream of peace, has ended, but the outer dream goes on icily. I hear a well-known voice, a single word, not commanding but short and muted, the morning command of Auschwitz, a foreign word that is dreaded and expected: "*Wstawać*" (rise).

Dov Paisikovic told me in 1968 that he frequently hits his wife in his sleep. "My worst dreams," he said "are those in which the mountains of corpses grow higher and start moving toward me." The dead bodies that he and the other members of the Sonderkommando had to take to the ovens and fiery pits of Auschwitz expanded in the heat, and consequently it was possible for these piles to set themselves in motion.

André Lettich, who came to the camp as a mature man and after the liberation practiced medicine in France again, told me in 1971 that he was repeatedly pursued by nightmares, even though the day before he had in no way been reminded of Auschwitz. The same thing was reported by Franz Danimann. As for me, I do not dream of the camp very often, and when I do, my dream is far less torturous—probably because I suffered much less than Guttenberger, Levi, or Paisikovic, perhaps because I repeatedly concern myself with this subject during the day. Most of my dreams about the camp relate to the bunker, where I was closest to death.

▪ Erich Gumbel, a psychoanalyst who gathered his material about this subject in Israel, writes that many former inmates lead a double life. Outwardly they appear to be normal, but in their dreams they continue to be persecuted; they suffer from feelings of guilt and cannot understand why they, of all people, survived the KZ. Gumbel adds that it is hard to help them. H. Bensheim, who examined patients in the General Workers' Hospital in Haifa, was also frequently asked, "Why did I survive?"

At the beginning of the war Ernst Papanek, who was living in Paris at the time, took care of Emil Geisler, who had fled there from Germany as a child because he was Jewish and therefore had to fear for his life. Geisler was deported to Auschwitz at the age of sixteen. He managed to escape from the extermination camp and thus was the only survivor of the seventy adolescents on his transport. When Papanek encountered him again in an Israeli kibbutz in 1956, Geisler was very pleased but strikingly taciturn. Papanek had an explanation for the strange behavior of Geisler, who was now a grown man: "Behind every question, no matter how innocent, they hear the voice of the investigating judge: 'Why did you survive and the others die? What did you do? What do you know?' And in the background of all these questions there is this one: 'Whom did you betray?'"

Like to many others, decades later Jean Améry is still distressed by the reproach that he did not take revenge on his tormenters. "That they and I did not rise up," he writes, "remains our very painful wound that keeps opening up." When the Dutchman Eduard de Wind entered the Birkenau camp complex after his liberation, he felt that he was a bad person. "What gives me the right to live? Why am I better off than the millions who perished?"

Elie Wiesel writes: "I am alive, therefore I am guilty. I am still here because a friend, a comrade, or an unknown person died in my stead." Wiesel has analyzed how this guilt feeling could arise. "The number alone, the quota, counted. Therefore an inmate who had been spared, especially after a selection, could not suppress a first reaction: a feeling of joy. After one moment, one week, or an eternity, this angst-laden joy was transformed into guilt. The liberating feeling of having been spared is tantamount to this confession: I congratulate myself on having made another inmate go in my stead."

At examinations of former KZ inmates, Paul Matussek got to hear statements like this one: "We Jews are guilty, too, and perhaps more than the others. We have failed."

Ella Lingens speaks for many who received preferential positions as Germans when she writes:

And doesn't every one of us repatriates walk around with a guilt feeling that our henchmen so seldom have and that derives from doubt? Am I alive because the others have died in my stead? Because I had my own bed with two blankets even though I knew that four women were lying in another bed with only one blanket and could never really sleep? Because I was able to eat a double ration of bread since the patient for whom the block had still received a ration was unconscious and at death's door and therefore unable to eat it? Because a grateful patient had "organized" warm felt boots for me from the property depot, while the vast majority of the women were rubbing their frozen feet raw in their heavy wooden shoes? Because I had a job that was part of the machinery created by the SS to keep the camp from sinking into a chaos from which no productivity of any kind could be extracted anymore? Because in all our wretchedness we were indispensable to the powers that be and our survival was important to them, because we thus constituted a little cog in this enormous machinery of destruction?

Simon Laks and René Coudy also write with unsparing frankness:

Only a very small number of KZ inmates returned. All those who survived Auschwitz owe this not just to luck, toughness, willpower, or resistance. These factors certainly contributed effectively to our rescue, but they would surely have proved inadequate if we had not recognized with lightning speed that we had to push aside a major part of our old morality, our "humanity," and all the benefits of our civilization to keep from going under in the camp—in short, that we had to use all our resources to integrate ourselves into the society of which we had become a part, to adapt ourselves to its mode of thinking, its customs, its views, its educational methods, and its laws. We are well aware that, given the extent to which we adapted both instinctively and knowingly, we all became more or less inhuman and therefore objectionable to the society to which we were fortunate enough to return. A deep abyss separates us from that society, possibly forever. Its literary, moral, emotional, and even humorous vocabulary is far too limited to speak in our favor. Even the most truthful reports and the most precise descriptions can never reproduce the reality to which we were exposed. We make no effort to fill up this abyss because we know that this would be impossible. We are a bit like Pirandello's characters in search of an author who could tell our story, but we are sure that we shall never find one.

Primo Levi speaks of the shame "felt by a righteous man, a guilt imposed on him by another that torments him because it exists, because it has been irrevocably brought into the world of existing things, and because his good will is worth little or nothing and not strong enough to prevent it." This shame beset Levi and his fellow sufferers when they were liberated by Russian troops "because we felt that there could never be anything good or pure enough to expunge our past and that the traces of sinfulness would remain in us forever, in the memory of those who experienced it, in the places where it happened and in the reports that we would make about it. For this reason—and this is the enormous privilege of our generation and of my people—no one has ever been better able than we to comprehend the incurable nature of sinfulness that spreads like a contagious disease."

In the fall of 1960 Imo Moszkowicz, who was interned as an adolescent, wrote to the Frankfurt court that he did not want to appear as a witness: "If I could present my nightmares in court, I would surely be an important witness. But, except for cold sweat, there is not much left in the morning. . . . I can't let the time in the camp erupt in me again. I have to forget it—otherwise, I'll eventually croak from it." Moszkowicz was interned as a teenager.

■ In 1967, when Michal Kula, a graduate engineer, was questioned by a Polish judge about his experiences in Auschwitz, he was fifty-six years old. The otherwise sober record concludes with these words: "At present my state of health is bad. The Auschwitz concentration camp branded me with the mark of fear, anxiety, and nervous breakdown. I often find myself on the verge of losing my will to live. I suffer from insomnia and often dream that I am in Auschwitz. Every time I wake up I am happy to be lying in my bed. Those nights are a nightmare for me." Kula died a year later.

Even as a young girl, Hermine Horvath had to endure persecutions and humiliations before she was deported to Auschwitz from southern Burgenland as a Gypsy in 1943. In 1958 she spoke about her fate in the Gypsy camp:

> I was often assigned to the night watch on Block 27. The tracks to the crematoriums were right next to our block. The oppressive stench of burned human flesh was constantly in the air. The distance between us and the crematorium was about 200 or 300 meters. Men had to dig a large pit there, and a fire burned in it. When I was on night watch again, all the blocks were ordered to be locked; no one was permitted to leave or even look out. This was the surest sign that thousands were being driven to their deaths again. I could hear terrible screams. These forced me to open the gate and look out, even though I knew that if I was caught, I would be put to death. What I saw was so horrible that I fainted. Live people were being thrown in the fire. Since that hour I have been suffering from epileptic seizures.

Frau Horvath has described her condition as follows: "The greatest desire would be to be able to work again, but I can't do it. If the sun shines on my head just a bit, I simply fall down. The physicians have no real understanding of any of that. They can't imagine what we lived through, and they may believe that I don't want to work." Frau Horvath died a few months later, not even thirty-five years old.

Many died untimely deaths even though they seemed to be relatively healthy right after their liberation. Dr. Joseph Heller, who examined deportees who had returned to France, reported that "one of the most astonishing phenomena noted in returnees from the camps was the premature aging of the former inmates."

C. B. was misused in Auschwitz by Horst Schumann for sterilization experiments and castrated. At that time he was not even twenty-five. In 1946 he gave this testimony in Nuremberg: "I feel very dispirited and am ashamed of my castration. The worst thing is that I have no future anymore. I eat very little and still grow fat." In the transcript it is noted: "While the witness is speaking, he starts to cry."

During the same experiments in Auschwitz, Benno C., twenty-one years of age, had one testicle removed. According to a medical report, in freedom he was unable to shed the feeling that this caused everyone to look at him. He was engaged to be married three times, but each time that C. told his fiancée about this operation, she broke the engagement. The physician's diagnosis was "psychological impotence."

The frequently cited Grete Salus has found valid words for another problem as well: "The proverb 'Time heals all wounds' seems to have been turned into its opposite among us. The greater the elapsed time and our distance from our experiences become, the more we seem to forget what value our bare lives used to have for us. We are becoming fastidious, perhaps too fastidious, as creditors of a debt whose collection is an almost hopeless undertaking. Some of us have become quite apathetic; many have returned to the past and wallowed in their pain; and still others despair and go farther and farther astray in a jungle with no exit."

■ It is, however, not my intention to paint a one-sided picture of all survivors of Auschwitz almost breaking down under the load of their memories. If an uninvolved person hears some conversations between Auschwitzers about the time they spent in the camp together, he may get the impression that they associate only cheerful memories with that place. "I remember primarily funny incidents in Auschwitz." This statement by Sonja Fischmann-Fritz applies not only to her.

When I was in Israel in 1968, I received an invitation from a woman I knew in Auschwitz. I asked her to invite friends from her time in Auschwitz as well because I was collecting material for this study and hoped that talking with them would give me valuable information. I knew that in Auschwitz she and her friends had been housed in the staff building, the home of members of the details that were doing clerical work for the ss. I shall always remember that afternoon in Ramla. Twenty women, almost all of them deported on the first transports from Slovakia, had gathered in the apartment. In deference to me they spoke German; after all, knowledge of that language had been required for an assignment to a good detail. Nevertheless, I received very little information for my work because they all talked at the same time, reminded one another of funny episodes, laughed, and had a rip-roaring good time. An unsuspecting listener might have believed that these women were exchanging beautiful memories of their youth.

The American psychiatrist Klaus D. Hoppe observed during serial examinations of survivors with marked psychological impairments that depressing experiences from the period of persecution were frequently minimized and limited in their significance—evidently because remembering them caused too much pain. There may be a simpler reason why accounts of funny episodes are dominant in many conversations between Auschwitzers. We need not remind each other of selections and mountains of corpses. To be sure, survivors of Auschwitz who had to exist there on the bottommost rung of the camp hierarchy have no memories that can provide amusement. Only those who were exempted from starvation can remember episodes that can afterward be laughed about.

Many feel a need to revisit the place where they had to experience so much. I know some Poles who live in the vicinity of Auschwitz and for a long time made pilgrimages to "their" Auschwitz every Sunday. On many occasions I observed that Auschwitzers behave strangely in the former camp. If one of them meets a stranger in that place, which is now the site of a museum, he acts like a host. Should one call what transpires when an Auschwitzer guides outsiders through "his camp" a kind of local patriotism or pride? I observed such a reaction in myself when I visited the camp again. Between 1954 and 1961, when I was the general secretary of the International Auschwitz Committee, I frequently went to Auschwitz, the place repeatedly chosen by the committee for its conferences. When our deliberations had been completed, I usually took a solitary walk through the camp—undisturbed because the museum was closed. It is hard to describe my feelings on such occasions. The present became unreal. Every corner stirred memories, but the past remained unreal as well. I felt as though I were walking between eras.

While Auschwitz acts like a magnet on many, others strive desperately to repress any memory of it. When I was looking for witnesses for the Auschwitz trial in Frankfurt and contacted two women who must have learned more in the camp than the average inmate, the replies I received were not from them but from their relatives. One went as follows: "She desires to have no more contact with Auschwitz because she hopes that this will cure her nervous condition." The husband of the other woman asked me not to write her anymore because she did not want to be reminded of the past, lived only for her children, and never talked about Auschwitz. I fear, however, that those two women exemplify what Gisa Landau says about herself: "I would like to forget the camp, but that can't be done."

Others have decided to continue occupying themselves with what happened in Auschwitz because they feel duty-bound to do so. With a self-sacrificing spirit that commands respect, Auschwitzers have been working for years in the camp museum, which includes an archive of great value for the study of contemporary history. They have taken it upon themselves to live in the camp area whose atmosphere surrounds them day and night. Henryk Porebski repeatedly went into the camp and did not let bureaucratic and technical impediments discourage him. Finally, in July 1961 the documents that the inmates on the Sonderkommando had buried—and that Porebski had known about— were found near the ruins of Crematorium III amid buttons, bottles, cutlery,

Hungarian, Czech, German, and Polish coins as well as other remnants from the property of murdered prisoners.

The fate of the prisoners in Auschwitz varied greatly, and so do the survivors' memories of their time in the camp. For the vast majority of them it meant a sum total of sufferings, humiliations, and shocks that is too great for their memory. To many Germans, Auschwitz is not merely a memory of terror and trouble; the time spent there was for them that epoch in their lives when they possessed an abundance of power they did not even come close to having in any other period of their lives. This is especially true of criminals who were despised and banished before and after the KZ but made everyone in the camp tremble. By virtue of their positions, they could indulge in pasha-like whims and humiliate people who would have avoided any contact with them in another situation. In fact they were courted by such inmates. In Auschwitz, and only during that period, they felt appreciated.

Not only German criminals and those who had adapted to them in an effort to join them at the top of the inmate hierarchy, but also German political prisoners, who clearly distanced themselves from the criminal upper crust of the camp, associate with Auschwitz the memory of a time when they were more important than in any other period of their lives. Even afterward they still feel superior to those who knew the camp from the perspective of an anonymous person among the gray mass of prisoners. In some of them this has reached the point where they like to play the role of an infallible expert.

Walter Petzold fancies himself in such a role. For almost four years he was a capo of various details. Because of his camp experience and good reputation as a political prisoner, he was appointed to an arbitration commission that was to make decisions in controversial cases involving former inmates who did forced labor for the Buna Works and after the end of the war demanded compensation from IG Farben. With great assurance Petzold rejected as incorrect the accounts by former inmates of Buna-Monowitz that did not accord with his recollection. Petzold did not believe that a certain factor applied to him—namely, that everyone has necessarily preserved in his memory a one-sided picture from his perspective and that no one could know everything about a camp from his own experience. He was also called to Frankfurt as a witness in the Auschwitz trial. After most of the eyewitness testimony had been given, the court went to Auschwitz for an on-site inspection. It turned out that Petzold's precisely presented testimony must have been erroneous because it was impossible to see from the place he had specified what he claimed to have observed from it. When the prosecutor in the Auschwitz trial in Vienna pointed out to him that some of his testimony was in contradiction to clearly documented facts, Petzold responded harshly, "Mr. Prosecutor, who was in Auschwitz, you or I?"

Before his detention in the κz, Ludwig Wörl had lived in rather modest circumstances in Munich. As the first camp elder with a red triangle in Auschwitz, a man who preserved his sense of political responsibility in this top position, he contributed a great deal to the improvement of conditions. After his liberation he could not resign himself to the fact that he was no longer the camp elder—that is, the top man. Having returned to his modest milieu, he felt misunderstood and insufficiently appreciated, and he indiscriminately attacked all comrades who had occupied a lower position in Auschwitz than he had but in freedom belonged to a higher social stratum. He wound up quarreling with God and the world. His bitterness developed into a persecution complex. When he fell ill, he resisted any medical treatment because he feared a physician might "inject" him—that is, kill him in the Auschwitz style. "He viewed himself as the great man of Auschwitz," said Werner Krumme, who was his friend in Auschwitz and afterward in Munich. "He thought he was the only authority on all matters involving Auschwitz. He probably imagined that he would be offered an important political position, though he had no qualifications for one." In Wörl's case, too, the effort to appear as an unimpeachable authority in all matters relating to Auschwitz resulted in having a part of his testimony in the Auschwitz trial disproved by an on-site inspection. With the exception of the statements given by Petzold and Wörl, nearly all of the other ones were confirmed by such inspections.

It was primarily Germans who remembered Auschwitz as their "great time," but they were not the only ones. At a conference Ella Lingens reported about an Austrian Jew who said the years he spent in Auschwitz were his last good period. He was on the staff of the infirmary there, which spared him the worst, and within modest bounds he had chances to help inmates he knew. After the liberation he was incapable of resuming a normal life.

■ For all those who survived the camp, Auschwitz has remained the central experience accompanying the rest of their lives.

The psychiatrist Eduard de Wind, who has experienced this in himself and in many patients, has come to this interesting conclusion: "I regard it as entirely possible that compulsive thinking about the camp, which so often appears in former inmates as a kind of obsessive-compulsive syndrome, and even nightmares about the camp actually have a consolatory function. A former inmate cannot think of the future without thinking of death, but when he remembers what he has suffered he also has the feeling that despite everything he did not die but instead pulled through. Thus the memory of his terrible experiences also has a consoling function."

Dr. Wanda Poltawska writes: "I want to forget, but I can't. This is not a problem of willpower; here the will alone is not sufficient. Perhaps one should do the opposite: not try to forget but always think of it, think of it so intensely that such situations will never be repeated for anyone. Would this relieve the tense anxiety states and horrible memories?"

Similar considerations influenced my decision to occupy myself for years with problems related to complex situation of Auschwitz and accept the fact that this does not diminish the distance between those leading normal lives and myself. I had to learn to avoid fine, big phrases like "never again." No matter how impressive these may sound, history since 1945 has shown that the possibility of repetitions cannot be easily excluded. For this very reason the study of interpersonal relationships in as extreme a situation as was deliberately created in Auschwitz appears to be especially important. It should serve as a warning by demonstrating what sorts of behavior patterns can be imposed on human beings.

The general statements that I have made about Germans in the camp apply to me as well. I did not wear the armband of a functionary, but in no other period of my life did I shoulder as much responsibility as I did in my two years in Auschwitz. In that sense Auschwitz was a "great time" in my life, too. One is flattered to be occasionally reminded of what even an inmate could achieve under exceptionally favorable conditions. Self-reproaches are the other side of the coin. I have been asked if this, that, or the other thing should not have been tried, whether I was not infected by the brutal harshness of the camp atmosphere. All things considered, I find that my constant occupation with this past has more of a consoling than a burdening effect on me.

When we, the survivors who have made it our task to acquaint coming generations with what became possible in Nazi extermination camps, want to present the facts to others, we have gotten into the habit—independently of one another and without any prearrangement—of saying nothing about our most horrendous experiences because they are beyond the human power of imagination. If knowledge of Auschwitz is to be beneficial, those who have experienced the camp must try to be considerate of those who learn about it many years later.

■ We have taken on a function that has been discussed by German psychiatrists: "Whether or not they know or want it, objective social reality has cast people who were once deprived of all rights in the role of prosecutors of all other people—especially Germans, of course." Many of us perform this function consciously. The impetus for the Auschwitz trials was provided by survivors of the camp. The same psychiatrists have also noted a certain social isolation, "a multilayered phenomenon that only partially derives from the sufferings in the camp and the transplantation to a new environment. Though these factors may be regressive, in many survivors the feeling of social exclusion increases, even if people around them are anything but uncomprehending and indifferent. Someone who was in a concentration camp is a marked man and uninhibited contact with him is more difficult in every instance." I can only confirm such insights.

Many physicians have studied the consequences of internment in an extermination camp. Psychiatrists who have themselves experienced such an imprisonment are in a much more advantageous position for this sort of study than their colleagues—not only because they can draw on their own experiences, but also because patients treated by them are more likely to shed the inhibitions caused by the fear that the physician might not believe everything they told him. Psychiatrists who lack the bond of a shared camp experience with their patients have complained about the inhibiting effects of this fear.

From his investigations Professor Leo Eitinger, who was himself in Auschwitz, gained the insight that survivors of the concentration camps cannot be compared with other patients who have been described in professional publications. German psychiatrists have confirmed this. "Unlike a returnee who was injured in the war, a survivor of a KL simply is not a returnee." Particularly those who were persecuted for "racial" reasons generally lost their families as well as the roots that had bound them to their homeland. Thus Ernst-Günther Schenck's comparisons with prisoners of war are not valid.

In support of his thesis, Eitinger points out that while history has recorded various forms of slavery as well as attempts by victors to exterminate defeated nations, the Hitler regime was the first to place the capabilities of modern technology in the service of the painstakingly planned extermination of human groups. Hence survivors from these groups offer an investigator two exceptional opportunities. Never before has a physician been able to examine so many individuals who were sentenced to death but who remained alive because the end of the war impeded the completion of the work of destruction. The families of those destined to die were murdered, their lives completely destroyed and their world reduced to rubble. As a result, they not only suffered a psychophysical shock of the greatest magnitude but afterward were isolated in the world without any anchorage. Since then, many of them have been living in "incurable loneliness."

Eitinger documents his findings with statistical material that he gathered in Israel in 1961 and 1962, when he questioned 554 former concentration camp inmates. Every one of them lost at least a close relative, and more than three-fourths were the only survivors of their families. When they were asked about their greatest shock, about one-third of them stated that it was the complete separation from relatives and friends.

German psychiatrists have come to the following conclusion:

The general attitude of distrust and embitterment that may be demonstrated in virtually all who suffered severe persecution derives from the destruction of the supporting foundation of human society. Experiences that cause the radical and protracted destruction of interpersonal relationships combine with the persecuted person's conflicted involvement with the world around him after his liberation and produce a pathological structure of relationships that is an important basic feature of the experiential personality change.

E. C. Trautmann, who made his observations in the United States, to which many survivors emigrated after their liberation, has noted an additional factor: an anxiety-producing condition of forlornness that was exacerbated by the unfamiliar language. Others speak in this connection of a depression caused by deracination. Professor Ulrich Venzlaff assesses emigration following confinement in a KZ and a stay in a DP (displaced persons) camp as a "psychic burden that many can no longer bear." He observed that after a certain latency period in the course of emigration there were severe nervous breakdowns.

Another frequently observed phenomenon, an overhasty marriage, can also be interpreted as a consequence of this rootlessness. Many survivors looked for some way to reestablish earlier bonds. Women frequently chose an older man who had known their murdered fathers. According to Trautmann's observations, in many instances "these attachments, born of distress, turned into an unsatisfactory marriage that was full of conflicts. This makes them an early example of the perpetuation of disturbed interpersonal relationships after the liberation in the form of an institutionalized permanent conflict."

Paul Matussek has found that "the choice of a spouse is clearly determined by the fate of persecution." He cites such statements as this one: "A person who was in a camp can only abide another former camp inmate as a partner. No one else understands what happened there." Thus the shared suffering becomes the basis of a matrimonial bond. Professor Ulrich Venzlaff has observed "a frequent rush into marriage between psychologically defective partners without an inner emotional relationship." And he adds: "It is a depressing fact that a particularly high percentage of the children from such marriages display behavioral disturbances and neurotic symptoms."

Not a single one of the 130 former KZ inmates whom Paul Matussek examined has come out of confinement without chronic disorders. Leo Eitinger examined survivors of Nazi concentration camps in two Israeli kibbutzim. All were able to work, but only three of them were healthy and fit. The two examinations were conducted without recompense for the subjects, thus eliminating symptoms that might resemble a compensation neurosis.

The previously mentioned team of Cracow physicians that examined seventy-seven former inmates of Auschwitz in the spring of 1959 reports that most of them claimed to have had no feelings of alienation in the camp; on the contrary, the help of comrades had uplifted them. Most of them did not develop feelings of alienation until after the liberation. The physicians emphasize that the men they examined were not *Muselmänner* in the camp; only four of them had been deported for reasons of "race." They have summed up their findings as follows:

> It should be noted that the majority of those examined believe that their time in the camp had a decisive effect on the further development and formation of their individuality. These are some of the effects they mentioned: difficulty in trusting people; difficulties in establishing contacts and at the same time a strong emotional attachment to former fellow inmates; heightened tolerance; placing a lesser value on unimportant matters. Many stated that since their liberation their emotional reactions have become blunted, that they can neither rejoice nor grieve as they did before. For many of them their stay in the camp has become an obsessive idea. . . . The most frequently mentioned pathopsychological manifestations include depression, a feeling of angst and constant danger, and an almost complete absence of the sex drive.

A premature weakening of the vital functions, early physical and psychological aging, and manifestations of typical geriatric disorders have been observed. More than one-third of the Frenchmen who returned from the camps in 1945 died within ten years. It may be assumed that the majority of the returnees were rather young, since few of the older inmates survived imprisonment in a camp. "Our clinical and statistical examinations of 500 former inmates," writes the German psychiatrist Walter von Baeyer, "turned up in about three-fourths of these cases not organically explainable, character-neurotic, psychopathic or experience-reactive abnormal attitudes, most of which must be regarded as having been caused completely or partially by persecution and the majority of which must be considered permanent."

Independently of one another, several experts have come to the conclusion that the results of their examinations, particularly of those former camp inmates who were interned in extermination camps under the special conditions of "racial" persecution, have deprived the psychiatrists' classic concept of causality of its general validity—the concept that says that every experience leaves a personality basically unaffected and only abnormal people react by becoming ill.

■ The Dutch psychoanalyst Tas wrote in June 1947: "I know people who came back from concentration camps where they had the most horrible experiences and, after a period in which they would not or could not say anything about those experiences, returned to a normal life with their family and their work. And yet it is impossible to speak of mental health in such cases. There is no doubt that large amounts of affect and aggression have been suppressed, but it is certain that these have not been assimilated. It is very probable that in the course of time this will lead to serious psychological disorders." In 1967 Tas's colleague Eduard de Wind referred to this statement and wrote: "After twenty years these words have been confirmed numerous times. Many former inmates who lived for years in an outwardly assimilated fashion in reality had an extremely regressive relationship to the world outside and harbored social, political, and other illusions that could never be gratified. A breakdown was unavoidable."

Dr. Wolfgang Jacob reports about a case that seems characteristic to him. Twenty years after his liberation from a concentration camp, a fifty-year-old patient suffered from high blood pressure as well as other complaints that were hard to diagnose. After his imprisonment he had quickly recovered, adapted well socially, and done successful work. At the examination this patient appeared quite composed and reserved. The physician finally referred to the years his patient had spent in a KZ. At first the patient blocked any talk about it, but then it burst out of him and over him. The memory was such a shock to him that it took six weeks of clinical treatment to restore him. "The tormentors have disappeared, but the torment remains."

French physicians also observed that in many survivors the consequences of their imprisonment in a KZ did not appear until later. After examining former deportees with lung diseases, they wrote: "We know many comrades who maintained an admirable composure during their entire detention but after their return suddenly seemed to have lost this balance—as if they had exhausted their entire reserves of energy! Perhaps there is a connection between this demoralization and their subsequent lung disease."

Delayed psychological effects are particularly noticeable in persons who were in a KZ as children. In her examination of "Auschwitz kids," Dr. Wanda Poltawska included those whose names and nationalities cannot be determined because they were small children in the camp. Even those who have no memory of Auschwitz suffer from anxiety attacks. "Suddenly, without knowing why, they greatly fear something. Only reluctantly and in moments of the utmost intimacy do they admit that they are afraid without any reason. They are afraid of dogs, uniforms, all people wearing any uniform, screams, white coats, and the German language." The closer the youths were to puberty at the time of their imprisonment, the more frequently did Dr. Poltawska encounter anxiety states and a morbidly enhanced memory of everything relating to the camp.

During a psychoanalytic treatment, Dr. H. Strauß observed that a patient who was in Auschwitz at the age of ten retained the idea of inferiority that had been forced on her so insistently in those days and believed that it was justified.

Hearing German speech again also caused anguish to persons who had been persecuted as adults. I repeatedly observed this when Auschwitzers visited me in Vienna. Jadwiga Landowska, a Polish woman, begged to be excused for this: "I know that people here are nice, but I can't help it." As soon as she heard German spoken in Vienna, she became afraid. This anxiety disappeared in conversations with me, even though they were conducted in German; evidently she regarded me as a companion in misfortune.

Alexander and Margarete Mitscherlich speak of indelible memory traces that sound an alarm at the slightest touch, and they document this phenomenon with the following case: "One of our patients, who had to live in a concentration camp for four years, is frightened by the sight of every German policeman. He knows that this is absurd, but the signal that once emanated from such a uniform is too powerful to be extinguished by relatively insignificant subsequent experiences."

Consequences of internment in extermination camps can be discerned even in the next generation. In Canada Dr. Vivian Rakoff observed depressions in children of Jewish immigrants who had been interned, but also aggressions and infractions of the law—evidently "because they are unable to abreact their generationally determined spirit of dissent, for the parents either idolized their children or were tired of reacting to the oppositional forces in any way. Thus the children's aggressions are vented outside the family." Added to such parental failings is their reluctance to speak with their children about the years of their persecution. This inhibition is particularly noticeable in Israel, where parents dread questions about their behavior as well as reproaches for having allowed themselves to be led to the places of extermination like sheep. Constantly evading this subject is bound to disturb a normal relationship between parents and children.

David Rousset is right: the fate of the survivors differs from that of all others through an experience that is impossible to communicate.

■ Strange though this may sound, the guards of Auschwitz apparently had a certain idea about this experience and this difference. There have been a number of reports that a member of the ss showed something like a kind of sympathy for an inmate he knew when he met him again in another camp.

In Groß-Rosen, Mieczyslaw Kieta reencountered the medic Josef Klehr, whom he had gotten to know all too well in Auschwitz. In accordance with regulations he greeted him by standing at attention and saying nothing. Klehr called out to him, "Hey, big fellow, wait a bit," asked him whether he had been in Auschwitz, and gave him a cigarette after Kieta had answered in the affirmative. Kieta had the impression that Klehr was pleased about this renewed encounter. In Auschwitz Teddy Pietrzykowski worked on a detail that was commanded by Franz Hössler, later the ss camp leader. When Hössler saw him again in Bergen-Belsen, he appointed him as senior capo and made him his *Kalfaktor* (handyman).

When Tadeusz Snieszko was transferred to a satellite camp at Ravensbrück, he was personally escorted by ss roll call leader Oswald Kaduk. During the trip Kaduk, an Upper Silesian, conversed with the inmate in Polish, asked whether he had been given food for the journey, and, after he had answered in the negative, gave Snieszko a can of sardines. At length he asked if Snieszko wanted something to drink. When the inmate answered that he had not drunk beer in a long time, Kaduk bought him beer. Snieszko mentioned this in his Frankfurt court testimony, but Kaduk denied everything. Even though Snieszko's story was virtually the only testimony from which the court learned about a humane action by Kaduk, Kaduk even claimed that he had not accompanied Snieszko on that trip. It seems that he was embarrassed in front of his comrades, now his codefendants, about his lack of discipline in dealing with this inmate.

In the courtroom the tormented reencountered their tormentors under completely different circumstances. When time had not yet been able to perform a healing or at least calming function, these renewed encounters were dramatic. I remember the atmosphere in the room when Höß was called to account in Warsaw in March 1947. The presiding judge tried hard to conduct the trial in an objective and sober manner, but the excitement of the audience in the large, overcrowded courtroom could be felt at all times. There I reencountered many acquaintances from Auschwitz who followed the trial every day.

The atmosphere at the Frankfurt trial was quite different from that at the Warsaw hearings, and not only because in the seventeen years between these two trials life had gone on; this time the trial was being conducted in Germany, the homeland of the victimizers (though, with some exceptions, not of the victims). Shivering and shuddering, and sometimes probably with some skepticism as well, the people attending the trial—primarily Germans, of course—experienced the necessarily inadequate reconstruction of the mechanism of destruction. The fact that school classes were taken to the courtroom indicated that Auschwitz had already become a factor in history.

For a year and a half I attended the trial in Frankfurt and observed the reactions of the witnesses as they encountered the defendants again. I empathized with the despair caused by their obligation to conjure up life in Auschwitz again in the atmosphere of a courtroom. All too often this despair was exacerbated by the fact that the questions of many members of the court demonstrated the inability of many German jurists to understand and make allowance for the situation of a former prisoner in a courtroom. In many instances it took a lot of urging on my part to make such a person decide to go to Frankfurt. I was not able to convince all of them of a survivor's duty to bear witness to the death of their comrades. More than once the fear of overstraining the nerves was stronger than all arguments.

For many their trip to Frankfurt marked their first renewed encounter with Germans since the liberation, a contact that they had avoided up to that time. Raya Kagan told me that on the plane taking her to Frankfurt she was impelled to scrutinize all German-speaking passengers of her generation and ask herself what one person or another could have been and could have done in those years.

All those who were called as witnesses were able to prepare themselves inwardly for testifying and encountering the defendants again, but what good was that when Auschwitz became such an uncanny presence in the courtroom?

Alex Rosenstock, a dentist who traveled to Frankfurt from Haifa, is an urbane and cultivated man. His testimony was passionate but self-controlled. When he had finished and was leaving the room he suddenly had to stop. He leaned against the wall and started to cry uncontrollably.

A Russian witness was supposed to identify the defendants about whom he was testifying. The ss men of yesteryear were instructed to stand in a semicircle behind the witness stand. When the Russian turned around and saw those twenty men in front of him, he instinctively covered his eyes with his hands. I was certainly able to empathize with this gesture.

Józef Gabis reported to the court that he saw the body of Lilly Toffler, who had been shot in the yard of Block 11 because a love letter from her to Gabis had been found. Gabis found out that Boger had killed his girlfriend. After the cross-examination Gabis was asked to identify Boger but said, "I would rather not look at the defendant." He left the courtroom without having looked at the dock.

When Filip Müller was giving his testimony, particular excitement could be felt in the courtroom, for the witness, who had been assigned to the Sonderkommando, was reporting about Hans Stark, whose cruel deeds were exceptional even in that trial. Stark's attorney tried to create doubt as to whether the evildoer described by Müller was identical with his client. At that point the witness, a Czech who spoke only broken German, gave such a precise imitation of the blustering, dialect-tinged tone of Stark's commands (the defendant had not yet spoken in the courtroom) that it became clear how vivid the past had remained to him.

Müller's testimony so stirred many witnesses that they were afterward impelled to speak with me, the only person they could expect to understand them.

Dr. Friedrich Skrein, a respected Viennese jurist, is familiar with the atmosphere in a courtroom. After his testimony he told me that he was nevertheless so disconcerted by the presence of the defendants, whom he knew from Auschwitz, that he forgot to give a substantial part of his prepared testimony.

As a block elder, the Pole Anna Palarczyk was able to observe many things with a greater inner detachment than an anonymous inmate possessed. Her testimony was matter-of-fact and devoid of emotion. On the next day she told me about an oppressive dream. She was alone in a big, empty room. The SS men on trial came in and approached her slowly but inexorably. She could not find an exit from that room.

Sometimes a reencounter after twenty years triggered different reactions. The Pole Erwin Bartel was eighteen when he worked under Hans Stark in the Admissions Department. After Bartel, who had gotten a degree in engineering, had finished his rather incriminating testimony, the defendant availed himself of his right to question the witness, something that he did not habitually do. "Does the witness still remember our confrontation in October 1959?" he asked Bartel. Stark had been arrested then, and Bartel had been invited to Frankfurt during the preliminary investigations. Bartel replied, "Yes, I remember. You said to me, 'Why didn't you say this ten years ago? Now I have a wife and a child.'" Stark continued: "At that time you said, 'We had a lot of good things when we worked for you, but so many bad things happened in Auschwitz that I have to tell everything.'" "Yes, that's correct," said Bartel. Stark's questions hardly diminished the witness's credibility; if anything, they enhanced it. I had the impression that Stark had not broken his usual silence toward incriminating witnesses in order to cast doubt on the testimony, but for another reason. It was as though he had felt a need to refer once more to the personal relationship developed in Auschwitz.

I have also heard about personal encounters between the guards and the guarded under radically changed circumstances after the end of the war. An inmate who was an expert on Persian lamb coats had to examine and work on such coats while on the Canada Detail. He helped the leader of this detail, SS Sergeant Otto Graf, to sell them on the black market, and in return the SS man made life more pleasant for the inmate. Graf had a bad reputation but was known to spare inmates who could be useful to him. Many years after the end of the war, the fur expert met Graf, a Viennese, at the race track in that city, and they discussed trading in Persian lamb coats.

Since 1955 I have increasingly concerned myself with the history of Auschwitz. I have spoken and corresponded with Auschwitzers, studied the pertinent literature, written and lectured about subjects connected with the camp, instituted legal proceedings, and conferred with judicial authorities. I thought that this activity had in the course of time given me an objective view of this part of contemporary history when to my surprise I was confronted with persons in Frankfurt whom I had known as ss men in Auschwitz. Dr. Viktor Capesius, the pharmacist in charge, was arrested in December 1959; and since he had denied any guilt and I happened to be in Frankfurt, he was brought face to face with me. When he entered the room, all of a sudden I vividly remembered details that I had not been able to recall during my conversation with the prosecutor a short time previously. Suddenly the past was in the room. I noticed that this surprising encounter had thrown Capesius off balance, too. Though he continued his denials even in my presence, his excessive sweating was visible evidence that he was lying. A short time later I was confronted with the medic Josef Klehr, whose murderous practices I tried to combat by notifying the ss garrison physician and who was finally transferred from Auschwitz. At the time I was well aware of the risk I was taking, particularly after I had noticed that he suspected I was working against him. I always had to be prepared for his revenge. Now a bailiff led him into the room by a chain attached to his wrist. His only response to my accusations was, "I know that Herr Langbein was not well disposed toward me even in Auschwitz." This renewed encounter was so ghastly that I was not able to laugh at his remark. At night I dreamed of him — not of the old, seedy Klehr whom I had confronted that day but of the medic at the zenith of his power.

I spent a sleepless night before testifying at the big Auschwitz trial in Frankfurt. Even when I had been called as a witness at the second Auschwitz trial, where my testimony was bound to have no particular significance, I was unable to sleep the night before. Kazimierz Smolen, the director of the State Museum of Auschwitz-Birkenau, occupies himself with events from the camp period more regularly than I do. While testifying against Dr. Horst Schumann in December 1970, he suffered a weak spell, which, as he told me later, he found difficult to conceal. Smolen had previously testified at all Auschwitz trials and associated no oppressive personal memories with Schumann.

In the course of my endeavors to reconstruct details of the history of Auschwitz, it frequently seemed appropriate to question former guards as well. For a longer period than was reasonable, I had compunctions about approaching such persons, even when I knew that they had tried to help the inmates in the camp. Even after I had overcome this reluctance, every encounter with a former member of the ss caused in me an emotional tension that is hard to describe.

In June 1967, when I was studying documents at the Institut für Zeitgeschichte in Munich in preparation of this study, I found a letter signed by Friedrich Entress, the camp physician of Auschwitz. When I suddenly saw the familiar signature again twenty-four years after encountering Entress for the last time, the elapsed time seemed unreal for a moment. To contain my trepidation I first had to remind myself that I was sitting in a reading room where I was treated courteously by cultivated people. I knew that Entress had been executed many years previously. Nevertheless, at that moment he was more present to me than those sitting beside me.

SS MEMBERS AFTER THE WAR

■ ■ ■

After the capitulation of the Third Reich, those bearing the greatest responsibility abandoned their subordinates to whom they had delegated the organization and execution of the mass murders. Hitler, Goebbels, and Himmler pointed the way with their suicides. Afterward, none of those who had given the commands to murder provided cover for those who had incurred guilt by executing their orders.

"I shall never forget my last report and farewell to the RFSS," wrote Höß. Along with other SS leaders from concentration camps, he had been summoned by Himmler, who had already withdrawn to Flensburg. "He was beaming and in the best of spirits, and yet the world, our world, had gone under. If he had said, 'All right, gentlemen, now it's over; you know what you have to do,' I would have understood, since it would have been in keeping with what he had preached to the SS for years: self-surrender to an idea. But this was his last order to us: Disappear into the Wehrmacht! This was our farewell to the man I had looked up to, in whom I had had such unshakable confidence, whose commands and utterances had been gospel to me."

The chief of the WVHA, SS General Oswald Pohl, did not take his life. In a Nuremberg prison he declared that he had never ordered or even encouraged anyone to beat inmates to death. On the contrary, he had opposed inhumane acts when he had heard of them. At the peak of his power, this same Pohl ordered all commandants of concentration camps to make the work assignments of the inmates "exhausting in the truest sense of the word." This can be read in black and white.

Others were cleverer than Pohl. They prepared their escape at a time when the idea of a German defeat was regarded as a capital crime, and not infrequently by those who were already mapping their own escape routes.

Adolf Eichmann escaped to Argentina. After he had had years of leisure to reflect on his actions, he thought that what he considered to be his defense was so important that he had it recorded on tape. "My subjective attitude to what happened was my belief in the national emergency preached by the leadership of the German Reich at that time. In addition there was my increasing belief in the necessity of a total war because to an increasing extent I always had to believe in the constant proclamations of the German Reich's leaders: 'Victory in this total war—or downfall of the German people.' Based on this mind-set I did my duty with a clear conscience and a trusting heart." Eichmann characterizes himself in these words: "I was nothing but a loyal, proper, correct, industrious member of the SS and the RSHA, who was filled only with idealistic feelings for my fatherland, to which I was honored to belong. I never was a *Schweinehund* or a traitor."

■ Equally typical as the substance and form of Eichmann's statement is the answer that Höß, in the Nuremburg prison, gave to the question of when he had first thought that he might be taken to court and sentenced: "At the time of the collapse—when the Führer died."

Ten months later Höß described his reaction more verbosely in his Cracow cell:

On the way (while fleeing with his family) we heard on a farm that the Führer was dead. When we heard that, my wife and I simultaneously had this thought: Now we have to go, too! The end of the Führer was also the end of our world. Did it make any sense for us to go on living? We would be pursued and sought everywhere. We were going to take poison; I had procured some for my wife so that she and our children would not be captured alive by the Russians if there was an unexpected advance. For the sake of our children, we did not do it and were willing to endure whatever might come. We ought to have done it, and later I always regretted that we did not do it, because we, and especially my wife and the children, would have been spared a great deal. And what will they still have to go through? We were tied and chained to that world, and it would have been our duty to go down with it.

Höß was content with pathos-filled words and until his arrest on March 11, 1946, lived on a farm near Flensburg with false papers provided by Himmler.

People such as Dr. Eduard Wirths and Dr. Hans Delmotte who had already attempted to distance themselves from the crimes while still in Auschwitz did end their lives.

Most members of the SS went underground, which was not too difficult after the capitulation and division of Germany into various occupation zones. They destroyed their pay books and in prisoner-of-war camps pretended to be members of the Wehrmacht, usually under false names. They soon noticed that it was practically impossible to check their false statements, and thus many of them became quite careless and audacious. Cases in point are Robert Mulka, the adjutant to Höß, who demanded (and received) compensation for his fictitious army service, or the block leader of the Auschwitz bunker, Bruno Schlage, who also passed himself off as a member of the Wehrmacht and, while he was at it, gave himself a higher rank than he had held in the SS because he expected that this would benefit him financially some day. The camp physician Horst Fischer felt so safe in the German Democratic Republic that he started a medical practice under his own name in a small town, where he was able to practice undisturbed for two decades. Dr. Horst Schumann, whose name had become public knowledge in the Nuremberg medical trial in connection with his sterilization experiments, had so much confidence in the authorities of the German Federal Republic that he lived there with his family without any attempt at camouflage and practiced medicine. He felt so safe that he applied for a hunting license in 1951, thereby challenging the authorities to concern themselves with him routinely. When the required certificate of good conduct was requested from Schumann's birthplace, the officials uncovered his past. But even then nothing was done to him because before any official action was taken Schumann was tipped off and bolted. Hans Anhalt, a former SS man who had been attached to the Canada Detail, relied on the fact that the authorities in the GDR did not conduct any systematic searches for Auschwitz guards. He kept taking to the pawnshop items that he had "organized" in Canada and sent home. Since the items were very valuable, this eventually aroused suspicion. When a search of his house turned up further property that demonstrably was from Auschwitz, he was finally taken to court in 1964.

Bernhard Walter of the Identification Service in Auschwitz had to take pictures of selections at the ramp even though a prohibition of photography was in force in the camp. He was so careless that he took along an album of his photographs at the evacuation of Auschwitz and did not destroy them when Germany capitulated. He does not seem to have realized the probative value of this series of photos.

■ When Allied troops saw at the liberation what crimes had been committed in the camps, they first arrested those whom they found there.

The most lasting shock among the general public was caused by the mountains of corpses of inmates who had starved to death, which the Allies encountered at the liberation of Bergen-Belsen. The first proceedings were brought in Lüneburg against guards of that camp. The Polish trial of guards in Majdanek, which had taken place before the end of the war and thus had attracted less attention, had been completed a long time before. At the head of the defendants before a British military court in Lüneburg was Josef Kramer, the last commandant of Bergen-Belsen and previously the commandant of Birkenau. Right after his arrest in April 1945, Kramer denied that there were gas chambers in Birkenau. Later, when he had to admit that there were, he was asked about the reason for his initial denial. Kramer replied that he had still felt bound by his oath to treat the extermination machinery as a secret and no longer felt bound by it only after learning of the deaths of Hitler and Himmler.

Kramer's attitude toward the prisoners was revealed when he was asked why, in his opinion, old and weak Jews were admitted to the camp even though they could no longer be forced to do work useful to the Reich. This was Kramer's answer: "The reasons why these people were sent to my camp were none of my business. My task was to accept them. Whether it was a political opponent or a Jew or a career criminal did not concern me. I accepted the bodies, and that was all."

After the glamour of the uniforms and insignia had faded, the SS men who had once brimmed with self-confidence presented a sorry picture. When they were confronted with crimes committed within their command, high-ranking officers of yesteryear claimed to have been double-crossed by their subordinates, and those accused of committing atrocities pointed to orders that they had to carry out if they did not want to risk their own lives. Hannah Arendt has summed up the behavior of the bigwigs of the machinery of extermination in these words: "In the completely changed atmosphere after the end of the war, not one of them had the guts to defend the Nazi Weltanschauung, though almost every one of them must have realized that there was no longer any hope for them."

When Maximilian Grabner was ferreted out in Austria, arrested, and confronted with me, I almost did not recognize him, though I remembered him all too well from Auschwitz. He was a yammering, groveling coward and kept asserting with a guileless look in his eyes that he had wanted only the best for the inmates. No one who heard his whimpering and begging could have imagined how much that man had enjoyed the terror that he spread as head of the camp Gestapo. After he had been extradited to Poland, he did so much moaning in a Cracow courtroom as he tried to deny any guilt that it became too much even for his codefendant, the former SS camp leader Aumeier. When the defendants were once again led out of the courtroom at the conclusion of a session, Aumeier gave Grabner, who was walking ahead of him, a kick as a sign of his contempt. Aumeier was the only one of the forty defendants at this Auschwitz trial in Cracow who did not try to minimize his responsibility for the crimes. Grabner attempted to make his judges believe that he participated because he could not change anything. He said that he was active in the machinery of extermination only out of consideration for his family and later was under irresistible compulsion and orders.

In late July 1945 Dr. Friedrich Entress testified as follows: "From the very first day, my service in the KL was spoiled for me by my obligation to attend all executions and the many minor incidents in the camp, including those among inmates, against which I was powerless. The greatest nervous strain began with the so-called Jewish transports." Entress had the following explanation for his killing of inmates by means of injections, allegedly only on orders: "No matter how great my guilt may now be because I executed these orders and how heavy the burden of my fate was during my service in the KL, I can only explain it all to myself today by pointing out that in the face of those mass deaths and masses of people we came to the bitter but true realization that under the necessarily prevailing circumstances these tormented people ought to be helped rather than harmed." Entress evidently realized that his arguments were not persuasive, and therefore he added: "The methods employed by the SS in the concentration camps had a completely deadening effect and caused us to have no scruples about our conduct anymore."

Anyone who was able to observe in Auschwitz the initiative displayed by Grabner and Entress, as holders of key positions in the machinery of destruction, and anyone who experienced how avidly these two tracked down any little attempt to lessen the omnipotence of the machinery of murder and how rigorously they hindered any mitigation of it will be shown by such statements to what degree a person can lie to himself. I state this because I do not believe that these men said these things only to put themselves in a better light before their judges. After feeling the revulsion aroused by their actions, they had a need to make excuses to themselves.

Along with Grabner and Aumeier, the SS camp leader Maria Mandel was sentenced to death in Cracow. Just before her execution she met in the bathroom of the prison a Polish woman whom she had known in Auschwitz, where that political prisoner had been an inmate functionary. Her nationalistic orientation after the liberation aroused the suspicion of the Russians, and thus she was imprisoned again in 1947. When the two were in the shower, Mandel approached the woman and asked her to forgive her, which would make her dying easier. The Pole said she forgave her, whereupon Mandel kissed her hand.

After the death sentence had been pronounced on Höß, he felt a need to justify himself to his family because he had to assume that they had learned about the monstrous deeds that had been the subject of detailed reports in the international press. Thus he wrote to his family: "As the commandant of the Auschwitz extermination camp, I was fully responsible for everything that happened there, whether or not I knew about it. I did not learn about most of the terrible and horrendous things that happened there until the examination and the trial itself. How people double-crossed me and twisted my orders, all the things they did, supposedly on orders from me—all this is indescribable. I hope that the guilty people will not escape judgment."

Oswald Kaduk, the SS roll call leader, took a more primitive path to self-justification. In the same year in which Höß wrote his letter, he defended himself before a Soviet military court with this argument: "I was a soldier and carried out all orders. More I was not able to do."

Pery Broad was shrewd enough to evade his judges, at least in the earliest and most critical period. He approached the administration of the British prisoner-of-war camp in which he was interned and on his own initiative gave a report about events in Auschwitz. When he was requested to do so, he put his report in writing and did not whitewash anything but said nothing whatever about his own role in the Political Department. "It was a kind of confession for him," said a Dutchman formerly employed in the interrogation section of that camp years later. Broad was given preferential treatment and was called in for the interrogation of other inmates—"in order to indicate to us which of them seemed suspect to him," as the Dutchman put it later. Finally, Broad, who had brought his knowledge of languages to the Political Department, was used as an interpreter in the Nuremberg trials.

■ Whom the Allies arrested shortly after the liberation of the camps and who remained undisturbed was decided in large part by chance, since documents had just begun to be utilized and the German population frequently behaved the way Boger later described it: "In Ludwigsburg I stayed for about three weeks in 1945 without registering with the police, but then I was betrayed by a former inmate of Auschwitz and arrested by the Americans." It is revealing that Boger uses "betrayed" for the action of a former prisoner. At that time Boger managed to escape from American captivity. He later testified about what happened afterward: "After escaping from captivity I was in hiding at the homes of relatives and friends in Württemberg without registering with the police. At that time it was still apparent that Germans stuck together because they all knew me and no one reported me."

Professor Friedrich Hacker has been trying to determine why the Germans behaved in this way, or in similar ways, at that time and why those who had to execute the crimes of Nazism go on living without pangs of conscience. He writes: "The Germans did not repress their bad conscience. Many of them have none. The projection of an enemy symbol spared them a repression. By now there are a sufficient number of investigations that prove that the Germans feel no more guilty than the American soldiers do in Vietnam. They simply regard their adversaries as lice or lemurs or subhumans, just as the Germans regarded Jews. Thus the whole brutal enterprise can operate under the designation 'extermination of vermin.' For this reason there is no point in digging out guilt feelings alleged to be buried. They do not even exist."

In the course of time this has become more and more clearly apparent, particularly after the Allied courts had long since suspended their activities and German courts began to conduct their own investigations after a long interval. With few exceptions the defendants regarded themselves as whipping boys, and in this they were confirmed by part of German society, which called the trials of Nazis a national humiliation.

The development of public opinion is clearly reflected in Boger's behavior. On July 5, 1945, when everyone was still under the spell of the crimes committed in the camps, crimes that had only recently become public knowledge, he testified as follows in American captivity: "Auschwitz! Unimaginable capital crime unique in the history of mankind! A big scientific investigation of this course of events by scholars from all over the world will find those who are truly guilty and absolve the German people in its totality as well as the mass of SS men, those pitiful slaves of the greatest sadist of all time, RFSS Himmler." Nineteen years later, when Boger was called to account by a German court in Frankfurt, his testimony was quite different. After a witness had described how during an "intensified interrogation" Boger crushed the testicles of a fellow prisoner, the defendant was told, "Surely you know that a prisoner who is so mistreated that blood flows from his trousers is eventually prepared to give any testimony. As an expert you ought to know that such a testimony is valueless." Boger responded self-confidently, "I am of a different opinion, and with specific reference to Auschwitz. It is also my view that in many cases corporal punishment would be appropriate even today—for example, in the current criminal law relating to juveniles." When this caused an audible disturbance in the balcony, Boger angrily yelled, "It's easy for you up there to laugh. You weren't there, were you?"

The Auschwitz trial in Frankfurt offered ample opportunities to observe the defendants. As in other trials of Nazis, they truly offered no picture of an elite, not even in the negative sense. Like most criminals, they worked at making excuses and did not spurn even the lamest ones. When they could no longer come up with excuses, one heard this hackneyed protestation: "Your Honor, try as I may, I cannot remember this after so many years!"

Willi Schatz, born in 1905, who had a doctorate in dentistry, stubbornly denied that he made any selections. When he was asked what he had done in Auschwitz, he responded, "I did my duty as a soldier."

When Johann Schobert, a low-ranking SS man in the Political Department, was asked whether the many dead bodies, which no one in Auschwitz could have overlooked, had not attracted his attention, he could only answer: "We didn't worry about them."

Heinrich Bischoff, a former block leader, was charged with several murders, and he also denied everything. When a flat denial seemed too implausible because too many witnesses had observed his shootings, he asserted that he was not a monster, that he had only administered coups de grâce. He was angry that he had been accused at all: "I've had heart disease for four years now. Up to now I've always led an honest life. But now such dirty tricks are meant to louse up the last days of my life."

Detlef Nebbe, the first sergeant in the commandant's office, was sentenced to a life term in Cracow and pardoned after nine years. When he was a witness in Frankfurt, he emphasized with obvious pride that he had served in the Waffen-SS in Auschwitz. Like virtually all the SS men in the camp, he did not spend a single day at the front. He gave the court a very detailed description of an episode in which an SS man helped an inmate escape. When he was asked why he recalled this particular occurrence so clearly, he replied: "The reason I can't forget this is that I knew what a soldier's duty was." Even during long years of captivity in Poland, that man did not reflect on human duties in an extermination camp.

Boger's life term had long since become final and he had already spent twelve years in prison when he was summoned to serve as a witness at another Auschwitz trial. "We were soldiers," he said, and by "we" he meant the guards in Auschwitz. In his case, too, his punishment had effected no remorse whatever.

Hans Stark was nineteen when he participated in the first gassings in Auschwitz. When a judge asked him about the feelings that motivated him then, he replied that he regarded the use of gas as unmanly and cowardly. That was evidently his only objection to the mass murder.

Here is Pery Broad's reply to the question of whether he regarded what happened in Auschwitz as appropriate: "You have to distinguish between what happened in the main camp and in the extermination camp. The idea of the main camp wasn't bad because there it was possible to make the inmates work. But then it was linked to the machinery of extermination."

As an SS major and the head of the Auschwitz administration, Wilhelm Burger also "administered" the poison gas. In Poland he was sentenced to prison, and after his discharge he was called to account in Germany. He hardly had to worry about the second trial, since the time served in Poland would be deducted from any new sentence. Still, the sexagenarian burst out in tears with or without a cause and made this lachrymose complaint: "This Auschwitz has been hanging on me for twenty years." In Dachau, where he lives, he had masses celebrated for a favorable outcome of his trial. From the records Burger knew that I had aided the prosecution by proposing witnesses and providing documents. From my own testimony he must have known my attitude toward the organizers of the mass murders in Auschwitz. On one occasion, when I was getting my overcoat after a session, he came running obsequiously to help me into it. He obviously did not consider how embarrassing this gesture was bound to be for me.

■ As soon as there was documentation of their crimes, former members of the SS pretended that as soldiers they had no alternative but to obey orders. Klaus Dylewski declared before his judges, "Refusing to carry out a command never crossed my mind. That wasn't in me." Mulka made this assertion: "I took care not to prepare my own death sentence by asking my superiors about the legality of the murders of prisoners that I had heard about. I bore a responsibility to my family and to myself."

The law expects no one to risk his own life to prevent a crime. If a soldier acts under Befehlsnotstand—the term used by jurists for a person who carried out a criminal command because he would otherwise have endangered his life —the law exempts him from punishment. Because defendants in Nazi trials repeatedly invoked Befehlsnotstand, experts have been asked to clarify this concept. Dr. Hans-Günther Seraphim has summed up this problem as follows:

> A refusal to obey an order to exterminate inmates is not regarded by Himmler as disloyalty in the context of the SS Weltanschauung and therefore is not deemed to be a capital crime. Rather, such a refusal ranked as "character weakness." This explains why it was not followed by any punishment. Himmler's statements also indicate that the extermination, the physical eradication, of the opponents of Nazism was regarded as a sign of a particular strength of character and a mind-set that was in keeping with the ideal image of the SS. To genuine SS men the orders to exterminate prisoners had to appear objectively justified, though there might be an inner struggle against them. In addition, campaigns of this kind had to be regarded by those who carried them out as special achievements and proofs of one's mettle that were appropriate for an elite.

Not all defendants in Frankfurt assumed from the beginning the stance that made one doubt during the trial that these people realized what they had done. After his surprising arrest in April 1959, Pery Broad in his first hearing admitted many things that he later stubbornly denied. For this reason the senior detective who had interrogated him was summoned to Frankfurt as a witness. "At his hearing Broad was perceptive," he testified. "We had a lengthy conversation. Afterward Broad was rather pleased that he had unburdened himself. He was relaxed and seemed liberated."

The same detective also examined Hans Stark shortly after his unexpected arrest, and the policeman made the following statement about him: "Stark was very forthcoming. He talked about some things that we did not know at the time." Stark's testimony in court years later was anything but forthcoming. In his closing speech he summed up his responsibility in these words: "I participated in the killing of many people. After the war I have often asked myself whether I became a criminal. I have not been able to find an answer to this question."

Only one of the least sophisticated men among the Frankfurt defendants,

Stefan Baretzki, found an answer to this question. When I visited him in the penitentiary after his sentence, a life term, had become final, he declared that he had been willing to accept this sentence right after it was pronounced. "After all, that's the only thing I could still do for the people," he said. However, his defense attorney and "the others," evidently his fellow defendants, obliged him to appeal the verdict, as the others did. Since he was in any case frequently snubbed by the others and was dependent on the support of wealthy fellow defendants and their contacts, he did not have the strength to insist on getting his way. This account by Baretzki indicates the possible origin of the uniformity of the defendants' defense that was evident in most of the Nazi trials.

A number of defendants told the court that they vainly attempted to get away from Auschwitz. The reasons they gave for these attempts are revealing.

Robert Mulka, the commandant's adjutant, claimed that the Auschwitz atmosphere disgusted him. "The things that transpired there shocked me from the beginning." When he was asked what transpired there, he replied, "Well, the people with the striped clothes." "Just the clothes?" asked the presiding judge, forcing Mulka to specify what had shocked him. "No, that wasn't all. I mean the whole tone. Just one example: I received my commission as a first lieutenant in 1922. If I had shown a young lieutenant this white sheet of paper in those years and had said, 'Isn't this a nice red sheet?' he would have responded, 'Yes, it's really a beautiful red. If you hadn't told me, I might have believed it was white.' If I had said something like that in the SS in Auschwitz, the reaction would have been 'What nonsense! That paper is white.' No, those men simply had no style."

Oswald Kaduk had other reasons for leaving Auschwitz. According to him, he was afraid of being done away with as a bearer of secrets. Josef Klehr was transferred from the infirmary in which he had administered injections of poison every day to the disinfection section, where he had no opportunities to kill inmates capriciously. In the courtroom there was a reading of a letter from him in which he regretted this transfer. When the prosecutor asked him about the reason for his dissatisfaction with this new assignment, Klehr replied: "Serving in the HKB was nothing special. But the work after that was much worse. As a disinfector I had to go into the contaminated barracks and was constantly at risk."

Several witnesses confirmed that, by contrast, his colleagues Herbert Scherpe and Emil Hantl killed enfeebled inmates with injections of poison only on orders and with obvious distaste. On one occasion Scherpe even refused to kill children. He was evidently embarrassed that this episode was discussed in front of his fellow defendants and former comrades. In the preliminary examination he had testified that he could not bear the injections "emotionally and morally any longer" and that his "nerves were completely shot"; but after witnesses had testified that he had broken down when he was supposed to kill children, he reacted by saying, "That's an exaggeration. That isn't true." It evidently was more important to him not to be considered *schlapp* (soft) by his erstwhile comrades than to gather extenuating circumstances for his sentence. All he said by way of a closing speech was "I am not aware of any personal guilt."

Hantl's situation before the court was even more favorable, for more witnesses testified in his favor than had supported Scherpe. He was charged with participating in selections made in the infirmary. "I only accompanied the SS physician," he said in his defense. "That was my duty, and I would do the same thing today." He indignantly rejected the assertion that he had administered injections of poison with his own hands. "I didn't do that. Was I supposed to let the infected patients breathe on me?" Even the man whom many witnesses credited with humane feelings could not give any other motives for restraint at the killings.

During the entire trial Bruno Schlage, the block leader of the bunker, denied everything with a pinched face, even when he must have noticed that no one could believe him any more. He read his well-prepared closing speech from a piece of paper. All he had to say about Auschwitz was this: "I had to do my duty the way it was demanded of me. We could not refuse to obey any orders while our fatherland was fighting a total war. I felt bound by my oath of loyalty to the commander in chief. We had no time to examine the orders because they had to be carried out immediately."

In the twenty months of the Auschwitz trial in Frankfurt, there were two occasions on which defendants' nerves gave out and they burst into tears. Kaduk and Bednarek wept when their own fate was discussed. "If an object of pity appears anywhere, it is usually one's own self." This observation by Alexander and Margarete Mitscherlich has been confirmed by the Auschwitz trial.

■ The German writer Martin Walser, who followed the trial with understanding and empathy, has this to say about the phenomenon of the memory of Auschwitz being a far greater burden for the victims than for the victimizers: "What Auschwitz was is known only by the 'inmates' and by no one else. When a former 'inmate' is unable to go on speaking in the courtroom; when it is hard for him to so much as look at his former tormentors to identify one of them; when he keeps repeating compulsively phrases of his torturers, twenty-year-old sentences, including things said by the tortured; when for a few minutes memory yields its dreadful substance in a simple and unprocessed form, a bit of Auschwitz becomes real."

On the other hand:

It is not the fault of the ss men but that of our human memory that they do not have to cry when they see the inmates again. To be sure, our memory continues to work in mysterious fashion on our experiences, which it absorbs, but when we recall a situation our memory first supplies an image of our role in that situation. Then, after newer insights, we can manipulate our role; we can regret it, deny it, disavow it. However, these commentaries that we now add to the memory material cannot attain real power over us. Thus one should not be too surprised that the accused frequently smile or give answers that almost seem ironic. That is not cynicism. Even today they cannot comprehend the Auschwitz reality of the inmates—because their memory has preserved an entirely different Auschwitz, their Auschwitz, that of the ss men.

That is why, when they returned from Auschwitz to their accustomed milieu, they did not seem to those around them to be criminals.

Hasheider, the Protestant parson of Uerdingen, certified after Klaus Dylewski's arrest that he had participated in the religious life of the congregation and was known to him from numerous pastoral conversations. "I believe I can vouch for Herr Dylewski," wrote this clergyman, "and affirm that he is today a person molded and bound by the Christian faith."

From 1950 to his arrest in October 1958, Wilhelm Boger was employed by the Heinkel Works in Stuttgart-Zuffenhausen. This firm gave him the following reference in 1959: "On the basis of his good performance, his ambition, his diligence, and his readiness for duty, he was promoted on March 1, 1956, to the position of senior stock clerk. Herr Boger has always performed the duties assigned to him to our complete satisfaction. His great interest in his work and his diligence have made him a very valuable member of our staff. His personal conduct toward his superiors and fellow workers has always been unobjectionable."

After he was pardoned in the GDR, Oswald Kaduk went to West Berlin and found a position as an assistant nurse in the Tegel-Nord Hospital. He became so popular with the patients that they called him "Papi" (Pop).

The lack of guilt feelings coupled with the publicity they received in the course of the trial caused many a former ss man to behave like a star. As a prisoner awaiting trial, Boger wrote his wife that he was sorry he had neglected to write his memoirs. When he had been sentenced and was supposed to testify in another trial, he stipulated that the interrogation had to take place in his penal institution because he would otherwise not be up to the excitement of a hearing. When the prosecutor got there, Boger emphasized that the only reason he was testifying was that the examiner was, like himself, a Swabian. He began his testimony by saying, "I feel neither guilty nor punished. I have to bear my fate."

When Oswald Kaduk had been sentenced and was taken to another trial as a witness, he looked around the courtroom with triumphant pride as if he wanted to say: "Look, it's me, the famous Kaduk!"

■ The manifestation of guilt feelings was the exception rather than the rule. Adam Rausch, a low-ranking SS man who was charged with killing inmates in the satellite camp Lagischa and had the revealing nickname "the Shooter," was supposed to have his first hearing in November 1971. On the eve of that hearing, he hanged himself without giving his family a reason for this act. Until then Rausch, who was transferred to Auschwitz as a very young ethnic German, had lived in Graz unmolested and without any manifestations of a guilty conscience.

The reaction of people who were only marginally involved with what went on in Auschwitz does not fundamentally differ from the behavior of those who were in the thick of it. Professor Günther Niethammer was given a very peculiar assignment. As an ornithologist he was attached to the SS in Auschwitz in order to watch the birds in the surrounding marshes. He did not deny that he knew what was done to the inmates, but he later asserted that it was impossible to do anything about it. He claimed that he gave the inmates bread and tobacco whenever he had a chance to do so and that he shifted his lookout to a spot from which no prisoners could be seen. In this way Professor Niethammer solved his personal Auschwitz problem. After the end of the war, he continued his scientific activities and did not concern himself with the Auschwitz episode any longer.

On the witness stand Max Faust, a professional engineer with the IG Works, was asked whether he had escorted Himmler through the Buna Works on his inspection tour of Auschwitz. Faust was offended and gave the following answer: "Yes, sir. But this came about only because the other managers of IG Farben happened to be away. That I gave the so-called RFSS a two-hour guided tour of the construction site has been since 1952 the pretext for all newspapers to print a photo that shows me with Himmler, often with the caption 'Murderers among us.' I am being written about, and I can't stop it. But I would like to take this opportunity to protest against it. Surely I can't be blamed for giving Herr Himmler a two-hour tour of a construction site."

Willi Hilse, a railroad official who managed the freight office in Auschwitz, also reacted in an irritable manner. Inmates were declared as "freight," and it was Hilse's job to supervise the cleaning and return of the cars that carried this "freight" to Auschwitz. As a witness he gave a businesslike account of the acceptance of these "transported goods" by means of a "big Wehrmacht waybill." One day a newspaper wrote this about his testimony: "To shunt the human freight conscientiously to Auschwitz was the task of Willi Hilse, now fifty-eight and a senior inspector of the federal railroads." Hilse felt offended in that he viewed himself as a proper official who was not to blame for anything.

Because of inadequate laws or an overly formal interpretation of the law, Kurt Knittel remained unmolested by the German justice system even though there is evidence that he shared the responsibility for the crimes of the guards in Auschwitz. This pedagogue was in charge of their indoctrination. After the end of the war, he managed to have an astonishingly rapid career in Baden-Württemberg. In 1957 he was appointed a *Rektor* (school principal) and just two years later was made a *Regierungsschulrat* (government education counselor). In addition he became director of the *Volksbühne* (theater) in Karlsruhe and ran for the position of city councillor as the candidate of the Free Democratic Party (Freie demokratische Partei, or FDP). After some interventions the ministry of culture in Stuttgart canceled his appointment as *Regierungsschulrat*. Knittel felt that he had been unjustly disciplined and brought suit against the administration. Stefan Baretzki was called as a witness in the trial and testified that when he and others asked why even Jewish women and children had to die, Knittel answered, "Because they are an inferior race." Baretzki concluded his testimony with these words: "After all, we learned how to murder from Herr Knittel's lectures."

The camp physician Bruno Kitt married Elfriede Maus, who was working in the Auschwitz SS infirmary as a laboratory assistant. Kitt was sentenced to death by a British military court for atrocities committed after Auschwitz and executed. For many years Frau Kitt-Maus fought for a posthumous rehabilitation of her husband, which meant an orphan's annuity for her son. She also sought to establish contact with me because she wanted me to certify that her husband did not participate in any crimes in Auschwitz. During a conversation with me, she tried to make me believe that she knew nothing of the extermination of human beings in Auschwitz even though she lived there for years. She claimed that her husband did not tell her about anything connected with the mass murders. When I pointed out that she ought to have smelled it, she answered that she did notice a peculiar sweetish smell but was told it was the smell of garlic from a sausage factory.

Adolf Prem, an Austrian, joined the NSDAP before the occupation of his homeland. As an SS sergeant in the SS storeroom in Auschwitz, he clashed with the leadership to such an extent that on November 30, 1944, he was convicted of prolonged military insubordination and assigned to a probationary unit. After the end of the war, he demanded to be recognized by the Austrian authorities as a victim of Nazism because of this sentence; and when he was turned down, he regarded it as an injustice. He did not consider the fact that he was a guard in Auschwitz for years an obstacle to a recognition that would have put him on a par with the surviving prisoners.

■ Only a very small number of former SS men had a different reaction to their past. Sepp Spanner, who was from Lower Austria, saw the ideal picture of Nazism that he had fashioned for himself sullied in Auschwitz, and he helped inmates wherever he could. After the war he made a living as a construction worker in Vienna. In 1967 he assured me that he frequently dreamt of episodes in Auschwitz that he did not remember by day. "After Auschwitz I did not have sexual intercourse with my wife for a year," he said.

Richard Böck from Günzburg, who had declared his inability to drive victims to the gas chambers in his LKW [truck], was the only former SS man who gave the Frankfurt court a straightforward description of the murderous methods of the SS and expressed his revulsion at them. He also agreed to speak on German television. When the question of extending the statute of limitations in the case of Nazi crimes was discussed in Germany and a telecast on the subject was being prepared, he appeared before the camera and spoke in favor of such an extension. Later, to be sure, he refused to make declarations on television again. Evidently the pressure to which he had been subjected after his first appearance had been too strong.

Wladimir Bilan has described how strong such a pressure can be. That man, whose conduct as an SS sergeant in Auschwitz has been praised by many former prisoners, told me that he was afraid the people in his new hometown, also a small town in Bavaria, might find out how he had helped inmates. If this became known, he would have to expect adverse consequences. That is why Bilan lived a very secluded life.

In the fall of 1963 I gave a lecture about Auschwitz in Munich. In the ensuing discussion a young man tried to cast doubt on the truth of the content of my remarks; he attempted to do so with the aid of quotations from neo-Nazi writings. Before I had a chance to respond to him, another member of the audience rose, identified himself as attorney Gerhard Wiebeck, turned to the young man, and said: "I was in Auschwitz as a leading member of the SS and can confirm that conditions there were much worse than what the lecturer described." Wiebeck had come to Auschwitz to investigate cases of corruption among the guards. He later told me that he had had a falling-out with his former SS comrades because he was not prepared to keep quiet about the crimes committed by the SS.

Spanner, Böck, Bilan, and Wiebeck kept away from the murderous doings to the extent that was possible for them. An SS man who had blood on his hands in Auschwitz cannot get over Auschwitz, either: Stefan Baretzki, who has been cited repeatedly as an exception from the rule. When I spoke with him in prison, he said that he was thinking of Auschwitz all the time. After answering my questions about details of the machinery of murder in Birkenau, he exclaimed: "I hope this will never happen again!"

CONCLUSION AND WARNING
■ ■ ■

For a long time the public balked at taking note of Auschwitz, and even those survivors who kept pointing out what had happened there could not change this situation. As warners, they remained the society's outsiders, as their experience of Auschwitz had made them.

To effect a change it took a new generation, young people who began to resist their fathers' tacit attempt to encumber them with such an oppressively heavy heritage. The Eichmann trial in Jerusalem and the big Auschwitz trial in Frankfurt provided the impetus for the public's abandonment of its resistance to learning the truth about Auschwitz.

A sober and objective position toward the Auschwitz phenomenon, however, is hardly possible in the lifetime of those who let themselves be induced to eliminate all natural inhibitions there, to deaden their conscience, to commit mass murder for years with the equanimity of exterminators of vermin, and at most to complain about the disagreeable work they had to do in the service of the nation. However, since this phenomenon challenges people to take a stand, they have usually taken their positions as factions, so to speak. One faction attempted to minimize what happened. This view is typified by the shameful discussion about the possible inflation of the number of victims in Auschwitz—as if the nature of the crimes would change if one million fewer human beings had been dragged to the gas chambers. This faction also zealously sought parallels to mass crimes of other peoples in an effort to conceal the fact that the Auschwitz phenomenon permits no comparison. Such efforts were resisted by another faction, which formulated confessions of guilt and accusations, though frequently in language that remained curiously abstract and thus had little expressivity. Even though no occurrence of the recent past constitutes a greater challenge to be analyzed, up to now no one has taken the initiative in producing a sober analysis of human reactions in the extreme situation of Auschwitz. This requires a generation who can look at Auschwitz with the detachment with which we view events of the nineteenth century.

This study is intended to facilitate the work of this generation. If it can also stimulate the younger people who have a personal relationship with Nazism through their fathers, that will be all the better.

I have always been aware, and no reader will have overlooked, that despite all my attempts at an objective viewpoint I have remained a partisan in this study. I hope, however, that my attempts at objectivity will not be overlooked, either. Some readers may even consider them exaggerated: for example, when I give a more detailed account of the behavior of the inmates who could be induced to tyrannize their fellow sufferers than of the conduct of the prisoners who remained comradely even as functionaries, or when there is a detailed examination of why members of the ss acted humanely toward the prisoners while less attention is paid to the guards who carried out every command to kill them. However, this is not only a result of the quest for objectivity of a person who was embroiled in the occurrences in Auschwitz. Exceptions always pose a greater challenge to an observer than the rule; an analysis of them can yield important insights into human reactions in an extreme situation. Added to this is the fact that the crimes of Auschwitz have already been documented. A recapitulation did not appear necessary.

■ Anyone who learns about the scope of the murders committed in Auschwitz will search for the culprits. My study should be understood as a warning against making a snap judgment. Innumerable people would not have behaved any differently from the majority of the guards if they had been ordered to go there, just as most of those who incurred guilt as cogs in the machinery of destruction would surely never have thought of murder and manslaughter if they had not been placed in the atmosphere of Auschwitz. This may be of only limited interest to jurists, for they must assess the actual guilt of an individual. However, anyone who knows how often chance decided who was assigned to participate in the mass crimes will not regard the standards of the legal system as sufficient. A Baretzki or a Neubert happened to be posted to Auschwitz. Dr. Wirths and Dr. Mengele would not have been transferred there if they had stayed fit for frontline service, and it was through a chain of circumstances that people such as Hans Stark and Irma Grese came under the discipline of the ss at a very early age. Anyone who learns this will know that it would be far too facile to put the blame for the mass murders only on those who committed them in the camp and on the handful of people who gave the orders. Did a few thousand willing recipients of these orders build in the strictest secrecy an organization of extermination that the population claims not to have known about? It was not that simple. Every serious analysis of the conduct of the murderers of Auschwitz goes beyond this group of people.

The clearest indication of how great the responsibility of the system for the guilt of an individual can be comes from studying the behavior of those who got blood on their hands while wearing the striped garb of the inmates. Who bears the responsibility for the monstrous deeds of a morally defective person — the habitual criminal who was given unlimited power over fellow human beings or the camp administration that rewarded him for giving vent to his rage and threatened to deprive him of his privileges if he behaved in a comradely way? I must also emphatically warn against making a rash judgment of those who had not come to the camp as criminals but could be turned into lackeys by the camp administration. Only someone who as a capo, a block elder, an inmate physician, or in a similar function experienced the pressure to which every functionary was exposed and was able to withstand it—as in the case of all temptations to make common cause with the masters (that is, the exterminators)—is capable of passing judgment on them. Many a survivor who did not abuse the power given him by the camp administration will hesitate to make such a judgment—precisely because he knows the situation.

The responsibility for the fact that there could be an Auschwitz in the twentieth century in a country with a proud cultural tradition must be borne by German Nazism as well as by those who helped make it possible for this regime to wield unlimited power. Only a totalitarian regime that attempted to bring all people into line could create in an alarmingly short time the prerequisites for a well-organized, undisguised genocide. Less than ten years after Hitler's accession to power in Germany, it had already become a daily routine to cram human beings into the gas chambers of Auschwitz. Only if democratic institutions are disparaged, the infallibility of the Führer is proclaimed, all critical voices are eliminated, and terror is installed can the ambition of types such as Höß and Mengele be channeled to such devastating effect. Only then can the command of an infallible Führer or an omniscient party deaden any normal sense of responsibility and create the conditions under which an Auschwitz can become reality.

And only a totalitarian system with its contempt for human beings includes genocide in its political plans with cool calculation. Hitler never denied this, and no one who voted for him could have any doubt about it. Auschwitz meant the realization of his slogan, which was screamed out numberless times: "Juda verrecke!" (Perish Juda/death to the Jews!).

Anyone who has seen how quickly a totalitarian regime can gain unlimited power over people under its domination will learn to appreciate the value of a democratic system, even if one is not prepared to overlook obvious weaknesses. Democratically organized communities have certainly also committed crimes. But many examples prove that if an injustice is committed, the voice of conscience cannot be permanently stifled. In a democracy an Auschwitz is inconceivable. Yet one can also draw on examples that show how every totalitarian system develops tendencies that point in the direction of Auschwitz.

The German people will for a long time have to bear the burden of what their government perpetrated in their name in the places of extermination. There is no doubt that there were typically German elements in the perfect organization of the machinery of murder. One can be certain that the military ideals of command and blind obedience, of the power of the uniform and the desire to roar a snappy "*Jawohl!*" — ideals that were more alive among the German people than among many others — aided the organizers of the genocide.

Nevertheless, one should be cautioned against the assumption that a totalitarian system could in no other country clear the way to a similar development; the recent past has too often proved how erroneous such a belief would be. It is not the details that are characteristic of Auschwitz but rather the principle that was put into effect there. Extreme contempt for people, thinking in terms of friends and foes, and absolute subordination to the will of a Führer — these elements are encountered in every totalitarian system. They led to the construction of the machinery of destruction for which the name Auschwitz has become a symbol.

A rather surreal vision that once flashed through my mind in Auschwitz has stuck in my memory. One day we were sitting in our inmate office in the ss hospital. We did not have much to do, and I leisurely clattered away on my typewriter. In the adjoining office of the ss, which was separated from ours only by a thin wall of boards, ss men were having a relaxed conversation about furlough problems and family matters. At that point I imagined that if everyone did not wear a uniform and were naked, no one would be able to distinguish the ss men from the inmates — that is, the masters from those doomed to die. That was not correct, of course. Not just the tattooed inmate numbers and the shaved heads or the haircuts would have distinguished the naked men from one another; the nutritional state of virtually all of them would have led to a clear conclusion as to which group any one person belonged. But that is not what my vision was about. The omnipotence and the total impotence that were connected with a uniform and that separated these people to such an extent that the whim of one who wore an ss uniform could mean the death of another who had to wear a prisoner's garb indicate the power of a system that turned human beings into wearers of uniforms in the most consequential way.

It is this system that we Auschwitzers got to know with greater clarity than anyone else. From the case of Dr. Eduard Wirths, the ss garrison physician, one can learn how easily a person could become a tool of Nazism. A bit of opportunism and the enjoyment of a fine uniform sufficed to put someone on a path on which every step made it harder to turn back and that eventually led to Auschwitz. From this and other examples one can learn how dangerous it is to devote oneself uncritically to an organization and what the consequences may be if one lets oneself be induced to make sweeping judgments of human groups. Then there will be a great temptation to condemn them, and everyone should always beware of doing this.

This is the lesson of Auschwitz: The very first step, the acceptance of a social system that aims at total control of human beings, is the most dangerous one. Once such a regime has conceived a plan to eradicate "subhumans" (they need not be Jews or Gypsies) and a person wears its uniform (which can be adorned with symbols other than the runes of the ss and the death's head), he has become a tool.

Like so many others, I dreamed in Auschwitz that mankind was going to draw its lessons from what became reality there, even though earlier everyone would have called that reality inconceivable and impossible. Will it learn these lessons?

BIBLIOGRAPHY

■ ■ ■

PUBLISHED SOURCES

Abada, Roger. "Organisation de la résistance au camp d'Auschwitz." In *Témoignages sur Auschwitz*. Paris: Édition de l'amicale des déportés d'Auschwitz, n.d.

Adelsberger, Lucie. *Auschwitz—ein Tatsachenbericht*. Berlin: Lettner, 1956.

Adler, H. G. *Gedanken zu einer Soziologie des Konzentrationslagers*. Meisenheim am Glan: Verlag Anton Hain, n.d.

———. *Theresienstadt, 1941 bis 1945: Das Antlitz einer Zwangsgemeinschaft*. 2d ed. Tübingen: J. C. B. Mohr (Paul Siebeck), 1960.

———. *Panorama*. Olten: Walter, 1968.

Adorno, Theodor W. *Erziehung zur Mündigkeit: Vorträge und Gespräche mit Hellmut Becker, 1959 bis 1969*. Edited by Gerd Kadelbach. Frankfurt am Main: Suhrkamp, 1970.

Alcan, Louise. "Sans armes et sans bagages." In *Tragédie de la déportation, 1940–1945: Témoignages de survivants de camps des concentration allemands*, edited by Olga Wormser and Henri Michel. N.p.: Hachette, 1954.

Altmann, Erich. *Im Angesicht des Todes: 3 Jahre in deutschen Konzentrationslagern Auschwitz—Buchenwald—Oranienburg*. Luxemburg: Verlag Luxemburgensia, 1947.

Améry, Jean. *Jenseits von Schuld und Sühne: Bewältigungsversuche eines Überwältigten*. Munich: Szczesny, 1966.

Anders, Günther. *Wir Eichmann-Söhne*. Munich: Beck, 1964.

Arendt, Hannah. *Elemente und Ursprünge totaler Herrschaft*. Frankfurt am Main: Europäische Verlagsanstalt, 1958.

———. *Eichmann in Jerusalem: Ein Bericht von der Banalität des Bösen*. Munich: R. Piper, 1964.

Aroneanu, Eugène. *Konzentrationslager: Tatsachenbericht über die an der Menschheit begangenen Verbrechen*. N.p.: Arbeitsgemeinschaft "Das Licht," n.d.

Auerbach, Hellmuth. "Die Einheit Dirlewanger." *Vierteljahreshefte für Zeitgeschichte*, no. 3 (1962).

"Aus der Anklageschrift gegen Maximilian Grabner und andere." In *Ewiges Gedenken*, edited by Adolf Rudnicki. Warsaw: Fremdsprachenverlag "Polonia," 1955.

Bacon, Jehuda. "Mit der Neugier von Kindern." In *Auschwitz: Zeugnisse und Berichte*, edited by H. G. Adler, Hermann Langbein, and Ella Lingens-Reiner. Frankfurt: Europäische Verlagsanstalt, 1962.

Baeyer, Walter von. "Auswirkungen rassischer Verfolgung und Konzentrationslagerhaft vom Standpunkt des Psychiaters." *Emuna: Horizonte* 5, no. 1 (January 1970).

Baeyer, Walter von, Heinz Häfner, and Karl Peter Kisker. *Psychiatrie der Verfolgten: Psychopathologische und gutachtliche Erfahrungen an Opfern der national-sozialistischen Verfolgung und vergleichbarer Extrembelastungen*. Berlin: Springer, 1964.

Baeyer-Katte, Wanda von. *Das Zerstörende in der Politik: Eine Psychologie der politischen Grundeinstellung*. Heidelberg: Quelle und Meyer, 1958.

Barcz, Wojciech. "Die erste Vergasung." In *Auschwitz: Zeugnisse und Berichte*, edited by H. G. Adler, Hermann Langbein, and Ella Lingens-Reiner. Frankfurt: Europäische Verlagsanstalt, 1962.

Baum, Bruno. *Widerstand in Auschwitz*. Berlin: Kongress, 1957.

Bendel, Sigismund Paul. "Le 'Sonderkommando.' In *Témoignages sur Auschwitz*. Paris: Édition de l'amicale des déportés d'Auschwitz, n.d.

Bergh, S. van den. *Deportaties: Westerborg, Theresienstadt, Auschwitz, Gleiwitz*. Bussum: (Uitg. Mij.) C.A.F. van Disboeck c.v., n.d.

Bernadac, Christian. *Les médecins de l'impossible*. Paris: Édition France-Empire, 1968.

Bernard, Marthe-Hélène. *Deux ans dans les camps de concentration nazis* [based on an account by Georges Wierzbicki, former political deportee]. Paris: Édité par "Le Déporté," 1957.

Betlen, Oszkár. *Leben auf dem Acker des Todes*. Berlin: Dietz, 1962.

Bettelheim, Bruno. *Aufstand gegen die Masse: Die Chance des Individuums in der modernen Gesellschaft*. Munich: Szczesny, 1964.

Bezwinska, Jadwiga, and Danuta Czech. Foreword to *Inmitten des grauenvollen Verbrechens: Handschriften von Mitgliedern des Sonderkommandos*. Oswiecim: Verlag staatliches Auschwitz-Museum, 1972.

Birnbaum, Suzanne (Luce). *Une française juive est revenue*. Paris: Éditions du Livre Français, n.d.

———. "Malla la Belge." In *Témoignages sur Auschwitz*. Paris: Édition de l'amicale des déportés d'Auschwitz, n.d.

Blécourt, André. *De la résistance au Bagne: Fresnes, Buchenwald via Auschwitz*. Collection Révélations, Petite Encyclopédie de la Résistance. N.p.: Fernand Nathan, 1945.

Blitz, Mirjam. *Auschwitz 13917: Hoe ik de Duitse concentratie-kampen overleejde*. Amsterdam: Elsevier, 1961.

Bloch, Claudette. "Les femmes à Auschwitz." In *Témoignages sur Auschwitz*. Paris: Édition de l'amicale des déportés d'Auschwitz, n.d.

Bonhoeffer, Emmi. *Zeugen im Auschwitz-Prozeß: Begegnungen und Gedanken*. Wuppertal: Johannes Kiefel, n.d.

Bornstein, Ernst Israel. *Die lange Nacht: Ein Bericht aus sieben Lagern*. Frankfurt am Main: Europäische Verlagsanstalt, 1967.

Borowski, Tadeusz. *Die steinerne Welt*. Munich: R. Piper, 1963.

Bramsted, Ernest K. *Goebbels und die nationalsozialistische Propaganda, 1925–1945*. Frankfurt: S. Fischer, 1971.

Brandhuber, Jerzy. "Die sowjetischen Kriegsgefangenen im Konzentrationslager Auschwitz." *Hefte von Auschwitz* 4 (1961).

———. "Vergessene Erde." *Hefte von Auschwitz* 5 (1962).

Brandt, Heinz. *Ein Traum, der nicht entführbar ist: Mein Weg zwischen Ost und West*. Munich: List, 1967.

Brinitzer, Carl. *Hier spricht London: Von einem, der dabei war*. Hamburg: Hoffmann und Campe, 1969.

Broad, Pery. "KZ Auschwitz: Erinnerungen eines SS-Mannes der Politischen Abteilung in dem Konzentrationslager Auschwitz." *Hefte von Auschwitz* 9 (1966).

Brol, Franciszek, Gerard Wloch, and Jan Pilecki. "Das Bunkerbuch des Blocks 11 im Nazi-Konzentrationslager Auschwitz." *Hefte von Auschwitz* 1 (1959).

Bruck, Edith. *Wer dich so liebt* . . . Frankfurt am Main: Heinrich Scheffler, 1961.

Buber-Neumann, Margarete. *Kafkas Freundin Milena.* Munich: Gotthold Müller, 1963.

Buchheim, Hans. *Totalitäre Herrschaft: Wesen und Merkmale.* Munich: Kösel, 1962.

———. *SS und Polizei im NS-Staat.* Duisdorf bei Bonn: Selbstverlag der Studiengesellschaft für Zeitprobleme, 1964.

———. "Befehl und Gehorsam." In *Anatomie des SS-Staates*, vol. 1. Olten: Walter, 1965.

Bulawko, Henry. *Les jeux de la mort et de l'espoir: Auschwitz-Jaworzno.* Paris: Amicale des anciens déportés juifs de France, n.d.

Chassaing, Thérèse. "27 avril 1944: Revier de Birkenau, femmes." In *Témoignages sur Auschwitz.* Paris: Édition de l'amicale des déportés d'Auschwitz, 1944.

Chowaniec, Tadeusz. *Epilog: Reminiscences of Former Auschwitz Prisoners.* Oswiecim: Verlag staatliches Auschwitz-Museum, 1963.

Cling, Maurice. *Testimony before the Kommission der Geschichte der Deportation.* In *Tragédie de la déportation, 1940–45: Témoignages de survivants des camps de concentration allemands*, edited by Olga Wormser et Henri Michel. N.p.: Librairie Hachette, 1954.

Cohen, Elie A. *Human Behavior in the Concentration Camp.* New York: Norton, 1953.

Comité International de la Croix-Rouge. *Vorläufiges Verzeichnis der Konzentrationslager und deren Außenkommandos sowie anderer Haftstätten unter dem Reichsführer-SS in Deutschland und deutsch besetzten Gebieten (1933–1945).* N.p.: Arolsen, 1969.

Czech, Danuta. "Kalendarium der Ereignisse im Konzentrationslager Auschwitz-Birkenau." *Hefte von Auschwitz* 2, 3, 4, 6, 7, 8 (1959–62, 1964).

———. "The Auschwitz Sub-Camps." In *History of KL-Auschwitz*, vol. 1. Oswiecim: Verlag staatliches Auschwitz-Museum, 1967.

———. "Most Important Events in the History of the Concentration Camp Auschwitz-Birkenau." In *History of KL-Auschwitz*, vol. 1. Oswiecim: Verlag staatliches Auschwitz-Museum, 1967.

———. "Deportation und Vernichtung der griechischen Juden im KL Auschwitz." *Hefte von Auschwitz* 11 (1970).

Delbo, Charlotte. *Aucun de nous ne reviendra.* Geneva: Éditions Gonthier, 1965.

———. *Le convoi du 24 janvier.* Paris: Éditions de Minuit, 1965.

Deschner, Günther. *Menschen vom Ghetto.* Foreword by Jean Améry. Gütersloh: Bertelsmann Sachbuchverlag, 1969.

Deutschkron, Inge. *. . . denn ihrer war die Hölle: Kinder in Gettos und Lagern.* Cologne: Verlag Wissenschaft und Politik, 1965.

Documents inédits sur les camps d'extermination nazis. Paris: Éditions Réalité, 1945.

Döring, Hans-Joachim. *Die Zigeuner im nationalsozialistischen Staat.* Kriminologische Schriftenreihe aus der Deutschen Kriminologischen Gesellschaft, vol. 12. Hamburg: Kriminalistik-Verlag, 1964.

Edel, Peter. *Schwester der Nacht.* Vienna: Erwin Müller, 1947.

Eichmann, Adolf. "Eichmann erinnert sich." In *Auschwitz: Zeugnisse und Berichte*, edited by H. G. Adler, Hermann Langbein, and Ella Lingens-Reiner. Frankfurt: Europäische Verlagsanstalt, 1962.

Eissler, K. R. "Weitere Bemerkungen zum Problem der KZ-Psychologie." *Psyche: Zeitschrift für Psychoanalyse und ihre Anwendungen* 23, no. 6 (June 1968).

Eitlinger, Leo. *Concentration Camp Survivors in Norway and Israel.* London: Allen and Unwin, 1964.

Elina, Odette. *Sans fleurs ni couronnes*. N.p.: Éditions J. F. Boulet, n.d.

Fajnzylberg (Feinsilber), Alter (vel Stanislaw Jankowski). "Aussage über seine Erlebnisse im Sonderkommando, 16. April 1945 in Krakau." In *Inmitten des grauenvollen Verbrechens: Handschriften von Mitgliedern des Sonderkommandos*. Oswiecim: Verlag staatliches Auschwitz-Museum, 1972.

Fantlova, Zdenka. "Long Live Life!" In *The Root and the Bough: The Epic of an Enduring People*, edited by Leo W. Schwarz. New York: Rinehart, 1949.

Feinstein, N. "Le Rire des bourreaux . . ." In *Témoignages sur Auschwitz*. Paris: Édition de l'amicale des déportés d'Auschwitz, n.d.

Fejkiel, Wladyslaw. "Typhus, Phenol, Gas." *Zycie literackie*, no. 52 (1960).

———. "Das Gesundheitswesen im Konzentrationslager Auschwitz I (Hauptlager)." *Przeglad Lekarski* 18, no. 2 (1962).

———. "Der Hunger in Auschwitz." *Hefte von Auschwitz*, no. 8 (1964).

———. "Medycyna za Drutami." In *Pamietniki Lekarzy*. Warsaw: Czytelnik, 1968.

Fest, Joachim C. *Das Gesicht des Dritten Reiches: Profile einer totalitären Herrschaft*. Munich: R. Piper, 1963.

Fichez, L. F., and S. Weinstein. "Die Tuberkulose bei den französischen Überlebenden der nazistischen Gefängnisse und Vernichtungslager." In *Andere Spätfolgen: Auf Grund der Beobachtungen bei den ehemaligen Deportierten und Internierten der nazistischen Gefängnisse und Vernichtungslager*, Medizinische Konferenzen der Internationalen Föderation der Widerstandskämpfer, vol. 2. Vienna: FIR, n.d.

Fiderkiewicz, Alfred. "Flecktyphus und Entlassung im Männerlager Birkenau." In *Erinnerungen Auschwitzer Häftlinge*. Oswiecim: Verlag staatliches Auschwitz-Museum, n.d.

———. "Erinnerungen an die Arbeit eines Häftlingsarztes in den Tuberkuloseblocks des Krankenbaulagers in Birkenau (während der Jahre 1943/44)." *Hefte von Auschwitz* 13 (1971).

Fijalkowski, Gracjan. "Man muß nicht sterben." *Hefte von Auschwitz* 5 (1962).

Frackiewicz, Jerzy. "Das Nebenlager Golleschau." *Hefte von Auschwitz* 9 (1966).

Fraenkel, Heinrich, and Roger Manvell. *Himmler: Kleinbürger und Massenmörder*. Frankfurt: Ullstein, 1965.

Frankl, Viktor E. *Ein Psychologe erlebt das Konzentrationslager*. Vienna: Verlag für Jugend und Volk, 1946.

Friedman, Filip, and Tadeusz Holuj. *Oswiecim*. Warsaw: Ksiazka, 1946.

Fryd, Norbert. *Kartei der Lebenden*. Berlin: Volk und Welt, 1959.

Furmanski, Jacques. "La première journée de travail." In *Témoignages sur Auschwitz*. Paris: Édition de l'amicale des déportés d'Auschwitz, n.d.

———. "19 janvier 1944: Camp de Birkenau, hommes." In *Témoignages sur Auschwitz*. Paris: Édition de l'amicale des déportés d'Auschwitz, 1944.

Garlinski, Józef. *Dramat i opatrznosc*. London: Gryfe Publications, 1961.

German Crimes in Poland. Warsaw: Central Commission for Investigation of German Crimes in Poland, 1946.

Geve, Thomas. *Youth in Chains*. Jerusalem: Rubin Mass, 1958.

Gilbert, G. M. *Nürnberger Tagebuch: Gespräche mit den Angeklagten*. Frankfurt am Main: Fischer-Bücherei, 1962.

Goldstein, Charles. *Leben ohne Stern*. Munich: R. Piper, 1964.

Golse, Dr. "Birkenau en 1943." In *Témoignages sur Auschwitz*. Paris: Édition de l'amicale des déportés d'Auschwitz, n.d.

Gradowski, Zelman. "Handschriften, bei dem Krematorium III in Birkenau am 5. März 1945 ausgegraben." In *Inmitten des grauenvollen Verbrechens: Handschriften von Mitgliedern des Sonderkommandos*. Oswiecim: Verlag staatliches Auschwitz-Museum, 1972.

Grass, Günter. "Schwierigkeiten eines Vaters, seinen Kindern Auschwitz zu erklären" [address given at the opening of an exhibition]. *Frankfurter Allgemeine Zeitung*, June 2, 1970.

Graumann, Samuel. *Deportiert!: Ein Wiener Jude berichtet*. Vienna: Stern, 1947.

Grossmann, Kurt R. *Die unbesungenen Helden: Menschen in Deutschlands dunklen Tagen*. Berlin: Arani, 1957.

Gumkowski, Janusz, Adam Rutkowski, and Arnfrid Astel, eds. *Briefe aus Litzmannstadt*. Cologne: Friedrich Middelhauve, 1967.

Gutman, Israel. "Der Aufstand des Sonderkommandos." In *Auschwitz: Zeugnisse und Berichte*, edited by H. G. Adler, Hermann Langbein, and Ella Lingens-Reiner. Frankfurt: Europäische Verlagsanstalt, 1962.

Hacker, Friedrich: "Gesetze sind aggressiv." *Der Spiegel*, October 26, 1970.

Haffner, Désiré. *Aspects pathologiques du camp de concentration d'Auschwitz-Birkenau*. Tours: Imprimerie union coopérative, 1946.

Hanack, Ernst-Walter. "Zur Problematik der gerechten Bestrafung national-sozialistischer Gewaltverbrecher." *Juristenzeitung* 10, no. 19 (May 1967).

Hart, Kitty. *Aber ich lebe*. Hamburg: Claassen, 1961.

Heiber, Helmut. *Reichsführer!: Briefe an und von Himmler*. Stuttgart: Deutsche Verlagsanstalt, 1968.

Heller, Joseph. "Betrachtungen über die wichtigsten Herz- und Gefäßerkrankungen bei ehemaligen Deportierten und Internierten: Die Aussichten ihrer Behandlung." In *Andere Spätfolgen — auf Grund der Beobachtungen bei den ehemaligen Deportierten und Internierten der nazistischen Gefängnisse und Vernichtungslager*, Medizinische Konferenz der Internationalen Föderation der Widerstandskämpfer, vol. 2. Vienna: FIR, n.d.

Henkys, Reinhard. *Die nationalsozialistischen Gewaltverbrechen: Geschichte und Gericht*. Stuttgart: Kreuz, 1964.

Herberg, Hans-Joachim. *Die Beurteilung von Gesundheitsschäden nach Gefangenschaft und Verfolgung*. Herford: Nicolaische Verlagsbuchhandlung, 1967.

Hill, Mavis M., and L. Norman Williams. *Auschwitz in England: A Record of a Libel Action*. London: Macgibbon and Kee, 1965.

Hirsch, Rudolf. *Zeugen in Ost und West: Aus dem Gerichtsalltag*. Rudolfstadt: VEB Greifenverlag, 1965.

Hochhuth, Rolf. *Der Stellvertreter*. Reinbek bei Hamburg: Rowohlt, 1963.

Holuj, Tadeusz ("Robert"). "Grupa Oswiecim: Jan Mosdorfs Waffenstillstand." In *Ewiges Gedenken*, edited by Adolf Rudnicki. Warsaw: Fremdsprachenverlag "Polonia," 1953.

Honel, Mira. "La libération du camp." In *Témoignages sur Auschwitz*. Paris: Édition de l'amicale des déportés d'Auschwitz, n.d.

Hoppe, Klaus D. "Psychosomatische Reaktionen und Erkrankungen bei Überlebenden schwerer Verfolgung." *Psyche: Zeitschrift für Psychoanalyse und ihre Anwendungen* 22, no. 6 (June 1968).

Höß, Rudolf. *Kommandant in Auschwitz: Autobiographische Aufzeichnungen.* Stuttgart: Deutsche Verlagsanstalt, 1958.

Huyskens, Pierre en de Mooij Theo. *De Gehavenden.* The Hague: Bond van Nederlandse Militair Oorlogslachtoffers, 1970.

Iwaszko, Emeryka. "Das Nebenlager 'Janinagrube.'" *Hefte von Auschwitz* 10 (1967).

Iwaszko, Tadeusz. "Häftlingsfluchten aus dem Konzentrationslager Auschwitz." *Hefte von Auschwitz* 7 (1964).

———. "Das Nebenlager 'Laurahütte.'" *Hefte von Auschwitz* 10 (1967).

———. "Das Nebenlager 'Günthergrube.'" *Hefte von Auschwitz* 12 (1971).

Jäger, Herbert. "Betrachtungen zum Eichmann-Prozeß." *Kriminologie* 3, no. 4 (1962).

———. *Verbrechen unter totalitärer Herrschaft: Studien zur nationalsozialistischen Gewaltkriminalität.* Olten: Walter, 1967.

Jazwiecki, Franciszek. "Erinnerungen." *Hefte von Auschwitz* 5 (1962).

Jezierska, Maria Elzbieta. "Eine Schachtel Brot." *Hefte von Auschwitz* 5 (1962).

Jong, Louis de. "Die Niederlande und Auschwitz." *Vierteljahreshefte für Zeitgeschichte,* no. 1 (1969).

Juvet, René. *Ich war dabei: 20 Jahre Nationalsozialismus, 1923–1943: Tatsachenbericht eines Schweizers.* Zurich: Europa, 1962.

Kagan, Raya. "Die letzten Opfer des Widerstandes." In *Auschwitz: Zeugnisse und Berichte,* edited by H. G. Adler, Hermann Langbein, and Ella Lingens-Reiner. Frankfurt: Europäische Verlagsanstalt, 1962.

Kaul, Friedrich Karl. *Schlußvortrag im Strafverfahren gegen Burger u. a.* ["Zweiter Auschwitz-Prozeß"]. Berlin: Druckhaus Norden, 1966.

———. *Ärzte in Auschwitz.* Berlin: VEB Verlag Volk und Gesundheit, 1968.

Kaul, Friedrich Karl, and Joachim Noack. *Angeklagter Nr. 6: Eine Auschwitz-Dokumentation.* Berlin: Akademie, 1966.

Kautsky, Benedikt. *Die psychologische Situation des Konzentrationslager-Häftlings.* Zurich, n.d.

———. *Teufel und Verdammte: Erfahrungen und Erkenntnisse aus sieben Jahren in deutschen Konzentrationslagern.* Vienna: Wiener Volksbuchhandlung, 1961.

Kempner, Robert M. W. *SS im Kreuzverhör.* Munich: Rütten und Loening, 1964.

Kielar, Wieslaw. "Edek und Mala." *Hefte von Auschwitz* 5 (1962).

Klein, Marc. "Auschwitz I." In *De l'université aux camps de concentration: Témoignages strasbourgeois.* Paris: Les Belles Lettres, 1947.

Klieger, Bernard. *Der Weg, den wir gingen: Reportage einer höllischen Reise.* Brussels: "Codac Juifs," 1957.

Klodzinski, Stanislaw. "Der Einsatz des polnischen Sanitätsdienstes bei der Rettung des Lebens der Häftlinge des KZ-Lagers Auschwitz." *Przeglad Lekarski* 18, no. 2 (1962).

———. "Verbrecherische Versuche aus dem Bereich der Tuberkulose in den nazistischen Konzentrationslagern." In *Unmenschliche Medizin,* edited by staff of *Przeglad Lekarski.* Warsaw: Internationale Auschwitz-Komitee, 1969.

Klusacek, Christine. *Österreichs Wissenschaftler und Künstler unter dem NS Regime.* Monographien zur Zeitgeschichte. Vienna: Europa, 1966.

Kogon, Eugen. *Der SS-Staat: Das System der deutschen Konzentrationslager.* Frankfurt: Europäische Verlagsanstalt, 1946.

Kohen, Guy. *Retour d'Auschwitz: Souvenirs de déporté 174.949.* Paris, 1945.

Kolb, Eberhard. *Bergen-Belsen*. Hannover: Verlag für Literatur und Zeitgeschehen, 1962.

Koprowska, Wanda. "Tage des Grauens." *Hefte von Auschwitz* 10 (1967).

Kosciuszkowa, Janina. "Kinderschicksale im KZ-Lager Auschwitz." *Przeglad Lekarski* 18, no. 2 (1962).

Kowalczykowa, Janina. "Die Hungerkrankheit im Konzentrationslager Auschwitz." *Przeglad Lekarski* 18, no. 2 (1962).

Kraus, Ota, and Erich Kulka. *Die Todesfabrik*. Berlin: Kongress, 1957.

———. *Massenmord und Profit*. Berlin: Dietz, 1963.

Kremer, Johann Paul. "Das Wesen und die Herkunft der mit der Zerstörung roter Blutkörperchen in Verbindung gebrachten eisenpigmenthaltigen Zellen der Milz." *Mikrokosmos-Jahrbuch* 36, nos. 6–7 (1942–43).

Kret, Józef. "Ein Tag in der Strafkompanie (Erinnerung)." *Hefte von Auschwitz* 1 (1959).

Kulka, Erich. *Utek z tabora smrti*. Prague: Nase Vojsko, 1966.

Küster, Otto. "Das Minimum der Menschlichkeit: Lehrprozeß für unsere Zeit" [summation before the Oberlandesgericht Frankfurt am Main in Wollheim/IG Farben case, given on March 1, 1955]. Special issue of *Freiburger Rundbriefe*, ser. 8, nos. 29–32 (1955).

Laks, Simon, and Coudy, René. *Musiques d'un autre monde*. Paris: Mercure de France, 1948.

Langbein, Hermann. *Die Stärkeren: Ein Bericht*. Vienna: Stern, 1949.

———. *Im Namen des deutschen Volkes: Zwischenbilanz der Prozesse wegen nationalsozialistischer Verbrechen*. Vienna: Europa, 1963.

———. *Der Auschwitz-Prozeß: Eine Dokumentation*. Vienna: Europa, 1965.

———. *Auschwitz und die junge Generation*. Vienna: Europa, 1967.

Lanik, Jozef. *Was Dante nicht sah*. Berlin: Verlag der Nation, 1964.

Laszlo, Carl. *Ferien am Waldsee: Erinnerungen eines Überlebenden*. Basel: Gute Schriften, 1956.

Laternser, Hans. *Die andere Seite im Auschwitz-Prozeß, 1963–1965: Reden eines Verteidigers*. Stuttgart: Seewald, 1966.

Lehrplan für die weltanschauliche Erziehung in der SS und Polizei. Prepared and edited by the SS-Hauptamt. N.p., n.d.

Lengyel, Olga. *Souvenirs de l'au-delà*. Paris: Éditions du Bateau Ivre, 1946.

Lesch, Franz-Xaver. *P. Maximilian Kolbe*. Würzburg: Echter-Verlag, 1964.

Lesniak, Roman, Jan Mitarski, Maris Orwid, Adam Szymusik, and Alexander Teutsch. "Einige psychiatrische Probleme des KZ-Lagers Auschwitz im Lichte eigner Untersuchungen (II. Bericht)." *Przeglad Lekarski* 18, no. 2 (1962).

Leszczynska, Stanislawa. *Bericht einer Hebamme aus Auschwitz*. Cracow: Przeglad Lekarski, 1965.

Lettich, André Abraham David. *Trente-quatre mois dans les camps de concentration*. Tours: Imprimerie Union Coopérative, 1946.

Leval, Eugene. *Black Book on the Martyrdom of Hungarian Jewry*. Zurich: Central European Times Publishing Company, 1948.

Levi, Primo. *Ist das ein Mensch?* Frankfurt am Main: Fischer Bücherei, 1961.

———. *Atempause*. Hamburg: Christian Wegner, 1964.

Levin, Meyer. *Eva: Ein Frauenschicksal*. Munich: Süddeutscher Verlag, 1959.

Lévy Jacques. *Auf der Suche nach dem Menschen: Tagebücher und Briefe.* Salzburg: Otto Müller, 1960.

Lévy, Robert. "Auschwitz II (Birkenau)." In *De l'université aux camps de concentration: Témoignages strasbourgeois.* Paris: Les Belles Lettres, 1947.

Lewental, Zelman. "Handschrift, am 17. Oktober 1962 bei einem Birkenauer Krematorium ausgegraben." In *Inmitten des grauenvollen Verbrechens: Handschriften von Mitgliedern des Sonderkommandos.* Oswiecim: Verlag staatliches Auschwitz-Museum, 1972.

Lewinska, Pelagia. "Vingt mois à Auschwitz." In *Tragédie de la déportation, 1940–1945: Témoignages de survivants des camps de concentration allemands,* edited by Olga Wormser and Henri Michel. N.p.: Hachette, 1954.

Ligeti, Hertha. *Die Sterne verlöschen nicht.* Bucharest: Espla Staatsverlag für Kunst und Literatur, 1959.

Lingens-Reiner, Ella. *Prisoners of Fear.* London: Victor Gollancz, 1958.

———. *Eine Frau im Konzentrationslager.* Monographien zur Zeitgeschichte. Vienna: Europa, 1966.

Lippe, Viktor Freiherr von der. *Nürnberger Tagebuchnotizen: November 1945 bis Oktober 1946.* Frankfurt am Main: Fritz Knapp, 1951.

Loewenstein, Rudolph M. *Psychoanalyse des Antisemitismus.* Frankfurt am Main: Suhrkamp, 1967.

Manvell, Roger, and Heinrich Fraenkel. *The Incomparable Crime.* London: William Heineman, 1967.

March, Hans, ed. *Verfolgung und Angst in ihren leib-seelischen Auswirkungen: Dokumente (Gutachten).* Stuttgart: Klett, 1960.

Martini, Emil de. *Vier Millionen Tote klagen an!: Erlebnisse im Todeslager Auschwitz.* Munich-Obermenzing: Hans von Weber, 1948.

Matussek, Paul. *Die Konzentrationslagerhaft und ihre Folgen.* Berlin: Springer, 1971.

Menasche, Albert. *Birkenau (Auschwitz II).* New York: Isaac Saltiel, 1947.

Minney, R. J. *I Shall Fear No Evil: The Story of Dr. Alina Brewda.* London: William Kimber, 1966.

Mitscherlich, Alexander. *Stenogramm zu Otto Köhler: Kongo-Müller.* Pardon-Dokumente. N.p.: Bärmeier und Nikel, n.d.

Mitscherlich, Alexander, and Mitscherlich Margarete. *Die Unfähigkeit zu trauern: Grundlagen kollektiven Verhaltens.* Munich: R. Piper, 1967.

Naumann, Bernd. *Auschwitz: Bericht über die Strafsache gegen Mulka u. a. vor dem Schwurgericht Frankfurt.* Frankfurt am Main: Athenäum, 1965.

Neumann, Robert. *Ausflüchte unseres Gewissens: Dokumente zu Hitlers "Endlösung der Judenfrage" mit Kommentar und Bilanz der politischen Situation.* Hefte zum Zeitgeschehen. Hannover: Verlag für Literatur und Zeitgeschehen, 1960.

Niederland, William G. "Diskussionsbeitrag zu E. de Winds 'Begegnung mit dem Tod.'" *Psyche: Zeitschrift für Psychoanalyse und ihre Anwendungen* 22, no. 6 (June 1968).

Novac, Ana. *Die schönen Tage meiner Jugend.* Reinbek bei Hamburg: Rowohlt, 1967.

Nyiszli, Miklos. *Auschwitz: A Doctor's Eyewitness Account.* New York: Frederick Fell, 1960.

Ostankowicz, Czeslaw. "Isolierstation: Letzter Block." In *Erinnerungen Auschwitzer Häftlinge.* Oswiecim: Verlag staatliches Auschwitz-Museum, n.d.

———. *Ziema Parujaca Cykonem.* Lodz: Wydawnictwo Lodzkie, 1967.

Ourisson (Wasserstrom), Dounia. *Les secrets du Bureau Politique d'Auschwitz.* Paris: Édition de l'amicale des déportés d'Auschwitz, n.d.

Paczula, Tadeusz. "Die ersten Opfer sind die Polen." In *Auschwitz: Zeugnisse und Berichte*, edited by H. G. Adler, Hermann Langbein, and Ella Lingens-Reiner. Frankfurt: Europäische Verlagsanstalt, 1962.

———. "Häftlings-Krankenbau." *Hefte von Auschwitz* 5 (1962).

Papanek, Ernst, with Edward Linn. "The Boy Who Survived Auschwitz." Special issue of *Saturday Evening Post*, 1964.

Pendorf, Robert. *Mörder und Ermordete: Eichmann und die Judenpolitik des Dritten Reiches.* Hamburg: Rütten und Loening, 1961.

Perl, Gisella. *I Was a Doctor in Auschwitz.* New York: International Universities Press, 1948.

Petit, Pierre. "Das war Bergen-Belsen." *Rappel—revue mensuelle de la L.P.P.D.* (Luxemburg), 1965–66.

Phillips, Raymond. *The Belsen Trial: Trial of Josef Kramer and Forty-four Others.* London: William Hodge, 1949.

Piper, Franciszek. "Das Nebenlager Blechhammer." *Hefte von Auschwitz* 10 (1967).

———. "Das Nebenlager Sosnowitz (II)." *Hefte von Auschwitz* 11 (1970).

———. "Das Nebenlager Neu-Dachs." *Hefte von Auschwitz* 12 (1971).

———. "Das Nebenlager Althammer." *Hefte von Auschwitz* 13 (1971).

Poliakov, Léon. *Auschwitz.* Paris: Collection Archives Julliard, 1964.

Poltawska, Wanda. "Kinder aus dem KZ." *Vorwärts* (Przeglad Lekarski), October 26, 1967.

Posmysz, Zofia. "Die 'Sängerin.'" *Hefte von Auschwitz* 8 (1964).

Rassinier, Paul. *Das Drama der Juden Europas.* Hannover: Hans Pfeiffer, 1965.

Rauschning, Hermann. *Gespräche mit Hitler.* Zurich: Europa, 1940.

Regau, Thomas. "Der Engel und die Feldwebel." *Die Zeit*, January 10, 1969.

Reichmann, Eva G. *Flucht in den Haß.* Frankfurt am Main: Europäische Verlagsanstalt, n.d.

Reitlinger, Gerald. *Die Endlösung: Hitlers Versuch der Ausrottung der Juden Europas, 1939 bis 1945.* Berlin: Colloquium, 1961.

Rousset, David. *L'univers concentrationnaire.* Paris: Éditions de Pavois, 1946.

———. *Les jours de notre mort.* Paris: Éditions du Pavois, 1947.

Rozanski, Zenon. *Mützen ab: Eine Reportage aus der Stafkompanie des KZ Auschwitz.* Hannover: Verlag "Das andere Deutschland," 1948.

Salus, Grete. *Eine Frau erzählt.* Bonn: Bundeszentrale für Heimatdienst, 1958.

Saurel, Louis. *Les femmes héroiques de la Résistance: Berthie Albrecht, Danielle Casanova.* Paris: Fernand Nathan, 1945.

Schnabel, Raimund. *Macht ohne Moral: Eine Dokumentation über die SS.* Frankfurt am Main: Röderberg, 1957.

———. *Die Frommen in der Hölle.* Frankfurt am Main: Röderberg, 1965.

Schoenberner, Gerhard, ed. *Wir haben es gesehen: Augenzeugenberichte.* Hamburg: Rütten und Loening, 1962.

Schuldig im Sinne des Rechts und des Völkerrechts: Auszüge aus dem Protokoll des Prozesses vor dem Obersten Gericht der DDR. Edited by the Arbeitsgruppe der ehemaligen Häftlinge des KZ Auschwitz beim Komitee der Antifaschistischen Widerstandskämpfer in der

DDR und dem Nationalrat der Nationalen Front des demokratischen Deutschland. Berlin, 1966.

Sehn, Jan. *Konzentrationslager Oswiecim-Brzezinka (Auschwitz-Birkenau)*. Warsaw: Wydawnictwo Prawnicze, 1957.

Skodova, Julia. *Tri Roky bes Mena*. Bratislava: Osveta, 1962.

Smolen, Kazimierz. "Die Widerstandsbewegung im Konzentrationslager Auschwitz." *Internationale Hefte der Widerstandsbewegung* 2, no. 3 (July 1960).

———. *Auschwitz, 1940 bis 1945*. Oswiecim: Verlag staatliches Auschwitz-Museum, 1961.

———. "Eine Laufbahn." *Hefte von Auschwitz* 5 (1961).

———. *The Concentration Camp Auschwitz: From the History of KL-Auschwitz*. Vol. 1. Oswiecim: Verlag staatliches Auschwitz-Museum, 1967.

Spritzer, Jenny. *Ich war Nr. 10291*. Zurich: Jack Schumacher, n.d.

SS im Einsatz. Edited by the Komitee der Antifaschistischen Widerstandskämpfer in der Deutschen Demokratischen Republik. Berlin: Kongress, 1967.

Stein, Georg H. *Geschichte der Waffen-SS*. Düsseldorf: Droste, 1967.

Steiner, Jean-François. *Treblinka: Die Revolte eines Vernichtungslagers*. Oldenburg: Gerhard Stalling, 1966.

Steininger, P. A. *Der Nürnberger Prozeß: Protokolle und Dokumente*. Berlin: Rütten und Loening, 1960.

Steinmetz, Selma. *Österreichs Zigeuner im NS-Staat*. Vienna: Europa, 1966.

Sternberg-Newman, Judith. *In the Hell of Auschwitz*. New York: Exposition Press, 1963.

Strzelecka, Irena. "Das Nebenlager Hindenburg." *Hefte von Auschwitz* 11 (1970).

Suhl, Yuri, ed. *They Fought Back: The True Story of the Heroic Jewish Resistance to Nazi Slaughter*. New York: Paperback Library, 1968.

Svalbova, Manca. *Vyharsnuté Oci*. Bratislava: Osveta, 1964.

Szmaglewska, Seweryna. "Rauch über Birkenau." In *Ewiges Gedenken*, ed. Adolf Rudnicki. Warsaw: Fremdsprachenverlag "Polonia," 1955.

———. *Uns vereint heiliger Zorn*. Warsaw: Fremdsprachenverlag "Polonia," 1955.

Szymanski, Tadeusz. "Nase." *Hefte von Auschwitz* 5 (1962).

Thümmler, Johannes. "Bericht des Kommandeurs der Sicherheitspolizei Kattowitz." In *Auschwitz: Zeugnisse und Berichte*, edited by H. G. Adler, Hermann Langbein, and Ella Lingens-Reiner. Frankfurt am Main: Europäische Verlagsanstalt, 1962.

Unger, Julien. *Le sang et l'or: Souvenirs de camps allemands*. Paris: Gallimard, 1946.

Vaillant-Couturier, Marie-Clause. *Mes 27 mois entre Auschwitz et Ravensbrück*. Paris: Éditions du Mail, 1946.

Vidor, Katalin. *Unterm Zeichen des Sterns*. Munich: List, 1963.

Vos, Leo. *Het Fluitje*. Rijswijk: V. A. Kramers, n.d.

Vrba, Rudolf. *Ich kann nicht vergeben*. Munich: Rütten und Loening, 1964.

Vrba, Rudolf, and Alfred Wetzler. "Ein geflüchteter Häftling berichtet." In *Auschwitz: Zeugnisse und Berichte*, edited by H. G. Adler, Hermann Langbein, and Ella Lingens-Reiner. Frankfurt am Main: Europäische Verlagsanstalt, 1962.

Waitz, Robert. "Auschwitz III (Monowitz)." In *De l'université aux camps de concentration: Témoignages strasbourgeois*. Paris: Les Belles Lettres, 1947.

Walser, Martin. "Unser Auschwitz." *Kursbuch* 1 (1965).

Wangh, Martin. "Diskussionsbeitrag zu E. de Winds 'Begegnung mit dem Tod.'"
Psyche: Zeitschrift für Psychoanalyse und ihre Anwendungen 22, no. 6 (June 1968).

Webb, Antony M. The Natzweiler Trial: Trial of Wolfgang Zeuss, Magnus Wochner, Emil Meier, Peter Straub, Fritz Hartjenstein, Franz Berg, Werner Rohde, Emil Bruttel, Kurt aus dem Bruch and Harberg. London: William Hodge, 1949.

Weijel, J. A., ed. De Vernietiging van de Joden in Polen: Ooggetuigeverslagen over Warschau, Lublin, Tremblinki, Belzec, Posen, Krakau, Auschwitz. Haarlem: Boom-Ruygrok, n.d.

Weiss, Reska. Journey through Hell. London: Vallentine-Mitchell, 1961.

Wellers, Georges. De Drancy à Auschwitz. Paris: Éditions de Centre, 1946.

———. "Sur la résistance collective et la 'cooperation' des victimes avec les bourreaux dans les camps d'extermination des Juifs." La Revue du Centre de Documentation Juive Contemporaine, no. 44 (October/December 1966).

———. "Auschwitz." La Revue du Centre de Documentation Juive Contemporaine, no. 56 (October–December 1969).

———. "Arbeit macht frei, ou le camp d'Auschwitz." In Pour la liberté. Paris: Édition U.N.A.D.I.F., 1971.

Wellers, George, and Robert Waitz. "Recherches sur la dénutrition prolongée dans les camps de déportation." Revue Canadienne de Biologie 6, no. 2 (1947).

Wielek, H. De oorlog die Hitler won. Amsterdam: Amsterdamsche Boek- en Courantmij, 1947.

Wiesel, Elie. Die Nacht zu begraben, Elischa. Munich: Bechtle, 1958.

———. Gezeiten des Schweigens. Munich: Bechtle, 1960.

———. Gesang der Toten. Munich: Bechtle, 1968.

Wind, Eduard de. Endstation . . . Auschwitz. Amsterdam: Republiek der Letteren, 1946.

———. "Begegnung mit dem Tod." Psyche: Zeitschrift für Psychoanalyse und ihre Anwendungen 22, no. 6 (June 1968).

Wolken, Otto. "Chronik des Quarantänelagers Birkenau." In Auschwitz: Zeugnisse und Berichte, edited by H. G. Adler, Hermann Langbein, and Ella Lingens-Reiner. Frankfurt am Main: Europäische Verlagsanstalt, 1962.

Wrobel, Haline. "Die Liquidation des Konzentrationslagers Auschwitz-Birkenau." Hefte von Auschwitz 6 (1962).

Zarebinska-Broniewska, Maria. Auschwitzer Erzählungen. Berlin-Potsdam: VYN, 1949.

Zieba, Anna. "Wirtschaftshof Budy." Hefte von Auschwitz 10 (1967).

———. "Wirtschaftshof Babitz—Nebenlager beim Gut Babice." Hefte von Auschwitz 11 (1970).

———. "Die Geflügelfarm Harmense." Hefte von Auschwitz 11 (1970).

Zywulska, Krystyna. J'ai survécu à Auschwitz. Warsaw: Éditions Polonia, 1956.

UNPUBLISHED SOURCES

Aumeier, Hans. Transcripts of hearings on August 10, 1945, and August 22, 1945, Oslo (in English). Curriculum Vitae dated September 17, 1947 (in German).

Bacon, Jehuda. Testimony recorded between February 13 and 22, 1959, in Jerusalem. Yad Vashem Archives, 03/1202.

Baer, Richard. Transcript made on October 10, 1961, by the Frankfurt District Court, 4KS 444/59.

———. Materials about Richard Baer compiled by the Auschwitz-Birkenau State Museum.

Baeyer, Walter Ritter von. "Über die psychiatrische Begutachtung von Gesundheitsschäden durch die nationalsozialistische Verfolgung."

Batawia, Stanislaw. Report about Rudolf Höß.

Baum, Bruno. "Bericht über die Tätigkeit der kommunistischen Partei im KZ Auschwitz." Vienna, July 5, 1945.

Begov, Lucie. "Ein Grab auf dem Zentralfriedhof."

Böck, Richard. Notes and talking points for the Auschwitz trial in Frankfurt (where Böck was called as a witness on August 3, 1964).

Boger, Marianne. Testimony as a witness. Stuttgart, October 27, 1958.

Boger, Wilhelm. Statements recorded in American captivity at Ludwigsburg on July 5, July 10, and August 30, 1945.

———. Reference for Wilhelm Boger by the Ernst Heinkel Aktiengesellschaft, Stuttgart-Zuffenhausen, October 1959.

Clauberg, Carl. Transcripts of hearings (2JS 248455) at Neustadt, December 3 to December 23, 1955, and at Kiel, August 6 to September 21, 1956.

———. Indictment of Dr. Carl Clauberg, dated December 14, 1956.

Claussen, Wilhelm. Report written in American captivity (in German). Ebensee, 1945.

———. Transcript of the Rudolf Höß trial, vol. 46, pp. 121–44 and 145–51.

Denser, Wolfgang. Statement about Dr. Eduard Wirths. Berchtesgaden, June 27, 1961.

Dürmeyer, Heinrich. Statement in his defense. Vienna, December 20, 1949.

Eggebrecht, Axel. Notes on the Bergen-Belsen trial in Lüneburg, September/October 1945.

Eichmann, Adolf. Text of the statements recorded on tape (*Sassen-Protokoll*), Argentina, 1957.

———. Text of the statements taped while awaiting trial in Israel. Mahana Iyar, May 29, 1960, to January 15, 1961. Copies made by Office 6 of the Israeli police.

Entress, Friedrich. Declaration made under oath. NI−6190.

Fajnzylberg (Feinsilber), Alter. Excerpt from his testimony in the Höß trial. Institut für Zeitgeschichte, Munich.

Faust, Max. Weekly report (126/127) covering the period from October 18 to October 31, 1943. IG Farben, Auschwitz.

Fischer, Horst. Testimony given in the criminal proceedings against Burger, Erber, and Neubert, 252A(S) 7/66 at the Municipal District Court Berlin-Mitte, February 22, 1966.

Frankfurter Schwurgericht. Verdict in the third Auschwitz trial, June 14, 1968.

Grabner, Maximilian. Texts of statements made at the police headquarters in Vienna on September 18, 25, 26, 1945, and December 21, 1945.

———. "Bericht über das Lager Auschwitz," Cracow, September 17, 1947.

Grönke, Erich. Text of statement made at Kenzingen on August 6, 1963. Frankfurt District Court, 4JS 1031/61.

Hodys-Mattaliano, Nora. Undated transcript, evidently made by the SS judge Wiebeck.

Höß, Rudolf. Transcripts of statements made on March 14, 1946 (NO 1210), and January 11, 1947.

———. Notes made in Polish captivity.

Hoffmann, Hanna. Notes on the children's block in the Theresienstadt family camp. Yad Vashem Archives, JM 2726, Jerusalem.

Horvath, Hermine. Report about her experiences in Auschwitz, 1958.

Idkowlak, Irene. Sworn statement about Dr. Eduard Wirths. Würzburg, October 27, 1945.

Joachimowski, Tadeusz. Description of conditions in the Gypsy camp, September 13, 1967.

———. Transcript of testimony given in Cracow on July 2, 1968.

Kaltenbrunner, Dr. Letter dated July 5, 1944, from the head of Gr. Inland II at the Foreign Office, Berlin, to SS Lieutenant General Dr. Kaltenbrunner, the chief of the security police and security service.

Kapp, Karl. Verdict of the Munich District Court II in the criminal proceedings against Karl Kapp, October 14, 1960.

Klehr, Josef. Letter to Martini. Auschwitz, April 15, 1943.

Kohlhagen, Erich. "Zwischen Bock und Pfahl: 22 Monate in den deutschen Konzentrationslagern erlebt und erlitten."

Krauch, Karl. Judgment of the American Military Court VI against Karl Krauch and others. Nuremberg, July 29, 1948.

Kremer, Johann Paul. Transcripts of hearings of Doctor Johann Kremer. Cracow, July 18, 1947, and July 30, 1947.

———. Transcript of the Kremer trial in Münster, November 14 to November 29, 1960, as compiled by Hermann Langbein.

Lachmann, Gerhard. Report about SS Sergeant Gerhard Lachmann by the Waffen-SS Dachau office charged with checking the health and fitness for duty of members of the SS. Dated June 18, 1943.

Lederer, Vitezslav. Letters to the author about Lederer's escape from Auschwitz. Prague, January 14 to 20, 1968.

Locke, Otto. Application for reinstatement. Berlin, May 17, 1960. (500) 2 PUS 1.56.

Mannheimer, Max. "Erlebnisbericht: Theresienstadt, Auschwitz, Warsaw, Dachau."

Morgen, Konrad. "Die Unrechtsbekämpfung in Konzentrationslagern durch SS-Richter." December 21, 1945. "SS—KZ—SS-Gerichtsbarkeit."

Nachemstein, Johanna. Testimony given as a witness on January 7, 1948, Berlin (Glowna Komisja Badania Zbrodni Hitlerowskich w Polsce).

Ortmann, Paul. Statement made under oath, NIK 12846.

Paiskovic, Dov. Text of his remarks about his experiences as a member of the Sonderkommando of Auschwitz. Recorded in Vienna on October 17, 1963.

Pohl, Oswald, and Hermann Hachmann. Statement made under oath at the Landsberg prison on September 3, 1949.

Prem, Adolf. Indictment against SS Sergeant Adolf Prem and warrant for his arrest. Kattowitz, 1944.

Pys, Edward. Statement for the Auschwitz-Birkenau State Museum. Rzeszow, September 1960, supplemented on October 7, 1960.

Rausch, Felix. "Bericht über Erlebnisse in Buchenwald und Auschwitz."

Rittner, Josef. Notes on his experiences in Auschwitz.

Scherpe, Herbert. Letter to Martini. Golleschau, April 29, 1943.

Schönberg, Arthur. Report about his experiences in Auschwitz.

Schuster, Heinrich. Sworn statement, NI—11862.

Spanjaard von Esso, Sara. Statement, NO 42646.

Steinberg, Samuel. Transcript of his testimony as a witness. Auschwitz, February 5, 1945.

Stromberger, Maria. Text of her testimony on the thirteenth day of the Höß trial in Warsaw, February 10, 1947.

Sussmann, Anna. Report about her experiences in Auschwitz.

Vesela, Sylvia. Testimony as a witness. January 15, 1957.

Vetter, G. Adolf. Letter to the author. Frankfurt, December 25, 1947.

Wellova, Nina. "Erinnerungen—71.978, Jude."

Widerstandsbewegung (resistance movement). Letters. Auschwitz-Birkenau State Museum.

Wirths, Eduard. Letter from the SS garrison physician of Auschwitz to the medic of the satellite camp Golleschau, November 16, 1943. Auschwitz-Birkenau State Museum.

———. Letters and notes of Dr. Eduard Wirths; his apologia, written after the war (undated).

Wolken, Otto. "Chronik des Lagers Auschwitz II (B II a)." Compiled from documents from the camp. Vienna.

INDEX

■ ■ ■

———